MW01044668

PRAISE FOR THIS BOOK

"I really like the way this book is not about just methods, it is about practice, and reflects my own approach to teaching evaluation: lots of real-world examples, methods that fit the contexts and feasibility, and a text that is both readable and builds on classic concepts."

—Jerry Hinbest, Vancouver Island University

"The editors and authors have made challenging evaluation concepts easy to understand, and available in one concise, well-written resource. Thank you for making this information available for students and practitioners alike!"

—Jennifer E. LeBeau, Washington State University

"This book provides valuable, relevant information that will help students learn to appreciate and utilize program evaluation as practitioners in various fields. The focus on collaboration makes it relevant to current real-world realities of organizations and systems."

—Skye N. Leedahl, University of Rhode Island

"This book is comprehensive and well-structured. The new models and ways of thinking introduced are refreshing, and the examples provided cover various settings and will resonate with readers from diverse backgrounds. I will definitely refer to this book when conducting the internal evaluation of our next grant, and I can't wait to share some of the take-aways with my students."

—Minjuan Wang, San Diego State University

The Practice of Evaluation

Sara Miller McCune founded SAGE Publishing in 1965 to support the dissemination of usable knowledge and educate a global community. SAGE publishes more than 1000 journals and over 800 new books each year, spanning a wide range of subject areas. Our growing selection of library products includes archives, data, case studies and video. SAGE remains majority owned by our founder and after her lifetime will become owned by a charitable trust that secures the company's continued independence.

Los Angeles | London | New Delhi | Singapore | Washington DC | Melbourne

The Practice of Evaluation

Partnership Approaches for Community Change

Editors

Ryan P. Kilmer
University of North Carolina at Charlotte

James R. Cook
University of North Carolina at Charlotte

Los Angeles | London | New Delhi
Singapore | Washington DC | Melbourne

FOR INFORMATION:

SAGE Publications, Inc.
2455 Teller Road
Thousand Oaks, California 91320
E-mail: order@sagepub.com

SAGE Publications Ltd.
1 Oliver's Yard
55 City Road
London, EC1Y 1SP
United Kingdom

SAGE Publications India Pvt. Ltd.
B 1/I 1 Mohan Cooperative Industrial Area
Mathura Road, New Delhi 110 044
India

SAGE Publications Asia-Pacific Pte. Ltd.
18 Cross Street #10-10/11/12
China Square Central
Singapore 048423

Copyright © 2021 by SAGE Publications, Inc.

All rights reserved. Except as permitted by U.S. copyright law, no part of this work may be reproduced or distributed in any form or by any means, or stored in a database or retrieval system, without permission in writing from the publisher.

All third-party trademarks referenced or depicted herein are included solely for the purpose of illustration and are the property of their respective owners. Reference to these trademarks in no way indicates any relationship with, or endorsement by, the trademark owner.

Printed in Canada

ISBN 978-1-5063-6800-9

This book is printed on acid-free paper.

Acquisitions Editor: Helen Salmon
Editorial Assistant: Kelsey Barkis
Production Editor: Gagan Mahindra
Copy Editor: Exeter Premedia Services
Typesetter: Exeter Premedia Services
Proofreader: Barbara Coster
Indexer: Exeter Premedia Services
Cover Designer: Rose Storey
Marketing Manager: Victoria Velasquez

20 21 22 23 24 10 9 8 7 6 5 4 3 2 1

BRIEF CONTENTS

DETAILED CONTENTS

CHAPTER 4 • Cultural Sensitivity and Responsiveness in Evaluation   56

CHAPTER 5 • Ethical Considerations   81

PREFACE

Over the last 21 years, we have worked together with community partners to help them increase their capacity to learn from their work and improve their practice. Many of our partnerships have spanned many years and multiple projects, and we highly value the relationships we develop with our partners, even when we may not work together for several months or even years. We have also built our graduate training programs in community psychology around this approach and regularly engage our talented graduate students in our ongoing partnerships for the mutual benefits inherent in this model.

As we conceptualize evaluation, it is never solely about merely "knowing"—it is always also about "effecting change"; improving practice and outcomes is always at the forefront. Because we recognize that, as "evaluators," we rarely have the power to effect change in the programs, organizations, or systems with which we work, the development of strong partnerships characterized by common interests, collaborative processes, and shared knowledge helps increase the likelihood that the evaluation findings are used to improve the program or the delivery of services and supports. This model has become our "standard operating procedure."

Although we prefer to conduct evaluation and applied research with community partners, it has also become clear this is not the approach employed by many. Many bright and talented researchers appear to not share our views regarding the utility and value of partnerships when conducting evaluation. Existing evaluation texts have largely not had this focus, so we undertook the development of this book to address this gap in the literature about evaluation: the limited coverage of the use of partnership-oriented approaches to evaluation to facilitate change. We want new and even more experienced evaluators to understand the value of evaluation practice in the context of a partnership, and to see how partnership principles, processes, and practices are useful in diverse settings and with a wide range of methodologies. In short, we wanted a book focused on the processes and practices involved in program evaluation and the diverse potential applications of the work.

Thus, the focus of this book is on evaluation in practice. As such, this volume provides foundational content regarding evaluation concepts, approaches, and methods, as well as applied, practical elements, with an emphasis on the use of evaluation to effect change. We have also worked to ensure that this book included coverage of topics that are often not included in evaluation texts, providing a means for students and professionals to have exposure to evaluative work—with diverse uses and goals—across settings and contexts.

In addition to providing key conceptual material (e.g., relevant terms and theory, design or methodological elements), chapters include at least one real example that illustrates these key ideas and concepts "in action," related to a specific topic, from organizational development or capacity building to program improvement or advocacy. For instance, rather than simply making reference in the narrative to how evaluation can support advocacy or policy-related work and leaving the reader unclear regarding how that might "look" in actual practice, we have included a chapter focused on this special topic—Melissa Strompolis and colleagues outline key concepts in the use of evaluation in advocacy efforts, including specific examples that take these ideas beyond the abstract discussion. Similarly, in another chapter, Katherine Strater Hogan, Virginia Covill, and one of the co-editors walk the reader through the different ways that evaluation capacity building and strategic partnership practices can support nonprofit organizational development work; and Greg Townley, in his coverage of geographic information systems (GIS), provides multiple examples of how partnership efforts drew on GIS data and participatory mapping strategies to address questions of interest and inform their work.

As a whole, the volume's authors focus on the application of varying designs or innovative methods and partnership strategies to maximize the rigor and utility of the work, including the ways findings can be used to support and effect change in programs, organizations, systems, and communities. Each chapter includes a discussion of actionable recommendations; common issues, barriers, and challenges to consider; and questions of relevance to the described example and, as appropriate, content regarding its generalizability to other settings. At each chapter's conclusion, authors also include a listing of references and resources for learning more about the content covered.

This work has been designed to serve as a core text for graduate-level courses in program evaluation across disciplines. It will likely hold particular relevance for those in psychology (especially community psychology or clinical-community psychology), social work, public health, public administration, and educational research. With its focus on the practice and application of evaluation, we see this text as particularly relevant for students and novice evaluators because it can help "connect the dots" between the methods or design strategies and the work's implications across diverse settings and contexts. One of our core goals for this text is to help make the methods, approaches, and strategies discussed "real," and the integration of detailed examples helps illustrate the topics, grounded in the experiences and real-world perspectives of the book's contributors. In addition, in our view, the use of a consistent format across chapters not only lends cohesion to the framing of an edited volume, it also supports students and early career professionals by structuring the communication of material. To support the text's use in training, each chapter includes an outline of learning objectives at the beginning as well as a listing of key terms and definitions and questions for reflection at the end of the chapter. Furthermore, we believe the consideration of a range of special topics—from the use of GIS or network analysis, to evaluation in healthcare settings or internal evaluation in the context of nonprofit organizations—distinguishes this text, and that the format employed can add value to the evaluation frameworks for readers at different levels of experience. While designed to be used by instructors and students in evaluation-focused courses, we also believe it could hold relevance for practitioners who engage in evaluation and its related applied work and their partners or potential partners.

With that as backdrop, our development of this text has been guided by two main notions:

1. The need for evaluators to engage partners—agency or system personnel, or other relevant stakeholders in the setting—at all stages of the evaluation process; we strongly favor a partnership-oriented, participatory approach.

2. The need for evaluation to be used to effect change, in programs, agency practices, system function, and the like. Rather than simply monitoring outcomes or being used to report program elements or agency activities to a funder,

a board, or other administrators or stakeholders, we believe evaluation should be integrated into improvement strategies across settings and contexts.

We believe evaluation should be viewed as a strategy to facilitate or effect change and should be approached intentionally and specifically as a means of effecting change. Well-designed and implemented evaluations can and should be used to improve programs or interventions and guide a range of action steps, from resource allocation to decision-making about implementation and strategies for scaling up the program. Even in programs that are functioning well and accomplishing their goals, evaluation, when done well, is not only to confirm the positive aspects of the program, but to identify ways that it can be implemented more effectively.

We have not attempted to create a "research methods" text; we assume that readers have at least a basic background in research design—or that they have access to a design-focused text. Instead, in our chapters and in those of our contributors, the focus is on the application of varying designs or innovative methods, challenges encountered, and partnership strategies to maximize the rigor and utility of the work. We seek to describe and highlight an approach that all program stakeholders, including funders, staff, and "clients," can back fully, because of the emphasis on the benefits to the programs' intended beneficiaries—the ultimate reason the programs are designed and exist. The emphasis is on how to apply basic research methods principles (consistent with a general quasi-experimental framework) to specific types of programs, settings, and situations. More broadly, though, the volume's focus is on pragmatic approaches to evaluation that balance the needs of different stakeholders in an ethical way, to provide useful, usable, and actionable information to enable program improvement.

At its core, this volume describes varying contexts for conducting evaluative research, different types and scales of evaluation, and the challenges and applications relevant to each, concretized via the presentation of actual examples. We have authored several chapters and have invited contributors to author chapters that align with their specialization and expertise. The perspectives and experiences of these experts enhance this volume and its value for readers, permitting coverage of evaluation, its practice, and its applications and implications across diverse settings and contexts.

We have structured the text into three parts. The chapters in *Part I—Evaluation to Support Change: Guiding Notions and Principles* lay the foundation for the book as a whole. This section underscores the basic premise that the primary purpose of evaluation is to help programs improve their capacity to effect positive change. To accomplish this goal, the evaluator must work in partnership with the program's stakeholders to develop a shared understanding of the program's intended outcomes and the strategies they use to effect these changes. The evaluator then supports program stakeholders in determining what they need to know to make sound decisions and helps them develop the best evaluation design possible (given resource and other constraints) to answer important questions. Consistent with this underlying theme, we authored Chapters 1 through 3 and framed relevant introductory content, including such topics as distinguishing between the "need to know" and what is interesting; balancing the needs of different stakeholders and evaluation demands; using logic models to clarify program theory and evaluation questions; maximizing trust and collaboration by focusing on meeting the needs of the program's intended beneficiaries; and basic elements of a partnership-based approach. Overall, these chapters outline the promise (as well as potential "pitfalls") in evaluation and put forth bedrock concepts for the book's focus on collaborative and partnership approaches. Chapter 4, authored by Cindy Crusto, Diane Purvin, Steven Hoffler, Michael Awad, and Osman Özturgut, addresses the need for culturally responsive methods and practices in evaluation, outlining crucial recommendations for action. This chapter is followed by Michael Morris's Chapter 5, centering on ethics in evaluation, including ethical considerations when faced with competing demands and goals. Chapter 6, Part I's final chapter, authored by the co-editors, underscores the necessity of conducting sound process evaluation when evaluating a program's effectiveness; process data (e.g., regarding implementation, the nature of what a program participant "received") are critical for understanding program outcomes, as well as pointing to areas for targeted improvements.

Building upon this initial framing, *Part II—Evaluation in Practice: Selected Strategies, Methods, and Applications* exposes readers to different strategies that enable partner organizations to understand how their programs work and the potential impact of those programs on different populations. For instance, in Chapter 7, an instructive contribution authored by Yolanda Suarez-Balcazar and Tina Taylor-Ritzler, readers will see how a partnership approach is used in assessing and building evaluation capacity. In Chapter 8, Pamela Imm, Mary Brolin, Janice Yost, and Opal Stone outline the conceptual underpinnings of empowerment evaluation and describe its use in planning and assessing a multi-component initiative to support re-entry (and reduce recidivism) for those in the criminal justice system.

Within Part II, the next cluster of chapters includes a focus on some newer methodologies in evaluation or specific approaches that we believe will be of interest to readers. In Chapter 9, Greg Townley describes the use of GIS in helping a partner evaluate a supportive housing initiative for individuals with serious mental illness and the use of participatory mapping in understanding the community support and daily activities of youth experiencing homelessness, in order to inform improvements in a partner's service delivery and outreach efforts. In Chapter 10, Andrew Case and Joy Kaufman discuss qualitative methods and draw on their work evaluating a publicly-funded mental health center. They describe the use of qualitative strategies to capture consumers' perspectives of the care environment and to support multiple programmatic goals, from engaging consumers to refining their service delivery. This focus on methodologies continues in Chapter 11, as Jennifer Watling Neal and Zachary Neal introduce network analysis and its use in evaluation. They describe how teachers' multiple networks affect their application of particular practices from a mental health service delivery model designed to address the needs of elementary school children with disruptive behavior problems. Then, in Chapter 12, Sarah Pettijohn and Joanne Carman provide an overview of cost-benefit and cost-effectiveness analyses, using specific examples from a nonprofit engaged in substance use prevention. While entire volumes have been written that focus on the specific topics addressed in Part II, these authors provide important conceptual overviews and describe useful examples that illustrate these methods and approaches in action. While these chapters are not designed to enable the readers to become experts on these topics, we hope that the descriptions of these methods, with particular examples of their use, can help readers identify opportunities for their use in their evaluation practice and resources they might seek to learn more about specific methods.

The chapters in the text's final section, *Part III—Evaluation in Action: Special Topics and Contexts*, focus on topics of potential interest and the use of a partnership-based evaluation approach in different settings and contexts. These works include a range of foci, beginning with Chapter 13, in which Katherine Strater Hogan, Virginia Covill, and one of the co-editors discuss evaluation as implemented by staff within a nonprofit organization, and the need for evaluation capacity enhancement and strategic partnerships to support organizational development. These authors draw on their specific work with a nonprofit that delivers integrated primary and behavioral health care, health education, and prevention programs and one that provides a range of school-based supports for youth, respectively. For Chapter 14's discussion of community–university partnerships, Lindsay Messinger collaborates with the co-editors to describe factors and characteristics of effective partnerships and uses case examples to illustrate a productive partnership and another, less successful partnership. In Chapter 15, Melissa Strompolis, Megan Branham, and Whitney Tucker write about data-guided advocacy and advocacy evaluation, using multiple case examples of varying scope to paint the picture of this work in action. For Chapter 16, Victoria Scott, Jonathan Scaccia, and Kassy Alia Ray focus on evaluation in healthcare settings and describe their key ideas in action in two case examples, one initiative involving an academic medical center and including assessments of organizations' readiness for integrated primary and behavioral health care, and the other a large-scale, community health coalition capacity-building project. In Chapter 17, Rebecca Campbell, Jessica Shaw, Hannah Feeney, and Debi Cain describe their use of participatory evaluation to assess and influence public policy, with a special emphasis on their multi-year efforts to improve criminal justice system response to sexual assault, particularly untested rape kits. We close out the book with an epilogue, synthesizing cross-cutting content, critical "lessons learned," and recommendations for evaluators going forward.

The 18 chapters cover important concepts in evaluation, illustrate evaluation in actual practice via real-world examples, and provide readers with fruitful considerations regarding the challenges of this work and recommendations for action. Taken together, these chapters point to the utility and implications of partnership-oriented approaches to evaluation and, of particular salience, how evaluation can support change in efforts across settings and contexts.

Ryan P. Kilmer
James R. Cook

TEACHING RESOURCES

This text includes instructor teaching materials designed to save you time and to help keep students engaged. To access these resources, search for this book on **sagepub.com** or contact your SAGE representative at **sagepub.com/findmyrep**.

ACKNOWLEDGMENTS

We would like to acknowledge some individuals without whom this volume would not have been possible. Thank you to Helen Salmon, Executive Editor at SAGE Publishing, for reaching out and inviting us to develop a text and for her enthusiasm, support, and guidance along the way. Thanks too to Chelsea Neve, Megan O'Heffernan, and Kelsey Barkis at SAGE for their efforts to support this book project and its many steps. Our sincere thanks also to the peer reviewers who offered their insights to strengthen this text:

- Viviana Andreescu, University of Louisville

- Kristin Bodiford, Dominican University

- Carrie Carmody, California Polytechnic University, Pomona

- Megan Delaney, Monmouth University

- Jerry Hinbest, Vancouver Island University

- Elaine T. Jurkowski, Southern Illinois University Carbondale

- Gabriel P. Kuperminc, Georgia State University

- Jennifer E. LeBeau, Washington State University

- Skye N. Leedahl, University of Rhode Island

- Victoria L. Lowell, Purdue University

- Hunhui Oh, St. Ambrose University

- Andy Sharma, Northwestern University

- Minjuan Wang, San Diego State University

We would be remiss if we did not acknowledge and thank the many community partners with whom we have worked as well as the students who have made significant contributions to the efforts of the Community Psychology Research Lab. Quite simply, our work would not be possible without our fantastic partners. Over the years, there are too many to name here, but we want to highlight the special contributions of Laura Clark, Virginia Covill, Rebecca Hefner, Katherine Strater Hogan, Kevin Markle, Lindsay Messinger, Libby Safrit, Jason Schoeneberger, Robert "Bob" Simmons, Emily Tamilin, Rosa Underwood, Sheila Wall-Hill, and Candace Wilson. It is also not possible to name all of our students in this brief space, but several have contributed meaningfully to the example evaluations described in our chapters, including Michelle Abraczinskas, Jaimelee Behrendt Mihalski, Virginia Johnson Covill, Andrew Gadaire, Victoria Galica Morris, Erin Godly-Reynolds, Katherine Strater Hogan, Jacqueline Larson, Eylin Palamaro Munsell, Alison Parrella, Khalil Salim,

Taylor Bishop Scott, Caitlin Simmons, Melissa Strompolis, Jacqueline Tynan, Tanya Vishnevsky, and Christine Zapata. Mentoring our students is greatly rewarding, and we have enjoyed seeing them grow and effect change in their communities.

Finally, it is crucial to mention our families. I (RPK) extend my deepest thanks to my wonderful wife, favorite collaborator (sorry, Jim!), and best friend, Sarah, for understanding what I do (including the long hours spent with a laptop seemingly attached as an appendage), for her extraordinary patience and good humor, and for her unwavering love and support. Thanks too to our children, Alex and Amelia, for their support—I have so enjoyed seeing them grow into the people they are and look forward to seeing what their next chapters will bring. In addition, I (JRC) would like to thank my dear wife, Lois, for her continuous support and encouragement throughout all these years of working with and for the community. She will be as happy as I am to see this volume completed, and I look forward to spending more time with her and less with the computer. I also wish to thank our children, Laura and Lisa, who have grown into wonderful adults and who continue to be supportive of my work.

Ryan P. Kilmer is Professor of Psychology and Director of the College of Liberal Arts and Sciences' Social Aspects of Health Initiative at the University of North Carolina at Charlotte, where he has been on the faculty since receiving his PhD from the University of Rochester in 1999. A community and child clinical psychologist, his work has focused on children and families and (1) using evaluation to refine programs, improve service delivery, and guide system change and local policy; and (2) understanding factors influencing the development of children at risk for emotional, behavioral, and/or academic difficulties, particularly risk and resilience and youngsters' adjustment to trauma.

Dr. Kilmer has partnered with diverse community stakeholders, directing or co-directing (with Jim Cook) projects that respond to community needs, functioning on collaborative teams, and mentoring early career professionals and students. His evaluation and applied research experience includes efforts funded by the National Institute of Mental Health and the Institute of Education Sciences and extends across areas and populations, including mental health, child welfare, education, public housing, early childhood, and integrated care. Across these efforts, many of them multi-year collaborations, he has sought to improve the services and supports provided to children and families, many of whom have traditionally been marginalized or underserved.

His broader professional involvements—including as President of the Global Alliance for Behavioral Health and Social Justice—demonstrate his investment in social justice and child and family well-being. At UNC Charlotte, he has been honored for his teaching, training, and community engagement with the Bonnie E. Cone Early-Career Professorship in Teaching, the Harshini V. de Silva Graduate Mentoring Award, and the Provost's Faculty Award for Community Engagement.

James R. (Jim) Cook, Professor of Psychology, has been on the faculty at UNC Charlotte since 1980, after receiving his PhD from Indiana University. Consistent with his identity as a community psychologist, he has worked to foster community change that improves the lives of people who (1) are economically and socially disadvantaged; and (2) have disabilities, with special emphasis on the needs of children and families. With faculty and students, he works in partnership with community programs, to help them collect, manage, and use data to improve their ability to address peoples' needs.

Dr. Cook has led government- and foundation-funded community–university partnerships that foster and sustain change efforts. He headed a HUD-funded Community Outreach Partnership Center and has co-led (with Ryan Kilmer) efforts to evaluate and support early childhood education, mental health, and neighborhood improvement programs. In addition, he led the effort to create the UNC Charlotte Institute for Social Capital, which brings together university researchers and community agencies to use data to inform and guide services.

In recognition of his efforts, Dr. Cook has received awards from local nonprofit organizations. He has also been honored with the UNC Board of Governors Award for Excellence in Public Service, for demonstrating "sustained, distinguished, and superb achievement in university public service and outreach ... improving the quality of life of the citizens of North Carolina"; the inaugural UNC Charlotte Provost's Faculty Award for Community Engagement, for work that embodies "the University's commitment to civic involvement"; and the Outstanding Educator Award from the Society of Community Research and Action, in recognition of "exemplary and innovative contributions to the education of students about community psychology and community research and action."

PART I

EVALUATION TO SUPPORT CHANGE

Guiding Notions and Principles

CHAPTER 1

EVALUATIVE RESEARCH

Key Concepts and Applications in Facilitating Change

James R. Cook and Ryan P. Kilmer

Learning Objectives

1. Understand the distinction between evaluation and research.

2. Describe questions that must be answered when planning an evaluation.

3. Outline steps in developing an evaluation.

4. Understand the potential benefits in taking a partnership-based approach to evaluation.

What is program evaluation? What can it do for me, my organization, my program, my partners, and my community?

When we talk about program evaluation or evaluative research, we need to be clear about what these terms actually mean. "Evaluation" and "research" are both words that can have some emotional loading or elicit strong reactions. The notion of being evaluated evokes among many a bit of anxiety, perhaps because of negative experiences they have had in the past or because they feel that evaluation means someone will be criticizing or diminishing what they are doing (for some, it may seem as if evaluation is spelled "e-v-i-l- ... "). In a somewhat different way, the notion of research is sometimes viewed with some hesitation. For some, it may call to mind prior training experiences in which research was equated with statistics and statistical tests, which some find aversive. Alternatively, for others, the idea of research may stimulate thoughts of being treated as "guinea pigs" or in a rather dehumanizing manner or, in other instances, of efforts that yield no practical utility.

When we, the authors of this chapter and the editors of this book, talk about program evaluation and evaluative research, we are talking about ways to answer questions of importance to you and the people around you. We would guess that you conduct research and evaluation in your everyday lives on a regular basis, even if you do not consider it as such. Imagine trying out a different route to work to see if you can get there sooner and comparing it to the typical way you travel. You might ask coworkers to suggest alternative routes and/or to collect data about how long it took them to get to work. Or perhaps you like to bake a favorite type of cake and you want to know if reducing the oil in the cake will result in a cake that is similarly moist and delicious. In each case, you might want to take some careful measurements (e.g., of the time of day at which you leave home and arrive at work, and the amount of oil you use) that would allow you to draw conclusions about what you would want to try next time. If the cake is dry and dense, or the new route takes an extra half hour to get to work, you would likely conclude that the "experiment" was unsuccessful, and either go back to the old ways of doing things or try out a different change that you could test. In each case, you are conducting evaluative research to answer questions of importance to you that will allow you to make decisions about how you proceed in the future.

For us, evaluation is a way of "doing business" and, more generally, a way of life. We try things out, we pay careful attention to what we do and how it turns out, we evaluate how well the process played out, and then we make decisions about what we want to do in the future. We do this at work and in almost every aspect of our lives. For some things (such as the driving to work example), the "test" is rather simple, with a clear process (a specific route) and outcome (time to work), although to address our question we do need to make sure that there was not a random accident that occurred on our new route or that differences in time to work did not simply reflect that we happened to be traveling at a time when school buses are dropping children off at school and blocking traffic. In some types of research, modifying or assessing the process is simple (reducing one-third cup of oil in the recipe), but gauging the outcome may not be as straightforward—for instance, you may like your cake a bit drier, but your family may like it more moist, or the cake may be really good when fresh, but the new version becomes drier and less palatable over time. As you try to gauge what is "good," involving others in the decision-making process can be very important, even imperative, unless you are the only one eating the cake!

> **A key to any evaluation is that we are trying to answer questions of importance to our partners and to us.**

These everyday examples point to some key elements that are applicable to more complex types of evaluation efforts. Programs often have multiple components, different types of people who participate in them, changing issues of focus or varying processes over time, and a range of outcomes that can be hard to measure. However, the key aspects of any evaluation, from our perspective, are that we are trying to answer questions of importance to our partners and to us. We work together to develop the questions and find ways to obtain the answers. The knowledge we gain allows us to move forward to better accomplish our goals.

While we have used program evaluation and evaluative research somewhat interchangeably in our discussion so far, there are times when it is important to make distinctions between what is defined as "program evaluation" versus "research." We will first outline the distinctions that are made and the reasons for those distinctions and the circumstances under which it is important to distinguish evaluation from other forms of research. We will then consider the key questions that must be answered when planning a program evaluation and discuss the ways that the answers to those questions have implications for how you would think about conducting an evaluation in the context of a partnership. Next, we will provide an overview of some major steps to take when starting to evaluate a program, policy, or practice. Lastly, we will describe some issues that you need to keep in mind to be able to successfully forge ahead with an evaluation effort while fostering and maintaining a partnership.

DEFINITIONS: EVALUATION VERSUS RESEARCH

Program evaluation is generally defined as a set of mechanisms for collecting and using information to (a) learn about projects, policies, and programs; (b) determine their effects, both intended and unintended; and (c) understand the manner in which they are implemented (Cook, 2014). This definition might sound to many like this is conducting research, and there is clearly important overlap among methods and processes used when doing evaluation and conducting research. In many instances, program evaluation is appropriately viewed as a type of research. However, it is helpful, and sometimes essential, to distinguish program evaluation from research (see Rogers, 2014, and Small, 2012, for brief summaries of the distinctions drawn).

Perhaps the main distinction that is used to distinguish between research and evaluation is the purpose of each. Whereas the primary purpose of research is viewed as the creation of generalizable knowledge, the purpose of evaluation is more typically seen as focusing on the effects of a particular program, policy, or practice, which may or may not be generalizable to other programs, settings, or populations. This distinction has been made by the Code of Federal Regulations (U.S. Department of Health and Human Services, 45 CFR 46.102(d)) relating to the Protection of Human Subjects, which defines *research* as "a systematic investigation, including research development, testing and evaluation, designed to develop or contribute to generalizable knowledge."

In this definition of research, evaluation can certainly be viewed as research if conducted to "contribute to generalizable knowledge." Certainly evaluation is a "systematic investigation," and most efforts to evaluate programs use research methods and analytic strategies that are often indistinguishable from those used when conducting research. Also, many evaluative efforts include a combination of research and evaluation (see Case Example: Combining Evaluation and Research: Evaluation of a System of Care—describing our evaluation of a local system of care—which was both).

Why does this distinction between evaluation and research matter? For individuals who work in universities or who receive federal funding for their work, the federal regulations cited earlier require that research involving human subjects be reviewed by an Institutional Review Board (IRB) to ensure that certain standards are met for protecting human subjects who participate in research. Program evaluation, which is not conducted to contribute to generalizable knowledge, and therefore not defined as research, is exempt from review by IRBs and not subject to the same requirements as research (e.g., participants in child and family teams did not have to review a lengthy informed consent statement, sign it, and give it to the researchers at every team meeting as would typically be required for "research"). Of course, program participants providing information needed to evaluate a program must be protected from harm, and their confidentiality should be protected; the central point here is that the rules are different and review requirements are different, based on how the work is defined.

Separate from the "legal" definition and the applicability of standards for protection of human subjects, there are other implications of making a distinction between research and evaluation, depending on the context in which the terms are used. For instance, in some academic settings, evaluation may be viewed as less important (or of lesser status) than research, meaning that applied researchers (particularly those who are more junior

CASE EXAMPLE: COMBINING EVALUATION AND RESEARCH: EVALUATION OF A SYSTEM OF CARE

We were the lead evaluators of a project designed to transform mental health care for children and families in our county. Funded by the Substance Abuse and Mental Health Services Administration (SAMHSA), our community developed a "system of care" for children with severe emotional disturbance and their families. One requirement of the funding was participation in the "national evaluation," a longitudinal effort designed to track changes in children and families resulting from system and community changes. Using protocols developed by a large research organization that coordinated the national evaluation, these data were then submitted to that organization and compiled across different sites throughout the country to help SAMHSA learn about the types of services and supports that contributed to child and family improvements. This, then, was generalizable research, to help understand the outcomes of these systems and what contributed to better outcomes and to guide future efforts. In addition to the "national evaluation," each site was encouraged to conduct "local evaluations" to help guide practice within that community. At our site, we focused on implementation of key components of a system of care, particularly the degree to which system practices and processes were in line with the practice model that had been adopted. That meant we collected data about the degree to which "child and family team" meetings— in which multiple parties develop a customized plan of care for the child and family—were conducted in a manner consistent with the program guidelines. We used those data to provide feedback to teams, supervisors, organizations, and the system to help the local community implement the program with fidelity and to see if better implementation led to better child outcomes. This local evaluation was viewed as "program evaluation," not research, because the focus was on the ways that we could help the program improve its functioning; we could not generalize our findings to other systems.

This distinction had important implications for the evaluation efforts. The local evaluation involved asking all the people participating in a child and family team meeting, including family members, professionals, and others who had an interest in helping the family, to complete brief surveys about the focus and function of the team meeting at the end of each child and family team meeting. The data were collected anonymously and used to inform team facilitators and system administrators about how well they adhered to specific principles. The focus was on improving services at that site, not generalized knowledge, and because of this, the participants in the child and family team meetings were not required to sign informed consent statements at each meeting, which might have taken more time to complete than the surveys themselves. A brief consent statement was included on each survey to ensure that each participant knew why the data were being collected, but there was no need for each participant to read and sign a separate form and no need for the evaluators to collect and store consent forms, making the process more manageable for the evaluators and the participants.

When we submitted the protocol for the evaluation efforts to our university's Institutional Review Board (IRB) for the Protection of Human Subjects, we made a clear distinction between the national evaluation research and the local evaluation efforts to improve service delivery. The IRB determined that the local "program evaluation" was not research, and thus did not fall under their purview.

in status) who do evaluation may be advised to describe their work as evaluative research (with the emphasis on "research"). In applied or program contexts, the term "evaluation" can have many meanings, including personnel evaluation, and may be viewed as a threat to individuals or programs. On the other hand, research is often viewed by program staff as esoteric and irrelevant.

These different views of program evaluation and research point to the importance of the context in which the work is being done. In different settings, with different funding, the same work may be (appropriately) referred to differently. This implies that we need to make sure that we use language that conveys the nature of the work in a way that avoids the negative connotations that may be present within a given context. It also underscores the need for clear, effective, and direct communication. Regardless of the label assigned to our work, we tend to emphasize the following key questions, upon which we will elaborate later:

1. *What do you/we need to know about the program and population of interest?* We tend to think of these as the "research questions" but, in some contexts, we refer to them as "evaluation questions" or merely "questions needing to be answered."

2. *What steps would we need to take in order to obtain answers to the questions of interest?* These are the methods we need to use to give us the most unequivocal answers possible.

3. *How would obtaining answers to those questions make a difference in how the program operates?* This is the "so what?" question that, for many, distinguishes evaluation from research. If the primary focus is on the specific program, policy, or practice that is being evaluated, and not on programs, policies, or practices more generally, then this is likely to be defined as program evaluation.

This latter question is critically important. As we conveyed in the Preface to this text, in our conceptualization of evaluation, it is never just about "informing" or "knowing" (i.e., documenting outcomes or impact or reporting on program elements to funders or other stakeholders); rather, our focus is on "effecting change" (e.g., in programs, agency practices, system function) via improving practices and processes and, in turn, outcomes. In our view, the primary purpose of evaluation is to improve programs and interventions, guide program changes, and make decisions about allocation of resources.

INITIAL STEPS IN THE DEVELOPMENT OF AN EVALUATION

Identify the research questions: What do you/we need to know about the program and population of interest?

Our questions shape the course and scope of the evaluation effort.

The identification of the research questions is much like specifying the destination before you begin a journey. If we do not know where we are trying to go, we may not know which route to take to get there, nor would we be able to tell if we have arrived at the right place. The questions must be clear because they necessarily shape the course and scope of the evaluation effort.

To gain a clear sense of the research questions requires first the identification of the critical people who have a stake in the success of the program (we will refer to them as *stakeholders*), including those who have the ability to act upon the findings. We need to spend time with them, understand their goals, and help them to specify what they want and need to know. This is generally an active process, whereby we attempt to put ourselves in the position of the stakeholder and ask ourselves what we would like to know if we were in their position.

It is important to underscore that the identification of useful research questions is not a simple process. You might think that all you need to do is ask the stakeholders what they need to know, they will tell you, and you proceed from there. However, in order for this simple process to work, you would need to have stakeholders who

- have spent a significant amount of time thinking about decisions that need to be made about the program;

- understand what information is needed in order to make those decisions; and

- understand the range of possible questions that can be answered.

In our experience, many program stakeholders have not had enough experience with evaluation design and implementation to know what the possibilities are—if someone is not aware of the different options that exist, it is not possible to make an informed decision about what one wants or needs. This would be like going into a restaurant and being invited to order your food without knowing what is on the menu. Our job, as evaluators, is to provide the "menu," explore with the stakeholders what they like (e.g., what level of spiciness do they want) or think they need, explain the trade-offs that exist in their decisions (some dishes take longer to prepare than others, some cost more than others; the decision about what to order will likely take into account how hungry they are and what their budget will allow), and help them make an informed choice about how to proceed. Making an informed decision requires that they have come to understand their needs, and can clearly articulate the options they have, based on the logistical constraints they face (or, more accurately, that we face together, because resources are always finite).

To determine what types of questions would be useful, it is crucial to gain an understanding of the program and what it is trying to do. This helps you think about the information needs from the perspective of the program and its multiple stakeholders. In particular, the evaluator will want to develop a good understanding of the following:

1. The program's intended beneficiaries (this term is used rather than "client" or "participant" because it reflects the fact that, often, programs are designed to benefit a range of people). In conceptualizing an evaluation and its questions, we want to be clear regarding who is expected to benefit from the program. While the expected beneficiaries are often those who directly participate in the program, in many programs there are others who are expected to benefit. For instance, the beneficiaries of a school-based social skills intervention could be the students who gain additional competencies, their classmates who have more positive interactions with the children who received the program, the classroom teacher who is able to spend more time teaching and less time intervening in disputes, and/or the parents who find their children to be better behaved and parenting to be more positive.

2. The program's expected benefits or results. Programs are generally created to contribute to or result in certain outcomes or benefits, although it is quite

common for programs over time to effect and/or identify other unintended consequences, positive and negative. Understanding those expected and unexpected consequences of the program or policy is important for developing an evaluation.

3. The actions taken by the program to effect those benefits. This refers to what the program does to bring about change. Rarely is there a single program element that effects change. Rather, change often comes from a complex set of interactions that include the identified program components, as well as multiple other actions that, while perhaps not the intended active elements, are critically important for effecting change. For example, a program to help educate new mothers about how they can take care of their infants may be created based on a belief that new knowledge is an important impetus for improved parenting. However, if the education is provided by visiting nurses or social workers, there may be important elements of skill building or role playing that occur, as well as social support that helps the mothers become more comfortable in their role and better able to parent (separate from the knowledge gained).

Sometimes the initial research questions from stakeholders are very basic and specific. We have heard program directors indicate that they wanted to know how many people they are serving in different ways. This is what we might describe as a "monitoring" question, rather than an evaluation question, and suggests a need for improvements in the program's internal data management capacity. If the program cannot answer a question as basic as that with its existing records, a first step before any real evaluation questions are answered would be to help them develop the capacity to reliably record and monitor their operations. Although this question is simple and not really a question of evaluation of the program, it opens the door to discover additional questions that may arise if the data were available to answer them. For example, it may be that there have been demographic changes in the program's "catchment area" (the geographic area served by the program) and program leaders wish to understand whether "newcomers" to the area are being served and what services they are utilizing. This could have important implications for outreach efforts or changes in the nature of the programs offered. Helping the program managers or other stakeholders move beyond "monitoring" questions is critical for knowing what data to collect and how to organize the information. It is important to think beyond the immediate question (e.g., monitoring) and imagine what other questions may be relevant, even if the program has no current capacity to answer the questions. Anticipating the questions that could be answered may stimulate simple changes in the data collected on an ongoing basis, enabling answers to relevant questions in the future.

As illustrated in Box 1.1, which outlines some common evaluation questions, program stakeholders are often interested in knowing how well the program is meeting the needs of the individual participants and/or "collaterals" (e.g., those connected with or related to the program "participants" or "clients," such as parents, spouses, neighbors, or coworkers) and/or the broader community. For example, programs may have high impact with a very small number of people, which may meet their individual needs, but if the goal is to address the needs of all (or a very significant subset) of those in the community, it would likely

BOX 1.1 COMMON QUESTIONS ADDRESSED IN EVALUATION EFFORTS

Monitoring: How many people are being served? In what ways? What are the characteristics of those being served? Is this the population the program intends to serve? Has that population changed over time and, if so, why? Are there beneficiaries besides the population being directly served?

Overall Impact Evaluation: How well does the program effect change among the intended beneficiaries? To what degree is it having the desired effects?

Differential Impact of Program for Different Participants: Does the program have different effects for different types of participants? Do some respond particularly well to the program, whereas others do not?

Fidelity of Implementation: Is the program (or its components) being implemented as intended? Are practices consistent with the model or plan that has been adopted?

Differential Impact of Specific Program Components: Do specific aspects of the program lead to different

outcomes? For different types of people? Do different amounts of treatment lead to different outcomes? Are there specific "doses" required to have the desired impact? How does the integrity or consistency of the implementation relate to outcomes?

Community Impact: What are the needs of the population being served? How well is the program able to address these needs? Is there a reduction in unmet need in the community?

Accessibility: Are the intended beneficiaries of the program able to access the program? Are cost, distance, transportation, culture, or other factors limiting the ability of some people to benefit from the program?

Cost Benefit or Cost Effectiveness: What is the return on the investment made in operating the program? How does the cost of implementing the program compare with the benefits obtained, for the participants or for the community? How does the return on investment compare with that of other programs with similar goals?

be necessary to determine the needs that remain or that are unmet by the program (with implications for improved efficiency or expansion).

When we are contacted by potential partners about an evaluation or decision makers are considering funding allocations, their questions about the effects of a program are often characterized as "does the program work?" This implies that there is a "yes" or "no" answer—we generally discourage people from thinking about programs in this way because it is rare that programs have no impact (particularly if they have been in existence for a long time). Rather, a focus on how well the program works, and potential variations across different subsets of participants, helps avoid the notion that a program is either a success or a failure. There are many levels of success, and it is important to try to sort out what is working well and for whom. In fact, well beyond framing a question or evaluation around whether a program works or not, when we engage in evaluative efforts, we typically approach them

> **Rather than framing an evaluation around whether a program "works" or not, we typically seek to employ data to improve program function and maximize the benefits to those enrolled.**

with the goal of employing data to improve program function and maximize the benefits to those enrolled.

This focus on conducting evaluation to make changes in the program is often referred to as a *"formative" evaluation* (see Chapter 16 for more information about formative, summative, and process evaluation). As the name suggests, a formative evaluation is most likely to occur when a program is new and developing, with the program using data on an ongoing basis to make corrective changes until it becomes established and stable. This is related to the notion of a *"process" evaluation* that focuses on how well the program is implemented in relation to its design and intent. This type of evaluation helps the program management make changes to improve its "fidelity" or consistency with the tenets of the program, practice framework, or curricular model. This focus on processes and making changes can be contrasted with the notion of a *"summative" or "outcome" evaluation*, which suggests that the purpose of the evaluation is not to improve the program, but to determine the effects of the program. This implies that the program has become stable and that the evaluation can be conducted over a sufficient time period to determine the effects of a particular, static program.

These distinctions between formative and summative, or process versus outcome, evaluations often are based on assumptions that we rarely see in practice. Most programs are not static, even after operating over many years. In fact, the longer a program has been operating, the greater the likelihood that the program has experienced some "drift" in its goals and/or operations; that is, the program's function or objectives have changed from what they were initially. Program operations may also change more deliberately, due to changes in resources, client needs, or staff capabilities. With the exception of the rare "controlled trial," in which the program is intentionally kept static while it is being evaluated, most programs undergo changes over time, which may not always be obvious to program management. Please see Case Example: Needs Assessment with a YMCA, which illustrates how broader community and contextual factors can be salient contributors to program evolution and change.

In addition, we often need to help the program's stakeholders get past an erroneous assumption that if the program is designed to do something, then it certainly must be doing that. Clearly, many (perhaps most) programs are not implemented as planned, and sometimes there is a major gap between the intended and the actual implementation of the program. Thus, the degree to which the program is implemented as designed and the relation between implementation and outcomes are often very important questions to answer, for both new and well-established programs. These answers can be crucial for making program-related changes, particularly given the growing evidence that program implementation is often highly related to the effectiveness of the program (Durlak & DuPre, 2008). Similarly, because programs rarely have all the resources they need, the efficiency of programs (i.e., their return on investment) is often important to assess (see Chapter 12 for a discussion of cost-benefit and cost-effectiveness types of evaluations).

Because program stakeholders often have not had the training or experience to readily articulate the range of questions that an evaluation might answer, it is useful for the evaluator to "put on the hat" of the program management and attempt to understand what questions might be of interest to them. In addition to the questions already mentioned, program leadership or other stakeholders may be concerned with the degree to which the intended beneficiaries of the program can access the program. This can mean that there

CASE EXAMPLE: NEEDS ASSESSMENT WITH A YMCA

We were once asked to help a YMCA undertake a needs assessment to determine what services the Y could provide to the surrounding community. The Y was originally created to serve the surrounding neighborhoods, and a main feature of the Y was its Olympic-sized swimming pool and strong competitive swim team. However, over the prior decade, the neighborhood had undergone significant changes, such that the largely white, working-class neighborhood had changed, with many families moving to other neighborhoods in more affluent suburban areas. Now the neighborhood surrounding the Y was largely populated by poor, minority families. Many of the families who had moved away continued to take advantage of the swimming program, and others from those more distant neighborhoods became members and used the Y. New leadership at the Y recognized that it was no longer meeting its mission of serving the local community, and they wished to learn from the neighborhood residents how the Y could best serve them so the Y could shift their programs to address their needs. Note that while the actual activities of the Y had stayed fairly constant over time, changes in the surrounding population resulted in it no longer achieving its goals. The needs assessment identified neighbors' needs and the potential barriers (e.g., financial, transportation) the neighbors would experience, and the Y made a major shift in their programs and fee structure to address these issues. They made a change to better serve their new neighbors and meet the needs of their changing context.

are concerns about distance and transportation, which may impede the intended beneficiaries' abilities to get to and use the program. However, access may also be limited by the cost of the program (families may not be able to afford the program), the hours of program operation (if it is only open from 8 to 5 on weekdays, working people may have difficulty getting off work to participate), and cultural appropriateness (the staff may not speak the language or may not be sensitive to the cultures of the intended beneficiaries). If a program is not accessible or acceptable to the intended beneficiaries, many will not use the program. In short, there are many questions that can arise in an evaluation of a program, and it is useful to explore the options with the program's stakeholders before proceeding too far.

As the questions evolve, it is useful to continue to ask what the stakeholders already know about how and how well the program benefits the population of interest and whether they see it as benefiting some more than others. These questions then generally lend themselves to asking about how they might know if the intended program benefits occurred. This then starts the journey into understanding what types of measurement and methods might be most useful for answering the research questions of interest. Before we propose to collect any new data, we want to know and understand the existing data collection efforts and how we can use the program's ongoing data management structures to evaluate the program.

This process of asking questions and working to understand what the program is trying to accomplish is the start of what we refer to as an articulation of the program's "theory of change." A theory of change describes the processes that the program has put in place to accomplish its goals. Specified within a theory of change are the program activities that are intended to effect certain short-term changes; these short-term changes are then prerequisites for later and/or larger changes that subsequently lead to the longer-term goals of the program. For example, the leadership and staff of a program designed to provide support to families of children with severe emotional problems recognized that they needed to be able to document the impact of their services and supports in order to sustain their funding. The program provided a range of services to the parents, the children with emotional problems, and their siblings, in order to strengthen the family and ultimately improve the mental health of the diagnosed child. To help clarify how these different activities were expected to lead to benefits for the parents or caregivers as well as improvements in the diagnosed child, a *logic model* was created that laid out, in a diagram, the program's theory of change. The creation of a logic model, to graphically illustrate how a program is expected to work, can be a critical tool for informing organizational and evaluation planning. The logic model can help frame an evaluation's focus and objectives, from its data sources to its key questions and indicators of outcome. A logic model is also very important for helping the different stake-holders, including the evaluator, be clear about the manner in which the different program components and goals logically fit together.

As seen in Figure 1.1, a de-identified and simplified logic model for this family support program, there were multiple ways that the different program components were expected to lead to improvements in children. Parent support groups were expected to lead to lower

Figure 1.1   A Logic Model of a Family Support Program

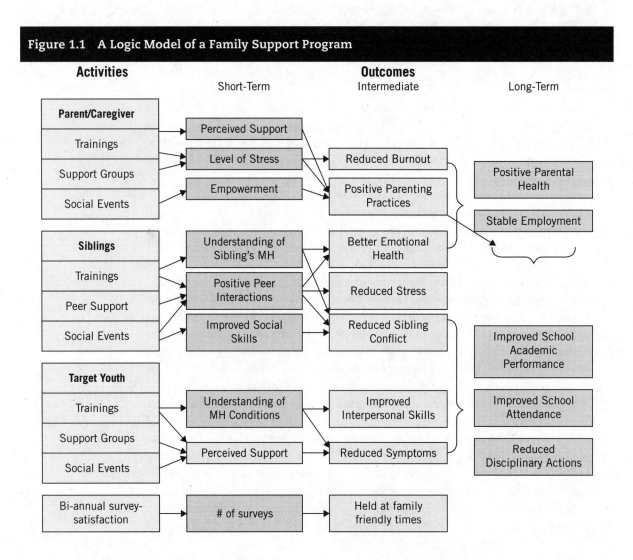

levels of stress among the parents, which would lead to more positive parenting and better child outcomes. Similarly, the activities provided for the siblings helped them to maintain a positive peer group and to understand the needs of their diagnosed sibling, leading to lower levels of conflict in the household and helping the sibling maintain emotional health. The activities for the child with the diagnosis (i.e., the target) were expected to help provide some respite for the parents and help develop greater social and interpersonal skills in the child. The collective impact of these different shorter-term outcomes was then expected to help reduce the symptomatology of the diagnosed child and increase his/her positive functioning at home and school. The logic model helped clarify the intermediate steps that contribute to better outcomes for the diagnosed child, and therefore helped identify the measures that needed to be used at different points in time to determine whether the program was having the desired results.

The logic model helps "connect the dots" between different program elements and describes how they contribute to different types of change in the (sometimes multiple) intended beneficiaries of the program. As a logic model is created and shared, the research questions can and should be refined, clarified, and prioritized as more is learned about the program and its operation. It is important to understand also that it is rare for a program to have the resources available to answer every question of interest in an evaluation, which means that the prioritization of the questions becomes increasingly important with more complex logic models.

Outline the methods: What steps are needed in order to obtain answers to the questions of interest?

The measures and methods need to follow the research questions. While this may seem to be an obvious statement, there are many times when people affiliated with programs identify a way of measuring something about the program, and then see it as a useful way to evaluate the program. Starting with the measure and allowing that to determine the nature of the evaluation is like the tail wagging the dog; the measurement used should always follow from discussion and understanding about what we want and need to know. The question(s) of interest should always guide the methods and measures of an evaluation. Remember that "not everything that can be counted counts, and not everything that counts can be counted" (Cameron, 1963, p. 13). It is critically important to have a clear understanding of what the program needs to know, and then focus the methods on obtaining answers to their important questions (please see Case Example: Ensuring Alignment Between Measures and Program Goals as an example).

> **According to Cameron (1963, p. 13): "Not everything that can be counted counts, and not everything that counts can be counted."**

Once we have reasonable clarity about what the program is trying to accomplish, its theory of change, and research questions of importance, decisions about the methods to use for answering the questions require some additional information.

What are the *sources of information* for answers to the questions? Program participants are often an important source, but there may be other people, such as parents, spouses, teachers, or supervisors, who may be able to shed light on whether the participants are changing in the ways intended by the program. The answers to questions may come from existing records kept for other purposes (e.g., attendance records or test scores in schools; crime reports; emergency room visits), and data may come not only from the people

CASE EXAMPLE: ENSURING ALIGNMENT BETWEEN MEASURES AND PROGRAM GOALS

We were once working with a senior center to help them evaluate the effects of an exercise program on the seniors who participated. While the program was primarily focused on improving or maintaining the seniors' quality of life, the county funders insisted that program staff assess weight loss. When the program leaders protested that many of the participants were fairly frail and should not lose weight, the county insisted that they have the seniors weigh themselves regularly and that the program track and report these weights. Since weighing the participants was not a costly endeavor and not viewed by the participants as a problem, the program leadership decided that they could easily satisfy the county's demand, but that they would still want to develop strategies to answer questions of importance to the program (e.g., how well participants could engage in activities of daily living). However, it would have been tragic if the county made its funding contingent on weight loss, when that was not a primary goal of the program and could potentially be hazardous to the participants. Alternatively, it may have required that the program recruit overweight seniors to "successfully" participate in the exercise program.

expected to benefit from the program, but also from others presumably not affected (a comparison group). The type of sampling is also a decision to make. For small programs, the "sample of the whole" may be appropriate, but for larger programs, a subset may be selected, and it is important to make sure that the sample is representative. As the sources of data become clear, the evaluator must almost certainly revise the questions to make them more specific and precise. Some questions may also be abandoned or revised based on the conclusion that there are no feasible mechanisms for answering the questions. For example, if an appropriate comparison group is available, a research question may shift from "how much do participants gain?" to "how much more do participants gain than the comparison group?" Please see Case Example: Evaluation of an Early Childhood Program as an example.

It is also necessary to determine the timeline under which the evaluation will be working. *When are results needed* and from what time period will the evaluation data be obtained? Sometimes answers to research questions are needed quickly, for example, when budgetary decisions about program funding are being made. In other instances, programs may have the luxury of collecting data over time to provide answers. The methodology of choice and, to some extent, the questions that can be answered are determined in part by the timeframe that is required. For example, if answers are needed quickly, then the evaluation may need to rely on records that are already available (known as *archival data*). Of course, without good records going back in time, it may be difficult to understand the longer-term effects of the program quickly; instead, it would likely be necessary to follow up or track the participants over time. That said, even if you do have data available over a period of time, the data may not capture the information that is wanted or needed. This can then require further revision of the questions to be answered to account for the constraints of data and time. When this type of shift occurs and the questions deemed important cannot be adequately answered, the evaluator and the program management

CASE EXAMPLE: EVALUATION OF AN EARLY CHILDHOOD PROGRAM

In our work with a large school system to evaluate an early childhood intervention program, we wanted to know whether children evidenced growth in their social–emotional skills as a result of the program. We identified measures for teachers to assess their students' social–emotional development and planned to have all teachers assess their students. However, the school administrators felt it was important to provide feedback to the teachers about their students' performance on the measure. We, as evaluators, noted that providing feedback would interfere with our ability to evaluate the program because this measure had not been used before and there were no plans in place to continue to use that measure. As such, the addition of feedback to teachers was a change in the program that would occur only during the evaluation and could potentially improve teachers' ability to educate their students, that is, the version of the program we were to evaluate might have better outcomes than the version of the program that had been in place (and would continue after the evaluation). In sum, we would not really know how well the program "as is" would do in the absence of the new "intervention" (teacher feedback). However, because the program was large with several thousand children, we proposed that we randomly select half of the teachers for a "feedback group," allowing us to determine the impact of the feedback on the students' development over the course of the year in the program compared to those students of teachers who did not receive feedback. Thus, we were able to respond to the questions and concerns of the program leaders by changing the research questions and the methods to include a good comparison group to answer questions of importance to the program. In addition, because the students in the "feedback" condition gained more than the students in the "no feedback" condition, we learned about a simple, inexpensive way to improve student learning (see Cook et al., 2014; Gadaire et al., 2020, for more).

must carefully determine whether the "new questions" are sufficiently important to warrant the time and energy that the evaluation would entail. If not, one option may be to retain the original evaluation questions and set up the data collection and management systems to allow answers at a future time. When using existing data, you also have to be careful to determine whether the data are accurate because they may not have been collected and recorded as consistently and carefully as needed. When you have the ability (and resources) to determine what data will be collected and how, you clearly have more latitude in answering the questions of greatest interest.

The timing of data collection is also important as you consider, in your theory of change, when you might expect to see program effects. If you collect data shortly after participants complete a program, you will only be able to assess the short-term effects of the program. If you anticipate that the effects take a longer time to be realized (or if longer-term effects would be most important, useful, or compelling to assess), then you will want to determine when you would best be able to measure those and collect data at an appropriate time (or at multiple times). Sufficient detail in your logic model/theory of change is important for determining when you need to collect data. A focus on longer-term changes will also generally require an investment in a longer-term evaluation in order to track and collect information over time. Without that commitment, the types of questions that can

CASE EXAMPLE: IMPORTANCE OF LONGITUDINAL EVALUATION METHODS

In the evaluation of a prekindergarten education program targeting 4-year-old children who were judged to be educationally "at risk," the school board wanted to know the degree to which the program resulted in educational gains for participants. In particular, it was hoped that the program would help the children become "ready" for kindergarten, and subsequently more successful in school over time. Outcome criteria of interest to the school system were the third and fourth grade end of grade tests. We designed an evaluation that would determine how these children improved in their verbal ability and in their social–emotional development over the course of the year and found that children in the program improved in their verbal and preacademic skills as much as children in a similar program that did not select children who were educationally at risk (the same social–emotional data were not available from children in the other program). Although the children made gains over their year in the program, the school system only funded the evaluation effort for 1 year, with no support to follow the children until third or fourth grade. Consequently, without follow-up, we could not really tell if any longer-term gains resulted from the program. We did, however, examine archival data from children who had been in the program in prior years and found that the gains made in the program year appeared to "wash out" by the time they took the third grade end of grade tests. We also looked at the quality of the schools they entered and found that those in lower performing schools were less likely to sustain their gains over time. Without the ability to follow up the children over time, we could not identify which aspects of the program (including implementation of the program's curriculum, which we assessed) were related to longer-term outcomes (nor explore the impact of social–emotional gains or whether they sustained, because the school system did not assess children's social–emotional functioning as a matter of course). While the use of the archival data provided information about the importance of the schools that the pre-K students entered, follow-up of the students would have provided a much more complete picture of the effects of the program.

On a different note, we do want to point out that a major concern with this evaluation was an attempt to evaluate a 9-month, pre-K program on its impact on third and fourth grade testing, when there are 4–5 years of classroom instruction and other life events that happen between the end of the program and these outcomes. Those test scores are quite distal outcomes! Since test scores are affected by many factors (e.g., teacher quality and school climate, parental education and involvement, traumatic experiences of children, test anxiety), it is probably not wise to evaluate a program serving 4-year-olds on these test scores without accounting for these other factors.

be successfully answered will be limited. (Please see Case Example: Importance of Longitudinal Evaluation Methods as an example.)

Identify how the evaluation (in particular, the answers to the research questions) will make a difference in program operation. As we indicated before, this is the key "so what?" question that, for us, defines evaluation (as opposed to research more generally).

The question of how the evaluation will be used to effect change in the program is perhaps the most important question of the three. We urge our partners to consider this question carefully because, if we cannot clearly identify how the results would translate into improvements in the program, it is hard for us to justify spending the time (and using the resources) necessary to do the work. Ideally, this question is being raised at every step along the way, helping ensure that you will not spend time working to answer questions

CASE EXAMPLE: REVISING RESEARCH QUESTIONS TO BE MORE "ACTIONABLE"

In a state-funded education program, program administrators wanted to know about the effects of a program. We learned that the state mandated the curriculum and dictated the processes for implementation. When we asked how different results would result in changes in the program, the administrators indicated that their hands were tied because they had no power to change it (although they could argue to the state to change its requirements). Upon further discussion, we asked if all program staff implemented the program in the same ways (it would be highly unlikely that they did) and, if they did not, did the differences in implementation result in different outcomes. Since they believed that there was variability in implementation and that this variability would likely affect outcomes, we revised the research questions, focusing on a careful evaluation of the variability of implementation across different sites, staff, and aspects of the program. This focus had clear implications for the administrators in that it would allow them to identify strategies for increasing quality control through changes in training and the supervision of their staff.

about which stakeholders do not really care or that would be "merely interesting." If we do not have clarity about how results would be used to effect change, we would suggest that the research questions need to be reformulated or the methods need to be revised to obtain "actionable" results (please see Case Example: Revising Research Questions to Be More "Actionable" for an example).

This example suggests the need to examine all three questions in a way that recognizes how the answers to each can affect the others. The specification of research questions should be made with a clear consideration of their implications for program improvement. Development of the methods to answer the questions often leads to revisions of the questions to match what is feasible, because we do not want to have research questions that cannot be answered. Then, changes in research questions must be re-evaluated to determine if they have important program implications and can inform action. This cycle of adaptation of one set of questions in light of the answers obtained for the other sets reflects part of the dynamic nature of evaluation that, at its core, involves capacity building among partners. That is, the different parties in the partnership must learn from one another, bringing their respective strengths to the table. Ultimately, through this iterative process of working through the different facets of the evaluation process, a set of methods is developed that can answer research questions that have important implications for improving the program.

We recognize that, when planning and conducting evaluations, the goal of having important research questions answered in the most unequivocal manner possible is often subject to compromise as practical considerations (e.g., availability of resources, such as funding and time) exert control over the process. Yet, at the same time, if the goal is to improve the program and its outcomes for participants, finding the right combination of salience and pragmatism is critically important. There is often a trade-off in designing evaluations between answering important questions with less robust methods versus answering less important questions with stronger methods. We believe that this trade-off should always lean toward answering important questions, as long as there is sufficient rigor of design to gain knowledge that can guide practice. There is certainly little to be gained by using strong (and often costly) methods to answer trivial questions about which nobody cares.

Throughout our discussion of the early steps in conducting an evaluation, the interactive nature of the process of making decisions should become obvious. As evaluators, we ask questions, sort through possible answers, revisit the questions, and continue to try to formulate a plan that will answer important questions and make a difference. As indicated by this book's title and its emphasis, this is work that is often conducted as part of a partnership, and we might argue is *best* conducted as part of a partnership. This focus on partnerships reflects a particular value orientation, one that is consistent with our training and perspective as community psychologists.

The Importance of Transparent Values in Evaluation

Evaluation is an endeavor that is steeped in values, which often become apparent in understanding the dynamic contextual and political processes that lead to the development of programs, their changes over time, and the decisions to evaluate them. Programs are created as reflections of peoples' needs to effect change. The goal or mission of the program is a reflection of what the founders, and hopefully the current leaders of the program, view as important. Similarly, the strategies used to accomplish the mission also reflect a set of values. It is important that we, as evaluators, see these program values as consistent with our own. Because the primary goal of evaluation is to help improve the program to better accomplish its mission, the mission of the program must be something we can actively support. Even if the current processes used to accomplish the mission are less than optimal, the evaluation should help the organization or program create processes that advance the mission as well as possible. For example, we have worked with the local school system to help it evaluate and improve its prekindergarten program (we discuss this partnership in more detail in Chapter 3). We made a point from the beginning that we were strong advocates for "high-quality pre-K programs" because the literature is clear that these programs can have important positive effects on children's growth and development. The goal of the evaluation, then, was to help determine the degree to which the program was implemented in a way consistent with what research would suggest is "high quality," and work to increase the likelihood that every child experienced a "high-quality" program. As seen in this example, we can easily evaluate the program while we advocate for the mission of the program, and work to help the program be successful, with the emphasis on ensuring that every child gets the best program possible. In a sense, when we align the mission of the program with part of our mission as evaluators, then the "client" of the evaluation is the "client" of the program. In the example of the pre-K program, we were always working for the best interests of the children and families being served and, because that was the espoused mission of the program, we could always focus on that when making decisions about how to proceed.

Thus, in our minds, evaluation is not a "value-free" practice or endeavor. Our approach to evaluation is also informed by our values. For instance, facilitating the participation of people in processes that affect them reflects a key part of our value orientation. This participatory orientation is part of a "capacity-building" focus of our work—we want people to participate in evaluation processes so that they can develop their abilities to critically examine what they do and, as a result, make efforts to effect positive changes (see Hogan et al., 2017, for background on how we train students to use a capacity-building approach in community work). As such, much of what we do in evaluation fits a *community-based participatory research model* (e.g., Viswanathan et al., 2004; also see Chapter 3), in which we involve the stakeholders in determining the questions to be asked, establishing the methods used to answer them, interpreting findings, and developing recommendations for action. Because our goal is to evaluate in a way that leads to action, and evaluators rarely have the power to change the program, it is critical to work together in partnership with program leadership to ensure that the evaluation is answering questions of importance to them and that they can see how answers point to specific changes they might make to improve the program. The buy-in of program leadership and stakeholders is critical for the action to occur because ultimately they are the ones with the power to effect change in the program.

Throughout the next chapters, we will build upon these themes and focus on the ways that we can build partnerships to conduct effective evaluation. While partnerships are not necessary for conducting evaluations (and many evaluators do so without developing partnerships), we find that partnerships are certainly helpful and make the work more rewarding. When conducting evaluation in the context of a partnership, it is much easier to bring together stakeholders, since you have built a relationship with them. We also find that stakeholders are more likely to be honest and forthcoming with information that can be useful for conducting the evaluation when they see the evaluator as an ally working toward a common set of goals. Some might argue that a partnership approach to evaluation runs the risk of evaluators becoming biased and losing their ability to report findings objectively and accurately and make difficult recommendations. However, if we are guilty of bias, it is bias toward making sure that the program is maximizing its benefit to the purported beneficiaries. We work to maintain our role as a critical friend (i.e., "a trusted person who … is an advocate for the success of that work," Costa & Kallick, 1993, p. 49) and work with our multiple stakeholders to understand the program and develop strategies for improving it. That is what we see as our role in partnership-oriented evaluations.

FURTHER READING

Association for the Study and Development of Community. (2001). *Principles for evaluating comprehensive community initiatives*. Author. http://www.racialequitytools.org/resourcefiles/CVP062001.pdf

Community Tool Box. *Developing a logic model or theory of change*. https://ctb.ku.edu/en/table-of-contents/overview/models-for-community-health-and-development/logic-model-development/main

Cook, J. R. (2014). Using evaluation to effect social change: Looking through a community psychology lens. *American Journal of Evaluation, 36,* 107–117 https://doi.org/doi:10.1177/1098214014558504

Hogan, K. S., Tynan, J. M., Covill, V. J., Kilmer, R. P., & Cook, J. R. (2017). A capacity building framework for community-university partnerships. *Collaborations: A Journal of Community-Based Research and Practice,* 1(1), 1–28. http://scholarlyrepository.miami.edu/collaborations/vol1/iss1/1

Logic Model Workbook, Innovation Network. http://www.nebhands.nebraska.edu/files/logic%20model%20workbook%20innovation%20network.pdf

The Pell Institute and Pathways to College Network. *Evaluation toolkit: Using a logic model.* http://toolkit.pellinstitute.org/evaluation-guide/plan-budget/using-a-logic-model/

W.K. Kellogg Foundation Logic Model Development Guide.
https://www.bttop.org/sites/default/files/public/

W.K.%20Kellogg%20LogicModel.pdf

KEY CONCEPTS

Archival data: Information and records that have already been collected or are available, prior to the initiation of an evaluation or a research effort.

Community-based participatory research (CBPR): "A collaborative research approach that is designed to ensure and establish structures for participation by communities affected by the issue being studied, representatives of organizations, and researchers in all aspects of the research process to improve health and well-being through taking action, including social change" (see Viswanathan et al., 2004).

Formative evaluation: A type of evaluation focused on making changes and refinements to the program. Most likely to occur when a program is new and developing, this evaluation uses data to make corrections or refinements until the program becomes established and stable.

Logic model: A graphic illustration of a program's theory of change or how the program is expected to work, used to help frame an evaluation's focus and objectives, from its data sources to its key questions and indicators of outcome. Also used to clarify the manner in which the different program components and goals logically fit together.

Outcome evaluation: Also referred to as a "summative" evaluation, the purpose of this type of evaluation is to determine a program's or initiative's effects.

Process evaluation: A type of evaluation that focuses on how well the program is implemented in relation to its design and intent. For instance, is the program being implemented with fidelity or in a way that is consistent with the methods specified as important for that program?

Program evaluation: A set of mechanisms for collecting and using information to (a) learn about projects, policies, and programs; (b) determine their effects, both intended and unintended; and (c) understand the manner in which they are implemented (Cook, 2014).

Research: "A systematic investigation, including research development, testing and evaluation, designed to develop or contribute to generalizable knowledge," as defined by the Code of Federal Regulations (U.S. Department of Health and Human Services, 45 CFR 46.102(d)) relating to the Protection of Human Subjects.

Theory of change: A description of what the program is trying to accomplish and the processes that are in place to accomplish these goals. This includes specification of the program activities that are intended to effect certain short-term changes; these short-term changes are then prerequisites for later and/or larger changes that subsequently lead to the program's longer-term goals.

QUESTIONS FOR REFLECTION

1. Consider the key questions and steps outlined in this chapter, that is, identifying the research questions, data sources, methods, timeline, and possible implications of the work. How are these steps interrelated? To what degree does the answer to one influence another?

2. As you consider a program or initiative with which you have familiarity, imagine yourself as a manager or director of the effort. What questions would drive your interest in evaluation? What kinds of indicators would be crucial to track?

3. What are the potential benefits of a partnership-based approach to evaluation? What might be some challenges inherent in this participatory, collaborative approach? How might a new

or novice evaluator get started with such an approach?

4. We note that, for us, evaluation is not "value free." As you think about your own work or programs you know, consider the alignment of your values with the effort or program. How did you navigate that relationship? If a program's mission did not align with your values, would you agree to serve as its evaluator? How would you approach that situation?

REFERENCES

Cameron, W. B. (1963). *Informal sociology: A casual introduction to sociological thinking.* New York: Random House.

Cook, J. R. (2014). Using evaluation to effect social change: Looking through a community psychology lens. *The American Journal of Evaluation, 36,* 107–117. doi:https://doi.org/10.1177/1098214014558504

Cook, J. R., Kilmer, R. P., with Tynan, J. M., Larson, J. C., Hogan, K. S., Scott, J. T. B., & Mihalski, J. L. (Contributors). (2014). *Evaluation of Bright Beginnings: Process and outcomes: Final report.* Community psychology research lab, University of North Carolina at Charlotte. https://www.cms.k12.nc.us/cmsdepartments/accountability/REA/Documents/Evaluation%20of%20Bright%20Beginnings%20Final%20Report%2011.2014.pdf.

Costa, A., & Kallick, B. (1993). Through the lens of a critical friend. *Educational Leadership, 51,* 49–51.

Durlak, J. A., & DuPre, E. P. (2008). Implementation matters: A review of research on the influence of implementation on program outcomes and the factors affecting implementation. *American Journal of Community Psychology, 41*(3-4), 327–350. doi:10.1007/s10464-008-9165-0

Gadaire, A. P., Armstrong, L. M., Cook, J. R., Kilmer, R. P., Larson, J. C., Simmons, C. J., Messinger, L. G., Thiery, T., & Babb, J. (2020). *Enhancing social–emotional development in pre-k: Using data to address students' needs* [Manuscript under review].

Hogan, K. S., Tynan, J. M., Covill, V. J., Kilmer, R. P., & Cook, J. R. (2017). A capacity building framework for community-university partnerships. *Collaborations: A Journal of Community-Based Research and Practice, 1*(1), 1–28. doi:10.33596/coll.10

Rogers, P. (2014). Week 19: Ways of framing the difference between research and evaluation. *Better evaluation: Sharing information to improve evaluation.* http://www.betterevaluation.org/en/blog/framing_the_difference_between_research_and_evaluation

Small, P. (2012). Four differences between research and program evaluation. *Blog: Nonprofit capacity building,* retrieved from https://managementhelp.org/blogs/nonprofit-capacity-building/2012/01/08/four-differences-between-research-and-program-evaluation/ on March 26, 2018.

U.S. Department of Health and Human Services. *Code of Federal Regulations.* 45 CFR 46.102(d), relating to the Protection of Human Subjects.

Viswanathan, M., Ammerman, A., Eng, E., Gartlehner, G., Lohr, K. N., Griffith, D., Rhodes, D., Samuel-Hodge, C., Maty, S., Lux, L., Webb, L., Sutton, S. F., Swinson, T., Jackman, A., & Whitener, L. (2004). *Community-based participatory research: Assessing the evidence.* Evidence Report/Technology assessment No. 99 (prepared by RTI-University of North Carolina evidence-based practice center under contract No. 290-02-0016). AHRQ publication 04-E022-2: Agency for Healthcare Research and Quality.

CHAPTER 2

PROGRAM EVALUATION
Promises and Pitfalls

Ryan P. Kilmer and James R. Cook

Learning Objectives

1. Learn the role(s) and benefit(s) of, and rationale(s) for, program evaluation.

2. Describe approaches, ideas, and alternatives to evaluation that reduce the likelihood that sound evaluation will occur.

3. Understand factors and conditions that can impact the degree to which evaluation data are used.

Evaluation can have many roles and purposes and can yield meaningful benefits. In Chapter 1, we outlined some basic parameters for evaluation (and what constitutes evaluation) and discussed some foundational content for thinking about this work, including some common questions addressed via evaluation. As we have underscored, for us, it is critical to use evaluation not just "to know" (i.e., documenting a targeted outcome or an unintended impact) but "to do" (i.e., effecting change, such as improving a program or intervention).

In this chapter, we will consider some of those roles and benefits in more depth. However, we would be doing a disservice to you, our reader, if we do not also engage some of the very real challenges faced by evaluators, ones that reduce the likelihood that a sound evaluation will be implemented or supported—or that impact the degree to which the evaluation and its findings even get used. We will start off by considering briefly some of the important roles and benefits of evaluation, including the rationale for conducting evaluation.

ROLES AND BENEFITS OF EVALUATION: WHAT IS THE RATIONALE FOR CONDUCTING EVALUATIONS?

This section outlines some of the major reasons for conducting evaluation—what it can "buy" an organization or program, how it can be used, and what its benefits might include. Throughout, we will discuss brief examples to help illustrate our key points.

Purpose of evaluation: Assessing program impact. Did it work? In recent years, there has been an increasing emphasis on "accountability" for public sector systems (such as our schools, child welfare agencies, and the juvenile justice system) as well as nonprofit organizations. That is, their funders and their stakeholders (boards of directors, community members, supporters, staff, and the intended beneficiaries of programming or services) want to know if the program or intervention "worked"; did it yield the impact, effects, or benefits that were desired or intended? Schorr (1997, p. 117) describes how the "public wants proof of results" and quotes Alice Rivlin (1971): "Effective functioning of the system depends on measures of achievement ... To do better, we must have a way of distinguishing better from worse." This "did it work?" question is addressed via *outcome evaluation*, and this objective likely reflects what most people think of when they consider "evaluation." However, we need to not only think about those intended (positive) results or outcomes, but also consider and assess possible unintended, negative consequences, known as *iatrogenic effects*. That said, it is difficult at best and impossible at worst to know if a program, intervention, or initiative "worked" without truly knowing what it involved and what was done in actual practice.

For example, the national evaluation of systems of care, also known as the National Longitudinal Study, examined a host of outcomes associated with efforts designed to revamp the system of services and supports provided to children with severe mental health difficulties and their families (e.g., Center for Mental Health Services, 2003, 2004; Holden et al., 2003). Over a period of years, various annual reports summarized results indicating a modest to moderate level of success, such as reduced need for special education, fewer suspensions from school, and decreased involvement in the juvenile justice system (e.g., Center for Mental Health Services, 2003, 2004; Cook & Kilmer, 2004; Holden et al., 2003). However, this outcome-focused work did not account for the variability across sites, from differential interpretation of key principles to very substantial differences in implementation (Cook & Kilmer, 2004, 2012; Kilmer & Cook, 2012). Funded communities were required to take part in this national evaluation, but they were not required to assess their *implementation fidelity*, including the degree to which they were putting key principles for the philosophy into actual practice (Kilmer & Cook, 2012; Kilmer et al., 2010). Data reported via various mechanisms, including reports to the U.S. Congress, would effectively summarize diverse outcome data—and, on a national scale, the outcomes from sites with strong implementation would be combined with those with middling to poor implementation, with the overall results suggesting modest to moderate positive changes. Site visitors conducting system-level assessments (Brashears et al., 2012) noted uneven implementation across key principles for these federally funded systems as well as meaningful variability in sites' quality improvement processes; however, that information was not integrated in the evaluation products describing outcomes nationally. For instance, it was not possible to examine effects separately for high- versus low-fidelity communities.

In our own community, we conducted a multicomponent evaluation in which we focused on what care coordinators and planning teams were doing (particularly in regards to key elements of the practice model they were to be implementing) and what children and families received and experienced through the system, as well as the required outcome-focused work. We found that, when youth were served via planning teams that engaged in high levels of implementation of the identified model, they improved more and at a greater rate than those whose planning teams did not (e.g., Haber et al., 2010; Hemphill et al., 2010; Johnson et al., 2011). Without taking into account what sites did—specifically, the degree to which their practices and processes aligned with the system of care philosophy and key practice models—it is impossible to truly judge the effectiveness of the approach or how well the program initiative "worked," since there were different versions of the approach being implemented in different locations.

We learn such information via a *process evaluation*, which focuses on monitoring the program and its implementation, assessing if it is being conducted as planned or in a manner that is consistent with a particular model. This degree to which a program evidences faithful replication or alignment to an intended model or program (e.g., Durlak & DuPre, 2008) reflects *implementation fidelity*. Quite simply, we need to know what the program or initiative is doing, and how those actions occur, in order to try to gauge its outcomes; without the process assessment, we may falsely conclude that the program as planned had particular effects, when we are really evaluating what may be a very different program (the version that was actually implemented). This brings us to our next major role for evaluation.

> **We cannot say "it worked" if we do not really know what "it" was. Process data are crucial for contextualizing outcomes. Without such information, the understanding or meaning we can make from the outcome data is more limited.**

Purpose of evaluation: Understanding outcomes. Do we know why it worked or did not work? Process-oriented information is critical for contextualizing outcome-related data—and helping to make sense of findings. If outcome data do not reflect the positive outcomes for which program leadership hoped, we need process data to understand why. Was it a problem of program theory? That is, were our ideas regarding how the program's actions would lead to the desired change (the theory of change) incorrect? Alternatively, was it a problem of implementation? That is, while a model may have evidence indicating its effectiveness, did our program staff not (or inconsistently) implement it with fidelity? Such linkages between process and outcome data will be discussed in detail in Chapter 6, but we will address these challenges briefly here.

As others have noted (e.g., Kloos et al., 2012), issues and errors in program theory led to some prominent programs (such as the Drug Abuse Resistance Education, or DARE, substance abuse prevention program) not having their intended effects. Another frequently cited example is Scared Straight. This program, intended to deter youth from engaging in delinquent or criminal behaviors, involved bringing groups of youth to prisons and having them see first-hand the consequences of these negative behaviors (e.g., Gilna, 2016). The program approach included incarcerated individuals relaying their stories, often including grim details, while yelling at or confronting the youth. The program was shaped by the idea that seeing this potential reality, and having the incarcerated individuals yell threats at the youth and try to frighten them, would shake the youth out of their rule-breaking ways (e.g., Gilna, 2016). This notion was not supported by research or evaluation; the program theory was incorrect. In fact, multiple studies found that program participants actually appeared to be at increased probability for committing crimes, and evaluation found that the program increased participants' risk for arrest, by unintentionally reinforcing attitudes and behaviors associated with breaking the law (e.g., Petrosino et al., 2005; 2013; also see Kloos et al., 2012). This is a clear example of an iatrogenic effect.

In other instances, the program theory is sound, and there may even be evidence to support its effectiveness, but it does not seem to "work" or yield the intended effects in a given setting. The issue in such cases may reflect problems of implementation—more specifically, the program's implementation may not be of the quality or dosage of the original or it may not align adequately with a model that has documented desired effects (e.g., Durlak & DuPre, 2008). We have seen many instances of how low-fidelity implementation—or not implementing the program or intervention in a manner that is consistent with the evidence-supported model—does not yield the desired effects. Issues of implementation have been discussed at length by many authors (see, e.g., Durlak & DuPre, 2008; Fixsen et al., 2005). In their review of five meta-analyses and 59 additional studies, Durlak and DuPre (2008) concluded that findings strongly supported the notion that "effective implementation is associated with better outcomes." Going further, these authors wrote:

> A major implication emanating from these findings is that the assessment of implementation is an absolute necessity in program evaluations. Evaluations that lack carefully collected information on implementation are flawed and incomplete. Without data on implementation, research cannot document precisely what program was conducted, or how outcome data should be interpreted.

Purpose of evaluation: Comparing models and assisting with model selection. When high-quality process and outcome data are collected, it is possible to compare the outcomes obtained via one program or intervention model versus another and inform the selection of a program model to utilize going forward. This could include comparing curricular models for a school-based program, deciding upon a framework for a community-based mentoring program, or assessing different home visiting approaches for families. The bottom line is that a careful analysis of the characteristics of programs as implemented can enable evaluation to support data-guided choices.

Purpose of evaluation: Informing changes. Should we do something differently? Providing information to improve programming or inform decision making about the program or initiative is a prime role of evaluation. This interest in using evaluation to improve programs is closely related to the objective of understanding outcomes; process data are absolutely necessary for guiding any kind of improvement or program refinement. Data can shed light on areas of strength and those that appear to carry weight in contributing to desired outcomes, as well as elements that warrant additional training or professional development, program components that do not "add value" in their current form, or gaps in a program model.

Sometimes these changes can be quite straightforward. As part of one evaluation, we provided early process feedback about how the pilot of a particular mental health, cross-system practice model was being implemented. We pointed to several specific areas in which implementation was going well and less well. After the meeting during which we shared these "early returns" with administrators and staff involved in the particular initiative, we had staff approach us and quietly disclose that they did not know what a particular intended program element was (we had noted the regular absence of this element in our discussion with the group). This suggested a need for additional training as well as supervision specific to the key practice model components. Without the process data—and a mechanism for providing feedback—this gap in implementation would have likely persisted. In this particular instance, the finding pointed directly to the need for resources dedicated to professional development and support.

In other instances, the circumstances are not as clear-cut or readily addressed. In another evaluation (in fact, in multiple related evaluations over multiple years), the data indicated that practices were not reflecting the cross-agency and cross-system collaboration thought to be crucial for the effort's success. Our data helped shape some strategies for addressing these issues, and some partners were interested in and willing to modify their actions. Unfortunately, all of the "players" did not share that sentiment, despite our use of diverse strategies to engage key leadership and staff, demonstrate how we could help support needed changes, and share a subset of results illustrating the potential benefits of the work when this collaboration occurred and the broader model was implemented effectively. These issues, in short, led to initiatives that underperformed and did not realize their potential—they did not have the intended benefits for the children and families served.

Purpose of evaluation: Informing resource allocation. Should we continue to fund it? How should we use the resources we have? Attesting to a program's effectiveness or impact can aid in deliberations about the use of public resources or the resources of a nonprofit or other organization. This is a central emphasis of much evaluation work and can relate directly to the degree to which a program, intervention, or initiative receives continuing funding, or funding to support its expansion. As we note in Chapter 3, we co-directed an evaluation of an early childhood education program that had sustained dramatic cuts to its funding shortly before we were engaged in work with the school system. The program and school system were hamstrung by the fact that they did not have rigorous data to support the program's effectiveness. During a time of resource strain and needed budget cuts, that lack of data did not serve the program well, and the program was targeted for major cuts. More broadly, the presence of evaluation data, with substantive information about program functioning and impact, can aid in deliberations about the use of public resources.

Such resource decisions are not limited to whether a program should be funded (or expanded) or not. Rather, evaluation data can be used to inform more fine-grained decisions, including about the use of professional development or training funds, the need for additional person power, the benefits of enhancing or augmenting a particular program element, and other decisions regarding program components. Evaluation can assess the "value add" of specific program components—or of innovations—and findings can also support the need for resources dedicated to enhance the implementation of those program elements. This may include additional support for consultants, coordinators, or coaches to help oversee or provide feedback regarding such elements as team planning meetings, group activities, program or classroom practices, or the informational support provided to parents. Alternatively, evaluation can help identify program components that are not adding to the overall value of the program, and may thus be either strengthened or eliminated. Chapter 12 provides an in-depth description of cost-effectiveness and cost-benefit analyses.

Purpose of evaluation: Support grant applications. In a similar vein, evaluation data—even a robust evaluation plan—can help an organization, program, or initiative to be competitive for grant funding. Rigorous evaluation data are viewed positively by funding entities; preliminary data can help demonstrate promise; and a well-designed evaluation plan can convey the value placed on data-guided decision making, accountability, and a culture of learning and improvement. Years ago, the leadership of a small local partner that provided family support services shared with us that our multiyear relationship (e.g., Cook et al., 2008; Kilmer et al., 2009), including our collaborative effort to develop a logic model, modify their data collection strategies, and build their evaluation capacity, was explicitly identified by a local funder as a key element in their positive funding decision. By her account, the funder saw those steps and the local partner's ongoing relationship with us as characteristics that helped set them apart in a competitive funding field.

Unfortunately, many applications submitted for program or initiative funding tend to frame evaluation as an afterthought, with underdeveloped plans or underfunded evaluations. In an optimal circumstance, the plan for evaluation would be developed hand-in-hand with the program's plan. Doing so—with an understanding of program objectives and how specific components are designed or intended to support program goals—would ensure targeted collection of process and outcome data and, more generally, access to the information necessary to answer questions of interest to the program or initiative leadership as well as key stakeholders or partners. The development of a rigorous evaluation plan can help establish trust with stakeholders, demonstrating an investment in quality programming, thorough understanding, and fiscal stewardship. It can also help improve program planning from the outset, by encouraging program planners to think in some detail about the ways they would detect changes, and the theory of change that would be expected to lead to those changes.

WHAT ARE BARRIERS TO EVALUATION? WHAT ABOUT WHEN THIS DOES NOT GO WELL?

Up to this point, we have described the manifold benefits of evaluation. Most critically for us, evaluation is necessary to improve, and optimize, the programs, services, and supports provided to the individuals, children, or families who are their intended beneficiaries. In addition, the groundwork for the evaluation should be linked inextricably to the development, planning, and implementation of the program. Given the clear benefits of evaluation, it would seem as if every program, initiative, or organization should be doing this, right? Unfortunately, however, "real" rarely aligns with "ideal," and many agencies, organizations, and programs do not have the capacity to support well-designed evaluation; they dedicate insufficient resources to support evaluation; or they operate as if evaluation is an "add on" or a "have to" that allows them to meet some reporting need (as if they are just checking a box). This section considers some factors and dynamics at play when strong evaluations are not sought or used—or their data are discounted.

A focus on outputs. In the place of an evaluation, many organizations track and report lists of the programs they have run, the number of people they have served, the presentations given, and other activities. We see this reliance on outputs or activities with some regularity—it often reflects the lack of dedicated resources to, or capacity for, evaluation. We have seen groups or organizations report that they conducted x number of programs in the community (sometimes including the number of people in attendance); disseminated x thousands of pamphlets or informational brochures; coordinated x number of program/support groups; or provided their program or intervention to x number of people. However, simply reporting such outputs does not provide any information regarding their effectiveness or impact. For example, we do not know if or how someone used the information provided, if they followed through on the referral made after the health risk screening, or if they attended to the discussion and used the material from the coping skills group. Based on these outputs alone, we cannot gauge if our actions constituted an adequate "dose" of the program or intervention, if we had the intended effects (or if there were unintended effects), or if the program was delivered with fidelity. We hope it is clear that this approach to "program evaluation," which would be more accurately referred to as program monitoring, is extremely limited. Tracking and reporting this information only permits the conclusion that the program or initiative did *something*, not that it made a difference.

The weight of political forces or reputation. Sometimes factors seemingly unrelated to the project or program come into play and influence the likelihood that evaluation findings will contribute to program improvements or that an evaluation will even occur. In some cases, when an effort or program has a powerful, well-known, or well-liked champion, founder, or director, that individual's political weight, popularity, or reputation can override evaluation findings or even lead to a conclusion that there is no real need for an evaluation. Sometimes systems or funders continue to fund efforts without requiring a critical evaluation of the work, believing that the work must be of value because it is associated with a particular champion or program director, even when there is no clear evidence that the program is having the desired effects. In other cases, programs are viewed positively because the work reflects values or goals that align with prominent or popular views (or, in some cases, social policy), or because the program is viewed as an "evidence-based program." However, being guided by admirable values and goals, having a well-known champion or leader, and using a program model found to be successful at another place and time do not necessarily translate into program success; evaluation is necessary to gauge the effort's effectiveness and identify strategies for its ongoing refinement.

We have encountered this issue in different forms. In one example—we will be intentionally vague here—we were brought in to evaluate an initiative that included a diverse range of stakeholders. We were invited to join the leadership and planning team, and we worked with the various players to understand the facets of the effort. We sought to partner and collaborate, but the nature of the relationships that emerged (and the collaboration that followed) varied substantially among the stakeholder groups and their organizations. Early on, the initiative hit some bumps, and the road was rocky—the nature of the work was new and different for the vast majority of the individuals being asked to implement the intervention and, notably, they regularly seemed to face challenges to their participation in this effort from their own agencies. We worked to provide balanced process-related information as well as specific, data-guided recommendations, with the goal of informing changes and shedding light on difficult areas that warranted additional attention or resources.

The initiative's leader had been active in the community for some time, was well connected, and, overall, had a positive reputation. Our experiences with this initiative leader during this specific effort led to a much different impression. Over time, as it became clear that there were major discrepancies between the actual initiative as implemented and the public description of the program, the initiative leader began to create roadblocks for the evaluation, from shifting established communication responsibilities and procedures to limiting access to needed data. She questioned every element of the evaluation and attempted to sow doubt about its methods, despite having been part of the discussions and processes through which the evaluation plan was developed. This individual met directly with the prime funder regularly and made sure the initiative had ongoing support; in that context (and others), we learned that she also made unfounded statements about us, our practices, and the evaluation. In the end, we tried multiple strategies to foster collaboration, to strengthen the broader effort via direct work with the partners who were interested, and to convey the initiative's challenges, the issues we were encountering, and some specific ways in which they could respond. Unfortunately, these attempts never gained sufficient traction to help the initiative turn a corner or to overcome the efforts by the initiative's leader to undermine the evaluation. Our final report documented the numerous and assorted challenges to the evaluation and drew on the data available to provide recommendations for modified practice. We also reported on outcomes—given that the practices did not align with the plan or the identified model for care, it is not surprising that the indicators of outcome suggested no benefit (and, in some cases, deterioration) for the children and families involved. Our contract was not renewed (much to our relief), and they identified and worked with multiple different evaluators over the years. The initiative's "champion" was powerful and well thought of enough that she was able to secure funding to sustain the initiative. Even now, years later, it has not achieved its potential. We will say more about this evaluation experience in the section below discussing "Organizational Factors" for why evaluation data do not get used.

Personal experience and testimonials. Many program staff and intervention providers will share stories regarding program successes and specific positive outcomes. When asked, they frame evaluation as unnecessary, given their experiences doing the work day to day. In fact, we have had some program staff or leadership literally say: "We just know it works." While some anecdotes of individual and family success can surely be compelling, and such testimonials are regularly used and can be helpful in fundraising, it is hard to know how representative they may be of program participants' experiences. In addition, we do not know what other resources, services, and supports may have contributed to the positive outcome or change in circumstance the staff witnessed. In brief: these experiences and stories do not take the place of an evaluation.

WHY DON'T EVALUATION DATA GET USED?

Sometimes an evaluation has been conducted, but the data or findings do not get used. A diverse range of factors can contribute to that outcome, some attributable to evaluators, some to organizations, and others to a variety of external influences.

Evaluator-related factors. There are times when the evaluator or evaluation team is responsible for their work not being used. Sometimes evaluation results are not provided in a timely manner, reducing their potential impact because they are delivered outside a useful time window, or other program or contextual changes have made them less representative of the program's current function. While we were not involved in the effort, we know of one such evaluation (we will be intentionally cryptic here): Despite describing the work and its design in various forums and settings, the evaluator missed deadlines for the project's report and other deliverables and did not provide findings to the program leadership in time to inform some key decisions about the program's future. In the end, very significant decisions were made, without empirical grounding, and the program and its delivery were changed meaningfully. The evaluator's lack of follow-through had repercussions for the program (and its intended beneficiaries) as well as the evaluator's reputation in the community.

In other instances, evaluator-related issues reflect challenges with communication. For example, the evaluator(s) may not have adequately conveyed the relevance of the findings to decision makers or other stakeholders (Kilmer, 2015). This can occur when reports or presentations are overly technical, they focus too heavily on statistics and effects, and their descriptions are jargon-heavy. Evaluators are better served when they can develop evaluation products that are tailored to the background and understanding of their audiences. Put frankly, evaluation findings will not be used if they are not communicated in a user-friendly manner that speaks to the concerns of the stakeholders (Kilmer, 2015). The technical elements (and reporting appropriate statistical approaches and their results) are important to be sure; it is also necessary to ensure that we as evaluators communicate "the story" of the evaluation and help readers understand the meaning of the results and their implications. In turn, in addition to the full evaluation report (perhaps with its most technical aspects in an appendix), we virtually always find it helpful to develop an executive summary or, in some instances, a one- or two-page brief of the evaluation's key findings and recommendations, to help ensure that the main points are more likely to be digested by critical stakeholders.

Organizational factors. Sometimes organizational leadership keeps evaluation findings at an arm's length because the results suggest that changes are needed. This behavior may reflect a fear of or discomfort with change or, more simply, organizational inertia. That is, it is easier for many in leadership just to keep programs and their procedures in place, to follow the path of least resistance and do nothing differently, regardless of the issues identified via evaluation. Some may say, regardless of findings, that the results confirm their expectations or "what we already know"; others, when learning of recommendations, say "that is what we already do." We have faced such situations, and in these circumstances it is difficult to gain momentum in working for change; we often find that the leadership did not seek evaluation of its own volition, but instead was strongly encouraged to do so by funders or others. In other instances, program leadership and staff may worry about negative findings and program problems coming to light, which may have the potential to impact negatively their funding or fundraising. Alternatively, the leadership may be concerned about the effects of any negative findings on the work or on staff morale. This aversion to any risk can undermine efforts to learn about the program and identify strategies for improvement.

Unfortunately, another phenomenon that we have encountered in the context of more than one evaluation is the desire to "look good" rather than actually "be good." This has occurred as part of higher profile efforts, sometimes with significant funding behind them, that have been undertaken with considerable fanfare. We will remain vague here for reasons we hope are evident. In the two most prominent examples of this issue that we have faced, the data, collected via multiple sources and using multiple methods, suggested that, at the core, those involved with the effort were not doing what they planned or said; the reality of implementation did not align at all with the model or plan. It likely goes without saying that outcomes mirrored those issues of process; that is, the obtained outcomes did not approximate the desired or hoped for outcomes nor those reported by similar initiatives. We provided process-related data for each of these initiatives, regularly reporting areas that could be addressed to help "right the ship." Despite our efforts to be balanced, to report areas of strength and those processes that were being implemented with fidelity as well as areas that needed attention, leadership for each initiative pushed back in multiple ways. It is not surprising, in such circumstances, to have program managers criticize the data, argue that the results are not representative of the program as a whole, assert that steps have already been taken to improve the processes in question, or say that those findings do not really matter anyway. We have learned that it is useful to have a fairly "thick skin" in evaluation work and to make sure that the evaluation data and processes are sound, to help counter such arguments.

This brings us back to the example we noted earlier in which the well-connected and well-liked initiative leader took multiple steps to impede the evaluation. In view of the issues at play, that experience warrants mention here. In fact, in a particularly striking incident, in a meeting preceding the release of an anticipated interim report about one of the efforts, we were asked "not to include" any content that could be perceived as "negative or that would raise questions" (the question was not asked by the initiative leader but by one of that individual's colleagues, and the leader was present). This request cuts to the core of an evaluator's professional ethics and integrity (see Chapter 5), and we conveyed directly that the data were the data and they "tell the story." We emphasized that, at that time, some indicators would be viewed as encouraging and others would be seen as pointing to clear issues, underscoring that we needed to gauge the quality or representativeness of the data, the degree to which caveats and qualifiers would be necessary (or if it was "too early" to report a given finding), and the like—but that those decisions would be our call. Given the context, it was necessary to assert ourselves and draw some clear lines regarding the integrity of the process. In that example, over time, the attempted partnership deteriorated; the initiative's leader chose to question the data and our methods and impugn our professionalism, rather than engage the findings thoughtfully or consider how to implement some of the strategies that we (and others) had communicated. Our contract was not renewed after the 1-year pilot, and the available data indicated that the initiative did not benefit.

This specific challenge, that is, when an organizational or initiative leader seems to care more about perception than about doing right by the work's intended beneficiaries, constitutes the most significant challenge that we face in our evaluations. In these instances, the leaders have not responded to clear and open communication nor to data- or logic-based rationales for needed modifications. Instead of framing the results as pointing to opportunities for change and improvement, they dug in and talked of the positive work being done. Of particular note, when this has occurred, the individuals heading the initiatives have evidenced a moral compass and sense of professional integrity that vary dramatically from our own. They have woven falsehoods about their own work as well as our evaluations (and us) and, in the end, they have done a disservice to the initiative's potential beneficiaries. These two efforts were opportunities lost.

External factors. Non-data-related factors can keep a program alive or hurt it and have substantive implications for evaluations. There are different perspectives, agendas, and stakes at play for the varied parties involved in the evaluation of a program or initiative. It can, at times, be challenging to navigate waters that may be experienced as politically treacherous. These waters can reflect resource strains or needed budget cuts as well as shifting policy interests and needs, especially during difficult budget years.

Shifting policy interests can sometimes reflect what some of our colleagues have deemed the "shiny penny" phenomenon, in which a new (or sometimes revisited) topic or initiative can capture the attention (and dollars) of local leaders or funders. In the short term, this can lead to interest in and support for evaluation of efforts or programs that function in this new area. However, the other side of that "coin" is that such shifting priorities can also lead directly to funds being diverted from other evaluation or program-enhancement efforts. Those functioning in areas that are no longer high priority can see their evaluation findings or recommendations fail to garner interest or, in some scenarios, can even experience the loss of expected funding. As we note in Chapter 3, we encountered this in our work with our local school system's early childhood program. In brief, even though the work had clearly been conceptualized as multiyear, system representatives conveyed in the latter part of year one that there would not be system resources to support the ongoing evaluation. This required the partners to seek other funds and led to a disruption of our work (also see Tynan et al., 2015).

WHAT YOU CAN DO

As we will discuss in the next chapter, there are steps evaluators can take to increase the likelihood that evaluation results will be used and have an impact, ideally by informing improvements in the program or initiative. A key is working with program leadership and staff, determining jointly the questions that will guide the evaluation.

Adopt a partnership-based approach to evaluation. This approach (see Chapter 3 for a detailed discussion) is foundational to this text. Creating an evaluation context centered on collaboration and learning (as opposed to "outsiders" coming in to judge, offer critical or punitive feedback, or put a program at risk) is crucial. Doing so can facilitate buy-in and participation across an organization, program, or initiative, which can yield better access to and quality of data. Working in partnership also increases the probability that the evaluation is experienced less as a "have to" or something "done to" the program and its staff, and more of an opportunity for us to learn about and maximize the impact of the program, thereby enhancing the likelihood that the evaluation (and its findings and recommendations) will be used.

Discuss concerns openly. Evaluators can set the stage for partnership by fostering open and direct communication—this is necessary for all relationships but holds particular salience when developing new ones. We can raise the possibility of and ask about risks or costs that may be eliciting concern. For instance, program leadership and staff may have concern about the evaluation's findings or the results' potential impact on their "bottom line." It can be useful to name the issues explicitly and then have the opportunity to address them head on. Sometimes it can be useful to acknowledge and appreciate the very real risks about which a program or organizational head may be concerned. Some concerns can also readily be reframed. For example, negative findings are a concern for potential funders, board members, staff, and other stakeholders if the organization chooses not to respond; however, when an organization recognizes that results do not align with the intended effects and demonstrates that they are seeking to improve the quality of their program, that focus on improvement can actually be of benefit.

Explore—and demonstrate—possible benefits. We recommend, early on, inquiring about questions of interest to program or initiative leadership. What do they want to know (but have not had the capacity to answer themselves)? How could the evaluation yield useful information that would help them improve their program? (See Chapter 1 for questions that programs might consider addressing in an evaluation.) When possible, it can also be illuminating to hear from program staff, ask about their questions, and learn their observations. In such discussions, it is helpful to underscore the importance of the evaluation for the intended beneficiaries of the effort—we try to emphasize the goal of optimizing the potential benefits for that targeted population (e.g., we want to maximize the strength and quality of the program for all of the enrolled children). Staff in social programs are generally drawn to that work because of their commitment to improving the well-being of the children, families, or other intended beneficiaries of the program. As such, they are often very receptive to evaluation efforts that can lead to improvements in their ability to benefit their clientele.

In addition, early on in an evaluation, there is utility in providing brief summaries of findings, in digestible formats. Compelling visuals or preliminary findings regarding possible trends can help those associated with the program have a more clear sense of what evaluation results could "look like" and how the data may be useful to them. For instance, summaries of the needs and challenges faced by intended program beneficiaries can help an organization's leadership and staff to define the scope of the problem(s) they are trying to address, and this information can be used in their grant applications and fundraising materials. It can also lead to program staff identifying additional questions that the data might answer, further investing the program staff and leadership in the evaluation efforts. A key is using early data to demonstrate the potential yield and usefulness, the promise, of the evaluation.

We have been able to see the fruits of demonstrating such promise or helping a program toward "small wins" repeatedly over the years. As one example, we have partnered (in various roles) for over a decade with a local agency that runs multiple different programs in our community. The director of the program that had the least information about its function and impact, and the least capacity to track and report data, consistently shared that she and her staff were not interested in an evaluation; they did not need it, they knew the program worked, and they did not want to subject their staff or program participants to evaluation processes. Over a period of years, our doctoral students (under our supervision) worked with the agency's other two programs, helping them develop or clarify logic models (see Chapter 1) and build capacity for tracking and reporting data that would be of interest to them. Agency leadership and the program directors shared their enthusiasm for their changes and the newfound capacity. In one meeting, with multiple diverse stakeholders present, the agency's executive director shared how, because of one of our student's efforts with one program and the new data to which this executive director now had access, he was making some changes in how he was allocating resources to the program. The data shed important new light on some person power needs and how they could make a difference. In fact, after this work with the agency's other two programs, the director of the third program evidenced a shift in her perspective—she became very interested in having one of our students work with her program, enhancing their capacity to track, use, and report data.

CLOSING THOUGHTS

While there are many challenges in doing community-based evaluation work, those challenges also yield opportunities for fruitful partnerships—and the chance to make a difference by facilitating needed change for social good. Evaluation offers some clear promise for having this kind of impact; however, all potential partners do not necessarily share this view, and all partnerships are not necessarily successful.

In this chapter, we discuss some of the common pitfalls that we and other evaluators encounter. Some of the issues can be readily addressed. For instance, an agency that focuses on outputs—and that has leadership and staff that want to learn and get better—is a well-suited candidate to expand their focus to questions about outcomes and, more broadly, for building evaluation capacity (see Chapters 7 and 13). Similarly, those who direct and run programming for which evaluation has been focused solely on outcomes will often have interest in how they can improve, how to "connect the dots," and how to capture the specific impact of their efforts. Those collaborations can be very positive.

It can be much harder to partner when critical leaders or staff are not interested or willing participants in the effort. There are multiple stakeholders and influences at play in any evaluation and any potential partnership. Every organization or program head does not really want to know or learn about what has gone well versus less well. As evaluators, we can communicate directly, work with stakeholders to design and conduct a strong evaluation, and consider data-guided actions to which the results point. However, as we have conveyed in this chapter, we do not always have control over (or access to needed) data or the degree to which our evaluation results and recommendations are used. Sometimes, difficult dynamics can create tensions (e.g., relationally, ethically) or raise concerns about the political or relational implications of our work and our own decisions and actions. In such circumstances, we need to stay true to our own values and moral code. Evaluation projects will come and go, but our integrity is the bedrock on which many relationships, and our careers, are constructed.

While every attempted partnership does not work and does not result in a successful collaboration, and those issues can impact our evaluations, we believe that it is important to keep trying. The opportunity to effect change and to influence the impact and reach of programs, organizations, and systems is a significant motivator, and evaluation is a prime mechanism for our communities to know how to allocate resources to address important issues. We have found that a partnership-based approach is particularly useful in facilitating evaluation-focused collaborations. The next chapter engages this topic in some detail.

FURTHER READING

Access Alliance Community-Based Research Team, in collaboration with Switzer, S., & Adams, M. (2012). *Community-based research toolkit: Resources and tools for doing research with community for social change.* http://communityresearchcanada.ca/wp-content/uploads/2018/05/Community-Based-Participatory-Research-CBPR.pdf

Centers for Disease Control and Prevention. *Introduction to program evaluation for public health programs: A self-study guide.* https://www.cdc.gov/eval/guide/introduction/index.htm

Heider, C. (2016). *What happens after the evaluation is completed?* Independent Evaluation Group/World Bank Group. https://ieg.worldbankgroup.org/blog/what-comes-after-evaluation-completed

Israel, B. A., Schulz, A. J., Parker, E. A., & Becker, A. B. (1998). Review of community-based research: Assessing partnership approaches to improve public health. *Annual Review of Public Health, 19*, 173–202.

Macfarlan, A. (2014). *Lessons learnt.* Post at BetterEvaluation.org. https://www.betterevaluation.org/en/evaluation-options/lessons_learnt

Also see the Community Toolbox, administered via the University of Kansas: https://ctb.ku.edu/en

KEY CONCEPTS

Iatrogenic effects: Possible unintended, harmful, or negative consequences.

Implementation fidelity: The degree to which the program or initiative is being conducted in a manner that is consistent with the model, intervention, or framework selected for the effort. When practices and processes align strongly with the planned model, the effort is said to have high implementation fidelity.

Outcome evaluation: An approach to evaluation that focuses on the program or initiative's effects, including potential benefits as well as unexpected or negative effects.

Partnership: Working relationship in which the parties involved identify and work toward common interests, build their efforts on the partners' complementary skills and perspectives, and develop processes and establish outcomes that yield mutual benefit.

Partnership approach to evaluation: An approach to evaluation in which the involved parties engage in open and direct communication, employ participatory practices, and ensure that the effort yields mutual benefits. In our view, this approach also uses evaluation to benefit programs, program participants/planned beneficiaries, and organizations.

Process evaluation: An approach to evaluation that focuses on how the program or initiative is operating. It involves monitoring and assessments of implementation. A particular emphasis is on whether the program is being conducted as planned.

QUESTIONS FOR REFLECTION

1. As you reflect on organizations or programs with which you have experience, consider the roles and potential benefits of evaluation for their programming. To what degree were they able to answer questions of interest to their stakeholders? In what ways would evaluation have been helpful?

2. What pitfalls or barriers to evaluation have you encountered in your own experiences or do you know of in your community? What dynamics and influences were at play? Why was evaluation not conducted or, if evaluation occurred, why were its findings not used?

3. Consider how the issues described in this chapter have arisen in your own work. Identify an experience or involvement that faced one or more of these challenges, and describe the strategies you employed—or could have employed—in trying to ensure the usefulness of your efforts.

4. More broadly, consider the nonnegotiable elements in your own approach. That is, what values, principles, or ethical codes guide your work? How do those relate to both the promise and potential benefits of evaluation as well as the possible pitfalls?

REFERENCES

Brashears, F., Davis, C., & Katz-Leavy, J. (2012). Systems of care: The story behind the numbers. *American Journal of Community Psychology, 49*(3-4), 494–502. doi:10.1007/s10464-011-9452-z

Center for Mental Health Services. (2003). *CMHS national evaluation: Aggregate data profile report—Communities funded from 1997 to 2000.* Atlanta, GA: ORC Macro.

Center for Mental Health Services. (2004). *Comprehensive community mental health services program for children and their families evaluation findings: Annual report to Congress 2004.* Atlanta, GA: Macro International.

Cook, J. R., & Kilmer, R. P. (2004). Evaluating systems of care: Missing links in children's mental health research. *Journal of Community Psychology, 32*(6), 655–674. doi:10.1002/jcop.20024

Cook, J. R., & Kilmer, R. P. (2012). Systems of care: New partnerships for community psychology. *American Journal of Community Psychology, 49*(3-4), 393–403. doi:10.1007/s10464-012-9516-8

Cook, J. R., Kothandapany, N., Weber, L. J., Wall-Hill, S., & Kilmer, R. P. (2008). Evaluation of a family organization: Integrating local and national evaluation data. In C. Newman, C. Liberton, K. Kutash, & R. Friedman (Eds.), *Agenda and Proceedings: 21st Annual Research Conference: A System of Care for Children's Mental Health: Expanding the Research Base* (pp. 185–186). Tampa, FL: University of South Florida, Louis de la Parte Florida Mental Health Institute, Research and Training Center for Children's Mental Health.

Durlak, J. A., & DuPre, E. P. (2008). Implementation matters: A review of research on the influence of implementation on program outcomes and the factors affecting implementation. *American Journal of Community Psychology, 41*(3-4), 327–350. doi:10.1007/s10464-008-9165-0

Fixsen, D., Naoom, S., Blase, K., Friedman, R., & Wallace, F. (2005). *Implementation research: A synthesis of the literature.* Tampa, FL: University of South Florida, Louis de la Parte Florida Mental Health Institute, National Implementation Research Network.

Gilna, D. (2016). "Scared Straight" programs are counterproductive. *Prison Legal News.* Retrieved from https://www.prisonlegalnews.org/news/2016/jun/3/scared-straight-programs-are-counter-productive/

Haber, M., Cook, J. R., Kilmer, R. P., & Hemphill, B. (2010, March). *Relationships of child and family team meeting processes to initial and long-term changes in youth functioning.* Paper presented at the 23rd Annual Mental Health Research and Policy Conference, Tampa, FL.

Hemphill, B., Cook, J. R., & Kilmer, R. P. (2010, March). *Child and family team processes as predictors of changes in youth functioning.* Paper presented at the 23rd Annual Mental Health Research and Policy Conference, Tampa, FL.

Holden, E. W., Santiago, R. L., Manteuffel, B. A., Stephens, R. L., Brannan, A. M., & Soler, R. (2003). Systems of care demonstration projects: Innovation, evaluation, and sustainability. In A. J. Pumariega & N. C. Winters (Eds.), *The handbook of child and adolescent systems of care: The new community psychiatry* (pp. 432–458). Jossey-Bass.

Johnson, V. A., Bishop, J. T., Malo, A., Lott, F. M., Wilson, C. A., Kilmer, R. P., & Cook, J. R. (2011, March). *Assessing the impact of family support programming in a system of care: Associations between type and intensity of support provided and family outcomes.* Poster presented at the 24th Annual Mental Health Research and Policy Conference, Tampa, FL.

Kilmer, R. P. (November, 2015). *Promises and pitfalls in program evaluation: Applied community research and … inaction.* Invited colloquium-Department of Psychology Excite and Engage Speaker Series, University of North Carolina at Charlotte.

Kilmer, R. P., & Cook, J. R. (2012). Moving forward with systems of care: Needs and new directions. *American Journal of Community Psychology, 49*(3-4), 580–587. doi:10.1007/s10464-012-9513-y

Kilmer, R. P., Cook, J. R., & Palamaro Munsell, E. (2010). Moving from principles to practice: Recommended policy changes to promote family-centered care. *American Journal of Community Psychology, 46*(3-4), 332–341. doi:10.1007/s10464-010-9350-9

Kilmer, R. P., Wall-Hill, S., Cook, J. R., Kothandapany, N., & Weber, L. J. (2009). Evaluating Parent-VOICE: Building family organization sustainability through family-university collaboration. In S. Swart, B. Friesen, A. Holman, & N. Aue (Eds.), *Building on family strengths: Research and services in support of children and their families* (pp. 164–168). Portland, OR: Proceedings of the Building on Family Strengths Annual Conference and State of the Science Report. Portland State University, Research and Training Center on Family Support and Children's Mental Health.

Kloos, B., Hill, J., Thomas, E., Wandersman, A., Elias, M. J., & Dalton, J. H. (2012). *Community psychology: Linking individuals and communities* (3rd ed.). Belmont, CA: Cengage Learning.

Petrosino, A., Turpin-Petrosino, C., & Buehler, J. (2005). "Scared Straight" and other juvenile awareness programs for preventing juvenile delinquency. *Campbell Systematic Reviews, 1*(1), 1–62. doi:10.4073/csr.2004.2

Petrosino, A., Turpin-Petrosino, C., Hollis-Peel, M. E., & Lavenberg, J. G. (2013). Scared straight and other juvenile awareness programs for preventing juvenile delinquency: A systematic review. *Campbell Systematic Reviews, 9*(1), 1–55. doi:10.4073/csr.2013.5

Rivlin, A. M. (1971). *Systematic thinking for social action*. Washington, DC: Brookings Institution.

Schorr, L. B. (1997). *Common purpose: Strengthening families and neighborhoods to rebuild America*. New York: Anchor Books, Doubleday.

Tynan, J. M., Larson, J. C., Mihalski, J. L., Bishop Scott, J. T., Hogan, K. S., Cook, J. R., & Kilmer, R. P. (2015, June). Translating research into action: Successes and barriers enacting recommendations within a school system. In J. C. Larson (Chair), *A partnership approach to evaluating a publicly funded pre-kindergarten program: Key findings and action steps*. Symposium conducted at the 15th Biennial Conference of the Society for Community Research and Action, Lowell, MA.

CHAPTER 3

SETTING THE STAGE

A Partnership Approach to Evaluation

Ryan P. Kilmer, James R. Cook, and Laura Marie Armstrong

Learning Objectives

1. Identify key practices that support a partnership-based approach to evaluation.

2. Become familiar with core elements of community-based participatory research.

3. Learn ways in which diverse stakeholders may benefit from a partnership-based approach.

4. Understand strategies for facilitating partnerships.

We have built this text around a partnership-based approach to evaluation. To us, this is just the way we do business. Besides the fact that we enjoy working with others, there are several reasons that we actively collaborate with partners on applied research and evaluation. First, we value working with others who share our interests in evaluation and want to improve their programs and communities. Second, the questions and issues we address and the efforts we evaluate are dealt with more effectively when we draw from our partners' different (often complementary) perspectives, skill sets, and experiences. Because the responsiveness and effectiveness of our systems, organizations, and programs depend on a host of factors that no single individual can fully understand and no one discipline can frame adequately, let alone change, it is critical to collaborate effectively with community partners who bring different perspectives, experiences, and backgrounds. Doing so maximizes our collective understanding of the program and its context and enables us to be more effective in helping it improve.

In our work, the partnership generally involves a combination of academics/researchers/evaluators and community stakeholders (not surprising because we are academics working in the community). These community stakeholders can vary, depending on the particular program or initiative and its context. Almost always, partners include program or initiative staff, from management to line workers, and those within a program, organization, or initiative who are charged with implementing any evaluation efforts. In addition, there are times when external funders of the program and/or the evaluation are partners, because they have a stake in ensuring the program is having beneficial effects and is operating efficiently. Other organizations or programs that work with the program or initiative of interest can be important partners, if they provide support to one another or have shared goals or clientele. The intended beneficiaries of the program can likewise be important partners, because they offer a unique and valuable perspective, they often have little say in the operation of a program, and they have the most to gain if the program works well (and the most to lose if it does not).[1]

The participatory nature of a partnership approach to evaluation, involving multiple stakeholders, enhances the work (and its potential impact). The evaluation effort benefits from the integration of the different perspectives and capacities of the partners. In our view, the creation of strong partnerships can yield (a) enhanced quality and availability of data; (b) questions that reflect both science and practice; (c) methods applied effectively within contexts and in work with specific populations; and (d) more useful science and more effective practice (Cook & Kilmer, 2008).

To obtain such benefits, we need to be clear about how we are approaching the work and our potential partners. For instance, as evaluators, we need to be mindful of our working knowledge and its limits. Let's consider an example. Years ago, we were asked to help evaluate the work of a grassroots organization that provided family support in multiple forms (e.g., Kilmer et al., 2009). With an eye toward their long-term sustainability, organizational leaders wanted evidence of their impact in helping families, as well as information to support other related goals (e.g., assessing if their efforts were improving family-centered practice in the mental health system). Of salience here, the organizational partners knew their families, their programs, their experiences, their needs and challenges, and their changes better than we did—unequivocally. They had access to the people involved and had questions borne of their practice, the work in which they engaged daily. We, as university partners, had greater expertise in design and analysis and knowledge regarding the broader system(s) (e.g., public mental health) in which they were functioning. We also had some knowledge of the literature on family support and had questions that grew from our knowledge of theory, systems, and the literature. Partnering and drawing on our shared expertise was critical to moving forward, both with that evaluation and with what evolved into a multiyear partnership focusing on building capacity to use data, strengthening programming, and working toward sustainability (e.g., Cook & Kilmer, 2008; Cook et al., 2007, 2008; Kilmer et al., 2009). The key point here is that we all needed to recognize one another's strengths as well as our own limitations. Considering one another's strengths and limitations can help ensure that there is a match between the needs present and the expertise and competence available (see, e.g., Cowen, 1985). Put simply: We have to be comfortable with what we know and, of equal importance, what we do not.

In addition, in considering the initiation or development of a partnership, it is important to underscore that a "partnership" is not reflected solely by the presence of a contract or a memorandum of understanding. There are countless instances of such structures or documents being in place and parties facing tremendous challenges in working together, because of disparate goals that interfere with implementation of coordinated efforts, limiting the progress made. Rather, partnerships need to identify and work toward common interests, develop processes that provide mutual

> At their core, partnerships are built around relationships. In turn, partnership-based evaluation is grounded in relationships.

---

[1] Please note that we use "intended beneficiaries," rather than "client" or "consumer," because there are potentially many intended beneficiaries who may not have direct contact with a program, and simply serving a person does not necessarily mean that person benefits from the program.

benefit, and build their efforts on the partners' complementary skills (Cook & Kilmer, 2012, 2016; Kilmer & Cook, 2015).

Partnership-based evaluation is grounded in the relationships developed among the partners. Whether discussing options in a planning meeting, considering evaluation questions and processes, or working to interpret findings, the quality of the relationship among the partners is paramount. This relationship is facilitated by several key practices:

1. *Engage in open, direct communication.* This is foundational, regardless of the content or focus of discussion. Whether talking or writing about goals, needs, and objectives or about what is working well versus not, the bedrock of a partnership relationship is honest, sound communication (e.g., Cook & Kilmer, 2012). Email or phone contact is often necessary and important, but in-person interaction is also crucial (Cook & Kilmer, 2012).

2. *Ensure that the partnership is mutually beneficial.* As part of building trust and developing partnership relationships, it is necessary for communication and activity to focus on identifying and addressing needs (in the short- and long-term) relevant to all partners (Cook & Kilmer, 2012). This can help all partners gauge the degree to which they can contribute to meeting those needs. While a focus on the partners' needs (e.g., documenting program effectiveness to funders) is important, perhaps even more important is sustaining a focus on accomplishing the goals of the program, which generally means meeting the needs of a program or initiative's intended beneficiaries. A focus on program goals can help ensure that the inevitable costs of evaluation efforts (e.g., resources needed to build capacity, time spent in collecting data) are viewed in light of a shared sense of mission to improve the outcomes for the organization or program's intended beneficiaries. This shared sense of purpose can be important in maintaining a sense of trust and a spirit of collaboration.

3. *Employ practices consistent with community-based participatory research (CBPR) or participatory action research.* CBPR has been defined as "a collaborative research approach that is designed to ensure and establish structures for participation by communities affected by the issue being studied, representatives of organizations, and researchers in all aspects of the research process to improve health and well-being through taking action, including social change" (Viswanathan et al., 2004). This approach is well suited to partnership-based evaluation to facilitate social change and impact. Core CBPR practices include shared governance of the effort; joint decisions regarding questions, measures, and methods; co-learning and reciprocal transfer of expertise; joint discussion of how to use and interpret findings; and mutual ownership of processes and products (see, e.g., Balcazar et al., 1998; Cook & Kilmer, 2008; Viswanathan et al., 2004). Thus, community partners are full and collaborative participants in all elements of the evaluation. Such steps put principles of partnership into actual practice and increase the likelihood that our evaluation products have an impact.

These steps are also consistent with prior recommendations to attend to "needs" and "contracts" (Cowen, 1985) in community-based work. Early on in the partnership it is useful to clarify the community partner's expertise relative to evaluation, the efforts they have made in the past to collect and utilize data, and the degree to which they have effected change based on data they have collected. In addition, it is important to understand the potential changes the partner might make to the program and the information you might need to understand the nature and extent of those changes. Keeping in mind that the goal of evaluation is to help the program or organization improve their ability to accomplish their mission, the partners must be clear regarding the needs (for the program, agency, neighborhood, or initiative); the evaluators must examine whether they have the relevant competencies, expertise, or interests to help the effort; and the partners need to negotiate a clear agreement about the specific roles and responsibilities for all partners (see Cowen, 1985 for more; also see Kilmer et al., 2018). This agreement should include an explicit understanding of what is needed to accomplish the evaluation—resources, access to data, facilitation of contacts, collection of data, cooperation of program staff, strategies for developing a shared understanding of and dissemination of findings, and the like—from all parties.

> **CBPR is a collaborative approach characterized by dual decision-making, shared governance, co-learning and transfer of expertise, and joint ownership of an effort's processes and products. See Balcazar et al. (1998) and Viswanathan et al. (2004) for more.**

It is important for evaluators to work with program leaders or stakeholders to understand the program's objectives and intended outcomes and the practices they use to accomplish those goals. This is part of the process of developing a logic model (which depicts the program's theory of change, as discussed in Chapter 1) to help ensure that all the partners are clear about how the particular program elements and activities are expected to contribute to accomplishing the program's mission. This then can help clarify the specific information that is required at each step of the program to identify and address questions of interest. The bottom line is that the partners work to ensure that program stakeholders will have the information they need in order to make sound decisions to improve the program. The partners then begin the specific work of developing a detailed plan for evaluation that accounts for the identified needs and resources.

The processes and specificity involved when negotiating an evaluation plan can vary considerably. For instance, agreement on the parameters of the work or on the elements of an evaluation contract can depend on how the partnership arose, the nature of the effort at hand, and the role for the evaluation team. Sometimes it is necessary to collect data and conduct a formal needs assessment or to hone in on the community partners' and stakeholders' needs through focus groups, meetings with stakeholder groups, or contacts with key personnel from the community setting; those efforts can be built into the evaluation plan. Regardless of the specific steps, the presence of dedicated funding, whether a grant or contract for a project or for an individual's time and expertise, typically necessitates an explicit and detailed scope of work that maps out the nature of the job at hand as well as key products or deliverables. Having a specific scope of work and a clear contract, with inputs and feedback from key parties (evaluator[s], community partners), can serve to protect the interests and resources of all parties and ensure that the partnership is mutually beneficial.

Throughout this text there are frequent references to a partnership-based approach, strategies to facilitate partnerships and mutual benefit, and the use of evaluation to benefit programs, program participants, and organizations. The next section of this chapter considers an in-depth example of one of our multiyear partnerships. This example illustrates many key notions for partnership-focused work.

AN EVALUATION PARTNERSHIP IN ACTION: A MULTI-YEAR PARTNERSHIP TO BENEFIT AN EARLY CHILDHOOD EDUCATION PROGRAM

We (RPK and JRC) have worked together for over two decades and, at the end of the day, a prime, cross-cutting goal of our collaborative efforts has been to improve programs, services, and supports for children and families, many of whom have experienced significant adversity, been marginalized, and/or faced socioeconomic disadvantage. We have chosen this specific evaluation partnership as our example here because it demonstrates the contextual influences that can serve as an impetus for evaluation (and influence the degree to which an evaluation's findings and recommendations are used), the partnership practices we employed, and the real-world relevance of the work. Over the span of this multiyear partnership, which has been supported by local and federal funds, we have presented components of this work and some of our core partnership practices at professional conferences (Cook & Kilmer, 2014; Kilmer & Cook, 2015; Kilmer et al., 2017, 2018; Larson et al., 2015; Mihalski et al., 2015; Tynan et al., 2015) and disseminated them via other outlets (Cook & Kilmer, 2012, 2014, 2017, 2018). This case description is an overview of our several years of collaboration and the partnership-oriented practices we employed.

Background and context. The program of focus is the Bright Beginnings Pre-Kindergarten Program, a publicly-funded early childhood education program of the Charlotte-Mecklenburg (NC) Schools (CMS). The program has two core curricular goals: (1) support the development of young children's language skills, literacy, and conceptual understanding; and (2) foster the development of their social–emotional skills (e.g., Cook & Kilmer, 2017; Kilmer et al., 2018). The program also aims to engage parents. Children are identified for the program via a multicomponent screening approach, with the main eligibility criterion that they are at risk for not being ready for kindergarten; that is, children score below their peers on aspects of cognitive, developmental, and/or preacademic functioning (see Cook & Kilmer, 2014).

Going back several years, the program was the target of considerable attention. In the face of budgetary challenges stemming from broader national and state economic conditions, school board members and system administrators were asking a range of questions. They wondered: "Does it 'work'?" "Is it effective?" "Is it worth the cost?" (Kilmer, 2015). Some wondered if funding the program was consistent with the school system's formal mission and charge, which focused on kindergarten through 12th grade education.

These issues came to a head in early 2011. The system leadership proposed dramatic cuts to Bright Beginnings, leading to noteworthy levels of advocacy work, media attention, and school board meeting time (Kilmer, 2015). Diverse community stakeholders advocated for maintaining the program and argued against the cuts in funding, speaking at school board meetings and writing letters to county commissioners, underscoring the potential benefits of quality early childhood education and the importance of evaluating the local effort in order to have evidence to support decision making (RPK gave one such talk and wrote a set of letters). What became clear over the course of weeks of discussion was that the system did not have research evidence to support the program's effectiveness. The need for evaluation was evident, exemplified by the statement of the school superintendent that, "at this time, there is not sufficient or valid evidence to support a funding decision on research from CMS" (Doss Helms, 2011, p. A1).

The school system did make major cuts to the program's budget, which included closure of dedicated early childhood centers that housed the program and the integration of the program classrooms into elementary schools. However, the budgetary debates, media coverage, and advocacy efforts led to calls for the school system and its Office of Accountability to initiate a dedicated evaluation of Bright Beginnings. The school system then issued a request for proposals to evaluate the program.

Our involvement: Initial steps. Beginning in 2012—and separate from the evaluation proposal process—we were asked to examine the system's archival data from multiple program years (i.e., students in prekindergarten from 2006 to 2008 and from 2011 to 2013). We analyzed student change during the prekindergarten program year as well as into elementary school. Our analyses compared children who had received the program to those who had not, and we also examined possible differences within the Bright Beginnings group. Analyses showed that children evidenced gains in the program but, of particular relevance for potential program improvement, that (1) the students' scores varied dramatically across program sites and (2) they were more likely to retain the gains they made in the program when they went to more proficient elementary schools; however, overall, program children were more likely to go to less proficient schools (Cook & Kilmer, 2014) . Our results pointed to the need for a prospective evaluation that focused on program processes and implementation in order to understand why children improved more in some classrooms. This information could then be used to help the program ensure a consistently positive experience for children.

Based, in part, on the initial work using the archival data and the recommendations regarding evaluation that we had made, we were asked to consider conducting a more extensive, prospective evaluation of the program. In initial meetings with leadership from the Office of Accountability and the Early Childhood Programs, we discussed their priorities for the evaluation, the nature of the data being tracked, and their concerns about the program. Given the program's difficult recent history, it was particularly crucial to ensure that we agreed about the importance of understanding both the processes and outcomes of the program, to support program improvements. These discussions led to a contract with CMS to evaluate the program in 2013–2014.

The initial evaluation. Once we had agreed upon a contract, our initial meetings with the director of the early childhood education department, her deputy director, and other program staff focused on clarifying what they wanted to know and what issues they wanted to address. These discussions were aided greatly by the clear and unwavering commitment of the early childhood director and her staff to do what was best for the children served by the program. They resonated with our desire to use the evaluation results to strengthen the program and clearly saw the potential benefits of using data to guide their decisions and to inform possible refinements or innovation.

We worked in partnership with the school system—including early childhood program leadership and staff and system researchers from their Office of Accountability—to clarify program goals and understand the program's curriculum and processes. These discussions informed the development of a logic model for the program (see Chapter 1) and were absolutely critical for the evaluation. For instance, we learned that one of the program's main goals was to enhance children's social and emotional development; however, the program had never systematically assessed this domain of functioning. Similarly, program leadership expressed their concerns about variability in curricular implementation, particularly given that the program was now being implemented in many different elementary schools. Such information was imperative to identifying our research questions and developing a well-targeted evaluation.

Collectively, the partners identified multiple goals for the evaluation, which would require substantial new data collection and work with archival data. We sought to

- examine implementation of the curriculum in the classroom;

- assess gains in verbal ability and social–emotional development;

- examine characteristics of teachers, schools, and parents and their relation to child gains; and

- identify strategies for improving outcomes for all students.

As the evaluation's central questions evolved, we identified or developed evaluation measures and processes together to ensure that the data collected could answer their questions. We collaborated in a time-intensive process of refining and pilot-testing observation measures and training our evaluation team to conduct classroom observations. We relied both on our search of the literature and our partners' vast experience and resources to identify and revise measures that would assess the dimensions that they viewed as most critical for student learning. Guided by insights from program leadership and staff, we conducted the initial training of our staff, followed by the assistant program director conducting classroom observations with our staff and debriefing with us to help us discriminate critically important classroom behaviors. This collaborative effort helped ensure that the methods had sufficient rigor and enhanced the credibility of the effort (the assistant director was able to report confidently to teachers that our student staff members were skilled in making appropriate classroom observations). We collectively determined the best sampling strategies, and they communicated with school administrators and program teachers to facilitate our entry into schools. They also worked to make sure we could access data collected by the school system (following appropriate review board approvals from our university and the school system).

The multicomponent evaluation design included the observation of 99 classrooms in late fall and late spring and teacher assessment of social–emotional development of all children in the program at the beginning and end of the year. We also surveyed teachers about their experience of school climate and support, conducted phone interviews with parents to gauge their impressions and satisfaction, and held focus groups with program "coaches" (who support teachers' implementation of the curriculum and early childhood best practices) to learn their views of their roles and program processes. All of these elements required close collaboration between the evaluation team and the program leaders, who encouraged teachers to complete the social–emotional measures and surveys and facilitated our contact with parents. These processes were planned in monthly "management team" meetings involving the evaluation and program staff, as well as representatives of the Office of Accountability, and while there were regular concerns about adding to the workload of teachers, at each juncture the program leadership determined that the data were essential for their operation and ongoing understanding of the program and its functioning.

It is beyond the scope of this chapter to describe the evaluation's findings in detail. In brief summary, the Bright Beginnings program students gained in verbal/receptive language ability and social–emotional development over the course of the school year— and they showed greater social–emotional growth when their teachers reported a positive school climate (Cook & Kilmer, 2014). We also found that there was significant variation in teacher implementation of the program curriculum and that better implementation of the program curriculum was associated with higher levels of improvements in children's social–emotional functioning.

Based on the evaluation findings, we, as a partnership, identified a set of actionable recommendations. They included the following:

1. Strengthen coaching of teachers to improve instruction, which should then contribute to greater student growth. This "enhanced coaching" would entail the use of structured observations to guide instruction and efforts to build stronger coordination with principals to provide consistent feedback to teachers.

2. Assess social–emotional development of students early in the year and provide teachers with feedback and guidance to help them individualize instruction and build on children's development.

3. Increase the Pre-Kindergarten Program's capacity to collect and manage data about parents and children in the program, with a particular emphasis on using screening data to improve instruction.

What happened next? The partnership team was disappointed to learn that the school system did not have funds allocated to continue the evaluative effort beyond that first year. Despite the lack of funding to support our work, we continued to collaborate with the early childhood program and the school system over the next 2 years via student-led projects (e.g., Tynan et al., 2017) and other efforts, including an exploration of chronic absenteeism (Messinger et al., 2017; also see Chapter 14). We then collaboratively worked to develop a proposal for federal funding (submitted by author JRC, Lindsay Messinger from the school system's Office of Accountability, and authors RPK and LMA, with program leadership as key senior personnel) that would help us further build the partnership and implement and evaluate the recommendations from the prior evaluation findings. This proposal was funded for 2016–2018 by the Institute of Education Sciences (IES) of the U.S. Department of Education.

At this point, the partnership took a rather different turn. Whereas the contract with CMS was clearly for the purpose of evaluating the Bright Beginnings program, the federal funding was explicitly designed to build upon the partnership (through strengthening the program's capacity to collect, manage, and utilize data) and develop, pilot, and evaluate changes in the program (such as helping teachers increase their focus on children's social–emotional functioning and developing enhancements to the coaching model that could support improved instruction). This connection between evaluation and action (and further evaluation … and action) is central to our work and approach.

Because of this shift in the nature of the partnership, we formalized the management team used in the prior evaluation efforts, which included university faculty and graduate students, early education program leadership and staff, and school system researchers. This group met regularly—typically monthly, but more frequently when it was necessary to establish and implement time-sensitive processes—and discussed the project's multiple goals, needed activities, questions and choice points, and action steps. This partnership management team worked out the logistics of the project's aims, balancing the goals of the partnership regarding the use of data, ongoing program practices and deadlines, and the task demands on teachers and program staff. These discussions and decisions were grounded in respect, appreciation of our different knowledge and skills, and openness to our varying perspectives. At the partnership management team's core was a mutual trust, with a clear understanding that we were all working together to increase the likelihood that all children in the program would receive the best instruction possible.

The importance of the partnership was apparent for each of the effort's three main components. In the focus on improving social–emotional development, the prior evaluation findings had suggested that teachers' receipt of feedback about children's social–emotional development was related to greater gains in their development. This led to our working with the program leadership and curricular specialist around assessing children's social–emotional functioning, sharing feedback with teachers and, as a new step, identifying and providing teachers with specific, individualized strategies that teachers could use in the classroom to help students make additional gains. As part of our ongoing evaluation of the broader work, teacher feedback about the process then led to the provision of feedback about students earlier in the year and the development of improved strategies that could address a broader range of behaviors (and build on foundational skills). The collective examination of the findings by the partnership led to collaborative efforts to improve the intervention. Our analysis of the impact of these changes is ongoing, but the available results suggest that, consistent with our findings from the 2013 to 2014 evaluation, program students improved in social–emotional functioning and students improved *more* when their teacher received feedback and strategies (see Gadaire et al., 2018, 2020); our analysis of the impact of the intervention modifications is ongoing.

For the enhanced coaching component of the project, the development of the enhanced coaching model was a collaborative, participatory process, involving program leadership, principals, and coaches (see Simmons et al., 2018, 2019, in press). While the enhanced coaching approach included multiple elements (including coaches providing key information to principals and increasing principal involvement), the data-guided nature of the coaching (based on structured observations) was the prime component of the resultant model. The observation measure used in the prior evaluation was shortened, based on data collected in the prior evaluation and input from program leadership and coaches, to make sure it focused on critical teacher behaviors. These classroom observations were coordinated such that two members of our evaluation team joined coaches to observe and rate the practices in each coach's classrooms. As we piloted the enhanced coaching model, we built in teacher self-assessments of their performance on the domains assessed by the observations, tracked the coaches' feedback to their teachers, assessed administrators' engagement, and provided coaches with feedback regarding teacher practices. Because coaches wanted to help teachers make mid-year corrections, we built in a mid-year observation so that coaches could provide feedback that could translate into possible improvements (and, ideally, a stronger program experience for children) by the end of the year (Simmons et al., in press). As of the writing of this chapter, analyses are ongoing regarding whether the self-assessments were associated with teacher improvements, the degree to which coaching emphases translated to differences in practice, and whether the enhanced coaching yielded "value add" above the standard coaching as usual as well as the social–emotional feedback intervention. Some early results suggest that children whose teachers received enhanced coaching evidenced significantly greater social–emotional growth than those whose teachers had coaching as usual, and that enhanced coaching led to greater absolute (but not significant) gains relative to the social–emotional feedback intervention. Clearly, the collaborative nature of the partnership led to changes that may have strengthened the program and improved outcomes, and we built in evaluation strategies to test their impact at each step.

Regarding the third aim, to increase the capacity of the program to collect, manage, and use data, the goals included improving program efficiency and the quality of the data collected, increasing the access to and utility of data for program staff, and facilitating future evaluation and research. Our efforts focused on the program's screening process used to select children for the program. At the time of our initial evaluation, screening measures were largely completed manually via pencil and paper, with scores calculated by screeners and results stored in paper files that accompanied children to their elementary school. These processes were slow, prone to calculation errors, and the resulting data did not appear to be used by teachers or administrators. Consequently, one of our graduate students, Drew Gadaire, met with the screening staff, learned their processes, and discussed with them ideas for how they might streamline their efforts. These discussions led to multiple steps, including migrating most screening measures to iPads and Google forms (informed by our findings and discussions, they had done this with some measures), automated calculation of scores, and improved management of more detailed, item-level information. Screening staff tested and provided feedback about proposed revisions and refinements of the processes and platform. Management team members also discussed how to share these data with the Office of Accountability and how they could be used by leadership and others to facilitate decision making or improve the program. These interactions contributed to a better process, with better data that could be disseminated to teachers and principals in a way that would facilitate better placements for children and increased support in the classroom. Involving all the relevant stakeholders in the process was critical to achieving a positive outcome, and these changes in their capacity to collect and manage data can persist beyond grant funding or involvement by the evaluation staff (with the exception, perhaps, of occasional consultation).

These changes in the screening data collection led to other modifications that enhanced the program's data capacity and processes. For example, beyond our team's efforts to help program staff identify some better screening measures, Mr. Gadaire also demonstrated new ways to use the screening data to calculate the eligibility "scores" required for assigning children to the program. He employed a multistep, data-guided approach, with participatory elements, to modify the program's use of data and identify a new eligibility formula to ensure that the children with the greatest need were selected for the program (see Gadaire, 2018, and Gadaire et al.,

2019 for more). In addition, we provided to Office of Accountability staff the code and data used to develop the feedback that we had provided to teachers regarding their ratings of children's social–emotional development. Their analysts subsequently built this feedback into the school system's data "portal," providing teachers and administrators the capacity to access the data at any time, without any involvement by the evaluation team. These modifications provided lasting improvements to the program's capacity to collect, manage, and use data for decision making.

Where are we now? The grant has ended, but analyses are ongoing, and we have reported much of the key findings to our partners in the early childhood program and Office of Accountability. We will continue to share our results and recommendations with our school system partners as well as with a broader audience. With the time-intensive "doing" of the project completed, we have shifted our emphasis to identifying the stories that have evolved and emerged out of this partnership and disseminating our findings and recommendations. Furthermore, we continue to work with our partners at the school system and submitted a federal grant to extend our partnership to address key school system needs and goals. Overall, in light of our ongoing relationship with the program and the school system, we can also continue to develop and test innovation, enhance capacity to track and use data, and conduct evaluative projects that have implications for local practice and policy.

Although the story of this partnership started with the school system and the community raising questions about the value of prekindergarten and why a public system should be responsible for "what parents should have done," this no longer seems to be a subject of debate. While we would like to be able to state that our evaluation findings contributed directly to greater interest in providing high-quality early childhood programming, in fact, the school system itself (not the pre-K or early childhood staff or accountability leadership and personnel) largely ignored the specific findings from the initial evaluation.

However, we have continued to work with the school system and other community partners on efforts using data to increase funding for pre-K programs, and to explore other evaluative research projects that benefit the program and the school system, while providing opportunities for our graduate students to gain valuable research experience. Our partners at the school system continue to make refinements in the program, in part due to the results of our evaluations, and remain committed to ensuring the quality of the prekindergarten experience for all program children.

PARTNERSHIP CHARACTERISTICS, GUIDING NOTIONS, AND STRATEGIES

As we reflect on our partnership with the early childhood education program and the Office of Accountability, there have been noteworthy strengths as well as challenges that bear mention. It has been a true collaborative partnership, with dual decision making and an inclusive partnership management team that functions well. The group's shared history and relationships enhance that functioning; our collective track records support a climate of trust and collegiality. We are able to have in-depth discussions, consider alternatives, and identify multiple strategies for analysis and action.

The partnership management team—and the partnership as a whole—has been characterized by strong relationships; regular, direct, and honest communication (and good listening!); and participatory research practices. Over the years, partners (whether from the school system or the university) have been flexible and responsive to changes as well as opportunities. Several aspects of the partnership helped it work particularly well. Because we used a shared governance approach; relied on joint decisions regarding questions, measures, and methods; drew on complementary perspectives and strengths and put co-learning into action; and fostered a spirit of mutual ownership of the partnership's processes and products, we were able to strike a balance between rigor and practicality (e.g., Balcazar et al., 1998; Kilmer et al., 2018). We worked well together and were able to integrate data collection into ongoing processes, providing means for supporting innovation and its evaluation.

That said, our partnership faced meaningful challenges. For instance, in this large system (upwards of 147,000 students in 176 schools; Charlotte-Mecklenburg Schools, 2017), there are diverse programs and a wide range of needs that have to be addressed, contributing to expectable strains in resources and person power as well as challenges in sustaining attention and focus. These kinds of concerns can slow progress and increase the difficulty faced by those working to effect change.

Nevertheless, this multiyear partnership has yielded short- and long-term benefits across levels and stakeholders. We have sometimes talked about seeking "wins" for all involved stakeholders (e.g., Cook, 2015; Cook & Kilmer, 2014), and this partnership yielded those multiple benefits. Let's consider:

Program leaders and staff. Program administrators received needed information about their program's effectiveness as well as data to guide practice-related decisions and test innovation. The partnership work also resulted in substantially enhanced capacity to track, manage, and report data about program children and the program's function, as well as strategies for building children's prosocial skills and strengthening coaching practices. Staff also obtained information to support or inform their practices, as coaches or classroom teachers. Because they resulted in a more user-friendly and efficient approach, the improvements to the screening process also led to a "win" for those staff in the screening office.

University students. Graduate and undergraduate students on our team gained applied experiences working on an evaluative effort with real-world implications, conducting observations, working with data, and attending meetings with partners. This was especially meaningful for our graduate students who took on project coordinator roles and had very substantive involvements, and was also a positive experience for our undergraduates who played key roles in classroom observations. Instead of *learning about* evaluation and participatory practices, they were engaged in *doing them*, growing their skills as they took on new roles. They were able to observe and participate, learn by doing, and develop their own repertoire of partnership-oriented skills. The data also provided the basis for student theses and student-led conference presentations and manuscripts, valuable products as they build their professional and scholarly records.

Faculty. In addition to being part of an important applied effort that they valued, faculty benefitted from the funds from grants and contracts, which also helped support several graduate students, and from the scholarly products that grew (and continue to grow) out of the work. In a similar vein, the partnership provided good opportunities for the faculty to mentor students in the context of an effective partnership. Such experiences to build practice competencies (in evaluation, CBPR, and work with partners more broadly) fit well with the faculty evaluators' approach to training and mentoring.

School system researchers. Our partners from the school system's Office of Accountability benefited as well. Their own capacity for future research was enhanced by the early childhood program's improved capacity to collect and use data. For instance, it will now be possible for them to draw on prekindergarten information in their own work, including exploring and testing predictive models. They also had the chance to contribute to a project and co-author presentations and publications with like-minded researchers, and the relationships developed have already led to subsequent collaborations.

The university. The university that employs us (and the graduate students) benefited from this partnership in multiple ways. Our grants brought in indirect costs, or overhead, and were in line with university goals to increase external funding. The work itself was also a visible effort in which the capacity and expertise of university faculty were being used to address community needs and support social change; this kind of involvement fits well with the university's growing interest in and support of community engagement. And, finally, the work, particularly the training opportunities yielded for our graduate students, was consistent with the university's mission as an institution of higher learning.

The community. The community also benefited from this partnership because it addressed a significant gap regarding the evaluation of the program with its initial work. Furthermore, because the partners worked to monitor and improve multiple elements of the program, this multiyear effort strengthened the quality of the program received by all enrolled children. The data about the program's effectiveness, as well as possible refinements or modifications, also contributed to the community's evolving discussion on early childhood education and its expansion.

Overall, this evaluation-focused partnership connected applied research and evaluation with real-world programming and used data to guide capacity building, modify practice, and contribute to local efforts to expand early childhood programs. In addition to the practices, strategies, and recommendations for partnership-oriented evaluation we have discussed throughout this chapter (including in the case example), we end our discussion with three key recommendations for facilitating partnerships:

1. *Creatively consider ways to build the relationship(s).* It can be useful to engage with one another outside of meetings, data collection, and the like. We have found real value in scheduling periodic informal or social times to interact and get to know one another and, in some cases, celebrate the partnership's work. If funding and schedules permit, it can also be fruitful to attend conferences together. Such settings provide opportunities for co-learning as well as informal interactions outside of sessions, at meals, or when traveling (Cook & Kilmer, 2012). Those interactions could include discussions of the partnership's work or simply be relationship enhancing.

2. *Think flexibly about ways to work together.* Given the partnership orientation of the team we co-direct, we are frequently exploring ways to work with our partners, even when there are not dedicated funds to support the work. This often starts with something as simple as an inquiry about other questions or needs our partners may have, followed by meetings to hone in on their goals and objectives. Once those are clear, they inform a discussion of options regarding various forms of action. In some cases, this has involved working with them without a contract or funding, simply because of our investment in the organization or program or in improving the education of our students (as a caveat: we recognize that this may not be a viable long-term strategy for many evaluators). Even in such cases, the involvement yielded mutual benefit because it (a) grew the depth

of our partnership and led to additional funded work down the line and (b) provided applied research and evaluation experience for our graduate students. Indeed, student projects—whether in the form of a program milestone project (such as a thesis) or a practicum for credit—can also be a means of maintaining a partnership when specific funding is not available. The student, working under our supervision, can engage in additional capacity building, evaluation, or data-guided program development or advocacy work (see, e.g., Hogan et al., 2017)—such experiences are crucial for the student's training and professional development and can also help as a bridge between contracts or funded projects.

3. *Go beyond the specific, expected task.* This notion clearly has applicability beyond work in evaluation. The principle of going above and beyond can certainly help convey an evaluator's commitment to the partnership and investment in the work. In addition, this recommendation holds relevance because of what is essentially a truism in the real world of community-based research and evaluation: these projects do not always unfold as planned. Rather, conditions or circumstances may change, additional questions of potential interest may emerge, or an evaluation's findings may be open to multiple possible interpretations. It can then be appropriate, even necessary, to go beyond the agreed-upon scope of work—to dig deeper, refine one's methods, and try to understand. This "going beyond" was apparent in our work with the prekindergarten program's screening office—one of our graduate students put in a great deal of time helping them modify and, over time, refine their screening work, automating processes, making changes to improve accessibility and utility, and fielding questions. Similarly, over the course of our work with our early childhood partners, we conducted focus groups or developed surveys that were not part of the initial plan of action, but they served us all well by lending an additional perspective to an issue or decision or increasing our understanding. These kinds of actions can improve the quality of one's work (as well as its practical applications), facilitate strong relationships with one's partners, and help build a reputation for quality work which can lead to other opportunities.

> **Recommended Strategies for Facilitating Partnerships**
>
> - **Creatively consider ways to build relationships.**
>
> - **Think flexibly about ways to work together.**
>
> - **Go beyond the specific, expected task.**
>
> **(Kilmer et al., 2018)**

These strategies and practices can serve to build the connections, relationships, and trust needed for effective partnership work. Those elements are the bedrock for sound evaluation partnerships, for novice and seasoned evaluators alike. We believe it is nonrandom that we have had many multiyear and multiproject partnerships: our partnership-oriented, participatory approach, with a focus on improving program practices, processes, and outcomes, increases the likelihood that the evaluation will (a) align with our partners' needs, wants, and goals; and (b) provide information that can and will be used to improve the program, service, or initiative in question. That is a critical "bottom line."

FURTHER READING

Cook, J. R. (2015). Using evaluation to effect social change: Looking through a community psychology lens. *American Journal of Evaluation*, *36*, 107–117.

Israel, B. A., Schulz, A. J., Parker, E. A., & Becker, A. B. (1998). Review of community-based research: Assessing partnership approaches to improve public health. *Annual Review of Public Health*, *19*, 173–202.

Ochocka, J., Moorlag, E., & Janzen, R. (2010). A framework for entry: PAR values and engagement strategies in community-based research. *Gateways: International Journal of Community Research and Engagement*, *3*, 1–19.

Viswanathan, M., Ammerman, A., Eng, E., Gartlehner, G., Lohr, K. N., Griffith, D., Rhodes, S., Samuel-Hodge, C., Maty, S., Lux, L., Webb, L., Sutton, S. F., Swinson, T., Jackman, A., & Whitener, L. (2004). *Community-based participatory research: Assessing the evidence*. Evidence Report/Technology Assessment No. 99 (Prepared by RTI-University of North Carolina Evidence-based Practice Center under Contract No. 290–02-0016). AHRQ Publication 04-E022-2. Agency for Healthcare Research and Quality.

Also See

Community-Based Research Canada https://communityresearchcanada.ca/

Community-Campus Partnerships for Health https://www.ccphealth.org/

Living Knowledge: The International Science Shop Network https://www.livingknowledge.org/

Society for Community Research and Action http://www.scra27.org/

KEY CONCEPTS

Community-based participatory research (CBPR): "A collaborative research approach that is designed to ensure and establish structures for participation by communities affected by the issue being studied, representatives of organizations, and researchers in all aspects of the research process to improve health and well-being through taking action, including social change" (see Viswanathan et al., 2004).

Logic model: A graphic illustration of a program's theory of change, or how the program is expected to work, used to help frame an evaluation's focus and objectives, from its data sources to its key questions and indicators of outcome. Also used to clarify the manner in which the different program components and goals logically fit together.

Partnership: A working relationship in which the parties involved identify and work toward common interests, build their efforts on the parties' complementary skills and perspectives, and develop processes and establish outcomes that yield mutual benefit.

Partnership approach to evaluation: An approach to evaluation in which the involved parties engage in open and direct communication, employ participatory practices (see *community-based participatory research* above), and ensure that the effort yields mutual benefits. In our view, this approach also uses evaluation to benefit programs, program participants/intended beneficiaries, and organizations.

Scope of work: An agreement that maps out the specific nature of the job/evaluation, the timeline and terms, and the key products or deliverables.

QUESTIONS FOR REFLECTION

1. Consider the case example. How did the university-based research/evaluation team take steps to support a partnership-based approach? What else could they have done to facilitate participation and engagement by the early childhood program's varying stakeholders?

2. What specific elements of CBPR are evident in the partnership described in the case example? How might they have been more participatory?

3. In thinking about the different elements of the partnership, consider the implications of their choices. Why do those partnership characteristics and practices matter? How might they influence the partners' working relationships, the evaluation's processes, the quality and usefulness of data, or the actions taken (or not) based on the evaluation findings? What might be the impact of a different approach (i.e., a non-participatory, non-partnership-based one) on those same elements?

4. Consider how you might apply these strategies in your own work. Identify an experience or involvement that may have been strengthened by the use of a partnership-based approach. How could you use these steps and strategies in your own evaluation work going forward?

REFERENCES

Balcazar, F. E., Keys, C. B., Kaplan, D. L., & Suarez-Balcazar, Y. (1998). Participatory action research and people with disabilities: Principles and challenges. *Canadian Journal of Rehabilitation*, *12*, 105–112.

Charlotte-Mecklenburg Schools. (2017). *About us. Fast facts.* http://www.cms.k12.nc.us/media-room/Documents/CMS%202017-2018%20Fast%20Facts.pdf

Cook, J. R. (2015). Using evaluation to effect social change: Looking through a community psychology lens. *American Journal of Evaluation, 36*, 107–117.

Cook, J. R., & Kilmer, R. P. (2008, June). *Using community-based participatory research to build capacity in family support organizations.* Paper presented at the 2nd International Community Psychology Conference, Lisbon, Portugal.

Cook, J. R., & Kilmer, R. P. (2012). Creating successful partnerships using applied community psychology research. *Living Knowledge: International Journal of Community Based Research, 10*, 16–17.

Cook, J. R., & Kilmer, R. P. (2014, April). *Using 5Win strategies to build strong community-university partnerships.* Paper presented at the 6th Living Knowledge Conference, Copenhagen, Denmark.

Cook, J. R., & Kilmer, R. P. (2016, June). *Building capacity for collaborative research and practice among students and community partners.* 7th Living Knowledge Conference, Dublin, Ireland.

Cook, J. R., & Kilmer, R. P. (2017, March). *Community-university partnerships to enhance educational outcomes for youth at risk.* Invited colloquium for North Carolina State University's Social and Behavioral Health Research Group, Raleigh, NC.

Cook, J. R., & Kilmer, R. P. (2018, April). *Evaluation of Bright Beginnings and NC PreK: Methods, findings, costs, and recommendations.* Invited Webinar for Early Childhood Executive Committee.

Cook, J. R., Kilmer, R. P., Wall-Hill, S., Weber, L., & Cable, E. (2007, September). *University-community partnerships to foster family support.* Paper presented at 3rd Living Knowledge Conference, Communities Building Knowledge – Innovation through Citizens, Science, and University Engagement, Paris, France.

Cook, J. R., Kothandapany, N., Weber, L. J., Wall-Hill, S., & Kilmer, R. P. (2008). Evaluation of a family organization: Integrating local and national evaluation data. In C. Newman, C. Liberton, K. Kutash, & R. Friedman (Eds.), *Agenda and Proceedings: 21st Annual Research Conference: A System of Care for Children's Mental Health: Expanding the Research Base* (pp. 185–186). Tampa, FL:

University of South Florida, Louis de la Parte Florida Mental Health Institute, Research and Training Center for Children's Mental Health.

Cook, J. R.., & Kilmer, R. P. Contributors: Tynan, J. M., Larson, J. C., Hogan, K. S., Scott, J. T. B., & Mihalski, J. L. (2014). *Evaluation of Bright Beginnings: Processes and outcomes: Final report.* Community Psychology Research Lab, University of North Carolina at Charlotte.

Cowen, E. L. (1985). Two little magic words. *Professional Psychology: Research and Practice, 16*(2), 181–190. doi:10.1037/0735-7028.16.2.181

Doss Helms, A. (2011). CMS finds success of pre-K hard to measure: As school board prepares to vote on $10.4M cut Tuesday, Gorman says research is inconclusive. *The Charlotte Observer*, A1, February, 6. (November 2, 2015).

Gadaire, A. (2018). *Assessing the predictive sensitivity of early childhood screening variables to improve pre-k eligibility decisions* [Unpublished master's thesis]. Charlotte, NC: University of North Carolina at Charlotte.

Gadaire, A., Simmons, C. J., Salim, K., Larson, J. C., Galica, V. L., Cook, J. R., & Messinger, L. (2018, October). *Using data and targeted teaching strategies to enhance social-emotional development in pre-k.* Paper presented at the Global Alliance for Behavioral Health and Social Justice's Coming Together for Action 2018 Conference, Denver, CO.

Gadaire, A. P., Armstrong, L. M., Cook, J. R., Kilmer, R. P., Larson, J. C., Simmons, C. J., & Babb, J. (2020). *Enhancing social-emotional development in pre-k: Using data to address students' needs.* Manuscript under review.

Gadaire, A. P., Kilmer, R. P., Cook, J. R., Quinlan, M. M., Babb, J., & Holcomb, C. (2019, June). Assessing the predictive sensitivity of early childhood screening variables to improve pre-k eligibility decisions. In K. Salim (Chair), *Applying community psychology principles to enhance public education.* Symposium at the 17th Biennial Conference of the Society for Community Research and Action, Chicago, IL.

Hogan, K. S., Tynan, J. M., Covill, V. J., Kilmer, R. P., & Cook, J. R. (2017). A capacity building framework for community-university partnerships. *Collaborations: A Journal of Community-Based Research and Practice, 1*(1), http://scholarlyrepository.miami.edu/collaborations/vol1/iss1/1

Kilmer, R. P. (2015, November). *Promises and pitfalls in program evaluation: Applied community research and … inaction.* Invited colloquium-Department of Psychology Excite and Engage Speaker Series, University of North Carolina at Charlotte.

Kilmer, R. P., & Cook, J. R. (2015, June). Facilitating student learning and sparking community change: How to develop and sustain successful community-university partnerships. In K.S. Hogan (Chair), *Creating capacity: Community-university partnerships as co-learning experiences.* Symposium presented at the 15th Biennial Conference of the Society for Community Research and Action, Lowell, MA.

Kilmer, R. P., Cook, J. R., Messinger, L. G., Armstrong, L. M., Gadaire, A., Larson, J. C., & Salim, K. (2018, May). *A community-university partnership to improve implementation and evaluation of an early childhood education program: Implications for practice and policy.* Paper presented at the 8th Living Knowledge Conference, Budapest, Hungary.

Kilmer, R. P., Gadaire, A., Messinger, L., Rios, F., Cook, J. R., Covill, V., Babb, J., Larson, J., Thiery, T., Godly-Reynolds, E., Day, P., & Simmons, C. (2017, May). *Supporting programs to foster student success: Community-university partnerships to benefit diverse youth at risk.* Team inquiry/symposium presented at the 2017 Community-College-University (C2U) Expo: For the common good, Vancouver, BC, Canada.

Kilmer, R. P., Wall-Hill, S., Cook, J. R., Kothandapany, N., & Weber, L. J. (2009). Evaluating ParentVOICE: Building family organization sustainability through family-university collaboration. In S. Swart, B. Friesen, A. Holman, & N. Aue (Eds.), *Building on family strengths: Research and services in support of children and their families. 2007 conference proceedings and state of the science report* (pp. 164–168). Portland, OR: Portland State University, Research and Training Center on Family Support and Children's Mental Health.

Larson, J. C., Bishop Scott, J. T., Tynan, J. M., Mihalski, J. L., Hogan, K. S., Kilmer, R. P., & Cook, J. R. (2015, June). Methodology of a publically funded pre-kindergarten program evaluation: A partnership approach. In J. C. Larson (Chair). *A partnership approach to evaluating a publicly funded pre-kindergarten program: Key findings and action steps*. Symposium conducted at the 15th Biennial Conference of the Society for Community Research and Action, Lowell, MA.

Messinger, L. G., Kilmer, R. P., Coughran, M., Larson, J., Hefner, R., Cook, J., & Avrin., J. (2017, May). *A district-city-university partnership to improve K-12 school attendance and reduce chronic absenteeism*. Roundtable presented at the 2017 Community-College-University (C2U) Expo: For the Common Good, Vancouver, BC, Canada.

Mihalski, J. L., Bishop Scott, J. T., Tynan, J. M., Larson, J. C., Hogan, K. S., Cook, J. R., & Kilmer, R. P. (2015, June). Key findings: Connecting the dots between the pre-kindergarten classroom processes, parent involvement, and students' performance. In J. C. Larson (Chair), *A partnership approach to evaluating a publicly funded pre-kindergarten program: Key findings and action steps*. Symposium conducted at the 15th Biennial Conference of the Society for Community Research and Action, Lowell, MA.

Simmons, C., Gadaire, A., Salim, K., Cook, J. R., Kilmer, R. P., Armstrong, L. M., & Messinger, L. (2019, June). Using an enhanced coaching model to improve pre-k teachers' instruction. In K. Salim (Chair), *Applying community psychology principles to enhance public education*. Symposium at the 17th Biennial Conference of the Society for Community Research and Action, Chicago, IL.

Simmons, C. J., Gadaire, A., Salim, K., Galica, V., Cook, J. R., Kilmer, R. P., & Messinger, L. (2018, October). *Strengthening support for pre-k teachers through an enhanced coaching model*. Paper presented at the Global Alliance for Behavioral Health and Social Justice's Coming Together for Action 2018 Conference, Denver, CO.

Simmons, C. J., Morris, V. G., Cook, J. R., Kilmer, R. P., Armstrong, L. M., Gadaire, A., Salim, K., Babb, J., Day, P., & Messinger, L. (in press). A community-university partnership to develop and implement an enhanced model of coaching for prekindergarten. *Collaborations: A Journal of Community-Based Research and Practice*.

Tynan, J. M., Cook, J. R., Kilmer, R. P., & Wang, C. (2017, June). *Social-emotional growth: How quality of teacher-child interactions in pre-k indirectly affect students' kindergarten achievement*. Ignite session presented at the 16th Biennial Conference of the Society for Community Research and Action, Ottawa, ON, Canada.

Tynan, J. M., Larson, J. C., Mihalski, J. L., Bishop Scott, J. T., Hogan, K. S., Cook, J. R., & Kilmer, R. P. (2015, June). Translating research into action: Successes and barriers enacting recommendations within a school system. In J. C. Larson (Chair). *A partnership approach to evaluating a publicly funded pre-kindergarten program: Key findings and action steps*. Symposium conducted at the 15th Biennial Conference of the Society for Community Research and Action, Lowell, MA.

Viswanathan, M., Ammerman, A., Eng, E., Gartlehner, G., Lohr, K. N., Griffith, D., Rhodes, S., Samuel-Hodge, C., Maty, S., Lux, L., Webb, L., Sutton, S. F., Swinson, T., Jackman, A., & Whitener, L. (2004). *Community-based participatory research: Assessing the evidence*. Evidence Report/Technology Assessment No. 99. Agency for Healthcare Research and Quality (Prepared by RTI-University of North Carolina Evidence-based Practice Center under Contract No. 290-02-0016).

CHAPTER 4

CULTURAL SENSITIVITY AND RESPONSIVENESS IN EVALUATION

Cindy A. Crusto, Diane Purvin, Steven Hoffler, Michael Awad, and Osman Özturgut

Learning Objectives

1. Understand the multiple dimensions that reflect culture and diversity and their relevance to evaluation.

2. Become familiar with the American Evaluation Association's Public Statement on Cultural Competence in Evaluation.

3. Become familiar with key ideas and concepts related to culture and context in evaluation.

4. Explore, identify, and critically reflect on issues of personal social position, power, privilege, and disadvantage to increase self-awareness and their potential influence in an evaluation process.

5. Describe questions that must be addressed for context-specific or contextually sensitive evaluation.

6. Understand essential practices for developing and implementing a culturally competent evaluation.

7. Describe key questions for evaluating the restorative justice nature of a program.

Behavioral researchers have historically failed to accept that all behavior occurs in the context of cultural values and norms. As a result, behavioral research has been defined, conducted, and interpreted as though culture did not matter (Segall, 1986). Evaluation has been no exception to this paradigm. However, over the past three decades, culture has moved from the periphery to the center of evaluation (Frierson et al., 2010; SenGupta et al., 2004), and more evaluators are accepting that culture influences evaluands, evaluation participants, and the evaluation process itself. More specifically, at a very basic level, evaluators have come to recognize that

1. culture fundamentally defines how people usually behave, think, feel, and relate in social interactions (Moleiro, 2018);

2. the dominant culture in the United States (primarily of Western origin) is, in fact, a culture but does not impact all cultural groups in a universal manner;

3. cultural groups have unique experiences and norms and ways of living that shape all aspects of their lives, including behavior, and that are fundamentally different from other cultural groups (Hopson, 2003);

4. evaluation must consider multiple contributors to or determinants of behavior, including culture, individual habit, or the effect of a program or service being evaluated (American Evaluation Association, 2011);

5. addressing cultural factors is not limited to describing the demographics of communities and programs, and requires addressing differences in values as well as considerations of power and privilege (Chouinard & Cram, 2020);

6. evaluators must critically review the Euro-Western positivist epistemological paradigm and methods for the ways in which it has historically oppressed and colonized certain groups. Further, they must be willing to use and integrate different paradigms, methods, and evaluation approaches (e.g., interpretive paradigm, transformative paradigm) to understand people's reality, motivations, and beliefs and to better account for context (Katz et al., 2016); and

7. culturally defined values and beliefs lie at the heart of any evaluative effort (Hood et al., 2015).

While more work must be done relating and applying evaluation theories to address culture and context (Chouinard & Cousins, 2009; Katz et al., 2016), the evaluation field can continue to benefit from illustrations of how culture and context are integrated into evaluation and how they strengthen current evaluation processes and products. This chapter provides (1) a conceptual discussion of culture and context in evaluation, including discussion of the American Evaluation Association (AEA) Public Statement on Cultural Competence in Evaluation as an organizing framework; (2) an overview of the Connecticut Deep End Diversion (DED) pilot project, a real-world example that illustrates key ideas and concepts related to culture and context in evaluation; and (3) a set of actions, issues, and questions that are relevant to the real-world example and its generalizability to other settings.

CULTURE AND CONTEXT IN EVALUATION: AN ORGANIZING FRAMEWORK

The AEA Public Statement on Cultural Competence in Evaluation (hereafter referred to as "the Statement"; AEA, 2011) is the organizing framework for this chapter. The Statement is grounded in and goes beyond the 2004 American Evaluation Association Guiding Principles for Evaluators (AEA, 2004), which guide ethical practice, to explore cultural competence and its significance in evaluation. It was crafted by the Cultural Competence in Evaluation Task Force of AEA's Diversity Committee and approved by the AEA membership in 2011. The Statement is important because it (1) affirms the importance of cultural competence as a criterion for assessing the quality of evaluation efforts, (2) indicates that the public should pay attention to cultural competence, (3) confirms the importance of practicing evaluators attending to relevant dimensions of culture, and (4) illuminates essential elements of cultural competence that are relevant to the interpretation and use of evaluation findings.

The Statement established that addressing culture, context, and common good are integral to ethical evaluation practice, the production of high-quality evaluations, and the use of evaluation findings (AEA, 2011, 2018; Centers for Disease Control and Prevention, 2014; Yarbrough, Shulha et al., 2010). The Statement presents and discusses key concepts and essential practices related to cultural competence in evaluation, discussed in greater detail below.

THE ROLE OF CULTURE AND CULTURAL COMPETENCE IN QUALITY EVALUATION

The Statement defines *culture* as "the shared experiences of people, including their language, values, customs, beliefs, and mores" (p. 2). In this way, the Statement challenges the traditional belief that evaluation is an objective, culture-free enterprise. Instead, it asserts that evaluation is culture-bound and values-based. Culture and the associated values of evaluators and of those sponsoring an evaluation influence every phase and all aspects of an evaluation, including what is being evaluated, how it is being studied, what data are collected, how the data will be analyzed and interpreted, and which groups are included or excluded from an evaluation process. Furthermore, these cultural values are used to make judgments about the merit or worth of what is being evaluated, whether one recognizes it or not.

According to the Statement, "Cultural competence is not a state at which one arrives; rather, it is a process of learning, unlearning, and relearning" (p. 3). *Cultural competence* is defined in relation to a specific context or location, such as geography (e.g., the Pacific Northwest vs. Central Texas), nationality (the place or country of citizenship or birth or the place from which a person descends shapes values, customs, beliefs), and history (e.g., past experiences such as abuses of groups of people influence their patterns of behavior such as adaptive cultural mistrust and parenting practices transmitted from one generation to the next). Thus, for each evaluation, a culturally competent evaluator (or evaluation team) must have specific knowledge of the people and place in which the evaluation is being conducted, including local history and culturally determined mores, values, and ways of knowing. Because each evaluation context is unique, an evaluator's competence in one context is not assured in another context. As a result, the process of becoming more culturally competent is continuous and has no endpoint—even if the evaluator shares a cultural background (or backgrounds) with those participating in an evaluation. At its foundation, cultural competence requires awareness of self, reflection on one's own cultural or social position/location (i.e., one's power, influence, advantages/privilege, and disadvantages relative to other groups within a social hierarchy), awareness of others' social positions, and the ability to interact genuinely and respectfully with others.

> **The process of becoming more culturally competent is continuous and has no endpoint.**

The Statement indicates that cultural competence is effectively a stance toward culture. For example, evaluators must not assume that they fully understand the perspectives of stakeholders whose backgrounds differ from their own; they must make a concerted effort to understand and reflect those perspectives in the work. Indeed, the most recent AEA Guiding Principles (American Evaluation Association, 2018) define the culturally competent evaluator as one

> [who] draws upon a wide range of evaluation theories and methods to design and carry out an evaluation that is optimally matched to the context. In constructing a model or theory of how the evaluation operates, the evaluator reflects the diverse values and perspectives of key stakeholder groups.

Evaluators have paid significant attention to defining and conceptualizing context and to its importance and role in evaluation practice (see Fitzpatrick, 2012, for a review). According to the AEA Guiding Principles (2018), contextual factors are "geographic location and conditions; political, technological, environmental, and social climate; cultures; economic and historical conditions; language, customs, local norms, and practices; timing; and other factors that may influence an evaluation process or its findings." In her call for context-specific evaluation, Rog (2012) indicates that context should be as much of a priority as methodology and that evaluators should explicitly consider context and should use this information to determine the most appropriate evaluation plan and design, including which questions to ask, whom to engage, which methods to use, and which strategies to employ for reporting results. Other factors that directly or indirectly affect the selection, design, and ultimate success of an evaluation include what is already known about the phenomenon or the problem that an intervention or program seeks to address (problem context); the structure, complexity, and dynamics of the program situation, such as the developmental stage of the intervention or program (intervention context); the identity of the decision makers that will use the evaluation results (decision-making context); the evaluation parameters such as budget or timeframe (evaluation context); and the broader setting (broader environment) in which the program is situated and operates. Thus, context must be considered in advance, rather than after the fact or when an evaluation does not proceed as expected or yields poor or unexpected results.

Why Cultural Competence in Evaluation Is Important

Cultural competence in evaluation is important because it reflects ethical practice, better ensures the validity and trustworthiness of the findings, and helps to uncover culturally embedded assumptions in the theories used. Cultural competence represents the intentional effort of evaluators to produce work that is valid, honest, respectful of stakeholders, and considerate of the general public welfare. Furthermore, culturally competent evaluation represents a commitment to fairness and equity for stakeholders. These ideas about ethical evaluation practice and research reflect and shape movement toward equity-, social justice- and human rights-focused evaluation. Because of their positions of influence on program improvement policies and practices, evaluators are well positioned to deal with inequities and power imbalances in society and, by extension, with social justice and the inclusion of marginalized groups, even if their programs do not explicitly focus on these issues (Rosenstein & Syna, 2015). Validity, or the degree to which an evaluation "got it right," demands cultural competence (AEA, 2011). To make valid inferences and conclusions, evaluators must ensure that they understand the cultural context and experiences of those participating in the evaluation.

According to the Statement, theories are inherently cultural in that "they reflect both implicit and explicit assumption of how things work." Theories reflect culturally based explanations or behavior and assumptions about how social problems come about and how they are addressed. They define which variables, factors, and processes are important and which are left out. Thus, the culturally competent evaluator should critically review theories used in their evaluations for culturally embedded assumptions and work to think through and, when possible, to correct how these assumptions might negatively impact the evaluation process and findings. For example, the culturally competent evaluator should seek to select and use theories that accurately reflect the experiences of the cultural groups involved in the evaluation.

Several types of theories are used in evaluation research, and these theories reflect and shape culture. In a review of sociological theories of crime and delinquency, Zembroski (2011) reminds the reader that "theories are shaped by the life experiences and the assumptions and worldviews of the theorists" (p. 253). Additionally, because theorists are embedded within larger societies, theories are shaped by the attitudes and beliefs of a point in time or a period of history. Theories often change over time due to the acquisition of new information or changes in prevailing attitudes. The programs and interventions that are the focus of evaluations often use theories, such as social science theories or locally derived understandings, to inform how the problem developed (i.e., what were the causal variables and processes) and how to best intervene (i.e., which variables and processes should be targeted to effect the desired changes).

The choice of theory for an evaluation has major implications. For example, if one uses some psychological theories (e.g., learning theory, developmental theory) versus sociological theories (e.g., opportunity theory, developmental life course theory) to explain crime and delinquency, the focus will be on individual or internal processes and individually focused interventions rather than social structural factors (e.g., neighborhood disadvantage) that impact crime and delinquency (Moore, 2011; Zembroski, 2011). Furthermore, the use of theories that fail to explicitly address the influence of social position factors, such as direct, indirect, vicarious, historical, and systemic/institutional racial and ethnic discrimination, to explain racial/ethnic minority child development, ignores a fundamental cultural-specific variable that has tremendous impact on physical and mental health of children (English et al., 2020; Fast & Collin-Vézina, 2019; Fisher et al., 2000; García Coll et al., 1996).

Program theory describes a program; identifies the program's goals, purpose, and desired outcomes; explains why a program's activities are supposed to lead to the desired effects; and identifies the conditions under which the outcomes will be attained (Chen, 2003; Sharpe, 2011). *Logic models* are a pictorial representation of a program's theory—how all program components (resources, activities/interventions, deliverables, and outcomes) work together to effect the desired changes (see Chapter 1). Although traditional logic models are widely accepted and used in evaluation, some in the field critique them because they reflect traditional Western, Eurocentric culture and may not reflect the cultural symbols, values, and traditions of the cultural group for whom they are being used (Jenkins et al., 2015). For example, in a description of ethical dilemmas arising from evaluation of a behavioral health intervention in an American Indian urban community, Julian et al. (2017) describe two versions of logic models guiding the project. The evaluator (from a non-Native American/American Indian, majority background) facilitated the development of the first logic model, which reflected a linear set of "if–then" statements in boxes. The second logic model, constructed by members of the tribal community without the presence of the evaluator, reflected deeper cultural values and used in circles, which are symbolic of equality and suggested that no one person is more prominent than any other person.

Essential Practices for Cultural Competence

The Statement describes practices that are essential for developing and implementing a culturally competent evaluation: (1) acknowledge the complexity of cultural identity; (2) recognize the dynamics of power; (3) recognize and eliminate bias in language; and (4) employ culturally appropriate methods. Each is described below.

1. *Acknowledge the complexity of cultural identity.* Although culture is often conflated with race and ethnicity, it refers to the sum of social identities (i.e., the categories which people are socialized to classify themselves and others) including age, ability status, class, gender, gender identity, political affiliation, religion, and sexual orientation (Halloran & Kashima, 2006). Based on the set of identities to which a person subscribes (or is prescribed by others), they may view themselves as composed of multiple identities that are simultaneously operating or they may experience conflicts in how they negotiate these multiple identities because of incompatible messages they receive from prevailing societal norms, cultural stereotypes, and self-perceptions. To this end, cultural identity is multidimensional and should not be conceptualized through a single lens. Layers of cultural differences exist within groups, such as skin tone variation within ethnic minority groups; different clans and clan systems within a single Native American/American Indian tribe; and differences in political perspectives, acculturation, religion, generational perspectives, and educational background within a single nationality. It is incumbent upon evaluators to be aware of and to elucidate these complexities. Evaluators must recognize that cultural identity is multifaceted and can defy precise categorization. The evaluator must consider the multiple identities that evaluation participants may have, including a recognition of issues of intersectionality (i.e., multiple dimensions of identity; potential inequities may be the result of multiple social locations, power dynamics, and experiences), diversity within and between groups, and the right of individuals to define their own cultural identities (e.g., Latino/Latina, Latinx, Hispanic, Chicano, or identification by nationality).

2. *Recognize the dynamics of power.* Evaluators should be aware of how their own cultural identities impact how they understand the world and how they approach the evaluation process. Evaluators should recognize the presence and dynamics of power (e.g., who holds power and how that power is used to influence the behavior of others) and privilege (advantages based on social identity) in all human interactions as well as the inferior social status and subordination that people experience based on their cultural identities. Evaluators should also recognize how these dynamics influence evaluation (e.g., inclusion or exclusion of certain stakeholders/participants in the evaluation process; decision-making authority; evaluators' own position of privilege and power within the evaluation). Because evaluation data and findings have the potential to contribute to structural change, evaluators should recognize the power of evaluation to illuminate experiences of marginalization and subjugation among socially "othered" groups and the subsequent role of evaluation for promoting equity and inclusion.

3. *Recognize and eliminate bias in language.* Because language is both intentionally and inadvertently used to denigrate oppressed groups, evaluators must recognize the critical use of language as a means for promoting social justice and must avoid using language that perpetuates stereotypes, bias, and social exclusion (e.g., "at-risk youth" vs. "youth at risk for poor developmental outcomes"). When used thoughtfully and purposely, language can contribute to a culturally competent evaluation by (a) respectfully communicating differences in key stakeholders' worldviews, (b) illuminating institutional bias and stereotypical practices, (c) capturing the nuance of participants' cultural identities in lieu of oversimplified social classifications, and (d) integrating participants' perspectives in their preferred language or mode(s) of communication.

4. *Employ culturally appropriate methods.* Evaluators should recognize that the common instruments and methodologies used in evaluation for data collection, analysis, and reporting are only optimally effective for the populations for which they were developed or normed. To use culturally appropriate methods, evaluators must (a) define constructs of interest based on how the groups being evaluated define, interpret, and understand them; (b) determine culturally informed methods to analyze/present findings and use or develop culturally validated measures; (c) engage in regular reflection on the ethical collection and use of data; (d) employ intermediaries for data collection in cases in which valuable perspectives may be lost due to barriers in language, abilities, or trust; (e) generate multiple reports that communicate findings at varying levels of comprehension; and (f) incorporate community feedback in the meta-evaluation process as a way to continue building cultural competence.

CASE EXAMPLE: CONNECTICUT DEEP END DIVERSION (DED) PILOT PROJECT

Background

As a real-world example of how culture and context were considered and addressed in an evaluation, we describe here the Connecticut DED pilot project. This project was initiated to reduce racial and ethnic disparities in the juvenile justice system by developing a unique diversion program within deep end congregate care facilities (residential treatment facilities, group homes, and high-security juvenile justice facilities). The project was developed in response to local data analyses, which found that the high number of arrests of youths living in juvenile justice congregate care facilities contribute to racial and ethnic disparities in Connecticut's juvenile justice system. Whereas youths who commit offenses while living in the community can participate in programs that divert youths from being arrested and charged, youths in the deep end of the juvenile justice system, who have been adjudicated delinquent and placed in juvenile justice facilities, do not have access to diversion programs for subsequent incidents. When these facilities contact local law enforcement to respond to a youth's behavior in the facility, the absence of a diversion mechanism increases the likelihood of an arrest, transfer to detention, and further penetration into the juvenile justice system (e.g., extended length of stay). Despite the impact of this gap in Connecticut and nationwide, there is almost no literature concerning the problem of incidents while in residential care and few successful strategies for addressing this problem.

Juvenile justice programs that adopt therapeutic treatment philosophies compared to control treatment philosophies are effective in reducing reoffense rates (Lipsey et al., 2010). One effective therapeutic model is the restorative justice model (Bouffard et al., 2017). The modern theory of restorative justice was developed in the 1970s in North America and is rooted in indigenous traditions in New Zealand and in North America. According to (Zehr, 2015),

> Restorative justice is an approach to achieving justice that involves, to the extent possible, those who have a stake in a specific offense or harm to collectively identify and address harms, needs, and obligations in order to heal and put things as right as possible. (p. 48)

Restorative justice engages those who are harmed (on a strictly voluntary basis), wrongdoers, and their affected communities in search of solutions that promote repair, reconciliation, and the rebuilding of relationships. While there has been much work done on restorative justice in schools (see Fronius et al., 2019, for a review) and in the community (Wilson et al., 2018) to reduce law enforcement referrals, there has been far less effort to extend these principles into congregate care settings, including high-security institutions, where they could reduce involvement with the juvenile justice system and help youths develop new skills to manage their behavior and relationships with others.

Work in Connecticut has resulted in systems change that reduced disproportionate minority contact with law enforcement and with the juvenile justice system at multiple points of contact or entry. However, the efforts to date have been unable to address arrests in congregate care facilities. Between October 2013 and December 2014, there were 461 arrests of youths in the facilities managed or contracted by State of Connecticut Department of Children and Families (DCF), the state department responsible for child welfare, juvenile justice, and children's mental health, and congregate care facilities; 76% were arrests of youths of color. The DED project's systemic reforms served youths living in congregate care facilities in Connecticut to address these issues. The goal of the project was to decrease arrests of youths in juvenile justice congregate care facilities in Connecticut by creating an innovative diversion mechanism inside these facilities. The pilot project's main objectives were to (1) work with a stakeholder group, which includes system-involved youth, to develop a DED model infused with restorative justice principles for juvenile justice facilities; (2) implement the DED model at the state's high-security juvenile justice facility and one juvenile justice residential treatment facility; (3) contract with an evaluator to conduct a formal evaluation of the implementation of the diversion model; (4) replicate the model in juvenile justice congregate care facilities throughout the state; and (5) produce an information brief on the model and disseminate the model developed from the pilot nationally. The timeline proposed in the original grant proposal specified the development of a restorative justice model within 6 months followed by the implementation of this model in two pilot sites and dissemination within 2 years.

Stakeholders and Partnership

The DED project represented a collaboration between several partners. The partners were the Center for Children's Advocacy (CCA), a children's legal rights organization (lead agency, project oversight and management); DCF, the state's child welfare, mental health, and juvenile justice agency (operator and contractor of congregate care facilities); the Center for Restorative Justice at Suffolk University, an entity to foster collaborative partnerships to build equitable and just communities and to institutionalize restorative practices (restorative justice/practices trainers and consultants); two congregate care juvenile justice facilities to develop and implement the intervention and participate in an evaluation; Community Mediation, Inc., a nonprofit organization that provides mediation and other conflict resolution services training to support inclusive communities whose members resolve conflict effectively (mediation trainers); The Consultation Center, Yale University School of Medicine (project evaluators); Southern Connecticut State University (project

Continued

coordination and evaluators); and the Institute for Community Research, a nonprofit organization that conducts research in collaboration with community partners to promote justice and equity (training and support in youth engagement). In most cases, senior leadership and managers/supervisors represented the organizations and designated frontline staff who had positive relationships with the youths. The project strategy made space for meaningful youth involvement in designing system reform. This unique component ensured the inclusion of youths who are isolated from society and typically disengaged or, even discouraged, from civic engagement. The CCA received funding from the Open Society Foundations to launch the project, and additional funding was secured from several regional and local foundations in Connecticut.

The relationships among partners within and outside of the initiative were essential to the development, implementation, and evaluation of the DED project. At the project's onset, there were historical trust issues because some partner organizations experienced historical "bullying" from other partner organizations. In addition, some members of the stakeholder group expressed a level of distrust toward other members of the stakeholder group because of their positional status, the level of power they held within the child welfare and juvenile justice systems, and the lack of transparency as perceived by some stakeholder members. Furthermore, some project partners were historically at odds. For example, the CCA, which fights for the legal rights of Connecticut's most vulnerable children, provides legal and advocacy services to prevent and divert children from involvement in the juvenile justice system and advocate for juvenile justice system reform. This reform work was often at odds with that of DCF, which maintains and contracts with the juvenile justice agencies. Some of the concerns about trust were expressed to the project coordinators and to the evaluation team privately and outside of stakeholder meetings. Thus, the project coordinators and the evaluation team became aware of some of the perceived power imbalances within the project relatively early in the project. The project coordinator and the evaluators then had to manage how to address these issues during the implementation phases.

Participating Facilities

Two facilities participated in the evaluation of the pilot intervention: the Connecticut Juvenile Training School (CJTS), the state's high-security juvenile facility, and Waterford Country School (WCS), a juvenile justice residential facility. These sites were selected for participation because they had the highest arrest rates of recidivism among the DCF facilities.

At the start of the project, CJTS was the only secure DCF-operated facility for treating youths who had been adjudicated by the courts as delinquent and committed to DCF. CJTS opened in 2001, and its mission was "to provide a safe, secure and therapeutic environment while providing opportunity for growth and success." CJTS used national best practices interventions and standards with the goal of reducing the risk of reoffending, preparing youths for community reentry, and developing positive youth outcomes. Admission to CJTS occurred through new commitments to DCF via the courts, parole violations, or congregate care (e.g., if a youth becomes too aggressive, picks up new charges, or is overall noncompliant in congregate care settings). For a majority of the project implementation, the CJTS facility was being rightsized, but not closed; however, the staff were under constant threat of layoffs and experienced anxiety regarding a rumored closing. CJTS had staff for collaborating on the project's implementation and evaluation. However, staff uncertainty and changes in staffing were consistent with the institutional history of CJTS. At the start of the project, CJTS had a very traditional, corrections-based approach to youth management and discipline, which was focused on strict and clear consequences for infractions. The historic and institutional factors operating in CJTS impacted the staff, and the youths, and stood in potential conflict with the trust- and community-building components of restorative approaches to juvenile justice. In the end, CJTS was scheduled to close on July 1, 2018 (after the DED project), after which adjudicated youths would be transferred from DCF to the judicial branch of the Court Support Services Division.

The pending closing of CJTS during the DED project posed trust issues because leaders from multiple organizations and decision-making bodies were involved in the project. CJTS staff had to reconcile being asked to participate in this reform effort while under the threat of potentially losing their jobs. The project coordinator and evaluation team worked closely to manage this distrust among the partners and CJTS staff by supporting the staff's legitimate concerns and the role of some partners. This required the project coordinators and evaluators to validate these concerns and manage distrust and anxiety among key stakeholders without breaching the confidence of those who shared these concerns on and off the record.

WCS is a nonprofit human service agency and a DCF-contracted agency dedicated to the special needs of children and their families. WCS provides services and programs to children and families at risk for poor outcomes and promotes overall well-being. WCS has a history of organizational stability and strong staff retention. Two WCS services and programs participated in the pilot project: residential treatment and emergency shelter. The residential treatment program provides a wide spectrum of therapeutic services to children and youths throughout Connecticut who cannot remain in their communities due to family issues, trauma, abuse, or serious behavioral problems. The emergency shelter provides emergency short-term placement for youths aged 10–18 years who need immediate services. Since 2009 and prior to the restorative justice intervention, WCS implemented an alternative model that replaced the traditional corrections-based approach. Because of this new model, WCS shifted its value system and grounded itself as a change-inducing practice before the DED pilot project. Although there were notable similarities between the alternative model and the restorative justice approaches, the WCS staff's positive experience with their existing model led to some resistance to a new model, including staff concerns about how this existing model would be affected by participating in this project.

Intervention

Following 15 months of training with stakeholders (i.e., management team, congregate care facility staff, youths, university-based evaluation team) and site visits to participating facilities by national restorative justice experts, the partners developed a model collaboratively. This model was composed of three main restorative justice practices, ranging from prevention of harm and conflict to mediation between parties. The first practice was talking circles/restorative dialogues, which are foundational and universal activities that impact the entire setting, building skills to better the entire environment/milieu, and bolstering relationships and social and emotional capacities among and between staff and youths. The second practice was problem-solving circles and restorative conversations, which are targeted activities often involving multiple youth peers and community members and used to manage problems and conflicts in the setting as they arise. The third practice was restorative conferencing, an intensive practice to repair serious harm when it happens. This practice brings together all the people who have been harmed and those who have harmed for a structured conversation to address and to repair the harm. Group conferences widen the participation of family members and other supportive community members, who gather to discuss the various impacts of the acknowledged harm.

The DED Evaluation

The evaluation sought to develop the methodology and to pilot the DED pilot project evaluation processes and procedures in anticipation of wider model dissemination in the state and nationally. The evaluation consisted of process and outcome evaluation and was conducted from April 1 through December 31, 2017. At the guidance of the management team, the project evaluation was guided by (Zehr's, 2015) six key questions for evaluating the restorative justice nature of a program: (1) Does the model address harms, needs, and causes? (2) Is it adequately victim-oriented? (3) Are offenders encouraged to take responsibility? (4) Are all relevant stakeholders involved? (5) Is there an opportunity for dialogue and participatory decision making? (6) Is the model respectful to all parties? These six overarching questions are standard guides in the implementation of the restorative justice model and evaluation of its effectiveness.

In addition to the AEA Public Statement on Cultural Competence in Evaluation described above and Zehr's six questions, the DED evaluation was guided by empowerment (Fetterman et al., 1996;

Continued

also see Chapter 8), participatory, and collaborative evaluation theories (Chouinard & Milley, 2016). The evaluation was designed to build the capacity of the two facilities to participate in a structured evaluation process and to take ownership of data collection for the new restorative justice intervention during and after the pilot project and to address the process of implementing the project as well as program improvement.

The evaluation team was composed of faculty, staff, and undergraduate students from two universities in Connecticut. The team was culturally diverse along several dimensions, including gender, race, ethnicity, sexual orientation, religious faith, professional discipline, and academic degree. The evaluation team's principal investigator (an African American woman) and coordinator (a Caucasian/White woman) were from Yale University. They developed the model and participated in all project training sessions that introduced the restorative justice framework. The first DED project coordinator, an African American male and licensed social worker with a doctoral degree and extensive experience working in the child welfare and juvenile justice systems, ultimately took a faculty position and joined the evaluation team. The evaluation team also contracted with an expert in qualitative methods to provide training to its members. All team members completed human subject protection training, including ethical considerations with vulnerable populations. All evaluation processes and procedures were reviewed and approved by the Yale University Institutional Review Board and by the Connecticut DCF Institutional Review Board.

Evaluation Design

We implemented a mixed-method evaluation study using qualitative (i.e., focus groups, individual interviews, and participant observation) and quantitative (i.e., surveys and process data collection forms) methods to assess Zehr's six questions and obtain a holistic picture of the project's implementation and outcomes. The process evaluation documented the implementation of the three different restorative practices (talking circles/restorative dialogues, problem-solving circles and restorative conversations, and restorative conferencing); the impact of implementing the intervention on programs and staff; and implementation barriers and challenges as well as facilitators and successes.

The outcome evaluation assessed the benefits of the intervention at the youth and facility levels. We initially planned a repeated measures design to assess the impact of the program over time. However, DCF indicated that it would only provide aggregate level data for youths participating in the intervention. Thus, using DCF and facility administrative data, we sought to track aggregate youth- and facility-level outcomes: rates of arrest, number of police calls, number of visits to the emergency department, average length of stay in each facility, significant incidents for which 911 was called, and number of restraints and seclusions. These data were collected from DCF, and administrative data were collected directly from the facilities. The goal was to obtain these data from DCF and the facilities for the 2 years prior to the start of this pilot project through end project implementation.

One youth focus group was conducted in person at CJTS with six males aged 16–17 years. Some of the youth focus group participants had participated in the management team, and all youths had participated in some aspect of the intervention (circles/dialogues, circles/conversations, conferences). Nine interviews were conducted and analyzed using a structured data analysis form to document themes. Notes taken by evaluation team members at stakeholder meetings provided an additional source of qualitative data to document the project's implementation and outcomes.

The timeline for developing and implementing the restorative justice model proved to be challenging due to the need to develop partnerships and the management team, to assess the milieu and context of the participating facilities for compatibility and readiness for the model, and to carry out the extensive training needed for all partners and facility staff in restorative practices. The project timeline, along with the time necessary to obtain all IRB and ethical approvals from the two entities, also posed challenges to the initial evaluation design.

Evaluation Findings

Despite their different barriers and supportive factors, both programs developed and implemented restorative interventions, and both saw positive impact on their overall programs, their staff, and their youths. Restorative circles were implemented with fidelity and were universally regarded as a successful and helpful intervention. Based on the data we collected, we addressed Zehr's six questions for evaluating the restorative justice nature of a program.

1. Does the model address harms, needs, and causes? Youths from CJTS and WCS reported that circles effectively managed and resolved conflicts that arose in group living situations. A WCS youth reported that when conflicts between co-residents arose, staff addressed them first privately among the affected parties, but then conflicts were brought to a circle to address the impact on the whole unit, and they discussed the particular conflict using a "talking piece" (a participant-chosen item used to designate the person who has the floor to talk at a given time within the circle session) to ensure that everyone participated and respected each other in the process. This youth felt that the structure of the circles made it "easier to open up" to the staff about concerns. CJTS youths reported that when they had a conflict, they knew they could bring it to one of the circles that were part of the different programs at CJTS and, depending on where it was going on, to "circle it out."

2. Is the model adequately victim-oriented? Based on interview data, the restorative conferences (the highest level of intervention within the restorative justice model) seemed to be adequately victim-oriented and restored the relationship between victims and those doing harm. One example took place at WCS, where a restorative conference was used to address an incident in which a group of program youths vandalized the office of an administrative assistant who had been with the program for many years. Staff participating in the conference reported that all parties seemed satisfied with the process and that it seemed to substantively change the relationship between the assistant and the youths for the better.

3. Are offenders encouraged to take responsibility? Although only two restorative conferences were held during the evaluation period, the data indicated that the conferences went extremely well and that offenders were encouraged to take responsibility for their behavior, and for at least one of the conferences involving youths, the benefits of the conferences extended to relationships in the youths' home community.

4. Are all relevant stakeholders involved (offenders, victims, all levels of settings, including leadership)? There was involvement of stakeholders at all levels in the development of the restorative justice model and in the oversight of the project implementation, including DCF leadership, leadership from CJTS and WCS, relevant partner agencies, youths, and the evaluation team. Although the youth participation component of the restorative justice initiative did not include a consistent core of youths fully integrated into the stakeholder group as designed, CJTS invited approximately four to six youths to participate in nearly every stakeholder meeting, with some specific individuals attending consistently. Beginning a few months into the project, CJTS youths facilitated the opening circle of each stakeholder meeting in which they participated. WCS supported the regular participation of one student in the stakeholder meetings and, on occasion, that of one or two others.

    All relevant parties, including staff from both facilities, were involved in the restorative practices. Youths reported that everyone had a chance to speak in the circles, and staff reported that youths participated appropriately. There were no reports of relevant stakeholders being left out of the restorative justice processes.

    All relevant stakeholders were involved in the model development, program oversight, and implementation of restorative practices, and both sites experienced systems-level change. Staff from both sites described reverberating positive effects that they attributed to the diffusion of "restorative thinking" that accompanied the incorporation of restorative circles into regular agency practices.

Continued

5. Is there an opportunity for dialogue and participatory decision making? Youths from both programs reported that everyone had a chance to speak in circles and conferences, even the youths who tended not to talk as much as others. All staff interviewed felt that youths appreciated the opportunity for a voice provided by the circles, and one WCS staff member reported that this led to a better culture in the agency. The youths reported that the structure of the circles and the use of the talking piece greatly facilitated youth voice and participation in the circles to share their concerns. Both programs used restorative circles to help start/reinstate regular youth council meetings, in which youths who met certain behavioral criteria were given a formal opportunity to provide input into program planning and policy.

Staff from both programs also described positive effects of staff being willing to share in circles with youths. These circles were encouraged and enabled by the initial successful deployment of restorative circles in staff-only spaces. Staff from both programs also reported extremely favorable views of the use of restorative circles and approaches for internal staff-only meetings within their agencies. WCS staff said that the intervention positively affected the program and improved relationships among and between staff members, sharing their decision to use restorative circles/processes in staff team meetings as an example. One WCS interviewee found staff leadership circles to be "more powerful than anticipated—the circle format creates opportunity for more profound communication." Acknowledging the morale issue confronting their staff in the face of layoffs and uncertainty, CJTS upper management allowed and supported the use of staff-only restorative circle processes before implementing such processes with youths.

6. Is the model respectful to all parties? Youths from both facilities reported that circles effectively managed and resolved conflicts that arose in group living situations. One youth reported that conflicts between co-residents were first addressed privately among the affected parties and then brought to a circle to address the impact on the whole unit. In the circle they discussed the conflict using a talking piece to ensure that everyone participated and respected each other in the process. This youth felt that the structure of the circles made it easier to express concern to the staff. Youths from both facilities overwhelmingly reported that they were treated with respect and given opportunities to participate. They reported this about their experiences with the stakeholder group, within training sessions and interactions with project coordinators, and within restorative circles and conferences. The seven youths interviewed were unequivocal on this point. When the facilitators in the CJTS focus group asked whether there were times the youths felt that interactions with staff had not gone well, one youth responded, "No, everyone listens and respects you, everyone speaks from their heart."

Line staff working directly with youths at both sites also uniformly reported full inclusion of youths in the program components and a belief that all youths were treated with utmost respect by staff within the restorative programs and processes. One CJTS staff person shared his belief that youth opinions, thoughts, and ideas were considered "as valuable, if not more, than the adults, as they were the ones it directly affected." Staff from both facilities also felt that the youths they brought to participate in stakeholder meetings had positive experiences. In the words of a WCS senior staff member, "Youth stakeholders were treated as equal partners."

With respect to juvenile justice-related outcomes, DCF provided aggregate risk management data for arrests, 911 calls, and emergency safety interventions (ESIs) for CJTS and WCS Residential Treatment Center for calendar years 2014–2017. All these metrics improved. There were 122 arrests of youths at CJTS from 2014 through 2017 (43 arrests per year in 2014 and 2015, followed by 15 in 2016 and 21 in 2017). As for 911 calls, there were 26 calls at CJTS from 2014 to 2017 and fewer than 10 calls in any year. The number of calls fell from nine in 2014 to three in 2017. There were 5,477 ESIs at CJTS across the four years and a decrease in all types of ESIs from 2014 to 2017. At the WCS site, there were a total of 54 arrests from 2014 to 2017, and despite fluctuations across the years, there was a decrease from 20 to three arrests per year during that timeframe. There were 253 police calls from WCS over this timeframe, with a decrease in the number of calls per year over this timeframe.

According to CJTS data, there was a reduction in incidents of staff assaults over the project period. For instance, the proportion of total incidents of staff assaults (criminal charges may not have been filed) relative to the number of youths served during a given calendar year decreased from 2014 to 2017. Additionally, the absolute number of staff assault incidents decreased over the four calendar years (2014–2017). The data also showed that the number and frequency of youth arrests trended downward over the four years and, since the initiation of restorative practices, there was a significant drop in unique youth arrests and staff assaults. Moreover, with respect to behavioral health symptomology,

since implementing the restorative practices, youths leaving CJTS endorsed a decrease in depression, anxiety, and oppositionality symptoms, and CJTS reported a reduction in the frequency of crisis and clinical safety watches.

While these changes are very promising, our understanding of the degree to which the changes can be attributed to the restorative justice intervention can be strengthened by collecting data at the individual youth level and staff level over time (i.e., examining pre-, post-, follow-up Global Appraisal of Individual Needs-Short Screener) and by using more rigorous methods (control and comparison groups). Additionally, it is important to note that historical events (such as CJTS rightsizing and downsizing) may have impacted the outcomes of the study (e.g., the unique characteristics of youths no longer at the facility or staff who were no longer employed may be related to the outcomes).

CASE EXAMPLE ANALYSIS

Ethics, Validity, and Theory

Ethics. The purpose of the DED project—to address disproportionate minority contact with the juvenile justice system—and the project partners' explicit commitment to social and racial justice compelled our evaluation team to join the project, despite very limited evaluation resources. Grounded in the fields of community psychology, social policy, and social work, our evaluation team was strongly committed to social justice, to equity, and to ensuring ethical and fair treatment of all individuals and groups participating in the evaluation. We anticipated and discussed the potential challenges of bringing a social justice and equity-focused evaluation to congregate care facilities due to the traditional control treatment philosophy that we assumed lay at the facilities' foundation. We learned that some of our assumptions were inaccurate given the diversity of treatment philosophies between and within the institutions. For example, some individuals were as committed to social justice as we were and worked within the juvenile justice system to effect change. We engaged allies at each institution to support the evaluation through our continuous and meaningful participation in the project; evaluation team members attended all training and project meetings and numerous on-site meetings about the evaluation.

We sought to protect the rights and fair treatment of three vulnerable groups participating in the evaluation: the youths involved in the evaluation, the parents/caregivers of youths participating in the evaluation, and the facility staff who would participate in the evaluation as participants and as data collectors. We protected the rights of participating youths in three ways. First, we obtained youth assent to ensure that youths were informed of the project evaluation and what their participation entailed. For CJTS, our evaluation team coordinated with the clinical social worker and the chaplain, who provided additional time with the focus group members explaining the consent form, prior to our team members spending additional time to engage them and create a level of comfort in participating while answering any questions and assuring anonymity. Second, we compensated the youths for their participation in the evaluation. From the beginning of the project, we had conversations with project stakeholders and representatives at each facility to determine policies and procedures for compensation. Together, we ensured that each youth participating in the management team and in the evaluation was compensated with a $10 Walmart gift card once they were released from the facility. The amount of compensation was determined by the facilities and was included as a line item in our evaluation budget. Third, we respected DCF's concern about sharing individual youth-level data (i.e., length of stay, reoffense data) with the evaluation team. We were never provided with an exact reason, but we presumed that the confidentiality of the participating youths was a concern. DCF was willing to provide aggregate-level data for each facility. This significantly impacted our original evaluation plan and design and the degree to which we could attribute any observed changes to the DED intervention. We had numerous conversations with key stakeholders to convey the limitations of this plan, but ultimately DCF's decision was paramount.

Our partnership with stakeholders in this project allowed our evaluation team to respect the rights of all parents/guardians/surrogates of youths participating in the evaluation (surveys, individual interviews, or focus groups and collection of administrative data). For CJTS, DCF leadership from central office played a key role in coordinating the parent permission process. Administrators and staff at each facility connected us to guardians/sponsors so that we could inform them about the study and obtain verbal parental permission for youths' participation in the evaluation. Some youths remained in the custody of their parents/guardians, while some were in the guardianship or custody of DCF; for the latter youth, we worked to secure permission from the surrogate (DCF), which was signed by the child's DCF social worker.

During the intervention, we came to realize that facility staff were typically lower-ranking members in very hierarchical systems, whose voices may have been less likely to be heard in process improvement and systems change processes. We had to understand their experience of the system as well as those of the young people. The first DED project coordinator spent considerable time with the staff addressing project-specific issues and allowing CJTS staff to process and talk about the rightsizing as well as its impact on them and their ability to participate in the project and the evaluation.

Validity is defined as the extent to which an evaluation "got it right" regardless of approach or paradigm (AEA, 2011). Valid inferences require shared understanding within and across cultural contexts. Shared understanding, in turn, requires trust that diverse voices and perspectives are honestly and fairly represented. Cultural competence fosters trustworthy understanding. To foster trust, we spent considerable time building and maintaining relationships with stakeholders, particularly staff at both facilities, the youths in the management team, and youths participating in the evaluation. Trust-building was integral to the project from Day 1, and members of the evaluation team attended all management team meetings, including those in which the management team was trained on restorative practices. The training was composed of didactic and experiential components and required active participation in trust-building activities and circles. Restorative circles were used during trainings to help build a cohesive and collaborative management team, teach about restorative justice theory and practice, and build the model. Thus, the management team experienced circles as the youths in the facilities would experience them from the start of the project. Participation in these meetings and trainings was critical for (1) understanding the role of each partner organization and partnership dynamics; (2) understanding the important contextual differences between the two facilities; (3) developing relationships with the individuals designated as the evaluation liaisons at each facility; (4) becoming familiar with restorative justice theory and practice, which was essential because this model had never been developed, implemented, or evaluated in deep end congregate care juvenile justice facilities; and (5) building trust through the co-learning and team-building exercises. The evaluation coordinator was thus very much a part of the project team and was present at all stakeholder meetings to receive direct updates on all aspects of the implementation process as they were shared by the project partners.

With respect to facility staff, the first project coordinator met with staff routinely about the project and, once he became a member of the evaluation team, he continued to meet with them to discuss the project and allowed them to process feelings about right-sizing that naturally emerged in just about every meeting. The project coordinator went well beyond his job description and partnered with the sites to coordinate transportation for the youths involved in the stakeholder group who were discharged to their communities. This also meant discussing the nature of the project with their family members or guardians and transporting them. On one occasion, the project coordinator and a representative from one of the sites had to intervene because a parent intercepted a stipend check designated for the youth as restitution for damage caused to the family's property. The project coordinator immediately replaced the youth's stipend when this was brought to the attention of the stakeholder group. Because this level of intervention could not be sustained due to lack of resources and because it was beyond the scope of the job description, youths were replaced and recruited from within CJTS, which resulted in the active participation of its youth council to resolve this issue.

The DED pilot project and the evaluation were guided by the cultural competence framework discussed above and the theory of restorative justice. The validity of what was being measured (i.e., the fidelity of the restorative justice practices and the victim-oriented and stakeholder involvement components of the practices) was evaluated using Zehr's (2005) six questions. There was a strong emphasis on the inclusion of voices who are marginalized (i.e., the youths themselves), frontline staff such as youth service officers, and direct care staff who were central to the research design and outcomes of the evaluation. Some theorists indicate that while reduced recidivism is likely a byproduct of restorative justice programs and is an important outcome, it is not the primary reason for operating restorative justice programs (Zehr, 2015), and it is only one of several objectives of restorative justice practices (Bazemore, 2001). Instead, restorative justice emphasizes the *process* of restorative justice, such as those experiencing harm being able to express their needs, and systemic change, such as changing the culture of organizations and how they respond to wrongdoing and harmful behavior to create safe, peaceful, just, and respectful environments.

This helped our evaluation team think more broadly about the importance of assessing culture and social context change before we could expect individual child-level changes. We planned facility-wide climate assessments from the perspective of staff and youths, but we were unable to carry them out because of the lengthy process of implementing restorative justice practices at both sites. Additionally, CJTS asked that we not collect these data during the rightsizing, which would likely result in negative perceptions and make it impossible to determine the impact of the restorative justice intervention.

Our evaluation was also guided by empowerment, participatory, and collaborative evaluation theories. Because each facility had experience with data collection and measuring outcomes, our goal was to foster buy-in and to establish the staffs' ability to collect data to evaluate restorative practices, which would require ongoing, daily documentation of key characteristics of restorative practices (i.e., which practices took place, fidelity assessments, and outcomes of practices implemented). In addition, consistent with many of the 10 principles of empowerment evaluation (Fetterman & Wandersman, 2007; see Chapter 8), we focused on program improvement, community ownership of the evaluation process, democratic participation in the evaluation process, social justice and racial equity, implementation of evidence-based strategies (restorative justice practices), community knowledge, capacity building, and organizational learning. Our work was also grounded in participatory and collaborative approaches to evaluation. According to Chouinard and Milley (2016),

> Participatory and collaborative evaluations are set apart from other approaches through the "relational and dialogic nature of the inquiry process," the involvement of multiple diverse stakeholders, the engaged position of the evaluator, and by the relationships that develop between stakeholders and evaluators. (p. 3)

Finally, although summative judgments were critically important to this project, we focused more on program improvement and identifying barriers and facilitators to implementing restorative practices than on summative judgments such as recidivism, reoffense, and length of stay data, consistent with participatory evaluation (Stufflebeam & Coryn, 2014).

ESSENTIAL PRACTICES FOR CULTURAL COMPETENCE

Acknowledge the complexity of cultural identity. We attended to three aspects of cultural identity in this evaluation project: organizational culture, youth culture, and the social identities of the youths participating in the project. The two congregate care facilities were selected for the pilot intervention based on data indicating that each had the highest rates of recidivism arrest among the DCF facilities. Although the two sites served similar populations, they had very different organizational structures, constraints, and histories, all of which influenced their approach to developing and to implementing the restorative justice intervention and to their participation in the evaluation. Our team had to manage the complexity of measuring two different sites, one private and one public; the continuum of care that existed at WCS versus the restricted environment at CJTS; different timelines and journeys from moving from more punitive to restorative justice models; significant workforce challenges (right-sizing) that impacted employee morale; and management of multiple groups within each institution (frontline staff, supervisors, leadership). Over the course of the project, we learned that some of our initial assumptions about the traditional treatment philosophies at each facility were inaccurate given the diversity of treatment philosophies at and within each institution. We engaged allies at each institution to support the evaluation through our continuous and meaningful participation in the project (i.e., evaluation team members attending all training and project meetings and numerous on-site face-to-face meetings about the evaluation).

The main barriers to creating a restorative environment within CJTS related to historical rightsizing and downsizing, which led to depressed staff morale, turnover among participating staff, and uncertainty about the commitment of upper management to the initiative. There were also challenges associated with staff resistance, high turnover of youths within the programs, insufficient staffing resources, and aligning restorative justice approaches to existing processes and procedures and to the CJTS behavior management system. WCS presented different challenges that required cultural consideration, including its private setting (in contrast to the public setting of CJTS) and workforce issues such as varied levels of employee morale and satisfaction, which presented challenges with commitment to data collection.

The second aspect of cultural identity to which we attended was youth culture. We had to understand the dynamics between the CJTS youths who resided in different towns. The serious conflicts among youths residing in different towns manifested in the facility and impacted whether youths could be housed together in CJTS or even participate in the same focus group for the evaluation. As the evaluation team, we had to respect the seriousness of this issue for the CJTS youths and for the staff and to think about ways to potentially alter the evaluation design to address this issue. The restorative justice intervention helped to address these longstanding, historical conflicts between residents of different Connecticut towns. The resolution of these issues within CJTS was one key indicator of success of the project.

Because the project emphasized the role of the youths, the project coordinator and the evaluation team worked closely with facility staff and with the management team to consider the format of the management team meetings to maintain youth engagement. The stakeholder meetings were 2 hours long and used a circle format. This format occasionally necessitated that we excuse the youths due to boredom or lack of attention. However, other attempts were made to maintain youth involvement. For example, we considered the possibility that youths would feel intimidated by the various stakeholders in a meeting that could be as large as 28–30 persons. To address this, the stakeholder meetings were broken into small discussion groups when appropriate. The youths also played leadership roles in the stakeholder groups using restorative practice methods that included sharing their culture through poetry, rap, and music. The youths were also involved in negotiating incentives for their participation. To their credit, the youths were instrumental in challenging program and residential policies, such as one allowing radios and music in their cells as an incentive. This policy was changed as the result of staff considering the role and voice of the youths when restorative justice was introduced. Lastly, the youths were empowered to use their creativity; they designed a restorative justice logo for the project that was adopted by the organization and included on agency letterhead in a common area along with other restorative justice symbols and messages.

The third aspect of cultural identity to which we attended was sexual orientation. We went to great lengths to allow young people to self-identify their sexual orientation. This self-identification was confidential, allowing for one male youth at CJTS to feel comfortable enough to identify as bisexual or gay in a culture that has not allowed expression of same-sex orientation, especially within youth and prison culture.

Recognize the dynamics of power. As evaluators and as individuals from an academic institution with a complicated history with the community, we were keenly aware of the position of power that we held or that might be ascribed to us by the partners. Fortunately, we had previously evaluated a different juvenile justice initiative with CCA and had a long-standing relationship with one of their staff persons. Thus, some partners were aware of our social justice orientation. We also made clear early in the project that we practice from empowerment, participatory, and collaborative evaluation frameworks. For example, we summarized these frameworks in our scope of work and routinely discussed our evaluation philosophy during the first few restorative justice trainings. While the power evaluators possess in any evaluation project can never be completely dismantled, we sought to foster trust, a shared commitment to promoting the well-being of youths involved in the juvenile justice system, and inclusive practice by attending every management and training meeting and by maintaining close connection with the project coordinator and staff at each of the facilities.

We carefully weighed the pros and cons of including the first project coordinator in the evaluation team once he transitioned to a faculty position. In the end, we felt that he was a crucial factor in promoting a project and an evaluation process that addressed the multiple trust issues and power dynamics that were present. We strategically decided that he and his team would collect data from the youths at CJTS and from some staff across the two facilities. Ultimately, we felt that the evaluation findings would be more valid and trustworthy because of the bond he had established with the youths and staff and the connection he had helped us develop with staff. We acknowledge that some would identify his transition from project coordinator to evaluator as an ethical conflict.

As discussed previously, many staff involved in the project were lower-ranking individuals in very hierarchical systems, who may have themselves been marginalized, especially given the lack of control in the systems change process or in the rightsizing process at CJTS. We noted that staff at the facilities were nervous about how any information reported to us might be used against them or their facilities. We regularly responded to these concerns. We believed that it was the ethical responsibility of the evaluators and of the evaluation process to help facilitate this social justice effort by providing data and information about mistrust and conflicts to the project coordinators. At CJTS, this involved building trust and fostering a strong partnership with the clinical director, who had positive relationships with the youths, staff, and senior leadership. As one of the few racially diverse leaders on the team, she led the efforts and bridged conversations with senior leadership due to her critical role in the system. She modeled restorative practices with the CJTS leadership team while engaging in these difficult conversations one-on-one with the superintendent and leadership team. This led to the superintendent playing a more active role in the project and managing the anxiety of his staff through the restorative work (i.e., participating in the training with his frontline staff). These processes, updates, and conversations were also included in the stakeholder meetings.

Recognize and eliminate bias in language. As individuals trained in the social sciences, all members of the evaluation team were accustomed to using person-first language. Person-first language is used to speak respectfully, appropriately, and in a humanizing and neutral manner about people with disabilities or those experiencing a health or other condition (e.g., an "individual experiencing homelessness" rather than a "homeless person" or a person diagnosed with schizophrenia vs. a "schizophrenic"). While we were sensitive to person-first language with respect to the juvenile and criminal justice system (e.g., saying "formerly incarcerated person" instead of "ex-con"), we were unfamiliar with language used in restorative justice theory. Prior to our involvement with the DED project, we used the terms "victim" and "offender." The term "offender" was not comfortable for us, but we did not have alternative language. Restorative justice theory uses the terms "individuals who have been harmed" or "individuals who have experienced wrongdoing" and "individuals who have engaged in harm" or "individuals engaging in wrongdoing." It took some time for us to consistently adopt this language in all forms of communication, but this was a crucial step in recognizing the dignity and worth of all involved parties.

Employ culturally appropriate methods. It was essential that we understand the perceptions, realities, and beliefs of the numerous stakeholder groups participating in the intervention and in the evaluation. While we had always planned a multimethod evaluation, we had to move to qualitative methods to understand the process of implementation and the impact from multiple perspectives due to the challenges associated with collecting data regarding key indicators of outcomes. The evaluation team used interview data and meeting notes to document the impact of the intervention on youths and facilities and they served to triangulate other qualitative and quantitative data. These notes include direct reports from staff and youths involved in the intervention at both sites, from different points in time as the intervention was being developed and implemented, as well as observations by the note-takers.

SET OF ACTIONS

The Connecticut DED pilot project addressed the issue of disproportionate racial/ethnic minority contact in the juvenile justice system, a significant social justice issue both in the state of Connecticut and across the United States. The case analysis used the key concepts and essential practices for culturally competent evaluation as described in the AEA Public Statement on Cultural Competence in Evaluation (AEA, 2011). The most important challenges inherent to this project were the limited funding for the evaluation and the very short timeframe for the project. These factors negatively impacted our ability to (1) increase rigor and the validity or trustworthiness of our data and conclusions, such as transcription of audiotaped interviews and focus group; (2) give more voice to the staff and youths, particularly regarding proximal outcomes (i.e., assessment of perceptions of organizational climate, collective self-efficacy, psychological sense of empowerment); and (3) implement additional essential practices for culturally competent evaluation (e.g., engage and consult with those groups who are the focus of the evaluation in the development of the logic model, and analysis and interpretation of data to address multiple perspectives). Furthermore, the resources were insufficient for us to conduct an evaluation from the empowerment, participatory, and collaborative evaluation frameworks, which require significant engagement with stakeholders. Despite this, we used these frameworks as our guide. Practically, this meant that the evaluation team provided a fair amount of in-kind work. More and more, evaluators are likely to be faced with the decision of whether to take on innovative pilot projects that address important social issues but have limited evaluation funding. The decision to support innovative and potentially impactful and far-reaching solutions to pressing problems despite limited resources represents an ethical dilemma that each evaluator and team will have to sort through. Each evaluation study represents unique considerations and trade-offs.

The DED project is representative of how the field of evaluation has moved toward evaluation as (1) a tool to effect change within programs and policies, (2) an improvement strategy across settings and contexts, and (3) a means to advance equity and to promote social justice. According to Rosenstein and Syna (2015), social justice is "a framework from which to address the evaluator's role in dealing with inequities and power imbalance among social groups in society" (p. 4). The authors also state that "the role of evaluation has expanded to include an almost 'watchdog' function of making sure that policy and programming protect the rights of all people and address issues affecting both marginalized and mainstream populations" (p. 4). Because of their positions of influence on program improvement policies and practices, evaluators are well positioned to deal with inequities and power imbalances and, thus, social justice and inclusion of marginalized groups, even if their programs do not explicitly focus on these issues. Thus, addressing culture, context, and common good and equity are integral to ethical evaluation practice, the production of high-quality evaluations, and the use of evaluation findings (AEA, 2011, 2018; Centers for Disease Control and Prevention, 2014; Yarbrough et al., 2010). This social justice movement in the field means that *all* evaluators will address complex social issues involving a multitude of stakeholders and cultural groups, whether or not they set out to do so (see Levin-Rozalis, 2015).

To prepare for this role, evaluators must become familiar with different evaluation theories, models, and frameworks that can guide culturally competent, culturally responsive, socially just, and equity-focused evaluation research and practice, including Multicultural Validity (Kirkhart, 2010), Culturally Responsive Evaluation (Frierson et al., 2010; Hood et al., 2005), Talent Development (Thomas & Stevens, 2004), Indigenous Evaluation Framework (LaFrance et al., 2012), Transformative Evaluation (Mertens, 2009), and Values-Engaged Evaluation (Hall et al., 2012), and the Centers for Disease Control and Prevention Framework for Program Evaluation in Public Health (Centers for Disease Control and Prevention, 1999). At the same time, evaluators must understand the limitations, critiques, and dangers of engaging in culturally competent and equity-focused work. For example, they must take great care not to perpetuate power differentials and colonization (Carey, 2015; Danso, 2018; Hopson et al., 2012; Milner, 2007). The first step to becoming a culturally competent evaluator is to "acknowledge the self." That is, the evaluator must critically assess their values, assumptions, and positions of power and privilege (both as a researcher in relation to the evaluation and in the broader society) and must understand how they impact the evaluation process. However, the work does not stop with assessment. Evaluators must interrupt negative biases that impact their ability to interact genuinely and respectfully with various stakeholders and cultural groups. This is a continuous, lifelong process.

FURTHER READING

American Evaluation Association. (2011). *American Evaluation Association public statement on cultural competence in evaluation*. Author.

Carey, M. (2015). The limits of cultural competence: An indigenous studies perspective. *Higher Education Research & Development*, *34*(5), 828–884.

Chouinard, J. A., & Cram, F. (2020). *Culturally responsive approaches to evaluation: Empirical implications for theory and practice* (Vol. 4). Sage.

Levin-Rozalis (2015). A purpose-driven action: The ethical aspect and social responsibility of evaluation. In B. Rosenstein & H. Desivilya Syna (Eds.), Evaluation and social justice in complex sociopolitical contexts. *New Directions for Evaluation*, 146, 19–32.

Milner IV, H. R. (2007). Race, culture, and researcher positionality: Working through dangers seen, unseen, and unforeseen. *Educational Researcher*, *36*(7), 388–400.

Williams, J. L., & Deutsch, N. L. (2016). Beyond between-group differences: Considering race, ethnicity, and culture in research on positive youth development programs. *Applied Developmental Science*, *20*(3), 203–213.

Zehr, H. (2015). *The little book of restorative justice* (Revised and updated). Simon and Schuster.

KEY CONCEPTS

Cultural competence: A stance toward culture that requires awareness of self, reflection on one's own cultural or social position/location, awareness of others' social positions, and the ability to interact genuinely and respectfully with others. In the context of evaluation study, the culturally competent evaluator (or evaluation team) must have specific knowledge of the people and place in which the evaluation is being conducted—including local history and culturally determined mores, values, and ways of knowing. The process of becoming more culturally competent is continuous and has no endpoint—according to the American Evaluation Association's Public Statement on Cultural Competence in Evaluation, it "is not a state at which one arrives; rather, it is a process of learning, unlearning, and relearning."

Culture: The American Evaluation Association's *Public Statement on Cultural Competence in Evaluation* defines culture as "the shared experiences of people, including their language, values, customs, beliefs, and mores."

Empowerment evaluation: This evaluation approach "aims to increase the likelihood that programs will achieve results by increasing the capacity of program stakeholders to plan, implement, and evaluate their own program" (Wandersman et al., 2005, p. 28).

Logic model: A graphic illustration of a program's theory of change, or how the program is expected to work, used to help frame an evaluation's focus and objectives, from its data sources to its key questions and indicators of outcome. Also used to clarify the manner in which the different program components and goals logically fit together.

Program theory: This describes a program; identifies the program's goals and purpose, and desired outcomes; explains why a program's activities are supposed to lead to the desired effects (e.g., how a program is expected to work); and identifies the conditions under which the outcomes will be attained (see Chen, 2003; Sharpe, 2011).

Restorative justice: "An approach to achieving justice that involves, to the extent possible, those who have a stake in a specific offense or harm to collectively identify and address harms, needs, and obligations in order to heal and put things as right as possible" (Zehr 2015). The approach engages those who are harmed (on a strictly voluntary basis), wrongdoers, and their affected communities in search of solutions that promote repair, reconciliation, and rebuilding of relationships.

QUESTIONS FOR REFLECTION

1. What are the benefits of employing culturally sensitive and responsive practices?

2. How might you take culture into account in developing a program's theory of change or logic model?

3. In what ways does a program's theory have implications for cultural competence and context sensitivity?

4. Consider the case example. What values and actions illustrate the partnership-focused orientation of the evaluation team?

5. When resources are strained (e.g., limited funding and/or person power), how can evaluators ensure that they are maximizing the effectiveness and utility of the evaluation, while engaging in culturally competent and partnership-based practices?

6. What steps can be taken to ensure the cultural competence of an evaluator or an evaluation team?

REFERENCES

American Evaluation Association. (2004). *AEA guiding principles*. Author. https://www1.eere.energy.gov/ba/pba/pdfs/drft_aeae.pdf.

American Evaluation AssociationAmerican Evaluation Association. (2011). *American Evaluation Association public statement on cultural competence in evaluation*. Author. https://www.eval.org/p/cm/ld/fid=92

American Evaluation Association. (2018). *American Evaluation Association guiding principles for evaluators*. https://www.eval.org/p/cm/ld/fid=51

Bazemore, G. (2001). Young people, trouble, and crime: Restorative justice as a normative theory of informal social control and social support. *Youth & Society, 33*(2), 199–226.

Bouffard, J., Cooper, M., & Bergseth, K. (2017). The effectiveness of various restorative justice interventions on recidivism outcomes among juvenile offenders. *Youth Violence and Juvenile Justice, 15*(4), 465–480. doi:10.1177/1541204016647428

Carey, M. (2015). The limits of cultural competence: An Indigenous studies perspective. *Higher Education Research & Development, 34*(5), 828–840. doi:10.1080/07294360.2015.1011097

Centers for Disease Control and Prevention. (1999). Framework for program evaluation in public health. MMWR.48 (No. RR-11). https://www.cdc.gov/mmwr/PDF/rr/rr4811.pdf

Centers for Disease Control and Prevention. (2014). *Practical strategies for culturally competent evaluation*. US Department ofHealth and Human Services.

Chen, H. T. (2003). Theory-driven approach for facilitation of planning health promotion or other programs. *The Canadian Journal of Program Evaluation, 18*(2), 91.

Chouinard, J. A., & Cousins, J. B. (2009). A review and synthesis of current research on cross-cultural evaluation. *American Journal of Evaluation, 30*(4), 457–494. doi:10.1177/1098214009349865

Chouinard, J. A., & Cram, F. (2020). *Culturally responsive approaches to evaluation: Empirical implications for theory and practice* (Vol. 4). Sage.

Chouinard, J. A., & Milley, P. (2016). Mapping the spatial dimensions of participatory practice: A discussion of context in evaluation. *Evaluation and Program Planning, 54*, 1–10. doi:10.1016/j.evalprogplan.2015.09.003

Danso, R. (2018). Cultural competence and cultural humility: A critical reflection on key cultural diversity concepts. *Journal of Social Work, 18*(4), 410–430. doi:10.1177/1468017316654341

English, D., Lambert, S. F., Tynes, B. M., Bowleg, L., Zea, M. C., & Howard, L. C. (2020). Daily multidimensional racial discrimination among black U.S. American adolescents. *Journal of Applied Developmental Psychology, 66* doi:10.1016/j.appdev.2019.101068

Fast, E., & Collin-Vézina, D. (2019). Historical trauma, race-based trauma, and resilience of indigenous peoples: A literature review. *First Peoples Child & Family Review, 14*(1), 166–181.

Fetterman, D., & Wandersman, A. (2007). Empowerment evaluation: Yesterday, today, and tomorrow. *American Journal of Evaluation, 28*(2), 179–198.

Fetterman, D. M., Kaftarin, S. J., Kaftarian, S. J., & Wandersman, A. (1996). *Empowerment evaluation: Knowledge and tools for self-assessment and accountability.* Sage.

Fisher, C. B., Wallace, S. A., & Fenton, R. E. (2000). Discrimination distress during adolescence. *Journal of Youth and Adolescence, 29*(6), 679–695. doi:10.1023/A:1026455906512

Fitzpatrick, J. L. (2012). An introduction to context and its role in evaluation practice. In D. J. Rog, J. L. Fitzpatrick, & R. F. Conner (Eds.), *Context: A framework for its influence on evaluation practice. New directions for evaluation* (pp. 135, 7–24).

Frierson, H. T., Hood, S., Hughes, G. B., & Thomas, V. G. (2010). Chapter 7: A guide to conducting culturally responsive evaluations. In J. Frechtling (Ed.), *The 2010 user-friendly handbook for project evaluation (Revision to NSF publication No. 02-057* (pp. 75–96). National Science Foundation.

Fronius, T., Darling-Hammond, S., Persson, H., Guckenburg, S., Hurley, N., & Petrosino, A. (2019). *Restorative justice in US schools: An updated research review.* WestEd Justice and Prevention Training Center.

García Coll, C., Lamberty, G., Jenkins, R., Crnic, K., Wasik, B. H., & Vázquez García, H. (1996). An integrative model for the study of developmental competencies in minority children. *Child Development, 67*(5), 1891–1914. doi:10.2307/1131600

Hall, J. N., Ahn, J., & Greene, J. C. (2012). Values engagement in evaluation: Ideas, illustrations, and implications. *The American Journal of Evaluation, 33*(2), 195–207.

Halloran, M., & Kashima, E. (2006). Culture, social identity and the individual. In T. Postmes & J. Jetten (Eds.), *Individuality and the group: Advances in social identity* (pp. 137–154). Sage.

Hood, S., Frierson, H., & Hopson, R. (2005). *The role of culture and cultural context in evaluation: A mandate for inclusion, the discovery of truth and understanding.* IAP.

Hood, S., Hopson, R., & Kirkhart, K. E. (2015). Culturally responsive evaluation. In *Handbook of practical program evaluation* (4th ed., pp. 281–317). Wiley Blackwell. https://doi.org/10.1002/9781119171386.ch12

Hopson, R. (2003). *Overview of multicultural and culturally competent program evaluation.* Social Policy Research Associates. http://www. calendow.org/uploadedFiles/Publications/Evaluation/Multicultural_Health_Evaluation/OverviewBook.pdf.

Hopson, R., Kirkhart, K. E., & Bledsoe, K. L. (2012). Decolonizing evaluation in a developing world: Implications and cautions for equity-focused evaluations.*Evaluation for Equitable Development Results*(pp. 59–82).

Jenkins, S., Robinson, K., & Davis, R. (2015). *Adapting the Medicine Wheel Model to extend the applicability of the traditional logic model in evaluation research.* Paper presented at the 2015 Federal Committee on Statistical Methodology (FCSM) Research Conference, Washington, DC. https://pdfs.semanticscholar.org/8d6c/73110b3eae786bf034f8b51de10233766451.pdf.

Julian, D. A., Smith, T., & Hunt, R. A. (2017). Ethical challenges inherent in the evaluation of an American Indian/Alaskan native circles of care project. *American Journal of Community Psychology, 60*(3-4), 336–345. doi:10.1002/ajcp.12192

Katz, I., Newton, B. J., Bates, S., & Raven, M. (2016). *Evaluation theories and approaches; relevance for Aboriginal contexts.* Social Policy Research Centre, UNSW Australia.

Kirkhart, K. E. (2010). Eyes on the prize: Multicultural validity and evaluation theory. *American Journal of Evaluation, 31*(3), 400–413. doi:10.1177/1098214010373645

LaFrance, J., Nichols, R., & Kirkhart, K. E. (2012). Culture writes the script: On the centrality of context in Indigenous evaluation. *New Directions for Evaluation, 2012*(135), 59–74. doi:10.1002/ev.20027

Levin-Rozalis, M. (2015). A purpose-driven action: The ethical aspect and social responsibility of evaluation. In B. Rosenstein & H. Desivilya Syna (Eds.), *Evaluation and social justice in complex socio-political contexts. New Directions for Evaluation* (2015, pp. 19–32). doi:10.1002/ev.20117

Lipsey, M. W., Howell, J. C., Kelly, M. R., Chapman, G., & Carver, D. (2010). *Improving the effectiveness of juvenile justice programs.* Center for Juvenile Justice Reform at Georgetown University. https://rhyclearinghouse.acf.hhs.gov/sites/default/files/docs/19740Improving_the_Effectiveness_of.pdf

Mertens, D. M. (2009). *Transformative research and evaluation.* Guilford Press.

Milner, H. R. (2007). Race, culture, and researcher positionality: Working through dangers seen, unseen, and unforeseen. *Educational Researcher, 36*(7), 388–400. doi:10.3102/0013189X07309471

Moleiro, C. (2018). Culture and psychopathology: New perspectives on research, practice, and clinical training in a globalized world. *Frontiers in Psychiatry, 9*, 366. doi:10.3389/fpsyt.2018.00366

Moore, M. (2011). Psychological theories of crime and delinquency. *Journal of Human Behavior in the Social Environment, 21*(3), 226–239. doi:10.1080/10911359.2011.564552

Rog, D. J. (2012). When background becomes foreground: Toward context-sensitive evaluation practice. In D. J. Rog, J. L. Fitzpatrick, & R. F. Conner (Eds.), *Context: A framework for its influence on evaluation practice* (135, pp. 25–40). New directions for evaluation.

Rosenstein, B., & Syna, H. D. (2015). *Evaluation and Social Justice in Complex Sociopolitical Contexts: New Directions for Evaluation, Number 146.* John Wiley & Sons.

Segall, M. H. (1986). Culture and behavior: Psychology in global perspective. *Annual Review of Psychology, 37*(1), 523–564. doi:10.1146/annurev.ps.37.020186.002515

SenGupta, S., Hopson, R., & Thompson-Robinson, M. (2004). Cultural competence in evaluation: An overview. *New Directions for Evaluation, 2004*(102), 5–19. doi:10.1002/ev.112

Sharpe, G. (2011). A review of program theory and theory-based evaluations. *American International Journal of Contemporary Research, 1*(3), 72–75.

Stufflebeam, D. L., & Coryn, C. L. (2014). *Evaluation theory, models, and applications* (Vol. 50). John Wiley & Sons.

Thomas, V. G., & Stevens, F. I. (2004). *Co-constructing a contextually responsive evaluation framework: The talent development model of school reform (No. 101).* Jossey-Bass.

Wilson, D. B., Olaghere, A., & Kimbrell, C. S. (2018). *Effectiveness of restorative justice principles in juvenile justice: A meta-analysis. Inter-University Consortium for Political and Social Research.*

Yarbrough, D. B., Shulha, L. M., Hopson, R. K., & Caruthers, F. A. (2010). *The program evaluation standards: A guide for evaluators and evaluation users.* Sage.

Zehr, H. (2005). *Changing lenses: A new focus for crime and justice* (3rd ed.). Scottdale.

Zehr, H. (2015). *The little book of restorative justice* (Revised and updated.). Simon and Schuster.

Zembroski, D. (2011). Sociological theories of crime and delinquency. *Journal of Human Behavior in the Social Environment, 21*(3), 240–254. doi:10.1080/10911359.2011.564553

CHAPTER 5

ETHICAL CONSIDERATIONS

Michael Morris

The collaborative approach to evaluation taken in this book is a compelling one. Indeed, meaningful engagement of stakeholders is consistent with the core values of the field as articulated in the Program Evaluation Standards authored by the Joint Committee on Standards for Educational Evaluation (Yarbrough et al., 2011). Challenges, however, accompany this orientation. Partnering with stakeholders to conduct evaluations that make a difference can be an exceedingly messy endeavor, both logistically (Shulha et al., 2016) and ethically (e.g., Tamariz et al., 2015). For example, in their examination of community-partnered research, Yonas and his colleagues observe that such research "raises particular ethical challenges as these studies often involve working together with various leaders and members from underserved, socially disadvantaged, or marginalized communities, communities whose backgrounds often are quite different from those of research investigators" (Yonas et al., 2016). This chapter will explore the ethical issues of which practitioners should be mindful when carrying out evaluations that are intended to be highly participatory in nature. The American Evaluation Association's (AEA's) *Guiding Principles for Evaluators* (AEA, 2018) will serve as the organizing framework for this analysis: Systematic Inquiry, Competence, Integrity, Respect for People, and Common Good and Equity. A detailed case example will then be presented, highlighting several ethical considerations, and will be followed by a discussion of general strategies that collaborative evaluators can use in addressing ethical issues in their work.

SETTING THE STAGE

What do we mean when we use the term ethics? As Campbell (2016) succinctly states, "The field of ethics examines right and wrong *conduct* (i.e., ideas into action, how we behave). ... In professional work, there are group-level norms and expectations establishing right

Learning Objectives

1. Become familiar with ethical challenges associated with partnership-based approaches to evaluation.

2. Understand how these challenges relate to the American Evaluation Association's Guiding Principles for Evaluators.

3. Identify and analyze the ethical dimensions of an evaluation case study from a partnership-based perspective.

4. Learn overall strategies for enhancing one's ethical practice in partnership-oriented evaluation.

and wrong conduct" (p. 295). In evaluation, the three major sources of ethical guidance in North America are the Guiding Principles for Evaluators (AEA, 2018), the Program Evaluation Standards (Yarbrough et al., 2011), and the Ethics statement of the Canadian Evaluation Society (Canadian Evaluation Society, n.d.). There are 5 AEA Guiding Principles, 30 Program Evaluation Standards, and 3 domains addressed by the CES Ethics statement. In this context, it is important to keep in mind that principles and standards are not the same as recipes and formulas. Dealing with ethical challenges in evaluation often involves the application of human judgment to complex situations in which reasonable—and moral—people can disagree over how a given principle or standard might apply (see Datta, 2002; Smith, 2002). Further complicating matters is the fact that, within the Guiding Principles, Program Evaluation Standards, and CES domains, there is little if any prioritization. This is a key issue, because in the discussion that follows it will become clear that principles and standards, and the values they represent, are not independent, and in some instances there may be tension among them. Maximizing the pursuit of one ideal or value might affect progress toward another. Thus, it is not uncommon to encounter circumstances in which a perceived conflict between two or more ethical principles produces what scholars refer to as an *ethical dilemma* (MacKay & O'Neill, 1992). These are particularly vexing from a decision-making perspective, given that the evaluator is likely to view himself/herself having to violate one valued ethical principle in order to achieve another.

APPLYING THE GUIDING PRINCIPLES

Systematic Inquiry

The core statement of Systematic Inquiry is that "evaluators conduct data-based inquiries that are thorough, methodical, and contextually relevant" (AEA, 2018, A). In order to fulfill this principle, evaluators should, among other things, "adhere to the highest technical standards appropriate to the methods being used" (AEA, 2018, A-1).

What ethical challenges might a collaborative evaluator face when attempting to engage in Systematic Inquiry? Perhaps the most prominent one involves the commitment to "highest technical standards." Evaluators typically have much more training in research methodology than the stakeholders with whom they work. They know what designs are likely to produce the most defensible conclusions regarding a program's impact, what data-collection strategies hold the greatest promise for obtaining valid evidence in a given context, and, overall, what the chances are that a particular evaluation can answer the fundamental questions that stakeholders bring to the project. Of course, these stakeholders may possess local knowledge and insight that can inform discussion of all these issues. As Ross et al. (2010b) note, "Community partners bring … knowledge of community needs, beliefs and interests, and practical knowledge regarding the community's social structure" (p. 23). However, it is naïve to think that there will never be circumstances when stakeholders advocate a course of action, during the planning or implementation of an evaluation, which the evaluator believes would seriously jeopardize the scientific integrity of the project.

This challenge can be especially daunting when the advocacy comes from powerful stakeholders. In his survey of AEA members using case vignettes, Azzam (2010) found that the more power or influence a stakeholder group was perceived to have over the logistics of an evaluation, the more willing the AEA respondents were to modify the evaluation's design to accommodate the stakeholder's concerns. This result suggests that the impact of stakeholder input on evaluation design may be less related to the technical merit of that input than it is to the political clout of those offering it. We thus have a cautionary tale. In theory, engagement-oriented evaluation approaches may strive to honor the contributions of all relevant stakeholders. In practice, however, it is probable that not all stakeholders are treated equally, a dynamic of which evaluators might not even be fully aware.

The other major ethical consideration raised by Systematic Inquiry involves the assertion that evaluators "communicate methods and approaches accurately, and in sufficient detail, to allow others to understand, interpret and critique their work … [and] discuss in contextually appropriate ways the values, assumptions, theories, methods, results, and analyses that significantly affect the evaluator's interpretation of the findings" (AEA, 2018, A-3, A-5). Stakeholders not only differ in their power, but also vary in their exposure to evaluation and to experiences (e.g., formal education) that can have implications for their ability to readily grasp the nuances of evaluation practice. These differences can place a significant communication burden on evaluators who are committed to substantively engaging a wide variety of stakeholders. Presentations may need to be modified for different audiences and include the preparation of multiple written reports of the same evaluation. For example, sophisticated statistical analyses that might be appropriate for professional stakeholders trained in quantitative methods would probably not be well suited to members of a grass-roots community advisory board participating in the same evaluation. A more valuable report for the latter group might emphasize the evaluation's major findings in the body of the document, with the appendix being used to delineate the specific analyses leading to those findings. Moreover, the logic underlying those analyses would need to be spelled out in a fashion that would not be necessary for audiences familiar with the relevant methodology.

The labor-intensiveness of these activities can tempt the evaluator to forego them, in the hope that a "one size fits all" approach will suffice. This hope is risky, however, unless it derives from experience working with the stakeholders in question. In the absence of such experience, using a standardized approach can estrange rather than engage the very groups with which one is attempting to collaborate. Thus, in the preceding example, a report that was not responsive to the advisory board's modest level of methodological knowledge would likely be confusing and intimidating to these stakeholders, who in turn might be reluctant to ask the evaluator questions that could lead to greater understanding. In these cases, the evaluator's "espoused theory" of collaboration is not consistent with his/her "theory in use" (Argyris, 1985), an inconsistency that has ethical significance in that it constitutes a failure to implement a core component of one's evaluation philosophy.

Competence

Not surprisingly, this principle asserts that "evaluators provide skilled professional services to stakeholders" (AEA, 2018, B). Toward this end, the evaluation team should possess "the education, abilities, skills, and experiences required to complete the evaluation competently" (AEA, 2018, B-1). The competencies that are most closely associated with evaluation tend to be methodological in nature, involving domains such as needs assessment, experimental and quasi-experimental designs, implementation monitoring, efficiency analysis, data-collection strategies, and logic models (topics discussed in other chapters of this text). Partnership approaches to evaluation heighten the salience of other skills that are more interactional in nature. For instance, managing relationships with and among stakeholders is a significant task in any evaluation, but it is likely to be especially challenging in evaluations having the goal of developing a collaborative network of stakeholders to carry out the project. At a minimum, one needs skills in the following areas:

- interviewing/reflective listening;

- group facilitation/team building;

- conflict resolution;

- negotiation;

- political networking; and

- cultural responsiveness (see Chapter 4 for an in-depth discussion of cultural sensitivity and responsiveness in evaluation).

To be sure, these skills are important for all evaluators (see King & Stevahn, 2013), but partnership-oriented evaluators have staked out a territory for their practice in which the cultivation of effective group and intergroup dynamics is crucial to success. An evaluator might legitimately claim, for example, that cost–benefit analysis was not part of his/her skill set, but a collaborative evaluator without distinctive expertise in group facilitation or conflict management would be practicing unethically. Thus, it is difficult to avoid the conclusion that, with respect to the Competence principle, requirements for the ethical practice of participatory approaches to evaluation are higher than for less engagement-oriented ones.

Participatory evaluators, for instance, take pride in bringing historically marginalized stakeholders to the table when planning an evaluation. In many cases, however, this step is insufficient to generate meaningful engagement, because these groups often do not view themselves as having the background or skills to contribute significantly to open-ended discussions that include individuals of higher status. In such circumstances, the former stakeholders are likely to be seen but not heard, and, in fact, see themselves as being set up for failure by the evaluator. A competent (and ethical) practitioner would need to employ group facilitation approaches (e.g., the Nominal Group Technique or focus-group methodology) that would minimize the salience of status differences and maximize the active participation of all stakeholders.

Against this background, it is noteworthy that endorsement of substantive stakeholder involvement in evaluation has grown substantially in recent years. Applications of Community-Based Participatory Research (CBPR), Participatory Action Research (PAR), and Empowerment Evaluation, for example, have become commonplace (see Fetterman et al., 2017; Lykes, 2017; also see Chapter 3 for more regarding CBPR and PAR and Chapter 8 for in-depth consideration of Empowerment Evaluation). Indeed, in its presentation of the Program Evaluation Standard of Responsive and Inclusive Orientation (P-1), the Joint Committee recommends that evaluators "identify stakeholders broadly, gather useful information from them, and include them in decisions about the purpose, questions, and design of the evaluation, so that they recognize the opportunity to participate as both a right and responsibility" (Yarbrough et al., 2011, p. 115). Normative statements such as these suggest that the field as a whole is moving toward a partnership-oriented philosophy. To the extent that this is the case, the ethical implications of the failure to possess the competencies reviewed in this section are likely to receive increased attention.

The Competence principle also states that evaluators "ensure that the evaluation team collectively possesses or seeks out the competencies necessary to work in the cultural context of the evaluation" (AEA, 2018, B-3). Given that Chapter 4 of this volume is devoted to this topic, we will simply note the obvious here: For all evaluators who claim to bring an engagement-oriented philosophy to their work, cultural competence is an ethical imperative.

Integrity

According to the Integrity principle, "Evaluators behave with honesty and transparency in order to ensure the integrity of the evaluation" (AEA, 2018, C). This principle applies the notion of transparency to every phase of the evaluation from entry/contracting through utilization of results. Stakeholders should have a thorough understanding of the major decisions affecting the design and implementation of the evaluation, the reasons for those decisions, and the consequences of those decisions. Furthermore, the results of the evaluation must be accurately reported and realistic steps taken to prevent those results from being distorted or misapplied by key stakeholders in the aftermath of the evaluation. In partnership-oriented evaluations, evaluators need to facilitate discussion of these considerations and their implications if truly shared decision making is to be achieved.

Ensuring the integrity of an evaluation is never a rote task, but in the case of collaborative evaluation, it can be especially challenging. Developing a high level of trust among participating stakeholders is essential and requires "relationship-building, spending time together listening to each other's concerns, interests, and needs, and incorporating them into the research agenda" (Ross et al., 2010b, p. 20). Consider, as an example, *conflicts of interest*. According to Ross et al., a conflict of interest occurs when "a primary interest (e.g., validity of research) is unduly influenced by a secondary interest (e.g., financial gain, academic success, community leadership)" (Ross et al., 2010c, p. 42). For instance, evaluating a program that is directed by a close friend would generally be regarded as a conflict of interest for the evaluator (and the director). Or consider an evaluator who expects that a lucrative new contract would be forthcoming if they produced a positive evaluation of a particular program. In both cases, it is reasonable to believe that the evaluator might be tempted to skew the study's findings (violating integrity and honesty) in order to maintain a personal relationship or produce financial benefits.

As the number of evaluation stakeholders increases and the networks within which they operate become more elaborate and complex, the "opportunities" for conflicts of interest to occur undoubtedly grow as well. Thus, virtually by definition, collaborative evaluations generate a landscape populated by stakeholders who are likely to see their vested interests linked to the evaluation. Community representatives on an evaluation advisory board, for example, might view themselves as potential staff members for an expanded program that could result from the positive evaluation of a pilot intervention.

Evaluators need to be sensitive to such dynamics as the evaluation proceeds. When it comes to monitoring possible conflicts of interest, this is a tall order, to put it mildly.

The existence of a conflict of interest does not necessarily mean that unethical behavior is inevitable, but it does set the stage for such behavior. Moreover, where conflicts of interest are involved, the appearance of impropriety can be as damaging to an evaluation as the reality of misconduct. Thus, the evaluator needs to ensure that measures taken to address conflict-of-interest issues are in fact viewed by stakeholders as credible.

It is almost certainly unrealistic to expect that a single evaluator, or evaluation team, can assume the full burden of managing conflict-of-interest issues in a wide-ranging, engagement-oriented evaluation. However, evaluators do bear a special responsibility for making sure that a process is established for dealing with such matters. Indeed, one of the Program Evaluation Standards (P-6) is wholly devoted to conflicts of interest, stating that "evaluations should openly and honestly address real or perceived conflicts of interests that may compromise the evaluation" (Yarbrough et al., 2011, p. 145). For example, if an evaluator believes that his/her judgment might be inappropriately influenced by relationships with key stakeholders, then having another evaluator, one unaffiliated with the project, review plans, designs, and report drafts could represent a wise investment that is likely to boost confidence in the integrity of the overall process.

Beyond conflicts of interest, the challenge of maintaining integrity in collaborative evaluations is highlighted by instances of stakeholder pressure on evaluators to misrepresent findings. Several studies indicate that such pressure is one of the most frequently encountered ethical conflicts in the work lives of evaluators (Buchanan & MacDonald, 2011; Morris & Clark, 2013; Morris & Cohn, 1993; Pleger et al., 2017; Turner, 2003). Not surprisingly, this pressure usually takes the form of being asked, subtly or not so subtly, to portray the program more positively, or less negatively, than the evaluator believes is warranted by the data. Although the evidence suggests that most pressuring episodes are resolved in a way that the evaluator sees as at least moderately satisfactory, it is clear that this challenge often generates ethical angst for the evaluator, given that in a substantial percentage of cases the evaluator believes that the stakeholder in question is motivated by an intention to deceive (Morris & Clark, 2013). To the extent that collaborative evaluations engage more stakeholders than other evaluations, the chances that misrepresentation pressure will occur during the communication-of-findings phase are multiplied.

One approach to the misrepresentation issue is to engage stakeholders in a discussion of hypothetical results during the entry/contracting stage of the evaluation. In essence, this involves asking stakeholders to react to a set of plausible but fictitious findings that the evaluator believes the stakeholders would perceive as disappointing. The evaluator can use this conversation to alert stakeholders to the challenges of reporting unwelcome results, and strategies that might be employed to be true to the data while being sensitive to stakeholders' concerns (e.g., highlighting alternative interpretations of results).

As the preceding recommendation implies, disagreements over how to interpret and report findings can occur in the absence of nefarious motives. As Ross et al. (2010b, p. 27) note:

> Research partners will sometimes have very different interpretations of the same data. ... the same data can be used to support or detract from the ability to procure

wanted services; in other cases, the data can be interpreted as promoting or detracting from social stereotypes and prejudices. When understanding and interests diverge, conflicts may arise regarding how the data are presented, the form in which the data are presented, and decisions about what data to publish.

Of the various lessons that can be drawn from this passage, perhaps the most telling one for our purposes is that an ethical mandate to display honesty and integrity can become much more intimidating when stakeholders disagree over what "honesty" would actually look like in a particular circumstance. Evaluators' responsibilities for facilitating effective communication among stakeholders become especially salient in these situations, even as they endeavor to examine critically their own understanding of the data. Emphasizing the formative rather than the summative uses of evaluation (distinctions described in Chapter 1) can be valuable here, helping stakeholders appreciate how a range of findings (positive, negative, in-between) can contribute to program development and improvement.

Respect for People

This principle states that "evaluators honor the dignity, well-being, and self-worth of individuals and acknowledge the influence of culture within and across groups" (AEA, 2018, D). This domain encompasses what most people think of when they contemplate research ethics and the protection of human subjects: risk, *informed consent*, confidentiality, *"do no harm," beneficence*, and so on. Of course, in collaborative evaluations the individuals to be respected generally extend far beyond the "human subjects" who participate in a typical clinical trial of a medical or mental health intervention. Thus, once again, the territory that evaluators traverse becomes more cluttered, not just in terms of the number of stakeholders but also their diversity.

Take the issue of informed consent, which refers to "agreement by the participants based on adequate information provided to them concerning their participation in a study" (Yarbrough et al., 2011, p. 289); this information "must address the risks and benefits that the research poses to the individual as an individual" (Ross et al., 2010b, p. 25). In some instances of collaborative evaluation, such as CBPR, obtaining informed consent at the group/community level—in addition to the individual level—may be necessary (see Ross et al., 2010b). The question of who, precisely, constitutes the "community" in a given circumstance can be a challenging one, however. Does one seek the approval of "official" representatives of the community in question? What if these representatives use a voting procedure with their constituencies to determine whether community consent is granted? Amidst all of these decision-making dynamics, it is important to keep in mind that individuals within a community can withhold their informed consent even when the larger groups they are a part of have provided approval in some fashion. That being said, such individuals might still experience real or imagined pressure to participate in the evaluation, raising additional ethical concerns. Conversely, someone might desire to participate in an evaluation that the larger community has chosen not to endorse (Ross et al., 2010b). These are all situations that are likely to require more detailed consideration of the informed consent process by the evaluator than would be the case in less collaborative endeavors.

A multistage approach is probably appropriate in many of these circumstances. Evaluators should first identify the most meaningful level of community that encompasses the study population in question and then determine what individuals/groups are likely to be seen as credible spokespersons for that level (e.g., a neighborhood's local citizen action committee, a housing development's resident board). Once contact is established with the appropriate spokespersons, the evaluator should seek input on appropriate ways to engage individuals represented by those stakeholders. This approach maximizes the likelihood that the thorough understanding needed for informed consent at various levels will be achieved.

Ensuring confidentiality can also become more complicated in participatory evaluations. The ranks of those who are enlisted as data collectors can expand to include agency practitioners (Shaw & Faulkner, 2006), indigenous fieldworkers (Alexander & Richman, 2008), and community members. As Ross et al. (2010b, p. 26) note, "Confidentiality of data may be more difficult to ensure when socially proximate individuals collect data from each other." It is not just the logistical challenge of protecting privacy that is involved here. Research indicates that community and agency stakeholders can differ from evaluators in how they conceptualize ethical issues (see Morris, 2015b), and these differences can have implications for the importance they assign to domains such as confidentiality. In these circumstances, care must be taken to provide appropriate education and training when initiating evaluation projects, leading to shared agreements about what is appropriate, acceptable, and just (see Yonas et al., 2016).

Another area of concern raised by the Respect for People principle is the management of risk. Consistent with the precept of "do no harm," evaluations should be conducted in a way that minimizes the risk of harm to participants while maximizing the likelihood of benefits ("beneficence"). In collaborative evaluations, the task of identifying potential risks and benefits can be intimidating. For example, risks can affect not only individuals as individuals, but also individuals as group/community members, as well as the group/community itself (Ross et al., 2010c). An evaluation of a program for low-income, single-parent families in a mixed-income community could contribute to the stigmatization of those stakeholders by increasing their visibility as "problem families" within that community. And at the community level, a serious disagreement within a grass-roots citizens group over whether or not to endorse a collaborative evaluation could damage the group's ability to advocate effectively for community interests in the future. Even in cases in which an enthusiastic consensus characterizes a group's decision to endorse an evaluation, harsh criticism of the group's decision can occur if the project later attracts negative publicity in the community. This is certainly a risk of harm of which group members should be made aware during the informed consent process.

It is not possible for evaluators to gauge precisely the magnitude of the myriad risks and benefits that are likely to be associated with a high-engagement, multiple-stakeholder evaluation, but a good-faith attempt to specify the nature of these risks and benefits at multiple levels is certainly warranted. Doing so would significantly reduce the unanticipated consequences of such ventures.

Common Good and Equity

According to this principle, "Evaluators strive to contribute to the common good and advancement of an equitable and just society" (AEA, 2018, E). This is probably the most wide-ranging of the Guiding Principles, given that it targets notions of the public interest and the public good. Of particular relevance to collaborative evaluation is the principle's assertion that "evaluators identify and make efforts to address the evaluation's potential threats to the common good especially when specific stakeholder interests conflict with the goals of a democratic, equitable, and just society" (E-3). The notion of social justice thus becomes salient here. From an evaluation perspective, Ross et al. argue that this concept encompasses

> ensuring that research priorities reflect the … needs of all socioeconomic communities, particularly vulnerable communities; and promoting institutions and social practices that support capacities for self-determination and ensure respectful interactions. This is best achieved if the individuals and communities who are the object of the research participate as partners at all stages of the research process. (Ross et al., 2010a, p. 6)

Viewed from a social justice vantage point, the Common Good and Equity principle puts forth an ambitious agenda, one that should be distinctively compelling to collaborative evaluators. In essence, evaluators are seen as having an ethical responsibility to engage stakeholders in ways that might extend beyond the narrowly defined parameters of a particular study and address the implications of that study for the achievement of positive community/social change. From a related standpoint, this can be regarded as a shift in emphasis from minimizing individual risk (i.e., do no harm) to "considering the benefits of evaluation to society" as a whole (Barnett & Camfield, 2016, p. 529).

Discerning these implications can be a difficult task, given the multiple stakeholders involved and the competing/conflicting interests they can represent. Indeed, extracting the nature of the overall public good in such circumstances is probably more of an ideological endeavor than an ethical one. What does seem clear, however, is that collaborative evaluators have embraced, ethically and otherwise, an orientation that is more rather than less inclusive with respect to defining the public good within the context of their work. At least this is what occurs at the level of espoused theory. The extent to which this emphasis is reflected in actual practice is an empirical question, one for which little beyond anecdotal data is available.

Collaborative evaluation, insofar as it entails the establishment of formal relationships between the evaluator and groups rather than just individuals, raises the possibility that group members who do not participate in an evaluation might nonetheless be affected by it. This is a matter clearly relevant to the Common Good and Equity principle. For example, a resident council within a low-income housing project might vote to participate in an evaluation of an intervention focused on certain subgroups within the project (e.g., families with children who are doing poorly in school). The publicity surrounding the evaluation could have a stigmatizing effect on *all* families with children in the housing project, even those not participating in the intervention. The operative word here is "could." There is no certainty that such stigmatization would occur, and even if it did, its magnitude might be negligible, given the level of stigma that could already be associated with living in the project. The key point, however, is that stakeholders who are not part of the intervention could be impacted by the decision of their representatives to engage with this study. This is precisely the sort of situation to which this principle is intended to alert evaluators.

The evaluator here should probably discuss the possibility of stigmatization with stakeholders during the entry/contracting phase of the project and monitor the ongoing evaluation for any signs of heightened stigmatization. This can be a challenging endeavor, given that the evaluator does not want to raise the issue in a way that contributes to stigmatization or provokes an undue sense of alarm. Not addressing the concern at all, however, would seem to be inconsistent with the Common Good and Equity and Respect for People principles.

CASE EXAMPLE: THE EVALUATION OF THE YOUNG SCHOLARS PROGRAM

The case that follows is fictitious. However, it depicts several ethical challenges that research indicates are relatively common in evaluation. Thus, the saga of the Young Scholars Program (YSP) is, in movie parlance, "based on true events."

Background

The YSP has occupied a special niche in Central City High School (CCHS) for over a decade. Founded by two CCHS teachers, the 2-year program annually recruits 20 students from the school's freshman class and provides them with a variety of enrichment experiences within and outside of the high school. These include, but are not limited to, museum trips, lectures, public presentations, and cultural events, as well as opportunities to take courses at a nearby magnet school specializing in the arts. The students meet as a group on a regular basis to discuss their experiences, and they write several reflection papers per term. Student participation in the program ends after their sophomore year.

The YSP represents a "labor of love" on the part of its two founding teachers, who continue to run the program with the help of several additional faculty who have joined CCHS over the years. No teachers are paid for the extensive work they put into the YSP, but the expenses associated with the activities engaged in by the students are covered by discretionary funds from the school's budget.

All CCHS freshmen are invited to apply to the YSP. Applicants submit an essay and are interviewed by one of the unpaid graduate student interns who work with the program. Because the time commitment required of YSP participants is substantial, the number of applicants each year is relatively modest. There are usually about 40 applications for the 20 slots. Applicant demographics are somewhat skewed. While the overall population of CCHS's freshman class is approximately 50% African American, 25% Hispanic, and 25% White, applications generally run about 40% African American, 15% Hispanic, and 45% White. YSP acceptance statistics closely reflect the application percentages.

Overall, the CCHS faculty and staff view the YSP with great pride, and the program has become a valued part of the school's culture. CCHS serves a largely low-income, marginalized segment of the city's population, and the YSP is regarded as a praiseworthy, albeit modest, attempt to do something "special" for those students who want to take advantage of it.

The Evaluation

Last year, a new principal arrived at CCHS, replacing the one who had served since the establishment of the YSP. She admires the good intentions behind the program, but believes that it is long overdue for a systematic evaluation. She obtains a small technical assistance grant from a local philanthropic foundation and proceeds to hire an external evaluator. The evaluator, who has a collaborative orientation, persuades the principal that it would be wise to establish an advisory committee for the evaluation that includes a variety of key stakeholders: the principal and assistant principal, a YSP teacher and a non-YSP teacher, two YSP alumni (a junior and a senior), the CCHS social worker, the CCHS guidance counselor, two YSP parents, and a representative from the cooperating magnet school.

The group assembles and the planning process begins. It quickly becomes apparent that conflicting perspectives exist among the stakeholders. For example, the principal wants to see what impact the YSP has, if any, on students' academic achievement during and after their participation in the program. Students, on the other hand, view the evaluation primarily as an opportunity to gather data on participants' satisfaction with current activities and suggestions for future activities. The parent representatives would like the study to determine how well the program succeeds in keeping participants "out of trouble" during their high school years. The teachers display little enthusiasm for the evaluation and appear suspicious of the principal's motives for seeking it in the first place. They believe that the YSP has been a CCHS "success story" for a decade. What is to be gained by subjecting this low-cost, well-received program to a formal evaluation? It is clear that the goals of the YSP are conceptualized differently by different stakeholders, a circumstance that is likely to have problematic consequences for the evaluation if not addressed early on by the evaluator.

The evaluator is not confident that it will be possible, given the resources available, to do justice to all of the agendas that have been put forth for the evaluation. Discerning the impact of the program on academic achievement might be particularly challenging, given the methodological constraints imposed by the YSP's selection process. However, it is the principal who hired the evaluator for this project. The evaluator ends up presenting the group with a design that reflects the principal's priorities to a greater extent than would have been the case if the principal had not played such a prominent role in commissioning the evaluation. The group respects the evaluator's expertise and agrees to the design, but the teachers remain disgruntled.

As the evaluation proceeds and implementation data are gathered on the program's activities, the evaluator notices a discrepancy: The attendance sheets for certain events indicate a significantly greater number of participants than is suggested by surveys of YSP students. Follow-up interviews with a subgroup of these students confirm that there are instances in which students are listed as having attended an event for which they were not present. Responsibility for recording attendance rests with the teacher(s) chaperoning the event, not the students.

As the evaluator delves further into the data, a pattern of inflated participation figures clearly emerges and is primarily associated with one teacher who has worked with the program for 3 years. The evaluator ponders how to handle this situation. Share the finding with the teacher and ask for an explanation? Share the finding with the YSP director, who is also a member of the evaluation advisory group? Simply include the finding in the final report of the evaluation without identifying the teacher in question? Something else?

The evaluator selects the first option and approaches the teacher, whose initial response is confusion. As the conversation proceeds, the teacher indicates that he must have occasionally filled out attendance sheets based on who had RSVP'd that they intended to participate in an event, rather than on who actually attended. The teacher's explanation for why he would do this was muddled and less than compelling; he suggested that the premature completion of attendance forms was somehow "more efficient" during busy times of the term. Solid data that could support or refute the teacher's account are not available, and the evaluator decides not to pursue this line of investigation any further. The draft of the final report submitted by the evaluator to the advisory committee recommends that steps be taken to ensure the accuracy of attendance figures for events, given that some inconsistencies in the data were discovered. The draft does not identify the teacher with whom the evaluator spoke.

This recommendation provokes little reaction from the group, but other parts of the draft report are not received so placidly. The report indicates that participating students and their parents view the YSP very positively, but that there is scant evidence to suggest that the program has a substantive impact on academic achievement. The teacher and student representatives are incensed, claiming that the report is disproportionately skewed toward grades, standardized test scores, and college attendance as measures of program effectiveness. They assert that the report should be "more balanced," and include more first-person accounts from students and others describing their experiences with the YSP. The principal and assistant principal are also unhappy. They are not surprised by the findings, but believe that the report needs to be stronger in terms of recommending fundamental changes in the program. From their perspective, the overriding goal of an intervention

Continued

such as the YSP should be academic success. As the principal states in an advisory committee meeting, "Our core mission at this school is to help young people develop their scholastic ability to the greatest extent possible. The evaluation results show that the YSP isn't contributing much to that goal, despite the time, effort, and resources we're investing in it. The report needs to send a much stronger message."

As the contentious discussion swirls around the room, the evaluator is wondering, "How am I going to handle this?"

Analysis of the Young Scholars Program Case

The first challenge presented in this case is one that is endemic to collaborative evaluation: If you seek to engage multiple stakeholders in planning an evaluation, do not be shocked if you find significant disagreement among them. Such disagreement raises a key ethical question: Whose views should the evaluator weigh more heavily in the event that a unanimously shared perspective cannot be achieved? The 2004 version of the Guiding Principles asserts:

> Evaluators necessarily have a special relationship with the client who funds or requests the evaluation. By virtue of that relationship evaluators must strive to meet legitimate client needs whenever it is feasible and appropriate to do so. However, that relationship can also place evaluators in difficult dilemmas when client interests conflict with other interests. (Morris, 2008, p. 210)

In this instance, it is the principal who has requested and (indirectly) funds the evaluation. Thus, one could argue that the evaluator should pay special attention to the principal's priorities for the project. However, a collaborative evaluator is also committed to giving a fair hearing to other stakeholder voices in establishing a project's direction. How can the evaluator be certain that a fair hearing has taken place in this case? Evaluators have a responsibility to point out the strengths and weaknesses (e.g., from a Systematic Inquiry perspective) of alternative visions for an evaluation's focus, but this process can be complicated when stakeholders of varying power advocate for competing visions that all have defensible rationales. Should the priorities of the primary client tip the scales in these situations? To what extent does a collaborative orientation carry with it a commitment to the empowerment, when feasible, of less powerful stakeholders? Insofar as such a commitment exists, does it exert ethical force or is it primarily a philosophical preference? These are questions that should inform the YSP evaluator's response to the challenge posed at the beginning of the case, and it would not be surprising if different commentators reached different conclusions about what the most appropriate course of action would be, especially in the absence of additional details about the case itself.

The YSP scenario highlights the challenge of dealing with stakeholders who voice conflicting views. But what if potentially key stakeholders have not participated in the evaluation? Morris (2015a) reports the case of a needs assessment focused on teachers' perceptions of their safety within public schools in a Northeastern city. The data revealed that teachers often felt threatened by the actions of their own students. Students had not been included as stakeholders in the study, and this finding did not result in their being solicited by the evaluators (or school system administrators) to become part of the project.

From a collaborative vantage point, one could see this omission having ethical significance: Those from a subgroup characterized as disruptive and dangerous were not given the opportunity to share their responses or concerns, producing a needs assessment that could be critiqued as highly skewed.

The second YSP challenge, involving the attendance records, raises questions concerning the handling of potentially volatile data. The evaluator decides not to pursue the matter further after hearing the teacher's explanation and simply notes the overall issue of accuracy in the final report. Should the evaluator have done more? To be sure, it would not be unreasonable to be at least a bit skeptical of the teacher's account and to imagine that the teacher was being intentionally deceptive in his record keeping. On the other hand, the evaluator has not been hired to function as a private detective, and it is not unusual for record-keeping discrepancies in social programs to have benign sources, as the teacher claimed this one was.

Does the Integrity principle require the evaluator to reveal details of the episode beyond what he/she has already done? Or to have a conversation with the teacher who directs the YSP? The following factors should probably be taken into account when answering these questions: The data here are directly relevant to the evaluation, and no mention has been made of confidentiality assurances that would constrain the evaluator's ability to share this information. It is not clear that any substantive evaluative purpose would be served by identifying the teacher in the report—after all, this is a program evaluation, not an individual performance appraisal—but in a conversation with the YSP director about this finding, the teacher's name would almost certainly come up. The Respect for People principle thus becomes relevant, given the admonition to "do no harm." It is possible that the teacher would be reprimanded in some fashion, or at least embarrassed, because of this revelation, but would this level of harm outweigh the importance of providing a full account of the attendance-recording issue to the director? Could subsequent data gathering on the part of the director lead to consequences that are more serious for the teacher, depending on what is discovered? If that occurred, to what degree would the evaluator be ethically responsible for those consequences? And would more serious consequences necessarily be unwarranted? Once again, evaluators might differ in the subjective cost–benefit ratios they calculate in this situation.

In the YSP case, the volatile data were "stumbled upon," as it were, by the evaluator. However, what should be done with information secretly presented to an evaluator by a stakeholder? During the latter stages of an accreditation site visit to a university, I (and several other members of the evaluation team) received a lengthy email from a faculty member at the institution. The message claimed that much of the testimony we had gathered during meetings with the faculty was suspect, because the faculty were intimidated by the school's president and senior administration and feared reprisal if their views of problems were shared with our team.

We discussed how this communication should be handled, a discussion that included consideration of our ethical responsibilities. We had attempted to be thoroughly collaborative throughout the site visit, providing all stakeholders, including faculty, with multiple opportunities to meet with representatives of the team. We assured participants in group meetings that their input would not be reported in ways that could be linked to them as individuals. With this background in mind, we decided not to incorporate the faculty member's concerns into our report. We did not make this choice in order to protect the individual's privacy. Rather, we believed that the climate of fear described in the email was not consistent with the other data we had obtained during the visit, and the content of the accusations did not point to anything beyond poor leadership on the part of the senior administration, a common complaint in organizational life. In our view, Systematic Inquiry would not have been served by including these outlier data that emerged from beyond the borders of our evaluation design.

Finally, there is the matter of the YSP draft report. This is typically a domain in which the Integrity and Common Good and Equity principles become salient. In general, evaluators believe that the public good is served when they author reports that accurately reflect their findings and conclusions, and they become greatly concerned when they feel pressured to do otherwise (Morris & Clark, 2013). Indeed, the Program Evaluation Standard of Transparency and Disclosure (P-5) stipulates, "Evaluations should provide complete descriptions of findings, limitations, and conclusions to all stakeholders, unless doing so would violate legal and propriety obligations" (Yarbrough et al., 2011, p. 139). In collaborative evaluations, the likelihood of experiencing pressure is enhanced, given the engagement of multiple stakeholders. In the YSP case, the teachers and students are calling for a "more balanced" report, while the principal and assistant principal want the evaluator to present recommendations that forcefully critique the program's performance.

It is possible, of course, for a stakeholder's suggestions for change in a report to be legitimate. Evaluators are not infallible, and their perceptions of what constitutes a valid representation of a program in a report can be flawed. (Early in my career, a key stakeholder chided me for writing an introductory summary for a high-profile evaluation report that read more like a sterile abstract for a journal article than a holistic, context-sensitive depiction of the evaluation. He was right.) In fact, a major strength of collaborative evaluation that is often cited is its ability to produce a more well-rounded portrait of a program than would be generated by a noncollaborative approach. The YSP evaluator must first attempt to minimize his/her defensiveness and assess the extent to which the stakeholders' claims have merit. Let us assume, however, that the evaluator concludes that the teacher/student recommendations would distort the major thrust of the findings and that the principal/assistant principal suggestions are not justified based on those findings. To what degree, if at all, should the evaluator agree to revise the report to make it more responsive to the stakeholders' concerns? Is it ethical to make *any* concessions?

The stakes involved here are not trivial. A report that glosses over the limitations of the program could forestall sorely needed changes, while one that is excessively harsh in its criticism could be used to undermine the program's core legitimacy and sustainability. YSP's stakeholders have vested interests that the evaluator would be wise to take into account when deciding how to proceed. Indeed, one of the Program Evaluation Standards (U-8) explicitly focuses on this issue: "Evaluations should promote responsible and adaptive use while guarding against unintended negative consequences and misuse" (Yarbrough et al., 2011, p. 65). The YSP scenario is one where such concerns are certainly relevant. Given the varied goals that different stakeholders appear to have for the program (academic achievement, school engagement, etc.), it might be possible for the evaluator to more explicitly link YSP's specific outcomes and accomplishments to those goals in the report. In this fashion, the report could address in a more fine-grained fashion the evaluation's implications for program modification. Of course, the task of prioritizing program goals, and the changes associated with them, would still need to be addressed by stakeholders, but a richer portrait of the YSP is likely to emerge, one that is more supportive of formative action.

The YSP Case and the Guiding Principles: A Summary

This section provides a recap of the implications of the Guiding Principles for the major ethical issues raised by the evaluation of the YSP and highlights the interrelated nature of the Principles.

Systematic Inquiry. This principle requires evaluators to "explore with primary stakeholders the limitations and strengths of the core evaluation questions and the approaches that might be used for answering those questions" (AEA, 2018, A-2), as well as to "make clear the limitations of the evaluation and its results" (A-4). These considerations come into play as the evaluator encounters the different priorities that various stakeholders have for the evaluation: impact on academic achievement (principal), satisfaction with program activities (students), and keeping kids out of trouble (parents). To what extent can a single, resource-constrained evaluation do justice to all three domains?

Not surprisingly, Systematic Inquiry is also relevant to the stakeholders' disparate reactions to the draft of the final report. Teachers and students call for a "more balanced" assessment while the principal and assistant principal desire a more hard-hitting set of recommendations for change. The evaluator must clearly communicate how the design and focus of the study have shaped what can be said with confidence in the report, thereby upholding the Systematic Inquiry principle of addressing the various factors that have influenced his/her interpretation of the findings.

Competence. The YSP case does not appear to engage any of the major components of this principle in a substantive fashion.

Integrity. This principle requires evaluators to "assess and make explicit the stakeholders', clients', and evaluators' values, perspectives, and interests concerning the conduct and outcomes of the evaluation" (AEA, 2018, C-4). Thus, it is crucial that the evaluator facilitate interaction between the YSP stakeholders in a fashion that contributes to a shared understanding and appreciation of the different priorities they bring to the evaluation.

The Integrity principle pertains as well to the issue of the inaccurate attendance sheets, given that the evaluator must "accurately and transparently represent evaluation procedures, data, and findings" (AEA, 2018, C-5). In short, the evaluator has to find an ethically appropriate way to report this sensitive finding.

Finally, accuracy and transparency are core concerns for the contested draft report. Ultimately, the evaluator must believe that the final report portrays the YSP in a holistic manner that fairly reflects the program's operations, its achievements, and its needs.

Respect for People. In stating that evaluators "strive to gain an understanding of, and treat fairly, the range of perspectives and interests that individuals and groups bring to the evaluation" (AEA, 2018, D-1), this principle underscores the importance of addressing the competing stakeholder priorities for the evaluation, as well as the differing views of the draft report that surface at the end of the case.

Respect for People is also the principle that most directly engages the vulnerability of the teacher who submitted inaccurate attendance sheets, given that it explicitly references "prevention of harm." The evaluator must be mindful of the welfare of this individual when sharing the finding with stakeholders.

Common Good and Equity. This principle calls for evaluators to "recognize and balance the interests of the client, other stakeholders, and the common good while also protecting the integrity of the evaluation" (AEA, 2018, E-1) and to "mitigate the bias and potential power imbalances that can occur as a result of the evaluation's context" (E-5). With respect to the YSP case, the distinctive contribution of this principle is that it focuses our attention on how competing stakeholder preferences, at both the beginning and the end of the evaluation, can have implications for how the evaluation serves the common good. For example, would an evaluation that heavily emphasized one set of outcome criteria, largely to the exclusion of others, be responsive to the multiple roles that a school-based intervention might need to play in a marginalized community? Would modifying the draft report to incorporate the sorts of sweeping recommendations for program change likely to be favored by the principal constitute a failure to mitigate power imbalances within the evaluation's context? Or could such revisions eventually lead to a stronger YSP that more effectively serves the common good? Of course, the Common Good and Equity principle, by itself, cannot answer these questions, but it does exhort the evaluator to consider them when making decisions during and after the project.

DOING THE RIGHT THING

What steps can collaborative evaluators take to maximize the likelihood they will behave ethically when working with stakeholders? In essence, they are probably the same steps that would benefit the practice of *all* evaluators. Thus, the following sections present recommendations that are intended to have generalized relevance, but will be explored from the perspective of evaluators who embrace a collaborative orientation.

Know the Guiding Principles, Program Evaluation Standards, and CES Ethics Statement

These three documents have foundational importance for the ethical practice of evaluation in North America. The Utility and Propriety Standards, for example, explore in detail evaluators' responsibilities to the stakeholders with whom they interact. They provide collaborative evaluators with a firm grounding in the overall domain of ethical stakeholder engagement, which can be supplemented with other resources more specifically attuned to the methodology of collaborative evaluation (e.g., Shulha et al., 2016).

As has been noted, principles and standards do not offer ready-made solutions to ethical challenges that evaluators might encounter. The nuanced, specific circumstances of a given case typically prevent such an automatic application (see Mabry, 1999). This is especially likely to occur in the complex network of relationships that high-engagement evaluations can engender. However, as an ethical "orienting device" (Morris, 2003), principles and standards can prove to be invaluable.

Stay Abreast of the Literature on Evaluation Ethics

Over the past three decades, the literature on evaluation ethics has grown substantially (for reviews, see Morris, 1999, 2015b). Research, commentary, and case-study analysis in this area have not neglected collaborative evaluation. Although it can be difficult for practitioners to find the time to review these resources, the resources themselves are relatively easy to access (e.g., the *American Journal of Evaluation's* ongoing series of articles on ethics) and they can help evaluators identify, predict, and respond to ethical conflicts in their work. Indeed, the Guiding Principle of Competence states that "evaluators should continually undertake relevant education, training or supervised practice to learn new concepts, techniques, skills, and services necessary for competent evaluation practice" (AEA, 2018, B-4). Viewed from this perspective, staying in touch with the current ethics literature is itself an ethical requirement in the evaluation field.

Maximize the Value of the Entry/Contracting Stage

The entry/contracting stage of the evaluation is when the shared understanding of, and expectations for, the project are developed among all key stakeholders, including, of course, the evaluator. It is hard to overstate how crucial this phase is in setting the stage for a successful evaluation. Evaluators should use the entry/contracting stage to educate stakeholders on the ethical issues that need to be addressed in the evaluation and draw their attention to challenges that the project might be particularly vulnerable to, given its context. For example, an evaluation that will produce a widely disseminated report in a highly politicized environment could easily generate strong pressures on the evaluator to misrepresent findings. Discussing strategies for how to handle this pressure, and perhaps even prevent or at least reduce it, would be far preferable to simply waiting for the pressure to occur much later in the project and then dealing with it (see Perrin, 2018).

In the YSP case, the failure to comprehensively address during the entry/contracting stage the stakeholders' views of program goals greatly complicated the evaluator's life when the time came to prepare the final report. A more in-depth discussion early on would, at a minimum, have generated a clearer set of expectations among stakeholders concerning the approach taken by the evaluator in the final report.

The entry/contracting stage is an ideal time for actively soliciting stakeholders' ethical concerns for the evaluation. This can be a challenging task because stakeholders' perspectives on ethics do not necessarily correspond closely with the categories that evaluators are accustomed to using. Rather than framing their inquiries specifically in terms of ethics, evaluators might be better served by using more general language when posing questions to stakeholders (e.g., "Are there any aspects of the evaluation that you're worried about?" "Do you think there is a risk of people's rights being violated or compromised during the evaluation?"). The overriding goal here is to surface as many relevant issues as possible before the evaluation actually begins. Doing so is likely to facilitate the development of the high level of trust that is needed for collaborative evaluation to succeed.

Consult With Colleagues

Obtaining input from respected colleagues is a time-honored method of enhancing one's ethical practice, inside and outside of evaluation. Such input can be valuable in at least two ways: (1) helping one reframe the nature of the ethical challenge and/or (2) expanding the number of options for dealing with the challenge. Evaluators should endeavor to cultivate a network of professional contacts who are "critical friends," that is, individuals who share their core values but might differ from them in terms of temperament, style, and preferences/attitudes concerning evaluation practice. Otherwise, one runs the risk of simply seeking advice from another version of oneself. The research evidence indicates that evaluators can disagree sharply over how to handle certain ethical issues, and it is important for evaluators to be aware of the range of perspectives that might be applied in a given circumstance. The EVALTALK listserv maintained by AEA is an excellent resource for contacts that one can engage in both online and offline discussions.

In the YSP scenario, seeking advice from an evaluator with experience in small-scale projects with multiple stakeholders in public school systems would certainly be recommended. Also, consulting with a public school principal or assistant principal in another community might help the evaluator more fully appreciate the perspectives of the various CCHS stakeholders and develop strategies for addressing them.

Know Thyself

Professional principles and standards are not the only value-laden resources that evaluators bring to the ethical challenges they face. Personal values relevant to equality, justice, independence, and compassion, for example, can play a key role in how evaluators view and respond to ethical problems in their work. The more self-aware evaluators are, the more effective they can be in integrating their personal and professional priorities in their work. For instance, if the evaluator in the YSP scenario was deeply committed to achieving equality and justice for marginalized populations, they might be more sensitive to calls from the teachers and students for greater balance in the final report than would otherwise be the case. Personal values can be especially useful when evaluation principles or standards offer conflicting advice, and thus do not provide a clear path for how to resolve the problem (see Newman & Brown, 1996).

CONCLUSION

The subfield of evaluation ethics has matured over the past several decades, as has the practice of collaborative approaches to evaluation. As both domains continue to evolve, their interaction will bring to light new challenges to work through, or at least revised versions of older ones. For example, this volume emphasizes the role of evaluation in bringing about community change. One can view this emphasis as an elaboration and extension of the utilization-focused orientation developed and championed by Patton (Patton, 2008). Indeed, one might ask if there are approaches to facilitating organizational and community change through collaborative evaluation that might be deemed ethically questionable. Datta (1999) has observed that "diverse evaluators *agree* that the evaluator should not be an advocate (or presumably, an adversary) of specific programs in the sense of taking sides"

(p. 84). Do collaborative evaluators run the risk of being perceived as advocates of specific programs or, as is perhaps more likely, advocates of specific *changes* in these programs (e.g., in the YSP case)? What are the consequences, ethical and otherwise, of being seen in this fashion? How can collaborative evaluators manage their role so that they are not regarded as crossing a line that separates appropriate from inappropriate professional influence in the name of change? Empirically, do we even have a clear grasp of where that line resides? Researchers in evaluation ethics should have a lot to keep them busy in the decades to come.

FURTHER READING

American Evaluation Association. (2018). *Guiding principles for evaluators*. http://www.eval.org/p/cm/ld/fid=51

Block, P. (2011). *Flawless consulting: A guide to getting your expertise used* (3rd ed.). Jossey-Bass.

Canadian Evaluation Society. (n.d.). *Ethics*. http://evaluationcanada.ca/ethics

Greene, J. C., & Lee, J. (2006). Quieting educational reform … with educational reform. *American Journal of Evaluation, 27*, 337–352.

Mabry, L. (1999). Circumstantial ethics. *American Journal of Evaluation, 20*, 199–212.

Morris, M. (Ed.). (2008). *Evaluation ethics for best practice: Cases and commentaries*. Guilford.

Newman, D. L., & Brown, R. D. (1996). *Applied ethics for program evaluation*. Sage.

Perrin, B. (2018). How to manage pressure to change reports: Should evaluators be above criticism? *American Journal of Evaluation*. https://doi.org/10.1177/1098214018792622

Yarbrough, D. B., Shulha, L. M., Hopson, R. K., & Caruthers, F. A. (2011). *The program evaluation standards* (3rd ed.). Sage.

KEY CONCEPTS

Beneficence: The ethical principle of having the enhanced welfare of study participants as a goal in research.

Confidentiality: The expectation that information provided by individuals to researchers will be shared with others in a way that protects the former's privacy.

Conflict of interest: A conflict between the private interests and official responsibilities of a person in a position of trust.

Do no harm: The ethical principle of striving to conduct research in a way that does not harm participants or at least minimizes the risk of harm.

Ethics: Dealing with what is good and bad in human conduct and with moral duty and obligation.

Ethical dilemma: A situation in which two or more ethical principles appear to offer conflicting recommendations for action.

Guiding Principles for Evaluators: Developed by the American Evaluation Association, the Guiding Principles provide a framework for the professional ethical conduct of evaluators. The five Guiding Principles are Systematic Inquiry, Competence, Integrity, Respect for People, and Common Good and Equity.

Informed consent: A voluntary agreement to participate in research in which the participant displays an understanding of both the research and its associated risks.

QUESTIONS FOR REFLECTION

1. If you were the evaluator in the YSP case, how would you respond to the concerns that stakeholders have with the draft report? What would be your reasoning? Would you invoke one or more of the Guiding Principles when explaining your response? If so, what would you say?

2. Overall, which one of the Guiding Principles do you think is most challenging to implement when taking a partnership-based approach to evaluation? Why? Which principle is least affected by such an orientation?

3. As a partnership-based practitioner, what ethical concerns would you be likely to emphasize in discussions with stakeholders during the entry/contracting phase of an evaluation?

4. The concluding section of this chapter raises the question: Can collaborative practitioners be so committed to partnership-generated community change that they jeopardize their role as credible evaluators? What's your opinion? How should evaluators deal with this possibility?

REFERENCES

Alexander, L. B., & Richman, K. A. (2008). Ethical dilemmas in evaluations using Indigenous research workers. *American Journal of Evaluation, 29*(1), 73–85. doi:10.1177/1098214007313023

American Evaluation Association. (2018). *Guiding principles for evaluators.* http://www.eval.org/p/cm/ld/fid=51

Argyris, C. (1985). *Strategy, change, and defensive routines.* Pitman.

Azzam, T. (2010). Evaluator responsiveness to stakeholders. *American Journal of Evaluation, 31*(1), 45–65. doi:10.1177/1098214009354917

Barnett, C., & Camfield, L. (2016). Ethics in evaluation. *Journal of Development Effectiveness, 8*(4), 528–534. doi:10.1080/19439342.2016.1244554

Buchanan, H., & MacDonald, W. (2011, November). *Anytime, anywhere, evaluation ethics do matter!* Paper presented at the meeting of the American Evaluation Association, Anaheim, CA

Campbell, R. (2016). "It's the way that you do it": Developing an ethical framework for community psychology research and action. *American Journal of Community Psychology, 58*(3-4), 294–302. doi:10.1002/ajcp.12037

Canadian Evaluation Society. (n.d.). *Ethics.* http://evaluationcanada.ca/ethics

Datta, L. (1999). The ethics of evaluation neutrality and advocacy. In J. L. Fitzpatrick & M. Morris (Eds.), *Current and emerging challenges in evaluation. New Directions for Evaluation, 82,* 77–88. doi:10.1002/ev.1139

Datta, L.-E. (2002). The case of the uncertain bridge. *American Journal of Evaluation, 23*(2), 187–206. doi:10.1177/109821400202300207

Fetterman, D. M., Rodriguez-Campos, L., & Zukoski, A. P. (2017). *Collaborative, participatory, and empowerment evaluation: Stakeholder involvement approaches.* Guilford.

King, J. A., & Stevahn, L. (2013). *Interactive evaluation practice: Mastering the interpersonal dynamics of program evaluation.* Sage.

Lykes, M. B. (2017). Community-based and participatory action research: Community psychology collaborations within and across borders. In M. A. Bond, I. Serrano-Garcia, & C. B. Keys (Eds.), *APA handbook of community psychology: Methods for community research and action for diverse groups and issues* (Vol. 2, pp. 43–58). American Psychological Association.

Mabry, L. (1999). Circumstantial ethics. *American Journal of Evaluation, 20*(2), 199–212. doi:10.1177/109821409902000203

MacKay, E., & O'Neill, P. (1992). What creates the dilemma in ethical dilemmas? Examples from psychological practice. *Ethics & Behavior, 2*(4), 227–244. doi:10.1207/s15327019eb0204_1

Morris, M. (1999). Research on evaluation ethics: What have we learned and why is it important? In J. L. Fitzpatrick & M. Morris (Eds.), Current and emerging challenges in evaluation. *New Directions for Evaluation, 82,* 15–24. doi:10.1002/ev.1133

Morris, M. (2003). Ethical considerations in evaluation. In T. Kellaghan & D. L. Stufflebeam (Eds.), *International handbook of educational evaluation (Part 1)* (pp. 303–328). Kluwer Academic Publishers.

Morris, M. (Ed.). (2008). *Evaluation ethics for best practice: Cases and commentaries.* Guilford.

Morris, M. (2015a). Professional judgment and ethics. In V. Scott & S. M. Wolfe (Eds.), *Community psychology: Foundations for practice* (pp. 132–156). Sage.

Morris, M. (2015b). Research on evaluation ethics: Reflections and an agenda. In P. R. Brandon (Ed.), Research on evaluation. *New Directions for Evaluation, 148,* 3–42. doi:10.1002/ev.20155

Morris, M., & Clark, B. (2013). You want me to do what? Evaluators and the pressure to misrepresent findings. *American Journal of Evaluation, 34*(1), 57–70. doi:10.1177/1098214012457237

Morris, M., & Cohn, R. (1993). Program evaluators and ethical challenges: A national survey. *Evaluation Review, 17,* 621–642.

Newman, D. L., & Brown, R. D. (1996). *Applied ethics for program evaluation.* Sage.

Patton, M. Q. (2008). *Utilization-focused evaluation* (4th ed.). Sage.

Perrin, B. (2018). How to manage pressure to change reports: Should evaluators be above criticism? *American Journal of Evaluation, 9*(Sept). doi:10.1177/1098214018792622

Pleger, L., Sager, F., Morris, M., Meyer, W., & Stockmann, R. (2017). Are some countries more prone to pressure evaluators than others? Comparing findings from the United States, United Kingdom, Germany, and Switzerland. *American Journal of Evaluation, 38*(3), 315–328. doi:10.1177/1098214016662907

Ross, L. F., Loup, A., Nelson, R. M., Botkin, J. R., Kost, R., Smith, G. R., Jr., & Gehlert, S. (2010a). Human subjects protections in community-engaged research: A research ethics framework. *Journal of Empirical Research on Human Research Ethics, 5*(1), 5–17. doi:10.1525/jer.2010.5.1.5

Ross, L. F., Loup, A., Nelson, R. M., Botkin, J. R., Kost, R., Smith, G. R., Jr., & Gehlert, S. (2010b). The challenges of collaboration for academic and community partners in a research partnership: Points to consider. *Journal of Empirical Research on Human Research Ethics, 5*(1), 19–31. doi:10.1525/jer.2010.5.1.19

Ross, L. F., Loup, A., Nelson, R. M., Botkin, J. R., Kost, R., Smith, G. R., Jr., & Gehlert, S. (2010c). Nine key functions for a human subjects protection program for community-engaged research: Points to consider. *Journal of Empirical Research on Human Research Ethics, 5*(1), 33–47. doi:10.1525/jer.2010.5.1.33

Shaw, I., & Faulkner, A. (2006). Practitioner evaluation at work. *American Journal of Evaluation, 27*(1), 44–63. doi:10.1177/1098214005284968

Shulha, L. M., Whitmore, E., Cousins, J. B., Gilbert, N., & Hudib, H. (2016). Introducing evidence-based principles to guide collaborative approaches to evaluation: Results of an empirical process. *American Journal of Evaluation, 37*, 193–215.

Smith, N. L. (2002). An analysis of ethical challenges in evaluation. *American Journal of Evaluation, 23*(2), 199–206. doi:10.1177/109821400202300208

Tamariz, L., Medina, H., Taylor, J., Carrasquillo, O., Kobetz, E., & Palacio, A. (2015). Are research ethics committees prepared for community-based participatory research? *Journal of Empirical Research on Human Research Ethics, 10*(5), 488–495. doi:10.1177/1556264615615008

Turner, D. (2003). *Evaluation ethics and quality: Results of a survey of Australasian Evaluation Society members.* Australasian Evaluation Society.

Yarbrough, D. B., Shulha, L. M., Hopson, R. K., & Caruthers, F. A. (2011). *The program evaluation standards* (3rd ed.). Sage.

Yonas, M. A., Jaime, M. C., Barone, J., Valenti, S., Documét, P., Ryan, C. M., & Miller, E. (2016). Community partnered research ethics training in practice: A collaborative approach to certification. *Journal of Empirical Research in Human Research Ethics, 11*(2), 97–105. doi:10.1177/1556264616650802

CHAPTER 6

EVALUATING PROGRAM EFFECTIVENESS
Connecting Process and Outcomes

James R. Cook and Ryan P. Kilmer

In Chapter 1, we described evaluation as a way to answer questions of importance to the program and its various stakeholders. (See Box 1.1 for a list of potential questions that might be answered.) More specifically, evaluation was described as a means to help improve the program so that it can maximize its ability to improve the lives of the purported beneficiaries of the program. In sum, evaluation is a set of procedures that are specifically intended to help the program do the best it can to produce its intended outcomes.

To understand how we might improve the program, we must first assess how well it is accomplishing its intended purposes. In general, we want to understand the degree to which our programs are causing the intended change. This, then, provides information needed to help the program increase its ability to benefit those who participate in it.

However, clear evidence that a program is causing the desired changes is often difficult to obtain, certainly for the vast majority of social programs. This is in part because our programs are never the sole "influencers" over their intended beneficiaries. The people that programs target are also affected by family members, friends, acquaintances, the media, other programs and policies, and their experiences in other settings. Therefore, change can be caused by multiple factors, and it may be difficult to conclude definitively that change was caused by the particular program in question or how much of the change was caused by the program, compared to other factors. This means that we need to develop programmatic strategies to help us draw conclusions about the causal impact of a program. Successful strategies recognize that programs must almost always strike a balance between the use of rigorous methodologies that can provide relatively unequivocal evidence that the program effects change and the need to operate a program in a manner that is consistent with its values, that uses resources wisely, and that collects and uses data to effect positive program change.

Learning Objectives

1. Identify strategies for understanding and assessing changes that occur among the intended beneficiaries of the program.

2. Identify strategies for understanding and assessing the degree to which a program is being implemented as intended.

3. Describe strategies for determining if changes in the intended beneficiaries are caused by the program.

4. Understand elements needed in a data management system to support evaluation.

We do not believe that we need to have unequivocal evidence about program impact to be able to understand how a program works and how the program can be improved. Using randomized experimental studies to examine the effects of a program can often provide important knowledge about the impact of a program, and such studies are often touted as the "gold standard" for research design. Yet, such studies are often difficult, if not impossible, to conduct in existing programs, given funding and other "real-world" practical limitations. Furthermore, implementing experimental designs can be sufficiently disruptive to the day-to-day operation of a program that they may, if implemented, result in the evaluation of a program that is sufficiently different from the typical ongoing operation of the program that any results obtained through such a design may have little generalizability to the program as it is implemented in practice. However, there are many research methods that can be used (see Shadish et al., 2001 as an excellent source for understanding a wide range of relevant research designs) to help us draw conclusions about the impact of a program.

In addition to having a design that will allow us to answer questions and draw conclusions, the program also needs to have a data management system that will enable it to collect, manage, and utilize data to support program decision making. Without a data management system in place, it is possible that programs will collect data that may be required by funders, but have very limited ability to translate those data into meaningful results that can inform program operations. There have been many instances in the past in which a program has asked us for assistance with evaluation, and their hope was that we could use the data that had been collected on paper forms that were piled in boxes in a closet (or otherwise unused and unusable). The program leadership had been told by their funders that they needed to collect data, but they had very little understanding of what they might do with it, and as a result, they collected information that did not help them answer questions of relevance to the program. In turn, it sat there in a form that was not particularly useful for much of anything. Creation of an effective data management system is an important component in evaluation capacity building (see Chapter 7). The next section considers the need for and role of data management systems.

DATA MANAGEMENT SYSTEMS

Data management systems range from the collection of information from program participants onto paper forms that is then tallied by hand, to the use of specialized applications on smartphones or computers that collect information directly from the intended program beneficiaries and then translate the raw data into answers to specific questions defined by the program administrators. Many organizations employ some electronic data recording, using a Microsoft Excel spreadsheet or a Google sheet, with the spreadsheet set up to tally totals, compute means, or otherwise provide some summary information. The development of a data management system should be clearly tied to the types of questions that the program needs to answer or would like to be able to answer in the future. For example, if a program had never been required to report the relative gains experienced by children from different neighborhoods or representing different racial or ethnic groups, it may not collect data about ethnicity or home address/neighborhood. However, if, in discussions with program partners, it was important to know these details about who was being served, then they would need to start collecting those data and recording them in a data management system to enable such disaggregation of the participants' data. Furthermore, it is critical to make sure that the racial and ethnic breakdown of importance for decision making is possible from the data recorded in their data management system.

To create a useful data management system, it is helpful to have some skills in working with spreadsheets. Most programs we have worked with have some capacity to use Microsoft Excel or Google sheets. While using a database program like Microsoft Access can be helpful, most programs do not have the ability to use and modify Access databases effectively (nor do we), so use of Access would require outside expertise to be consistently involved. This adds cost to the evaluation and is contrary to our general inclination to help programs develop the capacity to conduct their evaluations themselves with the need for minimal outside help or ongoing support.

In helping programs create a basic data management system, you need a clear idea of what questions need to be answered. There's no point in developing a complex system that can answer questions in which program stakeholders have no interest, because that will require more work and runs the risk of being confusing and underutilized. Yet, at the same time, the development of a data management system provides a good opportunity to revisit the current and potential needs for data. We try to put ourselves in the position of the program director and ask ourselves what we would like to learn from data if we were in their position. Then, we pose those questions, develop some sense of what it might cost (in time, effort, and money), and see if they have interest in developing the capacity to obtain those answers. Engagement with other stakeholders and partners can be useful to ensure that key variables and questions are not omitted, because it is easier to build capacity into the system at the outset than to revisit and revise later. At the same time, building a system that can be easily used and that answers questions viewed as important increases the likelihood that the data management system and the evaluation will be used, and revisions certainly can be made as the need for information grows. In fact, it is very common for programs to start small, collect and use a relatively small set of data to make important improvements in the program, and then ask for additional capacity, as their questions and need to know expand.

Key principles we find important in development of a data management system are as follows:

1. Assess the leadership and staff's capabilities and motivation early on to determine whether they have the necessary ability and willingness to change their processes for collecting and managing data. We can support skill building and technical competence enhancement, but an unwillingness to try something different can bring some challenge. One common circumstance we face is that, in some programs, the staff are clearly and unalterably opposed to using electronic devices to collect data when interacting with program participants, because they feel that it disrupts important relationship-building interactions. It can be useful to demonstrate to staff how they can become able to type or write on a tablet as easily as they can write on paper, but sometimes that does not overcome their reluctance. While direct entry can certainly save time, a compromise can be to have staff use paper when interacting with the program participants and then use what they have recorded on the

paper to enter the data into the tablet or a computer. Alternatively, program management may decide to shift responsibilities to enable those who are willing to enter data directly as they interact with participants to do so. Regardless of the strategy used, it is important to monitor the accuracy of the data and the impact on relationships to ensure that there are minimal negative side effects of changes in procedures.

2. Create a system that allows data to be recorded as close as possible to the time that the data are generated. Direct, electronic recording of the data at the time the data are being collected is certainly an efficient use of time, but it is also necessary to consider the impact of that on relationships and on the quality of the data more generally. In one setting, we urged staff to collect data from preschoolers using a tablet to allow the children to view and respond verbally to the stimuli, and the staff person would touch the screen to record the response. However, when the staff tried that approach, they found that the children would constantly try to touch the screen, often making responses that were inconsistent with their verbal responses, and they would then become upset when not allowed to touch the screen. This process became more disruptive and time consuming than desirable, so they reverted to paper versions of the stimuli, with staff keeping the tablet in their hands to record responses.

3. Record the most detailed, granular data possible. Although it is tempting to record data only in the form that is currently needed for decision making (e.g., if there are certain items that are summed into a scale, to only record the scale score that is used for a decision about a participant's progress), there are several reasons to avoid this practice. First, this often means that a staff person has to manually add up the scores and record the sum, and the more calculations the staff person has to make, the greater likelihood of errors. Second, sometimes it is useful to modify measures. It is not uncommon to find that measures have items that are not useful for a given set of circumstances, and using a smaller number of items may provide clearer results and save time (however, it is crucial to be judicious about modifying measures if they are standardized and you are trying to generalize to other populations based on that measure). In sum, collecting more granular data, with the management system manipulating it (via code, formulae, or functions) to create scores, provides more flexibility in the use of the data, at little to no extra cost, and sometimes with a reduction in the cost of data entry and use.

4. Use multiple sheets within the system to simplify its use and protect the data. For example, it is useful to have one or several sheets for data entry (different sheets might be used for different measures or different data collection periods), with data protections built in to help ensure that persons entering the data enter it accurately (using the data protection features of the software to create drop-down menus where possible). Other sheets can be used for formulae that compute scores as needed and for comparisons of different subgroups (e.g., males vs. females). Other sheets can be used to construct graphs or tables that can be directly copied and pasted into reports. For more sophisticated users, there are

"business intelligence" applications that can help create data dashboards that allow a snapshot of program statistics, but these can be more expensive in time and money than many smaller nonprofits are able to support.

The data management system provides the framework to enable the program to answer questions of importance. A good system allows the data to be collected with as little time and effort as possible and then automates the calculations and comparisons that are needed to answer questions. Summary statistics and graphs can then be provided in real time and copied and pasted into reports to share with stakeholders. Investing time and energy into the creation of a data management system that provides accurate and up-to-date information about the program can help the program answer questions about how effective the program is, as well as how its implementation contributes to its effectiveness (see following Case Example).

With a clear set of questions and a data management system that can help translate the data collected into useful information for the program, it is also critical to formulate a set of methods that can be utilized to yield the needed information to inform change efforts. This means we need to develop a set of procedures that enable us to answer the following questions:

- Does the desired change occur (regardless of our ability to determine the program's impact on that change) among the intended beneficiaries?

- Does the program do what it says it does (is it actually implemented as intended)?

- If change occurs, can we rule out other plausible alternative explanations (separate from the program) for that change, and therefore reasonably conclude that the program caused the change?

If, then, we can detect change and the program is being implemented consistent with its intent, in the context of a reasonable theory of change (stating how the program activities would be expected to lead to change), and we can rule out plausible alternative explanations for why the change would occur, we can have some confidence that the program is, in fact, causing the change to occur.

It should be clear that this is a deductive process, stepwise in nature. If we cannot detect change, then we will obviously not attribute change to the program. Similarly, if the program is not implementing the processes that its theory of change suggests would lead to the desired outcomes, then we would be skeptical of any conclusion that the program was effecting change, unless we can identify other potentially "change-inducing" processes operating within the program. That would imply the program is different from what we thought it was (and this sometimes happens). The next step of ruling out plausible alternative explanations is what then allows us to have a greater level of confidence that the changes we have detected are due to the program, and not to a wide range of other possible causal factors.

This deductive process then implies that we need to carefully consider these three steps that are essential in evaluation. We need to design an evaluation methodology that will enable us to answer these specific questions and ultimately draw conclusions about the program and its impact.

CASE EXAMPLE: IMPROVING SCREENING AND DATA MANAGEMENT IN A PRE-K PROGRAM

In Chapter 3, we described our work in partnership with a large school system and their prekindergarten program. That partnership holds relevance here as well. As part of basic program processes, a set of staff members assessed the children for entry into the program. Because children needed to meet certain developmental and educational criteria for being admitted, the assessment included a number of measures that assessed their verbal abilities, their social–emotional development, and other factors that were viewed as risk factors that suggested that the 4-year-old child was not prepared for and would not likely be successful upon entering kindergarten without additional help. The year-long program was designed to help the children become ready for school.

During our initial work with the program (which lasted for several years), we found that the screening data recorded were primarily summary scores, collected on paper, summed by the screener, and then the summary information was entered into a spreadsheet. Subsequently we learned that they changed their process to use tablets instead of paper measures (for some measures), and the staff recorded the information from each item into the tablet. However, they then manually added up subtotals for each scale and entered those scores into the tablet (the tablets had not been set up to calculate the summary scores, nor save those into a spreadsheet for data management). In sum, the tablets were being used in place of the paper measures to read the item and record the scores. They were clearly not using the tablets to their fullest benefit.

We spoke with the program management initially about the need for more granular data to serve as baseline data for evaluating the program and the recording of these data in a format that could be shared with the school system's office of accountability for research/evaluation purposes. Program management was very supportive of these goals. We then met with the screening staff, observing and assessing how they conducted the screenings, and jointly identifying and talking through ways that they might change their procedures to improve the ability to use the data and make the screening process more efficient for the screeners. We also assessed their familiarity with different data management structures (the school system tended to use Google forms and Google sheets). Based on this assessment, we developed some new procedures, pilot tested them among our staff, and then shared them with the screeners to obtain their views of how well it worked, what they would change, and any difficulties that they experienced or anticipated. We used Google forms for the measures and the initial data entry, and these data then were initially summarized in Google sheets. As the screeners were testing out the new "system," we were in close touch with the program administrators to ensure that the data reporting function of the system was meeting their needs and providing useful information without excessive detail they did not need. We then took the system to scale, with all the screeners using it and recognizing that it was easier, faster, and more accurate. Furthermore, the managers found that the data were easily understood and used for administrative purposes.

While all were happy with the improvements in this new data management system, additional possibilities became apparent. While the summary data for each child were intended to go to the pre-K teacher to help tailor classroom instruction to meet the needs of the child, it was on a paper form and often buried in the child's summary folder. The data management system was then refined to create individual reports for each child and then summary reports for each teacher and principal (showing the data for each child), to help the schools place students into classrooms and to help teachers group students for instruction and tailor the instruction to help meet each child's needs. This automated generation of the teachers' reports saved the management staff countless hours of time, provided better information to teachers, and was provided in a more accessible format for all teachers and their principals to use.

We will discuss each step in turn to provide a basic approach to evaluating program effectiveness. Note that this is not intended to be a comprehensive discussion of research methodology—that is not within the scope of this book or its objectives. Instead, we are outlining the general approach, which draws heavily from the works of Shadish et al. (2001). Furthermore, for an understanding of the factors that contribute to better implementation of innovations, we would urge you to look at work that has come to be called "implementation science," which focuses on ways to examine and improve implementation of programs (Fixsen et al., 2005). In addition, central to the partnership approach espoused in this volume, we will point out particular circumstances in which engagement of partners is helpful if not essential.

DOES THE DESIRED CHANGE OCCUR?

The first step in understanding the role the program might play in effecting change is to be clear about what change is intended, desired, and/or likely, given the program's logic model or the theory of change for the program (see Chapter 1). It helps if the theory of change is sufficiently detailed to specify the particular program elements or actions that are used to effect particular types of changes. Even when there is a fairly clear and specific theory of change or logic model, before developing an evaluation methodology it is important to clarify the specific desired outcomes expected by the program. It is also important to clarify what the most important potential outcomes of the program might be, because we rarely have sufficient resources to conduct a fully comprehensive evaluation that answers all the questions that stakeholders might have.

Having a good partnership with direct and open communication is particularly helpful at this point, to consider what program "effects" might occur under different sets of circumstances—for different participants, for those not directly participating in the program (e.g., parents might be affected by a program that is explicitly designed to improve the behavior of children), for those who are culturally different from the mainstream, or for participants of different genders or ages. Such discussions should lead to the identification or development of the specific indicators or measures to allow us to determine to what extent those changes are occurring. Measures need to be reliable and valid as much as possible (see Shadish et al., 2001 for thorough discussions of these constructs), with the recognition that there are times when a desired outcome is not easily measured and not clearly defined. For example, a program may want its participants to have a higher quality of life. The definition of "quality of life" may not be clearly specified nor widely agreed upon. This lack of specificity may lead to consideration of measures that do not capture the construct well, but are easy to administer. In Chapter 1, we included an example of a program for which the funder wanted a simple outcome measure (weight loss) that was not consistent with the program's goals, but was simple and easy to measure. There are surely other circumstances in which choices must be made between short and simple measures versus longer and more reliable and valid ones. We would argue that, if you need to make a choice, it is better to use measures that are closely related to the constructs of interest, even when measurement reliability and/or validity might suffer, than to use highly reliable measures that do not capture outcomes of importance.

An assessment of change generally implies that we measure the construct in question at least two times, so we can see if there is a difference between a "pretest" or baseline value and a "posttest" value. There are many variations on a pretest–posttest design that involve such measurement at two points in time and allow a direct assessment of change among the program participants. However, there are many cases when having a pretest does not make sense or is not possible. For example, if the program were teaching differential equations to high school students, asking in a pretest about something of which they have never heard and with which they have had no experience would not be productive. On the other hand, you may have a standard of learning that you want students to achieve, so an assessment of how well or how many of those students achieved that standard could be used as a measure of "change" (i.e., of the effect). Similarly, if we cannot conduct a pretest, we might compare students who received the training with a comparison group of those who did not (assuming the groups were similar), and that would provide us with a measure of differential learning that might reasonably be interpreted as change.

When assessing the difference between observations at different times (i.e., pre- vs. posttest) or among different groups (e.g., treatment vs. comparison group), it is desirable to determine if that difference is statistically significant, or not likely to occur simply by chance. The use of the term "desirable" is very deliberate, although some researchers would suggest that it is "essential," because without statistical significance, you should not consider the difference as a real difference. Since we assume that readers of this book have a basic background in research design and statistical analysis, we will not spend time explaining the meaning of statistical significance. However, it is important to recognize that there are many times when it is unlikely that a difference will be statistically significant, because of a low number of participants, unreliable measures or interventions (different participants get different "treatments"), highly variable samples of participants, or a host of other reasons (see Shadish et al., 2001 for a discussion of "statistical conclusion validity" and considerations in research design). In those cases, there may be a "real difference," not due to chance, but we just cannot detect it. Yet, if we have a sizably apparent (but not statistically significant) difference, under some circumstances this might be appropriately used by a program manager as a reason to modify the program.

For example, if a relatively small, low-cost change in a program were made in one site of a large, multisite program, and comparison of that site with others showed sizable but nonsignificant (perhaps because of the low number of participants in the evaluation) improvements, the manager may use that evidence to conclude that it is worthwhile to expand the change to more sites. In such a case, if the costs are low (considering both economic costs and potential disruption created by the change) and the potential for positive outcomes is reasonably high, the expansion to more sites could provide an opportunity to further evaluate the new change (and we would certainly argue for that next step of evaluation). The expanded use of the program change might provide sufficient power to discern a significant difference, which might then warrant taking the modification to scale. The point here is that we should not rigidly dismiss nonsignificant findings any more than we should act on statistically significant findings in which the actual difference (or "clinical significance") is minuscule. We recommend that you make a habit of discussing the possible meanings of any findings with your partners, to help everyone involved understand the limits of the knowledge, the possible changes to be made, and the potential costs and benefits of those changes.

HOW WELL IS THE PROGRAM BEING IMPLEMENTED?

If you are working with a program to help them clarify their theory of change, perhaps articulated in a logic model, program administrators can generally tell you how the program is supposed to work, including the specific actions staff take that are expected to effect changes in program participants. Program administrators may be very confident that the program staff carry out the program in the manner that they are trained and directed to do by the program administration. This certainty about the implementation of program activities may then lead to resistance by administrators to spend evaluation resources on a careful examination of the program's implementation. However, this belief—the program is described as doing something and therefore it must be doing it—is often in error, and empirical examination of implementation is an important and necessary part of program evaluation.

This is not meant to be an indictment of program managers, who may reasonably expect that staff follow their directions and implement the procedures espoused by the program. However, all staff may not implement all program elements with fidelity (i.e., in a manner that is consistent with the plan or an identified model). In addition, programs may change over time, due to new staff and variations in their training and competence (new staff may not have the same training that prior staff did, so their actions may be somewhat different), changes in the nature and needs of the clientele (old processes may not work well with the current level of clients' needs, resulting in changes in operations), changes in policy (Medicaid reimbursement rules may dictate changes in how the program works), or changes in the community (a growing immigrant population may require program changes to accommodate the broader cultural makeup of the community). These changes may be subtle and occur over time in ways that may not be readily observable. Hence it is important to assess the degree to which the program is implemented as planned, and it is important to critically examine and question, as needed, the appropriateness of the stated theory of change in the current context.

CASE EXAMPLE: USING REVIEW OF A LOGIC MODEL TO SHAPE THE DEVELOPMENT OF A PROGRAM

We were working with a community-wide effort to improve the community's ability to address the needs of children, with a particular focus on increasing school readiness. On the board was a leader in a local medical school's resident training program, who saw an opportunity to engage pediatric residents in the process of assessing the health of preschool children. While ensuring that children are healthy can certainly contribute to their readiness for attending school, the program was merely assessing the children, and not taking any tangible steps to actually address their health needs. As such, there was a greater benefit to the residents (who advanced their assessment skills) than to the children. We developed a logic model that clearly, graphically demonstrated the disconnect between this assessment and the goals of the initiative and elicited questions about whether this assessment was likely to contribute meaningfully to the children's school readiness. Upon review by the board, the board decided to remove the resident training experiences from the broader initiative, because it did not "logically" fit within or support the accomplishment of the initiative's goals.

When examining program implementation, it is useful to determine whether the program is implemented differently for different types of participants. For example, it is often the case that programs tailor the nature of the program to specific participants in an effort to meet their needs. Some participants with greater needs may remain in the program for a longer period of time. Others may require modifications because they are younger (may need more active approaches) or older (may need to reduce the physical demands of the program) than the average participant. Some participants drop out of services earlier than others or fail to regularly participate, leading to different "doses" of service across individual participants. Since different levels of dosage are likely related to differences in outcomes, data regarding the dose or the amount of the program (or of some aspect of the program) that the participant actually "receives" is important to record. These and other variations in program implementation are likely to lead to variations in program outcomes.

We occasionally hear program administrators suggest that, because their program is an "evidence-based program," there is no particular need for evaluation of its implementation. This is just another version of the "the program leadership says it does something and therefore it must be doing it" argument. Even if staff training is provided before the program is implemented, training does not ensure that the implementation is as specified, since time may pass, people may forget what they should do, or they may find that the prescribed implementation is difficult. And even if it is implemented according to the plan when the program starts, we have to be aware of the strong possibility that there is drift in implementation over time, with new staff, changes in clientele, shifting priorities and resources, and other factors. It is every bit as important to assess the implementation of "evidence-based interventions" as it is for any other programs.

Sometimes, in order to assess program implementation, a checklist is created, to indicate whether the specific actions and/or steps of the program are being taken. This may be a part of the program's ongoing recordkeeping, with program staff monitoring whether the requisite steps have been taken. We would advise caution in the use of such approaches to evaluating implementation without clear safeguards in place. First of all, the presence or absence of a step in the process is a really rough measure, without consideration of the quality of the implementation of that step. A pro forma indication that all the steps have been completed may tell us little about the quality of the implementation, and quality of implementation can certainly matter (Durlak & DuPre, 2008). In addition, if the people who are responsible for implementation of the intervention are also those who are asked to indicate the completion of the step or the quality of the implementation, biases or self-deception or a lack of understanding can lead to a conclusion that the program is being implemented well when it is not (see following Case Example).

We outlined briefly some important benefits of process evaluations of program implementation in Chapter 2; they warrant expansion here. The purposes of assessing program implementation are fourfold. First, if we say a particular program is effecting change in a population, it is important to know that the program's activities are actually the ones we think they are. In other words, if we are asked to evaluate a program designed to train people in job skills, we want to know that the program provides training, and the training is done in a way that could reasonably be expected to help participants develop those skills (e.g., not merely providing training in broader social

CASE EXAMPLE: ASSESSING IMPLEMENTATION IN WRAPAROUND SERVICES

As part of an evaluation of a System of Care for children's mental health, we attempted to assess the implementation of the wraparound services and supports which are a core part of the System of Care model. Wraparound is the prime practice model used in these systems, and wraparound services are designed to address the broad needs of the child with serious emotional disturbance and their family. These services and supports are developed and coordinated through the use of child and family teams (CFTs), which include the child, parents/caregivers, case managers and other service providers, and informal supports (i.e., people who are not formal mental health service providers but who provide support to the family, such as neighbors, extended family, friends, or teachers). The CFTs are expected to meet regularly, to plan and facilitate the provision (and/or to provide) assistance that is needed to help the family and child achieve success as they view it. A key aspect of wraparound is to ensure that the child and family receive support not just from professionals, but from the others in their lives who would continue to be involved with the family after the child's symptoms abate. Instead of focusing solely on problems or what is wrong with the child (the mental health or behavioral symptoms), the CFT is intended to also have a major focus on the child's and family's strengths, those enduring characteristics that they can use to help the family cope with and overcome the mental health problems and other challenges they were experiencing.

Our assessment of wraparound focused on the degree to which the implementation of the CFTs was consistent with "wraparound best practices" as described briefly above. To do this, we worked with system representatives (from multiple sectors, e.g., mental health, child welfare) as well as parents and other stakeholders to identify our approach and the key dimensions on which we would focus, as well as refine our measures. We developed forms for the members of CFTs to complete at the end of each meeting, including the date and time of the meeting and a listing of the participants in the meeting (to allow us to determine if the participants included informal supports or other professionals). We also developed a brief measure for the participants to complete at the end of each CFT meeting, specifying, among other things, whether the discussion focused on the strengths of the child and family and ways to capitalize on those strengths to improve the well-being of the child and family. We also had members of the evaluation team attend a sample of CFTs to provide an "outside" assessment of the CFT processes.

Our findings indicated that many of the CFTs were held with just the child, parent, and case manager; it was rare to have any input or support from other treatment providers or informal supports. Meetings were clearly not the inclusive process that was intended as part of wraparound practice. The meetings were held at irregular intervals, often with months between meetings, leading to difficulties in the team providing consistent support over time. Participants' responses to the surveys indicated that the meetings were viewed as focusing on and utilizing child and family strengths in the planning process. However, when members of our evaluation team attended meetings and used the same criteria for rating the meetings, they indicated that the team rarely focused on strengths. Rather than discuss strengths as assets to be used in the service plan (e.g., a child who liked and was really good with dogs could be a volunteer at an animal shelter as a mechanism for the child to develop responsibility and better skills in interacting with adults), team members tended to focus on physical characteristics (the child was pretty) or improvements in behavior (he did not "beat up" his brother as often), which do not readily lend themselves to strategies for engaging children in prosocial, beneficial activities. Overall, across indicators, the data indicated that implementation was not consistent with the wraparound practice model or the broader tenets of Systems of Care. In particular, the practices and processes of the CFTs (arguably the key system component for the wraparound model) did not align with multiple specific

Continued

aspects of wraparound. Their fidelity of implementation was generally quite low. When these findings were reported, together with very modest improvements in child behavioral outcomes, it became apparent that a focus on improving implementation could help improve child and family outcomes.

skills). We would want to understand the content of the training to ensure that we are assessing outcomes consistent with the types of jobs for which the training is provided. If we find that the program does not provide job skills, then it would be useful to refer to it as a different type of training program and adjust our measurement to ensure we are targeting appropriate outcomes. Second, if we wish to draw inferences about the program's role in causing desired outcomes, it is important to be able to have a believable process by which the program would cause those changes. This should be logically defensible and reasonably acceptable to the stakeholders of the program. If you cannot see how engaging in particular activities would lead to the desired outcomes, then it is hard to argue that the program (assuming it is implementing those activities) would cause the outcomes to occur. Third, examination of the levels of implementation can help us understand why we may not obtain the desired levels of change. For example, if the program does not actually implement activities (with sufficient dose and quality) that would be expected to cause the desired change, then we would not expect change among program participants. (Note, however, that different levels of implementation for different groups, whether for different segments of the population or at different program sites, can sometimes be used to better understand the causal impact of the program, since we might expect that the receipt of a higher dose is related to greater levels of change.) Fourth, because programs typically include multiple components designed to effect change in different ways, it is important to be able to link (in the logic model and in the data) the relationship between specific components and different types of outcomes. This is important because it provides useful information about what aspects of the program may need to be modified (i.e., if participants are not changing, we might want to improve the implementation of the program components expected to effect those changes to ensure they are being implemented with sufficient quality and dose). In addition, a careful examination of implementation and its relation to program outcomes can help you draw inferences about the causal relevance of aspects of the program. For example, if a component of the program is not being implemented well in one location, compared to implementation in a different site, and the setting with the higher implementation has better outcomes, you may have a higher level of confidence that the program (when implemented well) is causing change in the participants.

CAN WE RULE OUT PLAUSIBLE ALTERNATIVE EXPLANATIONS AND THEREBY INFER CAUSATION?

The final stage of our evaluation planning is to build into the evaluation procedures a set of strategies to help us determine how likely it is that the program was responsible for changes obtained. If we see changes occurring, and an assessment of program implementation indicated that there is a logical process occurring that would be expected to effect those changes, then we want to have evidence that the program was actually responsible for those changes.

It is extremely unlikely that all program participants demonstrate all the changes intended by the program. There will be variation as a function of the individual program participants, their experience of the program, and the implementation of the program. This implies that we will not likely be in a position to say "the program works as expected." Instead, we will be much more likely to conclude that certain parts of the program work better or worse for certain types of participants under certain types of conditions. We want to be able to examine the relationships among different types of variation, or variation on different factors or dimensions (participant characteristics, program implementation, participant changes), in order to help us understand the program and to be able to recommend specific improvements in the program. It is important, then, to try to anticipate the questions that we need to answer in order to infer causation, to help ensure that we have collected the data needed to answer those questions.

The process of identifying the answers to questions needed to make causal inferences about a program should draw upon both the literature about similar programs and the knowledge and experience of your partners. As a matter of practice, it can be helpful to ask those closest to the program why they think that some people in the program have better outcomes than others. Is it something about (1) their individual characteristics, (2) the context in which they live and the circumstances they encounter, or (3) the level and type of involvement in the program? In the paragraphs that follow, we will consider those three different reasons why people might improve when involved with a program.

Individual Factors

Some people involved in a program do very well simply because they were doing very well before they even started with the program. If a program attracts people who are already "successful" or, because of their attributes and characteristics, are likely to be successful on the dimensions that the program is attempting to foster, then the program will appear to be very good and successful, even if the program does not contribute much to their success. This is generally referred to as an issue of *selection* since participants who do well on outcome measures are selected (in some way, not necessarily deliberately) or select themselves into the program. Thus, there can appear to be a positive change in the participants, even if the program actually does not cause that change.

If it is plausible that such a selection effect results in the program appearing to be causing change (when it is not), then it is important to build into the evaluation design specific elements that will allow you to rule this out. For example, as an evaluator working with a program, you may help identify a comparison group, such as a waiting list of people interested in but not served by the program. You may collect information about potential participants when they express interest, and then follow them up to see if they change more or less than those in the program. Alternatively, you could make sure that the program's participants vary in their a priori "success" characteristics, and then compare those predicted to be successful with those who are not as likely to be successful. If the only participants who succeed are those who are already expected to be successful without the program, then we would want to discuss with our program partners whether they are using their resources wisely, and may want to consider ways to better structure the program to help those who are not likely to succeed without the program. Your community partners likely know the nature of the population being served, so they are your best asset in understanding the potential selection issues that might affect your ability to conduct an effective evaluation.

Other individual characteristics that could limit our ability to conclude the program is causing change include *regression* and *maturation*. If the participants are selected to be in the program because they have been judged to have high levels of need, then it is possible that, if we were to assess them again at the end of the program, they may appear to be better simply because of a type of measurement error referred to as *regression to the mean* This refers to the fact that if we select a group of people on a characteristic because they have very low scores on almost any criterion measure, when we measure them again on that characteristic (as in a posttest after the intervention), they are very likely to score closer to the mean (which would be a higher score than their prior scores). If we do not take into account this regression to the mean, we may erroneously conclude that the "improvement" was due to the program. Regression would then be a "plausible alternative explanation" for apparent improvement that we would want to rule out before we conclude that the program is causing the change we see. To address this, we may need a comparison group that has a similar level of need but that does not participate in the program or, alternatively, we could make sure that the participants in the program vary on the characteristic in question and see if those at the low end of the continuum are improving more than those at the higher end, suggesting that regression may be at work.

Maturation is another issue about which we have to be concerned, particularly when the program is serving a population that is likely to change over time in a way that would be consistent with and look like a "program effect." For instance, if a program is designed to tutor preschool children to help them improve their reading, we would want to know if their improvement is due to the fact that they are growing older and being exposed to more complex language, and therefore becoming better readers, regardless of their involvement in the program. We would need to rule out maturation as a "plausible alternative explanation" before we could conclude that the program is responsible for the improvement in reading. A discussion with your community partners of the likely types of maturation that might occur among the population of interest, within the timeframe of the evaluation, can help determine how much maturation is likely to be a "plausible alternative hypothesis" and what steps might be taken to rule it out so that you can evaluate the impact of the program.

We might also think we have a program effect when the change we see is the result of certain people dropping out of the program. Note that the degree to which this *attrition* is a problem depends on how many participants drop out and the characteristics of those who do drop out. Random attrition of a small number of people from a program may not be a significant problem, because this does not introduce bias into the evaluation process. Attrition in larger numbers or by certain program participants may suggest there are implementation issues that need attention (e.g., higher levels of attrition by a particular ethnic group may suggest that services are not being provided in a culturally appropriate manner). If those who are not responding well to the program are more likely to drop out, leaving only those who are being more successful, an examination of those who are left at the end may yield results that suggest there was a positive change due to the program, when in fact it may simply be that the average improvement is inflated by the attrition of those doing poorly. These issues and possibilities need to be clearly discussed with your partners before the evaluation is conducted to determine to what extent they are likely to be a problem and what steps need to be done to reduce the likelihood that attrition interferes with our ability to understand how the program is functioning and how it can be improved.

Contextual and Measurement Factors

If we are looking at change in participants over the time that they are participating in the program, we must recognize that there are contextual factors that will be affecting those participants, separate from the aspects of the program designed to effect change. We need to be attentive to those factors and identify those that might result in change that we could incorrectly interpret as a program effect or, alternatively, that might result in the program looking as if it made no difference when it did. We can make either of those errors when we draw conclusions about programs if we do not pay careful attention to these plausible alternative hypotheses.

The surrounding context of a program can affect program participants, possible program outcomes, and, in turn, the conclusions we might draw about a program in several ways. For example, if a program is developed to provide skills that would enable participants to obtain employment, we might evaluate the impact of the program based on how many participants obtain living wage jobs. While the program may provide needed skills, if a major employer in the community that would likely hire people with those skills shut its doors, then those participants may not be able to obtain employment, regardless of the levels of their skills they obtained in the program. This is an example of "*history*" (as labeled by Shadish et al., 2001), defined as a change in the context of the program that would affect the ability of the program to be successful, even when, in this example, the participants may have gained excellent skills. On the other hand, we might imagine that the opposite occurred. For example, if a new employer began hiring in a market with limited numbers of qualified employees, it is conceivable that all of the participants in the program (regardless of the skills they obtained) and many others beyond those in the program might be hired. In this case, the program might appear to be very successful, even if the program had no particular effect on the participants' ability to obtain employment. Or alternatively, if we were comparing the employment obtained by program participants with others in the community, the program may appear to have no effect, since the program participants may obtain employment at the same rate as those not in the program. In this case we may need to examine the type of employment (for instance, did program participants get better jobs, at higher pay, and remain at those jobs longer?) to obtain a clear understanding of how well the program worked. Such contextual factors are important to examine, and for most evaluators, particularly those who are not familiar with the local community, obtaining the input of the community partners to explore what contextual factors might be important, and in what ways, is an essential part of conducting an evaluation.

Among the many different factors affecting our ability to draw conclusions (Shadish et al., 2001) that we might need to consider, the types and quality of the measurement we use can be an important consideration. Failure to have sufficiently reliable measures will make it difficult to detect a difference, as we described above. In addition, it is critical that we are using measures that adequately address the constructs of importance to the program. It is not uncommon to find that a program staff member has seen a measure used by another program or a funder might suggest a specific measure, and the program then wants to use that measure to assess the impact of their program. While it is certainly possible that the measure they propose is highly useful and appropriate, we often find that a careful examination of the measure with program partners often reveals gaps between the measure and what the program is trying to accomplish. Perhaps this gap suggests that the measure needs revision, or perhaps we need an entirely different measure. We find that it is very common to have tension between the desire to have a longer measure of demonstrated reliability that captures the different aspects of what the program is trying to accomplish versus a shorter measure that is less reliable and/or that may only capture a small part of the desired change. Arguments for the shorter measure may include a desire to reduce the burden on staff and/or participants or to increase the likelihood that sufficient numbers of people respond. Finding a middle ground is an important discussion that evaluators often need to have with partners. Similarly, there are times when the program relies on parents or teachers to evaluate a child's behavior, rating specific behaviors over the course of a school year or time in a program. In these cases, the reliability of measurement may be extremely important, and steps must be taken to ensure that the ratings of the behavior are mostly determined by the child's behavior and not the teacher's other knowledge about, experience with, and/or predilection toward that child. In this case the teacher (together with whatever rating scheme is used) is a core component of the measurement. Their ratings may change over time as they get to know the child, and these changes may appear to reflect program changes. However, changes in the teacher's ratings may also be affected by the changes in the teacher's interpretation of the child's intent or ability to control behavior (even if the behavior remains essentially the same) and may be affected by the degree to which other children in the classroom become more or less affected by the child's behavior (if fellow students are no longer bothered by the behavior, it may be seen as less problematic, even if the actual behavior does not change). Therefore, teasing out the program effect versus the teacher change may be difficult. Again, it is important to work together with your community partners to determine ways to sort through the different factors that may contribute to the results obtained, and thus may result in erroneous conclusions about the program. Ideally this will happen throughout the process from the planning of the evaluation to the interpretation of results.

Level and Type of Involvement in the Program by Participants

Rarely is it the case that every participant receives exactly the same amount or "dose" of the program. If a program provides a series of trainings, it is certainly possible that some participants do not attend all the trainings because they are ill or they have transportation, childcare, or work issues that preclude their attendance. Alternatively, they may attend, but are spending time looking at their phones, sleeping, or otherwise not paying attention to the instructor. In either case, the program participants are not likely to receive the full benefit of the program. Alternatively, the instructors may vary, with some participants receiving a very thorough training because they have an experienced instructor who engages the participants, while others may have inexperienced instructors who are unable to provide an equally engaging experience for participants. In those cases, the participants are also not likely to obtain the full benefit of the program as it is intended.

It is important to build into a program's data management system a way to keep track of the dose experienced by each participant. This can mean tracking attendance, maintaining records of "engagement," or noting differences in the staffing of the program across different sites or times. Careful examination of the differences in the program outcomes as a function of the dose of the program can help reduce random error in the analysis when you examine the effects of the program (since the different levels of dose would be expected to add variability to the possible outcomes) and make it more possible to detect program effects. Furthermore, such tracking can also allow us to better understand the factors that might contribute to different levels of dosage and enable the program to make improvements in the program (e.g., only offer the program when there are experienced trainers available; provide incentives for regular attendance and program completion; and provide transportation or child care).

CRITICAL CHALLENGES TO CONSIDER

The quest for clarity about the degree to which the program is responsible for changes in program participants (and, potentially, others) is often a challenge. In our experience, most evaluations of programs focus on developing an understanding of the degree to which the program causes changes in the program participants, since, ultimately, most of the programs we encounter are designed to effect improvements in the lives of program participants. A major challenge in program evaluation is designing and enacting evaluation methodologies that enable us to demonstrate that (a) the participants change in the desired ways and (b) the program is responsible for that change. At the same time, we need to focus on understanding how the program is implemented, so we can have a reasonable understanding of the types of program activities that are likely to be causing the changes and some clarity about what program components might need to be changed to improve the program's outcomes. Essential to this effort is also careful attention to measurement, to ensure that our measures are sufficiently reliable and valid to be able to detect the desired changes, and a careful examination of an array of plausible alternative hypotheses, that can help us rule out other factors that may make it appear that the program has an effect or, alternatively, may make it appear that the program has limited or no effect. Understanding these key factors allows us to home in on the effects of the program and make clear recommendations about how to improve the program, working closely with our partners to gain their insights and perspectives about the program and its operations, its participants, and the contextual factors that affect our ability to determine the effects of the program. Furthermore, the development and use of a data management system is often a critical component that can enable the program and the evaluator to translate the data collected into useful, actionable knowledge about the program.

For partners who are not familiar with research design and measurement issues, it is important to be able to explain the multiple trade-offs that exist at every step. Measurement is generally more reliable if the measures include more items, but longer measures take more time and place a greater burden on the participants and staff who collect the data. Most programs expect to provide a number of benefits to participants, but assessing all the benefits (particularly in a reliable and valid way) of a program may be cost-prohibitive, requiring a prioritization of the program outcomes that can be examined in a given evaluation. As program administrators and other stakeholders become more involved in discussions of the questions they may want to have answered through an evaluation, it often becomes abundantly clear that choices must be made about which questions are most important, since there are seldom sufficient resources to answer all the questions of interest. Decisions about which "plausible alternative hypotheses" are critical, requiring methods designed to rule them out as well as discussions about how plausible those hypotheses are, which ultimately rely on the use of informed judgments, since there are no absolute answers. The use of comparison groups can entail higher levels of resources, but in some instances the absence of a comparison group makes it difficult to rule out important plausible alternative hypotheses. Similarly, careful examination of the implementation of a program requires that there is general agreement about what should be occurring, as well as a willingness to document carefully the different steps that take place. Each aspect of the evaluation requires negotiation, careful planning, and commitment to learning about the program. Although good partnerships may not be absolutely essential for these decisions to be made, there is no question in our minds that strong partnerships make the process easier and much more enjoyable—and result in better evaluations. In addition, because the evaluator is generally the expert in evaluation, it is important to help your partners understand the pros, cons, and trade-offs inherent at every decision point, so they can ultimately make decisions about what is important, what resources are to be expended in the evaluation process, and what information is needed to make decisions about potential changes in the program.

Of course, this discussion does not provide an exhaustive list of the types of factors you need to take into account. The resources listed in this chapter provide a more complete understanding of design issues, and there is no substitute for experience working with programs to help appreciate the complexities involved. However, we hope that this chapter conveys a sense of the importance of collaboration in the process, which is clearly deductive in nature. It is rarely the case that we have controlled circumstances that lend themselves to experimental designs, highly reliable and valid measurement, or clear definitions of the full set of outcomes desired by the program. Furthermore, we rarely have the ability to measure and evaluate everything we may want to assess. As such, we have to work carefully with our partners to determine the appropriate compromises that balance rigor with feasibility of the evaluation methods to ensure that we are providing accurate, useful, actionable information about the program.

FURTHER READING

Bansal, S. (n.d.). *Excel tips and tutorials*. Trumpexcel.com

Durlak, J. A., & DuPre, E. P. (2008). Implementation matters: A review of research on the influence of implementation on program outcomes and the factors affecting implementation. *American Journal of Community Psychology, 41*, 327–350.

Fixsen, D., Naoom, S., Blase, K., Friedman, R., & Wallace, F. (2005). *Implementation research: A synthesis of the literature*. University of South Florida, Louis de la Parte Florida Mental Health Institute, National Implementation Research Network.

Metz, A. (2015). *Implementation brief: The potential of co-creation in implementation science*. National Implementation Research Network. https://nirn.fpg .unc.edu/sites/nirn.fpg.unc.edu/files/resources/NIRN-Metz-ImplementationBreif-CoCreation.pdf

National Implementation Research Network. (2016). *Implementation brief: Active implementation practice and science*. https://nirn.fpg.unc.edu/sites/nirn.fpg.unc.edu/files/resources/NIRN-Briefs-1-ActiveImplementationPracticeAndScience-10-05-2016.pdf

Shadish, W. R., Cook, T. D., & Campbell, D. T. (2001). *Experimental and quasi-experimental designs for generalized causal inference*. Houghton Mifflin.

Also see The National Implementation Research Network (NIRN): https://nirn.fpg.unc.edu/national-implementation-research-network

KEY CONCEPTS

Attrition: The loss of data due to research participants dropping out of a research or evaluation study.

Data management system: A database or spreadsheet that facilitates data entry, management, and utilization by a program.

History: External events that occur between a pretest and a posttest that can effect change in program participants, making it appear as if the program had an effect.

Implementation: The processes that a program engages in to accomplish its goals; high-fidelity implementation implies that the program is implementing program processes in a way that is consistent with plans or expectations.

Maturation: Processes over time that lead to change in a program participant, such as aging or increased experience; maturation effects can erroneously lead to the conclusion that a program has effects.

Outcome evaluation: Evaluation of the degree to which a program results in certain effects or outcomes.

Plausible alternative hypotheses: A set of hypotheses about the degree to which factors, other than the treatment or program, are likely to cause program effects; ruling out plausible alternative hypotheses increases the ability to conclude that the program causes outcomes.

Process evaluation: Evaluation of the processes involved in a program, used to determine how the program is implemented and potentially to identify ways that the program implementation can be improved.

Regression to the mean: The tendency for measurement of extreme groups to, when measured again, appear as less extreme (or closer to the mean) as a result of unreliable measures and random error; regression to the mean can be mistakenly viewed as a program effect.

Reliability: The determination that a measure of a construct will be consistent over time or across raters.

Selection: The inclusion of participants in a program who already have characteristics expected after participating in a program, such that the program is erroneously viewed as having a positive effect, when it is merely a selection effect.

Validity (of measurement): The determination that a measure of a construct accurately measures the construct that it purports to measure.

QUESTIONS FOR REFLECTION

1. Given that there are multiple plausible alternative hypotheses that can interfere with our ability to accurately conclude that a program causes changes in participants, how can we possibly know which ones we need to take into account in designing an evaluation? What kinds of strategies can we employ to determine if the program caused changes in its intended beneficiaries?

2. In an assessment of the implementation of a program, how detailed should the assessment be, given that different staff might make many different (and even minute) actions in the daily implementation of a program with different participants? How would you approach decisions about understanding and assessing implementation with a community partner?

3. How do you negotiate the inherent trade-offs between measurement reliability and validity and ensure that the measures have sufficient quality to be able to detect meaningful results? How would you approach this with a partner?

REFERENCES

Durlak, J. A., & DuPre, E. P. (2008). Implementation matters: A review of research on the influence of implementation on program outcomes and the factors affecting implementation. *American Journal of Community Psychology, 41*(3-4), 327–350. doi:10.1007/s10464-008-9165-0

Fixsen, D., Naoom, S., Blase, K., Friedman, R., & Wallace, F. (2005). *Implementation research: A synthesis of the literature.* University of South Florida, Louis de la Parte Florida Mental Health Institute, National Implementation Research Network.

Shadish, W. R., Cook, T. D., & Campbell, D. T. (2001). *Experimental and quasi-experimental designs for generalized causal inference.* Houghton Mifflin.

PART II

EVALUATION IN PRACTICE

Selected Strategies, Methods, and Applications

CHAPTER 7

EVALUATION CAPACITY BUILDING

A Partnership Approach for Program Improvement and Social Change

Yolanda Suarez-Balcazar and Tina Taylor-Ritzler

Learning Objectives

1. Explain what evaluation capacity building is.

2. Understand individual- and organizational-level factors and indicators that define evaluation capacity.

3. Identify approaches and strategies to build evaluation capacity within community-based organizations.

4. Discuss examples of contextual and cultural factors that can affect evaluation capacity building.

SCENARIO

Staff at a community-based organization (CBO) serving individuals with developmental and intellectual disabilities and their families are preparing for a site visit from one of their funders who has requested in advance a copy of their outcome's logic model. Although they have developed a logic model, staff panic and rush to their evaluation partner for advice and feedback on their evaluation plan. The CBO staff want to ensure that they are tracking and measuring outcomes of interest to their participants and funders.

The scenario above is very common among CBOs. Identifying outcomes of interest to both participants and funders, and outcomes they can track, is often a challenge for CBOs. Partnerships with evaluation experts (possibly located in an institution of higher education) can help enhance their evaluation processes and outcomes. Budget cuts for social programs and pressure from funders and other stakeholders to demonstrate program effectiveness and accountability in order to receive new or continued funding place CBOs in challenging situations (Carman, 2007).

BACKGROUND

In 1993, the U.S. Government passed the Government Performance and Results Act (GPRA, P.L. 103-62), which holds CBOs accountable for how they spend federal, state, and private funds to improve the lives of the individuals they serve and to meet their goals. Although evaluation is an essential part of GPRA, many organizations struggle to demonstrate the impact of their programs on their participants, because of the many challenges they experience. One of these challenges, a lack of evaluation capacity, stems from limited training regarding (and, in turn, limited knowledge and skills about) how to evaluate their programs, identify and measure outcomes, and differentiate outputs from outcomes (Taylor-Ritzler et al., 2013). There is also a lack of institutional support and resources allocated to evaluation (Suarez-Balcazar et al., 2014). The result is a demand for *evaluation capacity building* (ECB) within CBOs and a growing need to foster partnerships with evaluators (e.g., institutions with expertise in evaluation). In this chapter, we will discuss a partnership approach to building evaluation capacity. Specifically, we will define evaluation capacity, discuss strategies for building evaluation capacity, and describe an exemplar of ECB based on the authors' partnership work with a nonprofit CBO.

WHAT IS EVALUATION CAPACITY?

Evaluation capacity refers to a set of competencies and practices related to the ongoing documentation of programs and use of data to inform understanding and improve the outcomes of social programs. Early definitions of evaluation capacity noted both the complexity and range of the factors to consider, as well as indicators of these. For example, Nye and Glickman (2000) mentioned that evaluation capacity consists of organizational, networking, programmatic, and political components that are in place to facilitate and promote program improvement. Hueftle Stockdill et al. (2002) defined evaluation capacity as "intentional work to continuously create and sustain overall organizational processes that make quality evaluation and its uses routine" (p. 14). Overall, these early definitions indicated that the desired outcome of evaluation capacity is that evaluation is an ongoing day-to-day activity in the organization (Hueftle Stockdill et al., 2002). According to Taut (2007), evaluation capacity is evident when organizations engage staff in ongoing documentation activities and use findings to improve their programs.

Several comprehensive models of ECB are available in the literature that further define evaluation capacity (e.g., Connolly & York, 2002; Cousins et al., 2004; Nielsen et al., 2011; Preskill & Boyle, 2008). Preskill and Boyle (2008), the most cited of these multidisciplinary models of ECB, focuses on the interaction between evaluation knowledge, skills, and attitudes and the transfer of learning through sustainable evaluation practices. The authors proposed that evaluation capacity is evident when organizational staff learn and adopt new knowledge, skills, and attitudes about evaluation and transfer these skills into improving their programs.

A synthesis of the ECB literature found that there is consensus that both individual and organizational factors are important indicators of evaluation capacity (Labin et al., 2012). Despite the presence of published ECB models, only a few are empirically validated and complemented with a corresponding assessment tool used to identify and measure indicators of evaluation capacity.

An empirically validated model and the corresponding evaluation capacity assessment instrument (ECAI) developed by Taylor-Ritzler et al. (2013) include important indicators of evaluation capacity, such as the degree to which evaluation is conducted routinely (mainstreamed) within the organization across programs, and evaluation findings are used to make program improvements. Further, Taylor-Ritzler et al. (2013) identified specific individual and organizational indicators of evaluation capacity that, in interaction, are predictive of evaluation mainstreaming and use. Table 7.1 depicts the different factors to consider at the individual and organizational levels and examples of the indicators that

Table 7.1 Evaluation Capacity Factors and Examples of Indicators

Factors	Indicators
Individual	
Attitudes	• Perceptions of evaluation (benefits, importance, drawbacks, uses) • Myths
Motivation	• Motivation to learn about, conduct, and support others to engage in evaluation • Readiness • Importance
Knowledge and skills	• Knowledge about evaluation plan, logic models, outcomes and outputs, how to collect data, analyze data, develop recommendations, and write an evaluation report
Organizational	
Leadership	• Leadership style • Communication • Leaders consider staff concerns, have realistic expectations of what staff can accomplish • Management policies • Commitment to evaluation • Clearly articulated goals • Managers supporting individuals and the organization to engage in evaluation
Learning climate	• Reflection, discussion, problem solving, respect • Opportunities for feedback and brainstorming
Resources	• Resources are allocated for evaluation related to: — Funding, time, people, space — Hardware, software, data management system — Training, consultation, and technical assistance • Accommodating the needs of people with disabilities and people from diverse ethnic/racial backgrounds

assess each factor (for a detailed description and full copy of the ECAI, see Suarez-Balcazar et al., 2014, Taylor-Ritzler et al., 2013).

Beyond identifying important indicators of evaluation capacity that help us to understand what it is and how to measure it, the validation study of Taylor-Ritzler et al. (2013) also showed that organizational factors mediate the relationship between individual factors, mainstreaming evaluation practices, and using evaluation findings. Having staff who are aware of the benefits of evaluation, are motivated to engage in evaluation, and have knowledge and skills of how to do so results in mainstreaming evaluation practices. Their work pointed to the salience of such factors as the support of organization's leadership, resources available to conduct evaluations, and an optimal organizational learning climate that prioritizes data-informed decision making and program improvement (Labin et al., 2012; Taylor-Ritzler et al., 2013). CBO staff might be motivated, knowledgeable, and skillful to engage in evaluation work; however, if the organization does not provide the necessary leadership, time, and supports, and foster a culture of learning, the motivation to engage in evaluation activities is thwarted and unlikely to result in program improvement or the social changes that the organization seeks to effect.

The importance of organizational factors in evaluation capacity cannot be overstated and, therefore, understanding these factors is essential to understanding and building evaluation capacity in CBOs. According to the model developed by Taylor-Ritzler et al. (2013), leadership entails communicating the importance of and a clear plan for evaluation, establishing realistic expectations, and understanding how evaluation fits into helping the organization fulfill its mission. In this model, resources and support entail allowing time, technical assistance, access to technology, training, and troubleshooting, as well as providing other supports needed to engage in evaluation. Creating a learning climate entails providing opportunities for staff to share and brainstorm together and have opportunities to openly discuss the findings of the evaluation and use them to improve programs. In all, research points to the importance of individual and organizational factors that lead to evaluation capacity outcomes (see Table 7.2 for examples of indicators of mainstreaming and use).

Table 7.2 Evaluation Capacity Outcomes and Indicators

Domain	Indicators
Mainstreaming	• Evaluation activities are integrated into day-to-day work of staff and management • Evaluation practices are used over time
Use	• Evaluation findings are used to meet internal and external needs and improve programs

APPROACHES AND STRATEGIES FOR BUILDING EVALUATION CAPACITY

How does an organization help individuals develop awareness of the benefits of evaluation, motivation to incorporate evaluation tasks and thinking in their work, and needed knowledge and skills? How does an organization improve its leadership for evaluation; commit adequate human, financial, and technological resources to evaluation; and create an organizational culture that values using data to learn and improve programs and services?

Different approaches to ECB have been suggested in the literature (see Hueftle Stockdill et al., 2002, for a brief summary); however, one frequently cited approach has been empowerment evaluation by Fetterman et al. (2014); see Chapter 8 for an in-depth discussion of empowerment evaluation). Empowerment evaluation assists communities in promoting social change and engaging in the process of program planning, implementation, and evaluation (Fawcett et al., 2003; Fetterman, 2001, 2005; Fetterman et al., 2014; Fetterman & Wandersman, 2004; Flaspohler et al., 2003; Wandersman, 2014). ECB is one of the core 10 principles of empowerment evaluation (Fetterman et al., 2014). In the process of building evaluation capacity, as part of the empowerment evaluation process, the evaluator assumes multiple roles—that of partner, coach, trainer, consultant, learner, and agent of change—to facilitate the institutionalization of evaluation practices within the CBO (Suarez-Balcazar et al., 2014).

One of the core goals of ECB is for staff to regularly document the implementation and outcomes of their programs and use the findings to strengthen program implementation, improve program outcomes, and meet the accountability requirements of funders and accrediting bodies (King, 2002; Preskill & Boyle, 2008; Taut, 2007). ECB practices generally involve an evaluator providing training, technical assistance, and/or consultation to one or more staff within an organization or system (Duffy et al., 2007; García-Iriarte et al., 2011). The training of evaluation skills is often grounded in transformative learning theories, which focuses on how gaining certain critical self-reflection skills could be used to improve programs, practices, and systems (Preskill & Boyle, 2008; Taut, 2007).

Partnerships between CBOs and evaluators, whether based at universities, evaluation firms, private practices, or community settings, can facilitate the process of building evaluation capacity. Institutionalization of evaluation practices is likely when partnerships focus on providing training, technical assistance tailored to the needs of the organization, consultation, and ongoing support to the CBO's staff.

Later we describe a partnership approach to building the evaluation capacity of one CBO. We described our work with this organization elsewhere within the larger framework of empowerment evaluation (see Suarez-Balcazar et al., 2014). In our view, ECB strategies represent the essence of empowerment evaluation, that is, building the capacity of the organization to achieve its goals and realize its mission. Here, we focus on how the partnership involved very specific ECB goals and activities intended to support the CBO to routinely document program impact and use program data to improve services.

CASE EXAMPLE: AN EVALUATION CAPACITY BUILDING PARTNERSHIP

Building Mutually Beneficial and Sustainable Partnerships

Background

During the last 15 years, the authors have had the opportunity to collaborate with a not-for-profit CBO that is in a predominantly Latino neighborhood in a large urban city. The CBO serves individuals with developmental and intellectual disabilities and their families and has programs that focus on employment training, vocational evaluation, adult day care, family respite care, and brain injury case management. Individuals with disabilities served by the CBO reside in community residences owned by the organization or with their families. The CBO receives funding from the state, United Way, and private foundations. The CBO is well known in the community and has strong relationships with

other agencies, a local alderman, and other institutions. The CBO has had a long history of supporting community-wide initiatives that target the Latino community, in general.

The first author is affiliated with an institution of higher education that has had a long-term relationship with the CBO that preceded our ECB work and continues today. In particular, the first author and the CBO have worked together on grants and action projects, and the CBO serves as a community practicum site for students from a variety of disciplines, including disability studies, nutrition, occupational therapy, and psychology. The partnership has been successful, mutually beneficial and characterized by a relationship built on trust, recognition of each other's strengths and expertise, respect for diversity, open communication, common goals, and other values of community-engaged research, as described elsewhere (see Suarez-Balcazar, 2005; Suarez-Balcazar et al., 2015; Thompson et al., 2003). The mutual benefits of the partnership have been many—the authors have provided training and ongoing technical assistance to the CBO and have learned a great deal about evaluation capacity and the effectiveness of ECB strategies in the process. In addition, the first author has involved generations of graduate students in ECB efforts with the CBO staff, providing these students with critical training experiences. The CBO staff have received evaluation training and technical assistance for over a decade, which has enhanced their ability to compete for competitive grants, develop their evaluation capacity, and improve their program processes, outcomes, and community impact. Members of the CBO are often invited as speakers in classes on topics related to disability and nonprofits and are collaborators on grants and publications.

Here we describe the ECB processes and activities that correspond to the individual and organizational levels that are at the core of the ECB model developed by (Taylor-Ritzler et al., 2013). We discuss the process of building evaluation capacity within a partnership approach.

The Process of Building Evaluation Capacity

In the section that follows, we frame six steps in the process of building evaluation capacity. These include (1) assessing ECB needs and readiness at the individual level, (2) assessing ECB needs and readiness at the organizational level, (3) implementing ECB activities, (4) attending to contextual and cultural issues that inform ECB activities, (5) assessing the impact of ECB activities, and (6) assessing program improvements and social change.

1. *Assess ECB needs and readiness at the individual level*

   To assess areas of evaluation capacity strength and weakness to inform ECB efforts, the evaluators reviewed program and agency reports and logic models, interviewed and administered the ECAI to the CBO leadership and staff, and conducted brainstorming sessions with groups of staff (see Suarez-Balcazar et al., 2014). From these assessments, it was clear that staff and leadership saw the need for ECB yet had little confidence in their level of knowledge or skills related to evaluation. Specifically, CBO's staff and leaders considered learning evaluation skills a necessity due

to a lack of staff with the evaluation knowledge and skills needed to meet funders' requirements and the accreditation guidelines for some of their programs. Even so, ambivalence about ECB was evident.

Early in the ECB process, staff at different levels of the organization expressed mixed views about becoming involved in evaluation activities. On the positive side, staff reported, for example, "I am very motivated to learn about evaluation," "It is important to do," "We need someone to help us who knows this stuff, we need a data person, I don't know how to do this [evaluation]," and "[Evaluation] helps you understand the relationship between what you do and the [program] goals." At the same time, other staff members were hesitant about their involvement in evaluation activities. For example, staff said, "It is time consuming and it takes us away from serving clients," "We were always motivated to do good work. We just didn't see the connection of paperwork with evaluation and program improvement." These staff thought that they did not have time for engaging in ECB activities. Furthermore, some staff eager to develop evaluation skills had attended United Way training or had limited previous experience with evaluation. In addition, each program had a team leader who, generally, was responsible for evaluation activities and therefore eager to develop needed knowledge and skills and receive technical support. Leaders at different levels of the organization worked hard to promote staff buy-in. The director of one of the programs said: "It is kind of a domino effect. You have to be very positive, present it in a good light so they are willing to follow … [by noting that evaluation can] keep you on track" and "It is an opportunity for feedback." The director of adults programs pointed out the need for supporting staff to transfer learning to what they do in their job:

> It is difficult to keep staff engaged and bought in to conduct evaluation activities. They [staff] see the importance, but when they go back to their job, they do the same thing they have been doing for years. It [evaluation] gives you a clear picture of what is expected of you and your program.

Continued

As such, organizational leaders faced the challenge of helping staff appreciate not only the benefits of evaluation thinking and processes in program improvement efforts, but also the challenge of supporting the transfer of learning. One-time evaluation training workshops do not necessarily produce changes in knowledge and skills; therefore ongoing support, technical assistance, training, and troubleshooting are critical for learning to occur.

Through the multiple assessment methods, we identified early in the process important areas of need for targeting with ECB strategies. These areas included helping staff to learn the difference between outputs and outcomes, identifying meaningful outcomes and outcome indicators, developing measures to document outcomes, promoting consistency in documentation practices across staff and programs, and developing processes for reviewing the relationship between program activities and outcomes.

2. *Assess ECB needs and readiness at the organizational level*

At the beginning of the ECB process, some staff shared organizational barriers to evaluation. For example, one staff said, "We have a high turnover at our organization that often obstructs continuation of evaluation activities," "Staff are overworked," "We don't have the right software/technology or funds to engage in evaluation," and "Other organizational priorities take over." These statements revealed that some staff perceived a lack of support for evaluation from agency leadership and a lack of communication about clear expectations for engaging in evaluation.

At the time that the authors were beginning the ECB process, the CBO was getting ready for two important site visits: one from a state accreditation body and a second from the United Way regarding a grant proposal that was under review. The first author had previously provided feedback on logic models and had sat in on site visits from United Way, one of their funders. In order to prepare for these site visits, the organization needed to have an evaluation plan in place, document program outcomes properly, and demonstrate how they were meeting their program goals. These external pressures for evaluation capacity contributed to organizational leaders'

motivation to engage in the ECB process and collaborate with the researchers who had experience with ECB.

3. *Implement ECB activities*

In our exemplar, we implemented ECB strategies to achieve three important partnership goals. First, we sought to develop the evaluation knowledge and skills of individual staff members. Second, we worked to develop organizational processes that would facilitate the staff's use of their evaluation knowledge and skills to mainstream evaluation practices into program operations and of their evaluation findings to improve services, helping the organization achieve its desired social impact. Third, we used multiple approaches to support sustained evaluation practice within the CBO. To achieve these goals, this partnership approach included the range of ECB strategies that have been discussed in the literature (see Preskill & Boyle, 2008), as described below.

(a) Develop evaluation knowledge and skills of individual staff. To build the evaluation knowledge and skills of CBO staff, the authors and graduate students engaged staff in ECB activities, such as discussion sessions about program goals, and provided staff with training, coaching, and technical assistance. Some ECB activities included all staff members, some included staff who worked in a specific program, and others included individual staff members. Group training sessions were on a range of topics, including introduction to evaluation, introduction to logic models and hands-on development of logic models, and development of outcome indicators and measures, among other topics. Training sessions included participatory processes and time for staff to practice applying the training topic to a specific program. However, recognizing that group-training sessions with hands-on practice built in are not enough to develop, transfer, or sustain evaluation skills, we followed group-training sessions with one-on-one technical assistance and coaching. A doctoral student with expertise in ECB provided some of this support by meeting weekly with a program manager to assist her in developing a working logic model, identifying indicators of outcomes of interest, and assessing outcomes and charting progress.

(b) *Develop organizational processes that support evaluation.* To support the development of organizational processes to allow staff to use their evaluation knowledge and skills, the partnership efforts targeted organizational processes beyond the efforts of individual staff members. Specifically, we focused on effecting change at the level of specific programs. We recognized that the transfer of evaluation competencies into program- or organizational-level practices often requires a catalyst approach wherein a person of influence within the organization becomes an evaluation champion who leads others in building organizational processes and practices that are necessary for evaluation capacity (see García-Iriarte et al., 2011). To facilitate the development of that champion, our graduate student and the second author met weekly with the program manager for 2 months to help her identify program-level strategies wherein she could use her leadership role to commit resources, such as allocating time for evaluation and giving priority to evaluation activities, thus creating a learning climate within the program. Other types of supports include helping the program manager establish an agenda for weekly staff meetings that included a focus on evaluation activities aimed at program improvement. This program manager became an evaluation champion and agent of change within the CBO through training and technical assistance. She assumed the role of catalyst for change by training others and providing staff with ongoing feedback. Early in this process, the program manager shared her own analysis of program data with staff to highlight challenges with the way the program was operating. When she was able to get her staff to focus on programmatic challenges, she trained her staff on new strategies for implementing services and methods for documenting their activities and outcomes. In later meetings, she reported to her staff on outcome data to engage them in the conversation about what was working and how they might refine their practices (see García-Iriarte et al., 2011).

(c) *Sustain evaluation practices over time.* To sustain the integration of evaluation thinking and activities into organizational practices and the use of evaluation findings to improve programs,

the partnership team engaged in ongoing evaluation activities. The first author continues to be available to provide support and technical assistance to the CBO, when requested. The support has included providing feedback on logic models and measurement protocols, participating in site visits from funders, providing feedback on an evaluation report, and discussing uses of evaluation findings. In addition, the first author teaches a program evaluation course in which she matches graduate students with community organizations seeking to enhance their evaluation skills. Students matched with the CBO in this exemplar had the task of providing feedback and/or assistance to develop evaluation plans, as needed. These students often continue with the evaluation effort beyond the class requirements by assisting in data collection and data analysis to support evaluation efforts. Given these multiple involvements, the evaluators and community partners have developed a strong relationship over the years and their ECB efforts have resulted in new grant funding to support healthy lifestyles programming at the organization. As the relationship shifted over time, researchers and students often provide technical assistance and consultation, as needed.

4. *Attend to contextual and cultural issues that inform ECB activities*

Evaluators need to consider culture, diversity, and contextual factors as they influence evaluation practices (see Chapter 4's in-depth discussion of cultural sensitivity and responsiveness in evaluation). Cultural and contextual factors were part of an early version of the model (see Suarez-Balcazar et al., 2010) developed and validated by Taylor-Ritzler et al. (2013). Thompson-Robinson et al. (2004) pointed out that "culture shapes values, beliefs and worldviews" and "evaluation is ... an endeavor of determining values, merit, and worth" (p. 6). As they noted, community programs are infused with cultural elements related to how the problem is defined and conceptualized and how and why they offer types of services. Likewise, evaluation activities also reflect cultural elements related to the approaches and the methods employed (LaFrance, 2004; Thompson-Robinson et al., 2004). It is critical to underscore the importance of cultural elements in carefully

Continued

matching ECB processes to organizations and communities.

Funders' demands, expectations, and deadlines; accreditation requirements; access to internet and overall technology for all staff; staff turnover; new funding opportunities and creation of new programs; and budget cuts are all contextual factors that influenced our ECB work with the CBO described in the example. We discussed many of these contextual factors and took steps to address them into the ECB efforts (e.g., funders' requirement); others surfaced as we moved along (e.g., organizational norms and culture).

In addition to these broad contextual factors, multiple diversity and cultural factors informed the ECB process, including diversity characteristics of participants served by the CBO (race, ethnicity, primary language); diversity characteristics of the staff (race, ethnicity, primary language, social class); accessibility issues according to type and severity of disability; and cultural, linguistic and accessibility/disability adaptations of tools and protocols. For instance, most evaluation protocols needed to be adapted to account for the challenges related to the disability experienced by the participants and translated to be available in Spanish, reflecting the literacy level, language, and specific characteristics of the community served. In this exemplar, partners gained information about contextual and cultural issues by asking relevant questions, observing programs, talking with participants and staff, attending fundraising and other community events hosted by the CBO, and reviewing existing documents.

5. *Assess the impact of ECB activities*

We used a variety of methods to assess the outcomes of the ECB partnership. Specifically, the evaluators administered the ECAI to the CBO leadership and staff, conducted interviews with key leaders and staff, and reviewed program reports and logic models.

To assess the evaluation knowledge and skills of individual staff, the researchers used two tools: the ECAI and an ECB checklist. We administered the ECAI a second time (see Suarez-Balcazar et al., 2014) and an ECB checklist that focused on staff members' level of mastery of relevant knowledge and skills. Findings from

the ECAI administration to staff indicated significant changes in staff motivation to engage in evaluation (see Suarez-Balcazar et al., 2014). A comment from a staff member supported this change: "I'm better prepared. I have more of a comprehensive understanding of how the process works. ... Before I thought, paperwork should be filled out and stored away. I am more excited about the process now."

We developed the ECB checklist in collaboration with the CBO's director and based on staff members' feedback. It provides another means of assessing staff members' knowledge and skills in multiple areas. Table 7.3 depicts the indicators of evaluation competence on the checklist. Like a report card, the ratings on the checklist include *Satisfactory, Inconsistent,* and *Does not exist.* We recommend using the checklist to assess for change and to identify areas of strength as well as those that warrant further attention.

In addition, to assess organizational processes to support evaluation, the partners used an interview format and direct observation of products and review of reports. The evaluators assessed the use of evaluation findings to improve programs as well as how evaluation activities were incorporated by staff into their daily programming. Leaders and staff reported evidence of building a learning climate that was conducive to evaluation. For example, the leader of adult programs said: "Staff began asking each other questions, ... helping each other, and now we have frequent staff meetings. A graduate student is now helping us on survey development and data analysis and interpretation." Similarly, a team member shared: "As a team member I now know how to support others in their [evaluation] efforts. I am trying to do innovative things and use our information in innovative ways. We do things in a team." Another team leader said: "I am a team sponsor and get to support others."

Two realities emerged in discussions of the importance of resources for evaluation. One related to the resource-limited circumstances that are salient for many CBOs. As one team member said: "Evaluation capacity is the ability to test efficacy and efficiency once additional resources are put in place. We do not have additional resources as of now; our resources have been substantially cut. Capacity

Table 7.3 Evaluation Capacity Building Checklist: Indicators of Evaluation Competence			
Rating Scale: Satisfactory: S; Inconsistent: I; Does Not Exist: D **INDICATORS of EVALUATION COMPETENCE RATING**			
Goals specify need and population			
Goals describe desired community impact			
Goals are SMART (specific, measurable, attainable, realistic, and timely)			
Logic model (or evaluation plan) includes goals, inputs/resources, outputs, outcomes, and outcome indicators			
Outputs indicate: # of participants or # of events or timeframe			
Outcomes indicate change (attitudes, behavior, knowledge, participant condition)			
Outcome measures are closely linked to the outcome indicator			
Outcome indicators are tracked			
Data are entered			
Data are analyzed			
Data and findings are discussed at staff meetings			
Findings are used to improve programs			

building is a solution to us." Another team member articulated the other reality, regarding how varying evaluation approaches and findings can be used: "Used process evaluation to reorganize program and outcomes to advocate for more staff and training." These staff members came to understand that they could use process and outcomes evaluation findings to advocate for needed resources, even in situations when resources were constrained (see Chapter 6 regarding the implications of employing process and outcome evaluation approaches in tandem).

The ECB effort and, in part, the empowerment evaluation approach utilized (see Suarez-Balcazar et al., 2014) resulted in important changes and improvements at the organizational level. For example, one noteworthy change was the increased involvement of staff in documenting participants' outcomes rather than just relying on the manager to do so. Moreover, staff were also more involved in discussions about recommendations for program improvement. Changes in practice were also apparent. For instance, we observed a clear match between client goals, activities,

and outcomes. Before we started the partnership, the staff matched client goals to outputs, not outcomes (e.g., how many clients attended the class on money management versus the client knowing how to count and manage money). In a similar vein, we also observed that staff were better able to match the outcomes they were measuring with state requirements. With additional consultation and training with our doctoral student, the CBO also developed a new consumer satisfaction survey that was accessible to people with disabilities from the Latino community (see Suarez-Balcazar et al., 2014).

6. *Assess program improvements and social change*

The desired outcome of ECB efforts is for programs to improve the quality and impact of their services. We aimed our approach to ECB at improving the CBO's capacity to serve people with intellectual and developmental disabilities from different racial, ethnic, and cultural backgrounds effectively. As such, many of the discussion sessions and trainings focused on the accessibility of services.

Continued

Accessibility of services considerations:

- Identifying and developing measurement protocols that are accessible to individuals with disabilities (e.g., using visuals when appropriate)
- Identifying outcomes that are doable and meaningful—and selected by participants, not by staff (e.g., learning how to take public transportation)
- Distinguishing outputs (e.g., how many people with intellectual and developmental disabilities attend a cooking class) from outcomes (e.g., people with intellectual and developmental disabilities can prepare their own meals) relevant to people with disabilities
- Engaging participants with disabilities in the evaluation process (e.g., participants selecting their own goals and ways to evaluate them)

The above considerations helped the organization achieve one of its goals—fostering self-determination among program participants.

Another important outcome that had spillover consequences across programs, and not just the programs on which the partnership concentrated, was the organizations' commitment to evaluation within the larger landscape of human service provision. To that effect, a leader said:

[Evaluation] ... is vital for Human Services as we are always in development. [Being involved in] capacity building ensures that we learn by our shared experiences and that we add to it by revisiting our current needs. Communities are also in development and their fluctuating needs drive services; if we fail to be sensitive to the changing needs of our customers, programs rapidly lose their effectiveness.

BUILDING PARTNERSHIPS THAT FOSTER EVALUATION-LEARNING COMMUNITIES

Our case example highlights critical aspects of the ECB process and points to opportunities that are inherent in a partnership approach to building evaluation capacity. Several issues merit further discussion, including the opportunities for building learning communities among partners. Evaluation processes implemented within a partnership approach must be relevant—staff must perceive value in attaining their programmatic goals and organizational missions to invest their already limited time and resources in evaluation activities. They must also appreciate the connection between their day-to-day service delivery activities and evaluation. As often said by staff: "How is this [evaluation] going to help me serve people better?" The collaborative and participatory approach embraced here facilitated the development of a learning community.

The mutually beneficial approach to building our partnership has created a win–win situation for both the evaluators (and their students) and the CBO. By no means have we created a relationship that depends on one partner only or limits the capacity of the CBO to engage in evaluation practices without the evaluators as partners. We have developed a relationship built on trust and common ground in which partners recognized and valued each other's assets and strengths. Yet, partnerships for evaluation are not without their challenges, which often present opportunities to strengthen the partnership.

Although the example here focused on a partnership between academic evaluators and a CBO, evaluation-learning communities can take place in between other types of partners, not necessarily university partners. For instance, multiple organizations—schools, city government, United Way, and nonprofits—may create learning communities and partnerships to promote evaluation practice. The presence of multiple community settings may enhance evaluation sustainability over time. Wolff et al. (2017) underscored the power of community coalitions to promote capacity building and social change.

It is important for evaluators to recognize that partnerships like the one described here take time and effort and that the long-lasting relationship with this CBO facilitated the engagement in evaluation activities. When such a strong relationship is not present, evaluators may need to spend time building trust with the CBO. A relationship can be built by getting to know the agency (staff, participants, and programs), offering voluntary services, visiting the agency, attending community events sponsored by the agency, and having informal conversations about the issues the agency faces when evaluating and documenting the impact of what they do (see Suarez-Balcazar et al., 2005).

The following four considerations facilitate the building and sustainability of evaluation capacity building partnerships.

1. *No room for linear thinkers.*

   Partnerships between evaluators and CBOs present a rich opportunity for creating evaluation-learning communities. However, evaluation-learning communities have little room for linear thinkers. Building and sustaining evaluation capacity at the organizational level is not necessarily an easy or straightforward task, given the challenges that CBOs experience such as staff turnover, budget cuts, priorities often dictated by state or funder regulations, and demographic changes, among others (Suarez-Balcazar et al., 2005). These challenges often require that the evaluators and their students go with the flow, are open minded, and are ready to accommodate last-minute changes to plans, training agendas, and project expectations.

   Given the changing world of human services, we found that CBO staff for the most part were not linear thinkers. They are used to social programs responding to several ongoing and last-minute changes and operating in the face of ambiguity. That said, for the CBO staff, the students' class schedule and academic calendar imposed challenges to scheduling meetings and training events.

   Despite these challenges, partnerships focused on capacity building and empowerment (see Suarez-Balcazar et al., 2014) can yield mutual benefits for those involved. Partnerships focusing on ECB are grounded in the belief that bringing together knowledge and expertise from diverse individuals can be transformative in improving the effectiveness of organizations in meeting their goals and achieving change. Thus, based on our experience we know that there is little room for linear ways of thinking in partnerships for evaluation.

2. *Defining and redefining boundaries between roles.*

   Building evaluation-learning communities also requires partners assuming different roles at different times in the process. Evaluation partners truly invested in creating evaluation capacity need to be ready to wear different hats and be flexible enough to change as needed. In this exemplar, both evaluation and CBO partners played different roles with ease. Evaluators became consultants, trainers, and instructors, yet were ready to be in learning mode at different points in the process, specifically as it related to strategies for measuring outcomes relevant to the disability and minority communities. Evaluators were also learners about disability accommodations and state accreditation requirements; cultural and political issues of importance to the community; and strategies for working with program participants.

The community partners felt empowered (see Fetterman et al., 2014; Suarez-Balcazar et al., 2014) to also function in different roles and establish their own boundaries. Mutually beneficial partnerships for evaluation foster the bringing together of diverse sets of skills and knowledge (evaluator and community partner) that need to be respected, listened to, and incorporated into the capacity building process to enhance sustainability. Being able to redefine boundaries and assume different roles requires flexibility and a collaborative participatory approach to the partnership.

3. *Stretching and maximizing resources.*

It is important to value and recognize the set of resources that each partner brings to the ECB. Recognizing, identifying, and celebrating resources and expertise brought by each partner aid in creating a balanced partnership. For instance, the evaluators brought students, easy access to technology, time, and funds to purchase refreshments for training activities. The community partners provided accessible space to run the training activities and access to people with disabilities and key informants about evaluation issues within the organization and vast knowledge of the community of interest. Nelson et al. (2001) allude to unbalanced relationships created when one of the partners controls all the resources or the most valuable resources, thus creating power struggles and often mistrust. In our case, the CBO realized that part of their commitment to evaluation implied allocating resources to support ECB activities; similarly, we committed resources to the partnership because we believed in what we could accomplish together and have benefited in the many ways explained here.

4. *What if the cup is half-empty?*

Overall, partnerships between evaluators and CBOs can become galvanizing movements that foster ECB learning communities and organizational transformation. Therefore, the cup will never be filled. There is no evaluation threshold to be achieved. There is always room for improving evaluation activities and building on the experience of putting into practice what is learned as the staff engages in evaluation. Mainstreaming evaluation practices results in a cycle of improving evaluation processes and evaluation outcomes in order to meet program goals and improve the lives of individuals with disabilities. Indeed, partners can build learning communities dedicated to documenting programs and utilizing findings that foster program improvement and social change (Suarez-Balcazar & Taylor-Ritzler, 2014). Ongoing brainstorming and reflection among partners must take place for the cycle to continue and for the learning community to thrive.

CONCLUSION

This chapter provides an overview of ECB through a partnership approach between evaluators and a CBO. Through the exemplar, we unpacked the essence of partnerships for evaluation. Partnerships for advancing evaluation practices provide a rich learning environment for students, faculty, CBO staff, and managers. Partnerships, as the one illustrated here, can become catalysts for social change and program improvement. Partners brought to the table unique sets of expertise that enabled the creation of a learning community about evaluation. We were fortunate to have a long-standing relationship before we began this ECB project. Partnerships take time and effort to build, yet they are essential in evaluation practices. If the evaluators do not have a well-established partnership with the community of interest, we advise taking time to develop trust by providing assistance as needed by the agency, participating in community events, attending community meetings, clarifying expectations, and developing common ground on evaluation issues. Before the onset of an ECB effort, we recommend establishing a strong communication and a mutually beneficial relationship with the partner (see Suarez-Balcazar et al., 2005).

This learning community is ongoing and, by underscoring the importance of a mutually beneficial reciprocal relationship, the interest in sustaining it is mutual. The sustainability of evaluation practices is happening because the CBO wants to improve program outcomes, achieve its goals, improve the lives of individuals with disabilities, and continue to obtain funding. The partnership has been successful, in part, because it is creating mutual benefits for both the organization and the university and has created a learning community that celebrates and takes pride in its shared accomplishments.

FURTHER READING

Community Tool Box. *Evaluating community programs and initiatives*. http://ctb.ku.edu/en

Kellogg Foundation. *Evaluation handbook*. http://www.capacity4health.org/resource/kellog-foundation-evaluation-handbook/

The Riley Institute. (n.d.). *Education policy*. https://riley.furman.edu/education/research-evaluation/about/evaluation-capacity-building/evaluation-capacity-building

Sastre-Merino, S., Vidueira, P., Diaz-Puente, J., & Fernandez-Moral, M. J. (2015). Capacity building through empowerment evaluation. In D. Fetterman, S. Kaftarian., & A. Wandersman (Eds). *Empowerment evaluation* (pp. 76–85). Sage.

University of Wisconsin-Extension. *Program development*. http://fyi.uwex.edu/programdevelopment/logic-models/

Urban Institute. *Building evaluation capacity*. http://www.urban.org/research/publication/building-evaluation-capacity

KEY CONCEPTS

Evaluation capacity building: Evaluation capacity refers to a set of competencies and practices related to the ongoing documentation of programs and use of data to inform understanding and improve the outcomes of social programs.

Individual-level capacity-building factors: Attitudes, motivation, knowledge, and skills are individual factors that affect ECB.

Mainstreaming evaluation: Making the process of documenting impact routine across programs.

Organizational-level capacity-building factors: Leadership, learning climate, and resources are organizational factors that affect ECB.

QUESTIONS FOR REFLECTION

1. Consider the scenario presented at the beginning of the chapter. How would you help the organization identify outcomes and outputs of interest to clients? What strategies can you utilize from this chapter?

2. Consider a community organization that you are familiar with in your community. What specific contextual and cultural issues need to be considered in the process of building the capacity of staff to evaluate their programs?

3. What do you think are some of the individual- and organizational-level challenges that community organizations experience when evaluating their programs routinely? Identify the challenges and potential solutions based on the information presented in this chapter.

REFERENCES

Carman, J. G. (2007). Evaluation practice among community-based organizations: Research into the reality. *American Journal of Evaluation, 28*, 60–75.

Connolly, P., & York, P. (2002). Evaluating capacity-building efforts for nonprofit organizations. *Organizational Development Practitioner, 34*, 33–39.

Cousins, J. B., Goh, S., Clark, S., & Lee, L. (2004). Integrating evaluation inquiry into the organizational culture: A review and synthesis of the knowledge base. *Canadian Journal of Program Evaluation, 19*, 99–141.

Duffy, J., Labin, S., & Wandersman, A. (2007, November). A review of research on evaluation capacity building strategies. T. Taylor-Ritzler (Chair), *Building and assessing capacity for evaluation: Creating communities of learners among service providers*. Symposium presented at the annual meeting of the American Evaluation Association, Baltimore, MD.

Fawcett, S. B., Boothroyd, R., Schultz, J. A., Francisco, V. T., Carson, V., & Bremby, R. (2003). Building capacity for participatory evaluation within community initiatives. *Journal of Prevention & Intervention in the Community, 26*(2), 21–36. doi:10.1300/J005v26n02_03

Fetterman, D. M. (2001). *Foundations of empowerment evaluation*. Sage.

Fetterman, D. M. (2005). Empowerment evaluation: From digital divide to academic distress. In D. M. Fetterman & A. Wandersman (Eds.), *Empowerment evaluation: Principles in practice* (pp. 92–122). Guildford Press.

Fetterman, D. M., Kaftarian, S., & Wandersman, A. (Eds.). (2014). *Empowerment evaluation*. Sage.

Fetterman, D. M., & Wandersman, A. (Eds.). (2004). *Empowerment evaluation: Principles in practice*. Guilford Press.

Flaspohler, P., Wandersman, A., Keener, D., Maxwell, K. N., Ace, A., Andrews, A., & Holmes, B. (2003). Promoting program success and fulfilling accountability requirements in a statewide community-based initiative. *Journal of Prevention & Intervention in the Community, 26*(2), 37–52. doi:10.1300/J005v26n02_04

García-Iriarte, E., Suarez-Balcazar, Y., Taylor-Ritzler, T., & Luna, M. (2011). A catalyst-for-change approach to evaluation capacity building. *American Journal of Evaluation, 32*(2), 168–182. doi:10.1177/1098214010387114

Hueftle Stockdill, S., Baizerman, M., & Compton, D. W. (2002). Toward a definition of the ECB process: A conversation with the ECB literature. *New Directions for Evaluation, 2002*(93), 7–26. doi:10.1002/ev.39

King, J. A. (2002). Building the evaluation capacity of a school district. *New Directions for Evaluation, 2002*(93), 63–80. doi:10.1002/ev.42

Labin, S. N., Duffy, J. L., Meyers, D. C., Wandersman, A., & Lesesne, C. A. (2012). A research synthesis of the evaluation capacity building literature. *American Journal of Evaluation, 33*(3), 307–338. doi:10.1177/1098214011434608

LaFrance, J. (2004). Culturally competent evaluation in Indian country. *New Directions for Evaluation, 2004*(102), 39–50. doi:10.1002/ev.114

Nelson, G., Prilleltensky, I., & MacGillivary, H. (2001). Building value-based partnerships: Toward solidarity with oppressed groups. *American Journal of Community Psychology, 29*(5), 649–677. doi:10.1023/A:1010406400101

Nielsen, S. B., Lemire, S., & Skov, M. (2011). Measuring evaluation capacity—Results and implications of a Danish study. *American Journal of Evaluation, 32*(3), 324–344. doi:10.1177/1098214010396075

Nye, N., & Glickman, N. J. (2000). Working together: Building capacity for community development. *Housing Policy Debate, 11*(1), 163–198. doi:10.1080/10511482.2000.9521366

Preskill, H., & Boyle, S. (2008). A multidisciplinary model of evaluation capacity building. *American Journal of Evaluation, 29*(4), 443–459. doi:10.1177/1098214008324182

Suarez-Balcazar, Y., Davis, M., Ferrari, J., Nyden, P., Olson, B., Alvarez, J., Molloy, P., & Toro, P. (2005). University-community partnerships: A framework and an exemplar. In L. Jason, C. Keys, Y. Suarez-Balcazar, R. R. Taylor, M. Davis, J. Durlak, & D. Isenberg (Eds.), *Participatory community research: Theory and methods in action* (pp. 105–120). American Psychological Association.

Suarez-Balcazar, Y., Harper, G. W., & Lewis, R. (2005). An interactive and contextual model of community-university collaborations for research and action. *Health Education & Behavior, 32*(1), 84–101. doi:10.1177/1090198104269512

Suarez-Balcazar, Y., Mirza, M. P., & Hansen, A. M. W. (2015). Unpacking university-community partnerships to advance scholarship of practice. *Occupational Therapy in Health Care, 29*(4), 370–382. doi:10.3109/07380577.2015.1037945

Suarez-Balcazar, Y., & Taylor-Ritzler, T. (2014). Moving from science to practice in evaluation capacity building. *American Journal of Evaluation, 35*(1), 95–99. doi:10.1177/1098214013499440

Suarez-Balcazar, Y., Taylor-Ritzler, T., Garcia-Iriarte, E., Keys, C. B., Kinney, L., Ruch-Ross, H., & Curtin, G. (2010). Evaluation capacity building: A culturally- and contextually-grounded interactive framework and exemplar. In F. Balcazar, Y. Suarez-Balcazar, T. Taylor-Ritzler, & C. B. Keys (Eds.), *Race, culture and disability: Rehabilitation science and practice* (pp. 307–324). Jones and Bartlett.

Suarez-Balcazar, Y., Taylor-Ritzler, T., & Morales-Curtin, G. (2014). Building evaluation capacity to engage in empowerment evaluation: A case of organizational transformation. In D. M. Fetterman, S. Kaftarian, & A. Wandersman (Eds.), *Empowerment evaluation: Knowledge and tools for self-assessment, evaluation capacity building, and accountability* (pp. 233–258). Sage.

Taut, S. (2007). Studying self-evaluation capacity building in a large international development organization. *American Journal of Evaluation*, *28*(1), 45–59. doi:10.1177/1098214006296430

Taylor-Ritzler, T., Suarez-Balcazar, Y., Garcia-Iriarte, E., Henry, D., & Balcazar, F. (2013). Understanding and measuring evaluation capacity: A model and instrument validation study. *American Journal of Evaluation*, *34*, 190–206.

Thompson, L. S., Story, M., & Butler, G. (2003). Use of a university-community collaboration model to frame issues and set an agenda for strengthening a community. *Health Promotion Practice*, *4*, 385–392. doi:10.1177/1524839903255467

Thompson-Robinson, M., Hopson, R. K., & SenGupta, S. (2004). *In search of cultural competence in evaluation: Toward principles and practices.* Jossey-Bass.

Wandersman, A. (2014). Getting to outcomes: An evaluation capacity building example of rationale, science and practice. *American Journal of Evaluation*, *35*, 100–106.

Wolff, T., Minkler, M., Wolfe, S., Berkowitz, B., Bowen, L., Butterfoss, F. D., Christens, B. D., Francisco, V. T., Himmelman, A. T., & Lee, K. S. (2017). Collaborating for equity and justice: Moving beyond collective impact. *Nonprofit Quarterly.* https://nonprofitquarterly.org.

CHAPTER 8

EMPOWERMENT EVALUATION

Pamela S. Imm, Mary Brolin, Janice B. Yost, and Opal R. Stone

Society has seemingly intractable problems. The proportion of the population living in poverty is increasing. Too many are hungry and lack access to affordable homes. Too many experience mental illness or substance use disorders and lack access to quality treatment and recovery services. After having served a sentence imposed by the criminal justice system, too many reoffend and are reincarcerated. These issues, and many others, persist despite the best intentions of government, nonprofit human service organizations, and healthcare providers. The government contributes billions of dollars collected from taxpayers, while individual donors, philanthropists, and foundations give generously, yet the problems continue unabated.

Programs to alleviate societal problems frequently lack a substantive evaluation component, as do some other large-scale initiatives. Too few resources are available to support a thorough planning process to design programs or interventions based on the priority needs identified. Process and outcome data are often haphazardly gathered. Continuous quality improvement (CQI) cycles of reflection and action are not the routine. Even programs that have powerful anecdotal examples of success do not always have the benefit of evaluation data that provide sufficient evidence to verify program outcomes. The lack of rigorous evaluation data and desired outcomes that can be broadly understood and accepted by a wide range of audiences prevents effective programs from being replicated and scaled up. Even effective programs typically struggle to maintain funding, often fading away until being reinvented. Empowerment Evaluation (EE) offers an approach to change this scenario, by engaging evaluators as partners in developing and monitoring program interventions and documenting the results (Fetterman et al., 1996).

Learning Objectives

1. Gain a basic understanding of how empowerment evaluation and the Getting to Outcomes® 10 accountability questions can be used in program evaluation.

2. Learn how empowerment evaluators can be engaged as partners in designing, monitoring, and evaluating program outcomes.

3. Identify how empowerment evaluators' partnership approach can add value in creating systems change to sustain effective programming.

BRIEF OVERVIEW OF EMPOWERMENT EVALUATION

Evaluators are frequently requested to utilize evaluation processes and methods to document the successes and outcomes of various programs, practices, and policies. A variety of evaluation methods and tools are available to answer specific evaluation questions to determine a program's value or worth. Many of these approaches and tools are implemented using traditional evaluation methods, which may be experimental or quasi-experimental in nature. Over the last 30 years, EE has become an increasingly well-known evaluation approach that has its roots in traditional evaluation as well as collaborative and participatory evaluation methods.

EE was initially described by David Fetterman in 1993 at the American Evaluation Association's (AEA) annual meeting (Miller & Campbell, 2006). The approach draws its origins from empowerment theory, community psychology, and action anthropology. An initial *EE* resource, *Empowerment Evaluation: Knowledge and Tools for Self Assessment and Accountability* (edited by David Fetterman, Shakeh Kaftarian, and Abraham Wandersman), was published in 1996 and offered examples of how evaluators used EE processes and methods in a variety of program and policy sectors. Since that time, the EE approach has blossomed to include additional volumes of books, resources, and tools for those interested in using EE as an evaluation approach. Innovative work and scholarship in recent years has contributed to EE being seen as a legitimate approach in professional evaluation circles and across settings (e.g., government, foundations). The AEA's Topical Interest Group (TIG) on Collaborative, Participatory, and Empowerment Evaluation has consistently increased its membership each year. Advocates of EE have also delineated it as theoretically different from similar evaluation approaches such as participatory evaluation and developmental evaluation (Wandersman et al., 2005).

In traditional evaluation processes, which are frequently conducted by an independent evaluator, collaboration may occur with key stakeholder groups to determine what is to be evaluated and suggest strategies for use. The extent of this collaboration varies widely on the following five dimensions: control of decision making, diversity among stakeholders who participate, power relationships among participating stakeholders, manageability of evaluation implementation, and depth of participation (Weaver & Cousins, 2004). EE places a strong emphasis on stakeholder control of the decision-making process and active engagement by stakeholders. There is also a focus on using data to facilitate *CQI*, that is, systematic cycles of collecting data and analyzing it in order to refine programming. Many organizations or groups that embrace EE over traditional evaluation processes appreciate the goal of building the capacities of program staff to conduct and use evaluation methods on their own. The use of EE in various types of organizations can facilitate longer-term systems-level change including building organizational learning through the use of data, informed decision making, and developing feedback loops for *CQI* (Lentz et al., 2005). Evaluators who utilize traditional evaluation methods do not typically view building an organization's evaluation capacity as a priority (Cox et al., 2009).

DEFINING AND OPERATIONALIZING EMPOWERMENT EVALUATION

Various definitions of EE have been offered including this initial definition provided by Fetterman et al. (1996): "the use of evaluation concepts, techniques, and findings to foster improvement and self-determination." More recently, EE has been defined as an approach that aims to increase the probability of achieving program success by (1) providing stakeholders with tools for assessing the planning, implementation, and self-evaluation of their programs and (2) mainstreaming evaluation as part of the planning and management of the program/organization (Wandersman et al., 2005). This most recent definition is not viewed as "new" but rather an expansion of the prior one with the goal of enhancing the overall clarity of EE (e.g., Fetterman & Wandersman, 2007). Both definitions have a strong emphasis on continuous learning and improvement and extend the traditional role of an evaluator to be one of a facilitator or coach. Moreover, the model explicitly states that the EE evaluator aims to aid the program (e.g., participants, staff) to achieve positive and/or successful outcomes as decided by the stakeholders (e.g., Wandersman et al., 2005). While detractors have used this core value to suggest that empowerment evaluators are more susceptible to bias in data collection and interpretation, the primary authors and champions of EE (e.g., Fetterman, Wandersman) have sought to refute these claims by underscoring EE as a credible and effective evaluation approach. These controversies are well documented and available in the literature (Fetterman et al., 2009), but are outside the scope of this chapter. It is noteworthy that the practice of EE is consistent with the AEA's Joint Committee on Program Evaluation Standards.

Methods for implementing EE strategies have also emerged over time. Fetterman (1994) highlights his *three step model for EE* to include these components: establishing the mission, taking stock, and planning for the future. The empowerment evaluator serves as a coach or a *critical friend* (i.e., a trusted person who asks provocative questions, provides data to be examined through another lens, and offers critiques of a person's work as a friend; Costa & Kallick, 1993) to help the community develop its missions. When taking stock, the empowerment evaluator assesses what existing efforts have already occurred. This is likely to include documentation of the project's baseline assessment. When planning for the future, the empowerment evaluator works with the community to set specific goals and uses evidence-based strategies or activities to accomplish the goals. Potential evaluation methods such as interviews or surveys may be used to test whether the strategies are working and allow for midcourse corrections. There are subsequent assessments of the activities comparing the findings to the baseline results to measure growth or change over time.

Wandersman and colleagues utilize a 10-step model for EE known as *Getting to Outcomes®* (Chinman et al., 1999; 2004). This model is built on a series of 10 accountability questions that integrates effective components of planning, implementation, and evaluation. The model and the manualized set of strategies were recognized as the Outstanding Publication by the AEA in 2008. The 10 accountability questions and related literatures for each of the 10 steps are presented in Table 8.1.

In 2009, Wandersman and his colleagues developed a document used by the Centers for Disease Control and Prevention on how to hire an empowerment evaluator (Cox et al., 2009). The document includes information about the skill sets and competencies an empowerment evaluator should have as well as specific hiring tools such as job descriptions and potential interview questions.

Table 8.1 *Getting to Outcomes® 10 Accountability Questions*[a]

Accountability Questions	Relevant Literatures
1. What are the underlying needs and conditions in the community? (*NEEDS/RESOURCES*)	Needs/resources assessment
2. What are the goals, target populations, and objectives (i.e., desired outcomes)? (*GOALS*)	Goal setting
3. Which evidence-based models and best practice programs can be useful in reaching the goals? (*BEST PRACTICE*)	Consult literature on science-based and best practice programs
4. What actions need to be taken so the selected program "fits" the community context? (*FIT*)	Feedback on comprehensiveness and fit of program including cultural competence
5. What organizational capacities are needed to implement the program? (*CAPACITIES*)	Assessment of organizational capacities
6. What is the plan for this program? (*PLAN*)	Planning
7. How will the quality of program and/or initiative implementation be assessed? (*PROCESS*)	Process evaluation
8. How well did the program work? (*OUTCOMES*)	Outcome and impact evaluation
9. How will continuous quality improvement strategies be incorporated? (*CQI*)	Total quality management; continuous quality improvement
10. If the program is successful, how will it be sustained? (*SUSTAIN*)	Sustainability and institutionalization

Source: Adapted from Chinman et al. (1999; 2004).

[a] Getting to Outcomes and GTO are trademarks registered by the University of South Carolina and RAND Corporation. It is noteworthy that, while GTO is trademarked, resources are available free of charge (visit http://www.rand.org/health/projects/getting-to-outcomes.html for access to manuals and other GTO tools and resources).

PRINCIPLES OF EMPOWERMENT EVALUATION

The *principles of EE* are outlined in the textbook *Empowerment Evaluation Principles in Practice*, edited by Fetterman and Wandersman (2005). To specifically illustrate the principles, each chapter provides a case study of the EE principles in practice. Table 8.2 outlines the *principles of EE* and a brief description of each. All principles are equal in importance and are not ordered by priority.

The *principles of EE* are defining characteristics, and those practicing EE are encouraged to utilize evaluation methods that include as many principles as possible. These principles, and the practice of EE, will certainly be more attractive to some organizations than to others. For example, a nonprofit organization whose mission may include social justice or community change may be interested in EE because of certain principles such as democratic participation, community knowledge, and community ownership. By working with empowerment evaluators, the capacities of organizations to adopt and integrate the principles can be improved over time.

Table 8.2 Principles of Empowerment Evaluation

Principle	Brief Description
Community ownership	EE places the primary responsibility and ownership for building the organization's evaluation capacity and evaluating the organization's strategies within the organization
Inclusion	EE involves the representation and participation of key stakeholders
Democratic participation	EE is a highly collaborative process. Every stakeholder's voice is to be heard and equally valued
Community knowledge	EE values and promotes the knowledge present within an organization and community in which they work. Community stakeholders are considered to be in the best position to understand the community's problems and to generate solutions to those problems
Evidence-based strategies	EE promotes the use of evidence-based strategies so that organizations can use their resources to select, implement, and evaluate strategies that have a high likelihood of success
Accountability	EE focuses on data that can be used to inform continuous program improvement and to determine whether a strategy has achieved the desired outcomes
Improvement	EE helps organizations to improve their strategies so they are more likely to achieve their stated goals and outcomes
Organizational learning	EE fosters a culture of learning within organizations. Stakeholders come to view all data (positive and negative) as useful information to inform improvement in strategies
Social justice	EE increases an organization's evaluation capacity to implement strategies that work to reduce health disparities that affect groups marginalized (Brennan et al., 2008) by discrimination, persecution, prejudice, and intolerance
Capacity building	EE builds individual and organizational evaluation capacity so that stakeholders are better able to conduct their own evaluations, understand the results, and use them to continuously improve their strategies

Source: Adapted from Fetterman and Wandersman (2005).

EVALUATORS AS PARTNERS TO SUPPORT SYSTEMS CHANGE

Using the EE approach, the evaluator is intentionally engaged as an active and integrated partner frequently beginning with the planning phase of the program/initiative. This is significantly different than the traditional model of how evaluators and funders frequently interact (Figure 8.1). Specifically, the organization (such as a grantee) typically has minimal involvement with the funder or the evaluator in the initial stages of evaluation planning. This traditional model assumes the grantee has selected interventions that are best practice or evidence-based and that the grantee has identified measurable objectives and valid measurement tools at the outset. The model also assumes that data are gathered methodically throughout the duration of the project, including the initial baseline data. All too frequently the traditional evaluation model concludes that the project's outcomes

Figure 8.1 Traditional Grant Evaluation Model

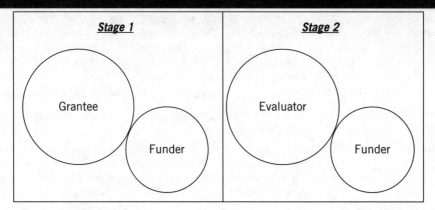

Source: This figure originally appeared in Fetterman et al. (2015). *Empowerment evaluation: Knowledge and tools for self-assessment, evaluation capacity building, and accountability, 2nd Edition* (p. 50). Sage.

cannot necessarily be attributed to the project's interventions. Such conclusions can often leave the grantee frustrated with the practice of evaluation and unable to gain support for sustaining the project. Moreover, the grantee, and the nonprofit sector in general, may become disillusioned about the value of pursuing new strategies and interventions in the future.

The EE partnership model depicted in Figure 8.2 reflects an interactive and collaborative partnership, which includes the funder (Yost, 2015). The partnership involves the evaluator as a meaningful partner who contributes to the program's planning and

Figure 8.2 Empowerment Evaluation Partnership Model

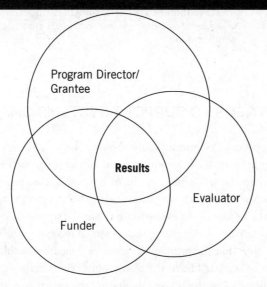

Source: This figure originally appeared in Fetterman et al. (2015). *Empowerment evaluation: Knowledge and tools for self-assessment, evaluation capacity building, and accountability, 2nd Edition* (p. 50). Sage.

monitoring as well as the documentation of its results. This collaboration allows for evaluators to share their perspectives and skills, adding value throughout the duration of the program and thereby increasing the likelihood of achieving results that can be attributed to the interventions. This collaborative partnership, consistent with the partnership-oriented emphasis of EE, is distinctly different from the traditional model of evaluation in which the evaluator is typically engaged in a separate function to assess a program after it has been implemented.

The EE partnership model may be used even if the funder partner cannot be actively engaged. However, funders who participate in cycles of reflection are likely to be better prepared to understand and authorize real-time decisions regarding programmatic or budget changes. In addition, funders may be in a position to attract others to cofund the program and may also assist in bringing the program to the attention of the media and public officials.

In the context of the EE partnership, the evaluator's role often includes the following:

- informing the planning process by assessing the selection of evidence-based strategies or best practices;

- adapting those selected strategies to the community and supporting implementation of strategies with fidelity;

- identifying valid measurement tools and assisting in the development of data gathering practices;

- fostering the monitoring of data collection to assist the process of *CQI* or cycles of reflection and action; and/or

- coaching the grantee on preparing credible progress and summary reports that can assist in securing future funding and institutionalizing the project.

In addition, the empowerment evaluator may embrace the role of teacher by intentionally working with the grantee to build the nonprofit organization's capacities to routinely practice high-quality evaluation beyond the specific grant project (Box 8.1).

BOX 8.1 SPECIFIC TASKS EMPOWERMENT EVALUATORS MAY PERFORM

- Help develop the theory of change or logic model.

- Help articulate clear goals and desired outcomes for the program, gather baseline data, and establish ways to measure the desired outcomes.

- Help identify promising or evidence-based practices that could be used to meet the goals and desired outcomes.

- Help strategize and plan evaluation implementation, including data collection

Continued

BOX 8.1 SPECIFIC TASKS EMPOWERMENT EVALUATORS MAY PERFORM   (CONTINUED)

methods and required approvals (e.g., Institutional Review Board approval).

- Monitor progress on goals and activities throughout the program period and advise on making adjustments.

- Assist in conducting periodic process evaluations.

- Participate in routine grant management team meetings (involving the program director/grantee partner, funder partner, and evaluator partner) to review progress and lessons learned and to revise program and evaluation components, and spending plans, as needed.

- Occasionally attend the program's steering committee and advisory group meetings and periodically gather their input and feedback on the program and the evaluation.

- Assist in preparing annual program summary reports by providing the program director with information related to the outcomes of the program.

- Assist in preparing materials or presentations regarding the program's outcomes that are suitable for communicating with varied audiences/stakeholders.

- Prepare a final evaluation report.

CASE EXAMPLE: EVALUATOR AS PARTNER— CRIMINAL JUSTICE REFORM THROUGH "A WISER APPROACH TO REENTRY (WISR)"

The Problem

In 2011, the Massachusetts Department of Correction reported that 44% of all individuals released from prison were incarcerated again within 3 years (Papagiorgakis, 2015). With reentry services spread across multiple state agencies and the needs of newly released individuals spanning multiple systems, reentry barriers for this vulnerable group were formidable. At an average cost of $53,000 per person per year, the cost to the state of this revolving door of incarceration was excessive. Beyond the financial cost to the state, the toll in human suffering associated with incarceration and recidivism was substantial.

Creation of the WISR Model

Intent on reducing reincarceration, increasing public health, and improving public safety, a group of criminal justice, mental health, and community health professionals came together to form the Re-entry Roundtable and develop the Worcester Initiative for Supported Reentry (WISR). The WISR program involved collaboration among community-based organizations including the Worcester Superior Court and District Court Probation Offices, Worcester County Sheriff's Office, Massachusetts Department of Correction, Massachusetts Parole Board, Dismas House, and the Edward M. Kennedy Community Health Center. From the beginning of the planning process, the partners within the Re-entry Roundtable aimed to institutionalize an evidence-based model for successful reentry. The implementation of the model was first led by Dismas House and then by Advocates, Inc., with a total of $1.9 million in funding from the Health Foundation of Central Massachusetts for planning (in 2011), piloting (2012), and fully implementing the WISR program (2013, 2016). Approximately 10% of the foundation's total funding for WISR went to support the work of the evaluation partner.

The primary purpose of the foundation's funding for large-scale projects is to ensure that its investment in evidence-based programs results in positive outcomes that have high potential to be sustained in communities. The foundation, classified by the IRS as a 501(c) (4), that is, a nonprofit social welfare organization that can engage in lobbying, provided that their lobbying efforts align with the stated purpose of the organization, works closely with its partners to ensure meaningful advocacy and policy-level changes to eventually sustain proven initiatives either locally or through state or federal commitments.

The EE Partnership Model

From the outset, the Health Foundation required the grant applicant to use the EE partnership model and recruited a select pool of evaluators with EE experience and content knowledge. The grant applicant, Advocates, Inc., and EE evaluators from Brandeis University (from this pool) became partners to plan, implement, and evaluate the WISR program. The evaluator partner from Brandeis contributed to the development of the initial planning grant application and all subsequent applications and process and outcome reports to the Foundation.

Advocates, Inc. was funded to implement the WISR program using a problem-solving framework similar to the collective impact model (see Kania & Kramer, 2011 for more) consisting of a common agenda, a backbone organization, mutually reinforcing activities, continuous communication, and a shared measurement system. As such, the Foundation required them, as the lead organization, to facilitate a collaborative effort, involving a structured process of planning, piloting, and implementing a set of interventions, with the end goal of changing systems to sustain evidence-based solutions. The evaluator partner participated with the grantee and funder partners in all stages of the process, which promoted a culture of shared-problem solving, ongoing and real-time data feedback, CQI, and accountability among all partners. While each of the partners had its own particular perspective, the EE model created opportunities for high levels of collaboration through collaborative planning, ongoing problem solving, and specific strategies for program enhancement. This occurred in a variety of ways including quarterly grant management team meetings for collaborative planning, participation in steering committee or advisory group meetings, and joint preparation of summary reports and presentations.

The expertise of each partner was shared in an interactive and ongoing manner that strengthened the program and its evaluation. The grantee brought deep knowledge of the problem in the community and gathered together the other relevant organizations to design a comprehensive program. The funder brought expertise in advocacy, an essential ingredient in creating systems change. The evaluator brought skills in identifying the theory of change and desired measurable outcomes, designing and monitoring the evaluation component, and then documenting the results in a final written report, which included an executive summary suitable for sharing with the general public and state policymakers.

Implementation of the EE Partnership

Planning and Grant Writing

With input from the Re-entry Roundtable and the empowerment evaluators, the grantee prepared a planning grant that addressed the first four accountability questions of the *Getting to Outcomes®* *empowerment evaluation* approach. This included identifying the needs to be addressed, the goals and desired outcomes of the initiative, and potential interventions to meet the goals. The empowerment evaluators contributed toward this effort by sharing information from a literature review with the Re-entry Roundtable to inform their planning.

Continued

In summary, the WISR program provided participants with intensive case management to support them with housing, employment, healthcare, and other key needs. Case managers met with participants 30–90 days before release, administered screenings and assessments to identify participants' strengths and service needs, and in partnership with the participants, developed individually tailored service plans to encourage smooth transitions to the community. Case managers coordinated services to ensure adequate supports were in place prior to release and as needed upon return to the community. Generally, participants accessed services for up to 1 year postrelease.

Throughout the planning process, the evaluators also facilitated discussions with the Re-entry Roundtable and the grantee to ensure that all of the collaborating agencies fully understood the needs of individuals reentering the community and the roles of each organization that worked with them such as the jail, the probation office, and community agencies. The empowerment evaluators also helped the team craft goals and program objectives that were measurable so they could track progress and outcomes. The partners used the planning grant to fully develop the WISR model for reentry and then tested and refined the model during a pilot grant year.

Developing Data Collection Systems

During the planning year, the empowerment evaluators worked with the grantee, particularly the case managers, to build on existing data collection systems (related to GTO questions #5–#7). The goal was to not only streamline data collection but also ensure that the data could be used for WISR program monitoring and outcome measurement. Together, the case managers and empowerment evaluators developed an Excel database to record data on program participants from intake to discharge. The database included information that the case managers needed for their own internal reporting, as well as for the WISR evaluation.

Using Data for Continuous Quality Improvement

All partners recognized that the grantee owned the data and that the grantee agency should understand how to use the data for their own monitoring and CQI. After completion of the dashboard to report progress, the lead agency submitted monthly data to the funder agency using the dashboard. The EE evaluators reviewed the monthly findings and ensured that the grantee was reporting the data accurately. The grantee, funder, and EE evaluators held quarterly meetings and used the monthly reports to track progress and identify areas for improvement (related to GTO questions #8–#10). These data were also shared periodically with the Re-entry Roundtable. When challenges arose, the EE evaluators would provide more in-depth analyses to facilitate CQI. For example, after studying several months of data, the partners noticed that a high percentage of participants were struggling to find employment. As a result, the grantee worked to ensure that all participants had sufficient access to the program component that focused on strategies to obtain employment.

Using Data to Assess Program Implementation and Outcomes

The grantee and representatives from other program providers serving on the Re-entry Roundtable partnered with the EE evaluators to design the process and outcome evaluations. Program partners also contributed to the process evaluation by sharing information, completing interviews, and participating in key meetings. The grantee and evaluator also cowrote the process evaluation sections of the biannual reports submitted to the funder. For the outcome evaluation, the Re-entry Roundtable helped define the recidivism outcome and the timeframe for analysis. Additionally, the Superior Court collaborated with the evaluators to obtain the recidivism data for the WISR participants and a comparison group randomly selected from a group of comparable men who would have been eligible for WISR but were released to probation before WISR started. This partnership resulted in a stronger evaluation design than would have been possible if designed and implemented by the evaluators or grantee alone, given the tight budget and the restricted access to recidivism data. The evaluators added value, however, because they were able to conduct a more detailed multivariate analysis than what would have been possible by the collaborating program providers. These analyses used multivariate models to control for moderating variables such as age, facility type (prison or jail), and race. These analyses helped to assess the strength of the WISR intervention on the main outcome (e.g., recidivism), while accounting for other variables.

Using Data to Advocate for Sustainability

The EE evaluators partnered with the lead agency and funder to share outcomes with policymakers throughout the project. Over a 2-year period, the partners engaged with selected policymakers, provided updates on *WISR*'s progress, and educated new policymakers as elections brought changes in legislators and committee assignments, as well as a party change in the executive office (from Democrat to Republican Party). Toward the end of the project, the grantee, funder, and EE evaluators participated in meetings with key groups of legislators and state agencies to establish a path for institutionalizing *WISR*. Although these meetings centered on the significant quantitative outcomes established through the rigorous evaluation, the partners also invited *WISR* participants to the meetings to share their personal experiences, which also had a strong impact on policymakers.

Additionally, the evaluators helped the grantee staff develop press releases and op-ed articles highlighting the program and its outcomes.

The Results

WISR resulted in a 47% reduction in recidivism 3 years postrelease, relative to a historical comparison group identified by the Massachusetts Superior Court Probation Office (Figure 8.3). This significant reduction contributed to increased safety of communities and reduced economic and social costs due to crime. Moreover, the reduction in recidivism yielded a 59% return on investment based on 1-year incarceration costs in Massachusetts (Figure 8.4; also see Chapter 12, which provides an in-depth overview of costs analysis in evaluation, including return on investment). Accounting for additional years of averted incarcerations would generate additional cost savings.

Figure 8.3   Reincarceration Rates by Years Post-Release

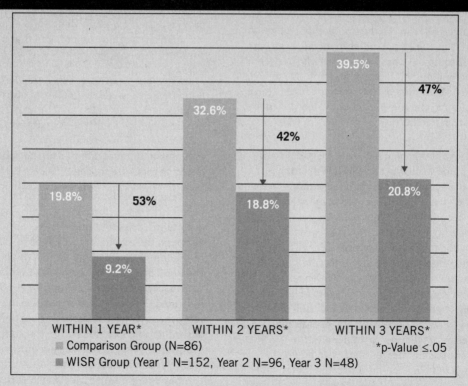

WITHIN 1 YEAR* WITHIN 2 YEARS* WITHIN 3 YEARS*
53% 42% 47%
19.8% 9.2% 32.6% 18.8% 39.5% 20.8%

■ Comparison Group (N=86)
■ WISR Group (Year 1 N=152, Year 2 N=96, Year 3 N=48)

*p-Value ≤.05

Continued

Figure 8.4 Cost Analysis of the WISR Model

WISR Costs		Incarceration Costs
Total (pilot + 3 years): $961,593		Average annual cost per person: $53,041
Average cost per person: $ 6,327		

Cost Analysis per 100 Participants

Averted incarceration costs:	$1,007,779
WISR Costs	$ 632,700
Net Savings	$ 375,079
Return on Investment (ROI): 59%	

Examples of How the EE Partnership Contributed to WISR Outcomes

WISR's outcomes can be attributed, partially, to effective use of the EE partnership model to engage partners throughout the planning of the program design, the ongoing monitoring and practice of CQI, and the documentation of program outcomes. These examples illustrate the particular value added by the evaluation partner:

- The EE evaluators worked with the staff of the grantee to conduct a search of existing literature for related best practices and evidence-based practices to inform the design of the program intervention. In the course of reviewing national and local programs, the lead agency staff also conferred with key service providers to identify interventions that would most ably address challenges in the local community. The providers identified local strengths and resources, and their ability to modify, when necessary, any operational policies or procedures to implement the evidence-based interventions with fidelity. Through ongoing one-on-one consultation and at grants management and steering committee

meetings, the evaluation team was an integral part of this decision making. Further, they provided their own knowledge and expertise gained from working on projects that used similar interventions.

- The EE evaluators worked with the Re-entry Roundtable to establish goals and outcomes that were generally accepted benchmarks for the criminal justice field. The 3-year, postrelease recidivism rate is the standard for measuring recidivism and was adopted as the primary outcome measure for the WISR.

- The research design was informed by practicality and affordability while also maintaining rigorous standards. For instance, although the evaluators would have preferred to randomly assign eligible individuals to the WISR program or a comparison group, conversations with the Re-entry Roundtable indicated that this was not feasible. However, representatives from Superior Court Probation agreed to pull a random historical comparison group based on the eligibility requirements for WISR participation, thus providing a rigorous comparison group. As mentioned earlier, the involvement with Superior Court Probation also allowed access to recidivism data that would have been difficult for the evaluators to access on their own.

- The evaluation partner worked to build the capacities of the grantee's staff to generate monthly dashboard reports to report "live data." These reports were shared with the steering committee and grants management teams and the Re-entry Roundtable, who collectively identified trends in recidivism, employment, housing, and access to primary health, mental health, substance use, and other services. This allowed the grantee to tap into the collaborative's resources to devise solutions to problems and enhance activities that showed positive trends. Timely access to these data helped the team to test different models and use data to develop and implement better systems.

- Specifically, ongoing data review of dashboard reports and interim process evaluation reports helped the WISR collaborating organizations identify problems and creatively address issues to strengthen program components. Early on, the process evaluation identified the immediate need for housing for some participants, and the budget was adjusted first to lease a few units and then later revised to provide "rent on demand" when appropriate. Similarly, the need for intensive employment support among many participants led to the creation of an employment specialist position. Continued gaps in employment then led to another redesign so that the responsibility for employment assistance was assumed by the case managers who had stronger relationships with the participants.

- Participation in CQI practices built the capacities of WISR leadership to generalize evaluation practices in other programming offered by the collaborating organizations. The evaluators' and key partners' involvement in the program design happened early on in the project's lifecycle and built a foundation for a culture of collaborative problem solving and ownership by all key stakeholders for CQI throughout the

project. As a result, when the grantee requested increased support from probation or approval of the Re-entry Roundtable for programmatic changes based on data-informed decision making, the partners supported these changes.

- The structure of the foundation's funding mechanism not only provided the project with the latitude to test new operational systems, but also required that it do so in order to fully vet and then implement the most efficacious set of services. The evaluation partner was instrumental in providing data to facilitate rapid cycles of reflection and action to ensure the program implemented the most effective services.

Effecting Systems Change

Throughout the WISR program years of 2011–2016, the grantee, funder, evaluation partner, and members of the Re-entry Roundtable worked to provide information to policymakers about WISR's impact on recidivism. Communications targeted public officials, primarily state legislators and key members of the administration, and were shared with the public through periodic media coverage. In April 2014, the foundation hosted a key public awareness event to introduce WISR and share its positive preliminary findings. Approximately 250 policymakers, including state legislators and representatives from key state agencies, representatives from the collaborating WISR provider organizations, and select community leaders attended. The event featured key speakers including the Executive Secretary of Public Safety, the Commissioner of the Department of Correction for Massachusetts, the Worcester County Sheriff, and the evaluation partner, who shared the promising preliminary results (Brolin & Dunigan, 2017).

In early 2017, armed with WISR's final results, the grantee, funder, and evaluation partner convened a series of meetings with leadership in the state legislature and the administration, including the lieutenant governor, to garner their support to sustain the WISR model through state funding. Additionally, court officers in the judiciary were identified as important individuals to educate and disseminate findings to colleagues in the legislature

Continued

to ensure ongoing financial support for the model. The evaluation partner's attendance at several of these key meetings brought attention to WISR's positive results and provided an opportunity for the evaluation partner to respond to questions, which strengthened the credibility of the findings.

The response was a broad-based and whole-hearted acceptance of the WISR model. Despite the state's limited capacity for funding new programs, key members of the administrative leadership agreed to begin to replicate the WISR model within the Massachusetts Department of Probation in its Office of Community Corrections, with 14 locations across the state. Then in 2018, the state approved substantive criminal justice reform, which included the provision of reentry services. By early 2019, the state had approved contracts totaling $7 million to pilot the services, based on the WISR model, in Worcester and Middlesex Counties through 2021. With the anticipation of significant reduction in recidivism rates resulting from the pilot, the intention is to then expand the reentry services throughout the state. As WISR scales up and becomes institutionalized across the state, the impact of the reduced costs of incarceration and improved public health and safety will benefit the entire Commonwealth. The use of the EE partnership model and ongoing engagement of the evaluation partner was integral to this significant achievement.

Deciding to Work With an Empowerment Evaluator

Program staff, program participants, and the community benefited by including the EE evaluators as partners in this complex initiative. By incorporating the evaluator as a meaningful partner, the collaborative developed a deep understanding of the needs of the population of focus and of those who are responsible for ongoing data collection.

For programs to benefit from EE, a concerted effort to identify and engage EE evaluators who bring content expertise to the efforts is warranted. Contract deliverables should include regular and frequent meetings with the EE evaluator to share evaluation data, identify areas in need of improvement, modify program approaches, and track results of these modifications. The EE evaluator can be a valuable partner in communicating results and advocating for sustained funding when the results are positive. By seeking and providing funding for an *empowerment evaluation*, funders and program providers have the opportunity to disseminate and sustain proven innovative practices rather than funding a one-time implementation of a new program model.

Considerations for the Novice Evaluator

There are a variety of issues to consider as one begins a career as a professional evaluator. First, become familiar with a variety of different evaluation approaches, knowing that there will be times when EE is not feasible or warranted. Certainly, the program staff or funder may not be interested in an EE approach given the significant investment of time required from various stakeholder groups. There are likely to be certain types of programs or situations in which EE might be more valuable than others. Some specific questions to address when considering an EE approach might be: Will a range of partners contribute to defining outcomes? To what degree is program staff interested in using evaluation findings for *CQI*? How willing are the program partners to build their own capacities to evaluate their own program? Be knowledgeable of a variety of evaluation models to ensure that choosing EE fits best with the situation. Second, the 10 *principles of EE* help to operationalize the model and distinguish it from other evaluation approaches. The principles were designed to communicate the underlying values of EE and guide the practice. While all of the principles are equally important, the work becomes more complex as each is integrated into an EE program design. What principles might be the most difficult or challenging to integrate into the practice of EE? What actions might be taken to help integrate these principles into the practice of EE? Do some appear to be more straightforward than others? Which might those be? Given the full set of EE principles, what strategies/processes might be useful in helping to build positive relationships including trust. Third, similar to all evaluation approaches, EE focuses on the ultimate results, which may require sophisticated measurement methodologies. Measuring changes in outcomes will require knowledge of quantitative data analyses, so novice evaluators will benefit from honing these skills. What qualitative data collection methods might be considered when using an EE approach? What qualitative data analysis procedures would best be used with these methods? Last, while EE continues to evolve and become refined in its approach, the concept of improvement has always been a central feature. EE has never been described as neutral. Given this commitment to improvement, what processes for feedback or *CQI* might be used? How might the program staff be involved to determine the best improvement strategies? What challenges might occur? The questions posed and issues raised in this section are meant to be thought provoking and provide constructive information for novice evaluators as they consider EE as an approach for their practice. The practitioners, researchers, and developers of EE have all grappled with these questions and continue to learn from each other. We look forward to you joining our community of learners.

FURTHER READING

General Information About Getting to Outcomes/Empowerment Evaluation

American Evaluation Association. (n.d.). https://www.eval.org/

BetterEvaluation: Sharing information to improve evaluation. (n.d.). https://www.betterevaluation.org/en

Fetterman, D. M., & Wandersman, A. H. (2007). Empowerment evaluation: Yesterday, today, and tomorrow. *American Journal of Evaluation*, 28, 179–198. https://www.researchgate.net/publication/234603883_Empowerment_Evaluation_Yesterday_Today_and_Tomorrow

Getting to Outcomes®: Frameworks for success for evidence-based programs. (n.d.). https://www.rand.org/multimedia/video/2017/06/12/frameworks-for-success.html

Getting to Outcomes®: Improving community-based prevention. (n.d.). https://www.rand.org/health/projects/getting-to-outcomes.html

Fetterman, D. M. (n.d.). Empowerment evaluation blog. https://www.betterevaluation.org/resources/website/empowerment_evaluation_blog

This blog, by Dr. David Fetterman, provides a range of resources on empowerment evaluation theory and practice. The blog includes links to videos, guides, and relevant academic literature that provide a detailed analysis and discussion of using empowerment evaluation.

Articles/Toolkits on Getting to Outcomes

Fetterman, D. M., Rodriguez, L. C., Wandersman, A. H., & O'Sullivan, R. G. (2014). Collaborative, participatory, and empowerment evaluation: Building a stronger conceptual foundation for stakeholder involvement approaches to evaluation. *American Journal of Evaluation*, *35*(1). 144–148.

Getting To Outcomes™ 2004: Promoting accountability through methods and tools for planning, implementation, and evaluation. (n.d.). https://www.rand.org/pubs/technical_reports/TR101.html[1]

Obteniendo Resultados 2004: Promoción de responsabilidad a través de métodos y herramientas de

planeación, implementación y evaluación. (n.d.). https://www.rand.org/pubs/technical_reports/TR101z1.html

Promoting Success: A Getting To Outcomes® Guide to implementing continuous quality improvement for community service organizations. (n.d.). https://www.org/pubs/tools/TL179.html

The Getting to Outcomes demonstration and evaluation: An illustration of the prevention support system. (n.d.). https://www.rand.org/pubs/external_publications/EP20080602.html

[1] The trademarks "Getting to Outcomes" and "GTO" are jointly owned by the RAND Corporation and the University of South Carolina.

KEY CONCEPTS

Continuous Quality Improvement (CQI): Systematic cycles of collecting data and analyzing it in order to refine and improve programming.

Critical friend: A trusted person who asks provocative questions, provides data to be examined through another lens, and offers critiques of a person's work as a friend.

Empowerment evaluation: An evaluation approach that engages evaluators as partners in developing and monitoring program interventions and documenting the results.

Empowerment evaluation partnership model: An interactive and collaborative partnership (that may include the funder) that utilizes the empowerment evaluation principles to plan, implement, and evaluate the program.

Getting to Outcomes®: One model to operationalize empowerment evaluation whereby the stakeholder groups (including the empowerment evaluator) address 10 accountability questions.

Principles of empowerment evaluation: The principles of empowerment evaluation that are inclusive of how the evaluator and stakeholder groups organize their work based on the local context and purpose of the evaluation.

Three-step model for empowerment evaluation: Fetterman's initial model of empowerment evaluation that includes the three components: establishing the mission, taking stock, and planning for the future.

WISR: The Worcester Initiative for Supported Reentry (WISR) that used the empowerment evaluation model to achieve positive program and systems-level outcomes.

QUESTIONS FOR REFLECTION

1. How does empowerment evaluation differ from traditional program evaluation? What are some of the strengths and challenges of each?

2. In what context or situations would program evaluation likely benefit from empowerment evaluators as partners? How might this contribution enhance program implementation?

3. What characteristics of a critical friend might be important in evaluation work? Would you be a good critical friend in an evaluation context? Why and why not?

4. Does the case study seem relatable to addressing other societal issues? If so, please identify some examples.

REFERENCES

Brennan, R. I., Baker, E. A., & Metzler, M. (2008). *Promoting health equity: A resource to help communities address social determinants of health.* Department of Health and Human Services. Centers for Disease Control and Prevention.

Brolin, M., & Dunigan, R. (2017). *A wiser approach to reentry: Three-year post-release evaluation findings for Worcester Initiative for Supported Reentry (WISR).* http://www.hfcm.org

Chinman, M., Imm, P., & Wandersman, A. (1999; 2004). *Getting to Outcomes: Promoting accountability through methods and tools for planning, implementation, and evaluation.* RAND Corporation. http://www.rand.org/publications/TR/TR101/

Costa, A., & Kallick, B. (1993). Through the lens of a critical friend. *Educational Leadership, 51,* 49–51.

Cox, P., Keener, D., Tifanee, L., Woodard, T., & Wandersman, A. (2009). *Evaluation for improvement: A seven step empowerment evaluation approach for violence prevention organizations.* Centers for Disease Control and Prevention.

Fetterman, D. M. (1994). Steps of empowerment evaluation: From California to Cape Town. *Evaluation and Program Planning, 17*(3), 305–313. doi:10.1016/0149-7189(94)90010-8

Fetterman, D. M., Kaftarian, S., & Wandersman, A. (Eds.). (1996). *Empowerment evaluation: Knowledge and tools for self-assessment and accountability.* Sage.

Fetterman, D. M., Kaftarian, S., & Wandersman, A. (Eds.). (2015). *Empowerment evaluation: Knowledge and tools for self-assessment, evaluation capacity building, and accountability* (2nd ed.). Sage.

Fetterman, D. M., Scriven, M., & Patton, M. (2009, August 24). "*Empowerment evaluation: Its promise (Fetterman) and pitfalls (Scriven & Patton).*" from the 2009 Claremont Evaluation Debates. Claremont Graduate University Lectures on Applied Psychology and Evaluation Science. http://ccdl.libraries.claremont.edu/cdm/ref/collection/lap/id/69

Fetterman, D. M., & Wandersman, A. (Eds.). (2005). *Empowerment evaluation principles in practice.* Guilford Press.

Fetterman, D. M., & Wandersman, A. (2007). Empowerment evaluation: Yesterday, today, and tomorrow. *American Journal of Evaluation, 28,* 179–198.

Kania, J., & Kramer, M. (2011). Collective impact. *Stanford Social Innovation Review, 9,* 36–41.

Lentz, B., Imm, P., Yost, J., Johnson, N., Barron, C., Lindberg, M., & Treistman, J. (2005). Empowerment evaluation and organizational learning: A case study of a community coalition designed to prevent child abuse and neglect. In D. M. Fetterman & A. H. Wandersman (Eds.), *Empowerment evaluation principles in practice.* Guilford.

Miller, R., & Campbell, R. (2006). Taking stock of empowerment evaluation: An empirical review. *American Journal of Evaluation, 27,* 296–319.

Papagiorgakis, G. (2015). *Three-year recidivism rates: 2011 release cohort*: Massachusetts Department of Correction, Office of Strategic Planning and Research. Retrieved September 15, 2016, from http://www.mass.gov/eopps/docs/doc/research-reports/recidivism/recidivism-rates-2011-releases-3year.pdf

Wandersman, A., Snell-Johns, J., Lentz, B. E., Fetterman, D. M., Keener, D. C., Livet, M., Imm, P. S., & Flaspohler, P. (2005). The principles of empowerment evaluation. In D. M. Fetterman & A. H. Wandersman (Eds.), *Empowerment evaluation principles in practice.* Guilford.

Weaver, L., & Cousins, J. (2004). Unpacking the participatory process. *Journal of Multidisciplinary Evaluation, 1,* 19–40.

Yost, J. (2015). Mission fulfillment: How empowerment evaluation enables funders to achieve results. In D. M. Fetterman, S. J. Kaftarian, & A. H. Wandersman (Eds.), *Empowerment evaluation: Knowledge and tools for self-assessment, evaluation capacity building, and accountability.* Sage.

CHAPTER 9

SURVEYING THE LANDSCAPE

Using Geographic Information Systems to Evaluate Community Programs and Facilitate Change

Greg Townley

Learning Objectives

1. Become familiar with core elements of Geographic Information Systems (GIS).

2. Understand how GIS concepts and strategies can be used to evaluate community programs and influence social change.

3. Consider challenges and limitations to using GIS, including generalizability across settings and privacy concerns.

4. Learn how to access GIS software and geospatial data, and how community–university partnerships can help facilitate this process.

Community-based organizations typically focus on specific regions or catchment areas with unique physical and social features that impact program success. As such, questions pertaining to space and geography, including the accessibility of services, the extent of program reach in the community, and the sociodemographic composition of neighborhoods within a service area, are often of primary interest. It can be daunting to collect, organize, and analyze the types of data needed to answer these questions, particularly in the face of competing demands for time and resources. However, emerging tools and technologies for examining the impact of geography and place are becoming more widely available and usable. This chapter will provide an overview of these approaches, along with specific examples of ways they can be used to evaluate programs and create change in communities.

GEOGRAPHIC INFORMATION SYSTEMS OVERVIEW

Geographic Information Systems (GIS) are computer-based programs used for cataloging, storing, querying, analyzing, and displaying geospatial data (Chang, 2013). At its most basic level, GIS is about making maps or spatial representations of reality that help us make sense of the physical and social world. We use mental maps to navigate our home and work environments, plan daily activities, and situate events that we learn about from friends, family, and news media (Campbell & Shin, 2011). We combine these mental maps with online and mobile phone mapping to tap into almost limitless possibilities for using and sharing geographic information. However, the capabilities of GIS extend beyond merely creating maps to represent the world around us. As will be described and illustrated throughout this chapter, the true power of GIS is in connecting data to geography to provide solutions for solving problems and guiding human behavior.

GIS can be used to examine social environments and community processes, including community health assessments, mapping of community resources, and community development (Jankowska et al., 2015; Linney, 2000; Luke, 2005). Despite its potential, GIS remains largely underutilized in community research and evaluation. The underutilization of GIS may be due in part to its reputation as a purely quantitative tool (Kwan & Knigge, 2006), and also because it has traditionally been in the domain of geographers and has only become more prominent in the social sciences in the last few decades. While researchers tend to utilize GIS software to conduct spatial analyses that rely on quantitative geographical information, this approach is a limited conceptualization of what the technology has to offer in terms of generating new knowledge and influencing social change. GIS can utilize diverse types of information, such as photographs, narratives, and other types of ethnographic materials (Kwan & Knigge, 2006). In line with the increasing recognition that multiple methods of inquiry are often necessary to address complex community phenomena, GIS can incorporate both quantitative and qualitative methodologies to accommodate multiple views of the physical and social world.

GIS has also been underutilized due to perceptions that it is too difficult and expensive to be used by people without training or expertise. While this may have been true at one time, the work of such geographers as Sarah Elwood has led to the proliferation of participatory GIS, which encourages individuals and social groups to participate equally in the collection, analysis, and communication of spatial data (Elwood, 2006). GIS technology has also become more user-friendly and capable of capturing and displaying a wider variety of data that is both relevant and important to diverse community stakeholders.

The advancements noted above, as well as the ability to synthesize different types of information across settings and time, makes GIS perfectly suited for use in program evaluation, including within partnership-oriented approaches. In particular, partnerships with universities where graduate students or faculty might have GIS skills and access to software provide an opportunity for community-based organizations to tap into innovative evaluation tools that may otherwise be outside their reach. Below, I will present GIS concepts and strategies that can be used to evaluate community programs and influence social change. While the capabilities and applications of GIS are vast, I will focus on (1) the creation of visual maps to display evaluation data; (2) the use of participatory mapping to engage diverse community stakeholders in the collection and display of data; and (3) the application of *activity space* methodologies to influence change in individuals and organizations. For each approach, conceptual discussion will be presented alongside real-world examples from research and evaluation conducted in collaboration with community partners. I will then highlight key issues, challenges, and questions of relevance to the use of GIS in program evaluation and discuss its generalizability across diverse community contexts.

CREATING VISUAL MAPS TO EVALUATE PROGRAM CONTEXT AND PERFORMANCE

Using GIS, evaluators can create maps that synthesize and convey information such as population health, sociodemographics, and program services data. This information can in turn help to engage stakeholders, focus or refine the evaluation design, track program changes, and triangulate findings across a variety of data sources to justify conclusions (Centers for Disease Control & Prevention, 2012). To create GIS maps for evaluation purposes, evaluators need datasets with *spatial* (i.e., location) data, such as county codes, zip codes, and street addresses; and attribute data, which represent descriptions, measurements, or classifications of the location data (e.g., county names, population data from the census, and distance between addresses). Evaluators will also need GIS software, such as ESRI ArcGIS (desktop or online versions), Quantum GIS (QGIS), or MapInfo. Collecting location data to be linked to relevant program variables is often the first step to any GIS analysis. This is typically done by converting addresses, zip codes, census blocks, and other locational features to longitude and latitude coordinates (a process called *geocoding*; Azzam & Robinson, 2013). Once location data are geocoded, they can be plotted onto digital maps obtained from GIS software or online databases and analyzed according to their attribute features. For example, the size of a mental health service catchment area can be measured to represent the population for which a community mental health service unit has responsibility; or more complex analytic operations involving *querying* can be used to identify locations where specific criteria are met (e.g., selecting only neighborhoods that contain a certain type of community resource, such as a library, school, or park; Lohmann, 2016).

In addition to knowing the location of resources in a community, evaluators are also often interested in understanding the sociodemographic composition of neighborhoods or city blocks where programs may be implemented. Linking project data to locational coordinates allows for nearly endless opportunities to access and display information about a project's setting, environment, and performance (Azzam & Robinson, 2013). For example, Figure 9.1 displays a map in which community centers have been geocoded and displayed

Figure 9.1 Diversity Index of Block Groups Surrounding Community Centers

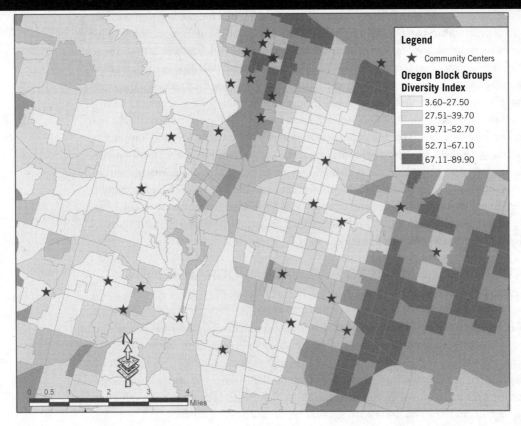

in relation to the racial diversity index of block groups (the smallest geographical unit for which the U.S. Census Bureau publishes demographic data) in Oregon. The diversity index calculates racial diversity within a population along a continuum of complete racial homogeneity (a score of 0) to complete heterogeneity (a score of 1; Lieberson, 1969). The map uses a *graduated color* scheme to visualize different levels of diversity. Specifically, the quantitative values for the diversity index are grouped into ordered classes, and each class is assigned a graduated color from smallest (in this case, least diverse) to largest (in this case, most diverse) values. In addition to better understanding the relative diversity of neighborhoods in which these community centers are located, we may also wish to examine their proximity to other resources, such as affordable housing. To accomplish this, we can *overlay* a map with geocoded affordable housing units on top of the map layers representing the location of the community centers and the diversity of block groups (Figure 9.2). By combining multiple data layers, we are able to examine multiple attributes of environments that impact population health and well-being. Below, I will provide additional examples of ways that maps can be used to better understand setting-level influences on community programs.

Figure 9.2   Proximity of Community Centers to Affordable Housing Units

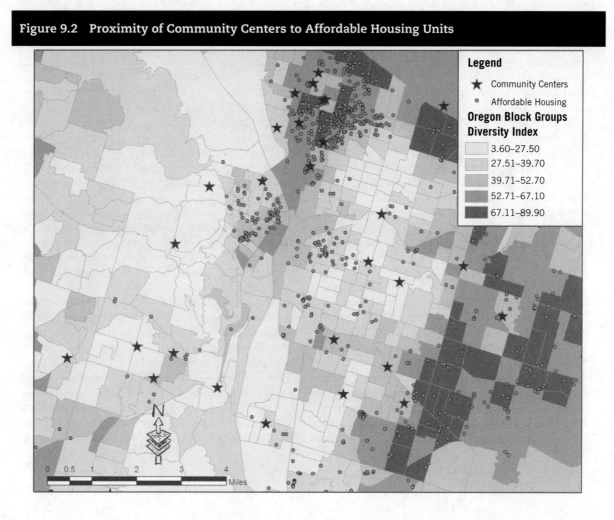

CASE EXAMPLE: THE ROLE OF GIS IN EVALUATING A SUPPORTIVE HOUSING PROGRAM

Since 2012, I have partnered with Cascadia Behavioral Healthcare (CBH) in Portland, OR, USA, to help them evaluate their independent supportive housing program for individuals with serious mental illnesses. I work closely with Jim Hlava, Vice President of Housing at Cascadia, to prioritize research goals, formulate evaluation questions, and select data collection measures. Cascadia was interested in updating their knowledge base concerning resident satisfaction, housing tenure, and service utilization. They were also interested in better understanding residents' perceptions of their housing and neighborhood environments (e.g., neighborhood safety and quality, relationships with neighbors), as well as their sense of community and ability to engage in community activities. In collaboration with Hlava, other CBH housing staff, and students at Portland State University, we developed an extensive survey which we administered to approximately half of the CBH independent housing residents ($n = 172$). Some of the specific programmatic components we evaluated included residents' perceptions of safety, their access to public transportation, and their use of high-cost health services (e.g., emergency room visits). Combining more traditional quantitative evaluation techniques with GIS approaches helped to triangulate findings and display information in a visually compelling and easily understandable way, as will be outlined below.

First, we found that residents in housing programs located in southwest Portland reported significantly higher perceptions of neighborhood safety ($M = 5.26$ out of 6, $SD = 0.76$) than residents in southeast Portland ($M = 4.32$, $SD = 1.2$) and northeast Portland ($M = 3.85$, $SD = 1.38$), $F(2, 162) = 14.17$, $p < .001$. This is an important finding, but given concerns about basing evaluation recommendations entirely on self-reported experiences, it is important to support this finding with more objective data. To do so, we obtained personal and property crime reports from the City of Portland Police Bureau and geocoded them alongside the CBH housing programs. In visually examining Figure 9.3, it becomes quite clear

that fewer crimes were reported in close proximity to the housing sites located in southwest Portland compared to those in northeast and southeast Portland. Please note that the easternmost housing site falls outside the Portland Police Bureau service area, and thus accurate crime reports were not available.

To quantify the magnitude of the difference in crime reports between the three regions, half-mile *proximity buffers* were created around each housing site using the ArcGIS proximity buffer tool. These buffers were joined with the crime report data layer to count the number of crimes occurring within a half-mile of each housing site (see callout box in Figure 9.3). This analysis revealed that a yearly average of 176 crimes occurred within a half-mile of the CBH housing programs located in southwest Portland, with yearly averages of 376 and 313 crimes occurring within a half-mile of the housing programs in northeast and southeast Portland, respectively, $F(2, 169) = 45.52$, $p < .001$. This finding corroborates the self-reported safety concerns among residents of CBH housing and is in line with the expectations and experiences of CBH staff. In discussing the implications of these findings, staff noted several potential targets of intervention for Cascadia, including working with the Portland Police Bureau to increase crime monitoring in these neighborhoods, implementing neighborhood watch programs, and hosting regular community meetings between residents and police to communicate their concerns. These findings also help Cascadia know which neighborhoods to target when considering the development of new housing programs.

Second, we found that a significantly higher percentage of residents in housing programs located in southeast Portland (38%) utilized emergency room services after moving into CBH housing than residents in programs located in southwest Portland (21%) and northeast Portland (9%), $F(2, 169) = 5.66$, $p < .01$. In mapping the proximity of CBH housing to hospitals (Figure 9.4), it became clear to us that the housing sites in southeast Portland were located more proximally to hospitals than the housing sites

Continued

Figure 9.3 Cascadia Behavioral Healthcare (CBH) Housing and Portland Police Bureau Crime Reports

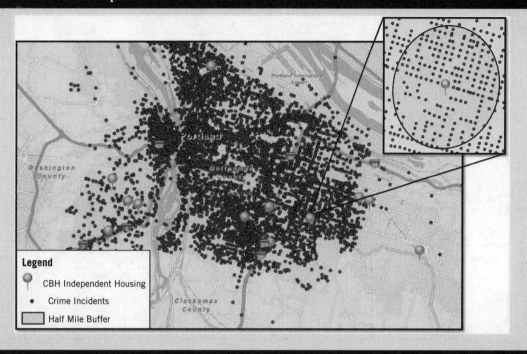

Legend

- CBH Independent Housing
- Crime Incidents
- Half Mile Buffer

Figure 9.4 Proximity of CBH Housing to Hospitals

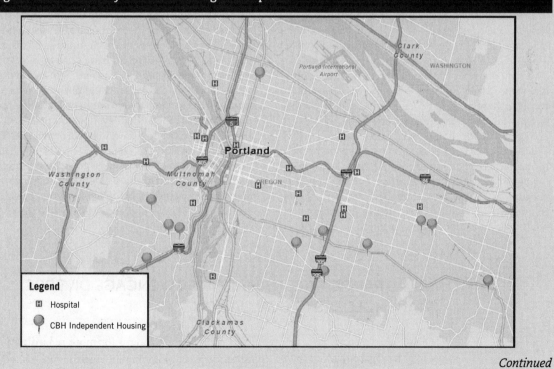

Legend

- Hospital
- CBH Independent Housing

Continued

Figure 9.5   Proximity of CBH Housing to Public Transportation

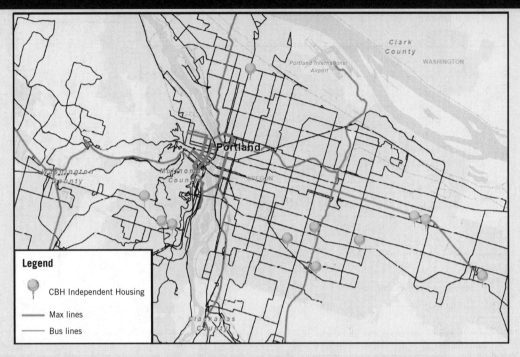

Legend

⊙ CBH Independent Housing

— Max lines

— Bus lines

in southwest and northeast Portland. Thus, it appears that accessibility may be at least somewhat responsible for the higher rates of ER use among residents in this region of the city. While healthcare access is a positive and often necessary feature of community residence for individuals with serious mental illnesses, these findings encouraged Cascadia to work with residents to identify less costly alternatives for those who may not necessarily need to access the ER for their health concerns.

Finally, 98% of residents reported being able to easily access public transportation, and 55% of residents said they never miss out on activities because of a transportation problem. Given how frequently individuals who utilize public mental health services report transportation as a barrier to

their community inclusion and well-being (Townley, 2015), it is encouraging that residents in CBH housing reported such strong perceptions of transportation access. These self-reports are augmented by visually examining a map of the housing sites in relation to public transportation (i.e., bus and light rail service; Figure 9.5). Hlava and other CBH staff were struck by how clearly the map illustrated their commitment to and success in locating new housing sites in areas where public transportation is readily available. This programmatic success, represented visually using GIS mapping tools, can be used to secure increased funding to expand their residential programs and offer opportunities to more community members who need affordable and accessible housing.

USING PARTICIPATORY MAPPING TO ENGAGE DIVERSE STAKEHOLDERS IN EVALUATION

Community-based participatory research (CBPR; see Chapter 3 for more regarding CBPR), which has had broad appeal in community psychology, public health, and related disciplines, aims to involve research participants and other stakeholders in the research process and ensure that they have a voice in the knowledge that is created (Israel et al., 1998). In geography, the trend toward more inclusive methods of research has led to an increased emphasis in involving local communities and individuals in a process called *participatory mapping* (Chambers, 2006). This method asks participants to identify the physical boundaries of their own neighborhoods and communities, as well as the important resources and the activities in which they engage (Coulton et al., 2013; Green & Kloos, 2009).

Some of the earliest work in this area was conducted by Kevin Lynch, an urban planner who was interested in how people organize spatial information about their environments. He asked respondents in three different cities to draw sketch maps showing significant features of their cities and discuss the importance of including these elements on the maps (Lynch, 1960). More recently, participatory mapping has been used to examine community integration among formerly homeless adults (Chan et al., 2014), map stakeholder perceptions of environmental problems (Forrester et al., 2015), and engage community members in HIV prevention research (Green et al., 2016).

In addition to being empowering and engaging, having people draw their own maps, as opposed to relying on census boundaries or predrawn maps, allows program evaluators to understand what types of resources and activities are most important to community members' functioning and well-being. Participatory mapping can also be useful in challenging assumptions and testing theories of what people appreciate in their communities and how they contribute to them (Townley et al., 2016). Additionally, when individuals are able to define their communities based on their own unique experiences and expertise, their perceptions of belonging to the community, as well as their intrinsic motivation to actively shape change efforts within their communities, are increased (Fernández & Langhout, 2014; Parker, 2006).

CASE EXAMPLE: PARTICIPATORY MAPPING WITH YOUTH EXPERIENCING HOMELESSNESS IN PORTLAND, OR

P:ear is a nonprofit community center in downtown Portland that focuses on building positive relationships with youth experiencing homelessness through education, art, and recreation. Recently, we collaborated on a project aimed at better understanding the community support networks and daily activities of youth experiencing homelessness in order to improve p:ear's service delivery and outreach efforts (see Townley et al., 2016, for a more extensive description of the project and methods). In addition to more traditional surveys and interviewing approaches, we used participatory mapping, a technique that tapped into youths' interests in artwork and self-expression and served as an empowering way for them to inform program evaluation and improvement. Youth were asked to draw maps of their communities, including places they spend time, engage in activities, and utilize services. Specifically, they were presented with a sheet of paper and colored pencils and asked, "Please use this sheet of paper to draw the places in your community that are important to you." Where necessary, we probed for specific activity locations, including activities of daily living, leisure and social activities, health service centers, employment/ education settings, and spiritual activities. Youth

Continued

Figure 9.6 Participatory Map Drawn by Homeless Youth—Example 1

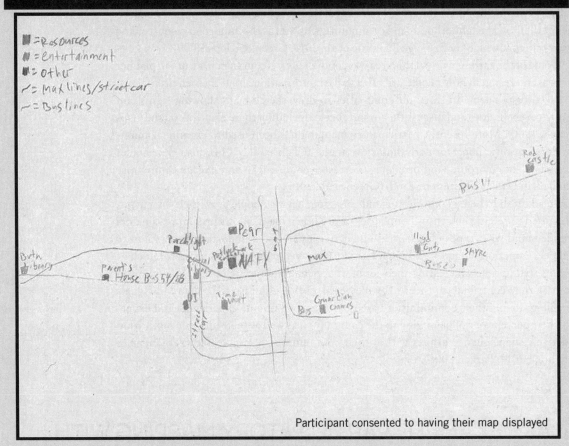

Participant consented to having their map displayed

were encouraged to draw the maps in a manner that was most conducive to narrating the personal meanings of their activity locations. See Figures 9.6 and 9.7 for examples of the types of maps youth drew to depict their activities and community experiences.

After participants drew their community maps, they were then presented with a Google map document and asked to locate their specific activity locations with as much precision as possible. This information was then used to geocode activity locations. Using GIS tools, spatial data can be displayed in a variety of ways and combined with symbols to provide information on the attributes of the mapped points. Staff at p:ear were particularly interested in knowing the types of activities in which youth

engage, and we worked with them to categorize the 90 unique activity points that youth reported into the following categories: *services* (e.g., locations that youth access to receive health services); *social* (e.g., parks and outdoor areas where youth gather); and *hobby/vocational/education* (e.g., local bookstores and locations where youth work or go to school). The activity locations were then given separate color symbols based on these categories (Figure 9.8).

Visually examining the maps allowed p:ear staff to learn more about the type, frequency, and location of youth activities. For example, they learned that the majority of service activity locations are clustered in downtown Portland, while youth participate in social and hobby activities throughout the

Figure 9.7   Participatory Map Drawn by Homeless Youth—Example 2

Participant consented to having their map displayed

Portland Metropolitan Area. This allowed them to begin thinking of ways to work with youth to make sure they have transportation to be able to access important social, vocational, and hobby-related activity locations in the broader metropolitan area. As displayed in the callout box in Figure 9.8, *proportional symbols* can also be employed to visually represent the activity locations that were most frequently visited by youth. Examining this map allowed p:ear staff to see which activity locations are most popular among youth, which will provide them with suggestions of where to target outreach efforts to other youth who may be experiencing homelessness. For example, numerous youth noted that a park along the waterfront is a common social gathering spot for homeless youth, so staff may begin canvassing this area to encourage youth who may benefit from their services to visit p:ear. By viewing the maps and reading quotes from qualitative interviews with youth, they also learned that youth spend the majority of their time engaged in homeless services (e.g., shelters, day programs, mental health service agencies) rather than in more normative daily activities (e.g., school, work, and recreation). Based on this finding, staff decided to focus on helping youth find a balance between activities that will help them integrate more fully into the community with those that they engage in out of necessity for daily survival.

Continued

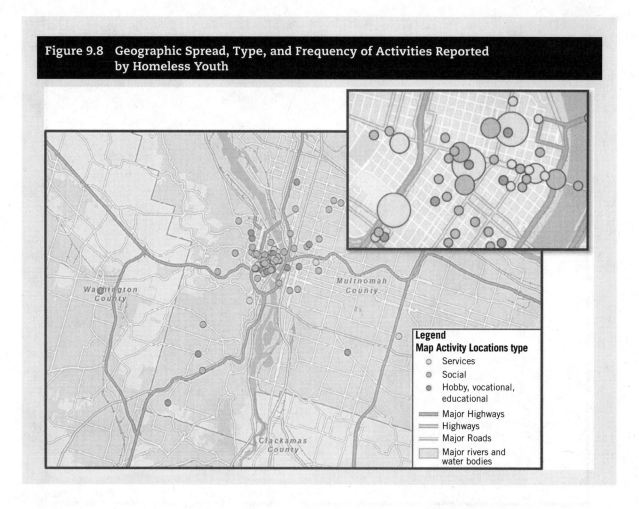

Legend
Map Activity Locations type
- Services
- Social
- Hobby, vocational, educational
- Major Highways
- Highways
- Major Roads
- Major rivers and water bodies

CREATING ACTIVITY SPACES TO EFFECT INDIVIDUAL AND ORGANIZATIONAL CHANGE

Recent work has expanded the participatory mapping technique by using GIS to create participant *activity spaces* (Chan et al., 2014; Townley et al., 2009). Activity spaces represent the manner in which individuals move about their communities in their day-to-day lives and can be used to measure geographic accessibility, mobility, and place identity (Gesler & Albert, 2000; Golledge & Stimson, 1987; Nemet & Bailey, 2000). They have been used as an analytic technique by evaluators working in various areas, including travel and transportation, city planning, crime statistics, and medical geography (Sherman et al., 2005). The size of the activity space is a quantifiable measure of community members' participation and engagement, and it has been found to be associated with quality of life, sense of community, and access to healthcare resources (Sherman et al., 2005; Townley et al., 2009).

Using GIS Activity Spaces to Illustrate the Activity Patterns of Youth Experiencing Homelessness

Expanding upon the participatory mapping project with youth experiencing homelessness discussed above, we applied the activity space methodology to further understand youths' activities and community experiences. Activity spaces were created in ArcGIS using the *standard deviational ellipse (SDE) method*, a bivariate statistical measure that provides an estimate of an individuals' activity space (Sherman et al., 2005). Using the designated geocoded points corresponding with each activity location that youth plotted on their maps (e.g., service-related activities, hobbies, and social activities), the SDE method calculates the standard deviation of the distances of the x- and y-coordinates of each individual point from the mean center of all points to define the major and minor axes for each individual's activity space. Once created, the ellipses represent a general distribution of activity locations/points in each participant's activity spaces (Figure 9.9). Using tools in GIS, it is also possible to calculate the square-mile area of each activity space that represents the geographic spread of community activities in which the individual reports engaging. The average activity space area for youth in this project was 6.57 square miles ($SD = 9.85$), with a range of 0.32–39.72 square miles (Townley et al., 2016).

Figure 9.9   GIS Activity Space Example

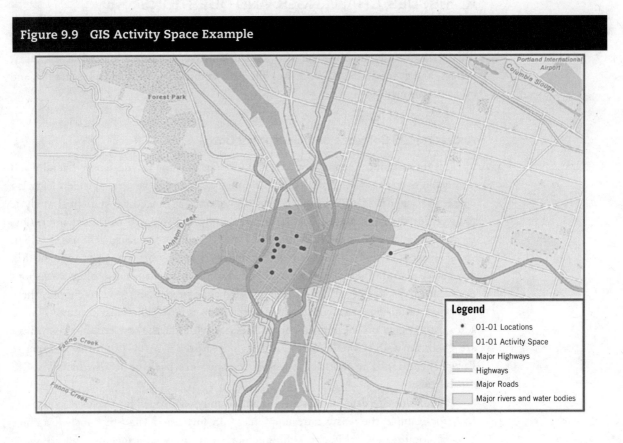

Legend

- • 01-01 Locations
- 01-01 Activity Space
- Major Highways
- Highways
- Major Roads
- Major rivers and water bodies

One particularly useful way that the activity space methodology can influence individual and organizational change is that health service providers can use it to help service users increase their activity and engagement. For example, if a treatment goal involves the service user engaging more frequently in community activities, the activity space method can be used to track client progress. Each time a service user visits a new activity location in the community (or stops regularly visiting a previous location), it can be added to (or removed from) the activity space, and the change in area can be calculated and interpreted as a reliable change index (Townley et al., 2009).

Returning to the supportive housing example discussed previously, the activity space method can also be applied to evaluations of housing and transportation programs. For example, if individuals in urban areas are shown to consistently have larger activity spaces than those in nonurban areas, this could point to the need to improve transportation access in nonurban settings or build more supportive housing sites in urban settings. The eye-catching and intuitive nature of activity spaces and other visual representations of geospatial phenomena make them well suited to share with a variety of community stakeholders when working to facilitate changes in individuals, organizations, and localities.

KEY ISSUES, CHALLENGES, AND QUESTIONS

In this section, I will discuss common issues, challenges, and questions that arise when using GIS. While these are certainly not exhaustive, questions around accessibility, privacy, and generalizability are among the most common ones faced by researchers and evaluators using GIS.

Accessing GIS Software and Geospatial Data

It is important to recognize that while GIS has become far more user-friendly and affordable over the past several years, it continues to require a fairly steep learning curve, particularly if evaluators wish to utilize more advanced geostatistical analytic tools rather than the more basic descriptive analyses discussed in this chapter. One recommendation is to enroll in an introductory GIS course focused on the use of GIS in social sciences. These are fairly prevalent in departments of geography, public health, and public planning. Some universities and community colleges also offer workshops or certificate programs. When deciding which type of GIS software to choose, there is a range of options with considerable variability in cost. The most commonly used software package on the higher end is ArcGIS, while at the low-cost/no-cost range are Quantum GIS, Google Earth, and many features of ArcGIS Online (Azzam & Robinson, 2013). The free and open-source software package R also includes GIS capabilities.

A wealth of GIS data can be accessed online and downloaded for free or at a licensing cost. For example, the census bureau provides GIS-formatted data which include a range of population demographics, including employment, household income, and ethnicity.

The Centers for Disease Control and Prevention (CDC) provides data on health-related variables that can be used in evaluations of health services and related interventions. Finally, many municipalities and local governments maintain publicly accessible databases containing spatial files ranging from crime reports and voting records to land use and zoning (Azzam & Robinson, 2013; Renger et al., 2002). For example, the City of Charlotte, in collaboration with Mecklenburg County and UNC-Charlotte, has an online "quality of life explorer" (https://mcmap.org/qol/); and the City of Portland maintains an online database of maps and geospatial data associated with neighborhood crime statistics, school information, and land use (https://www.portlandmaps.com/). In addition to secondary geospatial data, there is also an abundance of new technologies for collecting primary spatial data in the field. For example, a Global Positioning System (GPS) tracking device or GPS-enabled smartphone can be used to measure and track mobility, physical activity, neighborhood boundaries, and other program processes and outcomes (Jankowska et al., 2015).

Visually Representing Change

Depicting changes in program context and outcomes is of great importance to evaluators. While the maps displayed in this chapter illustrate cross-sectional snapshots of information, GIS can also be used to illustrate changes over time. For example, while Figure 9.3 represents crime points corresponding to one calendar year, we could create additional maps to visualize crime points for subsequent years and present them side-by-side to detect patterns of change. Changes can also be depicted on the same map. For example, data layers from an earlier time period can be overlaid and "subtracted" from a layer depicting a later time, and a graduated color scheme can be used to illustrate the degree of change (Renger et al., 2002).

Generalizability to Other Settings

In addition to considering the issue of representing changes in data over time, it is also important to consider the generalizability of GIS findings across diverse settings. As with any evaluation of a specific program or geographical context, the intent is often to understand and apply evaluation data locally rather than more broadly. However, in cases in which a program or approach is being transferred to another setting, it is necessary to examine how the unique environmental context may impact program adaptation and outcomes. Fortunately, geospatial data are collected and maintained fairly consistently across settings and can be easily accessed remotely. For example, an evaluator working in the southeastern United States who wishes to understand how a program may operate in other regions of the United States can access spatial files with sociodemographic information, community resources, and transportation networks by downloading shapefiles or geodatabases corresponding with other states, counties, or towns. Geospatial data are often large in size, but cloud-based file sharing programs allow for evaluators in different areas to communicate and share data easily and openly.

Evaluators collaborating with community partners in areas with a less well-developed geospatial infrastructure than we enjoy in North America will need to think more creatively, but there are certainly ways to tap into local resources to bridge these gaps. For example, in working to understand the link between health and place as it pertains to HIV prevention efforts in Kenya, Green and colleagues (2016) developed innovative mapping methods to engage youth in formative community-based evaluation. Because the community did not have accurate paper or digital maps, young people from the community were trained to use hand-held GPS devices to identify and locate community features that were used to create a digital basemap. Focus groups were then conducted to identify important places within the community, and this information was used to create digital "dot maps." Geocaching games were used to gather more detailed information from youths' perspectives about the locations identified during the focus groups. Finally, researchers used the compiled digital maps to create satellite imagery-assisted logs documenting times, spatial locations, and frequency of participants' involvement in HIV risk behaviors. While it was more difficult to utilize geospatial technologies in this low-resource setting, the innovative methods employed by the researchers provided a rich opportunity to engage the community and work together to create new knowledge about the local context.

Protecting Privacy

Finally, a fundamental concern when using GIS for evaluation purposes is the potential to invade personal privacy. Even if maps do not include identifying information, the viewer could still potentially locate individual households or other geocoded addresses. The most straightforward way to address this issue is by altering the presentation of data to display the location at a more generalized unit, such as a zip code, census tract, or cross-street (Azzam & Robinson, 2013). Offsets can also be used to displace or move a feature from its original location. For example, in the maps presented throughout this chapter, the latitude and longitude coordinates of each address were shifted by a random number ranging from 0 to 500 feet. Thus, the overall pattern of addresses remains visually similar but reverse geocoding cannot be used to determine the original location (Brusilovskiy & Salzer, 2012). Finally, data from individual participants across a study area can be aggregated and displayed as a single point at the centroid of the study area (e.g., a city, zip code, or neighborhood) rather than as separate points at the individual participant addresses. While there is no formal code of GIS ethics, it is imperative to consider all potential risks and benefits to individuals and communities when utilizing geospatial methodologies in research and evaluation.

CONCLUSION

GIS provides a wealth of possibilities for program evaluation and community change efforts. The power of GIS rests not only in its ability to depict complex information in a simple visual format, but also in its capacity for engaging diverse stakeholders in the collection, evaluation, and presentation of data. While GIS remains relatively underutilized among evaluators, this will most certainly change as GIS technologies continue to become more user-friendly, as cloud-based computing makes the sharing and displaying of geospatial data easier, and as innovative techniques emerge to facilitate the use of technology-based mapping tools even in low-resource settings. Maps created with GIS provide a powerful language for conveying information about program implementation, adaptation, and outcomes. They also act as a way of measuring and displaying changes over time and place. Perhaps most importantly, they allow us to make sense of the physical and social world and catalog the diversity of human experience that exists within and between our communities.

FURTHER READING

There are numerous books that provide good starting points for learning about GIS concepts and software. For example, *Introduction to Geographic Information Systems*, written by Kang-Tsung Chang and published by McGraw Hill, is a seminal textbook designed to provide beginners with a solid foundation in both GIS concepts and the use of GIS; and *Getting to Know ArcGIS*, written by Michael Law and Amy Collins and published by ESRI Press, is a comprehensive introduction to the features and tools of ArcGIS software. Numerous resources for getting started with GIS are also available online. *Essentials of Geographic Information Systems*, written by Jonathan Campbell and Michael Shin and published by the Saylor Foundation, is an open-source textbook that integrates key concepts of GIS alongside practical applications and real-world examples. ArcGIS Online (http://www.arcgis.com) allows users to make customized maps, analyze thousands of datasets, and save and share maps; and ESRI (www.esri.com) provides an array of online support pertaining to the use of ArcGIS, as well as resources for connecting with others using GIS (http://edcommunity.esri.com/).

There are also numerous online resources for teaching others how to use GIS. ESRI offers a free online course that provides strategies and sample activities for using GIS in the classroom: https://www.esri.com/training/catalog/57630436851d31e02a43f125/teaching-with-%20gis:-introduction-to-using-gis-in-the-classroom/. ESRI also provides YouTube playlists with tutorials for getting started with ArcGIS Online (https://www.youtube.com/playlist?list=PLGZUzt4E4O2IJt1O_OTDFR-3dUpiCZGKf) and case studies presenting GIS applications across a variety of industries and contexts (https://www.youtube.com/playlist?list=PLGZUzt4E4O2Jx5mFayHiw4k-fh7PpYwdg). Finally, *ArcGIS Online Five for Five* (https://www.arcgis.com/home/item.html?id=7ac4230f1b814eb7a51b0f044993c19c) is a helpful teaching resource that includes five short engaging activities that can be done with students.

KEY CONCEPTS

Attribute data: Characteristics which represent descriptions, measurements, and/or classifications of spatial (i.e., location) data (e.g., county names, population data from the census, distance between two addresses).

Community-based participatory research (CBPR): A research approach that aims to involve research participants and other stakeholders actively in the research process and ensure that they have a voice in the knowledge that is created.

Geocoding: A process of converting addresses, zip codes, census blocks, and other locational features into geographic coordinates (e.g., longitude and latitude).

Geographic Information Systems (GIS): Computer-based programs used for cataloging, storing, querying, analyzing, and displaying geospatial data in order to better understand the world and provide solutions for solving problems and guiding human behavior.

Graduated color map: A map on which a range of colors is used to indicate a progression of numeric values.

Overlay: The combination of two separate spatial datasets to create a new output dataset.

Participatory mapping: A group-based qualitative research method that asks participants to identify the physical boundaries of their own neighborhoods and communities, as well as the important resources and the activities in which they engage.

Proportional symbol map: A map on which the size of a simple symbol (e.g., a circle or star) is altered to indicate a progression of numeric values.

Proximity buffer: A zone (often a circle or polygon) drawn around a map feature measured in units of distance or time. It is often used in proximity analysis (i.e., an analysis used to determine the relationship between a selected point and neighboring points).

Querying: Using GIS software to ask and answer questions about geographic features, attributes, and the relationship between them.

Spatial data: Location data relating to a geographic coordinate with longitude and latitude. These can be points, lines, or areas associated with zip codes, census tracts, street addresses, and so on.

Standard deviational ellipse (SDE): A bivariate statistical measure that provides an estimate of an individual's activity space by calculating the standard deviation of the x-coordinates and y-coordinates from the mean center to define the axes of the ellipse.

QUESTIONS FOR REFLECTION

1. Consider the example provided about using GIS to evaluate a supportive housing program. How did the university-based research team use GIS in collaboration with their community partner to analyze and interpret their research findings? How might these findings inform the organizations' service delivery? What additional geospatial data might be important for them to consider as they evaluate their housing programs?

2. In each of the examples provided in this chapter, the university-based research team directed the process of using GIS approaches to evaluate community programs. How might the questions asked and methods used differ if they had originated from the partnering organizations instead of from the researchers? How could the research team have been more participatory in their approach?

3. How would you address some of the challenges and limitations to using GIS in your evaluation work? For example, how would you protect the privacy of individuals, organizations, and communities with whom you are working? How would you identify and obtain geospatial data that is relevant and applicable to the local context in which you are working?

4. Which of the GIS approaches discussed in this chapter do you think holds the most promise for partnership-based evaluation, and why? Which strategies are you most excited to use in your own evaluation work?

REFERENCES

Azzam, T., & Robinson, D. (2013). GIS in evaluation utilizing the power of geographic information systems to represent evaluation data. *American Journal of Evaluation*, *34*, 207–224.

Brusilovskiy, E., & Salzer, M. S. (2012). A study of environmental influences on the well-being of individuals with psychiatric disabilities in Philadelphia, PA. *Social Science & Medicine*, *74*(10), 1591–1601. doi:10.1016/j.socscimed.2012.01.033

Campbell, J., & Shin, M. (2011). *Essentials of geographic information systems*. Saylor Foundation.

Centers for Disease Control & Prevention. (2012, September). *Program evaluation tip sheet: Integrating GIS into evaluation*. https://www.cdc.gov/dhdsp/programs/spha/docs/tip_sheet_gis_evaluation.pdf.

Chambers, R. (2006). Participatory mapping and geographic information systems: Whose map? Who is empowered and who disempowered? Who gains and who loses? *The Electronic Journal of Information Systems in Developing Countries*, *25*(1), 1–11. doi:10.1002/j.1681-4835.2006.tb00163.x

Chan, D. V., Helfrich, C. A., Hursh, N. C., Rogers, E., & Gopal, S. (2014). Measuring community integration using geographic information systems (GIS) and participatory mapping for people who were once homeless. *Health & Place*, *27*, 92–101. doi:10.1016/j.healthplace.2013.12.011

Chang, K. T. (2013). *Introduction to geographic information systems*. McGraw-Hill Education.

Coulton, C. J., Jennings, M. Z., & Chan, T. (2013). How big is my neighborhood? Individual and contextual effects on perceptions of neighborhood scale. *American Journal of Community Psychology*, *51*(1-2), 140–150. doi:10.1007/s10464-012-9550-6

Elwood, S. (2006). Critical issues in participatory GIS: Deconstructions, reconstructions, and new research directions. *Transactions in GIS*, *10*(5), 693–708. doi:10.1111/j.1467-9671.2006.01023.x

Fernández, J. S., & Langhout, R. D. (2014). "A community with diversity of culture, wealth, resources, and living experiences": Defining neighborhood in an unincorporated community. *American Journal of Community Psychology*, *53*(1-2), 122–133. doi:10.1007/s10464-014-9631-9

Forrester, J., Cook, B., Bracken, L., Cinderby, S., & Donaldson, A. (2015). Combining participatory mapping with Q-methodology to map stakeholder perceptions of complex environmental problems. *Applied Geography*, *56*, 199–208. doi:10.1016/j.apgeog.2014.11.019

Gesler, W. M., & Albert, D. P. (2000). How spatial analysis can be used in medical geography. In D. P. Albert, W. M. Gesler, & B. Levergood (Eds.), *Spatial analysis, GIS and remote sensing applications in the health sciences* (pp. 11–38). Ann Arbor Press.

Golledge, R. G., & Stimson, R. J. (1987). *Analytical behavioural geography*. Croom-Helm.

Green, E., & Kloos, B. (2009). Facilitating youth participation in a context of forced migration: A Photovoice project in northern Uganda. *Journal of Refugee Studies*, *22*(4), 460–482. doi:10.1093/jrs/fep026

Green, E. P., Warren, V. R., Broverman, S., Ogwang, B., & Puffer, E. S. (2016). Participatory mapping in low-resource settings: Three novel methods used to engage Kenyan youth and other community members in community-based HIV prevention research. *Global Public Health*, *11*(5-6), 583–599. doi:10.1080/17441692.2016.1170178

Israel, B. A., Schulz, A. J., Parker, E. A., & Becker, A. B. (1998). Review of community-based research: Assessing partnership approaches to improve public health. *Annual Review of Public Health*, *19*, 173–202. doi:10.1146/annurev.publhealth.19.1.173

Jankowska, M. M., Schipperijn, J., & Kerr, J. (2015). A framework for using GPS data in physical activity and sedentary behavior studies. *Exercise and Sport Sciences Reviews*, *43*(1), 48–56. doi:10.1249/JES.0000000000000035

Kwan, M-P., & Knigge, L. (2006). Doing qualitative research using GIS: An oxymoronic endeavor? *Environment and Planning A: Economy and Space*, *38*(11), 1999–2002. doi:10.1068/a38462

Lieberson, S. (1969). Measuring population diversity. *American Sociological Review*, *34*(6), 850–862. doi:10.2307/2095977

Linney, J. A. (2000). Assessing ecological constructs and community context. In J. Rappaport & E. Seidman (Eds.), *Handbook of community psychology* (pp. 647–668). New York: Klumer Academic/ Plenum.

Lohmann, A. (2016). Geographic information systems. In L. A. Jason & D. S. Glenwick (Eds.), *Handbook of methodological approaches to community-based research* (pp. 93–102). New York: Oxford University Press.

Luke, D. A. (2005). Getting the big picture in community science: Methods that capture context. *American Journal of Community Psychology, 35*(3-4), 185–200. doi:10.1007/s10464-005-3397-z

Lynch, K. (1960). *The image of the city*. MIT Press.

Nemet, G. F., & Bailey, A. J. (2000). Distance and health care utilization among the rural elderly. *Social Science & Medicine, 50*(9), 1197–1208.

Parker, B. (2006). Constructing community through maps? Power and praxis in community mapping. *The Professional Geographer, 58*(4), 470–484. doi:10.1111/j.1467-9272.2006.00583.x

Renger, R., Cimetta, A., Pettygrove, S., & Rogan, S. (2002). Geographic information systems (GIS) as an evaluation tool. *American Journal of Evaluation, 23*(4), 469–479. doi:10.1177/109821400202300407

Sherman, J. E., Spencer, J., Preisser, J. S., Gesler, W. M., & Arcury, T. A. (2005). A suite of methods for representing activity space in a healthcare accessibility study. *International Journal of Health Geographics, 4*(1), 24–21. doi:10.1186/1476-072X-4-24

Townley, G. (2015). "It helps you not feel so bad—feel like you again": The importance of community for individuals with psychiatric disabilities. *Journal of Psychosocial Rehabilitation and Mental Health, 2*, 113–124. doi:10.1007/s40737-015-0036-3

Townley, G., Kloos, B., & Wright, P. A. (2009). Understanding the experience of place: Expanding methods to conceptualize and measure community integration of persons with serious mental illness. *Health & Place, 15*(2), 520–531. doi:10.1016/j.healthplace.2008.08.011

Townley, G., Pearson, L., Lehrwyn, J. M., Prophet, N. T., & Trauernicht, M. (2016). Utilizing participatory mapping and GIS to examine the activity spaces of homeless youth. *American Journal of Community Psychology, 57*(3-4), 404–414. doi:10.1002/ajcp.12060

CHAPTER 10

QUALITATIVE EVALUATION IN COMMUNITY PARTNERSHIP

Andrew D. Case and Joy S. Kaufman

Evaluators today enjoy a wide range of methodological options for assessing program quality. In fact, a 2001 review by Stufflebeam identified 22 distinct evaluation approaches. A subset of these that employs qualitative methods and methodologies is increasingly used by evaluators to illuminate the perspectives and experiences of individuals with diverse kinds of programs (Patton, 2015). With its focus on localized and in-depth knowledge, a qualitative evaluation approach is a natural fit with a community-engaged methodology, which positions community stakeholders to be meaningfully engaged in various facets of evaluation. Much has been written about qualitative evaluation generally, but far less attention has been given to implementing qualitative evaluation within community partnerships. In this chapter, we outline key considerations in selecting and implementing qualitative evaluation designs within the context of community partnerships.

This chapter is divided into two sections. In the first, we define qualitative inquiry. We maintain that designing and implementing appropriate qualitative evaluations depend on a keen understanding of qualitative inquiry (Patton, 2015; Ponterotto, 2005, 2010). Our definition outlines the assumptions that distinguish qualitative and quantitative inquiry and common qualitative methodologies and methods. With this foundation, we introduce key considerations for designing and implementing a qualitative evaluation within the context of a community partnership. These focus on the specific purposes, questions, and methodology and methods of the evaluation. To illuminate these considerations, we ground our discussion in an example.

DEFINING QUALITATIVE INQUIRY

Many descriptions of qualitative inquiry begin with a comparison between qualitative and quantitative "methods" (Bryman, 1984). In this contrast, quantitative methods are conceptualized as procedures

Learning Objectives

1. Identify the most widely used qualitative methodologies.

2. Describe the methods used in qualitative inquiry.

3. Understand how to determine whether qualitative inquiry is the most appropriate approach to answer a specific evaluation question.

4. Identify ways that a community partnership approach can enhance an evaluation utilizing qualitative inquiry.

that *quantify* a phenomenon in some way, usually via counts, distributions, or other statistical measurements or manipulations. Qualitative methods, in contrast, are procedures that *qualify* or characterize the essence of a phenomenon, often through "thick" narrative description (e.g., written accounts of behaviors and social interactions and their meanings within specific contexts). While this procedural distinction highlights an important difference between quantitative and qualitative approaches, it does not explain why and under what circumstances one would employ qualitative inquiry. Moreover, the procedural distinction overlooks fundamental differences between qualitative and quantitative approaches that are rooted in philosophy of science (Bryman, 1984). As Rist (1977) cogently argues,

> When we speak of "quantitative" or "qualitative" methodologies, we are, in the final analyses speaking of an interrelated set of assumptions about the social world which are philosophical, ideological, and epistemological. They encompass more than simply data gathering techniques.

Philosophy of science refers to the assumptions or beliefs that undergird the systematic quest for knowledge (Ponterotto, 2005). These assumptions fall under distinct branches of philosophy including ontology, epistemology, methodology, and methods (each of these will be defined and discussed below) and can be clustered to form distinct paradigms or worldviews that guide inquiry (Table 10.1 summarizes the central tenets of popular paradigms; Guba & Lincoln, 1994; Ponterotto, 2005). It is important to note that philosophy of science is applicable to both research and evaluation. Evaluation, like research, is a systematic quest for knowledge, though its objectives, audiences, standards for credibility, and priorities often differ from those of basic academic research (Balmer et al., 2016; also see

Table 10.1 Major Modern Paradigms and Assumptions in Inquiry (Guba & Lincoln, 1994; Ponterotto, 2005)

Paradigm	Ontological Positions	Epistemological Positions	Methodological Positions
Postpositivism	Reality governed by laws, imperfectly apprehended	Truth independent of inquirer and respondent; errors inherent in knowledge production	Hypodeductive (formulating hypotheses that can be falsified through observation; bias reduction; generalizability)
Constructivism/constructionism	Multiple realities; apprehended through mental constructions	Truth as co-construction of inquirer and respondent	Emphatic understanding through dynamic transactions between inquirer and respondent
Critical theory	Reality shaped by social forces	Truth a function of social position; values part of inquiry	Dynamic transactions; emancipatory aims

Chapter 1 for more on the distinction between evaluation and research). In this chapter, we use the term "qualitative inquiry" to denote the common philosophy of science that informs both qualitative research and qualitative evaluation.

The Ontological and Epistemological Basis of Qualitative Inquiry

Ontology is the branch of philosophy of science that deals with questions of the nature of reality. Qualitative inquirers investigate *qualia*, those aspects of reality that are subjective and that involve an element of *meaning making* on the part of individuals (Shweder, 1999). These include emotions, feelings, judgments, perceptions, and beliefs. As Denzin and Lincoln (2000) argue, the qualitative inquirer endeavors "to make sense of, or to interpret phenomena in terms of the *meanings* people bring to them" (p. 3). Bryman (1984) similarly notes that what distinguishes qualitative inquiry is "a commitment to seeing the social world from the point of view of the actor" (p. 77). Thus, qualitative inquiry is focused on capturing the meanings individuals give to their experiences.

Epistemology is the study of knowledge, including knowledge acquisition and justification and the relationship between knowledge and truth (Carter & Little, 2007). While there is variation in epistemological stances among qualitative traditions (Guba & Lincoln, 1994; Ponterotto, 2005), most share a *transactional-subjectivist* position. Within the constructivist/constructionist tradition, this means that knowledge is a co-construction between evaluation or research participant and inquirer (Guba & Lincoln, 1994).[1] Transactions are characterized by bidirectional, or mutual, influence. Thus, it is the transaction between the inquirer and the participant within the research relationship that gives rise to an understanding of participants' experiences. Within this transaction, the inquirer plays the role of an interpretive analytic tool (Ponterotto, 2005). The *critical* tradition, with its emphasis on illuminating the role of power in individuals' experiences as well as the inquiry itself, further assumes that the construction of knowledge is influenced by the social position (e.g., race, gender, socioeconomic status) and values of the inquirer and the participant. For example, as a user of mental health services, one's perception of whether those services are sensitive to issues of race and culture will depend, in large part, on whether one belongs to a nondominant racial-cultural group in that setting. Thus, the perceptions and experiences of racial-cultural sensitivity for an Afro-Caribbean person in a predominantly White mental health setting are likely to differ from those of a European American person in that same setting. In sum, qualitative epistemologies assume truth is dependent on the context of the inquiry in which it emerges. For this reason, qualitative inquirers consider the context of inquiry (e.g., population, setting) and the suitability of methodologies and methods to that context.

Methodologies in Qualitative Inquiry

A *methodology* is the logic and justification for using specific methods to produce knowledge (Carter & Little, 2007). A qualitative methodology provides a systematic way of capturing qualia that is consistent with specific philosophical premises. Ponterotto

---

[1] For discussions on epistemological positions that do not assume the co-construction of knowledge (i.e., dualist/objectivist position) in qualitative research, see Guba and Lincoln (1994) and Miles and Huberman (1984).

(2010) identified at least 20 qualitative methodologies. Among them, the most widely used are (a) ethnography, (b) grounded theory, (c) narrative inquiry; (d) phenomenology; (e) case study; and (f) participatory action inquiry (Carter & Little, 2007; Creswell, 2013). Below, we briefly define these methodologies. In addition, to elucidate how these methodologies can be used in evaluation and for what purposes, we describe implementing them in a similar context: a self-help group for persons in recovery from alcoholism.

Ethnography is one of the oldest qualitative methodologies and involves the immersion of the inquirer as a participant and observer within a group of interest in order to interpret shared patterns of beliefs, values, and behaviors (Case et al., 2014a; Emerson et al., 2011; Madison, 2012). The ethnographer spends an extended period of time within a setting or community conducting observations (and sometimes interviews) to answer a particular question. In evaluation, this methodology is particularly useful when the evaluation question involves trying to understand the shared social dimensions of a program (social interactions, roles, norms, relationships). In the context of an evaluation of a self-help group, one might use an ethnographic methodology to characterize the ways individuals support each other and the specific roles they play in the group.

In *grounded theory*, the inquirer uses prescribed procedures to translate descriptions of a phenomenon into explanations and theories of that phenomenon (Charmaz, 2006; Clarke, 2005; Glaser & Strauss, 1967). While some use grounded theory to analyze data, others maintain that the goal is not simply analysis (i.e., description) but *theory generation*. In fact, some argue that grounded theory is an optimal approach when there is no theory to guide (or constrain) the work. The data are drawn on to help establish a theoretical framework. In this sense, a grounded theory approach is most apt for evaluations focused on theory building such as determining what aspects of a program (from the perspective of participants) are responsible for the program's effectiveness. Interviewing is often the method of choice in this methodology, and interview transcripts are coded and compared in a systematic way. One might use a grounded theory methodology to generate a logic model (see Chapter 1 for an introduction to logic models) that postulates how the self-help group works to facilitate recovery.

Narrative inquiry involves giving an analytic and chronological accounting of a set of events or actions in an individual's life using spoken or written text (Creswell, 2013). As a methodology, it is best suited for capturing detailed stories in the life of an individual or a small group of individuals (Creswell, 2013). This approach, though not popular in evaluation, can be used to characterize the experience of someone in a program that is of evaluative or illustrative significance. For example, one could have participants journal their experiences with the self-help group and "re-story" those accounts in an analytic and chronological manner to elucidate the process of recovery in a self-help group.

The goal of *phenomenological* inquiry is to analyze individuals' experiences with a phenomenon to produce a generalizable description of the nature of that phenomenon (Garza, 2004). At its core, this approach is designed to help describe or explain a particular experience or set of experiences and the meanings attributed to them by individuals. However, unlike the narrative approach which utilizes the accounts of one or two individuals, this methodology assesses meaning across several individuals (Creswell, 2013). Phenomenological inquiry is especially useful when the goal is to have an in-depth and nuanced understanding of a shared experience among a group of individuals. This approach could be used to understand what recovery is like for individuals in the self-help group and different manifestations of recovery (e.g., abstinence, harm reduction, increased social contribution).

Case studies examine a particular *issue* within a case—a bounded system or set of systems (Stake, 1995; Yin, 2003). The "case" can be an individual, group, program, organization, society, and so on. Notably, some scholars do not consider the case study to be a methodology per se, but a level of analysis in inquiry (Stake, 2006). One type of case study, an intrinsic case study, is a natural fit for many evaluations (Stake, 2006) because the case is the issue of interest as it represents a departure from the norm. For example, one self-help group might evidence more favorable outcomes than others. A case study of that group might focus on what is unique about its functioning (e.g., policies, procedures, processes). In addition, if one adopts the view that a case study is a level of analysis, it is possible to embed one of the previously mentioned methodologies within it (e.g., ethnographic case study).

Last, *participatory action inquiry* is a methodology in which community members affected by an issue participate alongside academically trained inquirers to better understand and address that issue (Case et al., 2014b; Hall, 1992; Israel et al., 2001; Kidd & Kral, 2005). While this methodology is not exclusively qualitative in nature, adherents often use qualitative methods. In an evaluation, the goal of participatory action is not only to generate findings with the help of community members, but also to collaborate with those members in a process of reflecting and acting upon those findings to bring about changes that benefit their community. A participatory evaluation of a self-help group might examine structural barriers to recovery that exist within the program (e.g., strict rules, lack of employment resources). Importantly, this type of evaluation would involve participants of the group in various aspects of the evaluation such as identifying the questions of interest, creating an assessment instrument, collecting the data, and conducting the data analysis. Participants would also be involved in generating and implementing recommendations to improve the self-help group.

A Note on Mixed Methods Evaluation

Mixed methods evaluation designs incorporate qualitative *and* quantitative approaches. It represents a unique methodology grounded in the assumption that this approach counterbalances the weaknesses of quantitative and qualitative approaches while maximizing on their strengths (Johnson & Onwuegbuzie, 2004). Since this methodology is not distinctly qualitative and has its own unique philosophical underpinnings, a detailed description of it is outside the scope of this article. However, it is worth noting that in mixed methods, the qualitative approach is used alongside the quantitative approach for several different purposes (Creswell & Clark, 2017). For example, select interviews may be conducted to help explain and contextualize findings from a survey. Or, the results of a focus group may be used to inform the development of a quantitative instrument.

Methods of Qualitative Inquiry

Methods refer to the processes, procedures, and techniques of research. Methods are specified by the methodology utilized. As Guba and Lincoln (1994) argue, "Methods must be fitted to a predetermined methodology" (p. 108). As a case in point, given the close, prolonged engagement between inquirer and participants that is required by an ethnography, participant observations and interviews are the typical data collection methods used in this methodology. There is a wide array of methods in qualitative inquiry that fall under broad categories such as *sampling, data collection, analysis*, and *quality*. In Table 10.2, we provide a nonexhaustive list of qualitative methods and their descriptions. These methods are described in detail in texts dedicated to qualitative research or evaluation, such as Creswell and Poth (2018), Denzin and Lincoln (2018), and Patton (2015).

Quality criteria and procedures. These methods refer to the standards, measures, and procedures by which evaluators ensure the trustworthiness of their findings (Lincoln & Guba, 1986; Morrow, 2005). The choice of criterion is driven by the goals of the evaluation as well as philosophical considerations. For example, an evaluator working from a post-positivist paradigm might adopt *dependability*, a "parallel criterion" to reliability in quantitative research (Morrow, 2005). Dependability can be assessed through procedures such as interrater agreement (Cohen's kappa), whereby the agreement between two analysts coding the same data is measured. It can also be ensured through replicable, standardized

Table 10.2 Some Common Methods in Qualitative Inquiry (Guba & Lincoln, 1989; Patton, 2015; Suzuki et al., 2007)

Method	Definition
Sampling	
Convenience	Recruiting participants who are easily accessible
Purposive	Recruiting participants based on their potential to provide information that will be illuminative
Snowball	Recruiting new participants from current participants' social network
Data collection	
Participant observation	Inquirer takes part in meaningful activities while recording observations of participants taking part in those same activities
Interviews	Inquirer asks the participants questions while capturing their responses
Focus groups	Inquirer facilitates a dialogue with and among several participants while capturing their responses
Analysis	
Phenomenological	Describing and interpreting how a given person in a given context gives meaning to an experience
Thematic	Identifying and interpreting patterns of shared meaning across several participants
Discourse	Investigating meaning through linguistic patterns or the construction of language
Quality procedures	
Saturation	Having sufficient data to produce well-developed findings
Member checks	Interpretation of data presented to participants for feedback and refining
Peer debriefing	Sharing aspects of the inquiry with a peer or group of peers who then provide scholarly audit or challenge

methods (e.g., using the same interview guide across participants). From a constructivist position, an evaluator might pursue and assess *verstehen*, the extent to which participants' experiences are deeply understood (Morrow, 2005). Ensuring and assessing verstehen can be achieved through member-checking, the process of the evaluator soliciting feedback from participants on his or her interpretations of their responses. From a critical perspective, the evaluator may pursue consequential validity, which is the extent to which the findings and other products of the evaluation stimulate desired change.

There are two implications of a qualitative philosophy of science for qualitative evaluation. First, qualitative inquiry is best suited to answering specific types of evaluation questions, namely those concerned with the meanings participants ascribe to their experiences. Second, understanding the philosophy of qualitative inquiry can help the evaluator to determine which methodology and methods are best suited to an evaluation context.

DESIGNING QUALITATIVE EVALUATIONS

Qualitative inquiry can be an important tool for achieving evaluation goals (Patton, 2002). By evaluation, we refer to a specific type of inquiry that is conducted to (a) provide information to program administrators to determine whether to modify, expand, or end a program; (b) determine if a new program is meeting its objectives and being delivered as intended; (c) provide feedback with the goal of enhancing how a program is operating; or (d) provide data to the program funders to demonstrate implementation and effectiveness (Rossi et al., 2004). When determining whether qualitative inquiry is well suited, and which qualitative approach to use in a community partnership context, it is useful to consider some key issues related to qualitative philosophy of science. These are (a) the *purposes* of the evaluation; (b) the *questions* to be answered by the evaluation; and (c) the *methodology and methods* to be employed in the evaluation. While these questions are central for any type of evaluation, in our experience, facets of these questions are particularly relevant to qualitative evaluation in community partnership. We share an example to elucidate how a careful consideration of these questions can inform the design and implementation of a community-partnered qualitative evaluation.

CASE EXAMPLE: A QUALITATIVE EVALUATION: CONNECTICUT MENTAL HEALTH CENTER

During 2013 and 2014, we led an evaluation of the Connecticut Mental Health Center (CMHC), a large, urban, publicly funded community mental health center.[1] Established in the late 1960s during deinstitutionalization, CMHC is one of the oldest community mental health centers in the United States. The center provides individuals who have severe and persistent mental illness with acute

[1] This evaluation has been conducted 6 times with slightly different evaluation goals, questions, methods, and staff. The first author was involved during the second evaluation (2013–2014), while the second author, who is the lead evaluator, has been involved for the entire duration of the project. The information presented here comes from our recollections of events as well as interviews conducted with evaluation personnel and CMHC service directors for another report: Case et al. (2014b).

services, inpatient treatment, psychosocial rehabilitation, and outpatient care. Consumers of these services are predominantly persons of color, live below the poverty line, and have a history of inpatient and outpatient care across several centers.

As part of CMHC's ongoing performance improvement efforts, consumers complete annual satisfaction surveys. In 2012, a majority of them (92%) expressed high levels of satisfaction with the services they received and indicated that they would recommend the center to a family member or friend in need of services (Case et al., 2014b). Despite these high levels of reported satisfaction, the center's executive director (ED) desired to know why some consumers were not satisfied with services they received and how these services could be improved. In a conversation with Joy (second author), who oversees aspects of the quality improvement work at the center, the ED requested a more in-depth understanding of consumers' perspectives of the care environment.

Purposes

The first consideration in designing a qualitative evaluation is determining whether a qualitative approach is suited to the purposes of the evaluation. As noted above, evaluation can serve a number of purposes including monitoring outcomes, improving programs, informing decisions such as whether to fund or discontinue a program, encouraging democratic participation (House & Howe, 1998), promoting social betterment (Weiss, 1998), and empowering program participants (Fetterman & Wandersman, 2005). Chapters 1 and 2 provide an overview of some of these purposes.

Though a variety of goals can be addressed through qualitative evaluation, this approach is not suited to all evaluation purposes. Qualitative evaluation is most appropriate when the evaluation purpose requires an in-depth understanding of people's perspectives and experiences with a program, organization, or initiative. Purposes that readily align with a qualitative approach include (a) identifying people's needs in order to develop appropriate services; (b) determining the aspects of a program that are impactful in order to inform the development of a logic model; and (c) understanding

the limitations of current services so that they can be enhanced.

The primary purposes of the CMHC evaluation—that is, to understand consumer's *perspectives* of CMHC services and to identify areas for improvement—were consistent with the premises of qualitative inquiry. Evaluation efforts consistent with these purposes hinge on assessing the meanings participants ascribed to their experiences with the center, making this work well suited for a qualitative evaluation approach. There was also an alignment of secondary evaluation purposes with a *community-partnered* qualitative approach. These other objectives became clear through a number of meetings leading up to and during the evaluation, in which the center's ED revealed several additional implicit goals for the evaluation.

First, the ED wanted to increase the involvement of consumers in the center's operation. The center has traditionally followed a "recovery" treatment philosophy that stresses the need for consumers to have (a) a role in planning and directing the services they receive and (b) the opportunity to contribute meaningfully to their communities (Case et al., 2014b). The leadership of CMHC has worked to implement these aspects of a recovery model in a number of ways in the organization's functioning. For instance, it established a consumer advisory board that advises the ED on service delivery issues. The administration also invited consumers to participate on the CMHC performance improvement committee alongside clinic directors and other staff. Finally, the center hired consumers as peer leaders; these leaders are former and current consumers who are further along in their recovery and who assist consumers on their recovery journey. The ED hoped that the evaluation would serve as another mechanism through which consumers could be involved in directing and enhancing services at CMHC. Specifically, he wanted consumers to be involved in the evaluation effort beyond being a source of data.

In addition to creating opportunities for consumer involvement, the ED also hoped that the evaluation would "elevate" the status of consumers as individuals who make important contributions to the functioning of the center. This is a notable goal given that the mental health system has historically held a paternalistic stance toward consumers, effectively limiting their participation in service planning, research, and evaluation (Chamberlin, 2005; Craig, 2008). The ED hoped that consumer involvement in the evaluation would precipitate a shift in organizational culture, such that both staff and consumers would recognize consumers' role in CMHC as being more than service recipients.

Finally, the ED hoped that the evaluation would catalyze important changes in service delivery, which he envisioned as the ultimate impact of the evaluation. The leadership had been aware for some time of issues in the care environment, especially around cultural sensitivity. The ED hoped that challenging feedback from consumers would motivate staff to critically assess and modify their service delivery practices.

In collaboration with the ED, Joy determined that a qualitative community-based participatory research (CBPR; see Chapter 3 for more) methodology was optimally suited to the primary and secondary purposes of this evaluation. While this methodology was developed to pursue research goals (Israel et al., 2001; Patton, 2002), it can be utilized for evaluative purposes. Critically, this methodology emphasizes community partnerships and, when utilized effectively, affords consumers an opportunity to play a significant role in generating evaluative findings and recommendations. From a CBPR perspective, community members are not merely data points but coinquirers and partners with academically trained evaluators. In the context of the CMHC evaluation, consumers would be involved in data collection, analysis, interpretation, dissemination, and organizational change efforts.

Utilizing a community partnership approach to this evaluation was seen as advantageous for a number of reasons. Having consumers use their experiences with CMHC and familiarity with the target population would enhance the quality of the data collection and analysis as well as the overall implementation of the evaluation. Ultimately, we believed this partnership approach could generate actionable knowledge leading to organizational change. A community partnership approach would also satisfy the secondary purposes of the evaluation, specifically, creating opportunities for greater consumer involvement in the center's

functioning and elevating the status of consumers as co-evaluators and social change agents.

> *Community partnership* **approaches to evaluation increase**
>
> - **the quality of the data collected;**
> - **the validity of the results;**
> - **the likelihood that results will be actionable; and**
> - **opportunities for community members to be social change agents.**

Questions

The primary goal of any evaluation is to answer a question or set of questions posed by stakeholders about the program. In order to determine whether an evaluation question is most appropriately answered using qualitative methods, it is crucial to assess what you hope to learn from the evaluation. In the CMHC example, stakeholders wanted to explore consumers' perspectives of the care environment. In order to fully capture the richness of their experiences, it was important to collect open-ended responses to questions posed versus asking them to choose from predetermined response options. This distinction directed us to utilize qualitative methods.

Qualitative approaches yield data that allow the evaluator to understand the meanings program participants give to their experiences, perceptions, or motivations. The primary evaluation question for CMHC was: *What are consumers' views of the services they receive?* This overarching question elicited the positive and negative experiences consumers had with the center's services. The secondary evaluation questions were: *How can current services at CMHC be improved, and what additional services are needed?* Both sets of questions are answered by having consumers reflect on the treatment experiences they had at CMHC, while envisioning alternate possibilities for treatment. In this sense, the evaluation questions

Continued

required answers that were qualia or meaning-based in nature; these answers require qualitative methods.

Methodology and Methods

The third consideration in designing a qualitative evaluation is selecting a methodology and methods to accomplish a qualitative evaluation's purposes and to answer its driving questions. This selection involves sampling strategies, data collection methods, analytic strategies, and quality criteria. Table 10.3 provides an overview of the CMHC evaluation purpose and questions and includes the overall logic that guided our choice of methods. An additional step that is unique to community-partnered evaluation involves developing strategies and the necessary conditions to ensure an equitable partnership between consumers and academics as they engage in the evaluation effort. In determining the methods for the CMHC evaluation, we decided that hearing about the experience of receiving services at the center from a greater number of consumers had a higher probability of yielding the data needed to answer our evaluation questions than in-depth information gathered from fewer individuals. As such, our team decided to conduct focus groups instead of key informant interviews.

Enhancing Capacity and Fostering Partnership

A traditional CBPR approach stipulates that academic evaluators and community members engage the process as partners and coinquirers. Thus, our first task was to recruit consumers who would assist in the evaluation. We planned our budget so that we could hire four consumers and provide them with a stipend to compensate them for the time and expertise they would contribute to the project. To make the selection process open, transparent, and fair, Joy and a peer leader held a forum at CMHC and oversaw an application process. In this forum, Joy explained the primary purpose of the project and the role consumers would play in the effort. The forum was attended by approximately 70 consumers, 29 of whom applied to participate in the evaluation, with 17 subsequently interviewed by a peer leader and two academic evaluators (Case et al., 2014b). Four consumers who demonstrated a high level of motivation and interest in the project as well as necessary skills (e.g., communication)

were hired. Over the next 9 months, the consumers were trained by Joy in focus group methodology including protocol development (i.e., focus group questions), group facilitation, note-taking, data coding, and analysis (Kruger & Casey, 2015). In addition, the team was trained in methods to present the findings. Training for the second round of evaluations included Andrew (first author) and emphasized advanced moderation skills for leading focus groups. During the initial training, consumers attended weekly meetings during which they practiced the informed consent process, moderation of a focus group, and note-taking. In addition, during these meetings, consumers developed a focus group guide and the informed consent document. A benefit of the consumer involvement was that we were confident that these documents were accessible to the target population.

Sampling

The center and its satellite clinics consisted of several outpatient clinics that provide specialized treatment (e.g., substance abuse, young adult services, acute care). With the goal of representing the perspectives of consumers who had received a diverse array of services, we recruited a *typical cases* purposive sample (defined in Table 10.2 and described in Table 10.3). Specifically, one focus group was conducted for each of 13 clinics and service teams, resulting in a total of 106 participating consumers. In addition, we conducted a focus group for consumers who were deaf or hard-of-hearing. This sampling strategy allowed us to assess similarities and differences in perspectives across the clinics, which allowed us to provide general and specific findings and recommendations about CMHC services.

Data Collection

We collected focus group data to address the evaluation questions. An advantage of employing focus group discussions over individual interviews is that it allows participants to converse with each other and build on one another's responses, thereby enhancing the quality of the data collected (Patton, 2015). That is, through dialogue between participants, common, inaccurate, and extreme perspectives and experiences can be identified. We selected focus groups to identify the range of perspectives on

Table 10.3 Summary of Connecticut Mental Health Center's (CMHC) Evaluation Purposes, Questions, Methodology, and Methods

Component	Description/Application
Purposes	1. To better understand consumers' perspectives of CMHC and identify areas for improvement 2. Increase consumers' involvement in assessing and guiding care at CMHC 3. Elevate *status* of consumers at CMHC beyond simply being recipients of services
Questions	1. What are consumers' views of the services they receive? 2. How can current services be improved? 3. What additional services are needed?
Methodology	Community-based participatory research (CBPR). Consumers involved in all facets of the evaluation effort as co-evaluators. Consumers were selected after open forum and interviews and trained in focus group methods and thematic analysis. Consumers worked with academics to script the informed consent and interview guide; moderate the focus groups; analyze the data; and disseminate findings and recommendations
Methods	
Sampling	
Purposive (typical cases)	We recruited "typical" participants across clinics and clinical teams. The experiences of these participants with various services were assumed to represent the modal experiences consumers had at these clinics or with these services
Data collection	
Focus group	An open-ended interview with a group of people. Our focus groups ranged from 8 to 12 participants. Consumer evaluators moderated the groups and took notes. Academic evaluators audiotaped the interviews and compensated participants
Analysis	
Thematic (consensual)	A systematic approach to organizing and extrapolating shared meaning in the form of themes. Our consensus approach involved one consumer evaluator and one academic evaluator coding the focus groups separately, with specific attention paid to whether experiences and perspectives reported were positive or negative. A third evaluator was brought in to break any ties. Codes were presented to the entire team, who discussed them and generated themes. For example, codes around insensitivity from staff were combined into a "Lack of Respect" theme
Quality criteria and procedures	
Dependability	Consistency in study procedures. We used identical procedures to recruit participants across clinics, which included informing clinic directors and clinicians about the study and having them tell the consumers with whom they worked. In addition, we used a standard, structured interview protocol across all focus groups. In terms of analysis, we created an audit trail from coding to thematic analysis and a standard consensus process for resolving interpretive disagreements

(Continued)

Component	Description/Application
Table 10.3 (Continued)	
Verstehen	The degree to which the meanings consumers ascribe to their perspectives and experiences are keenly understood. The involvement of consumer evaluators in collecting and analyzing the data increased the team's capacity to deeply understand the data
Consequential validity	The extent to which the evaluation leads to important organizational change. Based on the recommendations from the first evaluation, CMHC established a primary care clinic and a gym, made the Patient Bill of Rights more visible, and launched a respect campaign. In the second evaluation, participants expressed satisfaction with these changes
Dissemination	Oral (PowerPoint-aided) and written reports

CMHC services among participants as well as to gain some consensus on the modal perception(s) of the center and its services.

> **Focus groups allow for a more efficient collection of data compared to interviews and provide opportunities for participants to build upon one another's responses.**

Focus groups also offer the advantage of increased efficiency of data collection compared to individual interviews (Kruger & Casey, 2015; Patton, 2015). In the time it takes to conduct one individual interview, focus group data can be collected from 8 to 10 participants. This was an important consideration in the CMHC evaluation as we had to maximize our human capital in the form of consumer time and effort, as well as the limited financial resources at our disposal.

To successfully conduct the focus groups, academic and consumer evaluators worked on different aspects of the effort. The academic evaluators oversaw efforts to publicize the focus groups, the recruitment and compensation of participants, and the audio recording of the groups' discussion, while the consumer evaluators carried out the data collection, consented participants, moderated the focus groups, and took notes on the discussion.

Analysis

Consistent with our community partnership approach, we needed to adopt an analytic strategy that would allow consumers and academics to partner in the endeavor. Our strategy was a multistep, group-based (i.e., consensus) thematic analysis (e.g., Hill et al., 2005; Schielke et al., 2009) through which we carefully reviewed the data to understand the meaning of what the focus group participants had shared and then collaboratively identified patterns that emerged from the data.

In the first step, the team worked together to develop a coding strategy. This was done through the group collaboratively coding two transcripts and coming to consensus on the codes. In the next stage, a consumer evaluator and an academic evaluator each coded transcripts of the remaining focus groups for positive and negative perspectives and experiences across several domains, including individual and group therapy, medication management, and overall treatment by staff. The two coders then discussed their codes to assess their degree of agreement and, as necessary, reconcile codes on which they had initially disagreed. In the event that a disagreement could not be resolved, a third person on the team would "break the tie." In the second step, we presented the data to the entire team in the form of excerpts that were organized by themes identified by the coders. Working together, the team carefully reviewed the coded excerpts and, through intense reflection on the data and discussion, identified the themes in the data and summarized these into a narrative that included actionable recommendations. Consistent with our CBPR approach, we deferred to the interpretation of the consumer evaluators who had greater knowledge of and experience with the issues highlighted in the data.

Quality Criteria

We employed three criteria in qualitative inquiry to ensure the quality of our findings and inferences: dependability, verstehen, and consequential validity. *Dependability* refers to consistency in how the evaluation is conducted across time and researchers, making the evaluation process explicit and reproducible (Morrow, 2005). To achieve dependability, we used a standard focus group guide and coding scheme. In addition, we created an audit trail from coding to analysis by carefully documenting the codes assigned by each coder, how consensus was reached when there were discrepancies, and how themes were identified from the data. Moreover, our multicoder system was based on a simple and repeatable "consensus" or "tie-break" process.

We also aspired to *verstehen* in our findings, which is having a deep understanding of the meanings consumer participants ascribed to their experiences and perspectives of CMHC. By having consumers involved in the evaluation, specifically in designing interview questions and in the collection and analysis of data, we believe we achieved a greater understanding of those meanings. The personal experiences of the consumer evaluators provided a unique lens through which we understood the focus group data, and the connection these evaluators had with the consumer participants helped to yield the rich data and findings in this evaluation.

In a similar vein, our evaluation project demonstrated a high degree of *consequential validity*, which means that the project led to important organizational changes (Morrow, 2005). After the first round of evaluation, several recommendations made by the team were implemented. First, in response to the desire for integrated care, the center opened an on-site primary care clinic so that consumers' medical and mental health needs could be addressed in one place. Second, a number of participants stated that they did not feel respected by some staff at the center. In the following year, "creating a community of respect" was the center's performance improvement

goal, and this objective preceded a number of initiatives and campaigns to increase respect within the center. Third, consumers stated that they did not know what their rights were as patients, that their clinicians did not always discuss these rights with them, and that they did not know where they could locate a copy of the Patient Bill of Rights. Moreover, a subsequent inquiry into this revealed that posted copies of the Bill were not always placed in a visible location. In response, the Bills were placed in more visible locations, clinical staff were reminded of the center's policy to discuss consumer's rights, and consumers were given a copy of the Bill of Rights during intake into services and during their semi-annual treatment planning sessions with their clinicians. What was striking to the team is that these issues, that is, desire for integrated care, not feeling respected, and not knowing their rights, were not raised by the focus group participants in the second round of the evaluation, indicating that the response of the center leadership to the recommendations made by the consumer evaluators effectively addressed the consumers' concerns.

Dissemination

We shared results and recommendations through two mechanisms: a written report and a set of oral presentations. An academic evaluator generated a report based on the thematic analysis findings and recommendations that emerged when the entire team met to analyze the data. In addition to describing findings and recommendations, the report detailed the primary purpose, questions, and methods that informed the evaluation, as well as the central role consumer evaluators played in the evaluation. This report was reviewed by the entire team and revised based on feedback. The team also gave oral reports (with the assistance of PowerPoint to add a visual component) to different CMHC clinics and teams. In these presentations, we highlighted general findings and recommendations as well as those that were specific to a given clinic or team. All oral reports were developed collaboratively by the team and delivered by a consumer evaluator. The reporting sessions were attended by both CMHC consumers and staff. Often, a larger discussion of findings, recommendations, and strategies for how (if feasible) to implement recommendations followed.

LESSONS LEARNED: CONSIDERATIONS FOR QUALITATIVE EVALUATION IN COMMUNITY CONTEXTS

A qualitative approach can be useful for addressing evaluation purposes that rely on an in-depth understanding of individuals' perspectives and experiences. In addition, a CBPR qualitative methodology has the added benefit of fostering important partnerships between academically trained evaluators and community members. These collaborative partnerships enhance the overall quality and utility of the evaluation, while empowering community members to engage in organizational change efforts (Case et al., 2014b). Any evaluation has the potential for conflict or divergent opinions. This is especially the case in CBPR, where differences in power, lived experiences, and pay are likely present between members of the team. Early in our work with the CMHC consumer evaluators, while developing the script that the consumer evaluators would use to introduce each focus group, the team encountered a major difference of opinion. The consumer evaluators felt it was important to say that they had been trained by *Dr.* Joy Kaufman while Joy requested that her professional title not be included. This disagreement provided the opportunity for a lengthy discussion of the differences in power and status between members of the team and the desire for this work to lessen the impact of these disparities. While Joy's desire to "level the playing field" was heard by the team, the consumer evaluators eloquently expressed that using Joy's professional title in describing who trained them helped to legitimize them and their expertise to conduct this work. In the end, the title stayed in the introduction, but more importantly, we believe the process of debating, authentically listening to each other, and resolving this difference helped to create a team dynamic in which everyone felt respected, knew that their opinions were valued, and felt safe to express themselves.

In our evaluation, we engaged in partnership at multiple levels using strategies that can hold value across contexts and populations of interest. First, we collaborated with the center's ED to identify primary and secondary goals, specific evaluation questions, and an appropriate evaluation methodology. Informed by our understanding of qualitative philosophy of science, we determined the appropriateness of a CBPR methodology, purposive sampling, and the focus group method for addressing the evaluation purposes and questions. Second, we partnered with consumers as coevaluators and partners in the evaluation process. Consumer evaluators helped to develop the informed consent document and interview guide, moderated the focus groups, assisted with data analysis, and presented findings and recommendations to key stakeholders. While not discussed in this chapter, we also collaborated with a variety of stakeholders (CMHC leadership, clinical staff, consumer evaluators; see Case et al., 2014b) in order to understand the various impacts the evaluation had on the organization.

The promises of qualitative evaluation in community partnerships are many. Consumer involvement in inquiry enhances the validity and usefulness of findings (Hancock et al., 2012; Linhorst & Eckert, 2002). When this potential is combined with in-depth and rich inferences gained through qualitative methodologies, there is opportunity for well-informed and insightful evaluative conclusions and recommendations. For example, we found in our evaluation that the consumer evaluators were more perceptive regarding themes of disrespect and marginalization than we were. In this sense, consumers can bring a different perspective to evaluation that leads to more nuanced understandings.

The consumer evaluators in our project were able to expand upon and provide context for the events, circumstances, and situations that participants referenced in the focus groups. Thus, consumers can enhance the capacity of the evaluation team to provide valid findings and make helpful recommendations.

There are challenges associated with community-partnered qualitative evaluation, and specifically partnerships with consumers of mental health services. Recruiting and selecting consumers to be evaluators can be difficult. While we wanted to be as inclusive as possible in our selection process, we also had to gauge whether a potential consumer evaluator possessed the basic capacities necessary for them to be successful in the project (e.g., communication and comprehension). We also sought to recruit consumers who were highly motivated to participate and who saw some value in participating beyond receiving a stipend.

One process that takes time and effort is recognizing and maximizing the strengths of consumers in ways that offset areas of potential challenge. For example, one consumer evaluator had led self-help groups and was an excellent oral communicator; however, he had difficulty reading due to a learning disability, which would make note taking and coding challenging. Another evaluator was a Certified Substance Abuse Counselor for many years and had recently become deaf. She was quite perceptive and had a keen understanding of the project. In a dyadic conversation, she was able to read lips and track a conversation well, but would have extreme difficulty tracking a conversation in a focus group setting in which multiple people spoke. Playing to their strengths, our excellent oral communicator moderated the majority of our focus groups with another member of the team taking notes. He did not code data. Our perceptive evaluator coded many of the focus groups and took a central role in the thematic analysis. She did not moderate focus groups. Thus, we had to be creative in how we guided the consumer evaluators to choose roles based on their strengths. This approach allowed us to conceptualize our team as one unit with individual members with complementary skill sets.

Qualitative evaluation yields data that allow for an in-depth understanding of the experiences and opinions of program participants. However, it is a methodology that is more labor intensive and often includes a smaller sample relative to efforts relying on quantitative evaluation. In deciding what methods to use in an evaluation, the first step is to work with program leadership to identify the evaluation questions (see, e.g., Chapters 1 and 3). If the questions include understanding the perspective and experiences of program stakeholders, the inclusion of qualitative methods in your evaluation design would be an effective method.

Qualitative evaluation situated within a community partnership approach has clear benefits and can fulfill a number of important explicit and implicit purposes within an organization. In deciding whether to use a community partnership approach, it is important to (a) review this option with program leadership to gain their buy-in; (b) include an evaluator on your team who has experience in engaging, training, and supporting community members; (c) invest time in recruiting community partners who have the skills, time, and desire to actively participate in the evaluation; and (4) make sure your evaluation budget includes appropriate remuneration for the community partners and allows for the extra time this approach requires. The effectiveness of qualitative evaluation within a community partnership approach is supported by an understanding of the purpose of a particular evaluation, knowledge of qualitative methods, and skills in fostering meaningful community partnerships.

FURTHER READING

Creswell, J. W., & Poth, C. N. (2018). *Qualitative inquiry and research design* (4th ed.). Sage.

Denzin, N. K., & Lincoln, Y. S. (2018). *Handbook of qualitative research* (5th ed.). Sage.

Krueger, R. A., & Casey, M. A. (2015). *Focus groups: A practical guide for applied research* (5th ed.). Sage.

Patton, M. Q. (2015). *Qualitative research and methods: Integrating theory and practice*. Sage.

KEY CONCEPTS

Consequential validity: A criterion of quality that is met through the inquiry stimulating valued social or organizational change.

Constructivism: A paradigm that assumes knowledge is actively constructed between inquirers and individuals with lived experience related to a particular phenomenon.

Dependability: A parallel criterion of reliability in qualitative inquiry that assumes quality is achieved through consistency.

Epistemology: The branch of philosophy of science that specifies the nature of knowledge, how it is acquired, and the relationship between knowledge and truth.

Focus groups: A data collection format in which an inquirer moderates a discussion with a group of inquirers who will illuminate a particular subject.

Ontology: The branch of philosophy of science that specifies the nature of reality.

Paradigm: A distinct cluster of philosophical assumptions and beliefs under which researchers and evaluators operate.

Participatory action inquiry: A distinct methodology concerned with generating knowledge to inform subsequent action to solve a localized problem.

Philosophy of science: The assumptions and beliefs that undergird the systematic pursuit of knowledge including ontology, epistemology, and methods.

Purposive sampling: A cluster of sampling strategies designed to recruit only participants who will provide information that is particularly illuminative.

Qualitative inquiry: A systematic approach to knowledge generation informed by a philosophy of science centered on making sense of the *meanings* people ascribe to their experience and their perception of the world.

Thematic analysis: A qualitative analytic approach in which the inquirer systematically searches for and interprets patterns of meaning across data provided by several participants.

Verstehen: A criterion of quality based on the notion that quality is achieved through "deep understanding" of the meaning of participants' perceptions.

QUESTIONS FOR REFLECTION

1. What other methods could have been used to gather consumer perspective of services offered at CMHC? What are the strengths and potential barriers of using these methods?

2. In thinking about the case example, identify an alternative evaluation question to explore aspects of the services received at CMHC. What qualitative methodology would be most appropriate to answer this question?

3. Think about a community service that you have some knowledge about. What are some evaluation questions that could be explored in understanding the services delivered at this program? Which of these questions could be answered with qualitative inquiry? For questions that can be answered with qualitative inquiry, what is the most appropriate methodology? What methods could you employ?

How might a mixed methods approach enhance your ability to answer this question?

4. How does a community partnership approach enhance an evaluation that is utilizing qualitative inquiry? What are some of the situations that need to be in place to support the partnership approach? What are the potential benefits and challenges of using a partnership approach?

REFERENCES

Balmer, D. F., Martimianakis, M., Rama, J. A., & Stenfors-Hayes, T. (2016). Using data from program evaluations for qualitative research. *Journal of graduate medical education, 8*(5), 773–774. doi:10.4300/JGME-D-16-00540.1

Bryman, A. (1984). The debate about quantitative and qualitative research: A question of method or epistemology? *The British Journal of Sociology, 35*(1), 75–92. doi:10.2307/590553

Carter, S. M., & Little, M. (2007). Justifying knowledge, justifying method, taking action: Epistemologies, methodologies, and methods in qualitative research. *Qualitative Health Research, 17*(10), 1316–1328. doi:10.1177/1049732307306927

Case, A. D., Byrd, R., Claggett, E., DeVeaux, S., Perkins, R., Huang, C., Sernyak, M. J., Steiner, J. L., Cole, R., LaPaglia, D. M., Bailey, M., Buchanan, C., Johnson, A., & Kaufman, J. S. (2014b). Stakeholders' perspectives on community-based participatory research to enhance mental health services. *American Journal of Community Psychology, 54*(3-4), 397–408. doi:10.1007/s10464-014-9677-8

Case, A. D., Todd, N. R., & Kral, M. J. (2014a). Ethnography in community psychology: Promises and tensions. *American Journal of Community Psychology, 54*(1-2), 60–71. doi:10.1007/s10464-014-9648-0

Chamberlin, J. (2005). User/consumer involvement in mental health service delivery. *Epidemiologia e Psichiatria Sociale, 14*(1), 10–14. doi:10.1017/S1121189X00001871

Charmaz, K. (2006). *Constructing grounded theory: A practical guide through qualitative analysis.* Sage.

Clarke, A. E. (2005). *Situational analysis: Grounded theory after the postmodern turn.* Sage.

Craig, R. (2008). *Empowerment and social work research-participatory action research and the relationship between the extent of mental health consumers' involvement in research and its capacity to serve an empowering function.* (Order No. AAIMR41394), Masters Abstracts International, 0167. http://search.proquest.com/docview/61379833?accountid=14553

Creswell, J. W. (2013). *Qualitative inquiry & research design: Choosing among five approaches* (3rd ed.). Sage.

Creswell, J. W., & Clark, V. L. P. (2017). *Designing and conducting mixed methods research* (3rd ed.). Sage.

Creswell, J. W., & Poth, C. N. (2018). *Qualitative inquiry and research design: Choosing among five approaches* (4th ed.). Sage.

Denzin, N. K., & Lincoln, Y. S. (2000). Introduction: The discipline and practice of qualitative research. In N. K. Denzin & Y. S. Lincoln (Eds.), *Handbook of qualitative research* (2nd ed., pp. 1–28). Sage.

Emerson, R. M., Fretz, R. I., & Shaw, L. L. (2011). *Writing ethnographic fieldnotes* (2nd ed.). University of Chicago Press.

Fetterman, D. M., & Wandersman, A. (2005). *Empowerment evaluation principles and practice.* Guilford Press.

Garza, G. (2004). Thematic moment analysis: A didactic application of a procedure for phenomenological analysis of narrative data. *The Humanistic Psychologist, 32*(2), 120–168. doi:10.1080/08873267.2004.9961749

Glaser, B. G., & Strauss, A. (1967). *The discovery of grounded theory.* Aldine.

Guba, E. G., & Lincoln, Y. S. (1989). *Fourth generation evaluation.* Sage.

Guba, E. G., & Lincoln, Y. S. (1994). Competing paradigms in qualitative research. In N. K. Denzin & Y. S. Lincoln (Eds.), *Handbook of qualitative research* (pp. 105–117). Sage.

Hall, B. L. (1992). From margins to center? The development and purpose of participatory research. *The American Sociologist, 23*(4), 15–28. doi:10.1007/BF02691928

Hancock, N., Bundy, A., Tamsett, S., & McMahon, M. (2012). Participation of mental health consumers in research: Training addressed and reliability assessed. *Australian Occupational Therapy Journal, 59*(3), 218–224. doi:10.1111/j.1440-1630.2012.01011.x

Hill, C. E., Knox, S., Thompson, B. J., Williams, E. N., Hess, S. A., & Ladany, N. (2005). Consensual qualitative research: An update. *Journal of Counseling Psychology, 52*(2), 196–205. doi:10.1037/0022-0167.52.2.196

House, E. R., & Howe, K. R. (1998). *Deliberative democratic evaluation in practice.* University of Colorado.

Israel, B. A., Schulz, A. J., Parker, E. A., Becker, A. B., ., & Community-Campus Partnerships for Health. (2001). Community-based participatory research: Policy recommendations for promoting a partnership approach in health research. *Education for Health: Change in Learning & Practice, 14*(2), 182–197. doi:10.1080/13576280110051055

Johnson, R. B., & Onwuegbuzie, A. J. (2004). Mixed methods research: A research paradigm whose time has come. *Educational Researcher, 33*(7), 14–26. doi:10.3102/0013189X033007014

Kidd, S. A., & Kral, M. J. (2005). Practicing participatory action research. *Journal of Counseling Psychology, 52*(2), 187–195. doi:10.1037/0022-0167.52.2.187

Kruger, R. A., & Casey, M. (2015). *Focus groups: A practical guide for applied research* (5th ed.). Sage.

Lincoln, Y. S., & Guba, E. G. (1986). But is it rigorous? Trustworthiness and authenticity in naturalistic evaluation. *New Directions for Evaluation, 30,* 73–84. doi:10.1002/ev.1427

Linhorst, D. M., & Eckert, A. (2002). Involving people with severe mental illness in evaluation and performance improvement. *Evaluation & the Health Professions, 25*(3), 284–301. doi:10.1177/0163278702025003003

Madison, D. S. (2012). *Critical ethnography: Method, ethics, and performance* (2nd ed.). Sage.

Miles, M. B., & Huberman, A. M. (1984). *Qualitative data analysis: A sourcebook of new methods.* Sage.

Morrow, S. L. (2005). Quality and trustworthiness in qualitative research in counseling psychology. *Journal of Counseling Psychology, 52*(2), 250–260. doi:10.1037/0022-0167.52.2.250

Patton, M. Q. (2002). *Qualitative evaluation and research methods* (3rd ed.). Sage. doi:10.1136/bmj.319.7212.774

Patton, M. Q. (2015). *Qualitative research and methods: Integrating theory and practice.* Sage.

Ponterotto, J. G. (2005). Qualitative research in counseling psychology: A primer on research paradigms and philosophy of science. *Journal of Counseling Psychology, 52*(2), 126–136. doi:10.1037/0022-0167.52.2.126

Ponterotto, J. G. (2010). Qualitative research in multicultural psychology: Philosophical underpinnings, popular approaches, and ethical considerations. *Cultural Diversity and Ethnic Minority Psychology, 16*(4), 581–589. doi:10.1037/a0012051

Rist, R. C. (1977). On the relations among educational research paradigms: From disdain to detente. *Anthropology & Education Quarterly, 8*(2), 42–49. doi:10.1525/aeq.1977.8.2.05x1394p

Rossi, P. H., Lipsey, M. W., & Freeman, H. E. (2004). *Evaluation: A systematic approach* (7th ed.). Sage.

Schielke, H. J., Fishman, J. L., Osatuke, K., & Stiles, W. B. (2009). Creative consensus on interpretations of qualitative data: The ward method. *Journal of the Society for Psychotherapy Research, 19*(4-5), 558–565. doi:10.1080/10503300802621180

Shweder, R. A. (1999). Quanta and qualia: What is the "object" of ethnographic method? In R. Jessor, A. Colby, & R. A. Shweder (Eds.), *Ethnography and human development: Context and meaning in social inquiry* (pp. 175–182). University of Chicago Press.

Stake, R. (1995). *The art of case study research*. Sage.

Stake, R. (2006). *Multiple case study analysis*. Guilford.

Stufflebeam, D. (2001). Evaluation models. *New Directions for Evaluation, 2001*(89), 7–98. doi:10.1002/ev.3

Suzuki, L. A., Ahluwalia, M. K., Arora, A. K., & Mattis, J. S. (2007). The pond you fish in determines the fish you catch: Exploring strategies for qualitative data collection. *The Counseling Psychologist, 35*, 295–327. doi:10.1177/0011000006290983

Weiss, C. H. (1998). *Evaluation* (2nd ed.). Prentice Hall.

Yin, R. K. (2003). *Case study research: Design and method* (3rd ed.). Sage.

CHAPTER 11

NETWORK ANALYSIS IN EVALUATION RESEARCH

Jennifer Watling Neal and Zachary P. Neal

Learning Objectives

1. Become familiar with evaluation questions that can be addressed using network analysis.

2. Learn how to identify and measure the relevant network for an evaluation research effort.

3. Understand how a network could be studied to address evaluation questions of interest.

4. Understand how network analysis can be integrated with participatory approaches to evaluation.

Suppose a community coalition that focused on improving children's mental health and well-being has been struggling to coordinate the organizations that provide services and programs. As a result, the coalition has decided to adopt a new organizing strategy designed to facilitate coordination of services by increasing the frequency with which these organizations share information with and refer children to each other (e.g., Lawlor & Neal, 2016). However, they do not know if the new organizing strategy is working, and have decided to undertake an evaluation that will inform their decision whether to continue along this path. This scenario represents an ideal evaluation context for applying network analysis. First, the strategy to be evaluated is designed to transform a network, in this example, of mental health services coordination. Second, it is clear who is in the network: the coalition's organizational members. Third, it is clear what kinds of relationships among these organizations are relevant: information sharing and referrals. The match of network analysis and evaluation research may not always be so clear, so the purpose of this chapter is to explore when and how network analysis can be useful for evaluation. By the end of the chapter, readers should be able to determine whether network analysis could be a useful evaluation tool, and if so, what the relevant network is and how it could be studied.

Network analysis is an approach to research that involves theory and methods designed to characterize and explain patterns of relationships (e.g., friendships, referrals) between a set of actors (e.g., people, organizations) in a system (e.g., workplace, coalition; Kornbluh & Neal, 2015; Marin & Wellman, 2011; Neal & Christens, 2014; Neal & Neal, 2017; Wellman, 1988). Network analysts start by operationally defining the actors and relationships within a particular system. Next, they collect network data that assess the relationships between each pair of actors in the system. Finally, they analyze these network data, calculating metrics that characterize patterns of relationships across the whole system (i.e., network-level metrics), relationships between pairs of actors (i.e., dyad-level measures), and/or different actors' network positions (i.e., actor-level metrics).

Network analysis can be particularly powerful for answering evaluation questions that are relational in nature and can be applied to both process evaluations of program implementation and impact evaluations of program effectiveness. In process evaluations, network analysis is useful when evaluators and their community partners have questions about how relationships affect program adoption or implementation. For example, a network analysis is particularly fitting for understanding how advice-giving among teachers in a school affects their use of innovative teaching methods (see Neal et al., 2011). In outcome evaluations, network analysis is useful when evaluators and their community partners have questions about how a program affects participants' relationships. For instance, a network analysis could help elucidate whether early career teachers are more likely to exchange advice with colleagues after participating in a professional learning community in their schools (see Shernoff et al., 2016). Network analysis can also be easily integrated with participatory approaches to evaluation that involve community partners in the framing of questions, evaluation design, data collection, and analysis (Burke et al., 2015; Kornbluh & Neal, 2015; Provan et al., 2005). For example, network analysis can be useful for collaboratively answering school principals' questions about whether they have selected teacher leaders who are optimally positioned to influence their colleagues' use of new teaching practices (see Burke et al., 2015; Kornbluh & Neal, 2015).

In this chapter, we first provide conceptual guidance on how to define, measure, and analyze network data in evaluation research. Next, for both process and impact evaluations, we explore possible questions and measures that adopt the lens of network analysis. We also highlight how network analysis can be integrated with participatory approaches to evaluation. Finally, we end with a real-world example of the use of network analysis in a process evaluation of *Links to Learning*, an alternative model of mental health service delivery for urban elementary school children with disruptive behavior problems (Atkins et al., 2015; Cappella et al., 2008; Neal et al., 2011).

DESIGNING EVALUATION RESEARCH THAT USES NETWORK ANALYSIS

Because network analysis is fundamentally relational (i.e., Wellman, 1988), it requires research designs, data collection methods, and analytic techniques that are different from those applied in standard quantitative approaches like regression or ANOVA that are designed to measure relationships between a set of variables (e.g., Kornbluh & Neal, 2015; Marsden, 1990; Neal & Neal, 2017). Therefore, evaluators and their community partners interested in applying network analysis should familiarize themselves with standard approaches to defining, measuring, organizing, and analyzing network data.

Defining the Network

Evaluators and community partners who plan to use network analysis in their work must first define their network of interest by answering three key questions. First, who are the people or what are the organizations or groups that interact with one another (i.e., the *actors*) in the evaluation? Second, which actors are members of the setting involved in the evaluation (i.e., *the system*) and should be included? Third, what are the theoretically or practically important types of interactions (i.e., the *relationships*) that should be measured between these actors in the evaluation?

Who or what are the actors? Network analysis aims to measure patterns of interactions among actors in a setting or system, but actors can be defined in different ways. In some cases, the actors may be people, while in other cases they may be whole organizations or other types of groups. When the actors are people, the method is often called *social* network analysis; however, because the actors in evaluation research are not always people, in this chapter we use the more inclusive term "network analysis." The first step in a network analysis involves determining who or what the relevant actors are, and at what level they should be measured. Butts (2009) offers some useful guidance, suggesting that actors "should be defined so as to include all distinct entities that are capable of participating in the relationship under study" (p. 414). Consider the case of examining patterns of communication among teachers in a school. It is possible to define "the first-grade teachers" as an actor, "the second-grade teachers" as an actor, and so on, thus constructing a network that captures, for example, whether the first-grade teachers communicate with the second-grade teachers. However, such an approach might hide a lot of detail because it treats all the first-grade teachers as a single actor. In this case, because each individual teacher is a distinct entity capable of participating in communication, it is better to define individual teachers as actors. Doing so makes it possible to construct a network that captures whether any particular teacher communicates with any other teacher, from which analysis could test whether first-grade teachers communicate with second-grade teachers. As a rule of thumb, care should be taken to define actors in the narrowest way possible and to avoid aggregating actors into groups.

Which actors? Once the relevant kind of actor has been identified, it is important to determine which specific actors are part of the network, which is sometimes called the boundary specification problem (adams, 2019; Laumann et al., 1983). Whole network analysis aims to measure and analyze all the relationships among all the actors within a given system, thereby capturing the whole system's structure.[1] Thus, whole network analysis requires having clearly defined system boundaries within which all actors can be identified. In some cases, systems have readily observable natural boundaries. For example, a school has clearly defined boundaries that include students, teachers, and staff at the school. Accordingly, the measurement of a whole network for the purposes of evaluating a school-based program might focus data collection on the relationships among students, teachers, and staff, but ignore any relationships they might have with others outside the school. In other cases, systems do not have natural boundaries, but the relevant sets of actors can still be identified. For example, the policy-making community is an amorphous set of people and organizations with fluid boundaries. However, measurement of a whole network for evaluating a specific policy may rely on concrete inclusion rules (e.g., people who have attended meetings about the policy) to draw an artificial boundary and identify

---

[1] We focus here on *whole network* analysis, which can be contrasted with *ego network* analysis. Ego network aims to examine the personal social network of a single individual or of a sample of individuals, but does not necessarily capture how those individuals are linked to one another. The types of analyses that can be conducted using ego networks are more limited, and their usefulness in an evaluation context is likely to be restricted to evaluating programs designed to impact individuals' personal social networks. For more information on ego networks, please see Marsden (2011) or Wellman (2007).

the most relevant actors. In still other cases, the system may simply be too large or ambiguous to practically define a boundary and identify all its actors (e.g., a city or town). In these cases, whole network analysis is generally not possible.

Which relationships? After identifying all the actors within the system, evaluators and/or community partners must determine which relationships among them are relevant. Relationships among the actors, and not the actors themselves, are the key building blocks of a network because they give the network its structure. Each type of relationship that is measured defines a separate network. For example, in a single school setting, it is possible to measure one network that captures "Who talks to whom?" (i.e., a communication relationship), and another network that captures "Who is friends with whom?" (i.e., a friendship relationship). Although these two networks involve the same actors, because they involve different types of relationships, they may or may not be the same.

In addition to identifying the relevant type of relationship, it is important to determine whether the relationship's directionality is relevant: Is "A communicates with B" different from "B communicates with A"? Likewise, it is important to determine whether a relationship's intensity is relevant: Is "A communicates with B frequently" different from "A communicates with B occasionally"? Each of these decisions, which should be guided by both theory and the purpose of the evaluation delineated by the evaluators and/or community partners, serves to shape the structure of the network and the techniques used for measuring and analyzing it.

Measuring and Analyzing the Network

Measuring the network. After determining which actors and relationships define the network, collection of whole network data is relatively straightforward. Data collection typically occurs by asking each actor in the system a name generator question of the form "With whom do you [relationship of interest]?" For example, to collect information for assessing a communication network among teachers in a school, one would ask every teacher, "With which other teachers in your school do you communicate?" It is important that actors be permitted to provide as many names in response to a name generator question as they wish; evaluators should avoid limiting the number of responses (Holland & Leinhardt, 1973; Kossinets, 2006; Neal, 2020). In cases in which there is concern that the actors will provide too many names, the name generator question can be narrowed, for example, "With which other teachers in your school did you talk about classroom behavior management last week?" In smaller systems, actors might be provided a roster of all other actors and asked to choose their responses from the list, while in larger systems for which a complete roster would be impractical, an open-ended free-response format is more useful.

Although direct data collection via name generator questions is common, network data can also be obtained from archival sources (Marsden, 1990). This can be a useful approach when the actors are not people, when the actors may have limited interest or time to participate in data collection, or when the system is too large for direct data collection to be feasible. Using archival sources requires that the relationship of interest be recorded in a document or other archival record. For example, it might be possible to construct a communication network from detailed meeting minutes or from records of sent and received e-mails. Similarly, it might be possible to construct an exchange network from records on patient referrals or accounting ledgers.

Figure 11.1   Example Network

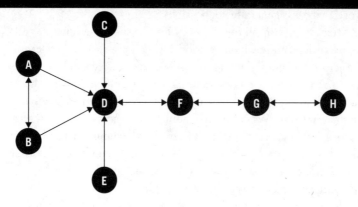

Whether whole network data are collected directly or indirectly, minimizing missing data is essential because many network analysis techniques have much lower tolerance for missingness than other data analytic techniques like regression (Kossinets, 2006). Although the amount of permissible missing data depends on the specific analysis employed, missing more than about 10% of the system's actors can sometimes have quite severe implications.[2] This lower tolerance for missingness is the primary challenge in network data collection. Evaluators and community partners seeking to use network analysis should bear this in mind and develop strategies to obtain complete data, for example, by using participation incentives and following up with non-respondents. In addition, some specialized data collection techniques have been developed to overcome the challenge of collecting complete data. For example, the cognitive social structures technique triangulates the structure of the whole network from multiple reporters (see Neal, 2008, for more), while the bipartite projection technique infers the structure of the whole network from actors' co-membership in groups (see Neal, 2014, for more). In addition, to ensure transparency and the quality of network data used in analyses, evaluators should report response rates for each of their networks (Neal, 2020).

Analyzing the network. Analysis of network data is possible at multiple levels (Kornbluh & Neal, 2015; Marin & Wellman, 2011). At the highest level, the structure of the network as a whole can be described by metrics like its *density* (i.e., how many relationships are present), *reciprocity* (i.e., if A → B, how often does B → A), and *transitivity* (i.e., if A → B and B → C, how often does A → C). For example, the simple network shown in Figure 11.1 has a moderate level of reciprocity because, of the actors that have a relationship, only half of these relationships are reciprocal (AB, DF, FG, and GH). Analysis at the network level can be useful for examining broad patterns of change in a system over time, for example, to evaluate whether a program intended to build relationships was effective. At a lower level, it is possible to explore how two actors are positioned with respect to one another in the network. For example, *geodesic distance* examines how far apart two actors are in the network. In the example network in Figure 11.1, A and B are quite close (geodesic distance of 1), while D and H are further away (geodesic

---

[2] A measure like degree centrality can tolerate higher levels of missingness, while a measure like betweenness centrality can be severely biased if even a single relationship is missing from the network.

distance of 3). *Structural similarity* examines how similar two actors are in terms of their network roles and, specifically, the extent to which they have the same pattern of relationships. In the example, A and B are very similar because their relationship patterns are identical: They have relationships with each other, and they each send to (but do not receive from) D. Analysis at the dyad level can be useful for thinking about how actors might affect one another. Finally, at the lowest level, metrics that characterize the position of individual actors can be examined. Here, the focus is often on actors' *centrality* or the extent to which they occupy an important position in the network. There are many different conceptions of what constitutes an important position, and thus many different measures of centrality, which make selecting the correct measure particularly important (Borgatti & Everett, 2006). For example, degree centrality views actors as important when they have relationships with many other actors, while betweenness centrality views actors as important when they are positioned between two otherwise disconnected other actors. In the example, D has a high degree centrality because it maintains relationships with many other actors, while F has a high betweenness centrality because it is the critical link between the actors on the left (A–E) and the actors on the right (G and H). Analysis at the actor level can be useful for identifying key individuals in a system, for example, to inform the selection of leaders to assist in promoting the use of a program.

While descriptive metrics at the network level, dyad level, or actor level can be helpful for characterizing the structure of a network and the position of actors within it, it is often necessary to use these metrics as variables in a statistical model. For example, an evaluation team and their school-based partners might want to know whether a teacher's centrality in a school advice network is associated with their frequency of use of a new teaching method or whether a new curriculum is more likely to be implemented when teachers are part of a dense network. Although the form of statistical models used for examining network statistics often resembles conventional statistical models (e.g., regression), methods for testing statistical significance do not. The relational nature of network data violates key assumptions of conventional statistical significance testing, most notably the assumption that observations are independent (Wellman, 1988). As a result, ordinary standard errors and p-values are invalid, and alternative tests of statistical significance that require fewer assumptions are necessary. Tests that are appropriate for network data are built into most network analysis software packages (see suggested resources at the end of this chapter), as well as many ordinary statistical analysis software packages.

NETWORK ANALYSIS IN EVALUATION

Network analysis can be usefully applied in the field of program evaluation (Durland & Fredericks, 2005). However, before embarking on a network analysis, evaluators and community partners should reflect on whether they have evaluation questions that focus on the pattern of relationships between actors and, therefore, that can be investigated using network analysis. These evaluation questions can be designed to assess how a program works (i.e., process evaluation; Dehar et al., 1993) or the extent to which a program works (i.e., impact evaluation; Khander et al., 2010). In addition, network analysis can be flexibly applied to evaluations with varying degrees of collaborative and participatory elements.

Process Evaluation and Network Analysis

Process evaluations provide information on how a program works, typically with the goal of understanding "how a program achieves what it does" (Dehar et al., 1993, p. 217; see Chapters 1 and 6 for more regarding process evaluation). While process evaluations can be used solely for explanatory purposes, they are also sometimes used for formative purposes to improve programs. Often process evaluations focus on aspects of program implementation including reach, dosage, contextual factors that influence program use, or fidelity. There are many process evaluation questions that are not relational in nature and do not require network analysis. For instance, an evaluator might be interested in understanding dosage by asking: *How often do participants attend program meetings?* The frequency of attendance of each participant at program meetings can be collected independently without relational information from any other participants, and thus this question can be answered without network analysis. In contrast, certain types of process evaluation questions are relational in nature and might benefit from a network analytic approach. For example, evaluators and/or community partners might be interested in asking: *Are participants more likely to attend program meetings if their friends also attend these meetings?* Answering this question involves collecting relational data on participants' friendships as well as friends' program meeting attendance. Some other examples of network-based process evaluation questions are provided below:

- To what extent does two-way communication occur between program providers during implementation (e.g., Burke et al., 2015)?

- How does the use of practices introduced in an intervention diffuse via participants' advice relationships (e.g., Neal et al., 2011), friendships (e.g., Long et al., 2014), or online communications (e.g., Kornbluh et al., 2016)?

- Who are the people and organizations that occupy important social positions that can influence others to use a program (e.g., Kornbluh & Neal, 2015; Provan et al., 2005)?

Each of these questions has the potential to offer insight into the role that relationships (i.e., two-way communication, advice, influence) play in how a particular program works. Understanding the extent of two-way communication in a network can help evaluators and their community partners identify the extent to which information about the program or practice can be disseminated to potential users. To measure the extent of two-way communication among program providers, a network-level measure like reciprocity would be useful (e.g., Burke et al., 2015). Exploring how a program diffuses among users can help evaluators and their community partners determine whether social networks in a setting facilitate or constrain its adoption and maintenance. To measure the diffusion of intervention practices, dyad-level measures like the presence or absence of a relationship, geodesic distance, or structural similarity are helpful (e.g., Neal, Neal, Atkins et al., 2011; Kornbluh et al., 2016; Long et al., 2014). Finally, identifying the influential people or organizations in a network can help evaluators and their community partners determine key partners that can help facilitate the dissemination and implementation of the program. To measure influential people and organizations that might influence program use, actor-level centrality measures are often employed (e.g., Kornbluh & Neal, 2015; Provan et al., 2005).

Impact Evaluation and Network Analysis

Impact evaluation provides information about the extent to which a program works (i.e., has an impact), typically with the goal of making an evaluative judgment about the program (Khander et al., 2010; see Chapters 1 and 6 for more regarding impact evaluation). The majority of impact evaluation questions do not require network analysis. For instance, an evaluator might be interested in asking: *Does a new phonics program improve students' reading scores?* Here, the outcome of interest—students' reading scores—can be collected from each program participant independently, without relational information from any other participants, and thus this question can be answered without network analysis. Network analysis is only relevant to impact evaluation in cases in which the evaluated program is expected to have an impact on the network or some feature of the network. For example, an evaluator might be interested in asking: *Does a new social skills program lead to classrooms with more friendships between students?* Here, the outcome of interest—classroom friendships—involves collecting relational data that enumerate who is friends with whom in the classroom. Some additional examples of impact evaluation questions that might benefit from network analysis are provided below:

- Does a coalition lead to increased organizational collaboration (e.g., Bess, 2015)?

- Does a new referral system increase the efficiency by which patients can link to appropriate providers (Bodenheimer, 2008)?

- Do participants in a leadership program form more advice-giving relationships in their workplace over time (McDade, 1994)?

Each of these questions focuses on a relational outcome (i.e., collaboration, referrals, advice-giving) and offers insight about the extent to which a particular program works. To assess whether a coalition leads to increased organizational collaboration, a network-level measure like density could be employed over the course of the initiative (e.g., Bess, 2015). Because density measures how many collaborative relationships are present across the coalition, it would provide evaluators and their community partners with information about whether organizations in the coalition become more connected (i.e., increase collaboration) over time. To assess whether a new referral system increases efficiency, evaluators and their community partners could assess dyad-level geodesic distance between patients and their providers over time. Because geodesic distance measures the number of steps between two actors in a network, if the system is working, patients should be able to link to the appropriate provider in fewer referral steps. To examine whether participants in a leadership program form more advice-giving relationships in their workplace, actor-level degree centrality is an appropriate measure. Because actor-level degree centrality measures an actor's number of relationships, it is an ideal way of assessing whether participants in the leadership program increased their advice-giving relationships.

Participatory or Partnership-Oriented Approaches to Evaluation and Network Analysis

Both process and impact evaluations can differ in the extent to which they employ participatory or partner-oriented approaches. Three dimensions of participatory evaluation identified by Cousins and Whitmore (1998) include partner selection (who participates?), depth of participation (i.e., the extent to which they participate), and control of the evaluation process (i.e., who makes the decisions?). Network analysis can be readily employed in process and impact evaluations that vary along each of these dimensions. However, when evaluators and their community partners adopt participatory or partner-oriented approaches, some special considerations are warranted.

Who participates? The selection of key community partners is an important consideration for participatory or partner-oriented approaches to evaluation (e.g., Cousins & Whitmore, 1998; Weaver & Cousins, 2007). In particular, it is important to consider whether partners represent the community of interest and have the influence and power to act on the results of the evaluation. Network analysis can shed light on both of these considerations and can therefore be a powerful strategy for identifying potential partners for participatory and partner-oriented evaluations. First, because network analysis assesses the relationships between all actors in a setting, it provides a map of all the different subgroups or cliques that exist within that setting (Fortunato, 2010). For participatory or partner-oriented evaluations, it may be helpful to ensure that partners are drawn from each of these subgroups. Second, network analyses can be useful for determining who has power (e.g., Neal & Neal, 2011) or influence (e.g., Neal et al., 2008; Valente & Pumpuang, 2007). These methods can be used to determine who the opinion leaders are in a setting that might be important to have on board as evaluation partners.

To what extent do they participate? Participatory or partner-oriented evaluations can involve community partners narrowly at only one or two stages of the evaluation (e.g., interpretation of results) or more extensively throughout the process of the entire evaluation (e.g., from framing the evaluation questions to disseminating the results; Cousins & Whitmore, 1998). When employing network analysis in participatory or partner-oriented evaluations, it is important to consider how and when community partners are involved and to take extra steps to ensure meaningful collaboration. For example, if community partners are involved in framing evaluation questions, evaluators may need to facilitate conversations about whether their interests focus on understanding individual actor attributes (e.g., teachers' level of experience) or relationships between these actors (e.g., teacher advice-giving). If the latter, evaluators would need to work with community partners to consider and select relevant network methods and analyses that match these partners' evaluation questions. Finally, evaluators should also provide community partners with information about logistical considerations and the feasibility of network data collection and analysis in the evaluation setting.

Who makes the decisions? Participatory or partner-oriented evaluations can also differ in the degree of decision-making control wielded by the evaluator or the community partners (Cousins & Whitmore, 1998). Providing training in network analysis to community partners can build their capacity to lead evaluation studies that involve the collection and analysis of network data.

CASE EXAMPLE: USING NETWORK ANALYSIS IN A PROCESS EVALUATION OF *LINKS TO LEARNING*

Network analysis offers promise for addressing relational process and impact evaluation questions and can be applied in participatory approaches to evaluation. However, for evaluators and community partners who are new to network analysis, it can be helpful to review some concrete real-world examples before conceptualizing and designing a network-based evaluation. In this section, we use a process evaluation of *Links to Learning*, an alternative model of mental health service delivery for urban elementary school children with disruptive behavior problems, to illustrate the major steps of network analysis and its application to program evaluation (see Neal et al., 2011). In this example, the *Links to Learning* evaluation team took the lead in defining, measuring, and analyzing the networks. However, it is important to note that an evaluation team and their community partners can also take these steps collaboratively.

Links to Learning and the Evaluation Question

Links to Learning leverages natural settings, including schools and homes, to provide mental health services to urban children living in poverty (Atkins & Lakind, 2013; Atkins et al., 2015; Cappella et al., 2008). In particular, the model includes a school-based component that involves consultation with kindergarten through fourth-grade teachers to encourage the use of both universal and targeted evidence-based practices focused on instruction, classroom management, and family outreach. For example, peer-assisted learning is a universal evidence-based instructional practice employed in *Links to Learning* in which teachers paired students with strong reading skills with students with weaker reading skills (e.g., Fuchs & Fuchs, 2005; Ginsburg-Block et al., 2006). These pairs of students then engaged in reading activities together, receiving small rewards for their participation. In addition, the daily report card is a targeted evidence-based practice employed in *Links to Learning* to encourage family outreach (Kelley, 1990). Using this approach, teachers and parents jointly identified academic and behavioral goals for

students, and teachers communicated student progress about these goals to parents on a daily basis.

Although *Links to Learning* involved school staff and mental health providers as partners in the intervention implementation, an evaluation team of researchers was primarily responsible for assessing its process and impact. As part of the evaluation of this school-based component of *Links to Learning*, members of this evaluation team were interested in answering the following question: How do participating teachers' existing advice networks influence their frequency of use of peer-assisted learning and the daily report card in their classrooms (Neal et al., 2011)? Based on existing theories of diffusion (e.g., Burt, 1987, 1999; Coleman et al., 1957), the evaluation team hypothesized two potential network mechanisms that might increase teachers' use of peer-assisted learning and the daily report card (Neal et al., 2011). First, the use of these practices may spread through direct contact with colleagues (i.e., a *cohesion* mechanism; Coleman et al., 1957). Second, the use of these practices may spread via colleagues who share similar network roles (i.e., *a structural similarity* mechanism; Burt, 1987; Burt, 1999). Exploring these mechanisms through a process evaluation provided insight into how existing teacher relationships in *Links to Learning* schools influenced their implementation of program practices (Neal et al., 2011). This was particularly important to the *Links to Learning* evaluation team, who were committed to finding effective strategies to facilitate the implementation of the program among participating teachers.

Defining the Networks in *Links to Learning*

Which actors? The evaluation was conducted in three public elementary schools participating in the first year of *Links to Learning* (Neal et al., 2011). Although the intervention only targeted kindergarten through fourth-grade teachers, the evaluation team decided to collect network data from all classroom teachers (prekindergarten through eighth grade) and ancillary teachers (e.g., art, physical education) in each of the three schools

Continued

($N = 28$, $N = 31$, $N = 28$). This expanded boundary was warranted because the kindergarten through fourth-grade teachers targeted by *Links to Learning* were likely to have relationships with teachers who were not targeted by the intervention. Therefore, assessing all classroom and ancillary teachers was important for accurate analysis of certain network features.

Which relationships? Because past research suggested the importance of advice networks for encouraging teachers' use of evidence-based practices targeting student mental health (e.g., Atkins et al., 2008), the evaluation team chose to focus on teacher advice networks (Neal et al., 2011). In particular, they measured different types of advice relationships among teachers including advice around family involvement and advice around instruction. Measurement of each type of advice relationship yielded a distinct directed advice network. To understand how participating teachers' existing advice networks influence their frequency of use of *Links to Learning* practices, the evaluation team decided to match the content of advice networks to the content of peer-assisted learning and the daily report card (Neal et al., 2011). Specifically, they examined the role of teachers' instructional advice networks in influencing the use of peer-assisted learning, which focused primarily on improving students' reading. In contrast, they examined the role of teachers' family involvement networks in influencing the use of the daily report card, which focused primarily on teacher–parent communication.

Measuring and Analyzing the Networks in *Links to Learning*

Measuring the networks. Prior to the introduction of peer-assisted learning and the daily report card to kindergarten through fourth-grade teachers, the evaluation team conducted 10- to 15-minute face-to-face interviews with all classroom and ancillary teachers in each of the three *Links to Learning* schools. These interviews included the following name generators that were relevant to addressing the aims of the evaluation:

- Please name the teachers in your school from whom you might seek advice <u>around instructional methods</u>.

- Please name the teachers in your school from whom you might seek advice <u>around involving families</u>.

The interviews used an open-ended, free-response format, and teachers were able to name as many or as few individuals as they chose for each name generator. Because the evaluation team was able to collect network data from all teachers and ancillary teachers in each school, there was no missing data.

Analyzing the networks. To examine whether cohesion or structural similarity mechanisms increased *Links to Learning* teachers' use of peer-assisted learning and the daily report card, the evaluation team used two dyad-level metrics to create different sets of potentially influential colleagues for each teacher in their sample (Neal et al., 2011). First, to measure cohesion, they used network analysis to determine, for each teacher, the set of colleagues that provided direct advice to them. Second, to measure structural similarity, they used network analysis to determine, for each teacher, a set of three colleagues whose position in the network was most similar to them. Next, for both peer-assisted learning and the daily report card, the evaluation team used lagged fixed effects regression models to determine whether the average frequency of use by teachers' cohesion set of colleagues and the average frequency of use by teachers' structurally similar set of colleagues predicted their own frequency of use (Neal et al., 2011). Findings demonstrated that only the average frequency of use by teachers' structurally similar set of colleagues predicted teachers' own use of *Links to Learning* intervention strategies. These results suggested that *Links to Learning* teachers' use of intervention strategies spread through colleagues who shared similar network roles rather than colleagues who provided direct advice. This finding mirrored findings in other settings with very different populations, including doctors (Burt, 1987) and lobbyists (Heinz et al., 1993; see Neal et al., 2011). The process evaluation findings described here are important because they have implications for natural change agents in schools who might be able to encourage the uptake and use of the *Links to Learning* intervention strategies. In particular, these findings can be used to inform future strategies for selecting teacher opinion leaders to support the implementation of *Links to Learning*. As the evaluation team concluded, it might be important to select some "key opinion leaders based on their patterns of connections to others" (i.e., structural similarity) to encourage the use of *Links to Learning* strategies (Neal et al., 2011, p. 284).

Lessons Learned From the *Links to Learning* Process Evaluation

The *Links to Learning* process evaluation offers three generalizable lessons that can be employed when considering the use of network analysis in evaluation research. Each of these generalizable lessons is identified and described in detail below.

Lesson 1: When bounding the network, it may be necessary to include actors beyond those implementing or receiving an evaluated program or practice. Evaluators and their community partners should carefully consider the "Boundary Specification Problem" in light of their proposed evaluation questions and network measures when determining who should count as an actor in their network data collection and analysis. The *Links to Learning* process evaluation focused on how networks influenced the implementation of practices by kindergarten through fourth-grade teachers targeted by the intervention. However, because kindergarten through fourth-grade teachers could give advice to or receive advice from anyone in their school, the evaluation team made the decision to bound the network more broadly around all classroom and ancillary teachers regardless of whether they were targeted by the *Links to Learning* intervention. In Figure 11.2, network sociograms depicting the teacher networks for advice around instructional methods and advice around involving families are presented for one *Links to Learning* school. In these sociograms, black circles represent kindergarten through fourth-grade teachers targeted by the *Links to Learning* intervention, and white circles represent all other teachers. Arrows indicate advice relationships and point from advice giver to advice receiver. Although the kindergarten through fourth-grade teachers targeted by the intervention tended to give advice to and receive advice from each other, they also clearly gave advice to and received advice from other teachers who were not targeted by the intervention. This confirms the importance of the evaluation team's decision to set a more expansive boundary for networks that included all teachers in the school rather than only teachers targeted by *Links to Learning*. Specifically, if the network were bounded more tightly around only the teachers targeted by *Links to Learning*, the evaluation team would have missed substantial parts of the network structure. This could lead to an inaccurate assessment of the network and, in particular, of structural similarity, a key concept in their evaluation, and could potentially result in misleading conclusions about the program.

Lesson 2: Pick network relationships that are relevant to the evaluated program or practice. Evaluators and their community partners should carefully consider how the network relationships that they plan to assess match the evaluated program or practice. In the *Links to Learning* process evaluation, the evaluation team matched the content of the network relationships to the content of particular *Links to Learning* practices (Neal et al.,

2011). Because peer-assisted learning focused on reading instruction, they assessed the diffusion of this practice through teachers' advice networks about instructional methods. Likewise, because the daily report card focused on teacher–parent communication, they assessed the diffusion of this practice through teachers' advice networks about involving families. The sociograms in Figure 11.2 suggest that, among the same set of teachers, advice networks about instructional methods and advice networks about involving families can be quite distinct. For example, the sociogram depicting advice around instructional methods is more densely connected and has fewer peripheral teachers than the sociogram depicting advice around involving families (Instructional Methods Density = 0.30; Involving Families Density = 0.17). Although harder to see in the visualization, the evaluation team discovered only modest overlap between these different types of networks in *Links to Learning* schools. Specifically, depending on the school, only 28%–36% of the relationships present in teachers' instructional advice networks were also present in teachers' family involvement advice networks (Neal et al., 2011). This suggests that teachers often gave advice to and received advice from different people depending on the advice content, justifying the decision to match the content of advice networks to the content of particular *Links to Learning* practices.

Lesson 3: Choose network analyses that map onto the evaluation question. Evaluators and their community partners should theoretically justify how their network analyses are fitting for their particular evaluation question. Specifically, before selecting a particular network-level, dyad-level, or actor-level metric, evaluators and/or community partners should ask themselves, "Why am I choosing this particular metric?" (Neal & Neal, 2017). In the *Links to Learning* process evaluation (Neal et al., 2011), the evaluation team articulated a clear evaluation question (i.e., How do participating teachers' existing advice networks

Figure 11.2 **Network Sociograms for Teachers in One** *Links to Learning* **School. Black Circles Represent Kindergarten Through Fourth-Grade Teachers Targeted by the Intervention and White Circles Represent All Other Teachers in the School. Arrows Point From Advice Givers to Advice Receivers**

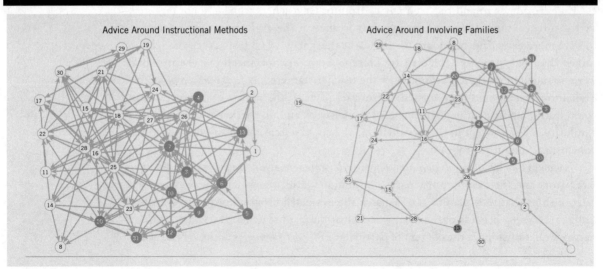

influence their frequency of use of peer-assisted learning and the daily report card in their classrooms?). They used preexisting theory to identify two contrasting network mechanisms that might predict teachers' use of peer-assisted learning and the daily report card: cohesion (i.e., diffusion through direct contact with colleagues) and structural similarity (i.e., diffusion through colleagues who share similar positions in the network; Burt, 1987, 1999; Coleman et al., 1957). Moreover, they selected specific dyad-level network analyses that mapped onto each of these two network mechanisms, thus tailoring their network metrics to their specific evaluation question and theorized mechanisms.

CONCLUSION

To conclude, network analysis has exciting potential for both process and impact evaluations focused on relational phenomena and can be applied in participatory approaches to evaluation. However, this paradigmatic approach requires research designs, data collection methods, and analytic techniques that differ from other non-relational approaches to evaluation. Evaluators and their community partners must think critically about who should be included as actors in the network, what relationships should be measured, and what network analyses should be conducted to address their evaluation questions. By doing so, they stand to gain new understanding of the relational factors that describe how or if a program or practice works.

FURTHER READING

Broad Book-Length Introductions
adams, j. (2019). *Gathering social network data*. Sage.

Borgatti, S. P., Everett, M. G., & Johnson, J. C. (2013). *Analyzing social networks*. Sage.

Neal, Z. P. (2013). *The connected city: How networks are shaping the modern metropolis*. Routledge.

Prell, C. (2012). *Social network analysis: History, theory, and methodology*. Sage.

Article/Chapter-Length Introductions
Kornbluh, M., & Neal, J. W. (2015). Social network analysis. In L. A. Jason & D. S. Glenwick (Eds.), *Handbook of methodological approaches to community-based research* (pp. 207–218). Oxford University Press.

Marin, A., & Wellman, B. (2011). Social network analysis: An introduction. In J. Scott & P. J. Carrington (Eds.), *The SAGE handbook of social network analysis* (pp. 11–25). Sage.

Marsden, P. (2011). Survey methods for network data. In J. Scott & P. J. Carrington (Eds.), *The SAGE handbook of social network analysis* (pp. 370–388). Sage.

Neal, Z. P., & Neal, J. W. (2017). Network analysis in community psychology: Looking back, looking forward. *American Journal of Community Psychology, 60*, 279–295. doi:10.1002/ajcp.12158

Software
R Igraph—https://igraph.org/

R Statnet—http://statnet.org/

RSiena—https://www.stats.ox.ac.uk/~snijders/siena/

UCINET—https://sites.google.com/site/ucinetsoftware/home

VISONE—http://www.visone.info/

KEY CONCEPTS

Actor(s): The people, organizations, or groups that interact with one another within a network.

Centrality: The extent to which a particular actor occupies an important position in the network. Actor-level metrics of centrality may vary and include, for example, degree centrality (i.e., actors are important when they have relationships with many other actors) and betweenness centrality (i.e., actors are important when they are positioned between two otherwise disconnected other actors).

Density: A metric in network analysis that describes the structure of the network as a whole. Density indicates how many relationships are present out of the possible total number of relationships in the network.

Name generator: A type of question used to collect data about the relationships in a network. These questions typically take the form "With whom do you [relationship of interest]?"

Network: A pattern of relationships (e.g., friendships, referrals) between a set of actors (e.g., people, organizations) in a system (e.g., workplace, coalition).

Relationship: The interaction between actors measured in the network (e.g., communication, advice, friendship). Relationships are the key building blocks of a network because they give the network its structure.

Structural similarity: A dyad-level metric in network analysis, indicating how similar two actors are in terms of their network roles and, specifically, the extent to which they have the same pattern of relationships.

Transitivity: A metric in network analysis that describes the structure of the network as a whole. Transitivity indicates the extent to which, if there is a relation between Actors A and B, and between Actors B and C, then there is also a relationship between Actors A and C (i.e., if A $\rightarrow$ B and B $\rightarrow$ C, how often does A $\rightarrow$ C).

QUESTIONS FOR REFLECTION

1. Consider the *Links to Learning* case example presented in this chapter. How did the evaluators define the network? What implications did their boundary specification have for their network analysis? How might their findings have changed if they had defined the network differently?

2. In the *Links to Learning* case example, what types of relationships did the evaluators measure? How did they decide which relationships to focus on and what implications does this have for their evaluation findings?

3. In the *Links to Learning* case example, what were the evaluation questions? How did the evaluators choose network metrics to map onto these evaluation questions?

4. Consider how you might conduct a network analysis in your own evaluation work. What process and impact evaluation questions do you have that might benefit from applying network analysis? How would you define the actors and relationships in your network? What types of network metrics would be necessary to answer your question?

REFERENCES

adams, j. (2019). *Gathering social network data*. Sage.

Atkins, M. S., Frazier, S. L., Leathers, S. J., Graczyk, P. A., Talbott, E., Jakobsons, L., Adil, J. A., Marinez-Lora, A., Demirtas, H., Gibbons, R. B., & Bell, C. C. (2008). Teacher key opinion leaders and mental health consultation in low-income urban schools. *Journal of Consulting and Clinical Psychology, 76*(5), 905–908. doi:10.1037/a0013036

Atkins, M. S., & Lakind, D. (2013). Usual care for clinicians, unusual care for their clients: Rearranging priorities for children's mental health services. *Administration and Policy in Mental Health and Mental Health Services Research, 40*(1), 48–51. doi:10.1007/s10488-012-0453-5

Atkins, M. S., Shernoff, E. S., Frazier, S. L., Schoenwald, S. K., Cappella, E., Maríñez-Lora, A., Mehta, T. G., Lakind, D., Cua, G., Bhaumik, R., & Bhaumik, D. (2015). Redesigning community mental health services for urban children: Supporting schooling to promote mental health. *Journal of Consulting and Clinical Psychology, 83*(5), 839–852. doi:10.1037/a0039661

Bess, K. D. (2015). Reframing coalitions as systems interventions: A network study exploring the contribution of a youth violence prevention coalition to broader system capacity. *American Journal of Community Psychology, 55*(3-4), 381–395. doi:10.1007/s10464-015-9715-1

Bodenheimer, T. (2008). Coordinating care—A perilous journey through the health care system. *New England Journal of Medicine, 358*(10), 1064–1071. doi:10.1056/NEJMhpr0706165

Borgatti, S. P., & Everett, M. G. (2006). A graph-theoretic perspective on centrality. *Social Networks, 28*(4), 466–484. doi:10.1016/j.socnet.2005.11.005

Borgatti, S. P., Everett, M. G., & Johnson, J. C. (2013). *Analyzing social networks*. Sage.

Burke, J. G., Lich, K. H., Neal, J. W., Meissner, H. I., Yonas, M., & Mabry, P. L. (2015). Enhancing dissemination and implementation research using systems science methods. *International Journal of Behavioral Medicine, 22*(3), 283–291. doi:10.1007/s12529-014-9417-3

Burt, R. S. (1987). Social contagion and innovation: Cohesion versus structural equivalence. *American Journal of Sociology, 92*(6), 1287–1335. doi:10.1086/228667

Burt, R. S. (1999). The social capital of opinion leaders. *The Annals of the American Academy of Political and Social Science, 566*(1), 37–54. doi:10.1177/000271629956600104

Butts, C. T. (2009). Revisiting the foundations of network analysis. *Science, 325*(5939), 414–416. doi:10.1126/science.1171022

Cappella, E., Frazier, S. L., Atkins, M. S., Schoenwald, S. K., & Glisson, C. (2008). Enhancing schools' capacity to support children in poverty: An ecological model of school-based mental health services. *Administration and Policy in Mental Health and Mental Health Services Research, 35*(5), 395–409. doi:10.1007/s10488-008-0182-y

Coleman, J., Katz, E., & Menzel, H. (1957). The diffusion of an innovation among physicians. *Sociometry, 20*(4), 253–270. doi:10.2307/2785979

Cousins, J. B., & Whitmore, E. (1998). Framing participatory evaluation. *New Directions for Evaluation, 80*, 5–23. doi:10.1002/ev.1114

Dehar, M-A., Casswell, S., & Duignan, P. (1993). Formative and process evaluation of health promotion and disease prevention programs. *Evaluation Review, 17*(2), 204–220. doi:10.1177/0193 841X9301700205

Durland, M. M., & Fredericks, K. A. (2005). An introduction to social network analysis. *New Directions for Evaluation, 107*, 5–13. doi:10.1002/ev.157

Fortunato, S. (2010). Community detection in graphs. *Physics Reports, 486*(3-5), 75–174. doi:10.1016/j.physrep.2009.11.002

Fuchs, D., & Fuchs, L. S. (2005). Peer-assisted learning strategies: Promoting word recognition, fluency, and reading comprehension in young children. *The Journal of Special Education, 39*, 34–44.

Ginsburg-Block, M. D., Rohrbeck, C. A., & Fantuzzo, J. W. (2006). A meta-analytic review of social, self-concept, and behavioral outcomes of peer-assisted learning. *Journal of Educational Psychology, 98*(4), 732–749. doi:10.1037/0022-0663.98.4.732

Heinz, J. P., Laumann, E. O., Nelson, R. L., & Salisbury, R. H. (1993). *The hollow core*. Harvard University Press.

Holland, P. W., & Leinhardt, S. (1973). The structural implications of measurement error in sociometry. *The Journal of Mathematical Sociology, 3*(1), 85–111. doi:10.1080/0022250X.1973.9989825

Kelley, M. L. (1990). *School-home notes: Promoting children's classroom success*. Guilford Press.

Khander, S. R., Koolwal, G. B., & Samad, H. A. (2010). *Handbook on impact evaluation: Quantitative methods and practices*. World Bank.

Kornbluh, M., & Neal, J. W. (2015). Social network analysis. In L. A. Jason & D. S. Glenwick (Eds.), *Handbook of methodological approaches to community-based research* (pp. 207–218). Oxford University Press.

Kornbluh, M., Neal, J. W., & Ozer, E. J. (2016). Scaling-up youth-led social justice efforts through an online school-based social network. *American Journal of Community Psychology, 57*(3-4), 266–279. doi:10.1002/ajcp.12042

Kossinets, G. (2006). Effects of missing data in social networks. *Social Networks, 28*(3), 247–268. doi:10.1016/j.socnet.2005.07.002

Laumann, E. O., Marsden, P. V., & Prensky, D. (1983). The boundary specification problem in network analysis. In R. Burt & M. Minor (Eds.), *Applied network analysis* (pp. 18–34). Sage.

Lawlor, J. A., & Neal, Z. P. (2016). Networked community change: Understanding community systems change through the lens of social network analysis. *American Journal of Community Psychology, 57*(3-4), 426–436. doi:10.1002/ajcp.12052

Long, J., Harré, N., & Atkinson, Q. D. (2014). Understanding change in recycling and littering behavior across a school social network. *American Journal of Community Psychology, 53*(3-4), 462–474. doi:10.1007/s10464-013-9613-3

Marin, A., & Wellman, B. (2011). Social network analysis: An introduction. In J. Scott & P. J. Carrington (Eds.), *The SAGE handbook of social network analysis* (pp. 11–25). Sage.

Marsden, P. (2011). Survey methods for network data. In J. Scott & P. J. Carrington (Eds.), *The SAGE handbook of social network analysis* (pp. 370–388). Sage.

Marsden, P. V. (1990). Network data and measurement. *Annual Review of Sociology, 16*(1), 435–463. doi:10.1146/annurev.so.16.080190.002251

McDade, S. A. (1994). Evaluating leadership development programs. *New Directions for Higher Education, 87*, 83–91. doi:10.1002/he.36919948710

Neal, J. W. (2008). "Kracking" the missing data problem: Applying Krackhardt's cognitive social structures to school-based social network research. *Sociology of Education, 81*(2), 140–162. doi:10.1177/003804070808100202

Neal, J. W. (2020). A systematic review of social network methods in high impact developmental psychology journals. *Social Development*. doi:10.1111/sode.12442

Neal, J. W., & Christens, B. D. (2014). Linking the levels: Network and relational perspectives for community psychology. *American Journal of Community Psychology, 53*(3-4), 314–323. doi:10.1007/s10464-014-9654-2

Neal, J. W., & Neal, Z. P. (2011). Power as a structural phenomenon. *American Journal of Community Psychology, 48*(3-4), 157–167. doi:10.1007/s10464-010-9356-3

Neal, J. W., Neal, Z. P., Atkins, M. S., Henry, D. B., & Frazier, S. L. (2011). Channels of change: Contrasting network mechanisms in the use of interventions. *American Journal of Community Psychology, 47*(3-4), 277–286. doi:10.1007/s10464-010-9403-0

Neal, J. W., Shernoff, E. S., Frazier, S. L., Stachowicz, E., Frangos, R., & Atkins, M. S. (2008). Change from within: Engaging teacher key opinion leaders in the diffusion of interventions in urban schools. *The Community Psychologist, 41*(2), 53–57.

Neal, Z. P. (2013). *The connected city: How networks are shaping the modern metropolis*. Routledge.

Neal, Z. P. (2014). The backbone of bipartite projections: Inferring relationships from co-authorship, co-sponsorship, co-attendance and other co-behaviors. *Social Networks, 39,* 84–97. doi:10.1016/j.socnet.2014.06.001

Neal, Z. P., & Neal, J. W. (2017). Network analysis in community psychology: Looking back, looking forward. *American Journal of Community Psychology, 60*(1-2), 279–295. doi:10.1002/ajcp.12158

Prell, C. (2012). *Social network analysis: History, theory, and methodology*. Sage.

Provan, K. G., Veazie, M. A., Staten, L. K., & Teufel-Shone, N. I. (2005). The use of network analysis to strengthen community partnerships. *Public Administration Review, 65*(5), 603–613. doi:10.1111/j.1540-6210.2005.00487.x

Shernoff, E. S., Frazier, S. L., Maríñez-Lora, A. M., Lakind, D., Atkins, M. S., Jakobsons, L., Hamre, B. K., Bhaumik, D. K., Parker-Katz, M., Neal, J. W., Smylie, M. A., & Patel, D. A. (2016). Expanding the role of school psychologists to support early career teachers: A mixed method study. *School Psychology Review, 45*(2), 226–249. doi:10.17105/SPR45-2.226-249

Valente, T. W., & Pumpuang, P. (2007). Identifying opinion leaders to promote behavior change. *Health, Education, & Behavior, 34,* 881–896. doi:10.1177/1090198106297855

Weaver, L., & Cousins, J. B. (2007). Unpacking the participatory process. *Journal of Multidisciplinary Evaluation, 1,* 19–40.

Wellman, B. (1988). Structural analysis: From method and metaphor to theory and substance. In B. Wellman & S. D. Berkowitz (Eds.), *Social structures: A network approach* (pp. 19–61). Cambridge University Press.

Wellman, B. (2007). Challenges in collecting personal network data: The nature of personal network analysis. *Field Methods, 19*(2), 111–115. doi:10.1177/1525822X06299133

CHAPTER 12

USING COST-BENEFIT AND COST-EFFECTIVENESS ANALYSES IN THE COMMUNITY CONTEXT

Sarah L. Pettijohn and Joanne G. Carman

Learning Objectives

1. Learn how to conduct cost-benefit and cost-effectiveness analyses.

2. Become familiar with the challenges inherent in cost-inclusive evaluations.

3. Understand strategies for facilitating evaluation partnerships.

Most evaluation research focuses on measuring and improving program outcomes, but it often fails to consider the costs associated with achieving those outcomes. However, cost analysis can enhance evaluations by examining the cost of a program relative to some benefit. Proponents of cost-inclusive evaluations argue that evaluations providing evidence of the program's success (i.e., it achieves intended benefits) *and* cost effectiveness have a better chance of securing scarce and limited resources. As policymakers, funders, and other stakeholders continue to demand efficient use of funds, cost-inclusive evaluations will become the new standard for evaluation practice (Crowley et al., 2018; Hausman et al., 2016).

Because many community-based organizations lack the capacity to conduct cost-inclusive evaluations, we suggest taking a partnership approach to this work. In most communities, there are resources available to assist with cost-inclusive evaluations. For example, universities and colleges have graduate students and faculty with these skills. Evaluation consultants also specialize in this area, and many government and philanthropic funders are interested in learning more about the return on their investments (Yates & Marra, 2017). In this chapter, we describe how evaluators and community-based organizations can work together, in partnership, to conduct cost-benefit and cost-effectiveness analyses.

UNDERSTANDING COST ANALYSIS

Before discussing cost-inclusive evaluations, it is important to understand the basics of cost analysis. In this section, we begin by discussing key concepts of two types of cost analysis: cost-benefit analysis (CBA) and cost-effectiveness analysis (CEA). To illustrate key concepts and components of CBA and CEA, we work though a cost analysis for

BOX 12.1 COST ANALYSIS IN ACTION

DFZ is considering purchasing a vehicle to transport participants to services at DFZ as well as its local partners. Currently, participants must provide their own transportation, which means those with limited transportation options often miss activities that are key to successful recovery. DFZ estimates that providing transportation to participants will increase the number of individuals enrolled to 550 from 400 (150 net gain); with a 35% success rate, DFZ estimates it will see the number of participants who enter and sustain recovery increase to 190 from 140 (50 net gain). Finally, individuals sustaining recovery, on average, have higher income compared to their counterparts, and DFZ estimates the increase in wage to be $3,240 per participant sustaining recovery.

DFZ funds this program through a state contract. The state reimburses DFZ for the cost of the program, $1,000 per participant.

Drug Free Zone (DFZ), a hypothetical nonprofit organization working to help individuals overcome addiction to substance use, throughout the chapter (Box 12.1).

Costs and benefits. Every program or intervention requires resources—financial, human, technological, and so on—to operate. *Costs* are simply these inputs monetized, while *benefits* are the outputs and outcomes quantified. Economists classify costs and benefits into three categories: *direct* or *indirect*, *tangible* or *intangible*, and *private* or *external* (Figure 12.1).

Costs and benefits in action. In our scenario, the costs of the vehicle, insurance, and fuel are directly related to the purchase of the vehicle, so these are direct costs of the proposed purchase. DFZ can quantify these costs using market prices, which means these costs are also tangible. The costs of the vehicle, insurance, and fuel are internal to DFZ (the organization making the decision), so these costs are direct, tangible, and private.

Figure 12.1 Categories of Costs and Benefits

Direct vs. Indirect Cost/Benefit	Tangible vs. Intangible Cost/Benefit	Private vs. External Cost/Benefit
Direct Direct result of the program or puchase	**Tangible** Cost/benefit can be quantified using market prices	**Private** Internal to decision-maker's organization
Indirect A by-product of the program or purchase May be an unintended cost/benefit	**Intangible** Not quantifiable using market prices Uses a proxy value or "shadow price"	**External** External to decision-maker's organization

DFZ will also experience indirect costs and benefits from the purchase of the vehicle. In our scenario, DFZ will provide services to an additional 150 individuals, which will likely require DFZ to hire additional program staff. The cost of hiring new program staff is an indirect cost of the vehicle, contributing to an increased number of program participants. Additionally, a net gain in the number of job opportunities available will result in an external benefit to the larger community through lower unemployment rates.

However, not all costs and benefits are easy to quantify. For example, most will argue that sustaining recovery is better for the individual and society, but to include this benefit in cost analysis, we must assign a dollar value to it. Quantifying intangible costs and benefits generally happens in two steps: (1) identify the quantity of the intangible cost and/or benefit; and (2) estimate a monetary value for the cost or benefit. In our scenario, we use a shadow price, or proxy value, to represent the wage difference between individuals sustaining recovery and those who do not to quantify the benefit of sustaining recovery when the individual has access to the services.

Many argue that selecting a proxy to quantify intangible costs and benefits is the most challenging step in cost-inclusive evaluations. While the shadow price varies based on the nature of the intangible cost or benefit in question, all techniques for selecting a shadow price focus on the willingness to pay (i.e., the maximum amount a person is willing to pay for something the individual wants) or willingness to accept principles (i.e., the minimum amount of money an individual is willing to accept for a less than ideal situation). In the situation above, we used the *revealed-preference valuation technique*, which uses observable data from the market to generate a proxy value for a benefit that has no market value (Zerbe, Jr. & Bellas, 2006). Here, we use the difference in wages between individuals sustaining recovery to wages of individuals not sustaining recovery to quantify the value associated with a benefit that has no market value, that is, access to services designed to help an individual sustain recovery. Another common technique for quantifying intangible costs and benefits is *stated-preference valuation* (Zerbe, Jr. & Bellas, 2006). Here, the evaluator surveys those with standing about their willingness to pay for certain benefits or their willingness to accept conditions that are less than ideal; both principles help analysts quantify intangible costs and benefits based on the stated value they have to individuals with standing.

Cost-benefit analysis. CBA is an economic evaluation that translates all costs and benefits into a common monetary value. CBAs were popularized during the 1970s, as the Nixon, Ford, and Carter administrations directed U.S. federal government agencies to consider the costs and benefits of different policy alternatives when making regulatory decisions (Shapiro, 2010). At its core, CBA requires the analyst to determine the costs and benefits of a program or policy alternative, compare the alternatives, and make recommendations or plans for action (Denhardt et al., 2016). When the analysis considers only private costs, it is called a financial CBA.

Historically, however, CBAs have been used to make programmatic and policy decisions to promote community well-being in a wide range of fields, such as education, foster care, crime prevention, healthcare, and substance abuse treatment (Institute of Medicine and National Research Council, 2014). When the analysis considers the external costs/benefits in conjunction with the private costs, it is called a social CBA. Many argue that there is an even greater interest and need for social CBAs today, as government agencies, philanthropic funders, and other nonprofit organizations[1] search for long-term, sustainable, community programs or initiatives that benefit the community at large (Agranoff & McGuire, 2004; Kania & Kramer, 2011).

Decision makers can use CBA before (*ex-ante*), during (*in medias res*), or after (*ex-post*) implementing a program to help stakeholders make decisions about starting or expanding a program. Typically, CBAs are conducted ex-ante to make decisions about implementing a new program or expanding an existing program by examining the potential benefits of the program and determining whether those benefits outweigh the costs. The goal is to ensure resources are used most efficiently (Boardman et al., 2001). However, in evaluations, it is more common for CBAs to be used ex-post, or after implementing the program. Regardless of when the CBA is performed, the formula is

$$Net\ Benefits = Total\ Benefits - Total\ Cost$$

CBA in action. In the DFZ example we described, if the benefits of the vehicle outweigh its costs (positive net benefits), the organization should move forward with its purchase. However, if the costs of the vehicle outweigh the benefits (negative net benefits), DFZ should not purchase it.

Cost-effectiveness analysis. CEA is also an economic evaluation that examines "the relationship between program costs and program effectiveness" (Yates, 1999, p. 3). This places an emphasis on scarcity and efficient use of resources. Accompanying the growing interest in cost analysis is a rising demand for evaluation research that documents the short- and long-term outcomes of community programs and initiatives (Thomas, 2016). Moreover, organizations, systems, and communities increasingly need to be able to make comparisons across community programs or initiatives to determine which proposed solution costs less but still achieves the desired outcome (Yates, 2009). CEA is a means for doing so.

For these analyses, the organization takes the key outcome it hopes to accomplish and assigns a dollar value to the cost (see Figure 12.1 for categories of costs) for each unit of outcome it plans to achieve, which Cellini and Kee (2015) call "units of effectiveness" (p. 493). Thus, the formula for CEA is

$$Cost\ Effectiveness\ Ratio = \frac{Total\ Cost}{Units\ of\ Effectiveness}$$

CEA in action. In the DFZ example, the "unit of effectiveness" is the number of individuals who are sustaining recovery. Thus, the cost-effectiveness ratio tells us the cost of one person achieving recovery.

As this brief overview suggests, both CBA and CEA require significant amounts of data. Therefore, it is essential for organizations to work in partnership with selected community agencies and evaluators to develop the capacity to collect data relating to all costs and benefits of a proposed program or purchase.

---

[1] In this chapter, we use the term "nonprofit organization" to refer to organizations that have been recognized by the Internal Revenue Service as being tax-exempt charitable organizations. For more information, see https://www.irs.gov/charities-nonprofits/charitable-organizations/exemption-requirements-section-501-c-3-organizations

PARTNERSHIP APPROACHES TO COST ANALYSIS

Given this volume's emphasis, the critical elements of partnership-based approaches to evaluation are discussed throughout the book (e.g., see Chapters 3 and 14). In reflecting on a partnership approach to evaluation, Malloy and Yee (2006) describe how *partnership evaluation* differs from traditional evaluation, writing:

> We attempt to move beyond the contractual business relationships that consultants have with their clients (i.e., vendor–consumer) to a place of partnership where we share resources and work collaboratively to gather information, answer critical questions, make decisions, and solve problems. These clients view us as integral members of their team, invested in their success; we see them as partners who contribute numerous assets to the evaluation process. (p. 68)

These qualities (and differences) have been highlighted by the examples integrated in this volume's chapters. Before going further with our discussion, it is important to recognize the antecedents to developing a successful cost-inclusive evaluation using a partnership-based approach. In this context, we recommend exploring the extent to which the evaluator, partner organization, and other interested stakeholders have a shared understanding about the purpose of the cost-inclusive evaluation and the intended use of the findings. The next step involves being strategic about developing the partnership relationship, recognizing that the roles and contributions of the partners will depend on the nature of the evaluation (Newcomer et al., 2015).

For example, it may be that the evaluator serves in a developmental or capacity-building role, bringing in the cost analysis expertise and relying on the partner organization to provide the data needed for the evaluation. Alternatively, it may be that the partner organization has the capacity to perform the cost analysis, and the evaluator serves more as a negotiator, convener, or facilitator for the evaluation (Cartland et al., 2008).

CONDUCTING A COST ANALYSIS IN PARTNERSHIP

Now that there is general understanding of the concepts involved, we can delve more deeply into how to conduct cost analysis. This next section outlines the six key steps for cost analysis.

Step 1: Define the analysis. The first step in any cost analysis is to define it. The audience, or the group of people who will use the results, can range considerably on any given cost analysis. For instance, the audience could be "thought leaders," that is, the people who will use the data to make decisions, such as elected officials, public administrators, nonprofit boards of directors, chief operating officers, and funders (Grob, 2015). The audience may also consist of other important stakeholders, such as program staff, program beneficiaries, journalists, social media outlets, and citizens at-large (Baxter & Braverman, 2004), representing diverse backgrounds with varying knowledge about the evaluation's specific focus, so you need to consider carefully how you present this information. It is likely that multiple groups will have interests in the results of the analysis, and it may be fruitful to develop different methods for presenting or disseminating the results of the analysis.

Table 12.1 Defining the Analysis

Perspective	Status Quo	Proposed Vehicle
DFZ		
Program participants		
Community partners		
State		
Timeframe	1 year	5 years[a]
Discount rate	0%	4%

[a] *Consumer Reports* notes the average life span for a vehicle is 8 years. However, this vehicle will be used more frequently than the average vehicle, so its life cycle is shortened to reflect the increased use.

In addition to communicating information to a broad audience, you must also be able to communicate the parameters of your cost analysis so the audience understands its limitations. Cost analyses require a number of estimates and assumptions to determine the net benefits (CBA) or cost-effectiveness ratio (CEA). These estimates and assumptions will significantly impact the results, which can inadvertently change the final decision and recommendation provided. We recommend using a template (Table 12.1) to present information to a wide audience with estimates and assumptions presented in a clear and concise manner. Specifically, you need to define the following:

a. First, the partners must decide on what type of analysis to do. That is, do you plan to conduct a *CBA*, *CEA*, or *both*? This decision is driven by the nature of the questions being asked, or the goal of the analysis. If the goal is to determine whether to purchase an item or implement or expand a program, you need CBA, but if you want to see how cost effective the item or program is, you need CEA. Additionally, if you are deciding between two options, CEA will provide more usable information.

b. You also need to determine who has *standing* in the analysis. Standing focuses on whose interests you are considering in the analysis. Cost analysis at the community level will require you to consider multiple *perspectives* of various stakeholders and not just those within your organization or the organization with which you are partnering. For example, in such circumstances, it is important to consider social costs and benefits. You can only include the costs and benefits to those that have standing in the analysis.

c. Additionally, you will need to specify the *alternatives or basis for comparison*. In cost analysis, you are deciding between at least two options: the status quo or a new purchase or program. However, other times you may be debating between two programs for implementation or two items for purchase, so you need to state clearly the nature of the comparison in the analysis.

d. Next, you must decide the *timeframe* for analysis and specify why it is appropriate. For instance, in general, a large purchase or program will operate over many years, so there will be costs and benefits associated with each year included in the analysis.

e. Along with the timeframe for analysis, you must determine a *discount rate*. Time value of money is an economic concept that assumes future money does not hold the same value as today's money (Office of Management and Budget, 1992). The purchasing power of money is reduced with inflation (it will be more expensive to purchase the same good or service in the future compared to today), so to complete the analysis, you need all dollar values converted to the *present value* to compare costs and benefits over multiple years using a common metric. Additionally, present values imply that the dollars are devalued each year in the analysis.

    While there are several methods for setting the discount rate, nonprofit organizations generally use one of two methods. First, if the purchase or project requires the organization to borrow money, you can use the cost of using the funds by taking the projected interest rate for a loan and discounting the future value of the costs and benefits at that rate. However, if the organization is not planning to borrow money or wants to consider other factors (e.g., opportunity costs), the organization can select an alternate discount rate. Organizations can select discount rates used by local, state, or federal levels of government. For example, nonprofits can find guidance in OMB *Circular* A-94, which discusses the discount rates for cost analyses conducted by the federal government. Since 1992, federal cost analyses have used "a real discount rate of 7%" (Office of Management and Budget, 1992).

Step 1 in action. Begin by creating a template to state assumptions and estimates clearly. DFZ and an evaluator (the partners) plan to conduct both CBA and CEA to examine whether it should move forward with purchasing a new vehicle. Table 12.1 presents a template to list key assumptions necessary to define the analysis. The first column lists whose interests "count," or whose perspective the partners—DFZ and an evaluator—will consider in the analysis; because DFZ is considering not only its own costs and benefits, it is conducting a social CBA. The next two columns illustrate the alternative to purchasing the proposed vehicle (maintaining the status quo). Finally, the last two rows outline the timeframe the proposed vehicle will be in operation, with justification for it in a footnote, and the discount rate to convert future dollar values into present value. In this example, we use a discount rate of 4%, which is the interest rate the bank will charge DFZ each year for a vehicle loan.

Step 2: List and monetize impacts (CBA) or quantify benefits by unit of effectiveness (CEA). Now you need to generate a list of costs and benefits from each perspective identified in Step 1. As Figure 12.1 outlined at the beginning of this chapter, costs and benefits can be direct/indirect, tangible/intangible, and private/external. In Step 2, you need to include all categories of costs and benefits. Then, once you have a list of the costs and benefits, you must monetize each impact (CBA) or quantify benefits by units of effectiveness (CEA). Note that the costs for CBA and CEA are the same, only the benefits are different.

We recommend allowing ample time to complete Step 2, which is typically the most challenging in cost analysis. Additional time will allow analysts from the primary organization to contact other individuals, groups, and/or organizations who have standing. This will help to ensure the list includes all relevant and appropriate costs and benefits. Additionally, when the cost or benefit is intangible, the partnership team will need to identify strategies for quantifying it, which will also require significant time and discussion among the partners. Finally, the partners will need to justify how they monetized the intangible cost or benefit.

Step 2 in action. Take the document created in Step 1 and include the costs and benefits (CBA) for each option (Table 12.2). The costs include the direct, tangible, and private costs of the vehicle and compounding interest ($38,700), vehicle maintenance (e.g., oil changes, brake repairs), operating costs (e.g., fuel and insurance), and overhead costs (e.g., overnight parking of the vehicle) as well as the cost for one additional employee to drive the vehicle. As a result of greater access, more individuals will be able to participate in services, which will require the state to reimburse DFZ for more participants. The analysis also considers two indirect and tangible costs external to DFZ: cost to program participants and cost to the state due to the wear and tear on roads from an additional vehicle.

The benefits, on the other hand, are all intangible, so we need to use a proxy to quantify ease of access, which is the goal of purchasing the vehicle. DFZ and its evaluator do this by calculating the difference in average wages between individuals using drugs and individuals not using drugs. This difference shows the average value a participant can expect by participating in the program, which is a direct result of the individual receiving services because they can access them via transportation in the new vehicle. Additionally, the analysis includes the cost savings (benefit) the state will receive by having fewer individuals receiving public assistance because individuals tend to be more productive in recovery.

It is important to note that there are a number of options evaluators can use to quantify intangible costs and benefits. For example, instead of using the revealed-preference valuation discussed earlier, we could have used a stated-preference valuation. This would require us to survey individuals with standing about their willingness to pay to reduce barriers for individuals attempting to access services (ease of access) and the value they place on an individual sustaining recovery (increased productivity). However, we decided to use the revealed-preference valuation technique because it uses observable data, which may reduce bias introduced by surveys (e.g., social desirability bias). Additionally, individuals who have standing are often involved with the program and, as such, may overvalue the benefits (and undervalue the costs) related to individuals sustaining recovery, which may lead to invalid and unreliable estimates. Thus, we recommend that evaluators should use the most objective, conservative estimates available to quantify intangible costs and benefits.

Finally, we do not include the additional revenue DFZ will receive from the state, which reimburses DFZ $1,000 per client, as a benefit in the CBA. That is, the community, which is the focus of this CBA, will not incur a real cost or benefit from the state transferring funds to DFZ. However, if we were to include this transfer as a benefit to DFZ, we

Table 12.2 Listing and Monetizing Impacts

Perspective	Status Quo	Proposed Vehicle
Costs to:		
DFZ		
Purchase price of vehicle	–	$7,740/year
Maintenance cost of vehicle	–	$3,000/year
Operating cost of vehicle	–	$2,000/year
Compensation for employee to transport	–	$31,200/year
Overhead costs (parking, etc.)	–	$4,500/year
Program participants		
Opportunity cost of participants' time	$1,250/participant	$1,250/participant
Community partners		
State		
Cost of drug treatment program	$1,000/participant	$1,000/participant
Increase use of public roads	–	0.0786/mile driven
Benefits to:		
DFZ		
More effective mission fulfillment	Benefit accrues to state	Benefit accrues to state
Program participants		
More access to program	$3,240/recovered participant	$3,240/recovered participant
Community partners		
More access for their clients referred to DFZ	Benefit accrues to participant	Benefit accrues to participant
State		
Productivity (cost savings in public assistance for people with drug addiction)	$8,726/participant	$8,726/participant
Timeframe	1 year	5 years
Discount rate	0%	4%

would essentially be saying there was no real cost to the community for serving additional participants. Only if the revenue to serve additional participants came from a source who did not have standing in the analysis would we consider it a real benefit. However, anytime you conduct CBA at the community level it is essential to exclude transfers (i.e., costs and benefits that shift from one partner to another partner included in analysis) to ensure the real costs and benefits to the community are depicted in the analysis.

Step 3: Discount future net benefits to determine present value. When determining present value, your analysis will include only the costs and benefits that exceed the status quo because the organization will incur certain costs and benefits even if it does not move forward with the proposed program or purchase. The total cost for the program or purchase is the difference between the full cost of the program and its current costs, and the total benefits for the program or purchase is the difference between the full benefits and its current benefits. Once you know the total cost and benefits, you can calculate the present value of net benefits. The formula for present value is

$$pv = \frac{(b_t - c_t)}{(1+i)^{t-1}}$$

where b = total benefits; c = total costs; i = discount rate; and t = time period.

The numerator requires you to determine the future value of the net benefits for each year (total benefits minus total costs). Then, the denominator discounts the future value of the net benefit to the present value of the net benefits for each year.

Step 3 in action. First, Table 12.3 illustrates how one could calculate the total costs and benefits of purchasing the vehicle by including only those costs and benefits that exceed the status quo. We begin by calculating the cost of owning, operating, and maintaining the vehicle for each year ($7,740 + $3,000 + $2,000 + $31,200 + $4,500 = $48,440). Our analysis should focus only on the 150 individuals who will participate (with 50 participants sustaining recovery) as a result of transportation to and from DFZ, so we calculate the costs to program participants ($1,250 × 150 = $187,500). To calculate the cost to the state, we assume the vehicle will result in an additional 40,000 miles of road use each year ($0.0786 × 40,000 = $3,144), which we add to the cost per participant the state spends on treatment ($1,000 × 150 = $150,000). Then, we use the same assumptions to calculate the benefits accrued to the 50 individuals sustaining recovery each year ($3,240 × 50 =

Table 12.3 Total Costs and Benefits Per Year

Perspective	Total Costs/Year	Total Benefits/Year
DFZ	$48,440	$0
Program participants	$187,500	$162,000
Community partners	$0	$0
State	$153,144	$436,300
Total	$389,084	$598,000

$162,000) and the state ($8,726 × 50 = $436,300). Thus, the cost of purchasing the new vehicle is $389,084 and the benefits are $598,300 for stakeholders with standing.

Now that we know the future value of the net benefits for each year, we can calculate the present value for each year (Table 12.4). Here, we calculate the net benefits ($598,000 – $389,084), which results in the future value of net benefits of $209,216 for each year DFZ uses the vehicle; this becomes the numerator for the present value formula outlined in Step 3. Now, we need to calculate the denominator $(1 + i)^t$, so we replace i with the 4% interest rate and t with the year in question. Thus, if we were calculating the present value of year 3, our formula would be

$$\text{pv}^{t=3} = \frac{(\$598,300 - \$389,084)}{(1 + .04)^{3-1}}$$

This results in a present value net benefit of $193,432. Here, we took the numerator of $209,216 ($598,000 – $389,084) and divided it by 1.0816, which is the square (3 − 1 = 2) of 1.04 (as reported in Table 12.4, year 3). Also, note in Table 12.4 that we separated financial benefits from societal benefits; we strongly recommend this separation for all CBA analysis. From Table 12.4, we can see there are no financial benefits that accrue to DFZ, but it will experience costs each year that it owns the vehicle. Thus, while the community as a whole benefits, it may not be financially feasible for DFZ to undertake the expense.

Step 4. Calculate net present value (CBA) or cost-effectiveness ratio (CEA). Now that the value of costs and benefits are in the present value, you can calculate the net present value (NPV) by summing the present value for each year of data. To calculate the cost-effectiveness ratio, we need to compute the present value of total costs, which is divided by the unit of effectiveness.

Step 4 in action. We add the values in the last column (net benefits, present value), which results in net benefits worth $968,648 in today's money, the NPV.

Next, we calculate the cost-effectiveness ratio. The total cost of the vehicle is $1,801,418 in today's dollar (Table 12.5). Because the benefits from the program will accrue over a 5-year period, and DFZ estimates that 50 participants will self-report that they are in sustained recovery each year, we divide the total cost by 250 participants. Therefore, the

Table 12.4 Expected Present Value of Net Benefits

Time period	Costs	Benefits		Net Benefits	
		Financial	Social	Future Value	Present Value
Year 1 (startup year)	$389,084	$0	$598,300	$209,216	$209,216
Year 2	$389,084	$0	$598,300	$209,216	$201,169
Year 3	$389,084	$0	$598,300	$209,216	$193,432
Year 4	$389,084	$0	$598,300	$209,216	$185,992
Year 5	$389,084	$0	$598,300	$209,216	$178,839

Table 12.5 Present Value of Total Costs

Time Period	Future Value Total Costs	Present Value Total Costs
Year 1	$389,084	$389,084
Year 2	$389,084	$374,119
Year 3	$389,084	$359,730
Year 4	$389,084	$345,894
Year 5	$389,084	$332,591
Total		$1,801,418

cost-effectiveness ratio is 1:$7,206. Put another way, it will cost the community $7,206 for a participant to sustain recovery if DFZ purchases the vehicle.

Step 5. Perform sensitivity analysis. Recall that the results of CBA and CEA are sensitive to the estimates and assumptions made at the beginning of the analysis. Before moving forward with a capital purchase or implementing a new program, you need to test whether your decision would change if the estimates used in the initial analysis differed meaningfully from reality. That is, in Step 5, it is particularly important to assess whether your decision would still be the same if conditions were worse than originally expected.

Step 5 in action. If we assume the bank was no longer able to offer a vehicle loan at a 4% interest rate, should DFZ move forward with its purchase of the vehicle? Using a 7% discount rate, we see that the present value of the net benefits decreases to $917,875. In this instance, the result of the CBA does not appear to be sensitive to the interest rate for the vehicle loan; that is, the benefits still outweigh the costs when using less favorable discount rates. When performing sensitivity analyses, you should vary the assumptions and estimates initially made to see if the benefits outweigh the costs, should the initial assumptions or estimates be too conservative.

Step 6. Make a decision and provide recommendation. If the benefits outweigh the costs of a project, you generally recommend the project move forward because the benefit to those with standing in the analysis will benefit from the project or purchase. That is, if the NPV is positive, you recommend moving forward; but, if the NPV is negative with the costs outweighing the benefits, you would not recommend the project move forward. If the initial NPV is positive but changes to negative during sensitivity analysis, you know the project is sensitive to the estimates used in the analysis, and you must caution decision makers about the conditions in which costs would outweigh benefits.

Step 6 in action. The NPV for the initial analysis is positive, even when performing sensitivity analysis. Thus, we would recommend that DFZ move forward with purchasing a vehicle and providing transportation for its drug treatment program.

Unlike CBA, there is no absolute decision rule associated with CEA. That is, you can only make decisions when comparing at least two options. If DFZ were debating between several vehicles, CEA could help leaders make the decision. Then, the decision rule for

BOX 12.2 SUMMARY OF SIX STEPS OF CBA AND CEA

Step 1: Define analysis.

a. Decide on type of analysis (CBA or CEA).

b. Identify standing and perspectives.

c. Specify alternatives or basis for comparison.

d. Report the timeframe for analysis.

e. Determine discount rate.

Step 2: List and monetize impacts (CBA) or quantify benefits by unit of effectiveness (CEA).

Step 3: Discount future net benefits to determine present value.

Step 4: Calculate NPV (CBA) or cost-effectiveness ratio (CEA).

Step 5: Perform sensitivity analysis.

Step 6: Make a decision and provide recommendation.

CEA is to choose the option that is *relatively* more cost effective compared to the other option. However, when only one option is considered, CEA is not helpful in making a decision about proceeding with the proposed purchase or program because CEA is about choosing the alternative that is most cost effective (Box 12.2).

CONNECTING COST ANALYSIS AND EVALUATIONS

Cost analysis is, in itself, an evaluation method. In the example we just worked through, DFZ is *evaluating* whether it is in the best interests of the community to purchase a vehicle. However, when we think about evaluations, we often think of those that assess the extent to which a program achieves its results *during* and *after* the program is complete (Poister, 2004), not before. In this section, we link cost analysis and evaluation, two complex concepts, together. After all, evaluations exist because of two factors, "first, the fact that there is not enough money to do all the things that need doing; and second, the realization that even if there were enough money, it takes more than money to solve complex human and social problems" (Patton, 1978, p. 16). These two factors are the foundation for cost analysis and evaluations, so when we combine evaluations and cost analysis, we have evidence and information about the effectiveness of the program as well as whether it was also cost effective, or worth the resources invested in it.

During an evaluation, we ask the organization(s) to describe its strategy for addressing the issue at hand in terms of a "theory of change" (see Chapter 1). In other words, we ask them to describe how and why they expect the program to achieve the intended outcomes or benefits (Weiss, 1995). In doing so, we identify the implicit and explicit assumptions behind the program or initiative (program theory or theory of change); quantify the resources that the program or initiative needs (inputs); identify the specific actions that will be implemented (activities); identify the measures that would be used to track the activities (outputs); and identify the benefits (outcomes). Using this information, we are able to create a logic model to provide guidance during both the evaluation (inputs, activities, outputs, and outcomes) and cost analysis (cost and benefits; Grantcraft, 2006; McLaughlin

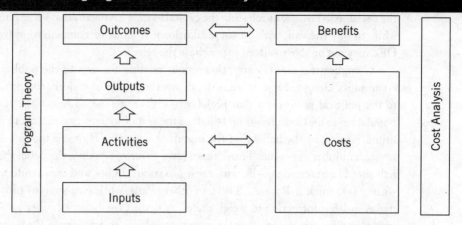

Figure 12.2 Connecting Logic Models to Cost Analysis

Program Theory

Outcomes ⟺ Benefits

Outputs

Activities ⟺ Costs

Inputs

Cost Analysis

& Jordan, 2016; Philliber, 1998; W. K. Kellogg Foundation, 2004; Chapter 1 includes additional information about logic models and an example logic model). This information allows us to link the inputs, activities, and outputs with the costs of the program and the outcomes with its benefits. Figure 12.2 illustrates the connection between these two concepts in practice.

Logic models and cost analysis are stronger when performed together, and neither carries much weight without the other. That is, the cost of a program only means something when we know whether the program is effective, and the effectiveness of a program means little when organizations cannot afford to implement it. By using the two in support of each other, a case can be made that the program works *and* is worth it, or that changes need to be made to improve its effectiveness or cost.

Making decisions. We design evaluations and cost analyses so they can be used to guide better decisions. Knowledge gained from evaluations can lead to decisions that improve service delivery, increase capacity, identify best practices, and create systemic change (Hatry et al., 2005). By including cost in the evaluation, we can also demonstrate how efficiently the program used resources, which may strengthen the case for policymakers to continue supporting the program. However, as we discussed earlier, careful attention must be paid to how the information is presented. Oftentimes, decision makers are faced with balancing different, and sometimes competing, values. The value that typically rises to the top among decision making criteria when operating in the public space is the standard of efficiency. Efficiency is the ability to perform a service well, without wasting public or scarce resources. At the same time, decision makers need to be sure services are delivered effectively (producing the desired result) and responsively (in a way that is received favorably or quickly; Denhardt et al., 2016).

Recall from the example that we recommended you separate financial and societal benefits from each other in CBA. This will provide decision makers with more information. When DFZ is contemplating purchasing the vehicle, the benefits outweigh the cost because societal benefits are included in analysis. However, DFZ will spend more than $220,000 (see DFZ costs in Table 12.1) over the life of the vehicle, but it receives no private or financial benefits from the purchase. This means the benefits accrued from purchasing the vehicle go to participants and the state. DFZ needs to understand the financial ineffi-ciencies of its decision to purchase the vehicle, especially because societal benefits tipped the decision in favor of purchasing the capital item. This means that while it may be worth-while to buy the van, without some additional revenue or compensation from the state, DFZ may not be able to afford to purchase the vehicle.

Complicating matters are other values relating to serving the public and creating community change. First, there is the democratic value of majoritarianism, which refers to the political philosophy that preference is given to the wishes of the majority of the population to make decisions on behalf of the rest of society. Second, there is the value of utilitarianism, or the belief that the morally responsible choice is the one that helps the greatest number of people. Third, there is the value of equality, the belief that all individ-uals should be treated equally with regard to status, rights, and opportunities afforded by society (Dubnick & Romzek, 1991). In other words, while cost analysis provides decision makers with information to weigh the costs against the benefits, other values may come into play when choosing what programs or policies to implement. Now, we present an example that links cost analysis with evaluations.

CASE EXAMPLE: UNDERSTANDING CBA AND CEA IN EVALUATIONS: AN EXAMPLE

Substance abuse is one of the costliest health prob-lems in the United States, costing more than $740 billion annually in costs related to crime, lost work productivity, and health care (National Institute on Drug Abuse, 2017). To combat the growing impacts of illicit drug use, many nonprofit organizations are implementing drug prevention programs. DFZ, our hypothetical nonprofit organization, also provides drug prevention services. In its most recent fiscal year, it provided drug prevention services to 100,000 participants through a $25 million contract with the state. The state has asked DFZ, in partnership with an evaluator, to assess the impact of this program, requiring an ex-post CBA and CEA. In the material that follows, we outline the evaluation and demon-strate how to integrate cost analysis in an evaluation.

Program Evaluation

The goal of DFZ's drug prevention program is to prevent an individual from engaging in substance abuse. To begin, the evaluation partnership must estimate the number of participants the program successfully deterred from abusing substances. During the intake process before participants began

the program, DFZ collected data on an individual's risk for drug use, which the evaluation team used to predict the propensity for an individual to abuse substances. Based on this information, the evalu-ation team estimated that approximately 9,000 of the 100,000 participants were at significant risk for abusing substances. Then, the evaluation team followed up with participants after the program ended to determine whether the participant was abusing substances. After following up with program participants, the evaluation team learned that 3,270 former participants were abusing drugs. This means that the program prevented 5,730 indi-viduals from abusing substances (9,000 – 3,270 = 5,730).

Cost Analysis

Just over 5,700 individuals not abusing substances can be attributed to DFZ's program. Now, the state wants the evaluation team to examine whether the cost of the program was worth it. To begin, Table 12.6 defines the analysis.

Once the evaluation team defined the anal-ysis, it listed and monetized the impacts (CBA) and

Table 12.6 Defining the Analysis

Perspective	Status Quo	Prevention Program
DFZ		
Program participants		
Community partners		
State		
Timeframe	1 year	1 year
Discount rate	–	–

quantified the benefits by units of key outcome for effectiveness (CEA). Recall the cost for both CBA and CEA are the same. It was relatively easy for the evaluation team to calculate the cost of the program because DFZ only used funds from its state contract for the program. The total costs for the program were $25 million. Since the program provided drug prevention services to 100,000 participants, the average cost per individual served by the program is $250 ($25 million/100,000 participants). However, as with most cost analyses, quantifying the benefits was more challenging. The evaluation team has limited the benefits it will consider to only those savings the state would have incurred had the drug prevention program not been offered.

To calculate the benefits, or cost savings, the evaluation team must determine the cost of state dollars spent on each person abusing substances. The state spends money related to the physical health and mental health of individuals who abuse substances, as well as child/family assistance programs. Additionally, the state spends funds on public safety and criminal justice issues related to illicit drug use, so the state will save money in these areas as well.

It is important to note that because the state defined benefits as only those that directly save the state money, many benefits are excluded from analysis. These indirect benefits include preventing the diseases spread through illicit drug use (e.g., HIV/AIDS, hepatitis C) and cost savings associated with negative effects on unborn babies. Moreover, the state's narrow definition of benefits excludes benefits produced from individuals who are drug free,

which can include lawful employment and entrepreneurship, income taxes paid on lawful income, and increased productivity at one's current job.

Physical healthcare costs for an individual abusing substances are $5,061, which includes drug treatment and medical services provided due to a drug-related injury or overdose. On average, the state spends $1,396 on mental healthcare and $1,571 per person abusing substances on assistance programs to provide food, housing, and disability support related to substance abuse. Additionally, because substance use results in other types of crime, the state spends, on average, an additional $698 on public safety and $2,269 to prosecute and jail persons abusing substances for drug-related crimes. This means the state benefits from cost savings of $10,995 for each year a person is not abusing substances—so, with 5,730 individuals deterred from abusing substances, the state's total benefits from the program were $63 million. These benefits ($63 million), minus the cost of the program ($25 million), resulted in a net savings of $38 million for the state. Additionally, the evaluation team provides information on the cost and benefits per program participant (total dollar amount/100,000 participants) and per case of substance abuse prevention (total dollar amount/5,730 participants deterred from substance abuse), which are presented in Table 12.7.

The state's $25 million investment in DFZ's substance abuse prevention program yielded more than $63 million in benefits, a net gain of almost $38 million. The evaluation team now wants to determine how cost effective the program was in

Continued

Table 12.7 Cost Analyses for DFZ's Drug Prevention Program

	Total	Per Participant (100,000)	Per Case Averted (5,730)
Costs			
Total estimated costs of DFZ program	$25,000,000	$250	$4,363
Benefits			
Health care	$29,000,000	$290	$5,061
Mental health	$8,000,000	$80	$1,396
Child/family assistance	$9,000,000	$90	$1,571
Public safety	$4,000,000	$40	$698
Criminal justice	$13,000,000	$130	$2,269
Total estimated benefits of preventing drug use	$63,000,000	$630	$10,995
Net benefits	$38,000,000	$380	$6,632

Table 12.8 Cost-Effectiveness Analysis for DFZ's Substance Abuse Prevention Program

Costs	
Total cost of DFZ program participant	$25,000,000
Benefits	
Estimated number of participants deterred from substance abuse (unit of effectiveness)	5,730
Cost-Effectiveness Ratio	**1:$4,363**

achieving its drug prevention goals. Once again, the key unit of effectiveness is the number of individuals prevented from abusing substances. Table 12.8 outlines the CEA for the DFZ's substance prevention program. It demonstrates that it costs the state $4,363 for each individual deterred by DFZ's substance abuse prevention program.

While many evaluations would have stopped after determining the number of participants the program prevented from becoming abusing substances (5,730), the evaluation team continued by also evaluating the cost of the services. The CBA revealed net benefits of nearly $38 million, and the CEA showed the cost of keeping one participant substance free is less than $4,500.

COST-INCLUSIVE EVALUATION: CHALLENGES AND RECOMMENDATIONS

In our experience, there are several challenges inherent in cost analysis that may be multiplied in an evaluation using a partnership-based approach. Most of these challenges are related to a lack of clarity surrounding the purpose of the project and the different partner roles; difficulties staying on track, time, and budget; data and measurement issues; and challenges associated with communicating the findings. With that in mind, we provide the following recommendations for those seeking to conduct cost-inclusive evaluations using a partnership approach to consider.

To clarify the purpose of the evaluation and establish shared ownership, the partners should develop a specific scope of work for the evaluation. The scope of work will vary based on the nature of the cost-inclusive evaluation, but it should include background information and contextual information about the project; a formal budget for the project with the planned expenditures; and a timeline with scheduled activities corresponding to each of the six steps. The scope of work should also identify and describe the expected contributions of each of the partners with respect to technical expertise to conduct cost analysis calculations. This includes noting who has the substantive expertise to provide context for the analysis, identify data sources, and inform decision making; who has the leadership capacity to ensure that stakeholders and those with standing are represented throughout the project; and who will provide the administrative support to ensure that the project moves forward on a timely basis. Each partner's contribution (technical expertise; substantive expertise; leadership; and/or administrative support) should be articulated for each of the six steps of the cost analysis project.

Once the partners have decided on the scope and goal of the cost-inclusive evaluation, many of the questions partners should address at the beginning of a cost-inclusive evaluation are considered in Step 1, defining the analysis. It is in this step that the partners agree on the type of analysis to conduct, who has standing, whose perspective to consider, alternatives or basis for comparison, timeframe of the program, and discount rate. Decisions made in this step define the analysis moving forward, which means partners should come to agreement on key elements of Step 1. If partners are unable to reach consensus in this step, we recommend additional sensitivity analysis in Step 5, which we discuss below.

When moving to Step 2, listing and monetizing the costs and benefits, we recommend that each partner create its own original list of costs and benefits. This will help ensure no costs or benefits are omitted, which could drastically alter the final results of the analysis. Additionally, this will help the partnership identify what costs and benefits are most frequently cited among partners and whether each partner values the costs and benefits in the same manner. This will help the partnership determine appropriate proxies to use for intangible costs and benefits, as it can help partners better understand the willingness to pay for other partners' preferences.

To list and monetize the costs and benefits, the partnership is likely to encounter data and measurement issues, as well as disagreements. It is important to acknowledge the potential issues relating to the identification and selection of the measures and assumptions related to the cost analysis. At the beginning of the evaluation, the partners should conduct an inventory of what data are available and what data are needed. Data to inform cost analysis will vary with different types of services or programs being evaluated, but it will likely come from existing agency records, forecasts or cost projections, previous cost studies, or those with technical or substantive expertise. Conducting sensitivity analyses (Step 5) and varying assumptions to produce higher and lower figures can help the partnership to review the potential range of the findings and choose among the different measures and assumptions. Additional sensitivity analysis may be necessary if the partnership is unable to agree on the assumptions and estimates, which may help build consensus among partners who value costs and benefits differently. All decisions should be well documented, transparent, and open, noting who made the decision (or decisions) and why. After all, cost-inclusive evaluations are only as strong as the assumptions and estimates used, so it is critical to be clear as to what assumptions were made and why.

The partnership team is not likely to experience challenges in Steps 3 and 4. In Step 3, the partnership team discounts future net benefits to present value, using the agreed-upon discount rate in Step 1 and, in Step 4, they calculate the NPV (CBA) or the cost-effectiveness ratio (CEA). While these steps are fairly straightforward, there are a few factors the partnership team should consider. First, CBA treats all decisions related to programs with a positive NPV the same, regardless of the magnitude of the positive net value result. That is, a program could have an NPV of $1 and it receives the same treatment (i.e., the decision to proceed with the program) as a program that has an NPV of $1 million. With scarce resources, the partnership should be aware of this limitation in CBA. Second, recall that CEA only examines costs of the program, not its benefits, because CEA assumes that differences in program effectiveness are negligible. The partnership should ensure that the programs being compared do in fact have similar levels of effectiveness. One program may be more cost efficient, but that same program may also not be as effective as a less cost-effective option.

In the presentation of the findings, the evaluation partnership needs to be sure to acknowledge any limitations associated with the analysis. These limitations might include weaknesses in the assumptions or the measures; a discussion of any relevant contextual factors; and a discussion about the implications of using alternative calculations. The evaluation partners should also consider the nature of the audiences when presenting the findings. Some stakeholders will be interested in greater levels of detail relating to the assumptions of the measures and each step of the analysis, while others will be more focused on the outcomes or the decision being made as a result of the cost analysis. Within the partnership, different stakeholders can also help to share and disseminate the findings to various audiences, if needed.

CONCLUSION

In summary, there are six steps to conducting cost analysis: defining the scope of the analysis; listing and monetizing the impacts (CBA) or quantifying benefits by the unit of effectiveness (CEA); discounting future impacts to determine present value; calculating the NPV (CBA) or cost-effectiveness ratio (CEA); performing sensitivity analysis; and making decisions and providing recommendations.

While the steps may seem straightforward, conducting cost-inclusive evaluations in the community context raises a number of issues. Typically, the values of efficiency and effectiveness are at the root of these types of CBA and CEA analyses, yet other factors may need to be considered when making strategic decisions about moving forward with a program, especially when the nonprofit's private costs outweigh its private benefits, which is why we recommend separating financial benefits from societal benefits (Table 12.4). Moreover, evaluators will need to assess the quality of the data with which they are working, given that some community programs will not have the capacity or the systems in place to help them to make reasonable calculations about the program's costs and benefits. Finally, given the wide range of potential stakeholders with standing, evaluators will need to tailor the presentation of the findings for different audiences and ensure that the assumptions, sensitivity, and limitations to the analyses are clear so that the stakeholders can make informed decisions.

FURTHER READING

Cordes, J. J. (2017). Using cost-benefit analysis and social return on investment to evaluate the impact of social enterprise: Promises, implementation, and limitations. *Evaluation and Program Planning, 64*, 98–104.

Keating, B. P., & Keating, M. O. (2017). *Basic cost benefit analysis for assessing local public projects* (2nd ed.). Business Expert Press.

Muenning, P., & Bounthavong, M. (2016). *Cost-effectiveness analysis in health: A practical approach* (3rd ed.). John Wiley & Sons.

Nas, T. (1996). *Cost-benefit analysis: Theory and application*. Sage.

PerformWell. (n.d.). http://performwell.org/.

Preskill, H., & Boyle, S. (2008). A multidisciplinary model of evaluation capacity building. *American Journal of Evaluation, 29*, 443–459.

Rogers, P. J., Stevens, K., & Boymal, J. (2009). Qualitative cost-benefit evaluation of complex, emergent programs. *Evaluation and Program Planning, 3*, 83–90.

Washington State Institute of Public Policy. (2017). *Benefit-cost results*. http://www.wsipp.wa.gov/BenefitCost

KEY CONCEPTS

Benefits: Monetary value of all resources produced or saved as a result of the program.

Cost-Benefit Analysis (CBA): Relationship between costs and benefits of a program.

Cost-Effectiveness Analysis (CEA): Relationship between costs and effectiveness of a program.

Costs: Monetary value of all resources required to implement a program.

Discounting: The process of converting future values into their present-day values by taking into account the time value of money.

Effectiveness: Results of the program in terms of units of effectiveness.

Net present value: The difference between the total discounted benefits minus the total discounted costs.

Present value: The present worth of future sums of money.

Proxy value/shadow price: The value assigned to intangible goods.

Sensitivity analysis: Efforts to measure how changes in the estimates and assumptions affect recommendations.

Theory of change: The assumptions about how and why a program will achieve the intended outcomes.

Time value of money: An economic concept that assumes future money does not hold the same value as today's money.

QUESTIONS FOR REFLECTION

1. Consider how you might apply cost-benefit or cost-effectiveness analysis in your own work. Identify a project that could benefit from using a cost-inclusive approach to evaluation. In what way or ways would this approach add value to the project?

2. How would you go about choosing a discount rate? What issues might you have when you try to monetize the costs and benefits? Why would you conduct a sensitivity analysis?

3. What challenges do you think you might encounter when adopting a cost-inclusive approach to evaluation? What strategies would you take to minimize these challenges?

4. What steps would you take to develop and facilitate an evaluation partnership for cost-inclusive evaluations?

REFERENCES

Agranoff, R., & McGuire, M. (2004). *Collaborative public management: New strategies for local governments*. Georgetown University Press.

Baxter, L. W., & Braverman, M. T. (2004). Communicating results to different audiences. In M. T. Braverman, N. A. Constantine, & J. K. Slater (Eds.), *Foundations and evaluation: Contexts and practices for effective philanthropy* (pp. 281–304). Jossey-Bass.

Boardman, A., Greenberg, D., Vining, A., & Weimer, D. (2001). *Cost benefit analysis: Concepts and practice* (3rd ed.). Prentice Hall.

Cartland, J., Ruch-Ross, H. S., Mason, M., & Donohue, W. (2008). Role sharing between evaluators and stakeholders in practice. *American Journal of Evaluation*, 29(4), 460–477. doi:10.1177/1098214008326201

Cellini, S. R., & Kee, E. (2015). Cost-effectiveness and cost-benefit analysis. In K. E. Newcomer, H. P. Hatry, & J. S. Wholey (Eds.), *Handbook of practical program evaluation* (4th ed., pp. 636–672). Jossey Bass.

Crowley, D. M., Dodge, K. A., Barnett, W. S., Corso, P., Duffy, S., Graham, P., Greenberg, M., Haskins, R., Hill, L., Jones, D. E., Karoly, L. A., Kuklinski, M. R., & Plotnick, R. (2018). Standards of evidence for conducting and reporting economic evaluations in prevention science. *Prevention Science*, 19(3), 366–390. doi:10.1007/s11121-017-0858-1

Denhardt, R. B., Denhardt, J. V., & Aristigueta, M. P. (2016). *Managing human behavior in public and nonprofit organizations* (4th ed.). Sage.

Dubnick, M. J., & Romzek, B. S. (1991). *American public administration: Politics and the management of expectations*. McMillan.

Grantcraft. (2006). *Mapping change: Using a theory of change to guide planning and evaluation*. http://www.grantcraft.org/assets/content/resources/theory_change.pdf.

Grob, G. F. (2015). Writing for impact. In K. E. Newcomer, H. P. Hatry, & J. S. Wholey (Eds.), *Handbook of practical program evaluation* (4th ed., pp. 739–764). Jossey Bass.

Hatry, H. P., Morely, E., Rossman, S. B., & Wholey, J. S. (2005). How federal programs use outcome information: Opportunities for federal managers. In J. M. Kamensky & A. Morales (Eds.), *Managing for results* (pp. 197–274). Rowman & Littlefield.

Hausman, D., McPherson, M., & Satz, D. (2016). *Economic analysis, moral philosophy, and public policy* (3rd ed.). Cambridge University Press.

Institute of Medicine and National Research Council. (2014). *Considerations in applying benefit-cost analysis to preventive interventions for children, youth, and families: Workshop summary.* The National Academies Press.

Kania, J., & Kramer, M. (2011, Winter). Collective impact. *Stanford Social Innovation Review,* 33–41.

Malloy, C. L., & Yee, P. A. (2006). Client relations: More than just "business". In G. V. Barrington & D. H. Smart (Eds.), *Independent evaluation consulting: New directions for evaluation, number 111* (2006, pp. 67–77). John Wiley & Sons. doi:10.1002/ev.198

McLaughlin, J. A., & Jordan, G. B. (2016). Using logic models. In K. E. Newcomer, H. P. Hatry, & J. S. Wholey (Eds.), *Handbook of practical program evaluation* (4th ed., pp. 62–87). Jossey Bass.

National Institute on Drug Abuse. (2017). *Trends & statistics.* https://www.drugabuse.gov/related-topics/trends-statistics.

Newcomer, K. A., Hatry, H. P., & Wholey, J. S. (2015). Planning and designing useful evaluations. In K. E. Newcomer, H. P. Hatry, & H. S. Wholey (Eds.), *Handbook of practical program evaluation* (pp. 7–35). John Wiley & Sons.

Office of Management and Budget. (1992). *Circular No. A-94 revised: Guidelines and discount rates for benefit-cost analysis of federal programs.* https://www.whitehouse.gov/omb/circulars_a094

Patton, M. Q. (1978). *Utilization-focused evaluation.* Sage.

Philliber, S. (1998). The virtue of specificity in theory of change evaluation. In K. Fulbright-Anderson, A. C. Kubisch, & J. P. Connell (Eds.), *New approaches to evaluating community initiatives, Vol. 2: Theory, measurement and analysis*(pp. 87–100). The Aspen Institute, Roundtable on Comprehensive Community Initiatives for Children and Families.

Poister, T. H. (2004). *Measuring performance in public and nonprofit organizations.* Jossey Bass.

Shapiro, S. (2010). The evolution of cost-benefit analysis in U.S. regulatory decision-making. *Jerusalem Papers in Regulation & Governance* [Working Paper No. 5]. http://regulation.huji.ac.il/papers/jp5.pdf

Thomas, J. C. (2016). Outcome assessment and program evaluation. In D. O. Renz & B. Herman (Eds.), *The Jossey Bass handbook of nonprofit management and leadership* (4th ed., pp. 444–479). John Wiley & Sons.

W. K. Kellogg Foundation. (2004). *Logic model development guide.* https://www.bttop.org/sites/default/files/public/W.K.%20Kellogg%20LogicModel.pdf

Weiss, C. H. (1995). Nothing as practical as good theory: Exploring theory-based evaluation for comprehensive community initiatives for children and families. In J. P. Connell, A. C. Kubish, L. B. Schorr, & C. H. Weiss, (Eds.), *New approaches to evaluating community initiatives, Vol. 1: Concepts, methods, and contexts* (pp. 65–92). The Aspen Institute, Roundtable on Comprehensive Community Initiatives for Children and Families.

Yates, B. T. (1999). *Measuring and improving cost, cost-effectiveness, and cost-benefit for substance abuse treatment programs: A manual.* Report prepared for U.S. Department of Health and Human Services (Report No. 99-4518). National Institute of Health. https://archives.drugabuse.gov/sites/default/files/costs.pdf

Yates, B. T. (2009). Cost-inclusive evaluation: A banquet of approaches for including costs, benefits, and cost-effectiveness and cost-benefit analyses in your next evaluation. *Evaluation and Program Planning, 32*(1), 52–54. doi:10.1016/j.evalprogplan.2008.08.007

Yates, B. T., & Marra, M. (2017). Introduction: Social return on investment (SROI). *Evaluation and Program Planning, 64,* 95–97. doi:10.1016/j.evalprogplan.2016.10.013

Zerbe, Jr., R. O., & Bellas, A. S. (2006). *A primer for benefit-cost analysis.* Edward Elgar.

PART III

EVALUATION IN ACTION

Special Topics and Contexts

CHAPTER 13

INVESTING IN NONPROFIT DEVELOPMENT THROUGH EVALUATION CAPACITY AND STRATEGIC PARTNERSHIPS
A Four-Tiered Model

Katherine Strater Hogan, Virginia Covill, and Ryan P. Kilmer

Nonprofit organizations in the United States are confronted with questions around the effectiveness, cost efficiency, and scalability of their services and programs, now more than ever. In response, nonprofits are investing in evaluation capacity. For some, the investment is made internally, by dedicating staff responsible for implementing data collection and reporting, while others contract externally with consulting firms, independent evaluators, or university faculty and research labs. Organizations with more defined evaluation and research agendas will often work in collaboration with community organizations and researchers to advance capacity.

Opportunities for nonprofit evaluation continue to grow as stakeholders, including boards of directors, funders and donors, government departments and administrations, and even service clients, become experienced with evaluation research and ask more complex questions of their services and systems. By internalizing evaluation capacity while leveraging partnership opportunities, nonprofits can extend beyond accountability requirements and support organizational growth and development, including strengthening the quality of services and programs, adopting new service models, communicating with stakeholders and funders, establishing linkages across the nonprofit ecological system, and enhancing the community's ability to address its most critical problems.

This chapter explores nonprofit evaluation using a four-tier model (Table 13.1), illustrating how evaluation, particularly when conducted in collaboration with community partners, can support the strategic evolution of a nonprofit. Each tier reflects advancing levels of evaluation capacity and organizational commitment and, subsequently, increasing levels of potential impact. Within each tier, effectively leveraged partnerships can enhance the quality of evaluation activities and the potential benefits for organizational functioning

Learning Objectives

1. Identify key internal evaluation and evaluation capacity needs within nonprofit organizations.

2. Become familiar with how evaluation can support organizational development.

3. Learn a four-tiered framework for conceptualizing nonprofit evaluation activities, reflecting different levels of organizational development and capacity.

4. Understand how partnership practices and partnership-based evaluation are relevant to each of the four tiers.

and community change. Goals and methods in each tier will be highlighted, with examples demonstrating the framework in practice.

THE NONPROFIT ACCOUNTABILITY MOVEMENT

Doing good for public good and passion for a cause are not enough in today's nonprofit sector. Citizens and legislators seek to maximize the impact of expenditures of public funds. In addition, nonprofit funders—corporate, family, and individual foundations, government agencies, philanthropists, and even small grant-making institutions—have increased their expectations, requiring data on the extent to which the programs they fund work and who they serve (Braverman et al., 2004; Carman, 2008; Cutt & Murray, 2000). Moreover, nonprofits are regularly pushed to reach new, larger audiences and grow their impact, typically with the same resources. The need for more advanced measurement, outcome reporting, and data-based strategic planning has spurred the growth of professional evaluation in the nonprofit sector (Boris & Winkler, 2013; Carman, 2007). Evaluation, however, is typically viewed as an administrative cost to be minimized in favor of service delivery. Without dedicated support for evaluation, nonprofits often rely on staff who may have limited experience with using data and lack access to technical assistance and resources (Morariu et al., 2016).

While there is abundant general literature on the topic, there are no integrated guidelines or expectations regulating nonprofit evaluation practices nor meaningful benchmarks to assess the effectiveness of evaluation activities (American Evaluation Association, 2007; Trochim, 2009). Insufficient resources and unclear standards have led to variability in the implementation and, consequentially, perceived value of nonprofit evaluation. Without clear objectives for evaluation, shared evaluation questions, and normative expectations for evaluation design, the full utility of this work remains unrealized among sector stakeholders (Liket et al., 2014). Surveying nonprofit executive directors, Carman (2011) identified diverse approaches to, and objectives for, evaluation, largely centered on securing and sustaining funding and public support. Nonprofit executive directors and managers often frame evaluation as a useful marketing and promotional tool or, at worst, a resource drain (Carman & Fredericks, 2008).

Consistent with a prime theme in this book, evaluation in a nonprofit does not simply attempt to prove that a project "worked," but it also informs how to improve outcomes. Applied strategically, evaluation can help an organization progress in its services and programs, administrative infrastructure, and application of data. For a nonprofit to evolve meaningfully and sustainably, evaluation is a necessary tool in the development and oversight of successful programs and the building of functioning, collaborative system partnerships. However, performance-based accountability requirements (i.e., numbers served, client satisfaction) have served to create a division between funders and nonprofits, as the capacity needed to improve community outcomes is not adequately supported (Carman & Fredericks, 2008; Mott, 2006). To date, the nonprofit–funder relationship remains largely transactional around outcome reporting, leaving nonprofits to determine how to incorporate these requirements, often the only evaluation they have the capacity to conduct, into strategic service refinement and enhanced organizational reach (Carman, 2007; Ebrahim, 2005; United

Table 13.1　A Four-Tiered Model of Nonprofit Evaluation Capacity

	Tier I Processes and Procedures	Tier II Outcomes and Impact	Tier III Models and Infrastructure	Tier IV Community Research and Expertise
Primary Goals	Measure the fidelity of program processes to expectations, best practices, or established protocols and fine-tune processes necessary for successful program implementation	Develop systems that reliably measure the constellation of relevant success indicators and outcome metrics at the right time and the right level and guide programmatic improvements	Translate and apply theory, best practice, and research by introducing, modifying, or expanding a nonprofit's internal components or programs	Evolve best practices, shape understanding of local and national trends, and develop and refine community-wide change strategies through interorganizational collaboration
		Ongoing application of Tier I & II activities supports expansion in Tier III & IV		
Roles of Evaluators and Evaluation Partners	Develop a data-guided culture Examine program functioning in comparison to expectations, benchmarks, or best practice Streamline and integrate data collection, reporting, and response to inform quality improvement Celebrate success	Develop capacity for routine, integrated outcome collection and reporting procedures Expand organizational communication and dissemination of evaluation findings locally and nationally Work across departments, programs, or service agencies to improve system functioning and enhance service experience	Build consensus among organizational staff, board of directors, and community partners regarding needs Identify and optimize drivers of success for a new program or organizational strategy Support program adaptations through Tier I & Tier II evaluation activity	Gather relevant research to demonstrate community need, build consensus over needed action, and support development of shared goals, action plans, and benchmarks Build, manage, or serve on funder collaboratives, collective impact initiatives, and community evaluation committees as principal investigators or research partners

(Continued)

Table 13.1 (Continued)

	Tier I Processes and Procedures	Tier II Outcomes and Impact	Tier III Models and Infrastructure	Tier IV Community Research and Expertise
	<u>University Partners/Consultants</u> • Graduate student training opportunities • Reduced costs associated with evaluation • Access to faculty expertise and resources • More objective "third-party" evaluation		<u>University Partners/Consultants</u> • Develop professional community capacity • Prevent costly challenges and delays • Seek grant or other resources	
	Ongoing development and expansion of data-based culture and engaged organizational partners →			
Capacity Builders	Change is accomplished through quality improvement processes encompassing incremental modifications to procedures, staffing, or program materials and resources. Accessible program data lend efficiency to organizational processes; strengthens grant applications, fundraising, and public communications; and ensures that those representing the organization and its programs have accurate information.		Change is accomplished by building the nonprofit's distinctive competencies and innovative, collaborative community service systems. New program models or collaborative research agendas help shift the nonprofit's ecological network, changing both the systems with which the nonprofit interacts and the positioning of the nonprofit itself in relation to other sector stakeholders.	

Way of America, 2000). Conducting longitudinal research on 200 nonprofits in the San Francisco Bay Area, Gammal et al. (2005) note, "Nonprofits often feel burdened by the overlapping and sometimes conflicting evaluation requirements of multiple grant makers who do not communicate with each other to determine a single set of requirements" (p. 40). Nonprofits with the capacity to apply research and evaluation in their strategic planning and decision making will more successfully adapt to changing political, economic, and community contexts.

NONPROFIT EVOLUTION AND DEVELOPMENT

Capacity and organizational development are areas of scrutiny in the nonprofit sector (also see Chapter 7). Nonprofits are composed of multiple subparts, including their programs and services, management, governance, available resources, and administrative systems, which may not always align in their functioning (Stevens, 2002). Often, capacity building focuses on organizational leadership (i.e., boards of directors) and management teams and is most often framed as technical assistance, strategic planning, or grant funding. While supporting leadership to use data in decision making and strategic planning is important, evaluation capacity can be leveraged beyond a "top-down" approach to strengthen and grow the nonprofit's various parts.

Understanding nonprofit capacity as a reflection of an organization and its parts along a developmental continuum can provide a useful lens for considering effective evaluation strategies. Stage theories classify nonprofits along a predictable continuum, beginning with initial phases of an *Idea* (i.e., a project proposal) and *Start-Up* (i.e., core staff and functions), followed by periods of *Growth* and *Maturity*, and in some cases, stages of *Decline*, *Turnaround*, or *Termination* (Stevens, 2002). During periods of growth, evaluation can be particularly useful in developing a nonprofit's "distinctive competencies" (Stevens, 2002, p. 32) that distinguish its work in the community. Because nonprofit evaluation necessitates navigating growth and change at the levels of the organization and its subparts, the work of an evaluator within one nonprofit, and even within one program area, may and should look different from the work within another due to variations in development and capacity. This chapter will delineate specific levels of evaluation activity that support a developmental framework, identify practices applicable throughout a nonprofit's lifecycle, and help nonprofit professionals more clearly articulate the organizational goals of evaluation.

The Nonprofit Ecological System

Conceptualizing a nonprofit as existing within its own unique environmental context, or ecological system (Figure 13.1), yields insight into its developmental evolution. A nonprofit's ability to achieve community impact depends greatly not only on internal drivers, but on external factors and conditions existing within its ecological system. These factors include the national, state, and local policies and priorities that influence regulations and public funding; accrediting and regulatory oversight committees and boards; public sector leaders; and collaborative partnerships within local nonprofit networks. An organization's position within this ecological system and its linkages with other entities

Figure 13.1   The Nonprofit Ecological System

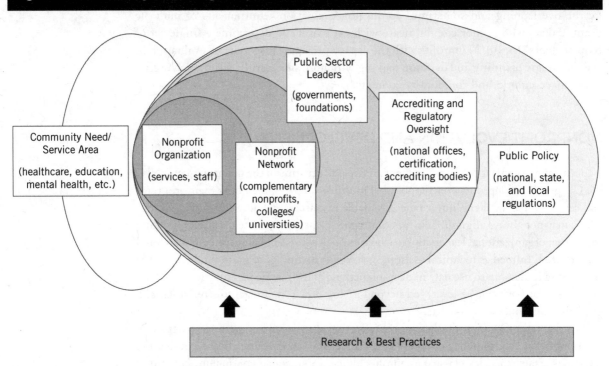

depend largely on the organization's ability to achieve growth and maturity. This position has implications for the organization's ability to draw on partners, resources, and funding to deliver effective, targeted interventions and ultimately accomplish its mission. Change or disruption in one layer of this ecological system can have a significant influence on the functioning and priorities of others. For example, changes in national policy can influence funding around particular health and human service needs, subsequently making regulatory and technical assistance programs more or less accessible to public sector leaders and nonprofit networks. How a nonprofit is situated within its system and the quality of its relationships across the nonprofit network, including public sector leaders and accrediting organizations, will predict how an organization sustains or grows its operations, particularly when disruptions occur. Nonprofits that have demonstrated the quality of their services and actively contribute back to this system through collaborative community change or knowledge expansion (i.e., around best practices or community needs) are best situated for long-term growth and sustainability.

Internal and Partner Evaluators

Discourse on nonprofit evaluation includes the potential role conflict, ethical dilemmas, and bias that internal evaluators may experience (Mathison, 1991), historically leading to a false conclusion that independent, external evaluation (e.g., university faculty, contracted consulting firms) is a best practice. Over time, this "forced choice" has limited the growth of nonprofits' evaluation capacity. Strategic application of both internal evaluation staff and external partners can be resource effective, depending on a nonprofit's objectives, and these roles should be considered complementary.

Nonprofits with available resources are internalizing their evaluation capacity by establishing staff positions and job responsibilities specific to evaluation (Morariu et al., 2016). With knowledge of the nonprofit's culture, policies, and context, internal staff can tailor evaluation designs and messaging (Love, 1991; Mathison, 2011). This knowledge aids in establishing well-targeted and sound performance management and quality improvement systems, helping to achieve critical outcomes. At higher levels of organizational capacity, internal staff trained in and dedicated to evaluation functions can help expand programs and services, enhance reputation, and establish new collaborative partnerships leveraging the work of multiple institutions toward shared community outcomes. In working with these partners, internal evaluation staff can translate the needs and goals of their own organization and its staff.

While internal evaluation staff can help facilitate a data-capable and responsive organization, partner evaluators can enhance the nonprofit's evaluation capacity at multiple levels. Evaluation-focused university partnerships provide nonprofits with access to skilled students to complete special projects or to the specialized expertise of faculty in key topic areas or advanced methods (see Hogan et al., 2017). Local universities often offer courses or programs that incorporate nonprofit evaluation (i.e., community psychology, nonprofit management, social work), and such work can yield substantive joint benefits. Consultation and technical assistance are also available through many local, regional, and national organizations, from hands-on contracted work to long-distance learning communities. Beyond those resources, evaluation partners in parallel service systems or organizations, including public schools, child welfare agencies, managed care organizations, and health and mental health systems, often maintain extensive data systems. Partnerships with targeted departments in such institutions can open dialogue and enhance data collection, providing access to information beneficial for program- and community-level evaluation efforts. Partnering with non-service delivery organizations, including advocacy or human rights organizations, provides additional capacity around data analysis and interpretation of results and can increase the momentum of community responses to evaluation findings. When strategically integrated, internal evaluators and external partners provide complementary capacity to a nonprofit. Through these partnerships, nonprofits can leverage their internal capacity, no matter how large or small, to advance their organizational development.

A FOUR-TIER MODEL OF NONPROFIT EVALUATION

This chapter describes a four-tier model of nonprofit evaluation practice that drives organizational evolution and development (see Table 13.1 for a description of this model). In this model, Tier I (Processes and Procedures) and Tier II (Outcomes and Impact) represent the most common and foundational conceptions of evaluation within nonprofits. The role of the evaluator in Tier I is to ensure that the organization is on a path to achieving desired outcomes by enhancing department, team, or program functioning through data-based feedback and modifications to procedures. The goal of Tier II evaluation is to assess and improve program outcomes and develop ways to communicate impact with community stakeholders. As organizations evolve, grow, and mature, Tier III evaluation (Models and Infrastructure) informs and facilitates adaptations to program models and expansion or termination of service lines. Finally, Tier IV (Community Research and Expertise) addresses how an organization can best position its services within its ecological system to foster systems-level change and access needed resources. Movement through each tier is not necessarily linear or cross-organizational; however, lower tier functions must be achieved and maintained before a nonprofit can commit to and leverage its capacity to advance to a higher tier.

To illustrate how evaluation teams, both internal evaluation staff and external evaluation partners, implement and leverage the evaluation tiers to support organizational development and evaluation capacity building, two nonprofits and their community partnerships will serve as case examples throughout this chapter. As a reflection of the diversity of organizational missions and infrastructures within the nonprofit sector, the examples reflect organizations serving the same community, Charlotte, North Carolina, through separate but parallel service systems—education (Communities in Schools; see Box 13.1) and health care (Teen Health Connection; see Box 13.2).

BOX 13.1 COMMUNITIES IN SCHOOLS (CIS) CHARLOTTE-MECKLENBURG

Working directly in more than 2,300 schools in 25 states, CIS is an organization that empowers all students to stay in school and on a path to graduation. CIS operates as a national federation of independent 501(c)(3) organizations, consisting of a national office, state and managing offices, and over 160 local affiliates. Case managers work in schools to serve at-risk students and families using an Integrated Student Supports (ISS) model, promoting academic success by assessing students' needs, connecting students and families with resources, and monitoring and adjusting supports through ongoing data tracking.

CIS Charlotte-Mecklenburg (CIS-CM) is an affiliate of the CIS network. Founded in 1985, it serves over 6,500 students annually in grades pre-K to 12. While the CIS National Office provides CIS affiliates with some evaluation tools and guidance, CIS-CM has invested in full-time internal evaluation for over 10 years. This has allowed the organization to develop evaluation resources tailored to local needs, establish capacity for ongoing practice refinement, and promote a culture that embraces data for continuous learning and improvement. The agency maintains a vice president of Research, Evaluation & Impact who reports directly to the chief executive officer and is responsible for evaluation design, oversight of cross-departmental initiatives, and external research collaborations. Additional department positions include a Research & Evaluation analyst, focused on internal "dashboard" reporting and external grant reporting, and a data support coach, overseeing data entry systems and quality improvement training. CIS-CM works closely with the Community Psychology Research Lab at the University of North Carolina at Charlotte (UNCC) to supplement selected efforts with external expertise and to contract with students and faculty on a part-time basis to implement evaluation activities. Data are routinely shared through a partnership between CIS-CM and the Charlotte-Mecklenburg Schools' Accountability Office to assess students' academic outcomes. Evidence of these outcomes supports the ongoing placement of CIS staff across public school locations.

BOX 13.2 TEEN HEALTH CONNECTION

Founded in 1992, the Atrium Health Levine Children's Teen Health Connection (Teen Health Connection) provides integrated health, mental health, and prevention services for adolescents. Teen Health Connection provides medical care through a community collaboration with a local hospital system, and its unique nonprofit extension supports an integrated care model, mental health services, prevention and outreach programming, and partnership capacities. The structure is innovative within traditional healthcare systems. While services are utilized by adolescents reflecting diverse contextual and socioeconomic backgrounds, the organization serves a predominantly high-risk population and over 65% of its patients are insured through Medicaid.

Beginning in 2010, Teen Health Connection partnered with UNCC's Community Psychology Research Lab to initiate evaluation of its integrated health care programs. Over several years, multiple program-specific (and mutually beneficial) student projects demonstrated to leadership the strategic advantage of incorporating internal evaluation staff responsible for working across programs and with community partners. The evaluation team consists of one director, full- or part-time research associates and consultants responsible for supporting the changing day-to-day evaluation functions (i.e., data entry and reporting) of distinct program areas, and graduate student interns through UNCC's Community Psychology Research Lab responsible for special projects. The team is involved across a variety of core agency functions, including strategic planning, development, marketing, and grant writing, and team members across the organization support and lead data collection and evaluation initiatives.

Tier I—Processes and Procedures

Tier I evaluation focuses on collecting, analyzing, and reporting data that will help fine-tune the processes necessary for successful program implementation. This includes measuring the fidelity of program processes to expectations, best practices, or established protocols and determining whether the procedures in place are necessary and sufficient for achieving expected results (see Chapter 6). Although Tier I activities are central to nonprofit evaluation, they may be misunderstood and underappreciated in organizations new to evaluation practice, in part because they are seen as reflecting program criticism, that is doubt or concern that the program is doing what it was designed (and supposed) to do. However, this level or type of evaluation is necessary for interpreting results from outcome evaluations (Tier II—Outcomes and Impact) and expanding or modifying programs (Tier III—Models and Infrastructure). By building this foundational evaluation capacity, subsequent evaluations are more likely to yield reliable and interpretable data, contributing to results that suggest a well-understood, well-functioning program.

Tier I: Goals and Evaluation Questions. Many nonprofits initially seek evaluation to answer questions related to a program's value before addressing Tier 1 evaluation's fundamental questions: "Is this program operating as intended?" and "Are there barriers to program processes?" At this level, nonprofit leaders need data related to a program's procedural elements to identify areas that are working as intended or that need improvement, recommend strategic modifications, and understand the impact of changes on program functioning. Evaluators help to establish thresholds for what is expected, monitor and modify procedures to better align with those expectations, and measure adherence in practice and over time. Engaging in Tier 1 evaluation in isolation is often a cost-effective means of driving implementation of a new service or engaging in quality improvement for existing programs. While it yields information on functioning, it cannot provide information on whether programs are effective, and in what dosage services achieve positive outcomes, the foci of Tier II activities.

Tier I: Tools, Techniques, and Implementation. Tier I evaluation activities are often referred to as formative or process evaluations and begin with outlining a program's "theory of change" and "logic model," the roadmaps of how program activities are implemented and their connection to desired short- and long-term outcomes (see Chapters 1 and 6). Data collection is tied to assessing the extent to which this roadmap is followed during service delivery, by staff, partner agencies, and service participants. As discussed elsewhere (see, e.g., Chapters 6 and 17), formative evaluation is designed to collect information relevant to modifying programs as they are developed, with the overall goal of improving outcomes (Royse et al., 2016; Stetler et al., 2006).

The data collected in Tier I focus on organizational and program outputs: number of people served; percent of the target population in services; participant retention, attrition, and completion rates; repeat visits; timelines of service delivery; costs per participant; program frequency and duration; staff productivity; and completion of program-specific activities included in the logic model (e.g., "homework" performed outside of the setting). Ultimately, this tier of evaluation is focused on collecting implementation data such as what services were provided, to whom, how often, and how well. This information identifies discrepancies in how the program is operating compared with target expectations or best practice.

Often, accurate data on basic program functioning indicators can be drawn from existing administrative functions, including basic record-keeping spreadsheets, employee time and effort reports, attendance sign-ins, appointment logs, and participant registration or referral forms. When the program utilizes an evidence-based or best-practice approach, fidelity measures should assess the extent to which the program adheres to the model guiding its development. In some cases, direct observation of service delivery is necessary to understand how a protocol is implemented. Checklists or reflections completed by program staff or service participants themselves, and direct interviews, focus groups, or surveys can illuminate strengths of program implementation and potential barriers to success, including those inherent in the program delivery (e.g., staff training), within the environment (e.g., transportation, perceived stigma), and reflective of individual performance (e.g., completion of "homework").

The exact tools, terminology, and techniques applied in Tier I may vary depending on the nonprofit sector. For example, health care organizations frequently utilize short turn-around, quality improvement tools that are reflective of core Tier I evaluation activity, including root-cause analysis, run charts, Plan-Do-Study-Act (PDSA) cycles (see Provost & Murray, 2011, and Chapter 16), and efficiency tools adopted from business management including LEAN (see Womack & Jones, 2003) and Six Sigma (see Pyzdek & Keller, 2009). These tools are suited to examine efficiently the unique time-bound procedures and volume of a health care environment. On the other hand, direct classroom observation, attendance logs, and teacher self-assessments are more common in educational research. When exploring potential tools in the development of Tier I evaluation initiatives, evaluators should explore resources across a range of industries.

Tier I: The Role of Partnership. Especially in Tier I, establishing trusting relationships between evaluators and program staff is essential. Much of the data collected directly reflect the degree to which program staff meet their own objectives, necessitating that evaluation is seen as an organizational improvement tool rather than a method of discipline. Program staff must trust that the evaluator has the content knowledge, expertise, and understanding of the program to interpret and report findings appropriately. In Tier I, evaluators should capitalize on opportunities to gain trust and buy-in from program staff by directly demonstrating how evaluation findings are used to promote program functioning, support organization-wide learning, and improve staff's own experiences with their work. Evaluators can support this data culture by documenting program successes and finding opportunities to recognize and celebrate program accomplishments.

Tier I evaluation activities represent an opportunity to improve programs while building evaluation capacity. With appropriate training and oversight, program staff can be trained to enter data, implement follow-up procedures, and assume basic reporting functions. Organization leadership and program managers can help identify and keep accountable those responsible for collecting and maintaining data, specify timeframes for collection, and centralize information for timely access. Once service metrics and data management procedures are developed and tested, some Tier I activities can be incorporated into staff routines. Frontline staff are also well connected to day-to-day program operations and have key knowledge of organizational realities; this ability to help interpret findings and implement changes make them critical Tier I partners.

While internal evaluators may be uniquely situated in terms of their organizational knowledge and rapport with staff, nonprofits with less evolved evaluation agendas are well suited to partner with local consultants or universities for low-risk, high-return collaborations. Through successful university collaboration, nonprofits are provided cost-effective evaluation capacity, and universities gain needed student training opportunities. These initial partnerships can lead to more substantive efforts and higher-level evaluation activity (see Hogan et al., 2017). Partnering externally around routine data collection, evaluation coordination, and analysis can also allow evaluation staff to attend to higher-level organizational functions and pressing needs.

Tier 1: Organizational Impact. Tier I evaluation supports the start-up and growth of an organization throughout its lifecycle. By implementing regular Tier I procedures, nonprofit staff, leaders, and governance can be responsive to program challenges and opportunities and ensure that programs operate as efficiently and effectively as possible. Organizations that routinely apply and, importantly, learn from this level of evaluation develop a strong data-guided culture. This culture can protect organizations from program decline and facilitate proactive response to turnaround.

This tier facilitates the development of capacity for advanced evaluation by building routine data monitoring systems and reporting procedures across programs. Formalized data collection processes and centralized "warehouses" of information increase the organization's capacity to fulfill basic accountability requirements of funders and boards of directors. Accessible program data can lend efficiency to organizational processes; strengthen grant applications, fundraising, and public communications; and ensure that those representing the organization and its programs have accurate, data-informed talking points. Over time, Tier I capacity helps evaluators support programs in other ways, such as focusing on expansion strategies or identifying relevant trends.

Until now, this discussion has conceptualized Tier I evaluation as a largely within-program or organization activity; however, when the processes and procedures under evaluation span multiple community partners or entire service systems, the organizational impacts of such evaluations can be profound. By evaluating the effectiveness of an organization's processes as they relate to the procedures of external partners, evaluators are positioned to make recommendations that could modify and enhance system-wide functioning. This can result in improvements in how systems and service-providing organizations interact and how they are experienced (see Case Example: Applying Tier I Evaluation for Programmatic Change).

CASE EXAMPLE: APPLYING TIER I EVALUATION FOR PROGRAMMATIC CHANGE

The Independent Psychological Assessment (IPA) program was designed in response to findings from the Mecklenburg County (NC) Child Fatality Prevention and Protection Team that improved mental health assessments and record reviews when youth entered foster care were needed. Due to its long-standing history of providing healthcare for this population, Teen Health Connection was approached to create and implement the comprehensive assessment protocol that would work efficiently with the child welfare system.

After 2 years of implementation (prior to internalizing evaluation capacity through staff positions), Teen Health Connection contracted with a student from the UNC Charlotte Community Psychology Research Lab to conduct an evaluation. Existing case management data and clinical reports were used to test assumptions about program volume, timelines, and comprehensiveness. Surveys, interviews, and focus groups were conducted with IPA staff and community partners, including district court judges, child welfare social workers and administrators, and guardians ad litem. The results confirmed the value and quality of the assessments; however, only 22% of youth entering custody were assessed, and the average time for report completion was over 3.5 months after a youth entered custody, at which time the utility of the assessment and its service recommendations was largely lost.

The final evaluation report included an extensive set of recommendations for changes to better ensure that assessments would be completed in a routine and timely way, consistent with best-practice parameters (Fostering Connections to Success Act of 2008). While some recommended changes were internal, including additional staff and modifications to case assignments, some required the cooperation of local partners, including the child welfare agency and public school system, to change their own procedures around information sharing.

Teen Health Connection leveraged positive findings around the perceived value of the IPAs to gain needed buy-in from district court judges and child welfare leadership. Increases in the availability of the IPA during court proceedings, combined with the utility of the report for understanding youth needs, led court judges and guardians ad litem to become strong advocates for the IPA program. Stemming from this evaluation, a database was created by the evaluation team and overseen by program administrators that allowed staff to enter, maintain, and retrieve case information more easily, facilitating a more responsive program.

Modifications continued over several years based on analysis of program process data and feedback sought from community partners. In 2018, the IPA program provided assessments for over 80% of age-eligible youth entering foster care, and 65% of these were completed early enough to be included in initial disposition and adjudication court hearings in which placement decisions and case plans are formulated. Because of built-in feedback procedures, upwards of 80% of assessed youth endorsed that they saw the IPA as contributing to a better understanding of who they are and believed that their needs would be better met by their foster parents, social workers, parents, and other key persons because of the assessment. Also, the local managed care organization began to expedite treatment authorizations stemming from the IPA. Psychologists conducting IPAs have since provided trainings on mental health assessments in collaboration with the managed care organization, the local Area Health Education Center, and other partners.

Simple tools transformed the IPA program from a good idea to a robust program on which many child welfare partners rely. A relatively low-cost Tier I evaluation yielded detailed information with which to make data-informed modifications to a service line that became a key component of the local child welfare system's ability to meet the needs of youth in its care.

Tier II: Outcomes and Impact

Nonprofit evaluation in Tier II focuses on defining service outcomes and measuring the impact of an organization and its programs. Again, to evaluate and interpret a program's outcomes accurately and attribute them correctly to the critical components of the program design, Tier I evaluation must be performed beforehand and/or concurrently. The combination of Tier I and Tier II evaluation is a foundational component of a nonprofit evaluator's work.

Tier II: Goals and Evaluation Questions. Tier II evaluation examines the extent to which a program or organization is having an impact on the community need that it was designed to address. Enhancing understanding of the outcomes associated with services (Tier II) and implementation of the programmatic factors necessary for achieving these outcomes (Tier I) are fundamental goals of nonprofit evaluation. Questions for evaluators in Tier II often focus on improvement in knowledge or awareness, behaviors, skills, or conditions at various units of analysis (individual, family, school, community, etc.). Tier II activities focus on identifying the constellation of success indicators and outcome metrics relevant to a particular program or set of programs and developing systems that reliably measure these indicators at the right time and the right level for the program's goals and state of functioning. With such information, evaluators can point to a program's successes or challenges, provide recommendations to guide implementation and build upon these outcomes, and develop differentiated messages for stakeholders to communicate and celebrate impact.

Tier II: Tools, Techniques, and Implementation. As in Tier I, this level of evaluation involves working first with program managers and staff to develop or review program logic models and theories of change (Chapter 1). This provides insight into possible data collection methods and opportunities to gauge service impact. While Tier I emphasizes the inputs, activities, and outputs within these program conceptualizations, Tier II includes a focus on short- and long-term outcomes and sets acceptable benchmarks by which to measure a program's incremental progress.

Evaluators should consider a range of indicators that assess the continuum of expected short- and long-term outcomes. Placing too much emphasis on one outcome metric (i.e., timeline to assessment completion) can be detrimental to understanding the full potential impact of the program (i.e., assessment comprehensiveness). Emphasis on too many outcomes can dilute important messages to stakeholders and unnecessarily complicate data collection. Furthermore, evaluators should remain aware of potential unanticipated outcomes, both positive and negative, and adapt methodologies over time to examine a shifting set of program indicators. Whenever possible, evaluators should work with other nonprofits or foundations to establish shared, community-level metrics, agreed-upon benchmarks, and collaborative data collection strategies.

While the results of Tier II evaluations can have significant implications for nonprofit organizations, they do not necessarily require substantial financial investment or staff burden to implement. In many cases, sources of important data exist, including health-care records, case notes, or student education portfolios and annual testing. Using existing data is advantageous as these data are precollected at regular intervals for the purposes of program functioning, minimizing the burden on program staff to access them. These data can also often be examined for periods of time predating the design of the evaluation or even the start of the program.

Before using these data, however, evaluators must fully understand why and how they were collected and the nature of data entry and management. Without this understanding, they may inadvertently apply inaccurate or misleading information. In many industries, there are strict protocols for the use of data collected during service delivery. Evaluators must obtain appropriate permissions from oversight committees, boards of directors, persons served by the program, and/or even full Institutional Review Boards. While such reviews can be tedious, many can be expedited due to the low levels of risk posed, and quality improvement around data collection can be performed internally prior to the approval of participant-level data analysis. Transparency in the use of these existing data is critical to ensure that they are properly managed and interpreted.

While existing data may be available, evaluators must often incorporate new methods into their evaluation designs to measure indicators of program processes or outcomes reliably or in a more targeted manner. This may include the introduction of new measurement systems such as pre- and/or post-surveys or client satisfaction measures. In most mental health or community-based programs, clinicians use some form of standardized measure of psychosocial, emotional, quality of life, or overall functioning to guide diagnosis and service recommendations. Readministering these same measures at additional time points can provide useful within-person, time-sequence information to evaluate the effectiveness of the service and to guide the intervention without burdening staff with a new procedure. When standardized or publicly available measures are available that reflect indicators of interest, it is in most cases advisable that these measures be used in lieu of new or adapted versions, unless the goals of the project or time constraints require otherwise. This allows greater confidence in the reliability of the results and facilitates potential comparison to other parallel programs and services. Relevant community data can also provide meaningful benchmarks against which to compare program outcomes in communications to stakeholders.

Whenever new data collection is introduced, evaluators and staff must work to ensure it does not disrupt program functioning. Unwieldy forms, additional procedures, and complicated data entry can frustrate staff, introduce errors, and deteriorate relationships. Ideally, platforms for data collection can facilitate and enhance program functioning by supporting program processes and providing real-time feedback to staff.

Tier II: The Role of Partnership. In Tier I and Tier II evaluations, evaluation staff within the organization are often well positioned to develop and implement detailed data collection protocols. They are knowledgeable about existing data sources (and their limitations) and can monitor data collection quality and fidelity closely. In addition, feedback may be better received when delivered by an internal employee; staff may be more likely to seek additional information, view findings as credible, or remain open to changes recommended by a familiar colleague. In response to recommendations, internal staff are positioned to monitor the initiation and effectiveness of changes over time.

While internal evaluators may possess this "insider knowledge," this added capacity is most critical for larger nonprofits with more complex infrastructure and evaluation agendas, where such streamlining can be truly advantageous and resource saving. This is not to say that partner-based evaluation is not sufficient or even preferred in many circumstances, particularly for nonprofits which may have a more limited budget or scope of ongoing evaluation needs. The Tier I and Tier II levels of nonprofit evaluation provide opportunities to connect with faculty at local universities and may be fruitful training experiences for graduate students, with faculty supervisors offering important expertise. Especially when conducted with a clear partnership orientation (see Chapters 3 and 14), collaborating with faculty and students at these institutions can offer crucial benefits for those involved, contributing cost-effective, valuable resources to the organization and supporting student development. Even for nonprofits with internal capacity for evaluation, these partnerships allow staff to attend to core activities critical for the strategic growth of the organization while facilitating ongoing monitoring and enhancement of individual programs. Moreover, the new and varied perspectives of students and faculty in the partnership can yield insights of relevance for the nonprofit. Beyond such benefits, external partnerships may also be necessary for more advanced evaluation designs (i.e., randomized controlled trials, large-scale/multisite survey research) or when an "objective third party" evaluation is a stipulation for funding or review. For example, research establishing a best-practice human service or mental health program, and many federal funding opportunities, require that evaluation be performed in partnership with external consultants or universities.

Collective impact evaluations that include the work of several nonprofits and sector partners often require very different approaches to evaluation. Traditionally, if operated by different nonprofits in the same community, programs addressing parallel community needs would be evaluated in isolation, providing each nonprofit with information specific to their services without incorporating the potential impact of parallel programs targeting a different audience (i.e., parents vs. their children) or social need (i.e., employment vs. housing). Assessing for collective impact through evaluations that encompass the work of multiple agencies is often best accomplished via partnerships involving agency-specific internal evaluators, knowledgeable of their own nonprofit's services, collaborating with an external team responsible for coordinating and communicating across organizations. Evaluating these programs in conjunction with each other can broaden understanding of the cumulative impact of complementary services, assessing for trends extending beyond individual consumers. For example, participation in a core set of programs may yield more positive outcomes than engagement in only one program, or streamlining of service duplication may improve resource division and participant experience.

Tier II: Organizational Impact. Both Tier I and Tier II evaluations have the potential to improve the functioning of an organization's programs and services through a PDSA, quality improvement approach. This capacity is salient throughout a nonprofit's lifecycle, helping it to transition from a start-up to a mature organization, experiment with the growth of new programs, and support organizational turnaround when necessary through targeted process and outcomes evaluation. Program staff, as the most direct link to service improvements, are critical recipients of evaluation findings. When staff are provided individual-level feedback (e.g., retention and attrition, consumer-level outcomes), they can offer their ideas about the factors at play and make direct and meaningful modifications to their interventions to achieve improved outcomes. Similarly, providing program managers with actionable reports about variations in staff productivity or outcomes can contribute essential coaching and supervision tools. It is crucial that evaluators establish clear guidelines about how data are used within the organization and make sensitive reports accessible only to those who can apply the information. Often, program managers and staff require more detailed data, broken down in ways that might differ from the level at which they are reported publicly. This type of knowledge allows staff to continue to implement the program with fidelity as well as articulate its benefits to potential consumers, funders, or other stakeholders.

Strategically communicating results of Tier II evaluation to stakeholder groups can provide opportunities for growth in an organization's resource development and governance. With actionable data, boards of directors can more effectively guide the work of nonprofit leadership and serve as advocates and financial stewards for the organization. Information about the functioning of services and their outcomes (or lack thereof) supports the board's ability to make decisions about funding, partnership, or expansion. Sharing evaluation results at this level can also help an organization reach new audiences, connect with leaders in their respective industries, and engage new and existing funders meaningfully in the nonprofit's work (see Case Example: Learning From Tier II Evaluation).

CASE EXAMPLE: LEARNING FROM TIER II EVALUATION

At CIS, focus groups with former CIS students suggested social–emotional learning was an important but unmeasured outcome for students receiving services. CIS outcomes had focused on attendance, behavior, and coursework improvement, but not the social–emotional skill building that anecdotally supported those changes. Evaluation staff worked with the programming team to adopt a measure of social–emotional functioning that would be first used during intake and could inform student-focused goal-setting and skill development, help program staff track individual student change over time, point to needed adaptations to case plans or intervention models, and provide data regarding overall program outcomes. The evaluators developed a tool that aligned well with program needs and provided valid and reliable indicators of social–emotional learning. In addition to creating the measure, the evaluators provided training on the assessment and integrated data collection within staff responsibilities. In this instance, the evaluators identified a gap in assessed program outcomes and implemented new data collection that supported an enhanced program model and delivery.

Tier III: Models and Infrastructure

In Tiers I and II, evaluation activities within a nonprofit are dedicated to documenting, monitoring, and understanding program and service outputs and outcomes. Change is accomplished through quality improvement processes encompassing incremental modifications to procedures, staffing, or program materials and resources. Tier III evaluation efforts enable nonprofits to go beyond quality improvement and make more significant adjustments to organizational operations and programming, including the creation of new programs or complete realignment (and even termination) of existing services.

Tier III: Goals and Evaluation Questions. After accumulating program data over time and building organizational evaluation capacity—work conducted in Tiers I and II—evaluators can begin more rigorous exploration and analysis of community needs and the organizational capacity to meet these needs. Tier III emphasizes how a nonprofit fundamentally allocates resources through the creation of new, or major modification of existing, service models or frameworks. Organizational goals relevant to Tier III evaluation are often created in response to data gathered from lower-tiered evaluation activities, including positive outcomes or unexpected trends that the organization can leverage for growth, or a lack of outcomes that might necessitate strategic turnaround or service termination. This level of work is also initiated in response to evolving community needs and priorities. As the underlying problems addressed by nonprofits are better understood and as organizations themselves grow their capacity, the strategies used inherently shift over time.

At Tier III, evaluators help nonprofits translate and apply theory, best practices, and industry research within the new program-specific context. This includes helping organizational staff, leadership, and boards of directors understand and apply changes to service models and ensuring that these changes align with the community needs or program findings. To ensure services remain effective and sustainable, evaluators also play a key role as everyday procedures transition, monitoring fidelity to service frameworks and the degree to which programs and services continue to meet goals and objectives, through Tier I and Tier II evaluation activities.

Tier III: Tools, Techniques, and Implementation. Methodologies at this level are focused on the interpretation and translation of research findings, both of multiprogram and multiyear evaluations and local and national research, into successful organizational adaptation (i.e., modifying, discontinuing, or expanding programs). At this level, evaluators can incorporate more advanced evaluation protocols and more sophisticated analytical techniques to better detect differential impacts of programs and services.

When learning from an organization's own programmatic data over time, Tier III methodologies are largely informed by implementation science practices. Implementation science helps organizations to adopt, refine, and sustain effective interventions (Fixsen et al., 2005) by identifying key "success drivers" across the organization, including competency factors (i.e., hiring and training practices), organizational factors (i.e., data resources and systemic support), and leadership factors (i.e., supervision and performance reviews; Fixsen et al., 2015). These "drivers" require modification as a program is adapted from best to routine practice within a nonprofit's applied setting. Evaluators may make recommendations about how a program should be modified in Tiers I and II; recommendations in Tier III revolve around adaptations beyond program functioning, such as additional organizational infrastructure, restructuring of departments, or new business practices and organizational procedures. Implementation science can guide the process of how those changes occur across the organization to accommodate the success of programs and services.

Engaging in this level of evaluation necessitates that nonprofit evaluators remain attuned to their local community and the larger nonprofit ecological system and service industries relevant to their work. Multimethod community needs assessments are useful tools to identify new opportunities to better address community concerns central to the nonprofit. Needs assessments can incorporate evaluator-led methods such as surveys (i.e., mail, phone, online) or focus groups with community members or clients, analyses of existing sources of private (e.g., healthcare records, educational records) and public data (e.g., census, government data, open access data), and reviews of current and trending literature across relevant areas and industries. Evaluators have the capacity to triangulate these data to maintain organizational sustainability in a changing ecological system, advise on changes before and as they are made, and determine whether adaptations lead to meaningful improvements in service experience and outcomes.

Tier III: The Role of Partnership. Adaptation of a nonprofit's models and infrastructure requires staff to translate a best practice into tangible process changes across an organization's departments and subparts (i.e., programs, resources, board of directors). Change processes associated with organizational growth at this stage can be challenging; staff may be asked to take on new responsibilities or practice in a new way, and inconsistency across and even within staff is inevitable. Navigating this process largely depends on the capacity and culture of the nonprofit, but it is often facilitated through a partnership approach incorporating technical assistance and feedback.

At this level of organizational development, it is critical that nonprofits have internalized evaluation capacity to support a strong, sustainable data culture, whether through evaluation-specific staff or routine data collection and reporting procedures. Evaluators, especially those internal to the organization, can identify and monitor key implementation drivers across the organization over time, as they often have more direct access to and influence over these practices (e.g., employee training in another department).

Introducing more complex organizational changes, however, often requires activities that fall outside of the day-to-day operations of nonprofits' core staff. These transitions often require skills in project management, business development, and rapid quality improvement cycles, for which many nonprofits lack internal capacity. Work with partner evaluators can help to reduce internal tensions associated with large transitions. Sound communication is a "must," and engagement with partners can help ensure transitions remain on schedule despite competing organizational needs. Partnering with outside consultants or university faculty in developing and implementing a strategic plan around these transitions can help to prevent costly challenges and delays. University faculty can help develop student internships or practicum placements and bring evaluative and content expertise to special topics.

Often the level of change required of Tier III activity requires additional work with a nonprofit's community partners to identify and work through procedural or structural barriers (e.g., billing, legal policies), collect data on participant outcomes, and ensure adapted programs are woven into local service networks. Multidisciplinary committees are useful when they are designed specifically to advise and support evaluation staff and leadership through the process of program or service adaptation. Advisory groups composed of community researchers, university faculty, content experts, and key organizational stakeholders, such as staff and clients, can provide perspective and resources to align programs, management, governance, resources, and systems as organizational changes occur. For example, partner agencies can access external data needed for enhanced outcome measurement, university faculty and their students can provide technical assistance, and board and staff members can support consistent messaging about organizational changes and serve as role models for the application of evaluation recommendations.

Tier III: Organizational Impact. Evaluation at this level is directly tied to advancing and guiding a nonprofit through its lifecycle (Stevens, 2002)—and it ultimately contributes to a nonprofit's relevance within its ecological system. This level of evaluation is particularly important during growth cycles, when new ideas and strategies for addressing community problems are added alongside a nonprofit's core programs and services. This tier should not be confused with mission drift, in which an organization, as a result of seeking resources, implements strategies or programs that do not align with its core objectives and mission (Weisbrod, 2004). Rather, as nonprofits develop distinctive competencies (Stevens, 2002), they define the community change strategies that they, as a result of their reputation, community context, and service array, can optimally deliver. Nonprofits may elect to, or even be asked to, reconfigure the strategies they apply to meet a community need.

This level of work may also be necessary when nonprofits are in decline, and the need for turnaround extends beyond a single program or department. To survive, organizations facing this challenge often publicly redefine priorities and make fundamental changes to their programs, leadership, or infrastructure. Tier III methods can help a nonprofit's staff and governance identify impactful strategies for turnaround that are aligned with the organization's mission and theory of change, establish meaningful benchmarks, and assess incremental progress.

The addition of new programs or service frameworks often corresponds with a shift in a nonprofit's ecological network, necessitating new partnerships and introducing public policy, legislation, regulatory oversight, and best-practice expectations by which the nonprofit was previously unaffected. Evaluation can help a nonprofit remain aligned with these new parameters during times of growth and expansion.

In this tier, it is particularly important to have clear messaging around the purpose and implications of organizational changes. Boards of directors must be confident that adapting service models will benefit the nonprofit and its clients and appreciate their role in supporting adaptation over time. Similarly, in the face of major programmatic shifts, funders, partners, community members, and clients may question the nonprofit's effectiveness or sustainability. Evaluators can support transitions by providing data about programs' evidence base and effectiveness, variance between anticipated and actual outcomes, and return on investment findings. Evidence of successful program functioning during transition improves confidence and can illustrate the benefits of changes (see Case Example: Tier III in Action—Adapting Trauma-Informed Services).

CASE EXAMPLE: TIER III IN ACTION—ADAPTING TRAUMA-INFORMED SERVICES

A strong national research agenda has resulted in improved awareness of the impact of trauma and adverse childhood events (ACEs). For instance, better understanding is emerging of trauma's direct and indirect health effects, and advanced evidence-based treatment options for individuals exposed to trauma are available. In 2017, a major community report outlined gaps in the local mental health system serving youth and families; primary among them was the availability of trauma-informed services. Evidence from Teen Health Connection's mental health clinicians and medical providers similarly suggested a high prevalence rate for trauma and trauma-related symptoms among the community's adolescents.

Based on this information, the evaluation team worked with the manager of mental health services to apply to the state's Trauma-Focused Cognitive Behavioral Therapy (TF-CBT) Learning Collaborative, documenting the local need for TF-CBT services and the fit and capacity of the nonprofit to provide them. Teen Health Connection clinicians were selected to undergo training to become certified clinicians in TF-CBT, a service delivery and billing requirement for this specialized treatment. Maximizing Teen Health Connection's integrated care approach, TF-CBT services were designed to target the high-risk population of youth served. To enhance identification and access, mental health clinicians worked with medical providers to screen medical patients using an ACEs checklist (Felitti et al., 1998; adapted by Burke Harris & Renschler, 2015), and mental health clinicians continued using the UCLA-PTSD Reaction Index (PTSD-RI; Steinberg et al., 2004) during intake assessments to assess for trauma exposure and symptom severity. Psychoeducation was provided to teens and families who reported exposure. For those who indicated trauma-related symptoms, mental health services were offered, and treatment options explored. Mental health clinicians providing therapy worked with medical providers to adapt their care for patients, particularly for those with chronic conditions such as asthma, diabetes, and gastrointestinal problems.

To recognize the achievement of the clinical team in implementing this screening process successfully, the evaluation team submitted the project for a quality improvement award through the local hospital, and Teen Health Connection, including direct program staff and managers, was publicly recognized by hospital leadership. Staff from the mental health team presented the work and provided education to hundreds of medical providers and hospital administrators on ACEs in healthcare and worked with the evaluation team to develop new improvement goals.

Expanding its work around trauma-informed care, a core team of staff participated in a local learning collaborative through the National Council for Behavioral Health. To support this work, Teen Health Connection contracted with a graduate student from the UNCC Community Psychology Research Lab. This student, in collaboration with the core team, led literature review and staff education, designed data collection to inform improvement efforts and measure progress (i.e., client perception surveys, environmental safety surveys), and made ongoing recommendations regarding practice improvements.

Staff from across the organization—the front desk registration team, medical providers and nurses, health education and prevention experts, and administration—were trained in applying trauma-informed practices. Ongoing evaluation examines the extent to which this organizational shift toward trauma-informed care influences preventive and mental healthcare service utilization and, ultimately, patient outcomes. Through its connections to community stakeholders, including funders, service providers, and government officials, and the purposeful application of local and national research, Teen Health Connection tailored its programs and its organizational infrastructure to align with trauma-informed principles and became local experts in the topic, routinely called on to provide community education.

Tier IV: Community Research and Expertise

In the highest tier of nonprofit evaluation and capacity development, evaluators evolve their focus from an organizational level to larger community needs and service delivery systems. Rather than modifying specific internal processes or adapting service lines in response to the nonprofit ecological system, this tier of evaluation seeks to contribute actively to that system. That is, in this tier, evaluators work to evolve best practices, shape understandings of local and national trends, and develop and refine community-wide change strategies. Engaging in community-level research in Tier IV is an opportunity for nonprofits to enhance understanding of the systems that seek to address community needs by leveraging expertise gained through their direct work with clients. Tier IV evaluation may seem beyond the scope and capacity of many internal nonprofit evaluation teams; however, the nonprofit sector is ripe with opportunities for evaluators to make substantial contributions to community-wide initiatives.

When nonprofits have the capacity to apply evaluation at this level, they can expand their scope of work beyond the delivery of their core services and programs to address systemic change efforts. Nonprofit evaluators can partner with others from the nonprofit sector, public systems, and, as relevant, universities, to develop a cohesive research or intervention plan. By applying their expertise to the community more broadly, nonprofits advance their own development by improving the systems (e.g., mental health, education, social services) with which they interact.

Tier IV: Goals and Evaluation Questions. In Tiers I–III, evaluators focus on organizational-level evaluation and program-specific evaluation design. While improving direct services is essential for meeting individual-level needs, systems-level problems continue to drive the demand for services. The level of community change inherent in Tier IV activity necessitates a cross-organizational, collaborative approach and occurs through many different forms of community system solutions and coalition building, including funder collaboratives (i.e., investors combining resources to address a common concern), collective impact initiatives (i.e., sector representatives agreeing to a common agenda, shared measurement systems, and aligned activities for solving a specific need), and public–private partnerships (i.e., collaborations between government and for-profit agencies organized around a community issue; Kania & Kramer, 2011; Wang et al., 2019).

These community-owned efforts often lack evaluation capacity, limiting their ability to translate research into practice or monitor their own processes, resulting in common complaints of ineffectiveness and attrition in members over time. The role of evaluation is critical to this work, and nonprofits with the capacity to provide evaluation assistance will be key stakeholders in their success. Evaluators in this tier are tasked with bringing relevant data and literature to shape dialogue and support development of shared goals, action plans, and benchmarks. Implementation strategies and service systems supported through these cross-agency initiatives take considerable consensus building to develop; evaluators can help demonstrate community need and provide evidence of the real or potential impact of these initiatives. Once strategies for action are identified, evaluators help to align activities within a valid theory of change and logic model, mapping how community partners and resources are aligned and communicating a cohesive community strategy across partners in the ecological system. Finally, evaluators help align an interorganizational evaluation and measurement strategy reflective of the collective impact model (Wang et al., 2019), helping to inform the common goals, benchmarks, and measurement processes that will assess incremental progress and overseeing data collection, analysis, and reporting.

Tier IV: Tools, Techniques, and Implementation. This tier is typically characterized by an increased focus on coalition building and developing a shared theory of change across the nonprofit network and ecological system. Rather than working within a nonprofit- or program-specific logic model, efforts focus on shifting how a community issue and the environmental factors surrounding it are understood and addressed.

Consistent with that approach, Tier IV methods fall along a continuum of organizational commitment and return. At one end of investment, an evaluator serves as an informational resource, responsible for the collection and reporting of organizational data or local trends in their client population to answer specific questions posed by members of the broader initiative. Nonprofits can contribute to these needs assessment efforts by providing their own data, or by implementing entirely new data collection efforts to gather information to guide a task force's planning and strategy development, including community surveys and focus groups. Evaluators on these collaboratives are often responsible, formally or informally, for staying up-to-date on current changes, trends, and dynamics across their relevant service system(s), interpreting the implications for their own organizational operations and for the larger change effort, and situating the findings from evaluations into a broader understanding of the evolving community need. To that end, evaluators can provide regular summaries of updated literature, best practices, and public policy to ensure the initiative remains informed of relevant changes.

At the highest end of the Tier IV continuum, nonprofit evaluators serve as community research scientists, leading community-wide collaborative endeavors and coordinating the efforts of task force partners into shared metrics, standardized data collection practices, and meaningful community indicators. In this role, evaluators must often navigate diverse governing entities to access needed data, including Institutional Review Boards and regulatory commissions, requiring preparation of application materials and detailed data protection and analysis plans. In this role, evaluators are also commonly the public face for a large portion of the work and must represent the initiative in public settings and engage in messaging beyond evaluation results. When an internal nonprofit evaluator serves in this role, it is critical that lower tier functions, including monitoring of service processes and outcomes, continue to be addressed and that the nonprofit remains a provider of high-quality services.

Tier IV: The Role of Partnership. A nonprofit's involvement in higher levels of community research requires an advanced internal evaluation agenda and evolved network of community partners. Evaluators participating in these initiatives must have an established level of credibility, gained through accumulated evidence that the nonprofit provides high-quality services or through the insights offered by their research, demonstrating a deep understanding of community trends.

At this level, nonprofit evaluation activity and oversight can be costly and time intensive. It is advisable (even necessary) that evaluation of complex or multi-level community initiatives be conducted through partnership, either via a network of nonprofit evaluators serving on a subcommittee of the change effort or by outsourcing significant responsibilities to community partners, including evaluation consultants, faculty evaluators, or evaluation teams from universities, including those able to employ and train skilled students. By creating evaluation subcommittees for community initiatives, nonprofit evaluators can accomplish substantial community-level research while providing critical evaluation-specific technical assistance to participating agencies.

Regardless of the composition of the partnership group, it is absolutely critical that members communicate openly about their respective goals, the roles they can assume, and the resources they can dedicate to the effort. While the larger community initiative may have a clear, overarching shared goal, direct discussion of the partners' varying objectives, interests, or agendas as well as delineation of the contributions they can make to the evaluation is of central importance. Such communication can increase the likelihood that evaluative efforts will yield findings that hold relevance for the participating stakeholders and organizations.

Tier IV: Organizational Impact. This tier has clear implications for organizational development during times of growth and maturity, when leaders can leverage their programs and staff toward community advocacy and policy. At a low end of return, evaluators can secure community data with direct implications for the nonprofit's funding, program decisions, and relationships with stakeholders in its ecological system. Evaluators engaged in this level of work can help establish links across key stakeholders within that network, including those conducting relevant research, involved in systems leadership, or responsible for advocacy or policymaking. When nonprofits connect with and influence their larger context in this way, they are more likely to have access to the resources and assistance needed to address complex, multidimensional problems.

By using evaluation to inform systems-level changes, a nonprofit alters how it operates relative to other organizations, funders, and government entities, positioning nonprofits to be contributors to community-l evel strategies beyond the delivery of their direct services. The positioning of an organization within its ecological system has significant implications for its ability to anticipate, respond, and adjust to changes and disruptions in that system, a critical test of its ability to survive. Altering where an organization "sits" in its ecological system can present a resource advantage for many nonprofits who are able to confront disruptions proactively by strategically expanding programs, applying for targeted funding, partnering with relevant stakeholders, or seeking technical assistance. By establishing a strong foundation of evaluation practice in Tiers I–III, nonprofits can advance to Tier IV evaluation activities that allow them to leverage their expertise across topics of community concern and inform local, regional, and national efforts directed at system change within their sector (see Case Example: Illustrating Tier IV—Collecting Community Data, and Case Example: Tier IV in Action—Informing Collective Impact).

CASE EXAMPLE: ILLUSTRATING TIER IV—COLLECTING COMMUNITY DATA

Teen Health Connection is home to a federally funded coalition aimed to prevent underage drinking and prescription drug misuse through teen-led community prevention. Several local community coalitions targeting different subpopulations exist. To research community trends in substance use, evaluate their interventions' effectiveness, and satisfy federal reporting requirements, these coalitions collaborate every 2 years to conduct the "Youth Drug Survey" of middle and high school students in the public school system. Teen Health Connection's evaluation team provides technical assistance around survey design and sampling, working with data analysts in the school system to identify a representative-stratified random sample that would allow for analyses of cultural and geographical subgroups.

The 2017 survey was completed by 11,050 students in 6th, 8th, 10th, and 12th grades. The final sample reflected school enrollments as well as the system's overall gender and racial makeup. External consultants are contracted to analyze the data and compile the final published report.

The ability to design the evaluation plan and collect data prior to contracting externally for advanced statistical analyses represents a cost savings for the coalitions and an opportunity to develop partnerships with school leadership and administration. By collecting these data together, the coalitions can ensure the availability of needed information and parcel out the data needed to meet funding requirements, monitor progress, and inform modifications to their respective prevention initiatives. Parallel indicators collected as part of evaluation for Teen Health Connection's community programs (i.e., past 30-day use, perceptions of risk) are compared with the Youth Drug Survey and other data sources, such as the Centers for Disease Control and Prevention Youth Risk Behavior Survey, to examine the relative impact of Teen Health Connection's programs against community benchmarks. Beyond the coalition-specific applications of these data, this survey yields data that allow the partners to gauge local trends and changes over time, and coalition partners make the information publicly available through reports and data requests.

CASE EXAMPLE: TIER IV IN ACTION—INFORMING COLLECTIVE IMPACT

In Charlotte-Mecklenburg (NC), it is unlikely that low-income children and youth can escape the cross-generational cycle of poverty. Of the 100 largest counties in the United States, Mecklenburg ranks 99th in upward mobility (Chetty et al., 2014). As a result of this finding, the Leading on Opportunity task force was born to explore and identify ways to improve local economic mobility. After months of interviews with local and national experts and stakeholders, the group crafted a summary report of findings and recommendations for action. The Charlotte nonprofit community mobilized around this issue, with organizations situating the services they provide within the context of the report and its recommendations.

The task force's work continued through the creation of an independent 501(c)(3) nonprofit organization and advisory board to implement the report's recommendations and design a community dashboard to gauge progress. With the investment of over a decade of evaluation capacity building, CIS Charlotte-Mecklenburg was positioned to advise and inform the community-wide effort and its assessment. CIS participated in multiple Leading on Opportunity (LOO) advisory groups for outcomes measurement and strategic planning. CIS also created several research briefs to inform key action areas for the LOO leadership and advised the groups regarding community dashboard indicators that could align with the initiative's outcomes of interest. Additionally, CIS created a Youth Advisory Board to provide input and guidance about the ongoing work and gather rich, qualitative feedback about youth perspectives. Thus, through an advisory capacity, and by introducing new mechanisms for community feedback, the organization was able to contribute directly to a systems-level change effort.

CONCLUSION: ISSUES, CHALLENGES, AND RECOMMENDATIONS

Public calls for accountability and transparency across the nonprofit sector have spurred evaluation activity. This activity, however, has not necessarily been applied strategically, focusing on satisfying short-term reporting requirements rather than long-term organizational development or community problems. By building evaluation capacity within nonprofits, these organizations can both meet accountability requirements and make progress through ongoing developmental challenges and stages. Unfortunately, despite the growing accountability and outcomes movement, evidence suggests that most nonprofits do not have the resources to advance their evaluation capacity due to a lack of investment across the sector. While partner evaluators, particularly local universities, can often provide long-term, cost-effective technical assistance, reliance on these arrangements has limited impact on organizational capacity building and widespread use of applied community research across the sector. Funding for evaluation capacity remains scarce. Funders' familiarity with direct programming and nonprofit operations, relatively limited experience with applied research and evaluation, and lack of clarity about the anticipated outcomes of evaluation activity lead to budgetary limits on these activities. Limited funding support in this area is a missed opportunity to align funders' good intentions for the organizations they support with the organizations' need for meaningful, ongoing development and improvement.

At the same time, the field of evaluation has not necessarily provided an optimal framework through which to understand the dynamic role evaluation can play in the growth and transition of the nonprofit sector. The applied work of evaluators currently in the field is helping shape how the nonprofit sector understands the needs of its communities, designs programs and services, interacts with other institutions, and evolves in its ability to accomplish its mission. Conceptualizing nonprofit evaluation along the four-tier model presented here provides a useful framework for funders, nonprofit leaders, boards of directors, and others to better understand the nature and value of evaluation work. Evaluation in Tiers I (Processes and Procedures) and II (Outcomes and Impact) can support meaningful organizational growth when metrics are selected through a collaborative, literature-informed process, and progress toward benchmarks is routinely reported. These types of evaluations have become common enough among nonprofits that many funders require an evaluation plan addressing these tiers in their funding applications and reporting templates. As a result, support for such activities can often be secured by outlining them in grant budgets; however, the scope of this work is typically limited to carrying out reporting requirements. In addition, while many nonprofit leaders have interest in improving program process, they may hesitate to share lessons learned or suboptimal findings (and their strategies to address them) out of concern that doing so may compromise their funding. The transactional nature of funder reporting can be changed through strategic investments in internal evaluation and supportive evaluation partnerships that can build capacity across each tier of evaluation activity to promote better services for clients, enhance organizational development, and inform community-wide systems change initiatives.

In general, the nonprofit sector is less familiar with the evaluation activities operationalized in Tiers III (Models and Infrastructure) and IV (Community Research and Expertise) and their potential to guide complex organizational shifts and enhance the collective capacity of nonprofits and community systems. Investing in the capacity for nonprofits to engage in more advanced tiers of evaluation can produce the benefits that nonprofit leaders and funding institutions expect and communities ultimately deserve. Strategic research agendas that leverage data collection across various tiers (e.g., applying screening data collected in Tier I or II to understand larger community trends in Tier III) have the potential to yield the most return for both individual nonprofits and the larger communities that the nonprofit ecological system serves. Understanding nonprofit evaluation according to this four-tier framework can aid the sector in adequately supporting and assessing the effectiveness of the work of evaluation professionals working internally within and in partnership with nonprofits. These tiers have the potential to introduce differentiated grant making and greatly improve the return on investment for the funding cycles of philanthropic institutions.

Even as nonprofits internalize the capacity for higher-level evaluation activities through improved data systems or internal evaluation staff, partnerships across the nonprofit network and ecological system remain crucial. As the examples throughout this chapter illustrate, all levels of evaluation can produce improved organizational and community outcomes if they are designed collaboratively, aligned with the nonprofit's developmental level, and effectively leverage community partnerships. Even novice evaluators and research agendas limited to Tier I or II can lead to organizational and system changes. Evaluation in the nonprofit sector will likely continue to experience growth in the foreseeable future—the four tiers described here are designed to help frame the development of a strategic, interconnected nonprofit evaluation agenda that contributes to the ongoing evolution and improvement of the organization, including its leadership and programs, as well as the collective capacity of nonprofit sector.

FURTHER READING

Crean, A., & Johnson, C. (2008). *Effective nonprofit evaluation: Through a "community of learners."* https://measureresults.issuelab.org/resource/effective-nonprofit-evaluation-through-a-community-of-learners.html

Knaflic, C. N. (2015). *Storytelling with data: A data visualization guide for business professionals.* John Wiley & Sons.

Langley, G. J., Moen, R. D., Nolan, K. M., Nolan, T. W., Norman, C. L., & Provost, L. P. (2009). *The improvement guide: A practical approach to enhancing organizational performance.* Jossey-Bass.

Love, A. J. (1991). *Internal evaluation: Building organizations from within.* Sage.

Ott, J. S., & Dicke, L. A. (2012). *The nature of the nonprofit sector* (2nd ed.). Westview Press.

Provost, L. P., & Murray, S. K. (2011). *The health care data guide: Learning from data for improvement.* Jossey-Bass.

Stevens, S. K. (2002). *Nonprofit lifecycles: Stage-based wisdom for nonprofit capacity.* Stagewise Enterprises.

Useful Resources

American Evaluation Association: https://www.eval.org/

Innovation Network: https://www.innonet.org/

Kansas University Community Toolbox: https://ctb.ku.edu/en/table-of-contents

National Council of Nonprofits—Evaluation and Measurement of Outcomes: https://www.councilofnonprofits.org/tools-resources/evaluation-and-measurement-of-outcomes

National Implementation Research Network: https://nirn.fpg.unc.edu/

KEY CONCEPTS

Collective impact: Cross-agency and cross-sector initiatives designed to address the most challenging social problems through inter-agency collaboration, common agendas, shared measurement systems, and aligned activities, programs, leadership, and procedures. Evaluating programs in conjunction with each other can broaden understanding of the cumulative impact of complementary nonprofit programs and assess for trends extending beyond individual consumers.

Distinctive competencies: The unique assets, skills, personnel, or programs of a nonprofit that distinguish its work in the nonprofit sector. Evaluation can help to fine-tune these competencies and can serve as a competency itself for organizations with more advanced capacity. As nonprofits develop distinctive competencies, they define the community change strategies that they can optimally deliver in their communities.

Evaluation capacity: The willingness and ability of an organization to ask questions and collect data on the functioning and value of its programs and effectively respond to internal evaluation and local and national research. Strong evaluation capacity is characterized by resources committed toward evaluation initiatives; internal staff dedicated to or trained in nonprofit evaluation practice; routine data collection procedures across programs and reporting procedures across key audiences; a culture of self-reflection, learning, and experimentation across nonprofit personnel; and the potential to apply data in ways that impact cross-agency or community-centered contexts.

Formative evaluations: Evaluations designed to collect information relevant to modifying programs as they are developed, with the overall goal of improving outcomes. These evaluations begin by outlining a program's "theory of change" and "logic model," monitoring the implementation of program activities, and assessing the connection of these activities to desired short- and long-term outcomes.

Four-tiered framework of evaluation capacity and activity: To guide funders, nonprofit leaders, boards of directors, and other stakeholders to better understand a nonprofit's nature and value, nonprofit evaluation can be considered along a continuum of capacity and activity spanning four distinct levels, or "tiers," including (I) Processes and Procedures, (II) Outcomes and Impact, (III) Models and Infrastructure, and (IV) Community Research and Expertise.

Implementation science: A practice that helps organizations to adopt, refine, and sustain effective interventions by identifying key areas across the organization that are tied to program functioning, including competency factors (hiring and training practices), organizational factors (data resources and systemic support), and leadership factors (supervision and performance reviews). The goal of implementation science is to promote successful program adaptation from best practice (i.e., research settings) to routine practice within nonprofit, applied settings (see Fixsen et al., 2005; 2015).

Nonprofit ecological system: The theoretical positioning of a nonprofit organization within the nonprofit sector, including its relationships and interactions with accrediting and regulatory oversight committees and boards; public sector leaders; and organizations across the local nonprofit network, and the national, state, and local policies and priorities that influence regulations and public funding. The ecological system of a nonprofit has implications for its ability to draw on partners, resources, and funding.

Nonprofit developmental lifecycle: Nonprofits begin with initial phases of an Idea (i.e., a project proposal) and Start-Up (i.e., core staff and functions), followed by periods of Growth and Maturity, and in some cases, stages of Decline, Turnaround, or Termination.

Nonprofit organizations: Nonprofits are tax-exempt organizations designed to address social needs and provide common goods that cannot be adequately or ethically addressed or provided through marketplace or government transactions. Nonprofit funds and resources are raised through a variety of sources (donations, grants, earned revenue, etc.) but must be directed toward activities aligned with its tax-exempt purpose and stated mission rather than distributed among stakeholders. Nonprofits are composed of multiple subparts, including their programs and services, management, governance, available resources, and administrative systems, which may not always align in their functioning and developmental level.

Outcomes: The benefit, profit, consequence, or impact (or lack thereof) of any undertaking, initiative, service, or program. Outcomes are intended and unintended and are operationalized differently, with different units of analysis, depending on the purpose of the undertaking and the goal of the evaluation. For example, outcomes may include the impact of an intentional change in program procedures on program functioning (i.e., time to service completion; Tier

I); changes in health status or behaviors of program consumers (Tier II); local systemic changes in response to new programs or treatment models, or the influence of cross-organizational "drivers" on program success (Tier III); and finally community-level and collective impact outcomes (Tier IV).

QUESTIONS FOR REFLECTION

1. Consider a nonprofit with which you are familiar. Assess the nature of the findings they report or the evaluation activities in which they engage. What tier of evaluation capacity do they reflect? What partnership activities or capacity-building steps might contribute to their development as an organization or the expansion of their role in the community?

2. In thinking about the chapter's varying examples, what specific roles did external consultants or university-based researchers/evaluators (or students) take to support the evaluative efforts? What partnership-based strategies did those involved employ? What were the mutual benefits from the collaboration?

3. Some funders and nonprofit leaders may be unfamiliar with evaluation's potential within the nonprofit sector. How can this chapter's four-tiered model inform an innovative grant proposal to a nonprofit funder supporting work to address a specific community need?

4. Evaluation and research agendas are important tools to ensure a nonprofit's evaluation capacity remains focused on critical areas of organizational growth. How can the four-tiered model described in this chapter be used to inform a strategic evaluation agenda for a nonprofit organization? How can the model be used by community evaluators to foster a culture of learning within a nonprofit? In what ways could a partnership-oriented approach to evaluation support their effectiveness in implementing portions of this agenda?

5. According to this chapter, prior to serving community-wide initiatives in an evaluation capacity (Tier IV), nonprofits must successfully implement lower tier activity and continue these efforts despite higher-level work. Consider the potential implications of skipping these tiers and attempting to engage in Tier IV work as a nonprofit new to evaluation. What are the potential downfalls of attempting such an approach?

REFERENCES

American Evaluation Association. (2007). *AEA evaluation policy task force charge*. http:// www.eval. org/EPTF.charge.asp

Boris, E. T., & Winkler, M. K. (2013). The emergence of performance measurement as a complement to evaluation among U.S. foundations. In S. B. Nielsen & D. E. K. Hunter (Eds.), Performance management and evaluation. *New Directions for Evaluation, 137*, 69–80. doi:10.1002/ev.20047

Braverman, M. T., Constantine, N. A., & Slater, J. A. (2004). *Foundations and evaluation: Contexts and practices for effective philanthropy.* Jossey-Bass.

Burke Harris, N., & Renschler, T. (2015). *Center for youth wellness ACE-questionnaire.* Center for Youth Wellness.

Carman, J. G. (2007). Evaluation practice among community-based organizations: Research into the reality. *American Journal of Evaluation, 28*, 60–75.

Carman, J. G. (2008). Nonprofits, funders, and evaluation: Accountability in action. *The American Review of Public Administration, 39*, 374–390.

Carman, J. G. (2011). Understanding evaluation in nonprofit organizations. *Public Performance & Management Review, 34*(3), 350–377. doi:10.2753/PMR1530-9576340302

Carman, J. G., & Fredericks, K. A. (2008). Nonprofits and evaluation: Empirical evidence from the field. *New Directions for Evaluation, 2008*(119), 51–71. doi:10.1002/ev.268

Chetty, R., Hendren, N., Kline, P., & Saez, E. (2014). Where is the land of opportunity? The geography of intergenerational mobility in the United States. *The Quarterly Journal of Economics, 129*(4), 1553–1623. doi:10.1093/qje/qju022

Cutt, J., & Murray, V. (2000). *Accountability and effectiveness evaluation in non-profit organizations.* Routledge.

Ebrahim, A. (2005). Accountability myopia: Losing sight of organizational learning. *Nonprofit and Voluntary Sector Quarterly, 34*(1), 56–87. doi:10.1177/0899764004269430

Felitti, V. J., Anda, R. F., Nordenberg, D., Williamson, D. F., Spitz, A. M., Koss, M. P., Koss, M. P., & Marks, J. S. (1998). Relationship of childhood abuse and household dysfunction to many of the leading causes of death in adults. The adverse childhood experiences (ACE) study. *American Journal of Preventive Medicine, 14*(4), 245–258. doi:10.1016/s0749-3797(98)00017-8

Fixsen, D., Blase, K., Metz., A., & Van Dyke, M. (2015). *Implementation science: International Encyclopedia of the Social & Behavioral Sciences* (2nd ed., pp. 695–702).

Fixsen, D. L., Naoom, S. F., Blase, K. A., Friedman, R. M., & Wallace, F. (2005). *Implementation research: A synthesis of the literature.* University of South Florida, Louis de la Parte Florida Mental Health Institute, The National Implementation Research Network.

Fostering Connections to Success and Increasing Adoptions Act of 2008, Pub. L. No. 110-351, 122 Stat. 3949. https://www.gpo.gov/fdsys/pkg/PLAW-110publ351/pdf/PLAW-110publ351.pdf

Gammal, D. L., Simard, C., Hwang, H., & Powell, W. W. (2005). *Managing through challenges: A profile of San Francisco bay area nonprofits.* Stanford Graduate School of Business.

Hogan, K. S., Tynan, J. M., Covill, V. J., Kilmer, R. P., & Cook, J. R. (2017). A capacity building framework for community-university partnerships. *Collaborations: A Journal of Community-Based Research and Practice, 1*, 1–28. doi:10.33596/coll.10

Kania, J., & Kramer, M. (2011). Collective impact. *Stanford Social Innovation Review, 9*, 36–41.

Liket, K. C., Rey-Garcia, M., & Maas, E. H. (2014). Why aren't evaluations working and what to do about it: A framework for negotiating meaningful evaluation in nonprofits. *American Journal of Evaluation, 35*, 171–188.

Love, A. J. (1991). *Internal evaluation: Building organizations from within.* Sage.

Mathison, S. (1991). Role conflicts for internal evaluators. *Evaluation and Program Planning, 14*(3), 173–179. doi:10.1016/0149-7189(91)90053-J

Mathison, S. (2011). Internal evaluation, historically speaking. In B. B. Volkov & M. E. Baron (Eds.), *Internal evaluation in the 21st century. New Directions for Evaluation, 132*, 13–23. doi:10.1002/ev.393

Morariu, J., Athanasiades, K., Pankaj, V., & Grodzicki, D. (2016). *State of evaluation 2016: Evaluation practice and capacity in the nonprofit sector.* Innovation Network.

Mott, A. (2006). Hand in hand: Evaluation and organizational development. *Nonprofit Quarterly, 13,* 42–47.

Provost, L. P., & Murray, S. K. (2011). *The health care data guide: Learning from data for improvement.* Jossey-Bass.

Pyzdek, T., & Keller, P. A. (2009). *The six sigma handbook* (3rd ed.). McGraw-Hill.

Royse, D., Thyer, B. A., & Padgett, D. K. (2016). *Program evaluation: An introduction to an evidence-based approach* (6th ed.). Centage Learning.

Steinberg, A. M., Brymer, M., Decker, K., & Pynoos, R. S. (2004). The UCLA PTSD reaction index. *Current Psychiatry Reports, 6,* 96–100.

Stetler, C. B., Legro, M. W., Wallace, C. M., Bowman, C., Guihan, M., Hagedorn, H., Kimmel, B., Sharp, N. D., & Smith, J. L. (2006). The role of formative evaluation in implementation research and the QUERI experience. *Journal of General Internal Medicine, 21*(Suppl 2), S1–S8. doi:10.1007/s11606-006-0267-9

Stevens, S. K. (2002). *Nonprofit lifecycles: Stage-based wisdom for nonprofit capacity.* Stagewise Enterprises.

Trochim, W. M. K. (2009). Evaluation policy and evaluation practice. In W. M. K. Trochim, M. M. Mark, & L. J. Cooksy (Eds.), *Evaluation policy and evaluation practice. New Directions for Evaluation, 123,* 13–32. doi:10.1002/ev.303

United Way of America. (2000). *Agency experiences with outcome measurement: Survey findings.*

Wang, R., Cooper, K. R., & Shumate, M. (2019). The community system solutions framework. *Stanford Social Innovation Review, 18,* 34–39.

Weisbrod, B. A. (2004). The pitfalls of profits. *Stanford Social Innovation Review, 2,* 40–47.

Womack, J. P., & Jones, D. T. (2003). *Lean thinking: Banish waste and create wealth in your corporation.* Simon & Schuster.

CHAPTER 14

COMMUNITY–UNIVERSITY PARTNERSHIPS TO PROMOTE CHANGE

Lindsay G. Messinger, Ryan P. Kilmer, and James R. Cook

Learning Objectives

1. Become familiar with the practices of community-based participatory research.

2. Understand factors that reflect readiness to engage in community-based partnerships.

3. Identify issues and behaviors that contribute to negative partnership experiences.

4. Understand practices that support successful community–university partnerships.

In light of the complex nature of the challenges our communities, systems, and families face, social problems are often better addressed collaboratively by multiple organizations than by any single organization alone. This collaborative approach, which may involve colleagues representing diverse disciplines, is used around the world (Vangen & Huxham, 2003) in many domains, from education (Hord, 2004; Leana & Pil, 2006; Pounder, 1998; Gajda & Cravedi, 2006; Teitel, 2008) to youth violence prevention (Gajda, 2006) and disease prevention and control (Elliott et al., 2014). We have learned that our collaborative style and partnership-oriented approach have proven well suited for the applied research and evaluation efforts in which we have been involved, and the views and expertise of colleagues from other university departments (e.g., communications studies, educational leadership) have strengthened a number of projects and initiatives.

In the context of evaluation, community–university (CU) collaborations, or *CU partnerships*, can prove quite fruitful. Indeed, as outlined earlier in this text (see Chapter 3), the central questions with which we will grapple as evaluators do not align solely with the focus of any specific discipline or domain, and, in fact, the complexity of the real-world questions we address requires effective collaboration among those—professionals and community stakeholders—who bring different (ideally complementary) perspectives and skills. In the case of CU partnerships, this approach to collaboration draws on the strengths of all partners from the university and the community.

This entire text is built around partnerships, and those partnerships can include varying parties and take different forms. Of particular relevance for this text, the evaluator partner may function in diverse roles or settings, ranging from a research and evaluation *team of one* at a nonprofit to an evaluation consultation firm or a faculty member who leads a team at a college or university. This chapter focuses on the latter. That is, while multiple chapters have described material relevant to such partnership-driven work (see Chapter 3 for key background), this chapter focuses on evaluators who work in higher education settings and who partner with stakeholders—nonprofit agencies, public sector system administrators, program leaders, county governments, neighborhood organizations—in the community. It holds relevance for students, faculty, and community stakeholders alike, given that we will consider practices to support effective, collaborative partnerships.

A CU partnership is a "collaboration between institutions of higher education and their larger communities for the mutually beneficial exchange of knowledge and resources in a context of partnership and reciprocity" (Tandon & Hall, 2015, p. 3). Through partnering with university faculty and students, community organizations can ultimately improve their capacity and, optimally, the outcomes of those they serve, while the university faculty (and their students) benefit from real-world applied research and evaluation opportunities. Faculty and students also increasingly are being encouraged to engage their communities, using the capacity and expertise on campus to address real-world challenges (e.g., Kilmer & Clark, 2017). Such partnerships can yield benefits to the university and the broader community, beyond those serviced directly by the community organization (see Cook & Kilmer, 2012, 2016; Cook & Nation, 2016). Using evaluation findings to improve organizational programming (Hoole & Patterson, 2008; Preskill & Boyle, 2008) may lead to social innovation (Janzen et al., 2012) that can benefit the entire community, of which both the evaluators and practitioners are a part.

The sections that follow will provide an overview of key models and concepts in CU partnerships, outline relevant examples, and conclude with a consideration of recommendations that are generalizable to other settings. An emphasis will be on a central collaborative methodology, community-based participatory research (CBPR). This approach or, alternatively, participatory action research (PAR), is foundational for collaborative evaluation work.

COMMUNITY–UNIVERSITY PARTNERSHIPS: KEY MODELS AND CONCEPTS

CBPR, defined as a collaborative approach to research in which stakeholders play an equitable role in the process of combining knowledge with action to ultimately achieve sustainable change (Israel et al., 1998; Minkler & Wallerstein, 2008), is arguably the prime means by which effective CU partnerships function. CBPR emerged in the 1980s and 1990s with the goal of engaging the individuals most affected by a problem to ensure that a community's health, mental health, or other needs are assessed and interventions to address these needs are implemented in partnership with community members (Israel et al., 2013; Minkler & Wallerstein, 2008; Viswanathan et al., 2004). Core tenets of CBPR include co-learning and the reciprocal transfer of expertise and knowledge (Viswanathan et al., 2004) through the creation of partnerships that promote mutual learning and benefit for all partners. That is, partners recognize what each brings to the table and the strengths of all partners are utilized. For example, while university faculty may have particular expertise in research design and analysis or the literature related to a specific area, members of the community are experts on their experiences, their contexts, their assets, and their needs. Thus, whether an individual is a caregiver of a child with a mental health diagnosis, a nonprofit organization executive director or staff member, or a neighborhood representative, that individual's knowledge, perspective, and insight are valued when identifying the questions to be addressed, deciding upon methods and measures, collecting data, making sense of findings, considering the implications of results, and establishing and working to enact plans for dissemination and action. In fact, when CU partnerships practice in a manner that aligns with a CBPR approach, they are characterized by shared decision making and dual ownership of the work's processes and products (see, e.g., Cook & Kilmer, 2008; Hogan et al., 2017; Viswanathan et al., 2004)

While a CBPR approach is distinct from Preskill and Boyle's (2008) *model of evaluation capacity building* (ECB; also see Chapters 7 and 13 for discussions of ECB), which has as its ultimate goal a method of evaluation that can be sustained by the partner/practitioner, they are similar in that they both advocate for university/community evaluators to ask questions that matter and use findings for decision making and action. Building on this capacity-building framework, Janzen et al. (2017) present three hallmarks of a community-based approach to evaluation. These three hallmarks align well with core elements of CBPR, that is, community-based evaluation (1) is community driven (e.g., is of relevance to the community, particularly those most affected by the issue, and community members have a voice throughout the process); (2) employs equitable participation (e.g., shared control of the research/evaluation design, implementation, and dissemination); and (3) is targeted toward action and change (e.g., cyclical and continuous change and reflection). To be sure, multiple frameworks share key "must have" elements as those that guide CU evaluations (see Hogan et al., 2017). The approach we employ is grounded in CBPR and it focuses on engaging partners, using participatory processes to enter into and maintain partnerships, and strengthening and deepening partnerships through our shared relationships and experiences.

Working for social change through partnerships and partnership-based approaches to evaluation are recognized as important (Andrews et al., 2007); yet, it can be difficult to gauge the degree to which university-based evaluators and researchers and community stakeholders are prepared to engage in partnership-based work and, in a given context, are on the same page for a potential collaboration. In fact, Andrews et al. (2012) have posited that the readiness of potential collaborating partners should be assessed.

To determine the key dimensions required for academic–community partnership readiness, Andrews and her colleagues conducted interviews and focus groups with academic and community participants who were experienced with CBPR partnerships. They defined CBPR partnership readiness as

the degree to which academic–community partners "fit" and have the "capacity" and "operations" necessary to plan, implement, evaluate and disseminate CBPR projects that will facilitate mutual growth of the partnership and positively influence targeted social and health needs in the community. (Andrews et al., 2012, pp. 558–559)

Ultimately, they developed the *CBPR Partnership Readiness Model*, which includes three major dimensions (and their indicators): (1) goodness of fit (shared values, compatible climate, mutual benefit, and commitment), (2) capacity (effective leadership, inclusive membership, complementary competencies, and adequate resources), and (3) operations (congruent goals, transparent communication, conflict resolution, and equal power). Andrews et al. (2011) created a toolkit that allows community and academic partners, ideally with the help of a facilitator, to assess their readiness.

> Some faculty act as though they prefer to do their work *to* a community organization rather than *with* the organization or community partner. Not all faculty employ practices that facilitate *partnership*.

These readiness resources (also see Darling et al., 2015; Woodland & Hutton, 2012) are intended to help gauge the readiness of both academic and community partners. Of salience, in our experiences, many faculty readily support the notion of collaboration and view it as valuable; however, some behave as though they prefer to do their work *to* a community organization rather than *with* the organization or community partner. While faculty engagement with communities is often lauded (or at least encouraged), not all faculty employ practices that facilitate *partnership*.

All partnerships are not created equal. Some work and are effective, sustaining, and successful. Timing and broader contextual factors are certainly of relevance. Relationships and partnership-focused practices are also key. The next section provides overviews of some examples of varying partnership experiences, with the goal of highlighting some prime qualities and characteristics for successful CU evaluation partnerships.

COMMUNITY–UNIVERSITY PARTNERSHIPS IN ACTION

Three main examples are provided here. The first two illustrate some important qualities of effective partnerships, and the third demonstrates some missteps and characteristics that may impede the work of partnerships.

CASE EXAMPLE: BRIGHT BEGINNINGS PREKINDERGARTEN EVALUATION

One positive example of a CU partnership relates to a multiyear collaboration between Charlotte-Mecklenburg Schools (CMS) and the University of North Carolina at Charlotte's Community Psychology Research Lab. Its focus has been on evaluating and improving the performance of the Bright Beginnings program, a publicly funded prekindergarten (pre-K) program serving approximately 2,300 4-year-olds whose family circumstances and individual skills and behaviors put them at risk for not being successful, either in or beyond kindergarten. In particular, program children have been found to

be performing at levels below their same-age peers and at risk of not being ready for kindergarten, based on a multicomponent screening process.

While this partnership was discussed at length in Chapter 3, it warrants mention here as a CU partnership. The partnership took root when the university evaluators (coauthors of this chapter, RPK and JRC) were asked to conduct some analyses using archival data, as part of the school system's effort to understand the Bright Beginnings program's potential impact. They were later asked to conduct a year-long evaluation of the program, which led to

Continued

the development of a 2-year project, funded by the Institute of Education Sciences (IES).

Based on the findings of the prior evaluation, the partners—including leadership from the school system's prekindergarten department, leadership from the school system's Department of Research, Evaluation, and Analytics (author LGM), and faculty and students from UNC Charlotte's Community Psychology Research Lab (RPK and JRC, their students, and child clinical psychologist Laura Armstrong)—developed a project with three primary foci. As part of the first aim, teachers assessed the *social–emotional learning (SEL)* of students and were provided with feedback about their students' social–emotional development through the school system's online data portal (Gadaire et al., 2020). Based on students' individual scores, teachers were also provided with suggestions for targeted interventions to help them promote students' social-emotional development. For the second aim, an enhanced, data-driven coaching model was developed to help improve teacher adherence to the program's curriculum as well as positive early childhood teaching practices (Simmons et al., in press). Among its central elements, the enhanced coaching involved the use of structured classroom observations to provide feedback to teachers and the involvement of school administrators in efforts to reinforce desired teaching practices. Two coaches and 26 teachers comprised the "enhanced coaching" group, which was to be compared to those relying on "coaching as usual." This implementation of the enhanced coaching model was being evaluated as a proof of concept study, to determine its impact on teaching behaviors and student development and assess the feasibility of its implementation across all Bright Beginnings classrooms. The effort's third aim focused on increasing the capacity of the Bright Beginnings program to be able to collect, manage, and use data for program improvement, evaluation, and research. To that end, the program's screening procedures and data collection have been automated (supported largely by the work of a university-based doctoral student, Drew Gadaire) to increase efficiency, accuracy, and the detail of the data being collected, particularly to be used to meet students' needs. In addition, the data are now being made available to the school system's Department of Research, Evaluation, and Analytics to facilitate ongoing evaluation and program improvement.

Several characteristics and practices of this partnership are consistent with key principles for research–practice partnerships (Coburn et al., 2013) and contribute to the fact that this partnership works well. For example, the partnership between CMS and the UNC Charlotte Community Psychology Research Lab has spanned many years, dating to 2012. Since its inception, the goal has always been to sustain the partnership across multiple units and individuals, regardless of the organization's leadership. Indeed, during a period of considerable transition in the school system, this partnership has endured, notwithstanding key personnel changes, including three different directors of Research, Evaluation, and Analytics and three different superintendents. This continuity has likely been possible because the focus of the partners has been on real problems of practice. Going back to its roots, the partnership was borne out of community concerns about potential (and subsequent) cuts in pre-K funding and the school system's need to evaluate its programs. Recommendations from an initial evaluation conducted by the UNC Charlotte-based faculty led to a funded IES grant to advance this applied research and evaluation partnership, build CMS capacity, and pilot efforts to improve the program.

In addition to the partnership's longevity, which can certainly contribute to growing trust and the valuing of the linkages and collaboration, the partners have implemented intentional strategies to foster partnership. For example, this project is participatory; that is, it is overseen by a management team of UNC Charlotte and CMS staff, with joint decision-making about questions, methodology, and project processes. At biweekly to monthly meetings, both organizations have evidenced an openness to flexibility (e.g., in scheduling regular meetings and classroom observations) and clear adaptability, a necessity and a notable strength in the regularly changing context of evaluation research within a large public system. The partners have also interacted with honesty (e.g., about goals and objectives and what is and what is not feasible) and communicated with transparency (e.g., related to data-sharing). Also supporting their connections and work together, multiple members of this management team are jointly involved in other initiatives and partnership efforts (e.g., with a local child advocacy and legal aid organization), thus enhancing their own understanding of system and community context and providing further opportunities to cultivate positive relationships within the community and among each other.

Finally, both groups are committed to mutualism and communicate directly about how to facilitate mutual benefits. The partnership has resulted in real improvements in CMS's pre-K practice and the ways that data are used by teachers and coaches. In addition to the increased ability of CMS staff to access and use the data, university faculty and students are then able to access the rich data collected by CMS, and undergraduate and graduate students' projects can ultimately serve multiple and mutually beneficial interests.

CASE EXAMPLE: STUDENT ABSENTEEISM PROJECT

A second example (described in part by Messinger et al., 2017) stems from the first and involves CMS, UNC Charlotte, and the City of Charlotte. Together, representatives of these entities are collaborating on a study of public school students' chronic absenteeism. The specific ongoing effort described here grew out of relationships built over the course of the Bright Beginnings evaluation, described above, as well as prior collaborations on committees or via interorganizational links. For instance, each author has also worked, in multiple other contexts, with a key partner representing the City of Charlotte, so it was a natural progression to build upon the relationships already in place. In fact, the occurrence of other, simultaneously occurring projects is a real boon for this project, because the partners see each other and interact on a regular basis and can answer questions and make decisions that can help keep this project moving along.

This project, quite simply, began with a question, asked by one of the university professors (and third author): *Do you have questions you would like to have answered, but you do not have the capacity or resources to pursue?* This question came up following a university-initiated meeting that was meant to brainstorm ways that the university might be able to address social good in the community, although most attendees and members of the audience thought of this in business terms. The group associated with this absenteeism project wanted to address an issue that was not related to profit but rather could directly benefit the larger community. While not an evaluation of a program per se, it is evaluative of the current city and school district practices related to multiple areas, such as neighborhood composition and housing, busing and transportation, and school attendance.

The study aims to examine the extent to which factors across different ecological levels contribute to absenteeism among elementary school students in CMS, a large, mostly urban school system in the southeast United States.

This particular project was chosen because of its relatively recent salience to the school district and its leadership. As of 2014, *chronic absenteeism* was defined (as missing more than 10% of total days enrolled) and added as a measure to the district's strategic plan (Charlotte-Mecklenburg Schools, 2014. Once the concept had been defined, it could be measured for individual students and aggregated at the school and district levels. School system researchers and leaders increasingly recognized the importance of this indicator and noted the literature on the topic, which we have summarized briefly below.

Quite simply, in order to succeed in school, children must be present. Yet, each year, an estimated 10% of U.S. students, or 7.5 million students, miss nearly a month of school (Balfanz & Byrnes, 2012), with serious detrimental effects. The lost instructional time can lead to high school dropout and achievement gaps, undermine the benefits of early education, and interrupt efforts for reading proficiency by the end of third grade (Ginsburg et al., 2014). Thus, one of the main threats to academic success is poor attendance. Poor attendance is negatively associated with school success, including academic achievement, promotion, high school completion, and future employment opportunities (Gottfried, 2009; Lehr et al., 2003; Steward et al., 2008). Of relevance given the current emphasis on accountability, students with higher rates of absenteeism have, on average, lower scores on national standardized tests (e.g., Ginsburg et al., 2014; Gottfried, 2009). Moreover,

Continued

the educational ramifications of missing school are exacerbated for students in urban settings (Balfanz & Legters, 2004).

Taken together, this growing body of research confirms the association between school attendance and subsequent student achievement and graduation outcomes and underscores the importance of intervening as soon as absences begin to add up. This is true whether the student is in elementary, middle, or high school. The "good news" is that attendance is actionable: Poor attendance can be turned around when states, districts, and schools enact policies and practices that encourage schools and communities to partner with families to monitor attendance patterns and intervene as necessary (e.g., Attendance Works and Everyone Graduates Center, 2017).

In light of its implications for students and their subsequent trajectories, efforts to understand and reduce absenteeism, especially chronic absenteeism, are of relevance to parents, teachers, school administrators, and communities. Findings to date suggest that the factors that contribute to absenteeism, in general, and chronic absenteeism, in particular, are diverse and multifaceted, often involving factors at multiple ecological levels, such as the student, family, classroom, school, and neighborhood. These factors include children's and parents' health (Balfanz & Byrnes, 2012), family mobility (Derien, 2016), poverty (Chang & Romero, 2008; Romero & Lee, 2007), lack of transportation (Balfanz & Byrnes, 2012), and neighborhood circumstances (Gottfried, 2014). Although the evidence points to the roles of factors reflecting multiple levels of students' ecologies, few research and evaluation efforts have examined these diverse contexts and their impact. This limitation is an important impetus for the partnership's work.

The school system-, university-, and city-based partners met regularly to identify the range of factors and variables to include and to refine the effort's aims and central questions. They decided to focus on students in early elementary school grades (kindergarten to third grade) because significant absenteeism occurs in early grades, early absenteeism predicts later absenteeism and academic outcomes, and absenteeism in early elementary grades may be more readily influenced by intervention and prevention efforts than in later grades (Blazer, 2011). The ultimate goal is to determine which factors could be addressed through school system or community efforts to promote attendance and positive student

outcomes and implement these types of interventions. This ongoing, collaborative study simultaneously examines factors at multiple ecological levels (i.e., child and family, classroom, home neighborhood, and school) that are relevant to absenteeism. Thus, a partnership between multiple organizations is necessary to use and understand the data at the various ecological levels. For example, CMS has data on students in the district, but the partnership with the city allows us to link to and make best use of the data contained in the Charlotte-Mecklenburg Quality of Life Explorer (https://mcmap.org/qol/), which is maintained by the City of Charlotte and contains data about housing and home ownership, crime and safety, higher education attainment, and health, among other variables that are relevant to this project.

One factor that contributes to the effectiveness of the partners' collaboration is the shared goal of supporting the school district's capacity to engage in sustained improvement efforts. Both CMS and City of Charlotte staff knowledgeable about the phenomena under study have provided data to inform analyses, while the university researchers (faculty and students) share practices and tools to bolster data for informed decision making. All of the partners have devoted staff and resources to ensure successful communication, trust, and collaboration among the participating entities. To date, the partner agencies have identified school absenteeism as the topic to be investigated, established the process for discussing and sharing findings and policy implications, and developed a plan for disseminating what is learned to a range of audiences (e.g., practitioners, policymakers, and researchers). Given that it was an "add on" to the partners' regular roles, it became challenging to maintain progress; it became clear that the group needed some dedicated person-power to help coordinate the project. Jacqueline Larson, a community psychology doctoral student working with the university-based faculty, made the decision to increase her role in the project, such as preparing materials to organize the discussion and inform the partners' choices (e.g., variable selection). In the end, in view of her leadership, she chose to develop the project as her dissertation, and this chapter's authors all are on her committee. As of the writing of this chapter, this study is in progress; it will continue, and the partners will attend to and identify actionable recommendations growing out of the results, as there is strong motivation to see reduction in student chronic absenteeism.

CASE EXAMPLE: LESSONS LEARNED FROM A PARTNERSHIP INITIATIVE

Another partnership, involving CMS (including the first author), university-based researchers/evaluators (including the chapter's other authors), and other parties, bears mention as an example of a collaboration that was less successful in terms of the experience of collaboration and "partnership." Thus, we have modified details from this example to reduce the likelihood that other parties may be identified. This project grew out of a grant-funded effort with local education-related programming and policy implications. It necessitated a significant evaluative effort to examine relevant data from multiple settings and grade levels. This example is shared to illuminate some lessons learned.

One of the three main arms of this project, a data and evaluation working group, was charged with determining whether children who attended an early education program with eligibility criteria related to income or developmental readiness for school had better kindergarten and third grade outcomes than a comparison group. This would allow the group to intuit that a future expansion of the program could have real benefits for the children involved. There were many individuals and organizations involved in the data working group: A local government agency was the grantee and hired a project manager; the school district was asked to share data for the original grant application and again after the grant was awarded, and two of its department directors were designated as chairs of two of the three working groups; an executive from a childcare agency oversaw the grant application and provided expertise on early childcare; staff who work with an integrated data system affiliated with the university provided key data needed to answer the research questions; three local university faculty conducted the analyses and shared expertise; two nonlocal university faculty shared their expertise in early childhood program research; and a consulting firm oversaw all aspects of the three main working groups of the project. While this project certainly had valuable aims and many of the "right" people involved, there were some feelings of frustration

because of a lack of true collaboration. We will relate and reflect upon some of these issues here.

As the grant was being developed, various parties were asked to provide information or draft narrative, often within a tight timeframe. Communication was limited in transparency (e.g., one partner was asked to provide a letter of support but shared, quite justifiably, that it was not possible to do so without seeing the proposal) and many stakeholders experienced the proposal development process as if this initiative were being done *to* them, as opposed to them being full partners and collaborating *with* those who were coordinating the effort.

While there were some initial kick-off meetings for the project, neither the roles of nor the mutual benefits to each party/person were clearly defined. This left many people wondering why there were so many people and organizations working on this project, what each was meant to do, how it might overlap with others' work (or other similar local efforts taking place at the same time), and to what end. This type of situation can be remedied through the use of multiple, basic partnership strategies. First, a substantial proportion of these issues could have been avoided via the use of participatory practices in the development of the grant proposal; stakeholders were called upon for answers but were not engaged and did not feel like partners. Second, this evaluative initiative would have been strengthened meaningfully if there had been discussion and consensus-building processes designed to outline roles, responsibilities, goals, and potential for benefits for all parties from the beginning, with regular reminders of the purposes (and the "so what?" implications, i.e., what it will really mean and how it might affect programming for children); this step can be particularly important if the group does not meet frequently or invites individuals to contribute who have a limited role or have not been involved from the beginning.

Issues of clarity regarding the nature of each member's role(s) and proposed interactions and responsibilities also stemmed from the grant writers'

Continued

inclusion of two nonlocal experts in the initiative. These external experts had been involved in early childhood evaluation and programming in other capacities; however, because local experts existed and were included in the project, their inclusion raised questions and led some to wonder whether enough and appropriate background information and context had been learned by those who had envisioned the project and written the grant. While additional knowledge shared by experts is always valuable, it is essential to recognize the salience of the local context and to prioritize the potential roles and contributions of local experts who are willing to participate and partner.

Another nonoptimal aspect of this project was that the consultants appeared to operate under the assumption that all of the others involved similarly had unlimited time to spend on this project. Unfortunately, the reality was that the vast majority of the people on the project had full-time jobs and, for many of them, this project did not buy out their time or provide them any additional funding. This contributed to tensions when the outside consultants proposed or attempted to hold the evaluation team members to deadlines that were not tenable. In multiple such instances, evaluation team members asserted themselves and explained the challenges inherent in the timeline; however, their views were not always valued equally. These types of conversations were initiated by representatives from the school system, two different university departments, and the institute that housed the integrated database. These dynamics contributed to generally lower morale and less traction for a project that actually had potentially significant implications locally; it was difficult to gain or sustain momentum because of regular problematic statements or other missteps made by the outside consultants. Even when processes were in place to try to secure needed data (and it was not yet possible to report on findings), they instituted weekly meetings or calls. As the project went on, these weekly meetings/calls were sometimes not well attended (especially in the 3–4 months that followed the initially identified deadline). The meetings were not always a good use of group members' time; in many cases, they had other important work that needed to take priority, either because it was already scheduled or because

it was more closely aligned to the person's job duties and, therefore, more crucial. While the intended outcomes of the project were ultimately met, as a result of these and other issues, the project took much longer to complete than the timeline originally allowed, and the consultants who were coordinating the efforts viewed the findings as proprietary and did not share the report with the participants, leading to frustration by many parties.

This example is shared not solely as a cathartic narrative about a project that did not go as well as it could have, but because we can often learn a great deal from projects that *do not* go as smoothly as one might hope. In such circumstances (or after such projects), lessons can be learned and recommendations put forth. For example, when the consultants placed expectations and deadlines on partners without consideration for their work demands and schedules, that may have been a time to raise the issue about the broader process and the lack of respect for the partners' time. In addition, while evaluation team members and others spoke up, it would have been important for the partners to speak up more readily and consistently, explaining the amount of time it would take to accomplish what was suggested as well as briefly describing concurrent demands. Doing so may have helped influence the interactions more than asserting themselves less consistently.

As another example, had we used a readiness assessment in the early stages of this project, we may have seen that we would have received low ratings in certain areas, such as in goodness of fit and, in particular, shared values. Goodness of fit is the key starting point to assess partnership readiness. If it is not present, perhaps the project should be delayed so that the potential partners can spend time to clarify the context and goals or even abandon the work entirely in favor of other projects to which the parties are better suited. In addition, the process of this evaluative research effort would have been more positive and productive had the parties who had the idea and developed the grant engaged in partnership-oriented practices. They did not set the stage effectively for collaboration from the earliest steps and, unfortunately, that tone, dynamic, and message carried through to the external consultant group and the project's subsequent elements.

Finally, at the conclusion of the project, partners who felt frustrated along the way could have facilitated a debriefing session (in the military, this is known as an "After Action Review") to openly discuss what did not go as planned or could have been improved. The entire group could then take these lessons forward to future projects. There will invariably be missteps, conflicts, and delays in this work; it is important to address them directly as well as recognize issues and learn from them going forward.

RECOMMENDATIONS FOR SUCCESSFUL CU PARTNERSHIPS

In the final section, some recommendations with brief explanation are offered in conclusion (see Figure 14.1).

1. Build Relationships to Help Develop Projects Collaboratively

In order to conduct research or evaluation that is of relevance to its intended users, we recommend taking steps to develop and sustain a partnership based on shared, mutual interests. It sounds simple, but building relationships is key. Of critical importance for any evaluator or university-based faculty member or student: You should not assume that just because you would like to pursue a project on a topic that you find interesting or that may fill a gap in the literature, that anyone at the community organization is interested in the topic in a practical way. If a given effort is framed or viewed as "your" project or "X University's" study, it is effectively done before you start. Thus, it is recommended that you work to cultivate relationships with individuals affiliated with organizations that are doing work you value.

A first meeting might involve a focus on a contact's interests and the priorities of the organization. Consider ways in which your skills and expertise, your experiences, or your resources (or connections to resources) may be able to help. (This is particularly true when partners are not from the same community. In this case, it is even more important to discuss shared goals and for the university students and faculty to have done their homework on the local community context and needs.) There may not be a clear next step on the basis of that first discussion; however, as time goes on and the relationship becomes stronger, you may see if there are areas in which an evaluation would be useful or where you can offer services, but this should always be in service to the community member's expressed needs. One pitfall to avoid: Do not approach your meeting with your contact at the organization with the goal of discussing a particular project that you have in mind, or worse, have already conceptualized and developed in isolation. Too often, our colleagues in public systems, nonprofits, and community organizations have reported the experience of being used by evaluators and/or university-based personnel, including ones who may have said the "right things" at the start, but who wound up morphing the evaluation to meet *their* needs and interests rather than those of the organization, system, or community stakeholders.

Building trust and relationships over time cannot be overstated, particularly in the field of evaluation, where practitioners may be apprehensive or resentful of having *their* (personal) program evaluated. It takes careful skill, best built on trust and transparency, to allow community staff to truly understand the benefits of evaluation while not feeling

Figure 14.1 Recommendations for Successful CU Partnerships

1. Build relationships to help develop projects collaboratively.

2. Engage in regular, direct communication.

3. Foster shared learning.

4. Remember that community organization leadership and staff already have full-time jobs with regular responsibilities.

5. Use dissemination and communication strategies and approaches that support and influence decision making.

as though they are personally being evaluated (or at least are prioritizing the benefit of the former over the potential discomfort of the latter). Regardless of whether their operating budgets come from donations or public funds, all community organizations are necessarily sensitive about how they are viewed and to the potential for "outsiders" to use limited data to make them look bad. They need to be able to trust that evaluation is used for the purpose of improving programs, services, and supports, to the benefit of those served and other stakeholders, and not used by the evaluator for a "gotcha" moment in which the evaluator can appear superior at the expense of the program. In fact, it may be the case that as you build a relationship with an individual at an organization over time, this person becomes a champion, helping to facilitate evaluation processes and decision-making for a given project. Word of mouth can be very powerful and, after you have developed a positive track record (characterized by respect, integrity, honest and direct communication, substantive professional expertise, and benefits for one's community partners and their programs), a champion can help promote positive partnership-oriented evaluation experiences in her or his organization as well as others.

The first author often sees this process unfold in a less-than-ideal way in CMS. As the director of Research, Evaluation, and Analytics, she oversees the process for and reviews all proposals to conduct research and evaluation projects in the school district. CMS allows qualified individuals and organizations to engage in professional research and evaluation projects that align with CMS's strategic goals and have the potential to improve learning conditions, student outcomes, and staff or program effectiveness in CMS. All persons interested in conducting research in CMS must go through an application process to obtain approval. The best case scenario is for university faculty and one or more district staff members to develop a project jointly. However, very often, the district is approached by researchers/evaluators who assume that a topic that is of great importance and value to them will also be very important to the district. If the project is *not* conceptualized and developed collaboratively, but has been developed independently, the researcher must be clear about how it will benefit the particular educational department, students, staff, and/ or the district, and so forth. There must be some tangible benefits in the short and longer term. It is important to identify short-term benefits (aside from simply adding to the literature; while practitioners certainly value this, it is not usually enough to get them to agree to participate in a program or research study).

There is no scarcity of evaluators and researchers interested in working with the district in various educational domains, so the district must be selective—not every proposed study is a "slam dunk", with certain approval. A case must be made, and the foundation for making the case must be built on the potential positive implications for the district and its students. Time and time again, the first author has been asked to grant permission for the district to participate in a research or evaluation project, where a relationship does not exist and when there has been no meaningful attempt to delineate the benefits for students. Figure 14.2 provides a fairly striking example of how *not* to establish a relationship with a potential partner. This is an actual email received by the first author, with all identifying information removed to protect the [non-] innocent. At the time of this email, its author had written several times to convey interest in working with CMS on an early education project, but the first author had never talked to nor met the person who wrote the email.

To eliminate studies that are not supported by, or in true service to, the school district, as of 2017, we require that evaluators have documented support from a central

---

Figure 14.2 An Email Example of How *Not* to Foster a Relationship With Current or Potential Partners

From: [Name of Researcher]
Sent: Friday, January 12, 2018 3:53 PM
To: Messinger, Lindsay
Subject: sorry, it's me again :)

Hi:

I'm so sorry. I'm diving deeper into the RFA and now realizing that it would be a partnership between CMS and [University X]. So, this is what I am thinking now:

- Only doing the [X intervention] model implementation in [grade-level] classrooms (RCT). We would provide the training to [X grade] teachers. It would be [intervention model] vs. control (no treatment) I think we would assign treatment by school to decrease contamination. We also could think about doing this in [another grade-level] instead.

- CMS would need to provide the data for analysis. I am thinking that we would need all [academic] data, [potential indicator of social-emotional functioning] data, suspension/expulsion data, office referral data, behavior incident data, absentee data, any teacher attitude data, and data related to teacher cultural competence. Also, school demographic data (e.g., free and reduced lunch, racial composition). I also would like data collectors to come into the classroom 1X per month to collect Behavior Incidents (using a measure developed by the [Project] and the [measure].

- I'm not sure who all would need to be involved from CMS — thinking [department], possibly [individual], measurement/research, [department] possibly.

So, just let me know what you think. I think this could be a really exciting partnership and really help kids. If you are interested, we really should move forward as quickly as possible. The application is due March 1. I'm really hoping to work with CMS, especially since [personal information about researcher].

Take care and have a great weekend.

office director prior to submitting an application. In fact, this documentation of support is now the first step in the application process so that neither the researcher/evaluator nor the district spends time unnecessarily developing or reviewing a research application for a project for which a solid relationship and interest does not exist.

In sum, new partnerships should first focus on building trust and relationships and emphasize creating mutually beneficial projects or studies that address short- and longer-term needs for all partners (Cook & Kilmer, 2012). This requires a *personal* relationship between faculty and key members of community organizations. We recommend that university faculty who are interested in conducting a program, research study, and/or a program evaluation partner with the relevant school district department's leadership, key staff at the nonprofit agency, or other community stakeholder prior to the development of the project. This will assist both the university faculty and the community agency in working toward a partnership that yields the greatest benefit.

2. Engage in Regular, Direct Communication

We recommend ongoing bidirectional communication throughout the application (for a grant, if relevant), planning, implementation, evaluation, and reporting stages. It is extremely important to be clear about the needs and responsibilities up front. From the community organization perspective, there is nothing worse than agreeing to something (no matter how potentially beneficial to your organization) and later feeling as though you have been hoodwinked when it becomes clear that much more is required. This usually takes the form of "small things" and generally minor requests that, over the course of an evaluation, add up to considerable time for the community member, such as compiling data or information about programs or previously completed studies (see Recommendation 4 below). Such materials can surely serve as relevant background information for the researcher, but they may not have been identified as useful up front. We recommend a contract, data-sharing agreement, or memorandum of understanding (MOU) that clearly identifies what the roles and responsibilities of each party will be (i.e., shared expectations; Cook & Kilmer, 2016) as well as the data to be shared. Partners should have a clear opportunity for informed consent regarding the nature of their potential involvement, the time commitment, and the like.

Once the partnership has been established and the agreement is signed by all parties, we recommend taking specific steps to maintain open communication. While regular communication via email and even phone calls can be useful, meeting in person regularly or via video conference is critical. The team should commit to and follow through on regular and scheduled-in-advance meetings to keep everyone in the loop. In our experiences, weekly meetings are probably too often (and not necessary) but quarterly is probably not often enough; we recommend monthly or bimonthly meetings. In advance of those meetings, create and share clear agendas so that participants are not left wondering what will be covered or why they are present, and make sure that the agenda addresses the concerns of all present (sharing draft agendas in advance with invitations to add or delete items can be helpful). During the meetings, work to create an environment in which everyone feels comfortable raising questions, bringing up their suggestions, and sharing information openly. After the meetings, to continue to maintain trust, you must provide action minutes/summaries and follow through on requests and agreed-upon action steps.

Throughout the project, we recommend that the evaluator provide opportunities for joint review and feedback of letters, reports, presentations, and other products.

Stability of community connection and support is important. We recommend having a clear go-to person on site (see Cook & Kilmer, 2012; Kilmer et al., 2013). To truly formalize this, if funding allows, it is useful to have a single person who is committed to the partnership and explicitly works for both teams, so that a single person has deep knowledge and understanding about the evaluation work and the community organization work. Therefore, we recommend requesting funds in grant applications to support a community partner-staffed research liaison who works closely with, for example, schools, district central office staff, and the research/data team as well as with the evaluation team at the university. This is especially beneficial when working with large school districts where individuals from the district's various departments/sites do not always work closely together or in the same office space. In smaller districts, these responsibilities may be carried out by a single person or certain positions may not exist (e.g., a research/data department). If it is not possible to support such a staff position, partnerships are facilitated by having continuity of contacts (e.g., university-based evaluators), a project lead (e.g., a graduate student project coordinator), and clear community leads for different aspects of the project. Doing so is not only important relationally and for partnership function, it reduces the likelihood of responsibility diffusion.

To summarize these first two recommendations, relationships are powerful and partnerships are strengthened when partners have developed a track record of communication and commitment. Yet, partners need to be honest with one another about what each party can accomplish and what is not feasible given time and resource constraints (Cook & Kilmer, 2012).

3. Foster Shared Learning

In order to establish working relationships among the partners, it is best to emphasize and foster shared learning. University faculty should not assume the role of *the singular* expert. After all, the community members (and potential partners) have diverse expertise, including the local or organizational context and its strengths and needs.

As discussed in Chapter 3, it is especially important for evaluators to recognize the capacity, skills, and expertise of community partners—and the limits of their own knowledge—and to appreciate the context for the work.

As one case in point, it is often necessary to strike a balance (or resolve a tension) between the rigor of an evaluation or research design and pragmatic factors. This issue can arise when university-based faculty evaluators do not consider fully the secondary effect of a suggested research design. For example, in the first author's experience, one evaluator suggested randomly assigning students to teachers for an intervention program that would be evaluated. While this gold-standard method is certainly the most desirable for the researcher, it was impractical for the district. First, the intervention would have started midway through the school year when students had already been assigned to classes (so this would be disruptive and, frankly, untenable as an approach). Second, this assignment method would not take into account matching the teacher with the personality style or resource needs of students (or other factors that school leaders and teachers take into account when establishing classroom groups). A community practitioner (i.e., the expert on the school context) would identify these issues to make placement decisions that would be most beneficial to the student. Because random assignment could not take these factors into account (and could even open the district up to risk if students with special needs are not appropriately served), it was not realistic and could not be implemented.

On the other side of the coin, community partners can benefit from applied research only when they are open to learning from a study's data and findings. They need to be ready to learn and to consider how they can respond to results that may not align with what they may have hoped to find (i.e., do not "look good" for the organization or program); it is critical that community staff approach evaluation as a means of identifying strategies to ultimately improve the program, agency, or system. While such decisions can be sensitive—and multiple factors and dynamics may be at play (see Chapter 2)—we must be able to put uncomfortable feelings aside and work to improve or decide to eliminate a program that is not best serving the needs of students/clients. In sum, sound partnerships tap into the complementary skills and expertise of both the community and university staff in order to work toward common interests. As emphasized in Chapter 3, it is important for evaluators to recognize the strengths and expertise of each member of the team and to engage in co-learning practices throughout the partnership's work.

4. Remember That Community Organization Leadership and Staff Already Have Full-Time Jobs With Regular Responsibilities

Arguably the most substantial obstacle for any community partner is the presence of competing priorities. The addition of a grant-funded project or evaluation is "one more thing" that gets added to their day-to-day responsibilities (typically, time cannot be bought out for salaried employees in community organizations); the time required to add another project gets added on to an already-full workload for salaried employees. This quickly becomes too much, and additional projects have diminishing returns because employees are spread too thin to adequately devote sufficient time to them. We recommend that university-based faculty and evaluators keep in mind that your given joint project is not the only project for the community partner, even though it may be the evaluator's only (or main) project. The new project may not be—or cannot be—a priority (Kilmer et al., 2009).

5. Use Dissemination and Communication Strategies and Approaches That Support and Influence Decision Making

At its core, CBPR is applied research. Thus, for any partnership to be truly successful, findings must be actionable. As a guiding notion for this book, we have asserted that all partners should focus on using data to *do*: to guide decision making and resource allocation, to improve practice, and to effect change. To that end, some suggest that collaboration between researchers/evaluators and practitioners ought to extend beyond the evaluation, such that researchers/evaluators are continuously engaged through the process of policy development (as discussed in Chapter 17; also see Maton, 2017). We concur and recommend bilateral engagement between researchers/evaluators and community practitioners (see Chapter 17; also see Miller & Shinn, 2005; Wandersman, 2003) to use evaluation evidence to develop public policy, whereby both groups plan, design, and conduct projects, and once the project is complete, the university social scientists have opportunities to provide input during the policy-making process. Yet, at the same time, university faculty must be sensitive to the public relations needs of community organizations (but not at the expense of sound, but practical, methodology; Cook & Kilmer, 2012). In sum, the goal of the partnership will be best served when the university evaluators can help guide action in a way that is aligned to the needs of the community organization, while upholding research/evaluation integrity.

CONCLUSIONS

CU partnerships can be advantageous to both organizations and have the potential to yield greater benefits than either could achieve alone. The partnership is meant to be a collaborative approach as part of the CBPR framework, whereby the community and university stakeholders play equal roles in the evaluation process. Two examples of successful partnerships are shared here along with one that can be used as a learning experience. Recommendations for extracting the most benefit and the least frustration from the partnership include building relationships and finding a champion, encouraging strong and open communication, fostering shared learning, recognizing that community organization staff are substantially burdened with their regular responsibilities, and working to disseminate findings to support and influence decision and policy making. Abiding by these recommendations will hopefully ease the inevitable challenges that arise in any cross-organization partnership.

FURTHER READING

Coburn, C. E., Penuel, W. R., & Geil, K. E. (2013, January). *Research-practice partnerships: A strategy for leveraging research for educational improvement in school districts*. William T. Grant Foundation.

Cook, J. R., & Kilmer, R. P. (2012). Creating successful partnerships using applied community psychology research. *Living Knowledge: International Journal of Community Based Research, 10*, 16–17.

Janzen, R., Ochocka, J., Turner, L., Cook., T., Franklin, M., & Deichert, D. (2017). Building a community-based culture of evaluation. *Evaluation and Program Planning, 65*, 163–170.

Ochocka, J., Moorlag, E., & Janzen, R. (2010). A framework for entry: PAR values and engagement strategies in community-based research. *Gateways:*
International Journal of Community Research and Engagement, 3, 1–19.

Viswanathan, M., Ammerman, A., Eng, E., Gartlehner, G., Lohr, K. N., Griffith, D., Rhodes, S., Samuel-Hodge, C., Maty, S., Lux, L., Webb, L., Sutton, S. F., Swinson, T., Jackman, A., & Whitener, L. (2004). *Community-based participatory research: Assessing the evidence*. Evidence Report/Technology Assessment No. 99 (Prepared by RTI-University of North Carolina Evidence-based Practice Center under Contract No. 290–02-0016). AHRQ Publication 04-E022-2. Agency for Healthcare Research and Quality.

Woodland, R., & Hutton, M. (2012). Evaluating organizational collaborations: Suggested entry points and strategies. *American Journal of Evaluation, 33*(3), 366–383. https://doi.org/10.1177/1098214012440028.

KEY CONCEPTS

Chronic absenteeism: A student's absences from school that exceed a particular threshold (often defined as missing more than 10% of school days enrolled, although there is no common definition in the United States).

Community-based participatory research (CBPR): A research approach that aims to involve research participants and other stakeholders actively in the research process and ensure that they have a voice in the knowledge that is created.

Community-university (CU) partnership: A collaborative effort between colleges and universities and their local communities to exchange knowledge, expertise, and resources in a context of partnership, often for the purposes of program evaluation.

Memorandum of understanding (MOU): A document that outlines a work agreement between two parties, clearly defining the purpose of the work and the roles and responsibilities of each party.

Model of Evaluation Capacity Building (ECB): A method of evaluation that is ultimately sustainable by the partner/practitioner. The evaluation method may be developed as a partnership, sometimes relying more heavily on the university faculty to develop the methods and instruments, but knowledge should be transferred throughout the project so that the community agency staff can sustain the evaluation over time.

Social-emotional learning (SEL): A set of critical skills and mindsets that enable success in school and in life by teaching children to recognize and understand their emotions, feel empathy, make decisions, and build and maintain relationships.

QUESTIONS FOR REFLECTION

1. Consider the case examples. In the third example, there are several examples of less-than-ideal interactions. What could the consultants have done to improve communication throughout the partnership? How about those on the local evaluation team or other local partners? What can you do if you are feeling frustrated with a partnership experience?

2. It is recommended that students are included in the management team of a community–university partnership. Such participation (e.g., as a project coordinator or evaluation staff member) can provide fruitful professional development opportunities and real-world experience. With which kinds of role(s) would you feel comfortable? In which roles would you need more support?

3. How can students, during internship, practicum assignments, or graduate assistantships, effectively set boundaries and expectations? Are there materials (such as a scope of work) that can be developed and used to facilitate these discussions?

4. Consider your experiences. How could you build on or leverage the relationships that you have to facilitate and maintain effective CU partnerships?

5. If you were engaging with a new potential partner, what kinds of practices could provide sound foundation for and facilitate the development of a positive partnership?

REFERENCES

Andrews, J. O., Bentley, G., Crawford, S., Pretlow, L., & Tingen, M. S. (2007). Using community-based participatory research to develop a culturally sensitive smoking cessation intervention with public housing neighborhoods. *Ethnicity & Disease, 17*(2), 331–337.

Andrews, J. O., Cox, M. J., Newman, S. D., & Meadows, O. (2011). Development and evaluation of a toolkit to assess partnership readiness for community-based participatory research. *Progress in Community Health Partnerships: Research, Education, and Action*, 5(2), 183–188. doi:10.1353/cpr.2011.0019

Andrews, J. O., Newman, S. D., Meadows, O., Cox, M. J., & Bunting, S. (2012). Partnership readiness for community-based participatory research. *Health Education Research*, 27(4), 555–571. doi:10.1093/her/cyq050

Attendance Works and Everyone Graduates Center. (2017). *Portraits of change: Aligning school and community resources to reduce chronic absence.* https://www.attendanceworks.org/wp-content/uploads/2017/09/Attendance-Works-Portraits-of-Change-Main-Document-Final-Sept.-1.pdf

Balfanz, R., & Byrnes, V. (2012). *Chronic absenteeism: Summarizing what we know from nationally available data.* Johns Hopkins University Center for Social Organization of Schools.

Balfanz, R., & Legters, N. (2004). *Locating the dropout crisis.* Johns Hopkins University.

Blazer, C. (2011). *Chronic absenteeism in the elementary grades.* Miami-Dade County Public Schools. http://files.eric.ed.gov/fulltext/ED536529.pdf.

Chang, H., & Romero, M. (2008). *Present, engaged, and accounted for: The critical importance of addressing chronic absence in the early grades.* Columbia University.

Charlotte-Mecklenburg Schools. (2014). *Strategic plan 2018: For a better tomorrow.* https://www.cms.k12.nc.us/communications/Documents/StrategicPlan2018%20rev%20063016.pdf

Coburn, C. E., Penuel, W. R., & Geil, K. E. (2013, January). *Research-practice partnerships: A strategy for leveraging research for educational improvement in school districts.* William T. Grant Foundation.

Cook, J. R., & Kilmer, R. P. (2008, June). *Using community-based participatory research to build capacity in family support organizations.* Paper presented at the 2nd International Community Psychology Conference, Lisbon, Portugal.

Cook, J. R., & Kilmer, R. P. (2012). Creating successful partnerships using applied community psychology research. *Living Knowledge: International Journal of Community Based Research*, 10, 16–17.

Cook, J. R., & Kilmer, R. P. (2016, June). *Building capacity for collaborative research and practice among students and community partners.* Presented at the 7th Living Knowledge Conference, Dublin Ireland.

Cook, J. R., & Nation, M. (2016). Community engagement: Universities' roles in building communities and strengthening democracy. *Community Development*, 47(5), 718–731. doi:10.1080/15575330.2016.1226912

Darling, M., Gonzalez, F., Graves, K., Sheppard, V. B., Hurtado-de-Mendoza, A., Leventhal, K-G., & Caicedo, L. (2015). Practical tips for establishing partnerships with academic researchers: A resource guide for community-based organizations. *Progress in Community Health Partnerships: Research, Education, and Action*, 9(2), 203–212. doi:10.1353/cpr.2015.0042

Derien, A. (2016). *People and places matter: Using integrated data systems to understand chronic absenteeism:* National Neighborhood Indicators Partnership. http://www.urban.org/sites/default/files/alfresco/publication-pdfs/2000699-People-and-Place-Matter-Using-Integrated-Data-Systems-to-Understand-Chronic-Absenteeism.pdf.

Elliott, L., McBride, T. D., Allen, P., Jacob, R. R., Jones, E., Kerner, J., & Brownson, R. C. (2014). Health care system collaboration to address chronic diseases: A nationwide snapshot from state public health practitioners. *Preventing Chronic Disease*, 11, 1–11. doi:10.5888/pcd11.140075

Gadaire, A. P., Armstrong, L. M., Cook, J. R., Kilmer, R. P., Larson, L. M., Simmons, C. J., Messinger, L. G., Thiery, T., & Babb, J. (2020). *A data-guided approach to supporting pre-k students' social-emotional development.* [Manuscript under review].

Gajda, R. (2006). Safe schools through strategic alliances: How assessment of collaboration enhances school violence prevention and response. *Journal of School Violence, 5*, 63–79.

Gajda, R., & Cravedi, L. (2006). Assimilating "real" teachers into pre-service teacher education: The benefits and limitations of a PDS course delivery model. *Action in Teacher Education, 28*, 42–52.

Ginsburg, A., Jordan, P., & Chang, H. (2014). *Absences add up: How school attendance influences student success.* https://www.attendanceworks.org/

Gottfried, M. A. (2009). Excused versus unexcused: How student absences in elementary school affect academic achievement. *Educational Evaluation and Policy Analysis, 31*(4), 392–415. doi:10.3102/0162373709342467

Gottfried, M. A. (2014). Chronic absenteeism and its effects on students' academic and socioemotional outcomes. *Journal of Education for Students Placed at Risk, 19*(2), 53–75. doi:10.1080/10824669.2014.962696

Hogan, K. S., Tynan, J. M., Covill, V. J., Kilmer, R. P., & Cook, J. R. (2017). A capacity building framework for community–university partnerships. *Collaborations: A Journal of Community-Based Research and Practice, 1.* doi:10.33596/coll.10

Hoole, T., & Patterson, T. E. (2008). Voices from the field: Evaluation as part of a learning culture. *New Directions for Evaluation, 119*(Fall), 93–113. doi:10.1002/ev.270

Hord, S. (2004). *Learning together leading together: Changing schools through professional learning communities.* Teachers College Press.

Israel, B. A., Eng, E., Schulz, A. J., & Parker, E. A. (Eds.). (2013). *Methods in community-based participatory research for health* (2nd ed.). Jossey-Bass.

Israel, B. A., Schulz, A. J., Parker, E. A., & Becker, A. B. (1998). Review of community-based research: Assessing partnership approaches to improve public health. *Annual Review of Public Health, 19*, 173–202. doi:10.1146/annurev.publhealth.19.1.173

Janzen, R., Ochocka, J., Turner, L., Cook, T., Franklin, M., & Deichert, D. (2017). Building a community-based culture of evaluation. *Evaluation and Program Planning, 65*, 163–170. doi:10.1016/j.evalprogplan.2017.08.014

Janzen, R., Seskar-Hencic, D., Dildar, Y., & McFadden, P. (2012). Using evaluation to shape and direct comprehensive community initiatives: Evaluation, reflective practice, and interventions dealing with complexity. *Canadian Journal of Program Evaluation, 25*, 61–88.

Kilmer, R. P., & Clark, L. Y. (2017, February). *Community-university partnerships: Putting good intentions into actual practice.* Opening plenary at the University of North Carolina at Charlotte's Engaged Scholarship and Community Partnership Symposium, Charlotte, NC.

Kilmer, R. P., Cook, J. R., & Brookins, K. C. C. (2013, June). *Facilitating student participation in service learning and applied research-based partnerships: Developing the capacity of a next generation of professional partners.* Roundtable presented at the 2013 Community-University Expo: Engaging Shared Words, Cornerbrook, NL, Canada.

Kilmer, R. P., Wall-Hill, S., Cook, J. R., Kothandapany, N., & Weber, L. J. (2009). Evaluating ParentVOICE: Building family organization sustainability through family-university collaboration. In S. Swart, B. Friesen, A. Holman, & N. Aue (Eds.), *Building on family strengths: Research and services in support of children and their families. 2007 conference proceedings and state of the science report* (pp. 164–168). Portland State University, Research and Training Center on Family Support and Children's Mental Health.

Leana, C. R., & Pil, F. K. (2006). Social capital and organizational performance: Evidence from urban public schools. *Organization Science, 17*(3), 353–366. doi:10.1287/orsc.1060.0191

Lehr, C. A., Hansen, A., Sinclair, M. F., & Christenson, S. L. (2003). Moving beyond dropout prevention to school completion: An integrative review of data based interventions. *School Psychology Review, 32,* 342–364.

Maton, K. I. (2017). *Influencing social policy: Applied psychology serving the public interest.* Oxford University Press.

Messinger, L. G., Kilmer, R. P., Coughran, M., Larson, J., Hefner, R., Cook, J., & Avrin., J. (2017, May). *A district-city-university partnership to improve K-12 school attendance and reduce chronic absenteeism.* Roundtable presented at the 2017 Community-College-University (C2U) Expo: For the Common Good, Vancouver, BC, Canada.

Miller, R. L., & Shinn, M. (2005). Learning from communities: Overcoming difficulties in dissemination of prevention and promotion efforts. *American Journal of Community Psychology, 35*(3-4), 169–183. doi:10.1007/s10464-005-3395-1

Minkler, M., & Wallerstein, N. (2008). *Community-based participatory research for health from process to outcomes* (2nd ed). Jossey-Bass.

Pounder, D. G. (1998). *Restructuring schools for collaboration: Promises and pitfalls.* State University of New York Press.

Preskill, H., & Boyle, S. (2008). A multidisciplinary model of evaluation capacity building. *American Journal of Evaluation, 29*(4), 443–459. doi:10.1177/1098214008324182

Romero, M., & Lee, Y. (2007). *A national portrait of chronic absenteeism in the early grades.* National Center for Children in Poverty.

Simmons, C. J., Morris, V. G., Cook, J. R., Kilmer, R. P., Armstrong, L. M., Gadaire, A., Salim, K., Babb, J., Day, P., & Messinger, L. (in press). A community-university partnership to develop and implement an enhanced model of coaching for prekindergarten. *Collaborations: A Journal of Community-Based Research and Practice.*

Steward, R. J., Steward, A. D., Blair, J., Jo, H., & Hill, M. F. (2008). School attendance revisited: A study of urban African American students' grade point averages and coping strategies. *Urban Education, 43,* 519–536.

Tandon, R., & Hall, B. (2015). *Institutionalizing community university research partnerships.* University of Victoria, PRIA, UNESCO.

Teitel, L. (Winter 2008/2009). School/university collaboration: The power of transformative partnerships. *Childhood Education, 85*(2), 75–80.

Vangen, S., & Huxham, C. (2003). Nurturing collaborative relations: Building trust in interorganizational collaboration. *The Journal of Applied Behavioral Science, 39,* 5–31.

Viswanathan, M., Ammerman, A., Eng, E., Garlehner, G., Lohr, K. N., Griffith, D., Rhodes, S., Samuel-Hodge, C., Maty, S., Lux, L., Webb, L., Sutton, S. F., Swinson, T., Jackman, A., & Whitener, L. (2004). *Community-based participatory research: Assessing the evidence.* Evidence Report/Technology Assessment No. 99 (prepared by RTI-University of North Carolina evidence-based practice center under contract No. 290-02-0016). AHRQ publication 04-E022-2: Agency for Healthcare Research and Quality.

Wandersman, A. (2003). Community science: Bridging the gap between science and practice with community-centered models. *American Journal of Community Psychology, 31*(3-4), 227–242. doi:10.1023/A:1023954503247

Woodland, R., & Hutton, M. (2012). Evaluating organizational collaborations: Suggested entry points and strategies. *American Journal of Evaluation, 33*(3), 366–383.

CHAPTER 15

DATA-DRIVEN ADVOCACY AND ADVOCACY EVALUATION

Melissa Strompolis, Megan Branham, and Whitney Tucker

Learning Objectives

1. Identify key components of advocacy efforts and tools to evaluate them.

2. Become familiar with unique challenges to evaluating advocacy efforts.

3. Learn ways in which strategic partnerships provide the foundation for action and change efforts within advocacy.

The field of evaluation uses a scientific approach to determine the worth or value of something—typically a program, project, or initiative. Evaluation has also evolved over time, moving from outcome and impact evaluation to assessments that include development, empowerment, and process (see Chapters 1, 3, and 8). The expansion of knowledge, skills, and tools within the field of evaluation has contributed to efforts to effect change at multiple levels, from data-driven decision making to improving interventions and scaling up programs in various settings and contexts. The focus of this chapter is evaluation within advocacy, with examples of how partnerships provided the foundation for action and change efforts in this space. The chapter begins with a short review of advocacy, then moves to using data and communication theory to drive advocacy efforts, and concludes with tools, methods, and challenges of advocacy evaluation.

UNDERSTANDING ADVOCACY

Effective advocacy work can address knowledge deficits, dispel misconceptions, and guide political action. With accurate information on trends and best practices, including knowledge from evaluation processes and activities, advocates can play a critical role in informing legislators so that they can create responsible, well-targeted policy. Moreover, advocates' data-driven influence can ignite legislative action.

Advocacy is an essential method for achieving social change because it has the potential to impact not only individuals and families but also communities and societies (Coffman, 2009). *Advocacy* is defined as "a wide range of activities conducted to influence decision makers at various levels" (Morariu & Brennan, 2009, p. 100). This expansive definition is intended to incorporate all potential advocacy-related activities, goals, and outcomes. Advocacy activities can include coalition or network building, earned or paid media, electronic outreach/social media, grassroots organizing and mobilizing, litigation, lobbying, marches, polling, petitions, public education, presentations, public service announcements, and rallies (Coffman, 2009; Morariu & Brennan, 2009).

The goal of advocacy, then, is to change social-, political-, or policy-related outcomes (Teles & Schmitt, 2011). For example, an organization may engage in grassroots organizing and secure paid media coverage as part of a strategy to decrease homelessness rates (social), elevate the platform of a candidate running for office (political), or streamline processes for paths to citizenship for immigrants (policy). The activities, goals, and intended outcomes of advocacy efforts are not prescribed; that is, there is no standard method or set of methods by which specific processes and operations are employed to meet certain goals or achieve particular outcomes. In a similar vein, advocacy is not a straightforward, linear process; it does not involve a sequenced set of ordered steps that are completed to accomplish a specified goal or outcome. In fact, organizations may try several different tactics, simultaneously or over time, to accomplish a difficult goal or outcome. Organizations involved in advocacy-related activities, therefore, face a number of challenges in demonstrating (e.g., evaluation efforts) that they are capable of effective advocacy and worthy of funding.

Influence on legislators can be achieved in a variety of ways (Jensen, 2007), further complicating efforts to gauge the impact of advocacy work. This fact contributes to difficulty in determining precisely what actions and strategies constitute effective legislative advocacy. Advocacy capacity assessments serve as tools to determine necessary knowledge and skills, and advocacy evaluation can shed light on effective tactics and activities to influence legislative policy (Egbert & Hoechstetter, 2006; Gerteis et al., 2008; Strong & Kim, 2012). Effective advocacy requires ongoing evaluation to ensure that advocate resources are appropriately allocated in order to guide legislators toward data-driven policy decisions.

USING DATA TO INFORM ADVOCACY EFFORTS

Before selecting an advocacy strategy, advocates must determine what data source(s) best informs the desired advocacy outcome. A plethora of data exist that are readily available in the public domain, and additional supporting data exist within the public (government agencies) and private (corporate) sectors; both typically require an application or special appeal for the data (sometimes in the form of a Freedom of Information Act request). Within the child well-being landscape, for example, the Annie E. Casey Foundation (Annie E. Casey Foundation, 2017) compiles data sources from across the country through their KIDS COUNT initiative. Multiple indicators exist for public access within categories of economic well-being, education, health, and family and community. Advocates must be able to mine these data to determine relevant indicators that bolster their message.

The process of deciding on the most applicable and appropriate data to inform an advocacy strategy should begin with the end in mind. That is, advocates should be working toward a final result or outcome at the conclusion of their advocacy efforts (i.e., *How will we know if we have been successful?*). This step is the first in a process known as *results accountability*, defined as "a disciplined way of thinking and taking action that can be used to improve the quality of life in communities, cities, counties, states, and nations" (Friedman, 2005, p. 11). Without data, advocates cannot monitor progress or improvements. It is important to note that advocates rarely have all the data they may need in the beginning of their advocacy process; however, starting with the best available data and continuing to gather data along the way, for example, through implementation or process evaluations, will further guide efforts. Additionally, data sources do not have to always include statewide or national data (including those from sources like KIDS COUNT); using localized data and/or basic data collection methods (e.g., survey) can provide a solid starting point.

Within *Trying Hard Is Not Good Enough*, Friedman (2005, p. 13) outlines key questions to answer within six areas when planning results accountability work: (1) results (*What are the conditions of well-being we want for our children, families, and community as a whole?*); (2) indicators (*How will we measure these conditions?*); (3) baselines (*What do the measures show about where we have been and where we are headed?*); (4) turning the curve (*What do successes look like if we do better than the baseline?*); (5) strategies (*What works to improve these conditions?*); and (6) performance measures (*How much did we do? How well did we do it? And is anyone better off?*). Importantly, the data must connect to the end desired result and inform strategies, not the other way around. After defining the end goal, advocates should follow where related data lead and design strategies to make measurable changes on key data measures subsequently impacting social outcomes. For example, if advocates seek to reduce the number of children within a state's foster care system, they should start by looking both at data trends over time as well as the current number of children in care. Advocates may then decide to further break down strategies by focusing on data within a subgroup of the larger population (e.g., children in care under the age of 14 or children in care for longer than 36 months). Strategies must align with those data points (e.g., policies that expedite adoption process) and clearly connect back to desired outcomes (reducing number of children in foster care). Advocates too often move forward with advocacy strategies on policy solutions that are not clearly linked to improving a result or conditions of a population. Data and strategies that are not linked to the end result will not result in the desired social change and may ignore or negatively impact vulnerable populations.

As one case in point, data disaggregation, by factors such as race or ethnicity, is a critical strategy used to better identify root causes of a variety of social issues, including disparities in health outcomes, education, and poverty (Annie E. Casey Foundation, 2016). The following brief case example illustrates this use.

CASE EXAMPLE: ADVANCING RACIAL EQUITY IN WASHINGTON STATE

Many organizations nationwide are using data disaggregated by race and/or ethnicity to inform policy work. Washington State has created a race equity and inclusion assessment checklist to guide decisions made in King and surrounding counties. The tool (Figure 15.1) combines community engagement and partnership strategies with the use of empirical data to address potential impacts on various forms of equity. The checklist outlines a process referred to as *Equity Impact Review* (EIR) and is separated into five phases to be completed in partnership with community stakeholders for

Continued

Figure 15.1   Race Equity and Inclusion Assessment Checklist

2015 Equity Impact Review Process Overview
Updated March 2016

The Equity Impact Review (EIR) process merges empirical (quantitative) data and community engagement findings (qualitative) to inform planning, decision-making and implementation of actions which affect equity in King County.

When conducting this review process, please a) consider organizational and cultural diversity, b) include members who regularly engage with communities or connect with key affected parties/stakeholders, c) involve managers and leadership, and d) engage subject-matter and feasibility experts.

Purpose: Ensure that equity impacts are rigorously and holistically considered and advanced in the design and implementation of the proposed action (plan/policy/program development, operations modification, capital programs/projects, etc.)

How and When to Use the EIR Process: It is expected that the Equity Impact Review is embedded within the development and implementation processes of the proposed action.

As a team, use the equity tools – Equity Impact Review process, Community Engagement and Language Access guides, and available data resources – to complete the EIR worksheets and understand how - and to what extent - your proposal impacts equity. The checklist on Page 2 will indicate successful completion of the EIR process.

REMEMBER: For each stage of the EIR process, consider how these frameworks of equity are being impacted.

Distributional equity—Fair and just distribution of benefits and burdens to all affected parties and communities across the community and organizational landscape.

Process equity—Inclusive, open and fair access by all stakeholders to decision processes that impact community and operational outcomes. Process equity relies on all affected parties having access to and meaningful experience with civic and employee engagement, public participation, and jurisdictional listening.

Cross-generational equity—Effects of current actions on the fair and just distribution of benefits and burdens to future generations of communities and employees. Examples include income and wealth, health outcomes, white privilege, resource depletion, climate change and pollution, real estate redlining practices, and species extinction.

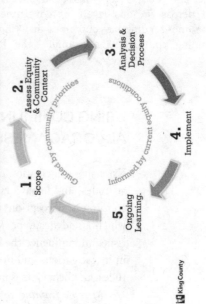

EQUITY IMPACT REVIEW PROCESS

1. Scope
2. Assess Equity & Community Context
3. Analysis & Decision Process
4. Implement
5. Ongoing Learning.

Guided by community priorities
Informed by current conditions

2015 Equity Impact Review Process
Updated March 2016

Phase 1: Scope. Identify who will be affected.
- ☐ Identify how your action will affect/serve people and places using demographic information. Consider in particular low income populations, communities of color, and limited-English speaking residents.
  - – Reach: which people and places will be affected by your action?
  - – Intensity: what effects, impacts and/or outcomes will your action have on people and places?
  - – Duration: how long will the action have an effect– short-, medium-, and/or long-term?
- ☐ Identify the group of stakeholders and affected parties – including those who have historically not been/felt included or engaged – and their roles in decision-making.

Phase 2: Assess equity and community context.
- ☐ Learn about affected communities', employees', and/or stakeholders' priorities and concerns. (Use the Community Engagement Guide to help with this.)
- ☐ Know which determinants of equity will be affected by your intended outcomes – both directly and indirectly. (Reference the Determinants of Equity report.)
- ☐ Know how your proposed course of action will affect known disparities within relevant determinants. (Use quantitative data and/or gather new information.)
- ☐ Identify potential unintended equity-related outcomes of this action.

Phase 3: Analysis and decision process.
- ☐ Project or map out how key alternatives will affect community and employee priorities and concerns.
- ☐ Evaluate each alternative for who will be disproportionately burdened or benefit - now and in the future. How will alternative actions differ in improving or worsening current equity conditions?
- ☐ Include upstream alternatives (and related costs) that target root causes to eliminate disproportionate impact.
- ☐ Prioritize alternatives by equitable outcomes and reconcile with functional and fiscal policy drivers.

Phase 4: Implement. Are you staying connected with communities and employees?
- ☐ Based on earlier use of Community Engagement Guide, communicate with communities, stakeholders and employees about how you will implement your action.
- ☐ Engage with affected communities and employees to guide successful implementation.
- ☐ Advance "pro-equity" opportunities when possible, i.e. contracting, hiring and promotion, materials sourcing, etc.
- ☐ Measure and evaluate your intended outcomes in collaboration with affected communities. Are there sufficient monitoring and accountability systems to identify unintended consequences? How will course corrections be handled if unintended consequences are identified?

Phase 5: Ongoing Learning. Listen, adjust, and co-learn with communities and employees.
- ☐ Evaluate whether your action appropriately responds to community priorities and concerns.
- ☐ Learn with the community to adjust your action as their priorities and concerns shift.
- ☐ Communicate progress to all stakeholders. Plan to include community feedback into future planning.

King County

King County

Source: From 2015 Equity impact review process overview, by King County, March 2016, http://www.kingcounty.gov/~/media/elected/executive/equity-social-justice/2016/The_Equity_Review_checklist_Mar2016.ashx?la=en. Copyright 2015 by King County Equity and Social Justice. Reprinted with permission.

successful determination and ongoing consideration of policies with potentially disparate and unjust outcomes, particularly for people of color, of low-income communities, and with limited English proficiency (King County, 2016).

In the first two phases of the EIR process, organizations undertaking the development of a policy or project partner with communities to identify relevant challenges and understand the context of their proposed work within that specific locale. King County created supplemental community engagement and language access guides to assist in this effort, helping organizations to reach and interact with traditionally overlooked and underserved populations to promote culturally appropriate and accessible opportunities for engagement and partnership in the review process. The second half of the EIR uses the information gleaned in the earlier phases to inform the analysis and implementation of proposed policies or projects. All potential decisions are prioritized by equity outcome, and community members are central partners, providing their input in the context of collaboration. Project developers are encouraged to further advance equity throughout the completion of any chosen initiative (i.e., through contract hiring and materials sourcing), and implementation steps are adjusted as community concerns arise or priorities shift (King County, 2016).

The EIR process tool has been successfully applied across various levels of government to promote more equitable outcomes in King and surrounding counties. For example, the budget process was updated to include equity impact considerations in department business plans, and the Department of Transportation used EIR guidelines when determining changes or improvements to public transit services before presenting to County Council. Additionally, the Department of Natural Resources and Parks made policy decisions to "keep selected parks open within the Urban Growth Area and invest in improving parks in underserved, low income, racially diverse communities to mitigate equity impacts" (King County, 2012, p. 1).

The tool is most successful when implemented as part of a strong partnership initiative, such as the youth outreach effort highlighted in the King County Community Engagement Guide (2011). The guide explains how King County Juvenile Justice and King County Superior Court partnered with county youth as well as the Office of Performance, Strategy, and Budget to determine a plan for reducing the detention time and number of warrants for failure to appear in court that disproportionately impacted youth of color (King County, 2011). These groups collaboratively developed a process for identifying the factors and conditions that prevented youth from appearing in court and garnered extensive feedback that they used to design a pilot program providing outreach to youth with histories of prior warrants. The success of this and similar racial equity and inclusion partnership initiatives has since informed the King County Equity and Social Justice Strategic Plan, a collaborative guide created to direct the county's equity policy efforts through the next 5 years.

USING COMMUNICATION THEORY TO FRAME ADVOCACY MESSAGING

Extensive information exists regarding the way communication influences perceptions, attitudes, and behaviors. Just as paid media advertisements have the potential to shape consumers' perceptions of and decisions about using products (Chang, 2007), the way in which an advocacy position is communicated can shape audience perceptions on social issues and influence the likelihood of behavioral action. A primary characteristic involved in investigations and evaluations of the impact of communications on perceptions, attitudes, and behaviors is message framing.

Message framing refers to the process whereby one message, among two or more messages with contrasting words or phrases, is preferred by individuals, even when the messages are logically equivalent (Druckman, 2001). In other words, message framing occurs when, given a consistent outcome across multiple messages, different words or phrases within the messages demonstrate predictable individual preferences among the messages (LeBoeuf & Shafir, 2003). In their now classic study, Tversky and Kahneman (1981) demonstrated the importance of this framing when they found that individuals have specific preferences when presented with a choice among multiple options, even when all choices have the same end result. Their results highlighted that the frame of the message that is communicated to individuals produces a preference for a message among multiple options with the same end result. Researchers have since studied message framing in many diverse contexts and conditions including consumer choices, evaluations of services and products, medical and clinical decisions, political perceptions, reactions to social problems, voting, and others (Lakoff, 2002; Levin et al., 1998; Schuck & de Vreese, 2009; Wong & McMurray, 2002).

Effective communication is the bedrock of successful advocacy work, making it possible to influence public discourse in a way that gives shape and substance to the policy landscape. Message framing is thereby important because it can provide the consumer with an alternative way of processing information and, ultimately, provide a signal for how the communicator feels about a given social situation (FrameWorks Institute, 2002). By understanding the context in which effective communication occurs, advocates and advocacy partners can align messaging and potentially have a positive effect on social issues via advocacy.

FrameWorks Institute in Washington, DC, has pioneered the approach known as *strategic frame analysis* that uses communications research to inform the framing of complex social issues to advance policy outcomes (FrameWorks Institute, n.d). This method encourages advocates to build communication efforts around "frames" such as culturally shared values and strategic visual cues to help audiences "assimilate new information ... by fitting it into the framework of something [they] already understand" (FrameWorks Institute, 2002, p. 2). As an example, the Center on the Developing Child at Harvard University (2015) created a simple message frame based on a commonly used visual cue (i.e., stop light) to convey meaning in regard to three types of stress. In the figure, "go/green" is used to symbolize positive stress, "yellow/slow down" is used for tolerable stress, and "red/stop" is used for toxic stress (see their visual at http://developingchild.harvard.edu/science/key-concepts/toxic-stress/). As another example, employing both strategic language and a strategic visual cue, the Institute has framed the concept of building resilience in children using the metaphor of an unbalanced scale, tipping toward either positive or negative development outcomes (Kendall-Taylor, 2012). This frame allows audiences to conceptualize resilience in the abstract while more concretely grasping the impact of policy advocacy efforts that "stack the scale" in promoting positive outcomes for children. Within this frame, work to promote early learning or increase access to services can be understood as counterbalancing negative factors (i.e., community violence or abuse) that might otherwise impact the trajectory of a child's life. This frame is a simple example of one way that effective advocacy can shift public perception. Given that communication is a key component within many advocacy strategies, advocates will want to be intentional with (e.g., test alternatives, use research-informed frames) the content of their communications to ensure strategic and effective framing to achieve their desired goals or outcomes.

Figure 15.2   Message Frame Manipulations

Goal Valence

Positive. Children First/Communities in Schools needs your help to improve the lives of children and families. Currently, our state uses a combination of state and federal funds to assist low-wage parents with the cost of child care – a cost that can exceed the price of college tuition. Despite a waiting list of over 35,000 children for the child care subsidy program, the North Carolina Legislature and Governor McCrory did not pass a budget with additional investments for child care subsidies. Families receiving child care subsidies may choose the child care program that best meets their needs and helps to ensure that the child care is safe, high quality, and dependable. The availability of child care subsidies also increases employment, job retention, workforce productivity, and the growth of businesses. With your help we can get more children into quality care programs and keep our parents in the workforce. Congress and President Obama just passed a budget that invests more federal dollars in early education. Please sign our petition asking North Carolina legislators to follow Congress' lead by increasing state funding for the child care subsidy program!

Negative. Children First/Communities in Schools needs your help to improve the lives of children and families. Currently, our state uses a combination of state and federal funds to assist low-wage parents with the cost of child care – a cost that can exceed the price of college tuition. Despite a waiting list of over 35,000 children for the child care subsidy program, the North Carolina Legislature and Governor McCrory did not pass a budget with additional investments for child care subsidies. Families who are not receiving child care subsidies cannot choose the child care program that best meets their needs and may not be safe, high quality, or dependable. The lack of availability of child care subsidies can decrease employment, job retention, workforce productivity, and the growth of businesses. Without your help we cannot get more children into quality care programs or keep our parents in the workforce. Congress and President Obama just passed a budget that invests more federal dollars in early education. Please sign our petition asking North Carolina legislators to follow Congress' lead by increasing state funding for the child care subsidy program!

Social Norm

Advocates who took action. Children First/Communities in Schools needs your help to improve the health of our community. Last year, 50 Children First/Communities in Schools advocates took action to support Medicaid expansions in our state. Although Governor McCrory and the NC Legislature blocked Medicaid expansion in North Carolina, we know that improving health outcomes for low-income parents will benefit the whole family. Additionally, if North Carolina does not expand Medicaid, fewer people will have higher costs for uncompensated care. We encourage you to join your fellow advocates to email Governor McCrory and your legislators and ask them to reconsider their decision to block the Medicaid expansion in our state. Please send your email now!

Advocates who did not take action. Children First/Communities in Schools needs your help to improve the health of our community. Last year, 690 Children First/Communities in Schools advocates did not take action to support the Medicaid expansions in our state. Although Governor McCrory and the NC Legislature blocked Medicaid expansion in North Carolina, we know that improving health outcomes for low-income parents will benefit the whole family. Additionally, if North Carolina does not expand Medicaid, fewer people will have higher costs for uncompensated care. We encourage you to buck the trend of your fellow advocates and email Governor McCrory and your legislators to ask them to reconsider their decision to block the Medicaid expansion in our state. Please send your email now!

Goal Setting/Behavioral Tracking

Specified goal and monitoring. Children First/Communities in Schools needs your help to improve the education of our children. At the Are you Smarter than an Elementary School Student? Event, we are trying to raise $10,000 to provide support for our after school Learning Center. The Learning Center is a safe haven afterschool program that provides academic assistance, healthy snacks, and enrichment activities for up to 60 at-risk children. The Learning Center strengthens the connections among student, school, teacher, parent, and community, a key element in helping an at-risk child succeed in school and prepare for life. We know you have attended a CF/CIS event in the past and we would love to see you at the Are you Smarter than an Elementary School Student? fundraiser as well!

Unspecified goal and monitoring. Children First/Communities in Schools needs your help to improve the education of our children. At the Are you Smarter than an Elementary School Student? Event, we are trying to raise money to provide support for our after school Learning Center. The Learning Center is a safe haven afterschool program that provides academic assistance, healthy snacks, and enrichment activities for up to 60 at-risk children. The Learning Center strengthens the connections among student, school, teacher, parent, and community, a key element in helping an at-risk child succeed in school and prepare for life. We would love to see you at the Are you Smarter than an Elementary School Student? fundraiser!

Figure 15.2 is referenced in CASE EXAMPLE: EMPIRICAL EXAMINATION OF ADVOCACY COMMUNICATION

Note: The message frame manipulations were tested by Strompolis (2015).

CASE EXAMPLE: EMPIRICAL EXAMINATION OF ADVOCACY COMMUNICATION

Evaluation of advocacy efforts is fraught with logistical challenges but is possible through the use of strategic partnerships and innovative methods. For example, as a community psychology doctoral student, Melissa Strompolis developed relationships with several members of the Society for Community Research and Action's (Division 27 of the American Psychological Association) public policy committee. One member, Dr. Jon Miles, provided Strompolis with an opportunity to work with him and a local nonprofit organization, Children First/Communities in Schools of Buncombe County (CF/CIS; North Carolina), in an effort to strengthen the impact of the organization's advocacy and policy efforts. Given the long-standing partnership that Miles had with CF/CIS, Strompolis was able to quickly develop a mutually beneficial partnership with CF/CIS's director of policy and build trust with the agency. In her examination of advocacy communication,

Strompolis (2015) utilized call-to-action emails from CF/CIS to its supporters to investigate the impact of varying message frames on advocacy-related behaviors, perceptions, and intentions. By manipulating the frame, that is, goal-valence, social norm, and goal setting/behavior tracking (Figure 15.2), of advocacy messages, Strompolis and CF/CIS were able to examine support for each frame among specific populations of advocates and college students. While the college students reported their perceptions and behavioral intentions in response to the frames, the examination of advocates involved real-world issues and real-time advocacy-related behavioral requests. The study findings were mixed regarding message frame preference and effectiveness; however, the project demonstrated how a strategic partnership led to a practical application of advocacy evaluation methods within a nonprofit setting.

CASE EXAMPLE: COALITION MESSAGE FRAMING

Building consensus around message frames can be difficult in large advocacy coalitions. One such group, the South Carolina Early Childhood Common Agenda (ECCA) coalition, utilized a collaborative communication approach with targeted outreach to craft and test new advocacy message framing. The ECCA was founded in 2014 by three partner organizations—Children's Trust of South Carolina, the Institute for Child Success, and United Way Association of South Carolina—and has since grown to include more than 50 partner organizations that offer policy recommendations to bolster the early childhood system in South Carolina. While the strength of the group as an advocacy force lies in its size and breadth of partnerships, in the early days of the collaboration, ECCA partners struggled to maintain a consistent advocacy message across sectors in regard to mutual policy

recommendations. Although each coalition member advocated for the same policies as the others, legislators reported being unaware that members were on the same side of an issue or working together. To address this, the coalition coordinator scheduled monthly in-person meetings in which partners would discuss not only the group's priority issues, but also the way in which all members would communicate about those issues. Several potential message frames were produced for each policy recommendation, and then partners would share the concept or phrase with key legislators, reporting back to the group on the messages that resonated with legislators. For example, when investigating message frames for establishing a South Carolina earned income tax credit (EITC), partners found that the phrase "tax credits for working families" was better received in the state's politically conservative

Continued

environment than the term "earned income." ECCA members incorporated this message framing into one-pagers for legislators, for policy briefs, and in social media outreach. Coalition members had been advocating for a state EITC for 2 years to no avail, but an EITC was established by the South Carolina General Assembly only 6 months after reframing the message. Legislative will and timing combined with an effective messaging frame can strengthen a coalition and can ultimately lead to a legislative win. Consistent communication among partners is key to building frames that are not only applicable across sectors, but also memorable and significant to decision makers.

EVALUATING ADVOCACY EFFORTS

Advocacy evaluation allows for the critical review of strategies to achieve advocacy- and policy-related results (Coffman, 2009). Similar to traditional assessment efforts, advocacy assessments can be used for both monitoring (i.e., formative or process evaluation) and evaluation (i.e., outcome and impact evaluation; Coffman, n.d), with monitoring focusing on measures of progress toward intended results, and evaluation focusing on a particular strategy's worth and/or achievement of intended results (Coffman, n.d).

Although advocacy evaluation is subject to the same accountability pressures (i.e., increasing demands from funders to demonstrate effectiveness and achievement of outcomes; Carman, 2010) as direct-service evaluations (Reisman et al., 2007), advocacy evaluation brings its own unique challenges (Teles & Schmitt, 2011) because of the nonlinear, ever-changing nature of advocacy. In their accountability efforts, providers of direct services must be able to show the nature and/or amount of services provided (e.g., 100 children completed social skills training program) and the effect of those services (e.g., disruptive behaviors in the classroom decreased by 25%). Similarly, nonprofit organizations and others engaged in advocacy must also be able to detail the advocacy activities the organization completed and document the effects of those activities (the effects can be particularly challenging to demonstrate when multiple advocates are working collaboratively or separately on a single issue). As funders increase interest in and financial support for advocacy-related activities, they want to know which advocacy efforts are a sound use of their resources and worth supporting (Teles & Schmitt, 2011).

In the face of these challenges, innovative capacity building and evaluation tools and methods need to be utilized to prepare for and examine the impact and effectiveness of advocacy. To begin, organizations with varied advocacy experience could benefit from completing an *advocacy capacity assessment* to determine strengths and areas for improvement in capacity to engage in and evaluate advocacy efforts. Bolder Advocacy (n.d.), an initiative of the Alliance for Justice, provides a free web-based and paper tool for this purpose, *Advocacy Capacity Tool (ACT!) for Organizational Assessment. ACT!* allows nonprofit organizations and other agencies to quantitatively examine four critical capacity areas, including advocacy goals, plans, and strategies; conducting advocacy; advocacy avenues; and organizational operations to sustain advocacy. Scores are provided for 18 indicators within the four capacity areas. The information can be used to determine if capacity exists to engage in advocacy, including coalition formation, messaging capability, and sustainability of efforts (Bolder Advocacy, n.d.).

Whether working with their own research and evaluation staff or partnering with an external evaluator, organizational leadership and staff must reflect upon their ability to track the necessary data accurately and create a manageable, resource-efficient advocacy evaluation (Coffman, 2009; Wiseman et al., 2007). To assess internal capacity, organizations need to gauge the level of funding, staff, and expertise required to conduct the evaluation (Reisman et al., 2007). *ACT!* can inform and guide decisions made to address deficiencies (e.g., lack of research or evaluation staff, capacity, or expertise), ensuring clear roles and responsibilities for staff and increasing the likelihood of achieving success in advocacy efforts.

Once an organization has assessed advocacy capacity (including establishing relationships with external partners) or made the decision to engage in advocacy efforts, several useful tools exist for structuring a plan to evaluate advocacy efforts. For example, the Harvard Family Research Project developed a *User's Guide to Advocacy Evaluation and Planning* (Coffman, 2009). The tool includes a four-step process for evaluating advocacy efforts: (1) focusing (evaluation audience, uses, and questions); (2) mapping (impacts and goals, activities, and interim outcomes); (3) prioritizing (essential components, timeframe, internal or external); and (4) designing (measures and methods). While the tool does not include who will complete the evaluation, implementation, analysis, or dissemination of evaluation results, the advocacy evaluation planning worksheet provides a user-friendly, concrete product and process for getting started with advocacy evaluation. To access the Advocacy Evaluation Planning Worksheet, you can download the *User's Guide to Advocacy Evaluation and Planning* at https://archive.globalfrp.org/publications-resources/browse-our-publications/a-user-s-guide-to-advocacy-evaluation-planning.

As another example, the United Nations International Children's Emergency Fund created the resource *Monitoring and Evaluating Advocacy: Companion to the Advocacy Toolkit* (Coffman, n.d). The toolkit includes an overview and description of distinctive features of monitoring and evaluating advocacy as well as five questions for planning advocacy monitoring and evaluation (*Who are the monitoring and evaluation users? How will the monitoring and evaluation be used? What evaluation design should be used? What should be measured? What data collection tools should be used?*). The toolkit provides context for each question along with relevant case studies and sample advocacy activities, outcomes, goals, and impacts in planning monitoring and evaluation activities for advocacy efforts. It also includes resources for capacity assessment and mapping (e.g., networking and system), continuous monitoring (e.g., media tracking and debriefs), collecting data on short-term and intermediate outcomes (e.g., surveys and interviews), and policy tracking. The toolkit is most useful after an organization has committed to, assessed readiness and capacity for, and dedicated resources for engaging in policy and advocacy efforts.

While the resources profiled above provide a useful starting point and overview of an advocacy evaluation process, the tools described do not provide a comprehensive examination of the types of measurements and outcomes that exist for advocacy evaluation. Given the inherent differences between traditional, program-oriented evaluation and advocacy evaluation, supplemental resources on measurement and outcomes would be beneficial to organizations engaging in advocacy evaluation. As one substantive example of such a resource, the AECF and Organizational Research Services developed *A Guide to*

Measuring Advocacy and Policy (Reisman et al., 2007) and identified six outcome areas at the individual, family, and community level that can be examined for changes as the result of advocacy work. The outcome areas include (1) shifts in social norms (e.g., changes in the importance of an issue and public behavior); (2) strengthened organizational capacity (e.g., improved abilities to manage, align, and communicate advocacy work); (3) strengthened alliances (e.g., strategic alignment of advocacy goals with other coalitions and organizations); (4) strengthened base of support (e.g., increased behavioral action by key champions and the general public); (5) improved policies (e.g., policy development, adaption, implementation, and enforcement); and (6) changes in impact (e.g., improved social conditions). These outcomes represent both short- and long-term indicators and include a wide range of potential areas to examine. Additionally, the Alliance for Justice (2011) developed benchmarks of advocacy effectiveness in their book *Investing in Change: A Funder's Guide to Supporting Advocacy*. The benchmarks, primarily focused on legislative advocacy, include five domains covering the executive, judicial, and legislative branches; the electoral process; and cross-cutting advocacy (see Case Example: A Survey to Increase Legislative Advocacy Capacity).

CASE EXAMPLE: A SURVEY TO INCREASE LEGISLATIVE ADVOCACY CAPACITY

Advocates often possess the knowledge and experience relevant to policy issues but struggle to increase the impact of their efforts on policymakers. Children's Trust of South Carolina (a nonprofit organization focused on strengthening families and leading communities to prevent child maltreatment and unintentional injuries) combated this issue within the state by partnering with 13 regional injury prevention coalitions to form Safe Kids SC. Children's Trust serves as the state office for Safe Kids SC, and members of the local coalitions rely on the statewide office to provide timely training, technical support, and resources to support community efforts to prevent childhood injury. In 2015, many local coalitions had positive relationships with state legislators but had failed to harness the collective influence necessary to effectively advocate for an update to the state's child passenger safety law. Children's Trust leveraged its policy, program, and research staff to partner with Safe Kids SC to assess the capacity of coalition partners and determine effective, consistent advocacy messaging to aid advocates in influencing childhood injury prevention policy discussions.

To learn how advocates could be more effective at engaging policymakers on prevention issues, Children's Trust gathered survey data from Safe Kids SC advocates, legislators, and legislative staff across four domains: knowledge of injury prevention, perceptions of injury prevention, advocacy capacity/impact, and community involvement (Strompolis et al., 2016). Gathering information from these four domains allowed Children's Trust to assess potential knowledge gaps and levels of perceived importance of injury prevention among Safe Kids SC advocates, legislators, and legislative staff; capacity to engage in advocacy efforts and levels of community involvement for Safe Kids SC advocates; and impact of advocacy efforts on legislators and legislative staff. Supplemental interview questions (Figure 15.3) were developed from the results of the survey to provide specific feedback on effective communication tactics with legislators. Findings from the survey were noted in questions to legislators and legislative staff, who were then solicited for advice to inform advocates moving forward (e.g., *District voters were rated as the highest influence for legislators—how does that information or influence get to you from voters in your district?*).

Continued

Figure 15.3 Legislator Interview Questions

Influencing Prevention Policy Through Effective Communications
With Legislators and Advocates

Context #1

In terms of general knowledge of injury prevention, advocates, legislators, and legislative staff
were asked questions related to motor vehicles, boats, all-terrain vehicles, safe sleep, and
firearms. Both legislators and advocates struggled with knowing key contributing factors and
consequences of motor vehicle safety – particularly, child passenger safety and distracted
driving.

1. Knowledge of injury prevention
   a. If the goal of a communication is to increase knowledge of the causes and
      consequences of motor vehicle safety, what is the most helpful way to
      communicate to you?
      Examples: email? Fact sheets? Events?

Context #2

In the survey, advocates, legislators, and legislative staff were asked to rate the legislative
priority level of injury prevention in general and cell phone use while driving, child passenger
restraint laws, and graduated drivers' licensing. Again, legislators and advocates thought all of
these areas were important; however, most were neutral on whether or not legislation would pass
in the next session to address some of these areas.

2. Perceptions of injury prevention
   a. What do you think it would take to make injury prevention a top priority of the
      South Carolina General Assembly?
   b. What would that effort look like for advocates of injury prevention?
      Examples: Town halls? Visits to the state house? Phone calls?

Context #3

In the last section of the survey, legislators and legislative staff were asked about various sources
of influence, such as voters, colleagues, the governor, and lobbyists. District voters and the
general public were rated as the strongest influences for legislators and legislative staff.

3. Sources of influence
   a. How does that information or influence get to you from voters in your district?
   b. How does that information or influence get to you from the general public?
   c. How could nonprofits be more effective in their advocacy efforts?

Findings from the surveys showed that advocates and legislators both considered advocates to have a greater understanding of most injury prevention issues than legislators, but the groups exhibited similar knowledge levels when assessed across prevention areas. They also showed similar priorities, rating child passenger safety as a very important injury prevention area and graduated driver's licensing as least important (relative to the other areas). Despite the attention given to child passenger safety, advocates and legislators both indicated little knowledge of best practices in this area. They were also incorrect in other aspects of motor vehicle safety, with coalition members consistently showing low levels of knowledge in the same areas as legislators and legislative staff. The authors suspected that similarities in the lack of knowledge between the groups may be the result of ineffective advocate education and/or poor communication, but additional study is necessary to uncover the root cause of this issue.

This work indicates that advocates may increase their impact by devoting additional time to ensuring their own expertise and developing relationships with policymakers, with the ultimate goal of cultivating reliable policy champions within the legislature's peer-to-peer support network. The authors also recommended that advocates collaborate with other nonprofit organizations to minimize time and effort devoted to local outreach while simultaneously increasing public and legislative interest and influence regarding their issue areas (Strompolis et al., 2016).

Based on the findings from the survey and responses from the legislative interviews, Children's Trust hosted a Safe Kids Advocacy Day at the South Carolina State House to provide Safe Kids SC coalition members an opportunity to gain experience in engaging legislators about injury prevention. The event consisted of a morning training session on effective advocacy techniques and an afternoon trip to the State House to discuss updating child passenger safety regulations with legislators. The advocacy training included a briefing on the survey and interview results as well as a discussion of current child passenger safety laws and the American Academy of Pediatrics recommendations. These overviews ensured that advocates tailored their message to legislative interests and were comfortable in their knowledge of appropriate child passenger safety regulations. Talking points about the issue were distributed to attendees along with tips for effective messaging. The advocacy efforts cultivated through this partnership were successful, and in 2017, a bill was passed in South Carolina updating the state's motor vehicle laws to reflect the child passenger safety recommendations of the American Academy of Pediatrics (Durbin, 2011).

CHALLENGES AND BARRIERS TO DATA-DRIVEN ADVOCACY AND ADVOCACY EVALUATION

Although advocacy evaluation can be problematic in a number of ways, evaluators can proactively address the challenges through early identification of potential barriers, such as the lack of a practical guide for conducting advocacy evaluation, different requirements by funding sources, varying perspectives regarding the role of evaluation, trouble identifying outcomes, and methodological issues (Reisman et al., 2007). Without practical guidance and resources for conducting advocacy evaluation, nonprofit organizations and other agencies often struggle to assess their advocacy efforts. Furthermore, funders struggle with evaluation requirements, often stipulating that the fundee limit the focus to solely outputs or impose overly aggressive outcome goals (e.g., achieving a policy change in a short period of time; Reisman et al., 2007).

Beyond varying requirements for evaluation, differences among funders add additional challenges for advocacy evaluation. For example, their diverse missions and practices lead both corporate and private funders to be involved in a wide variety of advocacy activities (Reisman et al., 2007), which can take place at multiple levels (e.g., local, state, national, international) and may seek to achieve many different goals (e.g., raise awareness of an issue, increase voting rates, change legislation). In addition, the alignment of funder preferences with the activities and objectives of an organization's advocacy efforts may be a difficult process. For example, funders and fundees may have different guidelines and policies on allowable advocacy activities, which can be a barrier not only to the strongest advocacy and policy tactics but also to the design of effective advocacy evaluations. Moreover, funders differ in their goals and emphases for evaluation activities; some focus exclusively on outcomes, others emphasize implementation, and still others prefer to assess the connections between the implementation of advocacy activities and outcomes, all while adhering to state laws and federal Internal Revenue Services (IRS) requirements for lobbying-related activities. State and federal IRS and ethics stipulations are another unique challenge that can impact advocacy evaluations as the design, process, and results must not violate any requirements. Clearly a one-size-fits-all approach to advocacy evaluation will not meet the needs of all funders (Reisman et al., 2007).

Another challenge to advocacy evaluation relates to varying perspectives regarding the role(s) of evaluation in this context. For instance, many organizations engaged in advocacy efforts view evaluation as reflecting opposition to their work. In a similar vein, the leadership and staff of some organizations may think their work cannot be evaluated and, in fact, believe efforts to conduct an evaluation can hamper advocacy efforts (Reisman et al., 2007). For example, in response to an initial plan, a funder may supply monetary resources for a social media advocacy campaign to address incarceration rates and an evaluation of the effort. During the course of the advocacy campaign, the organization may need to change tactics (e.g., using in-person advocacy meetings), but does not because they do not have the capacity to evaluate the change in tactics. Evaluations of advocacy may be labeled as unsuccessful if the efforts do not include prespecified activities or achieve predetermined outcomes, despite the variable nature of advocacy work and plethora of unpredictable policy influencers.

Determining outcomes represents another challenge to advocacy evaluation. Traditionally, projects are funded for short timeframes, usually 1–3 years; however, the goals or targeted outcomes of advocacy efforts often require a much longer timeframe (Reisman et al., 2007). Therefore, it is important to determine appropriate or flexible timeframes at the outset, noting that changes in outcomes and timeframes are commonplace in the advocacy and policy arena. Additionally, outcomes can be difficult to define when key contexts and stakeholders are changing due to political climate and election cycles. Flexibility is crucial in specifying variables and processes for advocacy evaluation, for both short-term and long-term outcomes (Reisman et al., 2007).

Finally, advocacy evaluation faces a number of methodological challenges. Challenges in this context include making accurate attributions (i.e., supporting that observed actions or changes reflect a specific effect of an individual, organization, effort, or activity); accounting for complexity (i.e., various methods are typically employed across different levels to achieve a single goal), organizational capacity, and engagement (i.e., evaluation experience and evaluation process buy-in of staff members); assessing and controlling for the role(s) of external forces (i.e., advocacy efforts, at various levels, working together (or against) the same goal); reconciling shifting strategies and milestones (i.e., shift in tactics to reflect change in advocacy context); and managing varying and often extended timeframes (i.e., amount of time needed for social, political, or policy change; Guthrie et al., 2005).

CONCLUSION

Effective advocacy work can change social outcomes and, therefore, holds value for organizations willing to invest in its strategic execution and evaluation (FrameWorks Institute, 2002; Teles & Schmitt, 2011). The nonlinear nature of advocacy efforts constitutes an imperative for organizations to guide their work with reliable data and assessment to ensure effectiveness and impact. Planning models such as results-based accountability and EIR can streamline advocacy work and help to keep data and equity outcomes at the forefront of strategic advocacy planning (Friedman, 2005). Given the nature of the work, message framing is also an important factor in the potential effectiveness of advocacy efforts and should be considered before launching any public campaign. The *Strategic Frame Analysis* developed by FrameWorks Institute (n.d) is one useful method for addressing existing mindsets around social issues and adapting advocacy messaging to fit within the current discourse. By appealing in this way to broader population-level values and understanding, advocates can coax support from groups that may traditionally have been reluctant to embrace their policy proposals. Measuring this engagement and other similarly vague indicators of advocacy effectiveness presents many challenges, however. Funders increasingly require that outcomes and achievements of advocacy work be quantified despite a relatively limited knowledge base for determining best practice in this area (Carman, 2010; Teles & Schmitt, 2011). While some tools do exist to assist organizations in the evaluation of their advocacy capacity (Bolder Advocacy, n.d.) and the assessment of advocacy efforts (Alliance for Justice, 2011; Coffman, 2009; Reisman et al., 2007), the field of advocacy evaluation is still relatively new. Additional study is required and anticipated in this area, as evaluators will need to continue seeking and using innovative methods to more accurately assess the work of shaping social perception and guiding political action. The systematic use of capacity assessments and evaluation tools and processes within advocacy will help address and prevent many social issues and build the capacity of community-based organizations and other workplaces engaging in advocacy work.

FURTHER READING

Bolder Advocacy, an initiative of Alliance for Justice. (n.d.). *Advocacy capacity tool for organizational assessment (ACT!).* http://www.bolderadvocacy.org/tools-for-effective-advocacy/evaluating-advocacy/advocacy-capacity-tool

Coffman, J. (2009). *A user's guide to advocacy evaluation planning.* Harvard Family Research Project. http://www.hfrp.org/evaluation/publications-resources/a-user-s-guide-to-advocacy-evaluation-planning

Coffman, J. (n.d.). *Monitoring and evaluating advocacy: Companion to the Advocacy Toolkit.* United Nations Children's Fund. https://www.unicef.org/evaluation/files/Advocacy_Toolkit_Companion.pdf

Gerteis, M., Coffman, J., Kim, J., & Marton, K. (2008). *Advocacy capacity assessment instrument*. Mathematica Policy Research. http://www.mathematica-mpr.com/~/media/publications/pdfs/health/cvc_instrument.pdf

Guthrie, K., Louie, J., David, T., & Crystal-Foster, C. (2005). *The challenge of assessing advocacy: Strategies for a prospective approach to evaluating policy change and advocacy*. Prepared for the California Endowment. The California Endowment. http://www.theoryofchange.org/wp-content/uploads/toco_library/pdf/2005_-_Guthrie_-_The_challenge_of_assessing_policy_advocacy.pdf

Organizational Research Services. (2009). *Ten considerations for advocacy evaluation planning: Lessons learned from KIDS COUNT grantee experiences*. Prepared for the Annie E. Casey Foundation. Organizational Research Services. http://orsimpact.com/wp-content/uploads/2013/08/ten_considerations_for_advocacy_evaluation_planning.pdf

Reisman, J., Gienapp, A., & Stachowiak, S. (2007). *A guide to measuring advocacy and policy*. Prepared for the Annie E. Casey Foundation by Organizational Research Services. The Annie E. Casey Foundation. http://www.aecf.org/resources/a-guide-to-measuring-advocacy-and-policy/

KEY CONCEPTS

Advocacy: A wide range of activities conducted to influence decision makers at various levels.

Advocacy capacity assessments: Tools to determine necessary knowledge and skills in order to engage in and evaluate advocacy efforts.

Advocacy evaluation: Critical review of strategies to achieve advocacy- and policy-related results.

Equity impact review: A tool that combines community engagement and partnership strategies with the use of empirical data to address potential impacts on various forms of equity.

Message framing: Process whereby one message, among two or more messages with contrasting words or phrases, is preferred by individuals, even when the messages are logically equivalent.

Results accountability: A disciplined way of thinking and taking data-directed action that can be used to improve the quality of life within a population (i.e., How will we know if we have been successful?).

Strategic frame analysis: Approach that uses communications research to inform the framing of complex social issues to advance policy outcomes.

QUESTIONS FOR REFLECTION

1. Consider the *Case Example: Advancing Racial Equity in Washington State*. What process and/or tool did King County use to better understand the relationship between policy and equity? What impact did this process have on various government departments and nongovernment partnerships?

2. The chapter reviews several tools and guides that assess organizational capacity. Think about the organization that you work for, an organization you have worked for, or a partner organization.

    What was that organization's capacity for evaluation, communication, and advocacy? How did those capacities impact the organization's ability to accomplish their mission? How could increasing internal capacity or external partnerships address issues of effectiveness?

3. Consider the *Case Example: A Survey to Increase Legislative Advocacy Capacity*. What advocacy elements were used in this example? In what way(s) were data and communication theory used to strengthen advocacy efforts? What additional

partnerships could have improved the effort? How would you evaluate the effort?

4. Think of a social issue that is important to you. Identify an outcome area you might change based on *A Guide to Measuring Advocacy and Policy*.

What led you to choose that outcome area? What partnership(s) could help strengthen your effort? What data would you need to inform your effort? What messaging theory would best communicate your effort? How would you evaluate your effort?

REFERENCES

Alliance for Justice. (2011). *Investing in change: A funder's guide to supporting advocacy*. Author. https://www.bolderadvocacy.org/wp-content/uploads/2012/02/Investing_in_Change.pdf

Annie E. Casey Foundation. (2016, August 8). *Taking data apart: Why a data-driven approach matters to race equity* [Blog post]. http://www.aecf.org/blog/taking-data-apart-why-a-data-driven-approach-matters-to-race-equity/

Annie E. Casey Foundation. (2017). *KIDS COUNT*. http://www.aecf.org/work/kids-count/

Bolder Advocacy. (n.d.). *Advocacy capacity tool for organizational assessment (ACT!)*. http://www.bolderadvocacy.org/tools-for-effective-advocacy/evaluating-advocacy/advocacy-capacity-tool

Carman, J. G. (2010). The accountability movement: What's wrong with this theory of change? *Nonprofit and Voluntary Sector Quarterly, 39*, 256–274. doi:%2010.1177/089976400833062

Center on the Developing Child at Harvard University (2015). *Key concepts: Toxic stress*. http://developingchild.harvard.edu/science/key-concepts/toxic-stress/

Chang, C. -T. (2007). Health-care product advertising: The influences of message framing and perceived product characteristics. *Psychology and Marketing, 24*(2), 143–169. doi:10.1002/mar.20156

Coffman, J. (2009). *A user's guide to advocacy evaluation planning*. Harvard Family Research Project. http://www.hfrp.org/evaluation/publications-resources/a-user-s-guide-to-advocacy-evaluation-planning

Coffman, J. (n.d.). *Monitoring and evaluating advocacy: Companion to the Advocacy Toolkit*: United Nation Children's Fund, United Nation International Emergency Fund. https://www.unicef.org/evaluation/files/Advocacy_Toolkit_Companion.pdf.

Druckman, J. N. (2001). The implications of framing effects for citizen competence. *Political Behavior, 23*(3), 225–256. doi:10.1023/A:1015006907312

Durbin, D. R. (2011). Policy statement – Child passenger safety. *Pediatrics, 127*, 788–793. doi:%2010.1542/peds.2011-0213

Egbert, M., & Hoechstetter, S. (2006). Mission possible: Evaluating advocacy grants. *Foundation News and Commentary, 47*, 38–46.http://www.bolderadvocacy.org/wp-content/uploads/2012/10/Mission_Possible_Evaluation_Advocacy_Grants.pdf.

FrameWorks Institute. (2002). *Framing public issues*. FrameWorks Institute. http://www.frameworksinstitute.org/assets/files/PDF/FramingPublicIssuesfinal.pdf.

FrameWorks Institute. (n.d). *Strategic Frame Analysis®*. FrameWorks Institute. http://www.frameworksinstitute.org/sfa-overview.html

Friedman, M. (2005). *Trying hard is not good enough.* Parse Publishing.

Gerteis, M., Coffman, J., Kim, J., & Marton, K. (2008). *Advocacy capacity assessment instrument.* Mathematica Policy Research. http://www.mathematica-mpr.com/~/media/publications/pdfs/health/cvc_instrument.pdf.

Guthrie, K., Louie, J., David, T., & Crystal-Foster, C. (2005). *The challenge of assessing advocacy: Strategies for a prospective approach to evaluating policy change and advocacy. Prepared for the California Endowment.* The California Endowment. http://www.theoryofchange.org/wp-content/uploads/toco_library/pdf/2005_-_Guthrie_-_The_challenge_of_assessing_policy_advocacy.pdf.

Jensen, J. L. (2007). Getting one's way in policy debates: Influence tactics used in group decision-making settings. *Public Administration Review, 67*(2), 216–227. doi:10.1111/j.1540-6210.2007.00708.x

Kendall-Taylor, N. (2012). *The resilience scale: Using metaphors to communicate a developmental perspective on resilience.* FrameWorks Institute.

King County. (2011). *Community engagement guide.* King County Equity and Social Justice. http://www.kingcounty.gov/~/media/elected/executive/equity-social-justice/documents/CommunityEngagementGuideContinuum2011.ashx?la=en

King County. (2012). *Using the equity impact review toolkit.* King County Equity and Social Justice. http://www.kingcounty.gov/~/media/elected/executive/equity-social-justice/documents/KingCountyEIRToolExamples.ashx?la=en

King County. (2016). *2015 Equity impact review process overview.* King County Equity and Social Justice. http://www.kingcounty.gov/~/media/elected/executive/equity-social-justice/2016/The_Equity_Impact_Review_checklist_Mar2016.ashx?la=en

Lakoff, G. (2002). *Moral politics: How liberals and conservatives think* (2nd ed.). University of Chicago Press.

LeBoeuf, R. A., & Shafir, E. (2003). Deep thoughts and shallow frames: On the susceptibility to framing effects. *Journal of Behavioral Decision Making, 16*(2), 77–92. doi:10.1002/bdm.433

Levin, I. P., Schneider, S. L., & Gaeth, G. J. (1998). All frames are not created equal: A typology and critical analysis of framing effects. *Organizational Behavior and Human Decision Processes, 76*(2), 149–188. doi:10.1006/obhd.1998.2804

Morariu, J., & Brennan, K. (2009). Effective advocacy evaluation: The role of funders. *The Foundation Review, 1*(3), 100–108. doi:10.4087/FOUNDATIONREVIEW-D-09-00031.1

Reisman, J., Gienapp, A., & Stachowiak, S. (2007). *A guide to measuring advocacy and policy. Prepared for the Annie E. Casey Foundation by Organizational Research Services.* The Annie E. Casey Foundation. http://www.aecf.org/resources/a-guide-to-measuring-advocacy-and-policy/

Schuck, A. R. T., & de Vreese, C. H. (2009). Reversed mobilization in referendum campaigns: How positive news framing can mobilize the skeptics. *The International Journal of Press/Politics, 14,* 40–66. doi:%2010.1177/1940161208326926

Strompolis, M., Branham, M., Tucker, W., & Aakjer, H. (2016). Influencing prevention policy through effective communication with advocates and legislators. *Global Journal of Community Psychology Practice, 7*(1). http://www.gjcpp.org/en/article.php?issue=21&article=123 doi:10.7728/0701201611

Strompolis, M. E. (2015). *They said what? How to communicate effectively with advocates* [Doctoral dissertation. ProQuest Dissertations and Theses database (UMI No. 3711898)].

Strong, D. A., & Kim, J. Y. (2012). Defining, building, and measuring capacity: Findings from an advocacy evaluation. *The Foundation Review, 4*(1), 40–53. doi:10.4087/FOUNDATIONREVIEW-D-11-00028

Teles, S., & Schmitt, M. (2011). The elusive craft of evaluating advocacy. *Stanford Social Innovation Review*, *9*, 40–42. http://www.ssireview.org/articles/entry/the_elusive_craft_of_evaluating_advocacy

Tversky, A., & Kahneman, D. (1981). The framing of decisions and the psychology of choice. *Science*, *211*(4481), 453–458. doi:10.1126/science.7455683

Wiseman, S., Chinman, M., Ebener, P. A., Hunter, S., Imm, P., & Wandersman, A. (2007). *Getting to Outcomes*™*: 10 steps for achieving results-based accountability*. RAND Corporation. http://www.rand.org/content/dam/rand/pubs/technical_reports/2007/RAND_TR101.2.pdf.

Wong, C. O., & McMurray, N. E. (2002). Framing communication: Communicating the anti-smoking message effectively to all smokers. *Journal of Community Psychology*, *30*(4), 433–447. doi:10.1002/jcop.10015

CHAPTER 16

USING EVALUATION TO PROMOTE IMPROVEMENTS IN HEALTH SERVICE SETTINGS

Victoria C. Scott, Jonathan P. Scaccia, and Kassy Alia Ray

Healthcare spending in America is enormous. Approximately $3.2 trillion, or about $11,172 per person, was expended on healthcare services in 2017 alone (Hartman et al., 2020). According to recent data, the United States spends nearly 50% more of its gross domestic product (GDP) on healthcare per year than other developed nations (Squires & Anderson, 2015). These alarming statistics exclude aggregate health service support system costs (i.e., dollars invested in building capacity for quality care and improved health outcomes), which are not tracked across systems. Despite the high healthcare costs, the United States ranks lower than many other countries on health outcomes and life expectancy rates (Davis et al., 2014). Additionally, there are vast disparities in health outcomes among marginalized populations in the United States (Artiga et al., 2020).

Improving return on the substantial investment in health service settings and population health requires greater coordination and collaboration among an interdisciplinary set of players dedicated to improving health, well-being, and equity. Health service settings vary by geography, population, health need, and a host of other characteristics. They are influenced by factors in the broader societal context as well as factors embedded within the health service context. For example, health service settings are likely to be impacted by the political climate and accessibility of healthcare as well as factors related to organizational readiness (capacity and motivation; Scaccia et al., 2015), which has real implications for implementation. The needs and complexity of health service settings bring emerging challenges, but also yield tremendous opportunities for evaluation professionals to contribute to health service improvement. For example, evaluators can work with health service professionals to identify, measure, and understand the confluence of factors and processes impacting service outcomes.

Learning Objectives

1. Describe the three main types of evaluation (summative, process, formative), including benefits and limitations associated with each type.

2. Become familiar with the role of the health service delivery system and health service support system.

3. Discuss specific strategies for befriending accountability.

4. Understand how the Inquiry-Observation-Reflection framework can guide evaluation efforts.

5. Provide specific examples of guiding principles/values for evaluation, and discuss how principles/values can inform the design and implementation of evaluations.

They can promote shared accountability among stakeholders for health service costs, methods, and outcomes by using evaluation methods that elicit data from multiple stakeholders. And they can build evaluation capacity in health service organizations by working with staff to evaluate their own programs.

In this chapter, we draw from our experiences in health service settings to discuss the value of a collaborative, improvement-oriented evaluation approach. We begin this chapter by providing a conceptual definition for health service settings. We then discuss the purpose of different types of evaluation approaches and how they relate to measuring accountability. We conclude this introductory section by emphasizing the utility of formative evaluation for capturing the complex, dynamic nature of health service organizations and sharing our own framework and operating principles for conducting evaluations.

In the second section of this chapter, we provide two real-world examples of our evaluation efforts and highlight how working closely in partnership with our stakeholders (implementation team, funders, program recipients) has strengthened the quality of our evaluations. The first example involves a capacity-building project that aims to facilitate the integration of behavioral health and primary care services (referred to as the Integrated Care Leadership Program; ICLP). The second example pertains to a national community health improvement initiative (referred to as Spreading Community Accelerators through Learning and Evaluation; SCALE). Both ICLP and SCALE illustrate how we have used a collaborative approach to evaluation within health service support systems (more about support systems in the next section), the primary focus of our work. We conclude the chapter with a discussion of lessons learned and reflections from our experiences as evaluators.

HEALTH SERVICE SETTINGS

Employment in the healthcare sector is projected to grow significantly between 2016 and 2026 and at rates faster than the rest of the economy (Martiniano & Moore, 2018). There is incredible diversity in the types of jobs within this field, though we can broadly categorize them as falling within one of two major types of systems: the Delivery System and the Support System (Wandersman et al., 2008; see Figure 16.1). Individuals and organizations in the *health service delivery system* (HSDS) provide services/interventions directly to patients/consumers. Different types of services/interventions include health promotion, prevention, and treatment (e.g., implementing nutrition-education programs, administering vaccines, and setting broken bones). Types of organizations within the HSDS are wide ranging. They include organizations in the for-profit (e.g., private physician's offices, natural birthing centers, private substance use rehabilitation centers), nonprofit (e.g., free clinics, hospital systems), and government sectors (e.g., state health departments, Women, Infant, and Children clinics, Veterans Affairs hospitals). The HSDS also includes settings that deliver patient care but are not solely healthcare facilities (e.g., schools, retail health clinics). The breadth of HSDS facilities is considerable.

The health service setting is also composed of individuals and organizations that influence population health outcomes by supporting healthcare delivery organizations.

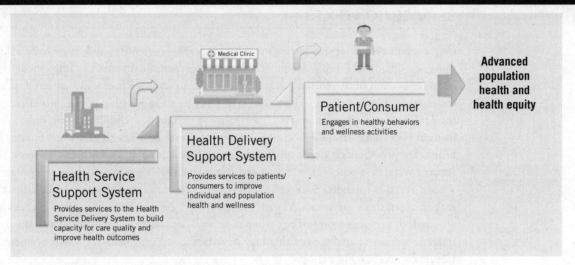

Figure 16.1 Health Service Settings Can Broadly Be Categorized Into Two Systems: Health Service Delivery Systems and Health Service Support Systems. Together, the Delivery System and the Support System Work to Promote Population Health and Health Equity

These individuals and organizations fall under the *health service support system* (HSSS) category. They provide services to healthcare organizations and healthcare providers, rather than directly to patients/consumers. Individuals in the HSSS aim to build the capacity of healthcare delivery systems and to improve the quality of care provided by healthcare organizations. HSSS organizations provide capacity-building resources (e.g., funding, educational materials, trainings, and technical assistance) to organizations in the healthcare delivery system. The Institute for Healthcare Improvement (IHI) is an example of an HSSS organization. IHI indirectly impacts health outcomes by promoting the use of evidence-based improvement methods like the Model for Improvement (Langley et al., 2009) in hospital and community health settings. Philanthropy organizations such as the Robert Wood Johnson Foundation (RWJF), March of Dimes, and Partners for Health are other examples of health service organizations within the support system. These HSSS organizations fund health promotion initiatives, facilitate partnerships among like-minded agencies and individuals, and actively disseminate practice-based evidence as means to promote health equity. Health-oriented professional societies such as the American Medical Association and the Alliance for Continuing Education in the Health Professions are also examples of HSSS organizations.

While organizations in the health service setting generally fall into the delivery system or support system category, some organizations provide both direct patient/consumer care services and capacity-building services to other healthcare organizations. For example, the Mayo Clinic provides clinical care to patients and is also committed to healthcare education and research. University-based medical departments also provide services characterized by both the delivery system and the support system. Despite the wide range of methods and interventions, organizations in the health service setting share the common interest of promoting individual and collective health and well-being.

COMMON CATEGORIES FOR EVALUATION IN HEALTH SERVICE CONTEXTS

Our work in health service settings involves process, summative, and formative evaluations (see Chapters 1 and 6 for more). *Process evaluation* documents the implementation of an innovation (intervention program, policy, or practice). Process evaluation data are collected to monitor the activities that take place as an innovation is put into effect. In the HSDS, the innovation might be a treatment program, a clinic standing order, or a medical procedure. In the HSSS, the innovation could be a health education course for healthcare providers or a new quality improvement approach. In both the delivery and support systems, a process evaluation can determine the extent to which an intervention was delivered as intended. It records the types of variations that occur and quantifies the magnitude of those variations. More than just auditing of services and outputs (a checklist approach to progress monitoring), when done well, a process evaluation helps to uncover implementation-related factors that may have facilitated or hindered the achievement of targeted outcomes. For example:

- How was implementation quality impacted by staff turnover, leadership buy-in, availability of resources, or the layout of the implementation facility?

- Was the dose of the intervention sufficient?

- To what extent did it reach the intended target group?

By addressing critical aspects of implementation, a process evaluation can help clarify the pathways from health service implementation to outcomes. For instance, is the primary care practice that is receiving subsidized federal funding serving the needs of the local population, as intended, or is it serving only a particular segment of the population? In this case, a process evaluation can be useful for measuring whether the healthcare practice is meeting the commitments made to an external funder.

While a process evaluation is highly useful for understanding implementation issues, by design, it does not measure outcomes associated with an innovation. Additionally, the practical value of a process evaluation may be limited if data analyses do not occur until well after implementation. Therefore, this type of evaluation is almost always used in conjunction with other methods (Rossi et al., 2018).

Summative evaluation is used to provide evidence about the worth or merit of an intervention and is typically conducted after an innovation has been implemented (Rossi et al., 2018). It focuses on products, results, or impact. A summative evaluation, when used in conjunction with process evaluation data, can also address the bottom-line question of how well an intervention worked. Addressing these bottom-line questions requires that comprehensive process and outcome data of high quality are available.

Summative data are critical for accountability. However, there can be major challenges in using summative evaluation in health settings, particularly for evaluations pertaining to delivery system services. For example, the complexity of the human condition makes it extremely challenging to isolate the effect of an intervention on an individual or population, given the multitude of factors that impact health and well-being. The types of evaluation designs that would allow one to examine such effects can be cumbersome, expensive, resource intensive, and in some cases, unethical (e.g., using a randomized control design that withholds a potential treatment from a group that could benefit from it).

Another significant consideration in health service settings is the time lag between health activities and health outcomes. We can measure what happened in a program, but may not be fully able to track whether or not the program ultimately made a difference in the target population without a significant investment in evaluation resources to track these changes over long periods of time. Potentially, it could be months or years before a program has its intended impact. Even in the interim, individual- and community-level influences could moderate the effectiveness of what was developed and implemented. Therefore, it becomes necessary in many cases to identify intermediate process and output measures as evaluation metrics. This challenge is further amplified when conducting large-scale evaluations across multiple health service organizations, each with their own contextual factors and influences.

Despite the limitations and challenges of summative evaluations, this type of evaluation bears its own merit. A summative evaluation answers the important question of "What actually works?," a critical input in promoting health outcomes and wellness. Using summative evaluation in many health services settings requires considering whether the goals of an initiative are feasible (i.e., Can these be achieved?), evaluable (i.e., Can we measure these?; see, e.g., Leviton et al., 2010), and plausible (i.e., Is the attribution chain between intervention and outcomes realistic?).

A *formative evaluation* is designed to create information that can be used for program improvement (Rossi et al., 2018). While a formative evaluation relies upon process evaluation data, it differs by objective. The aim of a formative evaluation is improvement, whereas the aim of a process evaluation is simply to monitor implementation activities. When done well, a formative evaluation illuminates areas and issues impacting outcomes as an intervention unfolds (Parry et al., 2013; Patton, 2011). A formative evaluation helps with identifying and addressing emergent challenges. As such, formative approaches are particularly useful for measuring and responding to the complexity of health service systems. Formative data can be collected and used by health service delivery and support systems to make evidence-informed decisions and midcourse corrections as needed. Formative evaluations can be used to complement process evaluations. For example, a process evaluation might first surface issues with implementation fidelity; then, a formative evaluation could be conducted with intervention stakeholders to identify opportunities for improvement.

A common formative evaluation method used in health service settings is Plan-Do-Study-Act (PDSA). Also referred to as a quality improvement method, PDSA involves engaging in rapid-cycle implementation, evaluation, and improvement activities (Langley et al., 2009). Evaluation data are collected during implementation and used in a timely fashion to guide improvements to the intervention. When using a formative approach, modifications to the theory of change or to the implementation plan are welcomed in the interest of achieving desired health service outcomes (Øvretveit et al., 2011). The chief limitation to conducting a formative evaluation is that it can be labor and time intensive, due to the rapid-cycle nature of this type of evaluation.

As participatory and empowerment evaluators (see Chapter 8 for more regarding empowerment evaluation) working in health service settings, we tend to focus on formative evaluations because the approach aligns with our interest in ongoing improvement and collaborative partnerships. However, we believe that all three types of evaluation (process, summative, formative) bear important measurement functions for accountability at various stages of implementation. Additionally, we recognize a blended approach is typically useful. Ultimately, the evaluation design should be informed by the type of questions being asked by stakeholders. Table 16.1 provides a comparison of the three types of evaluation methods and associated implications for accountability.

PROMOTING ACCOUNTABILITY IN HEALTH SERVICE SETTINGS

Broadly, accountability in health services refers to being responsible for meeting clinical care metrics (e.g., vaccination or hospital readmission rates) or health service program objectives (e.g., change in provider knowledge and attitudes). The term "accountability" can carry a punitive connotation and, in turn, raise fear and anxiety among health service professionals. As evaluators, we can help demystify accountability for health service professionals by clarifying the purpose and rationale behind the evaluation. Doing this involves raising awareness and being in conversation with health service professionals about the evaluation process and tools. Evaluators can also help health service professionals *befriend accountability* (i.e., become more comfortable with the concept of accountability) by involving practitioners in the development, implementation, and interpretation of evaluations. For example, we can work with health service professionals and other stakeholders to identify and develop metrics and to determine the best times for collecting health service performance data.

Framing evaluations in the spirit of improvement and demonstrating how evaluation data can be used to facilitate improvement in health service settings are additional ways to help health service professionals befriend accountability and focus on the needs of the patients and clients. An improvement-oriented frame to accountability drives conversations toward exploring future opportunities for growth, rather than focusing discussions on past missed or lost opportunities. This frame minimizes anxiety that a recipient might feel about receiving performance-based feedback. It also makes evaluation data more practically useful for practitioners.

OUR GUIDING PRINCIPLES AND VALUES FOR EVALUATION

Rooted in the disciplines of public health and community psychology and closely aligned with empowerment evaluation (Fetterman, 2015; see Chapter 8), the following key principles and values guide our work: *improvement*, *joint accountability*, *systems perspective*, and *social justice*.

Improvement: Many health service programs/interventions fail to achieve intended outcomes. In health service settings, where human health and wellness is of chief concern, evaluations should go beyond summative measures, to include formative

Table 16.1 Comparison of Key Evaluation Types: Summative, Process, and Formative Evaluation

Evaluation Type	Purpose	Implications for Accountability	Generic Sample Evaluation Question	Health Service Delivery System (HSDS) Sample Question	Health Service Support System (HSSS) Sample Question
Process evaluation	To document and monitor implementation of an innovation (e.g., health service program, policy, or practice)	*Advantages:* Can clarify the pathway between service implementation/delivery and resulting outcomes, including illuminating barriers and facilitators Can be useful for clarifying the impact of contextual factors and identifying implementation issues *Limitation:* Focuses on documenting rather than improving health service implementation	What activities were involved in program implementation/ service delivery? Was the intervention delivered as intended? What was the extent of any adaptation?	To what extent is the WIC clinic postpartum depression screening reaching the intended population of underprivileged mothers? To what extent is the screening protocol being implemented as designed?	What activities were used to train the local WIC clinic to screen for postpartum depression among underprivileged mothers? How many WIC clinics have been trained? How many clients do these WIC clinics serve monthly?
Summative evaluation	To measure the outcomes of an innovation	*Advantages:* Provides information on the impact of an intervention/health service *Limitation:* Does not shed light on the causal attributions of findings	In what ways was the intervention effective? How successful was the health service intervention?	To what extent did the WIC clinic postpartum depression screening improve the identification and referral of underprivileged mothers with postpartum depression?	To what extent did the postpartum training improve provider knowledge about and ability to implement postpartum depression screenings at the local WIC clinic?

(Continued)

Table 16.1 (Continued)

Evaluation Type	Purpose	Implications for Accountability	Generic Sample Evaluation Question	Health Service Delivery System (HSDS) Sample Question	Health Service Support System (HSSS) Sample Question
Formative evaluation	To facilitate improvements in the theory or implementation of an innovation	*Advantages:* Feedback is timely and near "real time," which allows for midcourse corrections *Limitation:* Time and labor intensive	What aspects of the program are going well? What aspects of the program can be improved? How can improvements be made?	What aspects of the new WIC clinic postpartum screening protocol are being implemented well? What aspects need to be modified and improved?	What aspects of the WIC employee postpartum training are going well? What improvements should be made to the remainder of the training?

approaches. As we noted earlier in this chapter, formative evaluations are essential for making midcourse adjustments to an intervention to increase the probability of achieving desired outcomes. In this way, evaluation can be both a method to examine an intervention and a means of facilitating outcomes. Notably, many organizations apply quality improvement methods to health settings (Leviton, 2011; Taylor et al., 2014). Therefore, there is potential to cultivate a learning culture in which an improvement mindset is applied to an intervention.

Joint accountability: Engaging partners with diverse perspectives deepens and expands our understanding of issues in context. This guiding principle speaks to not only the value of working in diverse evaluation teams, but also the importance of involving key stakeholders (e.g., funders, service providers, service end-users) across the stages of evaluation (i.e., design, implementation, data interpretation, information dissemination). For us, involving key stakeholders is more than simply keeping them informed. It means codesigning, inviting input, and using an iterative process to finalize evaluation materials and interpret evaluation results. We invite our stakeholders to use a "Venn diagram" approach to help to identify evaluation questions that are of interest to all. This specifically involves generating potential evaluation questions that are relevant to each stakeholder group, then categorizing and prioritizing the questions that satisfy the evaluation needs of multiple stakeholders (i.e., those at the center of the circle in Figure 16.2). In this way, we facilitate a collective discussion about the types of questions that will maximize the learning for all involved parties.

Systems (ecological) perspective: Health service systems are dynamic and often functionally and structurally complex organizations. Understanding the impact of a program or intervention in context requires an examination of individual factors (intrapersonal and interpersonal) and contextual factors (structural, functional, cultural issues within

Figure 16.2 Venn Diagram of Stakeholders

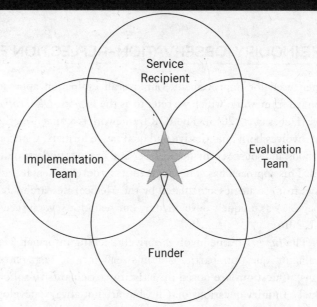

an organization, interorganizational issues, macro-level issues). It also requires understanding the downstream impact of HSSSs on HSDSs, and ultimately on individual and population health. Therefore, we find that our methods often have to cross multiple levels using mixed methods in order to capture how these different levels and factors interact and influence implementation. Simultaneously, while taking into account factors and influences across multiple levels of analysis, evaluation efforts should remain focused and prioritize metrics of greatest value to stakeholders. This is because evaluation resources are generally limited and, in turn, evaluators are often unable to assess all potential influential factors and conditions across all levels.

Social justice: This principle pertains to the broader social interest of promoting social justice (fair and just distribution of wealth, opportunities for personal activity and growth, and social privileges), specifically through the advancement of health equity (opportunity for all people to experience optimal health). It also relates closely to the principle of improvement. Providing evaluative feedback that supports health service organizations in making data-informed program or process improvements enhances the quality of services provided and healthcare quality. Broadly speaking, we want programs to achieve their goals of improved health, wellness, and equity, as these outcomes benefit the communities in which we live. Advancing *health equity*, or ensuring that all individuals attain their highest level of health regardless of their group membership or place of residency, is a critical goal for those with an interest in working toward social justice. Increasingly, health service settings aim to promote health equity on different levels and through different interventions.

Together, these principles inform the spirit of our evaluation designs. They are especially important in contexts such as health service settings, which are often characterized by high levels of volatility, ambiguity, uncertainty, and complexity. By allowing our questions, methods, and relationships with stakeholders to be grounded within fundamental ways of operation, we are able to conduct rigorous but flexible, methodologically sound evaluations that foster ownership and accountability among multiple stakeholders.

THE INQUIRY–OBSERVATION–REFLECTION FRAMEWORK

When used for improvement, our overall evaluation approach is guided by a three-pronged framework, which we refer to as the *Inquiry–Observation–Reflection (IOR) Framework* (Hayes et al., 2016). The IOR framework is a mixed-methods data collection design that involves both quantitative and qualitative formats. Using a variety of data collection methods and sources provides a richer and broader understanding of what is being evaluated. This approach has conceptual roots in developmental evaluation (Patton, 2011) and draws from strategies articulated by the Medical Research Council (Moore et al., 2015), though it was uniquely developed by our team for several recent evaluations (e.g., Hayes et al., 2016).

The *Inquiry* frame involves actively seeking information using an explicit, concise "evaluator question–participant answer" format (e.g., surveys and brief feedback forms). Questions are posed directly to participants to solicit information from individuals. Inquiry questions may be, but are not always, developed in collaboration with participants. The *Observation* frame involves collecting data on naturally occurring activities in the past or present (e.g., reviewing meeting products or observing a partnership meeting). In the Observation frame, the evaluators' questions may not be explicitly conveyed to activity participants in advance of the activity. Lastly, the *Reflection* frame encourages participants to reflect deeply on an issue or experience. It commonly uses a structured narrative approach (e.g., critical moments reflection methodology, case studies), in which the evaluator poses questions to elicit participant emotions, reactions, and beliefs on topics of interest. This may be in an individual (e.g., interview) or group (e.g., focus group) format. Reflection activities involving stakeholders are used to help structure personal reactions and experience to the data (e.g., What has been the most memorable moment or experience on this project? What about it made the moment so memorable? How did the moment affect you?). The data collection format of both inquiry and reflection frames can be similar (e.g., interview and focus groups). However, the two frames differ in the depth of content and richness sought. The reflection frame seeks to elicit richer, more personal, and meaningful content. The reflection component can be particularly valuable for engaging stakeholders in processing program improvement needs. It may be used to collaborate with stakeholders in a way that allows for understanding the meaning behind their perspectives.

The IOR framework can be used to help evaluators determine the best methods for understanding program implementation from diverse perspectives. We have found that involving stakeholders in the evaluation design and implementation strengthens the quality of our evaluations. More specifically, it has been mutually beneficial to have stakeholders (implementation staff, funders, program/service recipients) involved in the process of determining IOR strategies (e.g., conduct interviews vs. use an open-ended survey) and chiming in on how questions should be worded or which questions to include versus exclude.

All three of the IOR frames can be applied to each of the three types of evaluation (process, summative, formative) and used in conjunction with one another. For example, a process evaluation to monitor how physicians are implementing a new obesity healthcare protocol might include an assessment (inquiry approach) administered to individuals, a clinic visit (observational approach), and focus groups (reflective approach) to learn about physician experiences with the new protocol. And a summative evaluation of the impact of the new obesity protocol might draw from patient electronic health records (observational approach) to examine changes in weight, blood pressure, and body mass index and include patient interviews (reflective approach) to determine if the new obesity healthcare protocol is more patient-centric, as intended by design.

We now turn to two case examples of how we use the IOR frame and our guiding principles/values to promote accountability in two distinct health service settings.

HEALTH SERVICE EVALUATION FOR IMPROVEMENT IN PRACTICE

The applied examples shared in this section focus on evaluation of organizations within the HSSS, which is the focus of our work. The first example involves working with an academic medical center on an integrated care initiative. The second applied example pertains to a large-scale national effort to build capacity for community health improvement.

In both examples, we used a flexible model of organizational readiness (Readiness = Motivation × General Capacity × Innovation-specific Capacity, $R = MC^2$) that evaluates the motivation and capacities necessary to implement a new innovation with quality (Scaccia et al., 2015). This model aligns with our value of improvement because it provides targeted information about facilitators and barriers to implementation that can be addressed through coaching and technical assistance. Conceptual models help to frame and interpret the variety of factors that may impact program quality and outcomes (e.g., Campbell et al., 2000; Craig et al., 2008; Damschroder et al., 2009; Greenhalgh et al., 2004; Katz et al., 2013). We have found that models, such as $R = MC^2$, are useful for measuring and monitoring the complexity of health service settings.

CASE EXAMPLE: EVALUATING READINESS FOR INTEGRATING PRIMARY CARE AND BEHAVIORAL HEALTH

This first example of our work involves assessing organizational readiness for a new healthcare innovation, specifically an integrated care approach. Integrated care is a patient-centered approach to addressing the mental and physical needs of a patient population involving collaboration among behavioral health and primary care providers within a healthcare delivery system (Peek, 2013). This example draws from the lead author's (VS) work with the Integrated Care Leadership Program (ICLP).

About the Integrated Care Leadership Program

The ICLP is a multiyear initiative aimed at promoting integrated care in the United States, with a primary focus on the state of Georgia. The program emphasizes creation and advancement of opportunities for underserved, predominantly minority and low-income, patient populations and underresourced clinical settings to experience optimal health outcomes. The ICLP involves a multimethod model of capacity building for primary care sites consisting of (a) online training focused on enhancing leadership skills of healthcare professionals, improving care quality, and sustaining integrated practices; (b) technical assistance via structured monthly leadership development coaching calls, mentoring by other members of the practice community, monthly continuing education webinars, and site visits; and

(c) the opportunity to apply for an innovation award to pilot a site-specific quality improvement project intended to advance integrated practice. Led by the Satcher Health Leadership Institute at the Morehouse School of Medicine (SHLI/MSM), the ICLP involves a multisite partnership with the University of South Carolina and the University of North Carolina Charlotte. Members across the three institutions have worked closely, along with program recipients and funders, to design, implement, evaluate, and improve the ICLP. The following section focuses specifically on the collaborative nature of the ICLP evaluation. The ICLP is supported by Kaiser Permanente National Community Benefit and the RWJF.

Assessing Organizational Readiness for Integrated Care

A distinct aspect of the ICLP is examining and increasing organizational readiness for integrated care. We emphasized readiness because it is a major way to conceptualize the bridge between support and delivery systems in health services settings and to describe the conditions that will help facilitate quality implementation.

At the start of the ICLP, the evaluation team held a series of joint work sessions with the program staff to adapt a readiness assessment tool to the context of integrated care. Program staff feedback helped ensure that the measure assessed relevant aspects of integrated care and reflected the primary care context. Iterations of the assessment were also shared with and reviewed by physicians to make wording refinements. Once finalized, the assessment tool (referred to as the Readiness for Integrated Care Questionnaire, RICQ; Scott et al., 2017) was administered to participating healthcare organizations across multiple time points (at the beginning of ICLP and then at 6-month intervals). The RICQ is an example of the Inquiry frame within the IOR framework. We (the evaluators) worked with ICLP program staff (implementation team) to prepare site-specific readiness reports for each practice. In this process, the evaluation team took the lead on organizing, analyzing, and summarizing the data. The implementation team assisted with interpreting and adapting the report language to the context of clinical practice. The primary aim of the assessment reports was to facilitate practice improvement (for formative evaluation purposes).

Another method employed to assess practice readiness for integrated care was through in-person site visits. These half-day visits with participating practices involved an in-depth tour of their facilities (Observation frame of IOR) as well as meetings with practice members about integrated care implementation issues (Inquiry and Reflection frames of IOR framework). The clinic tours provided a first-hand sense of the clinical context, enriching understanding among implementation and evaluation team members of the issues that practice members encounter. In preparation for these resource-intensive visits, practice members were required to submit PDSA reports which documented their progress on a specific integrated care effort. The PDSA reports informed the focus of the site visits (e.g., it guided the nature of questions that we asked and the characteristics and conditions for which we looked during observational data collection). During the site visits, the PDSA reports were reviewed and discussed with practice members to facilitate reflection on what efforts were going well, areas that needed improvement, and next steps. Having the PDSA reports completed prior to site visits made it possible for us (the evaluation and implementation teams) to better prepare for site visits.

The readiness reports were paired with opportunities to reflect on the assessment results (Reflection frame of the IOR). For example, upon receiving baseline readiness data, the ICLP-Readiness Assessment team met individually with practice members to review and discuss their readiness results. We asked practice members a series of *reflective* questions

such as "How do the readiness trends fit with your recent experiences at work? What findings are you surprised by? Are there any findings you disagree with? Is there anything that has not been captured about the practice's readiness for integrated care that should be captured?" Engaging members from the program implementation team, the assessment team, and the participating practices (evaluation recipients) in these meetings was valuable for making sense of the findings and developing a shared understanding of the readiness trends. Additionally, the joint approach to data review and interpretation enriched conversations about potential next steps for practice-based improvements.

During the joint meetings, we (the evaluation team) also solicited suggestions for improving the readiness tool (e.g., Is the wording of any of the items unclear?) and invited suggestions for improving how the readiness assessment was administered. Practice member suggestions per the administration of the tool were especially useful for improving survey response times. For example, we learned that reminders to complete the assessment were more effective when delivered via personalized text messages or phone calls than when sent via email because providers spent the bulk of their workday with patients and only a modest amount of time during their day viewing emails. This process demonstrates that we not only attempted to use evaluation data to improve the readiness of sites to implement integrated care; we also used evaluation data to improve the evaluation itself.

All four guiding principles (improvement, collaboration, social justice, and systems perspective) were highly salient to how we designed the implemented readiness assessments with the practices and their staffs. For instance, by design, the RICQ takes a systems perspective by including a broad set of organizational constructs (e.g., workplace culture and climate, availability of resources). The assessment tool includes specific items that measure communication quality among practice members, the adequacy of resources, the extent to which the practice's vision and mission are clear to its members, and other salient organizational issues. Through these items, the tool encouraged practice members to think systemically about integrated care efforts. The site visits (described above) are another example of how we incorporated a systems perspective in our data collection. They provided a clearer understanding of the practice environment (operations, culture, physical layout).

CASE EXAMPLE: EVALUATING A NATIONAL CAPACITY-BUILDING INITIATIVE FOR HEALTHY COMMUNITY COALITIONS

The second example of our work describes how formative evaluation was used to assess implementation of a national capacity-building initiative for community health coalitions. The example draws from the authors' work with the Spreading Community Accelerators through Learning and Evaluation (SCALE) initiative. It is an example of how data collected are used to provide ongoing guidance for implementation improvement.

About the Spreading Community Accelerators Through Evaluation and Learning Initiative

SCALE was an RWJF-funded capacity-building initiative led by the IHI. SCALE was designed to accelerate communities' progress toward a Culture of Health (Plough, 2015)[1] and a goal of 100 Million Healthier Lives by 2020. The overall goal of SCALE was to build readiness and enhance the capability of 24 community coalitions across the country to improve health, well-being, and equity through the use of improvement methods and the establishment of a peer-to-peer system to spread good ideas.

The program included a multilevel support system designed to increase use of improvement methods and facilitate dissemination of ideas and approaches among peer networks. SCALE communities participated in four Community Health Improvement Leadership Academies (CHILAs). CHILAs were in-person, multiday training sessions designed to build relationships between communities, build skills in community health improvement leadership, and facilitate learning across community coalitions. In between each CHILA, community coalitions received intensive coaching support and additional training. Specifically, participating community

coalitions were grouped with a Peer Community Team (PCT). Each PCT was composed of five community coalitions and one improvement coach. As part of the PCT, community coalitions participated in monthly calls with coaches and other members of their PCT. Community coalitions were also provided with the opportunity to join monthly webinars designed to provide additional training on specific content areas, engaging diverse community stakeholders, measuring outcomes, and sustainability. Throughout program delivery, community coalitions were also provided access to an online learning platform called "Healthdoers." The primary function of Healthdoers was to provide an online space for sharing learning and providing support to members of the SCALE community. Healthdoers also provided a resource library of tools.

Use of a Formative Evaluation Approach to Guide Implementation Improvement

We used formative evaluation in SCALE[2] to guide learning about what works and what does not work to build a culture of health and to provide ongoing feedback for program improvement. A formative evaluation approach was ideal for SCALE for several reasons: (1) Though IHI has tremendous experience working in health service settings, their efforts thus far have primarily been situated in healthcare organizations. SCALE was among the first community-based initiatives for IHI. (2) Furthermore, while community capacity-building initiatives have been previously developed, there are few (if any) examples that attempted capacity building at a national scale. Thus, SCALE was uncharted territory for IHI. SCALE also had the challenge of implementation in many diverse settings. The aim of SCALE was to build a system for spreading capacity for improvement methods nationally by enhancing the ability of an

---

[1] A *Culture of Health* is defined as one in which good health and well-being flourish across geographic, demographic, and social sectors; fostering healthy equitable communities guides public and private decision making; and everyone has the opportunity to make choices that lead to healthy lifestyles.

[2] The SCALE evaluation was the recipient of the American Evaluation Association's Outstanding Evaluation Award for 2017.

already existing infrastructure for health services: community coalitions. As with many health service settings, community coalitions have their own needs and resources when it comes to health. Implementation of a capacity-building innovation and, as a result, the evaluation of such an initiative, would need to be flexible to adapt to changing needs across context and time.

The evaluation was informed by multi-stakeholder perspectives, including the evaluation team, IHI, and community partners (Communities Joined in Action, The Collaborative Health Network, and Community Solutions, referred to as the "implementation team"), RWJF (funder), and participating community coalitions (program recipients; see Figure 16.3). Early on, it became clear that stakeholders had similar goals when it came to the evaluation of SCALE; all parties had an interest in helping SCALE to succeed and using the tools of evaluation to monitor progress to that end. Interestingly, the use of formative evaluation paralleled the focus in IHI, which was on the use of improvement science (Langley et al., 2009) to promote data ownership and utilization.

Consistent with a partnership-focused evaluation approach, our core evaluation questions were developed collaboratively with key stakeholders (Box 16.1). An evaluation approach was needed that answered questions while embracing the complexity of SCALE. Specifically, SCALE was a complex intervention (involving a comprehensive, multilevel support system) delivered in the context of complex systems (i.e., community coalitions). Adding further complexity, the theory of change for the initiative and the specific intervention components were not fully conceptualized at the start of the initiative and thus were evolving over time. The evaluation team looked to evaluation models designed to measure complex interventions in complex settings, such as Developmental Evaluation (Patton, 2011), Learning Evaluation (Balasubramanian et al., 2015), and FORE-CAST (FORmative Evaluation Consultation and Systems Technique; Katz et al., 2013). These models use formative approaches that adapt with the intervention and context as changes occur over time. They informed our mixed-method, multilevel formative evaluation strategy.

Throughout implementation, cycles of (1) question definition, (2) method development, (3) IOR, and (4) sense-making were applied. During the question definition phase, implementation activities were described and process questions were created. We

Figure 16.3   A Multi-stakeholder Perspective on the Evaluation of SCALE

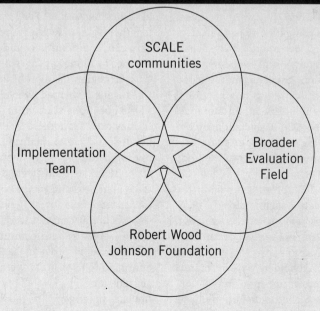

Continued

BOX 16.1 CORE EVALUATION QUESTIONS FOR THE SCALE FORMATIVE EVALUATION

1. What are the accelerators and inhibitors of progress in communities across the phases of the SCALE project? (process evaluation)

   a. What are the criteria and associated indicators of readiness and capability (capacity and motivation) to assess performance of communities? (formative evaluation)

   b. How can we use these indicators to monitor and predict progress? (formative evaluation)

2. How are these accelerators and inhibitors influenced by other aligned initiatives in a community? (process evaluation)

3. What are the facilitators and inhibitors of intercommunity spread under the SCALE approach? (process and formative evaluations)

4. How can the SCALE approach be improved to increase effectiveness and efficiency of spread? (formative evaluation)

5. What can we say about the contribution of the SCALE approach to progress? (summative evaluation)

6. How do we synthesize, document, disseminate, translate, and support implementation lessons learned from SCALE to facilitate spread across additional communities in the future—to make progress toward 100 Million Healthier Lives and a Culture of Health? (summative evaluation)

selected methods to answer process questions, using evidence-based approaches and tools (e.g., validated psychometric measures) when they were available. Data were then collected using inquiry (e.g., an electronic community survey), observation (e.g., observations of monthly webinars), and reflection (e.g., critical moment reflection sessions that elicited implementation team member reflections on critical moments in delivery of the intervention) methods. Upon data synthesis, the SCALE evaluation team used a combination of mechanisms to share and generate meaning from results (i.e., sense-making). SCALE data were shared on an ongoing basis during the initiative (see Table 16.2 for an example of the frequency of evaluation data dissemination).

Strong partnerships among the evaluation team, implementation team, funder, and community stakeholders were critical for making the evaluation a success. Importantly, stakeholders were intimately involved in the evaluation's design, implementation, and analyses. During the question definition phase,

evaluation and implementation team members worked together to identify key activities involved in implementation. For example, teams worked together to clarify the purpose of meetings held between community coalitions and improvement coaches to define key ingredients of implementation. Using the identification of activities, process questions were developed by evaluation team members. These questions were guided by process evaluation frameworks (Saunders, 2015) that focus on dose, fidelity, reach, and quality, and the questions were reviewed and refined by members of the implementation team. Methods were developed by evaluation team members and vetted and refined by implementation team members. Inquiry methods, including the community survey, were pilot tested and refined using feedback from community participants who volunteered to provide feedback before they were administered. As data were collected and results shared, findings were processed among stakeholders to engage in collaborative sense-making

Table 16.2   Frequency of Disseminating Evaluation Results

Type of Reporting	Frequency	Description
Informal updates	Weekly	Updates shared by evaluation team members to implementation team; purpose was to share real-time feedback and proactively identify areas for improvement
Interim reports	Approximately every 30–45 days	Brief, structured reports disseminated to implementation team stakeholders during the implementation of action phases (i.e., periods of coaching and technical assistance) to share updates on community progress
Comprehensive reports	Approximately every 70 days	Extensive, structured reports disseminated to project stakeholders (funders, implementation team, community participants) following the completion of critical events (e.g., completion of CHILA) and/or action phases

of findings. For instance, as reports were shared with implementation team members, we processed the results during structured *Reflection* activities. These sessions not only provided an opportunity to engage fully with the data, but in several cases, critical implementation issues were raised that were not otherwise captured by our other evaluation methods. In this way, the stakeholders were able to appropriately weight evaluation findings in a way that informed improvements in the evaluation plan and implementation.

Part of the SCALE design included a focus on building readiness and capability for using quality improvement methods to improve community health. Because the evaluation team fostered joint accountability and an improvement orientation with our stakeholders, we were able to advocate for a model of readiness rooted in the joint expertise of all stakeholders. This model was incorporated in various ways into evaluation and implementation processes. For example, the evaluation team worked with the implementation team to develop the initial application process based on the readiness framework. This enabled the implementation team to select community coalitions who were most likely to benefit from the SCALE initiative. Throughout implementation, community coalitions were asked to complete the Readiness Monitoring Tool (RMT), which was designed to assess community coalitions' readiness to use SCALE methods for community health improvement. Findings from this assessment were incorporated into

tailored reports that were disseminated to community coalitions to guide improvement specific to their work. Findings from this readiness assessment were also shared with funder and implementation team stakeholders; results highlighted the variability in community readiness and informed the delivery of implementation supports that were intended to meet community coalitions at different stages of readiness.

A formative evaluation was critical to the successful implementation of SCALE. Both the SCALE theory and support model adapted and changed over time to meet emergent needs at the community and program level. A summative approach would not have captured these changes and, as a result, the evaluation would likely have been irrelevant. By using a formative approach, we were able to adapt our evaluation plan so as to work with changing program needs. Additionally, the formative evaluation likely strengthened program impact by identifying areas for improvement during implementation. A formative approach was essential to evaluating this initiative and it is unlikely that a traditional approach would have provided an evaluation of comparable quality and facilitated the acquisition of meaningful learning for all stakeholders.

A prime example of this was the shift in focus to health equity after the second CHILA event. At the time, community stakeholders (the program recipients) began to express concerns that the CHILA content did not adequately cover health equity. Health equity was a major concern for both participating community coalitions and the

Continued

implementation team, so this mismatch was disconcerting. Our evaluation captured this issue and subsequently informed significant changes to the program theory and curricula. Health equity was prioritized as a top-level aim, and the content of the third CHILA was organized specifically around health equity. Had a formative approach not been used, health equity may not have been addressed adequately in the initiative.

The evaluation approach used in SCALE was grounded in the guiding principles we identified earlier. Joint accountability and improvement were inherent throughout the evaluation; all stakeholders viewed themselves as being equally accountable for informing the design, implementation, evaluation, and improvement of SCALE to ensure that it was effective at building community capacity for health improvement. A systems perspective was also critical. The evaluation needed to not only consider the complexity of the intervention, but also capture how that intervention was influenced by the diverse systems in which it was implemented. A multilevel perspective was integrated throughout to ensure that a systems perspective was adequately captured. The evaluation also sought to promote social justice through a focus on health equity and through use of empowerment evaluation principles (see Chapter 8) to ensure that data were meaningful and immediately useful for guiding implementation.

CONCLUSIONS, APPLICATIONS, AND REFLECTIONS

We recognize that the health services sector is enormous, and no one evaluation approach or set of principles is likely to be applicable to all settings. Within this reality, we provide some general guidance on building evaluation capacity for complex community and practice-based interventions as an important contribution to improving outcomes for people most in need. We also include questions to facilitate thinking about evaluation in health and human service settings. These questions can serve as useful guides regarding questions and issues to consider. In addition, they can be useful in thinking about the different elements of an evaluation in the context of a specific and familiar initiative (program, policy, practice) that is being implemented in a health and human service setting.

Promoting Joint Accountability Through Stakeholder Engagement

Regardless of the evaluation type (formative, process, and/or summative), we find it necessary to consider the evaluation needs of all relevant stakeholders. This involves including participants, to the extent that this process is feasible, in the development and prioritization of the evaluation questions and methods. Ideally, considering the needs, values, and questions pertinent to all stakeholders is done at the beginning of the evaluation.

Specific to formative evaluation, staying attuned to what stakeholders find useful within the evaluation makes it possible to continue to maximize the value of the evaluation. Emerging results may suggest new questions, new directions, and, subsequently, new areas of investigation. This is entirely appropriate in formative evaluation because stakeholder needs can change over time.

While desirable, the reality is that a highly collaborative evaluation may not always be possible or align with funder goals or priorities. We believe the Venn diagram approach is best practice; however, the weight attributed to inputs from different stakeholder perspectives (e.g., funder vs. health service organization staff, vs. health service recipient) is expected to vary based on the initiative and characteristics of the collaboration. On some initiatives, funder input might be weighted more heavily. On others, the perspective of health service program staff may matter most. Ideally, an initiative advisory board would help to provide guidance and clarify the relative importance of different needs. Regardless, we encourage evaluators to make a good faith effort to use a collaborative approach. This facilitates joint accountability and stakeholder engagement. It also helps to ensure that the evaluation methods and results have relevance to those who will be influenced by the evaluation findings.

Several questions can inform one's approach to stakeholder engagement:

- Who are the key stakeholders involved in the initiative? Which stakeholders are major influencers? Are there stakeholders that should be engaged who are currently not involved?

- How well are stakeholders aligned in their view of the initiative's evaluation approach? Where is there most and least alignment?

- What structure and processes are in place to facilitate joint accountability for initiative outcomes?

- What crucial (important but difficult) conversations would be useful for advancing stakeholder engagement and accountability? Who should be involved in those conversations?

Using Mixed Methods to Reflect System Complexity

Health systems are extraordinarily complex. Conducting evaluations in these settings can seem daunting, even for seasoned evaluators. We find that the use of mixed methods, as represented by the IOR framework, allows us to both gather diverse types of data and elicit stakeholder perspectives on the meaning of that data. Through this mixed-method approach, we have greater confidence that the data accurately represent the stakeholder experiences and the context of study.

Additionally, we find putting the concept of organizational readiness (motivation × capacity) front and center in our evaluations is useful for dissecting and understanding the complexity of factors influencing health service organizations. In our evaluations, organizational readiness is viewed as a dynamic construct that is expected to fluctuate over time. As such, we measure and monitor readiness across multiple time points. We believe measuring readiness is a key aspect of formative evaluations.

In considering an evaluation's approach and design, keep in mind these key questions:

- What are the key issues impacting that initiative? Make a list of the issues. For each issue: How is evaluation being used to monitor and address those issues?

- Thinking along the IOR framework, are there any shifts in the evaluation design (e.g., how evaluation data are collected) that might make the evaluation data more useful?

- What elements of organizational readiness for change (e.g., organizational culture, staff capacity, leadership effectiveness) have greatest impact on decisions about evaluation?

Fostering Improvement Through the Use of Evaluation

With improvement as a guiding value, we strive to integrate formative evaluation where possible to optimize the implementation of interventions. Formative evaluation is not a magic bean that ensures problem-free implementation. In fact, the premise for formative evaluations assumes just the opposite: implementation commonly bears a host of anticipated and unanticipated challenges. Formative evaluations provide a mechanism for identifying implementation issues as they arise. Because so many health outcomes have a long lag time between cause, intervention, and effect, the ability to make midcourse data-informed improvements enables more proactive use of resources and increases the likelihood of achieving targeted outcomes. While the value of formative evaluations is conceptually tangible for staff in health and human service settings, this type of evaluation may be viewed by staff as supplemental to process and summative evaluations. Our experience has taught us that initiating conversations early on (e.g., during grant writing or initiative development stages) and engaging multiple stakeholders in these conversations (e.g., funders, implementation staff, evaluation team, service recipients) about anticipated costs and benefits associated with conducting formative evaluations are helpful planning steps.

These questions can be useful to consider when considering formative strategies:

- What are perceived costs and benefits across key stakeholders to using formative evaluations in the selected health and human service setting?

- What open-ended evaluation questions do you think would benefit health setting stakeholders at this time?

FINAL THOUGHTS

When working in health service settings, problems and solutions are rarely straightforward, even when evidence-based interventions are used. In order to improve the effectiveness of these interventions, learning systems must be implemented alongside the intervention so that adjustments can be made to improve the likelihood of success. We believe using an improvement-oriented, collaborative approach to evaluation is critical for working with health service organizations to improve health, well-being, and equity outcomes.

ACKNOWLEDGMENTS

Insights from case examples provided in this chapter were made possible through our involvement in the ICLP and SCALE initiative and funding provided by the RWJF. We are tremendously grateful for the challenges, insights, and joys that emerged from evaluation of those initiatives. We are also grateful for the critical comments provided by Dr. Rohit Ramaswamy on an earlier version of this chapter.

FURTHER READING

Chandra, A., Miller, C. E., Acosta, J. D., Weilant, S., Trujillo, M., & Alonzo, P. (2016). Drivers of health as a shared value: Mindset, expectations, sense of community, and civic engagement. *Health Affairs, 35*(11), 1959–1963. https://www.healthaffairs.org/doi/full/10.1377/hlthaff.2016.0603

Hayes, H., Scott, V., Abraczinskas, M., Scaccia, J., Stout, S., & Wandersman, A. (2016). A formative multi-method approach to evaluating training. *Evaluation and Program Planning, 58,* 199–207.

Katz, J., Wandersman, A., Goodman, R., Griffin, S., Wilson, D., & Schillaci, M. (2013). Updating the FORECAST formative evaluation approach and some implications for ameliorating theory failure, implementation failure, and evaluation failure. *Evaluation Program Planning, 39,* 42–50.

Lavizzo-Mourey, R. (2014, December 10). *Building a culture of health.* http://www.rwjf.org.

McDowell, C., Nagel, A., Williams, S. M., & Canepa, C. (2005). Building knowledge from the practice of local communities. *Knowledge Management for Development Journal, 1,* 30–40.

Moore, G. F., Audrey, S., Barker, M., Bond, L., Bonnell, C., Hardeman, W., Moore, L., O'Cathain, A., Tinati, T., Wight, D., & Baird, J. (2015). Process evaluation of complex interventions: Medical Research Council guidance. *British Medical Journal, 350,* 1–7.

Ramaswamy, R., Reed, J., Livesley, N., Boguslavsky, V., Ellorio, E. G., Sax, D. H., Kimble, L., & Parry, G. (2018). Unpacking the black box of improvement. *International Journal for Quality in Health Care, 30*(s1), 15–19.

Scanlon, D. P., Alexander, J. A., Beich, J., Christianson, J. B., Hasnain-Wynia, R., McHugh, M. C., Mittler, J. N., Shi, Y., & Bodenschatz, L. J. (2012). Evaluating a community-based program to improve healthcare quality: Research design for the Aligning Forces for Quality initiative. *The American Journal of Managed Care, 18,* s165–s176.

Scott, V. C., Kenworthy, T., Godly-Reynolds, E., Bastien, G., Scaccia, J., McMickens, C., Rachel, S., Cooper, S., Wrenn, G., & Wandersman, A. (2017). The Readiness for Integrated Care Questionnaire (RICQ): An instrument to assess readiness to integrate behavioral health and primary care. *American Journal of Orthopsychiatry, 87,* 520–530.

Scott, V., Scaccia, J., Alia, K., Wandersman, A., Ramaswamy, R., Stout, S., & Leviton, L. (2019). Formative evaluation and complex health improvement initiatives: A learning system to improve theory, implementation, support, and evaluation. *American Journal of Evaluation,* 41(1), 89–106. doi.org/10.1177/1098214019868022

Wandersman, A., Alia, K., Cook, B. S., Hsu, L. L., & Ramaswamy, R. (2016). Evidence-based interventions are necessary but not sufficient for achieving outcomes in each setting in a complex world: Empowerment evaluation, getting to outcomes, and demonstrating accountability. *American Journal of Evaluation, 37,* 544–561.

Wandersman, A., Alia, K. A., Cook, B., & Ramaswamy, R. (2015). Integrating empowerment evaluation and quality improvement to achieve healthcare improvement outcomes. *British Medical Journal, 24,* 645–652.

KEY CONCEPTS

Befriend accountability: The process of becoming comfortable with the concept of accountability.

Formative evaluation: A type of evaluation designed to facilitate program improvement.

Health equity: A social condition in which all individuals can attain their highest level of health regardless of their group membership or place of residence.

Health service delivery system (HSDS): An entity that provides health services/interventions directly to patients/consumers to improve individual and population health and wellness.

Health service support system (HSSS): An entity that provides services to healthcare organizations and healthcare providers (HSDS) to build capacity for care quality and improve health outcomes.

Inquiry–Observation–Reflection (IOR) framework: A mixed-methods (quantitative and qualitative) data collection approach that involves the use of inquiry, observation, and reflection strategies to ascertain

a rich and broad understanding of a particular set of evaluation issues.

Plan-Do-Study-Act (PDSA): A quality improvement method that involves rapid-cycle implementation, evaluation, and improvement activities.

Process evaluation: A type of evaluation that measures the implementation of an innovation.

Summative evaluation: A type of evaluation that measures the worth or merit of an intervention.

QUESTIONS FOR REFLECTION

1. Define the three main types of evaluations (summative, process, and formative). What are the benefits and limitations of each type?

2. What is the distinction between the HSDS and the HSSS? Provide three sample evaluation metrics for each health service system.

3. Review the suggestions for working with health service providers to befriend accountability. Create a list of the suggestions and add any of your own ideas for working with health service providers to be more comfortable with evaluations. Looking at the list of suggestions and ideas: which resonate more versus less with you, and why?

4. In thinking about the Inquiry–Observation–Reflection framework and its associated evaluation methods (e.g., focus groups, interviews, archival data, surveys), do you think there are particular methods that are more suitable for each of the three types of evaluation (summative, process, and formative)? Why or why not?

5. Select one of the case examples described in this chapter. In what ways did the evaluation reflect the guiding principles of improvement, collaboration, social justice, and systems perspective? What other guiding principles/values seem apparent, but not explicitly named? What would your own set of guiding principles/values for evaluation look like?

REFERENCES

Artiga, S., Orgera, K., & Pham, O. (2020, March). Disparities in health and health care: Five key questions and answers. In *Disparities policy*. Retrieved from: https://www.kff.org/disparities-policy/issue-brief/disparities-in-health-and-health-care-five-key-questions-and-answers/

Balasubramanian, B. A., Cohen, D. J., Davis, M. M., Gunn, R., Dickinson, L. M., Miller, W. L., Crabtree, B. F., & Stange, K. C. (2015). Learning evaluation: Blending quality improvement and implementation research methods to study healthcare innovations. *Implementation Science, 10*(1), 1–11. doi:10.1186/s13012-015-0219-z

Campbell, M., Fitzpatrick, R., Haines, A., Kinmonth, A. L., Sandercock, P., Spiegelhalter, D., & Tyrer, P. (2000). Framework for design and evaluation of complex interventions to improve health. *British Medical Journal, 321*(7262), 694–696. doi:10.1136/bmj.321.7262.694

Craig, P., Dieppe, P., Macintyre, S., Michie, S., Nazareth, I., Petticrew, M. (2008). Developing and evaluating complex interventions: The new Medical Research Council Guidance. *British Medical Journal, 337*, a1655. doi:10.1136/bmj.a1655

Damschroder, L. J., Aron, D. C., Keith, R. E., Kirsh, S. R., Alexander, J. A., & Lowery, J. C. (2009). Fostering implementation of health services research findings into practice: A consolidated framework for advancing implementation science. *Implementation Science, 4*(1), 1–15. doi:10.1186/1748-5908-4-50

Davis, K., Stremikis, K., Squires, D., & Schoen, C. (2014). Mirror, mirror on the wall. In *How the performance of the US health care system compares internationally*. The Commonwealth Fund.

Fetterman, D. M. (2015). Empowerment evaluation: Theories, principles, concepts, and steps. In D. M. Fetterman, S. J. Kaftarian, & A. Wandersman (Eds.), *Empowerment evaluation* (2nd ed.). Thousand Oaks, CA: Sage.

Greenhalgh, T., Robert, G., Macfarlane, F., Bate, P., & Kyriakidou, O. (2004). Diffusion of innovations in service organizations: Systematic review and recommendations. *The Milbank Quarterly, 82*(4), 581–629. doi:10.1111/j.0887-378X.2004.00325.x

Hartman, M., Martin, A. B., Benson, J., Catlin, A., & National Health Expenditure Accounts Team. (2020). National health care spending in 2018: Growth driven by accelerations in Medicare and private insurance spending. *Health Affairs, 39*(1), 8–17. doi:10.1377/hlthaff.2019.01451

Hayes, H., Scott, V., Abraczinskas, M., Scaccia, J., Stout, S., & Wandersman, A. (2016). A formative multi-method approach to evaluating training. *Evaluation and Program Planning, 58*, 199–207. doi:10.1016/j.evalprogplan.2016.06.012

Katz, J., Wandersman, A., Goodman, R. M., Griffin, S., Wilson, D. K., & Schillaci, M. (2013). Updating the FORECAST formative evaluation approach and some implications for ameliorating theory failure, implementation failure, and evaluation failure. *Evaluation and Program Planning, 39*, 42–50. doi:10.1016/j.evalprogplan.2013.03.001

Langley, G. J., Moen, R. D., Nolan, K. M., Nolan, T. W., Norman, C. L., & Provost, L. P. (2009). *The improvement guide: A practical approach to enhancing organizational performance.* John Wiley & Sons.

Leviton, L. (2011). Reconciling complexity and classification in quality improvement research. *Quality and Safety in Health Care, 20*(Suppl 1), i28–i29. doi:10.1136/bmjqs.2010.046375

Leviton, L. C., Khan, L. K., Rog, D., Dawkins, N., & Cotton, D. (2010). Evaluability assessment to improve public health policies, programs, and practices. *Annual Review of Public Health, 31*, 213–233. doi:10.1146/annurev.publhealth.012809.103625

Martiniano, R., & Moore, J. (2018). *Health care employment projections, 2016-2026: An analysis of the Bureau of Labor statistics projections by setting and by occupation.* Center for Health Workforce Studies, School of Public Health, SUNY Albany.

Moore, G. F., Audrey, S., Barker, M., Bond, L., Bonell, C., Hardeman, W., Moore, L., O'Cathain, A., Tinati, T., Wight, D., & Baird, J. (2015). Process evaluation of complex interventions: Medical Research Council guidance. *British Medical Journal, 350*, h1258–7. doi:10.1136/bmj.h1258

Øvretveit, J., Leviton, L., & Parry, G. (2011). Increasing the generalisability of improvement research with an improvement replication programme. *BMJ Quality & Safety, 20 Suppl 1*(Suppl 1), i87–i91. doi:10.1136/bmjqs.2010.046342

Parry, G. J., Carson-Stevens, A., Luff, D. F., McPherson, M. E., & Goldmann, D. A. (2013). Recommendations for evaluation of health care improvement initiatives. *Academic Pediatrics, 13*(6 Suppl), S23–S30. doi:10.1016/j.acap.2013.04.007

Patton, M. Q. (2011). *Developmental evaluation: Applying complexity concepts to enhance innovation and use*. Guilford Press.

Peek, C. J., The National Integration Academy Council. (2013). *Lexicon for behavioral health and primary care integration: Concepts and definitions developed by expert consensus (Report No.13-IP001-EF)*.Agency for Healthcare Research and Quality.

Plough, A. L. (2015). Building a culture of health: A critical role for public health services and systems research. *American Journal of Public Health*, *105*(S2), S150–S152. doi:10.2105/AJPH.2014.302410

Rossi, P. H., Lipsey, M. W., & Henry, G. T. (2018). *Evaluation: A systematic approach* (8th ed.). Sage.

Saunders, R. P. (2015). *Implementation monitoring and process evaluation*. Sage.

Scaccia, J. P., Cook, B. S., Lamont, A., Wandersman, A., Castellow, J., Katz, J., & Beidas, R. S. (2015). A practical implementation science heuristic for organizational readiness: R = MC². *Journal of Community Psychology*, *43*(4), 484–501. doi:10.1002/jcop.21698

Scott, V. C., Kenworthy, T., Godly-Reynolds, E., Bastien, G., Scaccia, J., McMickens, C., Rachel, S., Cooper, S., Wrenn, G., & Wandersman, A. (2017). The Readiness for Integrated Care Questionnaire (RICQ): An instrument to assess readiness to integrate behavioral health and primary care. *American Journal of Orthopsychiatry*, *87*(5), 520–530. doi:10.1037/ort0000270

Squires, D., & Anderson, C. (2015). US health care from a global perspective: Spending, use of services, prices, and health in 13 countries. *The Commonwealth Fund*, *15*, 1–15.

Taylor, M. J., McNicholas, C., Nicolay, C., Darzi, A., Bell, D., & Reed, J. E. (2014). Systematic review of the application of the plan-do-study-act method to improve quality in healthcare. *BMJ Quality & Safety*, *23*(4), 290–298. doi:10.1136/bmjqs-2013-001862

Wandersman, A., Duffy, J., Flaspohler, P., Noonan, R., Lubell, K., Stillman, L., Blachman, M., Dunville, R., & Saul, J. (2008). Bridging the gap between prevention research and practice: The interactive systems framework for dissemination and implementation. *American Journal of Community Psychology*, *41*(3-4), 171–181. doi:10.1007/s10464-008-9174-z

CREATING COLLABORATIVE PARTNERSHIPS THROUGH PARTICIPATORY EVALUATION TO SHAPE PUBLIC POLICY

Rebecca Campbell, Jessica Shaw, Hannah Feeney, and Debi Cain

In 1973, Carol H. Weiss forewarned that "evaluation is a rational enterprise that takes place in a political context," and in the "rough and tumble" world of politics, evaluation findings may have limited influence in shaping public policy (pp. 37, 38). Decades later, Weiss and colleagues (2008) noted that the "dream of evidence-based policy" is not yet widespread reality, as evaluative evidence is not routinely used in the policy-making process (p. 29). This *science–practice gap* is well documented in multiple policy arenas, such that research/evaluation findings are not known and used by policymakers (e.g., Lum et al., 2012; Makse & Volden, 2011). A promising strategy for closing the science–practice gap has been strengthening linkages between researchers, policymakers, and practitioners through building collaborative partnerships (Kazdin, 2008; Kennedy, 2011; Klofas et al., 2010; Miller & Shinn, 2005; Wandersman, 2003; Weiss et al., 2008). Moving away from a model of unilateral dissemination of research findings (Mrazek & Haggerty, 1994; O'Connell et al., 2009) to bilateral engagement between researchers/evaluators and practitioners/policymakers (Miller & Shinn, 2005; Wandersman, 2003) may help promote the use of social science evidence in the development of public policy. This bilateral engagement would include practitioners and policymakers in the process of planning and conducting research and evaluation projects and allow researchers and evaluators to have opportunities for input in the policymaking process.

In this chapter, we will examine how we can build these collaborative partnerships to bring practitioners and policymakers into the world of evaluation and to find ways that we can be part of their world of social policy. For our evaluation work, we utilize Cousins's practical participatory evaluation theory as a framework for planning, implementing, and utilizing evaluation findings as it provides guidance for how to involve diverse stakeholders throughout this process (Amo &

Learning Objectives

1. Become familiar with the defining features of Cousins's practical participatory evaluation theory.

2. Identify multiple forms of use that may result from evaluation.

3. Understand the importance of collaborative partnerships when trying to impact public policy through evaluation.

Cousins, 2007; Cousins, 1996, 2003; Cousins & Chouinard, 2012; Cousins & Earl, 1992; Cousins & Whitmore, 1998). Our work is also informed by participatory policy analysis models for ways of creating space for researchers/evaluators in the policy arena (deLeon, 1992; Durning, 1993; Laird, 1993; Maton, 2017).

We have drawn upon these models throughout a multiyear collaboration with state-level policymakers to improve the criminal justice system response to sexual assault. Sexual violence is a pervasive social problem, as national epidemiological data indicate that 17%–25% of women are sexually assaulted in their lifetimes (Breiding, 2014); however, the vast majority of sexual assaults that are reported to the police are never prosecuted by the criminal justice system (Lonsway & Archambault, 2012). In this chapter, we describe a long-term collaboration between researchers/evaluators (Campbell, Shaw, and Feeney) and a policymaker (Cain) to address how law enforcement personnel investigate reported sexual assaults. We will begin with a brief discussion of practical participatory evaluation in a policy context and then present a real-world example of our work on the criminal justice response to sexual assault. Then, we will describe the policy actions that have stemmed from this collaborative partnership.

PARTICIPATORY EVALUATION IN A POLICY CONTEXT

Cousins's *practical participatory theory of evaluation* provides a conceptual framework for engaging diverse stakeholders to develop and implement an evaluation (Cousins, 1996, 2003; Cousins & Chouinard, 2012; Cousins & Earl, 1992; Cousins & Whitmore, 1998). A "participatory" approach to evaluation means that practitioners need to be directly involved in the planning and execution of the evaluation and, to that end, Cousins outlines three dimensions of that involvement. First, with respect to *stakeholder selection*, evaluators and their community partners need to decide who will be involved in the planning and execution of the project. Some participatory models mandate inclusion of a broad range of stakeholder groups (e.g., community members at-large; Patton, 2008), but practical participatory evaluation projects tend to limit involvement to program staff and other immediate users, as this will often (though not always) promote use of the evaluation findings. If, however, utilization will require the buy-in and involvement of more diverse groups, then the project should include more stakeholders. Second, with respect to the *control of the evaluation process*, practical participatory evaluation projects vary as to whether the evaluators or practitioners hold more control over the process. Cousins's theory does not stipulate whether one group should have more (or less) control, but rather emphasizes the importance of open communication about control of the project and finding ways to ensure participation from all groups. Finally, practical participatory evaluations vary in *depth of participation*, such that stakeholder involvement ranges from a consultant-type role (e.g., no decision-making responsibility) to deep participation (e.g., involvement in all aspects of the evaluation, including dissemination and utilization). In some projects, program staff might be quite hands-on and actually conduct much of the evaluation themselves and, in other contexts, it might be more useful for program staff to advise evaluators on these tasks and focus their attention elsewhere. Cousins's theory does not prescribe what mode of participation is "right;" instead, stakeholder engagement should be tailored to the specific project to promote local use of the evaluation findings.

Cousins adds "practical" as a prefix to participatory evaluation to signal the importance of addressing the specific, immediate information needs of local practitioners. Whereas many research/evaluation projects seek to identify cross-cutting issues that generalize across multiple settings and sites, Cousins encourages evaluators to focus on addressing local problems by crafting local solutions. Those solutions may indeed have applicability and utility in other settings, but the primary goal should be addressing pressing needs of the community in which the evaluation is being conducted. This "ground-level" targeted approach is consistent with the values and methods of community-based participatory action research, which also emphasize the utility of locally situated projects that seek to address an immediate problem in a specific community through pragmatic, collaborative problem solving (Greenwood & Levin, 2006; Kemmis & McTaggart, 2005; Wallerstein & Duran, 2008; also see Chapters 3 and 14). Multiple disciplines have been finding success with this practical approach to problem solving. For example, in the field of criminal justice, Kennedy (2011) noted that evaluations are most successful in promoting criminal justice policy change when they "stick close" to the problem at hand and identify concrete operational steps *that will get us from here to there* . . . and actually solve the problem" (pp. 210–211, emphasis in original).

Cousins emphasizes that engaging multiple stakeholders in a participatory manner and focusing on local, immediate needs will help stakeholders become invested in the evaluation and, therefore, they will be more likely to use the findings to promote change. Cousins defines multiple types of "use" that could result from a practical participatory evaluation project (Amo & Cousins, 2007; Cousins & Chouinard, 2012, Cousins & Whitmore, 1998; see also Patton, 2008). First, *process use* refers to the changes *within* program staff (e.g., knowledge, skill development) and organizations (e.g., culture shifts) that stem from participating in an evaluation. This type of use is often referred to as the development of "evaluative thinking." Second, *instrumental use* is when the evaluation findings are directly used to inform a decision or contribute to solving a problem. In this type of use, there must be a clear, discernible link between the substantive results and a programmatic change (e.g., "because we found *this*, we decided to do *that*"). Finally, *conceptual use* is when the evaluation findings change how stakeholders think about a program or policy in a more general way (e.g., a new insight, a deeper understanding, new questions; see also Weiss et al., 2005). In practical participatory evaluations, the goal is that all forms of use (process, instrumental, and conceptual) occur, but in a policy context, there is particular emphasis on promoting instrumental and conceptual use, as they are critical for policy change (Weiss et al., 2005). For example, instrumental use may allow stakeholders to continue integrating structural changes after the evaluation has ended, while conceptual use may lead to deeper understanding of the issues being addressed.

For instrumental and conceptual use to occur, policymakers need to be aware of evaluation findings and their implications. In practical participatory evaluations, stakeholders have been involved in the process of generating the work, but that is still no guarantee that the findings will be acted upon to generate change. To that end, bilateral models of engagement call for researchers to be embedded in policy work (see Maton, 2017). This same idea has been percolating in policy studies since the 1990s when the concept of *participatory policy analyses* was introduced as a way of making public policy more relevant and responsive to needs of citizenry (deLeon, 1992; Durning, 1993; Laird, 1993). Laird (1993) argued that public participation is critical to the success of a policy, and the scientific community is one sector of the public that often has relevant, empirically-based information to guide policy development. Thus, the collaboration among researchers, practitioners, and policymakers must extend beyond the evaluation itself and create ways for researchers/evaluators to continue to be engaged throughout the next phases of policy development and implementation (Maton, 2017). This engagement can take many forms (e.g., participation in policy work groups, providing testimony in legislative hearings), and identifying and sharing successful strategies of such collaborations remains a pressing need in policy scholarship.

PRACTICAL PARTICIPATORY EVALUATION IN ACTION: ADDRESSING THE CRIMINAL JUSTICE SYSTEM RESPONSE TO SEXUAL ASSAULT

Developing a Collaborative Partnership

Practical participatory evaluation projects take time to develop relationships with stakeholders, engender trust and respect, establish areas of expertise, and identify projects for collaboration. In this real-world example, our policy partner was the Michigan Domestic & Sexual Violence Prevention & Treatment Board ("the Board"). The Board was established by state legislation in 1978 to respond to the needs of domestic violence and sexual assault survivors throughout Michigan. As part of the Department of Health and Human Services, the Board develops and recommends public policy and legislation regarding gender-based violence; provides technical assistance and training to an array of stakeholders and audiences; and administers state and federal funding for domestic and sexual violence services. The executive director of the Board, Debi Cain, has long recognized the value of research and evaluation in public policy and social services and has actively used her role to seek out advice and consultation from experts at nearby institutions, like Michigan State University. Over a span of many years, trust was built between these two entities, and these small requests developed into more substantial collaborations. Eventually, a solid working relationship was established whereby Cain and the Board have partnered with multiple faculty members at Michigan State University, through our PhD graduate program in Ecological-Community Psychology and our multidisciplinary Research Consortium on Gender-Based Violence. Our (Campbell, Shaw, and Feeney) collaborations with the Board (Cain) have spanned multiple projects pertaining to community services for sexual assault victims, particularly in regard to the criminal justice response to rape and post-assault medical care for victims. Sexual assault victims are often advised to have a medical forensic exam (MFE), including the collection of a sexual assault kit (SAK) in order to preserve forensic evidence of the crime (Department of Justice, 2013). A SAK (also termed a "rape kit") contains biological evidence collected from victims' bodies after the assault (e.g., semen, blood, saliva) that can be analyzed for DNA and entered into the federal criminal DNA database, CODIS (Combined DNA Index System). DNA matches in CODIS can be instrumental in solving crimes, prosecuting rapists, and preventing future attacks.

Over a 10-year collaborative partnership, Campbell's research teams and Cain's Board members and staff have worked on various projects to improve survivors' experiences with seeking post-assault MFEs and reporting to the police. For instance, we collaborated on a number of formative evaluations that included participatory process and outcome evaluations of specialized sexual assault nurse examiner (SANE) programs that provide comprehensive healthcare and advocacy services for victims (Campbell & Cain, 2014; Campbell et al., 2008, 2012). We also redesigned and evaluated a new official SAK for the state of Michigan for state-of-the-art forensic evidence collection and compassionate care for survivors (Shaw et al., 2016).

This context regarding the Board's role in state policy and social services and our prior work together on the criminal justice system response to rape is critical background for understanding the real-world case example that is the focus of this chapter. In August 2009, the city of Detroit discovered ~11,000 SAKs in a remote police property storage facility, some dating back to the 1980s. When pressed for details about the status of these rape kits and whether they had been tested for DNA, police officials were not able to verify how many had been submitted for forensic testing. Police officials also could not tell how many of these reported rapes had been investigated and prosecuted. Based on what little information was available, it appeared that most of these rape kits had never been tested for DNA and these cases had not been investigated. These actions—or rather, inactions—threatened public safety, as potentially thousands of rapists had not been apprehended for their crimes, and eroded public trust, as thousands of sexual assault victims had come forward to report violent crimes and little had been done to help them. In time, it would become clear that Detroit was actually one of hundreds of U.S. cities that had large stockpiles of SAKs in storage, most untested and not investigated (Campbell et al., 2017). Conservative estimates suggest that there are 200,000–400,000 untested rape kits in police storage throughout the United States (Campbell et al., 2017; Strom & Hickman, 2010). The national problem of untested rape kits has garnered the attention of Human Rights Watch (2009, 2010, 2013) as a violation of international human rights laws that require police to investigate reports of sexual violence and take steps to protect individuals from sexual assault. Likewise, Department of Justice's (2015) report, *Gender Bias in Law Enforcement Response to Sexual Assault*, specifically highlighted the problem of untested rape kits as an example of biased and discriminatory police practices.

In 2009, though, when Detroit discovered their stockpile of untested rape kits, they were one of the first U.S. cities to confront this issue, and it was a staggering and overwhelming problem to surmount. The Elected Prosecutor of Wayne County (which includes the city of Detroit) reached out to the Board, as a key resource on sexual assault policy, and Cain and her staff sought emergency funding through the federal Department of Justice, Office of Violence Against Women, to conduct an independent review of the Detroit rape kits. The 400 Project was formed as a multidisciplinary team of practitioners from law enforcement, prosecution, forensic science, forensic nursing, and victim advocacy, with advisory input from MSU researchers (Campbell and the MSU Center for Statistical Training and Consultation's Dr. Steven Pierce). The goal of The 400 Project was to randomly select 400 SAKs from the population of SAKs in the police property storage facility and to provide comprehensive, victim-centered, multidisciplinary investigation and support services in response to the sexual assault cases corresponding to each selected SAK. This involved submitting each selected SAK for DNA testing; compiling and reviewing corresponding police, medical, and forensic records (if any) for each case; and notifying victims about their case status and next steps (when applicable). The 400 Project also provided critical insight into the scope of the problem of the full population of ~11,000 SAKs in the police property storage facility. The 400 Project multidisciplinary team learned that most of the 400 randomly selected rape kits had probably not been tested for DNA and that most of these reported assaults had not been thoroughly investigated. In generalizing these findings to the full population of SAKs in Detroit, it became clear that the city of Detroit needed to develop long-term plans for resolving thousands of cases.

In fortuitous timing, the National Institute of Justice had released a funding announcement to support action research projects on untested SAKs just as the preliminary findings from The 400 Project became available. The Elected Prosecutor of Wayne County decided to apply for these funds, in collaboration with the Board and practitioners from law enforcement, forensic science, forensic nursing, and victim advocacy, with Campbell as the formal research partner. The Detroit collaborative was awarded these funds, and the action research project was tasked with identifying the underlying reasons why Detroit had so many untested kits and developing long-term strategies for testing, investigation, prosecution, and victim notification and advocacy. For this chapter, we focus on this NIJ Sexual Assault Kit Action Research Project and a Process Evaluation of The 400 Project Data. It is important to note that the Process Evaluation of The 400 Project Data is separate and distinct from the initial 400 Project. Whereas The 400 Project was developed to respond to the discovery of the SAKs in real time, the Process Evaluation of The 400 Project Data was implemented several years later in order to learn more from these invaluable data. These two initiatives—the NIJ SAK Action Research Project and Process Evaluation of The 400 Project Data—as well as the original 400 Project (led by the Board, and described above) overlapped in chronology and in key personnel. This is common in policy work, yet challenging to describe in the kind of linear sequence typical in academic writing. Thus, we have organized our discussion around two key substantive issues: (1) how research/evaluation could help Detroit stakeholders make decisions regarding testing previously unsubmitted rape kits (drawing on work from the NIJ SAK Action Research Project, led by Campbell); and (2) how research/evaluation could help illuminate broader problematic practices in how sexual assault cases are investigated by the police (drawing on the Process Evaluation of The 400 Project Data, led by Shaw).

Using Research and Evaluation to Develop a Plan for Testing Rape Kits

Consistent with a practical participatory approach to evaluation, we began the Detroit SAK Action Research Project by considering *stakeholder selection* and outlining a participatory group process for our work together. Our key task was to develop a testing plan for these old rape kits, and the group readily decided that broad-based stakeholder engagement was necessary. Though stakeholders from one specific discipline—forensic science—would be doing the actual work of testing the kits, many disciplines had been/would be involved in the collection of those kits, investigating leads from those kits, presenting the evidence from within those kits in court, and explaining testing findings to sexual assault survivors. Thus, the work group included frontline practitioners as well as senior organizational leaders from law enforcement, prosecution, forensic science, forensic nursing, and victim advocacy. This multidisciplinary team met in person at the prosecutor's office twice a month from 2011 to 2015; phone/in-person meetings and off-site retreats were held as needed to attend to urgent issues. Team meetings were facilitated by a grant-funded project coordinator, who was a representative of the prosecutor's office; the researchers and practitioners decided that the coordinator role should be filled by a member of the community (not a researcher) in order to build local capacity for long-term sustainability of the initiative after the initial grant funding ended. Decision making was participatory as all disciplines had input into the issues at hand, though final authority typically rested with the senior-most official within each organization (e.g., Elected Prosecutor, Police Chief), given the complex legal issues inherent in this project. To ensure a fair and transparent work process, the researchers and practitioners established memoranda of understanding outlining roles and responsibilities; data use agreements; privacy and confidentiality practices; guiding ethical principles; conflict resolution strategies; and release of information/dissemination agreements (including provisions to co-publish and co-present).

As this multidisciplinary group began discussing the work at hand, it became clear very quickly that stakeholders had strong differences of opinion as to whether all of these rape kits *should* be submitted for forensic DNA testing. Some stakeholders argued that *all* kits should be tested for DNA to seek justice for victims and honor promises made to them to test the evidence from their kits. Others contended that only *some* rape kits merited testing. Some team members argued that only the rape kits associated with stranger-perpetrated sexual assaults should be tested, as DNA evidence could potentially reveal the identity of the offender. In sexual assaults committed by someone known to the victim (e.g., an acquaintance, friend, co-worker, neighbor, dating/intimate partner, family member), the offender's identity was not in question, so some stakeholders argued that DNA testing was not necessary in these cases. Other members of the group countered that argument by noting that DNA testing could be helpful in non-stranger sexual assault cases because it would confirm offender identity and might reveal DNA matches to other crimes (through the federal DNA database, CODIS) committed by the offender. The action research project members could not reach consensus on this central issue, so the research team explained how these debates could become empirical evaluation questions. We could test a sample of SAKs that included both stranger- and non-stranger-perpetrated sexual assaults and then compare the utility of the information provided by the testing. The action research project team agreed to this plan, but given the contentious debates about this issue, we mutually decided that the *control of evaluation* should rest primarily with the research/evaluation team, as we were perceived as an outside objective party. As to the *depth of participation* among stakeholders in this evaluation, the group wanted input into formulating the evaluation questions (below), but then would step back to allow the evaluators to collect and analyze the data independently. The whole group would then come back together to review the results, interpret the findings, and decide on next steps.

For this component of the action research project, we had three primary evaluation questions: (1) What proportion of kits would produce a DNA match in the federal DNA CODIS database (a "CODIS hit"), indicating that police likely needed to reopen and reinvestigate a case; (2) Would CODIS hit rates significantly differ between stranger-perpetrated and non-stranger-perpetrated sexual assaults, informing decisions about whether all kits should be tested; (3) How many CODIS hits would link to other criminal cases, indicating a pattern of serial offending and a potentially urgent public safety threat? To address these questions, we used a complex stratified random sampling design to select 1,595 SAKs for forensic testing (see Campbell et al., 2015, for details).

The results for our first evaluation question were startling: 785 SAKs yielded DNA samples that were eligible for upload into the federal criminal DNA database, CODIS (i.e., these rape kits tested positive for DNA, and the DNA met the federal standards for inclusion into the national database). From those uploads, there were 455 CODIS hits, meaning there was a match to an offender's DNA profile (i.e., potentially solving or confirming the offender's identity). Practically, these results meant that 455 cases needed to be reopened and reinvestigated. To answer our second evaluation question, we compared the CODIS hit rates for SAKs associated with stranger-perpetrated sexual assaults and non-stranger-perpetrated sexual assaults. We used continuation ratio modeling and equivalence testing methods to compare our forensic outcomes (e.g., CODIS hit rates) as a function of the relationship between the victim and offender (e.g., stranger vs. non-stranger). Briefly, there are several stages in SAK DNA testing; continuation ratio modeling and equivalence testing methods (see Agresti, 2002; Barker et al., 2002; Hosmer et al., 2013; Tunes da Silva et al., 2009) allowed us to examine how many SAKs reached each new stage, based on the number of SAKs in the prior stage. We found that CODIS hit rates were statistically equivalent between stranger and non-stranger SAKs—they were equally likely to produce a CODIS hit (Campbell et al., 2016).

Finally, for our third evaluation question, we examined whether DNA testing could establish linkages across multiple criminal cases (i.e., serial offenders). Of the 455 CODIS hits in this project, 127 were hits to another sexual assault case, meaning that there were DNA matches across multiple sexual assault cases and the offender was a suspected serial rapist. We had multiple instances in which the DNA from a stranger-SAK hit to non-stranger-SAK, and vice versa (Campbell et al., 2018). Practically, this meant that police had 127 suspected serial offenders to investigate, and many of them had patterns of raping both strangers and people known to them.

When the full action research project team came together to review and discuss these results, stakeholders were stunned by these results, as they did not expect that so many kits would produce CODIS hits, investigation leads, and suspected serial sexual offenders. Some stakeholders had argued that kits in non-stranger rapes case should not be tested, and instead the results indicated that CODIS hit rates were equivalent—and non-stranger cases might connect to other unsolved stranger-perpetrated sexual assault cases. The action research project team recommended that all of the previously unsubmitted SAKs should be tested as a matter of public safety and judicial integrity in the event there had been wrongful convictions of innocent individuals who could now be cleared by DNA testing. While the broader team readily agreed with this overall plan, establishing a process by which this recommendation could be carried to completion proved more daunting and complicated than first anticipated. Later in this chapter, we will return to how local-, county-, and state-level officials leveraged resources to act upon this recommendation.

Using Research and Evaluation to Identify Problematic Practices in Police Investigations

The focus of the NIJ SAK Action Research Project was to understand how and why Detroit amassed so many untested rape kits and to develop long-term plans for testing these kits and notifying victims (see Campbell et al., 2015). The SAK, though, is just one part of a larger criminal investigation. The accumulation of untested SAKs over time begs the question as to what happened in each of these cases, beyond the mishandling of the SAK. The initial review of police records in The 400 Project and NIJ SAK Action Research Project suggested that other aspects of the criminal investigation, in addition to how kits were handled, were problematic. A separate empirical investigation, focused explicitly on examining the police records associated with the untested SAKs in the police property storage facility, could provide additional information regarding what happened in these police investigations. The 400 Project records were an ideal data source for such inquiry as the detailed records collected for that project would allow for a more in-depth examination of the broader investigative context to understand police practices in sexual assault cases. As previously described, The 400 Project cases were a random sample from the full population of unsubmitted SAKs in this community; thus the findings from the empirical examination of these records could be generalized to the full population, providing critical information on how police investigate sexual assault cases, and how policy and practice change might improve them. And though these records were already reviewed by the Board-led multidisciplinary 400 Project team, a second look at these records in the form of a systematic process evaluation could identify empirically patterns in police (in)action and decision making.

For this Process Evaluation of The 400 Project Data, *stakeholder selection* was limited to the Board. The Board maintained The 400 Project records and expressed interest in wanting to learn more about how these police investigations progressed. Though other stakeholders—such as the police—played a major role in the *evaluand* for this project (i.e., the subject/focus of the evaluation, in this case, the police investigations), it was not feasible to ask them to participate in this project at the same time that they were deeply entrenched in the work of the larger NIJ SAK Action Research Project. Additionally, the Board was likely to be the immediate user of the findings that resulted from this inquiry, using them to inform their policy and training initiatives. The Board's position in the state, as well as in the NIJ SAK Action Research Project, also made it possible for them to share and promote use of the evaluation results with all relevant stakeholders when politically feasible to do so.

Accordingly, the researchers (Shaw and Campbell) worked with the Board (Cain) to develop a more nuanced understanding of what policymakers hoped to learn from a second look at The 400 Project data: The Board wanted to know more about *how* police responded in these cases and *why* they responded in the way that they did. To ensure open and transparent communication throughout this evaluation project, and that the researchers and the Board were in agreement as to how raw data and evaluation findings would be shared, handled, and used, a memorandum of understanding was established between the researchers and the Board. The researchers and the Board agreed that the operational *control of the evaluation* would be primarily with the researchers/evaluators. Given what was already known about the police response to sexual assault in this community and across the country, it was likely that the evaluation findings would be unflattering and perhaps contentious; thus it was critical that the evaluation was handled by an outside entity—outside of the immediate circle of Detroit and state-level stakeholders. However, because this evaluation would not be possible without the Board granting access to the data, the Board exercised equal control in major decisions (e.g., setting the parameters of the evaluation). The Board's *depth of participation* varied across the project: They played a critical role in shaping the evaluation questions; stepped back during data analysis; and played an equal role in disseminating the findings, coauthoring and copresenting alongside the researchers.

Ultimately, the evaluation was designed to answer three focal questions: (1) What happened in these investigations and how thorough was the police investigative response? (2) To what extent did police provide explanations for their investigative response and what specific beliefs and attitudes appeared in their explanations? and (3) To what extent did the investigative responses and explanations provided vary across cases? (Shaw, 2017; Shaw et al., 2015). To answer these questions, the process evaluation took the form of a *sequential exploratory mixed-methods multistudy* (Shaw, 2014). In this approach, the multistudy sequence begins with exploratory qualitative work to learn about the phenomenon of interest. Findings from this phase of work are then used to inform the subsequent quantitative investigation (see Campbell et al., 2017). For this process evaluation, directed and conventional content analyses were used to code actual police case records for explanations provided by police for their response to sexual assault (Shaw, 2014; Shaw et al., 2017). Then, path analysis was used to examine empirically the relationships between the investigative response, the explanations provided by police for the investigative response, and specific case variables (Shaw, 2014; Shaw et al., 2016). Briefly, path analysis is a flexible approach that allows for the empirical examination of theorized models that explain how variables relate to one another by constraining and relaxing parameters within the model, assessing for improved model fit along the way (see Barrett, 2007; Bollen, 1989; Byrne, 2012). We used this analytic method to examine the explanations provided by police as predictors of the police response; the relationship between the different types of explanations provided by police and the police response; and the impact of victim and perpetrator sex, race, and age, as well as the number of perpetrators, on both the explanations provided by police and the police response.

In response to our first evaluation question, analyses revealed that police completed an average of 3.4 out of 10 possible investigative steps on each case (e.g., canvassing the area; photographing the crime scene; obtaining a statement from the victim); that the vast majority of cases were never referred by police to the prosecutor's office for the consideration of charges; and that the likelihood of case referral increased as more investigative steps were completed (Shaw, 2014; Shaw et al., 2016). As for our second evaluation question, content analyses resulted in the identification of three different types of explanations provided by police for their investigative action (or rather, inaction). This included statements that denied the assault based on specific circumstances (e.g., the victim is not upset enough; termed "circumstantial statements"); justified or denied the assault based on specific victim characteristics (e.g., the victim is a drug user; termed "characterological statements"); or blamed victims for the way police responded to the assault (e.g., the victim is uncooperative; termed "investigatory blame statements"; Shaw, 2014; Shaw et al., 2017). Finally, in regard to the third evaluation question, we found that the type of explanation provided by police varied based on the race and age of the victim, as well as the number of perpetrators. However, none of these variables directly predicted the police investigative response; all relationships between such variables and the investigative response were fully mediated by the statements police made.

ACTION

Acting on Evaluation Findings: Developing a Plan for Testing All Rape Kits

Given that results of the NIJ SAK Action Research Project indicated that most of the Detroit kits had never been tested for DNA and that useful information could be learned if they were tested, a key next step was to secure resources to fund testing, investigation, prosecution, and victim advocacy services for all of these kits/cases. The Wayne County Prosecutor's Office, together with the Board, secured funds from the state Attorney General's Office (with the support of the Governor's Office) to test all remaining previously unsubmitted Detroit SAKs. The Wayne County Prosecutor's Office received multiple federal Department of Justice grants to create a cold case investigation and prosecution unit. The original Detroit SAK collaborative continues to meet bimonthly now as the Wayne County Sexual Assault Kit Task Force to process CODIS hits, victim notifications, investigations, and prosecutions. The Task Force partnered with the Michigan Women's Foundation and the Detroit Crime Commission to create Enough SAID (Enough Sexual Assault in Detroit) to raise public awareness and additional funds for investigation, prosecution, and victim services.

Local, county, and state policymakers also wanted to take steps to ensure that the problem of untested rape kits did not happen again in Detroit or any other Michigan jurisdiction. Thus, the Board partnered with the Prosecuting Attorney's Association of Michigan to draft legislation to mandate SAK testing. The Michigan Sexual Assault Kit Submission Act (MCL 752.931-935) stipulates that all SAKs that have been released by victims for forensic DNA testing must be submitted to a forensic crime laboratory for testing. The law provides specific timeframes regarding when police must be notified that a SAK is ready for transport, when police must pick up the SAK, when the SAK must arrive at the crime laboratory, and when SAK testing must be completed. A companion law was also passed, the Michigan Sexual Assault Victim's Access to Justice Act (MCL 752.953), which stipulates victims' rights to information and access to sexual assault MFEs and evidence collection.

The Process Evaluation of The 400 Project Data was not completed until after the Michigan Sexual Assault Kit Submission Act and the Michigan Sexual Assault Victim's Access to Justice Act were passed. Thus, the evaluation findings did not directly inform the creation of this legislation, but they do provide empirical confirmation and justification for the implementation of these new policies. For example, the Process Evaluation of The 400 Project Data highlighted that police frequently attributed the omission of investigative steps—such as submitting the SAK to the crime lab—to an "uncooperative victim," and that Black victims, as well as victims over the age of consent, were more likely to be deemed uncooperative (Shaw, 2014; Shaw et al., 2017). Furthermore, the evaluation found that as more investigative steps (like submitting the SAK) were omitted, and once a victim was deemed "uncooperative," the case was significantly less likely to reach prosecution. By implementing the Sexual Assault Kit Submission Act, law enforcement can no longer simply deem the victim "uncooperative" as justification for an unsubmitted SAK. They must submit it, which, according to the Process Evaluation of The 400 Project Data, should increase the likelihood of the case reaching prosecution and help mitigate differential treatment of the victim based on age or race.

To help other jurisdictions throughout the United States that also have large numbers of untested SAKs, we documented lessons learned from these evaluation projects to share with other cities and states. For each major phase of work, we created "Step by Step Guides" that outlined each decision point in the process, a summary of relevant research to inform discussions about the issue, and the final decisions reached by the Detroit team. We also created "Lessons Learned" infographics to highlight strategies for successful multidisciplinary team partnerships. These practice resources were released nationally through the National Criminal Justice Reference Service (https://www.ncjrs.gov/pdffiles1/nij/grants/248680.pdf). Moreover, the NIJ Communications Department developed several policy and practice dissemination products, including an interactive web feature story *"Sexual Assault Kits: Using Science to Find Solutions"* (http://nij.gov/unsubmitted-kits/Pages/default.aspx), and a series of four NIJ policy bulletins on untested rape kits (https://www.ncjrs.gov/pdffiles1/nij/249233.pdf; https://www.ncjrs.gov/pdffiles1/nij/249234.pdf; https://www.ncjrs.gov/pdffiles1/nij/249153.pdf, https://www.ncjrs.gov/pdffiles1/nij/249232.pdf).

Acting on Evaluation Findings: Improving Police Sexual Assault Case Investigations

The 400 Project and the NIJ SAK Action Research Project indicated a pressing need for training and policy reform on law enforcement practices in sexual assault case investigations. The Board knew that Michigan did not have a cohesive, statewide resource for law enforcement agencies regarding best practices for investigating sexual assaults. Thus, to rectify this, the Board decided to establish a multidisciplinary team to develop a model policy for statewide use by law enforcement investigating adult and young adult sexual assault cases. Given the longstanding partnership between the Board and MSU researchers, and the Board's commitment to evidence-based social policy, Cain invited a researcher to participate in this policy workgroup (Feeney).

The model policy had four main goals as a statewide resource for law enforcement: (1) ensure that all sexual assault cases in the state are properly and ethically investigated; (2) reduce the secondary trauma to the victim by responding in a compassionate manner; (3) incorporate investigative practices that focused on the actions and choices of the offender, rather than the victim; and (4) encourage a coordinated community response to sexual assault. The workgroup brought together professionals from a number of disciplines (e.g., law enforcement, SANEs, lawyers) to review and ultimately develop the final model policy. To help accomplish these tasks, the head of the working group compiled a number of informational resources for the committee's review, such as other states' model policies and policy suggestions from Human Rights Watch (HRW) and End Violence Against Women International (EVAW). In the role of a research consultant to the group,

Feeney participated in these workgroup meetings by bringing current findings from the *academic* literature for the group's consideration. At times, stakeholders from differing disciplines held varying opinions regarding best practices, and having a research consultant present at these meetings allowed the group to turn to the academic literature and consider a more holistic and empirically grounded position. For instance, if the model practice being suggested was in direct conflict with the existing literature, the research partner (Feeney) would bring this information to the group for immediate consideration. After many months, the model policy was published as *The Michigan Model Policy: The Law Enforcement Response to Sexual Assault* (Michigan Domestic and Sexual Violence Prevention and Treatment Board, 2015). It was shared with all law enforcement agencies in the state in an effort to provide easily adaptable steps for completing a consistent, thorough, trauma-informed, victim-centered, and offender-focused sexual assault case investigation.

Like the SAK and victims' rights legislation passed in Michigan, the model policy was developed before the Process Evaluation of The 400 Project Data was completed; thus its findings could not directly inform the model policy development and instead provided empirical support for its implementation. For example, the Process Evaluation of The 400 Project Data findings showed that as more investigative steps were completed on a given case, the case was more likely to progress in the criminal justice system, suggesting that any standardized effort to increase systematically the number of investigative steps taken on a case—like the model policy—will increase the number of cases that reach prosecution. Indeed, the Board uses these evaluation findings and specific case examples from the evaluation when training new communities on the model policy (see Krieger et al., 2017; Shaw et al., 2015).

To help other jurisdictions improve sexual assault investigational practice, the model policy and training materials (i.e., a training video on "Sexual Assault: A Trauma Informed Approach to Law Enforcement First Response," https://www.youtube.com/watch?v= gtWD1XJrhNo; and a 2-day curriculum on non-stranger sexual assault) have been shared with other states and federal clearinghouse resources on gender-based violence and the criminal justice system. The findings of the Process Evaluation on the 400 Project Data have also been shared to help inform policy conversations at the national level, including at the White House Domestic Violence Awareness Month Roundtable (Shaw, 2015) and at the U.S. Department of Justice, Office on Violence Against Women Roundtable on Identifying and Preventing Gender Bias in Policing (Martinson & Gamache, 2016; Shaw, 2016).

For evidence-based social policy to become a widespread reality (Weiss et al., 2008), we must develop sustainable partnerships between researchers/evaluators and practitioners/policymakers. To a new evaluator, the partnerships, projects, and impacts described in this chapter may seem as though they came together with ease. For others, our story and presentation of the material may be overwhelming and suggest that such work is best left to those with extensive experience in the policy world. However, it was by drawing upon Cousins's practical participatory evaluation theory and participatory policy analysis models that our team established successful multiyear collaborations with state-level policymakers. These frameworks provide necessary specificity, yet allow for adequate flexibility in regard to which stakeholders we select as partners in evaluation, their level of involvement, and with whom decision-making power lies, allowing for broad application of participatory approaches to evaluation. We hope to highlight, through this approach, that such partnerships are built only through time, trust, and mutual appreciation and that both new and experienced evaluators are able, with practice, to exercise the type of commitment and skill necessary to develop and foster such relationships (see Weiss, 1973). Our long-term collaborations have informed various policies, training initiatives, and future projects and while development can take significant effort, the resulting partnerships can help create essential, sustainable changes for communities.

FURTHER READING

Background on and Examples of Practical Participatory Evaluation

American Evaluation Association Theories of Evaluation Topical Interest Group: http://www.eval.org/p/cm/ld/fid=11

Cousins, J. B., & Chouinard, J. A. (2012). *Participatory evaluation up close: An integration of research-based knowledge.* Information Age Publishing.

Cousins, J. B., & Whitmore, E. (1998). Framing participatory evaluation. *New Directions for Evaluation, 80,* 5–23.

Shaw, J., Campbell, R., Hagstrom, J., O'Reilly, L., Kreiger, G., Cain, D., & Nye, J. (2016). Bringing research into practice: An evaluation of Michigan's pilot sexual assault kit (SAK). *Journal of Interpersonal Violence, 31,* 1476–1500.

Wharton, T., & Alexander, N. (2013). Evaluating a moving target: Using practical participatory evaluation (P-PE) in hospital settings. *American Journal of Evaluation, 34,* 402–412.

Substantive Findings Referenced Herein

Campbell, R., Feeney, H., Fehler-Cabral, G., Shaw, J., & Horsford, S. (2017). The national problem of untested sexual assault kits (SAKs): Scope, causes, and future directions for research, policy, and practice. *Trauma, Violence, & Abuse, 18,* 363–376.

Campbell, R., Shaw, J., & Fehler-Cabral, G. (2015). Shelving justice: The discovery of thousands of untested rape kits in Detroit. *City & Community, 14,* 151–166.

Shaw, J., Campbell, R., & Cain, D. (2016). The view from inside the system: How police explain their response to sexual assault. *American Journal of Community Psychology, 58,* 446–462.

Shaw, J., Campbell, R., Cain, D., & Feeney, H. (2017). Beyond surveys and scales: How rape myths manifest in sexual assault police records. *Psychology of Violence, 7,* 602–614.

KEY CONCEPTS

Community-based participatory action research: An array of approaches to research that prioritize participatory and collaborative processes, multiple ways of knowing, reflection, pragmatic problem-solving, and action.

Conceptual use: Changes in how stakeholders think about a program or policy more generally as a result of the evaluation.

Control of the evaluation process: A defining dimension in a practical participatory evaluation that refers to who has decision-making power throughout the evaluation process. This may range from full control with the evaluators, with the stakeholders, or somewhere in between.

Depth of participation: A defining dimension in a practical participatory evaluation that refers to the level of involvement among the selected stakeholders. This may range from selected stakeholders being involved in every aspect of the evaluation to participating in select aspects of the evaluation process.

Evaluand: The subject or focus of an evaluation.

Instrumental use: Direct use of the evaluation findings to inform a decision or contribute to solving a problem.

Participatory policy analysis: Policy analysis that supports the participation of stakeholders so that their insights may inform public policy.

Practical participatory evaluation: An evaluation approach that prioritizes engaging stakeholders in the evaluative process and practical use of the evaluation process and findings.

Process use: Changes within program staff and organizations that stem from participating in an evaluation.

Science–practice gap: Contexts in which practice or policy development operates independently of relevant research or evaluation.

Sequential exploratory mixed-methods design: A mixed-methods design in which exploratory qualitative data are collected and analyzed first, followed by quantitative data collection and analysis.

Stakeholder selection: A defining dimension in a practical participatory evaluation that refers to the intentional selection of stakeholders to be involved in the evaluation process. This may range from all individuals with any stake in the evaluand, to a select subgroup of stakeholders.

QUESTIONS FOR REFLECTION

1. Consider the case example. What was unique about the relationship between the evaluators and the policymaker that allowed the described projects to progress as they did?

2. Cousins's practical participatory evaluation theory outlines three dimensions related to practitioners' involvement in evaluation: stakeholder selection, control of the evaluation process, and depth of participation. How did these dimensions vary in relation to the two key substantive issues addressed in the case example? How might have use of the evaluation findings been impacted if different decisions were made in regard to stakeholder selection, control of the evaluation process, and depth of participation?

3. In the case example, some policy decisions were made before the evaluation was completed.

Because the evaluation findings supported decisions already made, the findings were used to reinforce their importance. What could the evaluators have done if the findings suggested a different policy solution? How might the evaluators' decisions on what to do next be influenced by, and impact, their relationship with the policymaker?

4. Consider how you might apply these strategies in your own work. Identify a public policy topic that would benefit from evaluation or evaluative insight. What stakeholders should be involved in the evaluative effort (i.e., stakeholder selection)? Who should have control and decision-making power over the course of the evaluation process (i.e., control of the evaluation process)? In what ways should the stakeholders be involved (i.e., depth of participation)?

REFERENCES

Agresti, A. (2002). *Categorical data analysis* (2nd ed.). John Wiley & Sons.

Amo, C., & Cousins, J. B. (2007). Going through the process: An examination of the operationalization of process use in empirical research on evaluation. *New Directions for Evaluation*, 116, 5–26. doi:10.1002/ev.240

Barker, L. E., Luman, E. T., McCauley, M. M., & Chu, S. Y. (2002). Assessing equivalence: An alternative to the use of difference tests for measuring disparities in vaccination coverage. *American Journal of Epidemiology*, *156*(11), 1056–1061. doi:10.1093/aje/kwf149

Barrett, P. (2007). Structural equation modeling: Adjudging model fit. *Personality and Individual Differences, 42*(5), 815–824. doi:10.1016/j.paid.2006.09.018

Bollen, K. A. (1989). *Structural equations with latent variables.* John Wiley & Sons.

Breiding, M. J. (2014). Prevalence and characteristics of sexual violence, stalking, and intimate partner violence victimization. *Morbidity and Mortality Weekly Report.* Surveillance Summaries, 63.

Byrne, B. M. (2012). *Structural equation modeling with MPlus: Basic concepts, applications, and programming.* Routledge.

Campbell, R., & Cain, D. (2014, June). *A multidisciplinary response to sexual violence. Current research findings on the effectiveness of sexual assault response teams (SARTs).* Paper presented at the Battered Women's Justice Project Annual Conference, New Orleans, LA.

Campbell, R., Feeney, H., Fehler-Cabral, G., Shaw, J., & Horsford, S. (2017). The national problem of untested sexual assault kits (SAKs). *Trauma, Violence, & Abuse, 18,* 363–376.

Campbell, R., Feeney, H., Pierce, S. J., Sharma, D. B., & Fehler-Cabral, G. (2018). Tested at last: How DNA evidence in untested rape kits can identify offenders and serial sexual assaults. *Journal of Interpersonal Violence, 33*(24), 3792–3814. doi:10.1177/0886260516639585

Campbell, R., Fehler-Cabral, G., Pierce, S. J., Sharma, D., Bybee, D., Shaw, J., & Feeney, H. (2015). *The Detroit sexual assault kit (SAK) action research project (ARP), final report. U.S. Department of Justice:* National Institute of Justice.

Campbell, R., Patterson, D., Adams, A. E., Diegel, R., & Coats, S. (2008). A participatory evaluation project to measure SANE nursing practice and adult sexual assault patients' psychological well-being. *Journal of Forensic Nursing, 4*(1), 19–28. doi:10.1111/j.1939-3938.2008.00003.x

Campbell, R., Patterson, D., & Bybee, D. (2012). Prosecution of adult sexual assault cases: A longitudinal analysis of the impact of a sexual assault nurse examiner (SANE) program. *Violence Against Women, 18*(2), 223–244. doi:10.1177/1077801212440158

Campbell, R., Pierce, S. J., Sharma, D., B., Feeney, H., & Fehler-Cabral, G. (2016). Should rape kit testing be prioritized by victim-offender relationship?: Empirical comparison of forensic testing outcomes for stranger and nonstranger sexual assaults. *Criminology & Public Policy, 15,* 555–583.

Campbell, R., Shaw, J., & Gregory, K. A. (2017). Giving voice—and the numbers, too: Mixed methods research in community psychology. In M. A. Bond, I. Serrano-Garcia, & C. B. Keys (Eds.), *APA handbook of community psychology: Volume 2, Methods for community research and action for diverse groups and issues.* American Psychological Association.

Cousins, J. B. (1996). Consequences of researcher involvement in participatory evaluation. *Studies in Educational Evaluation, 22*(1), 3–27. doi:10.1016/0191-491X(96)00001-6

Cousins, J. B. (2003). Utilization effects of participatory evaluation. In T. Kellaghan & D. L. Stufflebeam (Eds.), *International handbook of education evaluation.* Kluwer.

Cousins, J. B., & Chouinard, J. A. (2012). *Participatory evaluation up close: An integration of research-based knowledge.* University of Illinois-Champaign: Information Age.

Cousins, J. B., & Earl, L. M. (1992). The case for participatory evaluation. *Educational Evaluation and Policy Analysis, 14*(4), 397–418. doi:10.3102/01623737014004397

Cousins, J. B., & Whitmore, E. (1998). Framing participatory evaluation. *New Directions for Evaluation, 80,* 5–23. doi:10.1002/ev.1114

deLeon, P. (1992). The democratization of the policy sciences. *Public Administration Review, 52*(2), 125–129. doi:10.2307/976465

Department of Justice. (2013). *A national protocol for sexual assault medical forensic examinations: Adults & adolescents* (2nd ed.).

Department of Justice. (2015). *Identifying and preventing gender bias in law enforcement response to sexual assault and domestic violence.*

Durning, D. (1993). Participatory policy analysis in a social service agency: A case study. *Journal of Policy Analysis and Management, 12*(2), 297–322. doi:10.2307/3325237

Greenwood, D. J., & Levin, M. (2006). *Introduction to action research* (2nd ed.). Sage.

Hosmer, D. W., Lemeshow, S., & Sturdivant, R. X. (2013). *Applied logistic regression* (3rd ed.). John Wiley & Sons.

Human Rights Watch. (2009). *Testing justice: The rape kit backlog in Los Angeles City and County.*

Human Rights Watch. (2010). *"I used to think the law would protect me" Illinois's failure to test rape kits.*

Human Rights Watch. (2013). *Capitol offense: Police mishandling sexual assault cases in the District of Columbia.*

Kazdin, A. E. (2008). Evidence-based treatment and practice: New opportunities to bridge clinical research and practice, enhance the knowledge base, and improve patient care. *American Psychologist, 63*(3), 146–159. doi:10.1037/0003-066X.63.3.146

Kemmis, S., & McTaggart, R. (2005). Participatory action research: Communicative action and the public sphere. In N. K. Denzin & Y. S. Lincoln (Eds.), *The Sage handbook of qualitative research* (3rd ed., pp. 559–604). Sage.

Kennedy, D. M. (2011). *Don't shoot: One man, a street fellowship, and the end of violence in inner-city America.* Bloomsbury.

Klofas, J., Hipple, N. K., & McGarrell, E. (Eds.). (2010). *The new criminal justice: American communities and the changing world of crime control.* Routledge.

Krieger, G., Cain, D., & Shaw, J. (2017). *Making a difference for sexual assault victims: Lessons from Michigan.* Paper presented at the Battered Women's Justice Project's Conference: What Works: Identifying and Preventing Gender Bias in the Criminal Justice System Response to Domestic Violence and Sexual Assault, Jacksonville, FL.

Laird, F. N. (1993). Participatory analysis, democracy, and technological decision making. *Science, Technology, & Human Values, 18*(3), 341–361. doi:10.1177/016224399301800305

Lonsway, K. A., & Archambault, J. (2012). The "justice gap" for sexual assault cases: Future directions for research and reform. *Violence Against Women, 18*(2), 145–168. doi:10.1177/1077801212440017

Lum, C., Telep, C. W., Koper, C. S., & Grieco, J. (2012). Receptivity to research in policing. *Justice Research and Policy, 14*(1), 61–95. doi:10.3818/JRP.14.1.2012.61

Makse, T., & Volden, C. (2011). The role of policy attributes in the diffusion of innovations. *The Journal of Politics, 73*(1), 108–124. doi:10.1017/S0022381610000903

Martinson, R., & Gamache, D. (2016, August). *Ending gender bias in the law enforcement response to sexual assault and domestic violence: Report on the OVW Roundtable*: Battered Women's Justice Project.

Maton, K. I. (2017). *Influencing social policy: Applied psychology serving the public interest.* Oxford University Press.

Michigan Domestic and Sexual Violence Prevention and Treatment Board. (2015). *Michigan model policy: The law enforcement response to sexual assault.*

Miller, R. L., & Shinn, M. (2005). Learning from communities: Overcoming difficulties in dissemination of prevention and promotion efforts. *American Journal of Community Psychology, 35*(3-4), 169–183. doi:10.1007/s10464-005-3395-1

Mrazek, P. B., & Haggerty, R. J. (1994). *Reducing risks for mental disorders: Frontiers for preventive intervention research*. National Academies Press.

O'Connell, M. E., Boat, T., & Warner, K. E. (2009). *Preventing mental, emotional, and behavioral disorders among young people: Progress and possibilities*. The National Academies Press.

Patton, M. Q. (2008). *Utilization-focused evaluation* (4th ed.). Sage.

Shaw, J. (2014). *Justifying injustice: How the criminal justice system explains its response to sexual assault* [Unpublished doctoral dissertation]. Michigan State University.

Shaw, J. (2015). *The police response to sexual assault*. Paper presented at the White House Domestic Violence Awareness Month Roundtable, Washington, D.C.

Shaw, J. (2016). *Documenting gender bias in the police response to sexual assault*. Paper presented at the Office on Violence Against Women Roundtable on Identifying and Preventing Gender Bias in the Policing, Washington, D.C.

Shaw, J. (2017). *The view from inside the system: How police explain their response to sexual assault*. Paper presented at the Battered Women's Justice Project's Conference: What Works: Identifying and Preventing Gender Bias in the Criminal Justice System Response to Domestic Violence and Sexual Assault, Jacksonville, FL.

Shaw, J., Cain, D., Krieger, G., & Campbell, R. (2015). *Understanding and improving law enforcement's response to sexual assault*. Paper presented at the International Association of Chiefs of Police, Chicago, IL.

Shaw, J., Campbell, R., & Cain, D. (2016). The view from inside the system: How police explain their response to sexual assault. *American Journal of Community Psychology, 58*(3-4), 446–462. doi:10.1002/ajcp.12096

Shaw, J., Campbell, R., Cain, D., & Feeney, H. (2017). Beyond surveys and scales: How rape myths manifest in sexual assault police records. *Psychology of Violence, 7*(4), 602–614. doi:10.1037/vio0000072

Shaw, J., Campbell, R., Hagstrom, J., O'Reilly, L., Kreiger, G., Cain, D., & Nye, J. (2016). Bringing research into practice: An evaluation of Michigan's sexual assault kit (SAK). *Journal of Interpersonal Violence, 31*(8), 1476–1500. doi:10.1177/0886260514567964

Strom, K. J., & Hickman, M. J. (2010). Unanalyzed evidence in law-enforcement agencies: A national examination of forensic processing in police departments. *Criminology & Public Policy, 9*, 381–404.

Tunes da Silva, G., Logan, B. R., & Klein, J. P. (2009). Methods for equivalence and noninferiority testing. *Biology of Blood and Marrow Transplantation, 15*(1 Suppl), 120–127. doi:10.1016/j.bbmt.2008.10.004

Wallerstein, N., & Duran, B. (2008). The theoretical, historical, and practice roots of CBPR. In M. Minkler & N. Wallerstein (Eds.), *Community-based participatory research for health: From process to outcomes* (2nd ed., pp. 25–46). Wiley.

Wandersman, A. (2003). Community science: Bridging the gap between science and practice with community-centered models. *American Journal of Community Psychology, 31*(3-4), 227–242. doi:10.1023/A:1023954503247

Weiss, C. H. (1973). Where politics and evaluation research meet. *Evaluation, 1*, 37–45. doi:10.1037/ort0000356

Weiss, C. H., Murphy-Graham, E., & Birkeland, S. (2005). An alternate route to policy influence: How evaluations affect D.A.R.E. *American Journal of Evaluation, 26*, 12–30.

Weiss, C. H., Murphy-Graham, E., Petrosino, A., & Gandhi, A. G. (2008). The fairy godmother and her warts: Making the dream of evidence-based policy come true. *American Journal of Evaluation, 29*, 29–47.

CHAPTER 18

EPILOGUE

Ryan P. Kilmer and James R. Cook

The 17 preceding chapters underscore two key propositions put forth from the outset of this book: evaluation can (and, to us, *should*) be used to facilitate critical social change, and these efforts to effect change are best done in partnership with key stakeholders. Evaluation planning should include such goals as improving programs, guiding the use of resources, contributing to policy efforts, enhancing practice, or informing organizational action or system change. In sum, evaluation data should be used to effect social change (e.g., Cook, 2015). It is not just "to know"; it is "to know" *and* "to do, change, or improve," and the examples throughout this text highlight how that is possible across different settings and contexts. They shed light on evaluation in practice, in the context of major systems (such as the schools, mental health, or health systems, e.g., Chapters 3, 6, 11, 14, and 16), nonprofit organizations or their programs (e.g., Chapters 1, 7, 12, and 13), ongoing partnerships and initiatives (e.g., Chapters 8–10), and even advocacy and policy work (e.g., Chapters 15 and 17). This is, of course, a nonexhaustive list, and multiple chapters can be framed as reflecting more than one of those contexts.

We maintain that evaluation work is best done in partnership, and the contributions in this book illustrate how a partnership-based approach can be effective. Key to any partnership is ensuring that there are clear common interests and mutual benefits (e.g., Cook & Kilmer, 2012; Kilmer & Cook, 2015). While this may seem somewhat obvious, we have heard too often of evaluators shifting an evaluation's foci to pursue their own agenda, reducing the scope of an effort so that it did not yield the data or results necessary to inform the work of a program or organization, or expanding an evaluation's objectives to such a degree that it left the organization or program staff feeling as if it was the evaluator's "research project." Open and direct communication is a must for any partnership to be successful; if an evaluator's ideas about the scope or focus of the evaluation do not align with those who sought the evaluation, this discrepancy must be addressed. That said, in reality, it regularly occurs that the leadership of a program or organization asks for an evaluation to do "X," but the evaluator may determine that they really need "X" and "Y" or "Z," given their expressed goals. In such instances, it is incumbent on the evaluator(s) to ask questions and explain options to help walk our partners through the choice points and their implications, helping them see what "Y" or "Z" might yield relative to "X." The decisions must be joint and collaborative. Otherwise, the evaluation process will likely be less successful, and key stakeholders will not be pleased with the questions that have been addressed, the process of the evaluation, or the core findings. Such issues must be resolved early on in order for the evaluation to be useful for facilitating change.

As we highlighted in Chapter 3, it is imperative that we are attentive to process as we work with partners, that we are intentional in our efforts to foster trust and build a relationship, and that we communicate transparently. It is necessary to be participatory in approach—in turn, we must appreciate the expertise, strengths, and capacity of our partners and know what we do not know. This collaborative approach will often take longer than if the evaluator was simply trying to design an evaluation on his or her own—there will need to be discussions of objectives, goals, priorities, data sources, and possibilities; there will be some back-and-forth, steps, and missteps; and there will necessarily be a fair number of meetings and conversations (e.g., Kilmer et al., 2009). However, while this process is more time intensive, it is crucial for building a foundation for the evaluation (and, perhaps, a longer-term partnership). Moreover, this participatory approach will lead to better questions, higher quality data, strengthened (and contextually-grounded) evaluations, and a greater likelihood that recommendations are translated to action (e.g., Cook & Kilmer, 2008). In other words, it can foster buy-in and yield better science, a better evaluation, which then has implications for action. We must always strive for mutual benefit.

The work is surely not without its challenges. Notwithstanding contracts, memoranda of understanding, and other "best laid plans," terms and circumstances can and do change. Political dynamics can influence the group, new needs will emerge, key contacts will transition to other roles, or other broader ecological factors may impact access to data, timelines, design options, and the like. Resource limitations (such as person power, funds available, time, and data capacity) must always be taken into account, and budget constraints, or changes, will sometimes meaningfully impact evaluation planning or activities.

With these notions as backdrop, some key take-home points emerge for evaluators (and those in training) going forward:

> **Evaluators must be flexible and adaptable—and adept at "code-switching."**

- *Be flexible.* Evaluators must be flexible and adaptable—and able to tolerate ambiguity. We must be respectful of and sensitive to varying, or changing, priorities and agendas. We need to understand the larger context and the other potential factors and forces at play.

- *Build skills for communicating with diverse partners and stakeholders.* We have underscored that relationships and communication are key—sometimes, as an evaluator works across stakeholders, systems, and partners, they need to be skilled at code-switching. That is, we need to be facile with different languages, both in listening to our partners and others and in communicating our thoughts, findings, and recommendations. We would necessarily discuss an evaluation and its findings differently with a group of researchers than we would a nonprofit board of directors or a lay audience—and we should develop materials for dissemination that are targeted appropriately to diverse audiences as well.

- *Anticipate and prepare for conflict.* In the context of our partnerships, we need to expect the inevitable conflicts or disagreements—and even plan for them. These can happen despite the best efforts and intentions of those involved; they can also come up in response to a host of different factors and dynamics (see Chapter 2). In our experiences, we have typically been able to have parties come together to discuss their different viewpoints openly and arrive at either consensus or a workable compromise. However, in some cases, that is not always possible, or a vocal minority digs in and appears unwilling to work toward consensus. As a matter of practice, it can be helpful to establish processes for resolving disagreements or disputes before they occur; then, the parties have a mechanism through which they can work through the challenge. Particularly on larger-scale projects, we find that it greatly facilitates the work of the evaluation to establish a partnership management team or advisory group, with leaders or representatives from salient constituencies. Such a team's regular meetings (often more frequent at the initiation of an effort or at critical time points) can serve as a means for supporting shared decision-making processes, including key voices, helping arbitrate disagreements, and ensuring accountability and progress for the evaluation project overall.

- *Acknowledge that there will be a tension between rigor and practicality.* We discussed this notion in Chapters 1 and 14, but it warrants revisiting here. We must always consider the data and sources of information that would be helpful and take steps to minimize the burden on a program's intended beneficiaries or staff. In thinking through and planning an evaluation design, a randomized trial can help maximize rigor, but that may not be a tenable option in the context of the program, with the population being served, or in the face of the problem being addressed. In our experiences, the most rigorous possible option is unlikely to be realistic or reasonable, or ethically or politically feasible. Again, decisions about design and evaluation procedures—and their implications—should be discussed among the partners and made jointly.

- *Recognize that evaluation is not value free.* While the data should tell the story, this work is not value free (see Chapter 1). Our values influence our choices about the groups with which we work (e.g., based on their missions or areas of focus) and the way we approach evaluation. Our participatory, partnership-based approach and our objective to use evaluation to support social change are grounded in our values as professionals and as people. Some findings will be favorable for our partners, some will look less positive; we unequivocally must report the findings of the evaluation accurately and objectively. Our values drive our emphasis on using those findings to support change. Our values lead us to work passionately to strengthen our local systems, improve programs in our public systems or nonprofit sectors, guide practice, and effect change in policies locally and beyond.

> **The data are what they are, and evaluation findings tell the story—but evaluation is not value free.**

In developing this text, we have thought often of the new or novice evaluator, with a goal of illustrating evaluation's potential and how it can be used to support action-able recommendations. However, we also recognize that some of the examples, whether growing out of multiyear partnerships or described by seasoned evaluators, may not align with the experience or opportunities of an early career professional or someone new to a particular community. In such circumstances, what can you do?

Our clear message: Invest and engage—get involved in your community. In partic-ular, seek opportunities to volunteer or otherwise connect with nonprofits or programs that have missions you value. Reach out and strive to learn about what they do. Serve on committees (e.g., evaluation, policy) that play to your strengths and can help meet a need. If there are coalitions or initiatives that align with your topical interests, your expertise, or your values, explore how you can get involved and contribute. Some possibilities will be "behind the scenes" but critically important, such as helping a program or nonprofit build evaluation capacity (see Chapters 7 and 13) or working with a program, organization, or initiative on their theory of change or logic model (see Chapter 1). Such involvements help you to contribute and make a difference when there is not a contract or grant on the line. They provide an opportunity to invest and commit to a potential partner. You will build relationships as you connect with the others involved, and those relationships can grow over time. You will also develop a better understanding of the community's broader ecological context, including prominent issues that are salient for community members (or subgroups of the community), political dynamics you may need to navigate, strengths and needs of public systems and nonprofit organizations, and the like. In addition, if you are in or affiliated with a university, it may be possible to involve students in the evaluation efforts, in a way that both contributes to the overall goals of the evaluation and contributes to the development of a growing cadre of evaluation professionals who can also use evaluation to effect change. Furthermore, through your involvement(s), you may link up with others who share your views and values who also want to make a difference and effect change.

It goes back to the "so what?" question we noted in Chapter 1—Will the evaluation effort yield information, guide recommendations, or help generate support to make a difference and facilitate community change? Will it be used to do something? We hope this text helps demonstrate how evaluation can support such goals and effect change.

REFERENCES

Cook, J. R. (2015). Using evaluation to effect social change: Looking through a community psychology lens. *American Journal of Evaluation, 36*, 107–117.

Cook, J. R., & Kilmer, R. P. (2008, June). *Using community-based participatory research to build capacity in family support organizations.* Paper presented at the 2nd International Community Psychology Conference, Lisbon, Portugal.

Cook, J. R., & Kilmer, R. P. (2012). Creating successful partnerships using applied community psychology research. *Living Knowledge: International Journal of Community Based Research, 10*, 16–17.

Kilmer, R. P., & Cook, J. R. (2015, June). *Facilitating student learning and sparking community change: How to develop and sustain successful community-university partnerships.* In K. S. Hogan (Chair), *Creating capacity: Community-university partnerships as co-learning experiences.* Symposium presented at the 15th Biennial Conference of the Society for Community Research and Action, Lowell, MA.

Kilmer, R. P., Wall-Hill, S., Cook, J. R., Kothandapany, N., & Weber, L. J. (2009). Evaluating ParentVOICE: Building family organization sustainability through family-university collaboration. In S. Swart, B. Friesen, A. Holman, & N. Aue (Eds.), *Building on family strengths: Research and services in support of children and their families* (pp. 164–168). 2007 Conference Proceedings and State of the Science Report. Portland State University, Research and Training Center on Family Support and Children's Mental Health.

GLOSSARY

Actor(s). The people, organizations, or groups that interact with one another within a network.

Advocacy. A wide range of activities conducted to influence decision makers at various levels.

Advocacy capacity assessments. Tools to determine necessary knowledge and skills in order to engage in and evaluate advocacy efforts.

Advocacy evaluation. Critical review of strategies to achieve advocacy- and policy-related results.

Archival data. Information and records that have already been collected or are available, prior to the initiation of an evaluation or a research effort.

Attribute data. Characteristics which represent descriptions, measurements, and/or classifications of spatial (i.e., location) data (e.g., county names, population data from the census, distance between two addresses).

Attrition. The loss of data due to research participants dropping out of a research or evaluation study.

Befriend accountability. The process of becoming comfortable with the concept of accountability.

Beneficence. The ethical principle of having the enhanced welfare of study participants as a goal in research.

Benefits. Monetary value of all resources produced or saved as a result of the program.

Centrality. The extent to which a particular actor occupies an important position in the network. Actor-level metrics of centrality may vary and include, for example, degree centrality (i.e., actors are important when they have relationships with many other actors) and betweenness centrality (i.e., actors are important when they are positioned between two otherwise disconnected other actors).

Chronic absenteeism. A student's absences from school that exceed a particular threshold (often defined as missing more than 10% of school days enrolled, although there is no common definition in the United States).

Collective impact. Cross-agency and cross-sector initiatives designed to address the most challenging social problems through inter-agency collaboration, common agendas, shared measurement systems, and aligned activities, programs, leadership, and procedures. Evaluating programs in conjunction with each other can broaden understanding of the cumulative impact of complementary nonprofit programs and assess for trends extending beyond individual consumers.

Community-based participatory action research. An array of approaches to research that prioritize participatory and collaborative processes, multiple ways of knowing, reflection, pragmatic problem-solving, and action.

Community-based participatory research (CBPR). "A collaborative research approach that is designed to ensure and establish structures for participation by communities affected by the issue being studied, representatives of organizations, and researchers in all aspects of the research process to improve health and well-being through taking action, including social change" (see Viswanathan et al., 2004). This helps ensure that participants and other stakeholders have a voice in the knowledge that is created.

Community-university (CU) partnership. A collaborative effort between colleges and universities and their local communities to exchange knowledge, expertise, and resources in a context of partnership, often for the purposes of program evaluation.

Conceptual use. Changes in how stakeholders think about a program or policy more generally as a result of the evaluation.

Confidentiality. The expectation that information provided by individuals to researchers will be shared with others in a way that protects the former's privacy.

Conflict of interest. A conflict between the private interests and official responsibilities of a person in a position of trust.

Consequential validity. A criterion of quality that is met through the inquiry stimulating valued social or organizational change.

Constructivism. A paradigm that assumes knowledge is actively constructed between inquirers and individuals with lived experience related to a particular phenomenon.

Continuous Quality Improvement (CQI). Systematic cycles of collecting data and analyzing it in order to refine and improve programming.

Control of the evaluation process. A defining dimension in a practical participatory evaluation that refers to who has decision-making power throughout the evaluation process. This may range from full control with the evaluators, with the stakeholders, or somewhere in between.

Cost-Benefit Analysis (CBA). Relationship between costs and benefits of a program.

Cost-Effectiveness Analysis (CEA). Relationship between costs and effectiveness of a program.

Costs. Monetary value of all resources required to implement a program.

Critical friend. A trusted person who asks provocative questions, provides data to be examined through another lens, and offers critiques of a person's work as a friend.

Cultural competence. A stance toward culture that requires awareness of self, reflection on one's own cultural or social position/location, awareness of others' social positions, and the ability to interact genuinely and respectfully with others. In the context of evaluation study, the culturally competent evaluator (or evaluation team) must have specific knowledge of the people and place in which the evaluation is being conducted—including local history and culturally determined mores, values, and ways of knowing. The process of becoming more culturally competent is continuous and has no endpoint—according to the American Evaluation Association's Public Statement on Cultural Competence in Evaluation, it "is not a state at which one arrives; rather, it is a process of learning, unlearning, and relearning."

Culture. The American Evaluation Association's *Public Statement on Cultural Competence in Evaluation* defines culture as "the shared experiences of people, including their language, values, customs, beliefs, and mores."

Data management system. A database or spreadsheet that facilitates data entry, management, and utilization by a program.

Density. A metric in network analysis that describes the structure of the network as a whole. Density indicates how many relationships are present out of the possible total number of relationships in the network.

Dependability. A parallel criterion of reliability in qualitative inquiry that assumes quality is achieved through consistency.

Depth of participation. A defining dimension in a practical participatory evaluation that refers to the level of involvement among the selected stakeholders. This may range from selected stakeholders being involved in every aspect of the evaluation to participating in select aspects of the evaluation process.

Discounting. The process of converting future values into their present-day values by taking into account the time value of money.

Distinctive competencies. The unique assets, skills, personnel, or programs of a nonprofit that distinguish its work in the nonprofit sector. Evaluation can help to fine-tune these competencies and can serve as a competency itself for organizations with more advanced capacity. As nonprofits develop distinctive competencies, they define the community change strategies that they can optimally deliver in their communities.

Do no harm. The ethical principle of striving to conduct research in a way that does not harm participants or at least minimizes the risk of harm.

Effectiveness. Results of the program in terms of units of effectiveness.

Empowerment evaluation. An evaluation approach that engages evaluators as partners in developing and monitoring program interventions and documenting the results.

Empowerment evaluation partnership model. An interactive and collaborative partnership (that may include the funder) that utilizes the empowerment evaluation principles to plan, implement, and evaluate the program.

Epistemology. The branch of philosophy of science that specifies the nature of knowledge, how it is acquired, and the relationship between knowledge and truth.

Equity impact review. A tool that combines community engagement and partnership strategies with the use of empirical data to address potential impacts on various forms of equity.

Ethical dilemma. A situation in which two or more ethical principles appear to offer conflicting recommendations for action.

Ethics. Dealing with what is good and bad in human conduct and with moral duty and obligation.

Evaluand. The subject or focus of an evaluation.

Evaluation capacity. The willingness and ability of an organization to ask questions and collect data on the functioning and value of its programs and effectively respond to internal evaluation and local and national research. Strong evaluation capacity is characterized by resources committed toward evaluation initiatives; internal staff dedicated to or trained in nonprofit evaluation practice; routine data collection procedures across programs and reporting procedures across key audiences; a culture of self-reflection, learning, and experimentation across nonprofit personnel; and the potential to apply data in ways that impact cross-agency or community-centered contexts. Evaluation capacity enables the use of data to inform understanding and improve the outcomes of social programs.

Focus groups. A data collection format in which an inquirer moderates a discussion with a group of inquirers who will illuminate a particular subject.

Formative evaluation. A type of evaluation focused on making changes and refinements to the program. Most likely to occur when a program is new and developing, this evaluation uses data to make corrections or refinements until the program becomes established and stable.

Four-tiered framework of evaluation capacity and activity. To guide funders, nonprofit leaders, boards of directors, and other stakeholders to better understand a nonprofit's nature and value, nonprofit evaluation can be considered along a continuum of capacity and activity spanning four distinct levels, or "tiers," including (I) Processes and Procedures, (II) Outcomes and Impact, (III) Models and Infrastructure, and (IV) Community Research and Expertise.

Geocoding. A process of converting addresses, zip codes, census blocks, and other locational features into geographic coordinates (e.g., longitude and latitude).

Geographic Information Systems (GIS). Computer-based programs used for cataloging, storing, querying, analyzing, and displaying geospatial data in order to better understand the world and provide solutions for solving problems and guiding human behavior.

Getting to Outcomes®. One model to operationalize empowerment evaluation whereby the stakeholder groups (including the empowerment evaluator) address 10 accountability questions.

Graduated color map. A map on which a range of colors is used to indicate a progression of numeric values.

Guiding Principles for Evaluators. Developed by the American Evaluation Association, the Guiding Principles provide a framework for the professional ethical conduct of evaluators. The five Guiding Principles are Systematic Inquiry, Competence, Integrity, Respect for People, and Common Good and Equity.

Health equity. A social condition in which all individuals can attain their highest level of health regardless of their group membership or place of residence.

Health service delivery system (HSDS). An entity that provides health services/interventions directly to patients/consumers to improve individual and population health and wellness.

Health service support system (HSSS). An entity that provides services to healthcare organizations and healthcare providers (HSDS) to build capacity for care quality and improve health outcomes.

History. External events that occur between a pretest and a posttest that can effect change in program participants, making it appear as if the program had an effect.

Iatrogenic effects. Possible unintended, harmful, or negative consequences.

Implementation fidelity. The degree to which the program or initiative is being conducted in a manner that is consistent with the model, intervention, or framework selected for the effort. When practices and processes align strongly with the planned model, the effort is said to have high implementation fidelity.

Implementation. The processes that a program engages in to accomplish its goals; high-fidelity implementation implies that the program is implementing program processes in a way that is consistent with plans or expectations.

Implementation science. A practice that helps organizations to adopt, refine, and sustain effective interventions by identifying key "success drivers" across the organization, including competency factors (hiring and training practices), organizational factors (data resources and systemic support), and leadership factors (supervision and performance reviews). These "drivers" require modification as a program is adapted from best to routine practice within a nonprofit's applied setting (Fixsen et al., 2005; 2015).

Individual-level capacity-building factors. Attitudes, motivation, knowledge, and skills are individual factors that affect ECB.

Informed consent. A voluntary agreement to participate in research in which the participant displays an understanding of both the research and its associated risks.

Inquiry–Observation–Reflection (IOR) framework. A mixed-methods (quantitative and qualitative) data collection approach that involves the use of inquiry, observation, and reflection strategies to ascertain a rich and broad understanding of a particular set of evaluation issues.

Instrumental use. Direct use of the evaluation findings to inform a decision or contribute to solving a problem.

Logic model. A graphic illustration of a program's theory of change, or how the program is expected to work, used to help frame an evaluation's focus and objectives, from its data sources to its key questions and indicators of outcome. Also used to clarify the manner in which the different program components and goals logically fit together.

Mainstreaming evaluation. Making the process of documenting impact routine across programs.

Maturation. Processes over time that lead to change in a program participant, such as aging or increased experience; maturation effects can erroneously lead to the conclusion that a program has effects.

Memorandum of understanding (MOU). A document that outlines a work agreement between two parties, clearly defining the purpose of the work and the roles and responsibilities of each party.

Message framing. Process whereby one message, among two or more messages with contrasting words or phrases, is preferred by individuals, even when the messages are logically equivalent.

Model of Evaluation Capacity Building (ECB). A method of evaluation that is ultimately sustainable by the partner/practitioner. The evaluation method may be developed as a partnership, sometimes relying more heavily on the university faculty to develop the methods and instruments, but knowledge should be transferred throughout the project so that the community agency staff can sustain the evaluation over time.

Name generator. A type of question used to collect data about the relationships in a network. These questions typically take the form "With whom do you [relationship of interest]?"

Net present value. The difference between the total discounted benefits minus the total discounted costs.

Network. A pattern of relationships (e.g., friendships, referrals) between a set of actors (e.g., people, organizations) in a system (e.g., workplace, coalition).

Nonprofit developmental lifecycle. Nonprofits begin with initial phases of an Idea (i.e., a project proposal) and Start-Up (i.e., core staff and functions), followed by periods of Growth and Maturity, and in some cases, stages of Decline, Turnaround, or Termination.

Nonprofit ecological system. The theoretical positioning of a nonprofit organization within the nonprofit sector, including its relationships and interactions with accrediting and regulatory oversight committees and boards; public sector leaders; and organization across the local nonprofit network, and the national, state, and local policies and priorities that influence regulations and public funding. The ecological system of a nonprofit has implications for its ability to draw on partners, resources, and funding.

Nonprofit organizations. Nonprofits are tax-exempt organizations designed to address social needs and provide common goods that cannot be adequately or ethically addressed or provided through marketplace or government transactions. Nonprofit funds and resources are raised through a variety of sources (donations, grants, earned revenue, etc.) but must be directed toward activities aligned with its tax-exempt purpose and stated mission rather than distributed among stakeholders. Nonprofits are composed of multiple subparts, including their programs and services, management, governance, available resources, and administrative systems, which may not always align in their functioning and developmental level.

Ontology. The branch of philosophy of science that specifies the nature of reality.

Organizational-level capacity-building factors. Leadership, learning climate, and resources are organizational factors that affect ECB.

Outcomes. The benefit, profit, consequence, or impact (or lack thereof) of any undertaking, initiative, service, or program. Outcomes are intended and unintended and are operationalized differently, with different units of analysis, depending on the purpose of the undertaking and the goal of the evaluation. For example, outcomes may include the impact of an intentional change in program procedures on program functioning (i.e., time to service completion; Tier I); changes in health status or behaviors of program consumers (Tier II); local systemic changes in response to new programs or treatment models, or the influence of cross-organizational "drivers" on program success (Tier III); and finally community-level and collective impact outcomes (Tier IV).

Outcome evaluation. Also referred to as a "summative" evaluation, the purpose of this type of evaluation is to determine a program's or initiative's effects.

Overlay. The combination of two separate spatial datasets to create a new output dataset.

Paradigm. A distinct cluster of philosophical assumptions and beliefs under which researchers and evaluators operate.

Participatory action inquiry. A distinct methodology concerned with generating knowledge to inform subsequent action to solve a localized problem.

Participatory mapping. A group-based qualitative research method that asks participants to identify the physical boundaries of their own neighborhoods and communities, as well as the important resources and the activities in which they engage.

Participatory policy analysis. Policy analysis that supports the participation of stakeholders so that their insights may inform public policy.

Partnership. A working relationship in which the parties involved identify and work toward common interests, build their efforts on the parties' complementary skills and perspectives, and develop processes and establish outcomes that yield mutual benefit.

Partnership approach to evaluation. An approach to evaluation in which the involved parties engage in open and direct communication, employ participatory practices, and ensure that the effort yields mutual benefits. In our view, this approach also uses evaluation to benefit programs, program participants/planned beneficiaries, and organizations.

Philosophy of science. The assumptions and beliefs that undergird the systematic pursuit of knowledge including ontology, epistemology, and methods.

Plan-Do-Study-Act (PDSA). A quality improvement method that involves rapid-cycle implementation, evaluation, and improvement activities.

Plausible alternative hypotheses. A set of hypotheses about the degree to which factors, other than the treatment or program, are likely to cause program effects; ruling out plausible alternative hypotheses increases the ability to conclude that the program causes outcomes.

Practical participatory evaluation. An evaluation approach that prioritizes engaging stakeholders in the evaluative process and practical use of the evaluation process and findings.

Present value. The present worth of future sums of money.

Principles of empowerment evaluation. The principles of empowerment evaluation that are inclusive of how the evaluator and stakeholder groups organize their work based on the local context and purpose of the evaluation.

Process evaluation. A type of evaluation that focuses on how well the program is implemented in relation to its design and intent. For instance, is the program being implemented with fidelity or in a way that is consistent with the methods specified as important for that program?

Process use. Changes within program staff and organizations that stem from participating in an evaluation.

Program evaluation. A set of mechanisms for collecting and using information to (a) learn about projects, policies, and programs; (b) determine their effects, both intended and unintended; and (c) understand the manner in which they are implemented (Cook, 2014).

Program theory. This describes a program; identifies the program's goals and purpose, and desired outcomes; explains why a program's activities are supposed to lead to the desired effects (e.g., how a program is expected to work); and identifies the conditions under which the outcomes will be attained (see Chen, 2003; Sharpe, 2011).

Proportional symbol map. A map on which the size of a simple symbol (e.g., a circle or star) is altered to indicate a progression of numeric values.

Proximity buffer. A zone (often a circle or polygon) drawn around a map feature measured in units of distance or time. It is often used in proximity analysis (i.e., an analysis used to determine the relationship between a selected point and neighboring points).

Proxy value/shadow price. The value assigned to intangible goods.

Purposive sampling. A cluster of sampling strategies designed to recruit only participants who will provide information that is particularly illuminative.

Qualitative inquiry. A systematic approach to knowledge generation informed by a philosophy of science centered on making sense of the *meanings* people ascribe to their experience and their perception of the world.

Querying. Using GIS software to ask and answer questions about geographic features, attributes, and the relationship between them.

Regression to the mean. The tendency for measurement of extreme groups to, when measured again, appear as less extreme (or closer to the mean) as a result of unreliable measures and random error; regression to the mean can be mistakenly viewed as a program effect.

Relationship. The interaction between actors measured in the network (e.g., communication, advice, friendship). Relationships are the key building blocks of a network because they give the network its structure.

Reliability. The determination that a measure of a construct will be consistent over time or across raters.

Research. "A systematic investigation, including research development, testing and evaluation, designed to develop or contribute to generalizable knowledge," as defined by the Code of Federal Regulations (U.S. Department of Health and Human Services, 45 CFR 46.102(d)) relating to the Protection of Human Subjects.

Restorative justice. "An approach to achieving justice that involves, to the extent possible, those who have a stake in a specific offense or harm to collectively identify and address harms, needs, and obligations in order to heal and put things as right as possible" (Zehr, 2015). The approach engages those who are harmed (on a strictly voluntary basis), wrongdoers, and their affected communities in search of solutions that promote repair, reconciliation, and rebuilding of relationships.

Results accountability. A disciplined way of thinking and taking data-directed action that can be used to improve the quality of life within a population (i.e., How will we know if we have been successful?).

Science–practice gap. Contexts in which practice or policy development operates independently of relevant research or evaluation.

Scope of work. An agreement that maps out the specific nature of the job/evaluation, the timeline and terms, and the key products or deliverables.

Selection. The inclusion of participants in a program who already have characteristics expected after participating in a program, such that the program is erroneously viewed as having a positive effect, when it is merely a selection effect.

Sensitivity analysis. Efforts to measure how changes in the estimates and assumptions affect recommendations.

Sequential exploratory mixed-methods design. A mixed-methods design in which exploratory qualitative data are collected and analyzed first, followed by quantitative data collection and analysis.

Social-emotional learning (SEL). A set of critical skills and mindsets that enable success in school and in life by teaching children to recognize and understand their emotions, feel empathy, make decisions, and build and maintain relationships.

Spatial data. Location data relating to a geographic coordinate with longitude and latitude. These can be points, lines, or areas associated with zip codes, census tracts, street addresses, and so on.

Stakeholder selection. A defining dimension in a practical participatory evaluation that refers to the intentional selection of stakeholders to be involved in the evaluation process. This may range from all individuals with any stake in the evaluand, to a select subgroup of stakeholders.

Standard deviational ellipse (SDE). A bivariate statistical measure that provides an estimate of an individual's activity space by calculating the standard deviation of the x-coordinates and y-coordinates from the mean center to define the axes of the ellipse.

Strategic frame analysis. Approach that uses communications research to inform the framing of complex social issues to advance policy outcomes.

Structural similarity. A dyad-level metric in network analysis, indicating how similar two actors are in terms of their network roles and, specifically, the extent to which they have the same pattern of relationships.

Summative evaluation. A type of evaluation that measures the worth or merit of an intervention.

Thematic analysis. A qualitative analytic approach in which the inquirer systematically searches for and interprets patterns of meaning across data provided by several participants.

Theory of change. A description of what the program is trying to accomplish and the processes that are in place to accomplish these goals. This includes specification of the program activities that are intended to effect certain short-term changes; these short-term changes are then prerequisites for later and/or larger changes that subsequently lead to the program's longer-term goals. In sum, it describes the assumptions about how and why a program will achieve the intended outcomes.

Three-step model for empowerment evaluation. Fetterman's initial model of empowerment evaluation that includes the three components: establishing the mission, taking stock, and planning for the future.

Time value of money. An economic concept that assumes future money does not hold the same value as today's money.

Transitivity: A metric in network analysis that describes the structure of the network as a whole. Transitivity indicates the extent to which, if there is a relation between Actors A and B, and between Actors B and C, then there is also a relationship between Actors A and C (i.e., if A → B and B → C, how often does A → C).

Validity (of measurement). The determination that a measure of a construct accurately measures the construct that it purports to measure.

Verstehen. A criterion of quality based on the notion that quality is achieved through "deep understanding" of the meaning of participants' perceptions.

INDEX

Michigan Sexual Assault Kit Submission Act, 341
Microsoft Access program, 105
Mixed methods evaluation, 181
Morris, M., 92
Multicomponent evaluation, 23–24

Name generator, 199, 206
Narrative inquiry, 180
National Criminal Justice Reference Service, 342
National Longitudinal Study, 23
Network analysis
    actors, 198
    boundary specification problem, 198
    centrality, 201
    data collection, 196, 199–200
    density, 200
    descriptive metrics, 201
    evaluation questions, 201
    geodesic distance, 200–201
    and impact evaluation, 203–204
    Links to Learning process evaluation, 205–207
    outcome evaluations, 197
    partnership-oriented approaches, 204–205
    and process evaluation, 202–203
    reciprocity, 200
    relationships, 199
    sociograms, 208f
    statistical models, 201
    transitivity, 200
    whole network analysis, 198
NIJ Sexual Assault Kit Action Research Project, 336
    control of evaluation, 337, 339
    depth of participation, 337, 340
    DNA CODIS database, 337–338
    empirical investigation, 339
    kit testing plan, 341–342
    Michigan Sexual Assault Kit Submission Act, 341
    path analysis, 340
    police sexual assault case investigations, 342–344
    sequential exploratory mixed-methods multistudy, 340
    stakeholder selection, 336–337, 339
    Wayne County Sexual Assault Kit Task Force, 341
Nonprofit developmental lifecycle, 242, 356
Nonprofit Ecological System, 241–242
Nonprofit evaluation
    capacity building, 241
    ecological system, 241–242, 242f
    four-tier model. *See* Four-tier model of nonprofit
        evaluation
    funding, 262

internal evaluation staff and external partners, 242–243
national policy changes, 242
nonprofit accountability movement, 238, 241
nonprofits, 241
stage theories, 241
stakeholders, 237
Nonprofit–funder relationship, 238
Nonprofit organizations, 237
Nye, N., 125

One size fits all approach, 83
Ontology, 179
Organizational leadership, 30–31
Organizational learning, empowerment evaluation, 145
Organizational-level capacity-building factors, 125–127
Outcome evaluation, 23
Overlay, 161

Participatory action inquiry, 181
Participatory action research (PAR), 40, 84
Participatory mapping, 164–168
Participatory policy analyses, 333
Partnership-based approach, 32
    community, 50
    community-based participatory research, 40
    community stakeholders, 38
    cost analysis, 218–226
    early childhood education program, 42–48
    faculty, 49
    geographic information systems, 159
    mutually beneficial, 39
    network analysis, 204–205
    open and direct communication, 39
    participatory nature, 39
    partners, 38
    program leaders and staff, 49
    recommended strategies, 50–51
    school system researchers, 49–50
    shared governance approach, 49
    university, 50
    university students, 49
Partnership building
    community-based organization, 124
    evaluation capacity building
        boundaries and roles, 135–136
        competence evaluation, 133
        contextual and cultural issues, 131–132
        empowerment evaluation approach, 133
        evaluation knowledge and skill development, 130
        evaluation-learning communities, 135

Kassy Alia Ray is the founder and CEO of Serve & Connect, a nonprofit organization focused on igniting positive change through police–community partnerships. A graduate of the University of South Carolina with her doctorate in clinical–community psychology, Dr. Alia Ray founded the organization after her husband, a police officer, was shot and killed in 2015. Under her leadership, the organization has grown from a hashtag to a movement dedicated to creating change. Her work bridges the gap between law enforcement and the communities they serve, drawing on her personal experiences related to the loss of her husband combined with her expertise in community psychology. She speaks regularly across the United States on topics related to collaboration, grief, empathy, and reimagining police and community relationships, and her work has been recognized nationally, including a feature on NBC's Today Show and in *Time Magazine*, for its impact.

Laura Marie Armstrong is an Assistant Professor in the Department of Psychological Science and graduate faculty in the Health Psychology and Public Health Sciences PhD programs at the University of North Carolina at Charlotte. She is also a Licensed Psychologist in North Carolina. She earned her PhD in clinical psychology from the Pennsylvania State University and completed a 2-year postdoctoral fellowship at Brown University Medical School. The goals of her research are to understand and improve children's lives by working to support the multiple systems (i.e., parent, family, school, and cultural contexts) that influence children's health and development from conception to adolescence. She has specific interests in parent and teacher contributions to children's social–emotional development, as well as predictors of family engagement in mental health and school-based programs that support behavior change. She also examines conditions that can undermine children's healthy development, including parent psychopathology, poverty, and trauma.

Michael Awad is a Postdoctoral Associate in the Department of Psychiatry at the Yale School of Medicine. As an Evaluation Consultant with YaleEVAL, he provides program evaluation services to nonprofits, schools, and community agencies. He is the Chair of the New Haven Prevention Council, a community-based coalition that coordinates substance abuse prevention and health promotion initiatives for adolescents in New Haven Public Schools. Dr. Awad served as Policy Fellow in the Office of Behavioral Health Equity at the U.S. Department of Health & Human Services, where he led numerous projects focused on reducing behavioral health disparities and improving the provision of culturally and linguistically appropriate care.

Megan Branham is the Vice President of Policy and Advocacy Programs at North Public Relations and has spent more than 15 years advocating in the nonprofit sector to improve the lives of children and youth. Since completing her Master's in social work at the

University of South Carolina, Megan has advanced legislation and policies improving child well-being during her time at the Children's Trust of South Carolina and the Palmetto Association for Children and Families, implemented programs to improve maternal and child health with the South Carolina March of Dimes, and facilitated community efforts to prevent teen pregnancy at Prisma Health. Megan is a graduate of the Annie E. Casey Foundation's Leadership Institute for State-based Advocates with an emphasis on results-based leadership. Megan currently serves as Chair of the Sisters of Charity Foundation of South Carolina's Kinship Council and is a member of the SC Children's Justice Act Taskforce.

Mary Brolin is a Scientist within the Institute for Behavioral Health, Schneider Institutes for Health Policy at the Heller School for Social Policy and Management, Brandeis University, and has worked in the behavioral health field for more than 30 years conducting health services research and evaluating community-based prevention and treatment programs. Her research interests focus on the intersection of behavioral health services with other service systems, including the criminal justice, housing, and primary care systems. She conducts mixed methods research on behavioral health services for Medicaid populations, low-income people, chronically homeless people, criminal justice populations, youth and young adults, and other vulnerable populations. Dr. Brolin teaches the Capstone Seminar for students completing the Master's degree in public policy at the Heller School at Brandeis University.

Debi Cain is the Executive Director of the Michigan Domestic and Sexual Violence Prevention and Treatment Board and Director for the Michigan Division of Victim Services. She worked for 15 years as founding Executive Director of HAVEN, a suburban Detroit area sexual assault and domestic violence agency. She then directed the Sexual Assault Prevention and Awareness Center at the University of Michigan. Ms. Cain has a Master of Science in administration and a Bachelor of Science in psychology and political science. A founding member of the Michigan Coalition to End Domestic and Sexual Violence, Ms. Cain has served as a consultant, author, and/or editor for a number of publications related to violence against women and children. She has been involved in developing training curricula for diverse professionals (e.g., judges, police, child welfare staff, domestic violence and sexual assault program staff) and has been honored for her contributions to the field.

Rebecca Campbell is a Professor in the Department of Psychology and a Presidential Advisor in the Office of the President at Michigan State University. Her research examines how contact with the legal and medical systems affects sexual assault victims' psychological and physical health. Most recently, she was the lead researcher/evaluator for the National Institute of Justice-funded Detroit Sexual Assault Kit Action Research Project, which was a 5-year multidisciplinary study of Detroit's untested rape kits.

Joanne G. Carman is an Associate Professor in the Department of Political Science and Public Administration at the University of North Carolina at Charlotte. She teaches in the Master of Public Administration program and has served as Coordinator for the Graduate Certificate in Nonprofit Management for 15 years. Over the course of her career,

Joanne has worked with dozens of public agencies and nonprofit organizations conducting program evaluation and applied research. The overarching goal of her research and evaluation is to improve the way public and nonprofit services are provided by focusing on organizational capacity building, program evaluation, leadership, and governance. She currently serves on the editorial board for *Nonprofit Management and Leadership*, and she previously served on the board of directors for the Association for Research on Nonprofit Organizations and Voluntary Action. In 2020, Dr. Carman was awarded UNC Charlotte's Bonne E. Cone Professorship in Civic Engagement.

Andrew D. Case is an Assistant Professor of Psychology and Health Psychology at the University of North Carolina at Charlotte. He earned his doctoral degree in clinical and community psychology from the University of Illinois at Urbana-Champaign and completed a predoctoral internship in prevention and community research at Yale University and a postdoctoral fellowship in health psychology at Duke University. As part of his applied work, he conducts evaluations with nonprofit organizations and social service agencies that provide services to underserved communities. He specializes in utilization-focused evaluations that emphasize partnership and cultural humility.

Virginia Covill serves as the Vice President of Research, Evaluation and Impact for Communities In Schools (CIS) of Charlotte-Mecklenburg. Dr. Covill earned her PhD in the community psychology concentration of the Health Psychology doctoral program as well as her M.A. in clinical and community psychology at the University of North Carolina at Charlotte. Her research collaborations with child welfare agencies, mental health organizations, and education partners have focused on informing system and policy changes for children who are at-risk for emotional, behavioral, or academic difficulties. Prior to joining CIS Charlotte-Mecklenburg in April 2016, she worked as Vice President of Evaluation for Thompson Child & Family Focus, a mental health and early childhood provider. She also currently serves on the research committees of the Council for Children's Rights, READ Charlotte, the Leading on Opportunity Data Collaborative, and the Institute for Social Capital.

Cindy A. Crusto is an Associate Professor of Psychiatry (Psychology Section), Yale School of Medicine, and the Director of Program Evaluation and Child Trauma Research at The Consultation Center. She is a noted expert in addressing culture, context, and human diversity in clinical work and community-engaged research and program evaluation. She has held leadership roles in the American Evaluation Association, including chairing a task force that developed practice guidelines for addressing culture and context in the profession and in the provision of evaluation services to the public and to evaluation consumers. She is the Assistant Chair for Diversity in the Department of Psychiatry, with responsibilities for diversity, inclusion, and equity initiatives. Dr. Crusto is known for her work in community-engaged research, program evaluation and research, and intervention work in the area of children's exposure to psychological trauma and its impact on their health and well-being.

Hannah Feeney is a Research Public Health analyst in RTI International's Division of Applied Justice Research. Dr. Feeney conducts research on violence and the victimization of marginalized communities, and her areas of expertise include community and systems' response to victimization and help-seeking behavior in survivors. Dr. Feeney has extensive experience with quantitative and qualitative methods, data management, and policy development. Dr. Feeney is well versed in developing and supporting research partnerships with key stakeholders, including policymakers, law enforcement personnel, nonprofit organizations, and other victim service providers. This work has included training and technical assistance to practitioners.

Steven Hoffler is an Assistant Professor in the Department of Social Work at Southern Connecticut State University. He currently serves as a consultant for the Connecticut Department of Children and Families, Hartford Healthcare, and Yale University School of Drama on workforce development and diversity, equity, and inclusion efforts. Dr. Hoffler's research and interests include child welfare, juvenile justice, and mental health in the black community. His practice experience has also included clinical, supervisory, and administrative positions at Yale New Haven Hospital, the Connecticut Department of Children and Families, and the Annie E. Casey Foundation through Casey Family Services where he served for 10 years as the Deputy Division Director with administrative and clinical oversight of its foster care, post-adoption, reunification, and community involvement programs. At Southern, Dr. Hoffler serves as a faculty liaison to the Multicultural Center and an advisor to Brotherhood of Scholarship and Excellence.

Katherine Strater Hogan served as the first member of Teen Health Connection's research and evaluation team, overseeing the department's development since 2014. Dr. Hogan earned her MA in clinical and community psychology and PhD in community psychology from the Health Psychology program at the University of North Carolina at Charlotte. During her graduate studies, she worked closely with faculty and students to evolve the program's applied research, community practice, and student training frameworks. Dr. Hogan continues to collaborate across Teen Health Connection's departments and internal evaluation staff as an outside consultant to evaluate and enhance its integrated care frameworks. As a consultant, Dr. Hogan works with nonprofit organizations, providing evaluation and strategic planning services. Her work across healthcare, mental health, child welfare, and other community systems leverages a collaborative capacity-building approach designed to link nonprofits with tools, skills, and partners to engage in ongoing organizational learning and development.

Pamela S. Imm is a Community Psychologist with extensive experience in the areas of program development, program evaluation, and applied research. She received her doctorate in clinical–community psychology from the University of South Carolina and is currently affiliated with LRADAC and the Wandersman Center. Her research and practice areas include the prevention of high-risk behaviors, coalition effectiveness, evidence-based practice, and models of technical assistance and organizational readiness. Dr. Imm has worked and published in the area of empowerment evaluation throughout her career. She and her colleagues developed the Getting to Outcomes framework which is currently used in various communities, state agencies, and foundations. The Getting to Outcomes framework was awarded Outstanding Publication by the American Evaluation Association in November 2008. In 2015, the Society for Community Research and Action, Division

27 of the American Psychological Association, recognized Dr. Imm for her distinguished contributions to the practice of community psychology.

Joy S. Kaufman is a Professor of Psychiatry at Yale University School of Medicine and Deputy Director of The Consultation Center where she directs the areas of Program and Service System Evaluation and Evaluation Research. Trained as a clinical and community psychologist, Dr. Kaufman conducts large-scale, multi-level evaluations of health service delivery systems, provides consultation to governmental and community organizations regarding these evaluations, and carries out related research. These evaluations take place in under-resourced communities; involve close partnerships with state and municipal governments, community organizations, and other public stakeholders; and generate data that inform program and policy development. A unique feature of her work is the training of public stakeholders to evaluate the services they receive or to utilize data so that they can provide rigorous and systematic feedback to improve services and participate in decision-making about their community.

Lindsay G. Messinger is the Director of Research, Evaluation, and Analytics at Charlotte-Mecklenburg Schools. Her work focuses on equity and breaking the predictive link between demographic characteristics and achievement outcomes. She also studies risk and protective factors for student achievement, including research and evaluation to assess the effectiveness of school-based interventions and measurement of social-emotional learning and mental health services for K-12 students. Dr. Messinger also teaches at the University of North Carolina at Charlotte. She earned her MA and doctorate in Applied Developmental Psychology from Fordham University and BA in Psychology from New York University.

Michael Morris is Professor Emeritus of Psychology at the University of New Haven. His 1993 study, "Program Evaluators and Ethical Challenges," was the first national survey examining the ethical conflicts faced by evaluators. A member of the Task Force that revised the American Evaluation Association's *Guiding Principles for Evaluators* in 2018, his book *Evaluation Ethics for Best Practice* (Guilford Press, 2008) has been widely used in evaluation education and training. Dr. Morris's research on evaluation ethics and other topics has appeared in many journals, including the *American Journal of Evaluation (AJE)*, *Evaluation Review*, *Evaluation and Program Planning*, *American Journal of Community Psychology*, *Sociology and Social Research*, and *The American Sociologist*. The author of a number of handbook chapters on ethical issues in evaluation, he was editor of *AJE*'s "Ethical Challenges" column from 1998 to 2004 and is currently on the Editorial Advisory Board of *New Directions for Evaluation*.

Jennifer Watling Neal is an Associate Professor of Psychology at Michigan State University. Her research focuses on understanding how social networks are associated with children's and educators' behavior in schools, and she addresses questions like (1) How can social networks be leveraged to improve educators' access to and implementation of evidence-based programs and practices? (2) How are relationships in childhood and adolescence associated with aggression, prosocial behavior, and personalities?, and (3) How do children and teachers perceive classroom relationships and how "accurate" are they in these perceptions? She has collected social network data in a range of urban, suburban, and rural school settings. Moreover, she has experience collecting and analyzing many different types of network data including self-report, peer-report, teacher-report observational, and relational chain data. Dr. Watling Neal is the recipient of the 2016 American Psychological Association Division 27 Early Career Award and is currently an Associate Editor for *Social Development*.

Zachary P. Neal is an Associate Professor of Psychology at Michigan State University. His research focuses on how networks structure everything from neighborhood social relations, to public school decision-making, to global transportation and economic transactions. He is also interested in developing new metrics for network characteristics like centrality and small worldliness. He has taught network analysis several times, at both the graduate and undergraduate levels, and has developed software to analyze networks in both R and STATA. Dr. Neal is the recipient of the 2017 American Psychological Association Division 27 Early Career Award and the 2016 Freeman Award from the International Network for Social Network Analysis and is currently an Associate Editor for *Journal of Urban Affairs*, *Global Networks*, and *Evidence & Policy*.

Osman Özturgut is the Dean of Extended University and Associate Vice President for International Programs at California State University-Channel Islands (CSUCI). He is responsible for providing chief administrative oversight to all self-support academic programs and responsible for broad academic affairs and university-wide initiatives including leadership of international programs. Prior to arriving at CSUCI, Dr. Özturgut was the Dean of Research and Graduate Studies at the University of the Incarnate Word (UIW) in San Antonio, Texas. At UIW, he provided leadership in policy development, support for implementation, and assessment of policies related to research and graduate education, including masters, doctoral, and professional programs. Dr. Özturgut's current research focuses on cultural competency across multiple disciplines. He taught courses in entrepreneurship, program evaluation, cultural competency, international communication, and research methods. He has numerous publications and presentations in the field of education, cultural competency, international development, and leadership.

Sarah L. Pettijohn is an Assistant Professor in the Department of Political Science and Public Administration at the University of North Carolina at Charlotte. Dr. Pettijohn teaches courses in nonprofit management in the Gerald G. Fox Master of Public Administration Program. Her research focuses on the role, capacity, and financial well-being of nonprofit organizations in the United States. Prior to joining UNC Charlotte, Dr. Pettijohn was a research associate in the Center on Nonprofits and Philanthropy at the Urban Institute in Washington, DC. In addition to her research work, Dr. Pettijohn provided support to the National Center on Charitable Statistics and assisted with data requests and the National Fundraising Survey administered by the National Research Collaborative.

Diane Purvin is an independent policy and evaluation research consultant based in New Haven, CT. As an evaluation consultant to The Consultation Center at Yale University School of Medicine, she coordinated the evaluations for Connecticut's Deep End Diversion juvenile justice initiative and Rhode Island's SAMHSA-funded Systems of Care

Expansion Cooperative Agreement. In her prior role as a Senior Research Associate at the Annie E. Casey Foundation, she focused on evaluating outcomes for youth in long-term foster care, the impact of state-level policies on vulnerable communities and populations, and engaging community stakeholders in public/private evaluation partnerships. In addition to her doctorate in social policy from the Heller School at Brandeis University, Dr. Purvin completed a NICHD-funded postdoctoral fellowship in child and adolescent development at the Wellesley Centers for Women, Wellesley College.

Jonathan P. Scaccia is the Principal of the Dawn Chorus Group. He has extensive experience helping organizations select, adapt, implement, and evaluate community-based improvement interventions. Dr. Scaccia was one of the initial developers of the $R = MC^2$ readiness model. His current research focuses on developing comprehensive methods to evaluate quantitative and qualitative differences in organizational readiness and enhancing strategies that can help to build readiness. Dr. Scaccia works toward developing practical implementation science techniques that are usable by front-line practitioners through facilitating the use of evidence-based implementation support strategies. Dr. Scaccia also founded the research synthesis website PubTrawlr. He received his PhD in clinical–community psychology from the University of South Carolina and completed a research fellowship in the U.S. Department of Health and Human Services, Office of the Assistant Secretary for Health's Public Health Systems, Finance, and Quality Program.

Victoria C. Scott is an applied, interdisciplinary social scientist and community psychologist with formal training in community psychology, clinical psychology, and business administration. She holds an academic appointment at the University of North Carolina at Charlotte as an Assistant Professor of Psychological Science and Affiliate Faculty of Public Health Science. Her research focuses on promoting health equity and fostering collective wellness through systems-level (organizational and community) capacity-building efforts. With a particular interest in health and human service settings, Dr. Scott develops and studies approaches to implementing, evaluating, and improving multifaceted, complex interventions. The impact of her contributions to the community of scholars and practitioners has been recognized through the *Society for Community Research and Action Early Career Award*, the *Don Klein Publications Award*, and the *American Evaluation Association Outstanding Evaluation Award*.

Jessica Shaw is an Assistant Professor in the Community and Prevention Research Program of the Psychology Department at the University of Illinois at Chicago (UIC). She is trained as a community psychologist with specializations in evaluation and organizational change and development. She earned her PhD in ecological–community psychology from Michigan State University in 2014. Prior to joining the faculty at UIC, Dr. Shaw spent a year as a Visiting Fellow with the U.S. Department of Justice, National Institute of Justice, and several years on faculty in the Boston College School of Social Work. Dr. Shaw's research focuses on improving within and between system responses to sexual assault by relying on community partnerships to facilitate empirically-informed practice and policy change. Most often, her research and evaluation projects are developed and implemented in collaboration with community practitioners and policymakers to produce relevant and timely information that can be put to use.

Opal R. Stone is the Director of Reentry Services at Advocates, a behavioral health service provider that supports more than 20,000 individuals annually in Central and Eastern Massachusetts. She oversees Advocates Reentry Services programs, including having led the *Worcester Initiative for Supported Reentry*, a project that achieved a 47% reduction of recidivism among medium- to high-risk citizens returning to the community from prison and jail. She has also directed three federally-funded reentry and specialty court projects, work which incorporated Risk Needs Responsivity principles and partnered closely with the courts, Probation, Parole, Sheriff's offices, and the Massachusetts Department of Correction. Ms. Stone has presented at local and national behavioral health and drug court conferences about building criminal justice and behavioral health collaborations to achieve effective, integrated programming. She has been actively involved in Massachusetts criminal justice policy reform and has consulted on strategic and operational analysis projects in jails.

Melissa Strompolis is the Chief Strategy and Implementation Officer at Children's Trust of South Carolina, a statewide organization focused on the prevention of child maltreatment. Dr. Strompolis works with her team to lead and build systems and infrastructures for population health programming, community coalitions, prevention trainings, and prevention-oriented research and evaluation. Additionally, she is an adverse childhood experiences (ACEs) master trainer, has numerous publications and presentations on ACEs, and sits on many advisory boards, committees, and councils. She is also a guardian ad litem, a volunteer that advocates on behalf of a child referred by family court, and a member of the Society of Community Research and Action (SCRA), Division 27 of the American Psychological Association. Dr. Strompolis received her PhD in community psychology from the University of North Carolina at Charlotte and holds a Master's degree from the University of West Florida.

Yolanda Suarez-Balcazar is a Professor and Head of the Department of Occupational Therapy and Affiliate Faculty in the Department of Disability and Human Development and Department of Psychology at the University of Illinois at Chicago. Trained as a community psychologist, Dr. Suarez-Balcazar studies the nexus between race, culture, disability, and health disparities. Her current funded scholarship aims at identifying social determinants of health impacting children with disabilities and their families and designing, implementing, and evaluating culturally relevant community-level interventions to promote healthy lifestyles and prevent obesity among this population. Her evaluation scholarship has focused on building the capacity of community service providers to evaluate their program outcomes and engage in empowerment evaluation in partnership with communities of color. Dr. Suarez-Balcazar is a Fellow of the American Psychological Association and the Society for Community Research and Action (SCRA; Division 27). In 2017–2018, she served as president of SCRA.

Tina Taylor-Ritzler is Professor and Chair of the Department of Psychology and also serves as the Director of the Social Justice and Civic Engagement Minor at Dominican University. Dr. Taylor-Ritzler completed her PhD in community psychology at the University of Illinois at Chicago. Her work is aimed at conceptualizing, building, and measuring organizational capacity related to cultural competence and program evaluation to promote the inclusion and participation of all community members, in particular those who are marginalized because of systems of oppression related to race, ethnicity, disability, gender, and immigration. Dr. Taylor-Ritzler's work focuses on using data to inform and evaluate programming to improve equity in disability nonprofits and in higher education. Her current work is focused on improving educational outcomes in Hispanic Serving Institutions and is funded by grants from the U.S. Department of Education, Title V Office, and the National Science Foundation.

Greg Townley is an Associate Professor of community psychology at Portland State University and director of research for the Homelessness Research & Action Collaborative. His research focuses primarily on community inclusion of individuals with serious mental illnesses, homelessness, and sense of community among marginalized groups. In his work, Dr. Townley uses a variety of social–environmental research methods, including geographic information systems, neighborhood assessments, and ethnographic approaches. He works closely with the Temple University Collaborative on Community Inclusion of Individuals with Psychiatric Disabilities and served on the qualitative evaluation team for the At Home/Chez Soi project, the largest research trial of Housing First. He also has extensive experience working with consumer-run organizations and community mental health centers to implement and evaluate supported housing and peer support programs.

Whitney Tucker works to advance public policies that enable children to meet their full potential. As Policy Director, she leads policy development, analysis, and advocacy strategy at NC Child—a statewide, multi-issue child advocacy organization based in Raleigh, NC. She engages in direct advocacy and policy research, focusing on issues of economic security and advancing racial equity. She has presented and published on issues ranging from Adverse Childhood Experiences (ACEs) to Medicaid coverage and children's enumeration in the U.S. decennial census. She is a primary contact regarding child well-being for legislative and executive branch agencies across NC. Ms. Tucker chairs the national steering committee of the Annie E. Casey Foundation's KIDS COUNT data program and sits on several NC policy, data, and evaluation councils and committees. She holds a Master of Public Health degree from the University of South Carolina and a bachelor's degree in public policy from Vanderbilt University.

Janice B. Yost has been serving as founding President of The Health Foundation of Central Massachusetts since 1999. The Foundation's grantmaking focuses on multi-year projects, which employ an empowerment evaluation approach to develop evidence-based strategies that are taken to scale by advocating for systems change to sustain the strategies. With these grants totaling $31 million, projects have achieved substantive public policy accomplishments and secured over $69 million in direct sustained funding to date. Dr. Yost previously served as the founding President of Mary Black Foundation and her community service included serving as a Trustee on the Board of the Spartanburg Regional Hospital System in South Carolina. Her earlier career as a high school teacher and then as a college professor and administrator included serving as Associate Chancellor for University Relations at the University of South Carolina-Spartanburg campus. She earned a doctorate in speech education from the University of Georgia.